MEAT GRINDER

OSPREY
PUBLISHING

DEDICATION

For Tom Saunders

MEAT GRINDER

THE BATTLES FOR THE RZHEV SALIENT
1942–43

PRIT BUTTAR

OSPREY PUBLISHING
Bloomsbury Publishing Plc
Kemp House, Chawley Park, Cumnor Hill, Oxford OX2 9PH, UK
29 Earlsfort Terrace, Dublin 2, Ireland
1385 Broadway, 5th Floor, New York, NY 10018, USA
E-mail: info@ospreypublishing.com
www.ospreypublishing.com

OSPREY is a trademark of Osprey Publishing Ltd

First published in Great Britain in 2022

© Prit Buttar, 2022

A catalogue record for this book is available from the British Library.

ISBN: HB 978 1 4728 5181 9; PB 978 1 4728 5182 6; eBook 978 1 4728 5183 3; ePDF 978 1 4728 5178 9; XML 978 1 4728 5179 6

22 23 24 25 26   10 9 8 7 6 5 4 3 2 1

Maps by Prit Buttar
Index by Zoe Ross
Typeset by Deanta Global Publishing Services, Chennai, India
Printed and bound in Great Britain by CPI (Group) UK Ltd, Croydon CR0 4YY

Osprey Publishing supports the Woodland Trust, the UK's leading woodland conservation charity.

To find out more about our authors and books visit **www.ospreypublishing.com**. Here you will find extracts, author interviews, details of forthcoming events and the option to sign up for our newsletter.

CONTENTS

LIST OF ILLUSTRATIONS

German general Walter Model (in vehicle holding map) led Ninth Army from January 1942 until September 1943. He would play a leading role in the battles around Rzhev. (Nik Cornish at www.Stavka.org.uk)

Generalmajor Walter Hörnlein commanded Panzergrenadier Regiment *Grossdeutschland*. In 1943, he was awarded the German Cross in Gold and the Knight's Cross with Oak Leaves. (Photo by ullstein bild/ullstein bild via Getty Images)

Overall command of the German Army was in the hands of Field Marshal Walther von Brauchitsch (seen here with Romania's leader Marshal Ion Antonescu to his right). In reality, however, he was little more than a messenger between Hitler and the army group commanders. (Nik Cornish at www.Stavka.org.uk)

General K. K. Rokossovsky and G. K. Zhukov had both fought in dragoon regiments during the First World War. (Courtesy of the Central Museum of the Armed Forces, Moscow via Stavka)

Lieutenant General P. A. Belov's I Guards Cavalry Corps operated behind enemy lines in one of the most prolonged and remarkable such episodes of the war. (Photo by: Sovfoto/Universal Images Group via Getty Images)

Politically astute Marshal A. M. Vasilevsky rose to be Deputy Defence Minister in October 1942 but has rarely received the recognition that is due to him. (Courtesy of the Central Museum of the Armed Forces, Moscow via Stavka)

Lieutenant General A. A. Vlasov commanded Second Shock Army during the siege of Leningrad. He was captured in July 1942, and agreed to fight against Stalin as commander of the *Russische Befreiungsarmee*. (Nik Cornish at www.Stavka.org.uk)

The muddy conditions on both sides of the front line created an environment that would have been familiar to older combatants or their fathers during the First World War. (Nik Cornish at www.Stavka.org.uk)

Beautifully posed, a Soviet unit advances through deep snow. From this image it is clear how well the camouflage suits blend in. (Courtesy of the Central Museum of the Armed Forces, Moscow via Stavka)

A Soviet river crossing by pontoon is completed by horse power. Often, unseasonable rains made rivers almost impassable. (From the fonds of the RGAKFD in Krasnogorsk via Stavka)

Bread for the Soviet front-line troops being delivered by sledge. By the time it arrived it would be frozen solid. (Courtesy of the Central Museum of the Armed Forces, Moscow via Stavka)

A German supply column made up of commandeered local farm carts that proved more efficient when drawn by hardy local horses than the much heavier horses and wagons issued by the *Heer*. (Nik Cornish at www.Stavka.org.uk)

A company runner delivers a message to his HQ. Such men were obvious targets for Soviet snipers and suffered accordingly. (Nik Cornish at www.Stavka.org.uk)

A German NCO peers cautiously over the lip of a trench while the cameraman nestles under cover. (Nik Cornish at www.Stavka.org.uk)

A German flamethrower team advances cautiously through heavily wooded terrain. When identified, the operator became a priority target for any enemy infantrymen. (Nik Cornish at www.Stavka.org.uk)

A Soviet sub-machine-gun unit advances towards the enemy. They are wearing waist length, quilted *telogreika* jackets, felt *valenki* boots and the *ushanka* imitation fur cap. (Courtesy of the Central Museum of the Armed Forces, Moscow via Stavka)

A German machine-gun team keeps a careful watch, with a mix of grenades close at hand. (Nik Cornish at www.Stavka.org.uk)

Soviet infantrymen moving up to the lines. A farmer's cart has been pressed into service for transport duties. (Courtesy of the Central Museum of the Armed Forces, Moscow via Stavka)

Troopers of the I Guards Cavalry Corps charge into action. The Red Army raised a large number of cavalry units during the Second World War, many of which fought with distinction in a theatre where there were few continuous lines and mobility was vital. (Courtesy of the Central Museum of the Armed Forces, Moscow via Stavka)

A Ju 87 awaits maintenance. The intensive efforts of the Luftwaffe greatly hindered the Soviet's attempts to exploit their successful attacks in August 1942. (Nik Cornish at www.Stavka.org.uk)

An unidentified radio team checks in. The efficiency of German communications was vital to their defensive operations. (Nik Cornish at www.Stavka.org.uk)

Panzerbefehlswagen III Ausf. H command tanks such as this one carried extra wireless equipment that replaced the main armament. (Nik Cornish at www.Stavka.org.uk)

Heavy artillery was Stalin's 'god of war'. This is a 152mm M1935 (Br-2), which had a rate of fire of one shot every two minutes. (Courtesy of the Central Museum of the Armed Forces, Moscow via Stavka)

The iconic Russian-made Maxim M1910/30 heavy machine-gun in a support role. Used in both world wars, it remains in service today. (Courtesy of the Central Museum of the Armed Forces, Moscow via Stavka)

Minefields caused substantial losses on both sides. Here a Soviet operator uses a VIM-203 mine detector, attached to his Mosin rifle. (Nik Cornish at www.Stavka.org.uk)

A Soviet partisan scout, high in the trees. Clashes with partisans often resulted in widespread punishments by the Germans – such as the burning of villages and mass executions. (Courtesy of the Central Museum of the Armed Forces, Moscow via Stavka)

A lonely and dangerous duty: German sentries were frequently taken by Soviet patrols for interrogation. Victims were known as 'tongues' to their captors. (Nik Cornish at www. Stavka.org.uk)

Soviet intelligence officers interview a captured German 'tongue' in this picture. However, the position of the POW's Iron Cross seems a little odd. (Courtesy of the Central Museum of the Armed Forces, Moscow via Stavka)

A Red Army man moves from his foxhole as supporting artillery fire bursts on enemy lines. Hedgehog anti-tank defences are visible in the distance. (Courtesy of the Central Museum of the Armed Forces, Moscow via Stavka)

The dreadful muddy conditions caused massive transport problems not just for the Germans, as seen here, but for both sides during the more clement days of winter. (Nik Cornish at www.Stavka.org.uk)

A Panzer IV crew keeps up with the never-ending maintenance regime. One consolation is that their main armament is short barrelled. (Nik Cornish at www.Stavka.org.uk)

A T-34 with 76mm gun on fire. Most tank brigades had a mix of vehicles, and the T-34s often suffered substantial losses before the heavier KV-1s arrived. (Nik Cornish at www.Stavka.org.uk)

A Soviet gun crew firing a captured German 75mm Pak 40. Ammunition and spares shortages limited the value of such 'trophy' weapons, however. (From the fonds of the RGAKFD in Krasnogorsk via Stavka)

A wounded German is supported by his fellow soldiers. Soldiers on both sides at Rzhev endured one of the most brutal and prolonged phases of the Second World War. (Nik Cornish at www.Stavka.org.uk)

Civilians also suffered terribly during the Rzhev fighting. (Courtesy of the Central Museum of the Armed Forces, Moscow via Stavka)

Red Army men advance towards a church in this atmospheric shot. The winter camouflage overall was such a treasured item of clothing that injured men would apologise for their bloodstains. (From the fonds of the RGAKFD in Krasnogorsk via Stavka)

Two exhausted German infantrymen catch a few moments' rest during the bitter fighting. (Nik Cornish at www.Stavka.org.uk)

Eternal rest in no man's land. (Nik Cornish at www.Stavka.org.uk)

LIST OF MAPS

DRAMATIS PERSONAE

GERMANY

Arnim, Hans-Jürgen von, Generaloberst – commander XXXIX Panzer Corps

Becker, Carl, Oberst – commander 18th Grenadier Regiment

Bieler, Bruno, General – commander VI Corps

Bittrich, Wilhelm, Brigadeführer – commander SS Cavalry Division

Bix, Hermann, Feldwebel – tank crewman

Blumentritt, Günther, Oberst – chief of staff, Fourth Army, later Chief Quartermaster of the Army

Bock, Fedor von, Field Marshal – commander Army Group Centre

Bodenhausen, Gustav Freiherr von, Oberst – commander 31st Panzer Regiment, 5th Panzer Division, and eponymous battlegroup

Brauchitsch, Walther von, Field Marshal – commander-in-chief German Army

Bundrock, Georg, Oberst – head of intelligence, Ninth Army

Burdach, Karl, Generalmajor – commander 251st Infantry Division

Canaris, Wilhelm, Admiral – head of the *Abwehr*

Cetto, Walter, Oberst – commander eponymous battlegroup, 5th Panzer Division

Chevallerie, Kurt von der, General – commander LIX Corps

Eberbach, Heinrich, Oberstleutnant – panzer regiment commander, 4th Panzer Division

Elverfeldt, Harald Freiherr von, Oberst – chief of staff, Ninth Army

Esebeck, Hans-Carl Freiherr von, Generalmajor – commander 2nd Panzer Division

Fegelein, Hermann, Standartenführer – commander SS Cavalry Brigade

Fehn, Gustav, Generalleutnant – commander 5th Panzer Division

Fretter-Pico, Maximilian, General – commander XXX Corps

Frydag, Harro Freiherr von, Hauptmann – commander motorcycle battalion, 1st Panzer Division

Gablenz, Eccard von, Generalleutnant – commander XXVII Corps

Gehlen, Reinhardt, Oberst – head of *FHO*

Grossmann, Horst, Generalmajor – commander 6th Infantry Division

Guderian, Heinz, General – commander Second Panzer Group

Halder, Franz, Generaloberst – chief of the general staff, *OKH*

Harpe, Josef, General – commander XLI Panzer Corps

Heinrici, Gotthard, General – commander XLIII Corps, later commander Fourth Army

Heusinger, Adolf, Generalleutnant – head of operations staff, *OKH*

Hilpert, Carl, General – commander XXIII Corps

Hitter, Alfons, Generalmajor – commander 206th Infantry Division

Hobe, Cord von, Major – senior staff officer, *Grossdeutschland*

Hoepner, Erich, Generaloberst – commander Fourth Panzer Group

Holste, Rudolf, Oberst – commander eponymous battlegroup, 1st Panzer Division

Hörnlein, Walter, Generalmajor – commander *Grossdeutschland* Division

Huppert, Helmut, Hauptmann – commander panzergrenadier battalion, 1st Panzer Division

Jodl, Alfred, General – chief of operations staff, *OKW*

Kassnitz, Erich, Oberst – commander Fusilier Regiment, *Grossdeutschland* Division

Kauder, Richard – head of *Dienststelle Klatt*

Kinzel, Eberhard, Oberst – head of *FHO*

Kluge, Günther von, Generaloberst – commander Fourth Army, later commander Army Group Centre

Knobelsdorff, Otto von, Generalmajor – commander 19th Panzer Division

Köhler, Otto, Oberst – commander Panzergrenadier Regiment, *Grossdeutschland*

Krebs, Hans, Oberst – chief of staff, Ninth Army

Krüger, Walter, Generalmajor – commander 1st Panzer Division

Kübler, Ludwig, General – commander Fourth Army

Lindig, Max, Generalleutnant – chief of artillery, Ninth Army

Longin, Ira Fedorovich – member of the 'Max' spy network

Lorenz, Karl, Major – commander of combat engineer battalion, *Grossdeutschland*, subsequently commander of eponymous battlegroup

Lüttwitz, Heinrich Freiherr von, Generalmajor – commander 20th Panzer Division

Manstein, Erich von, Generaloberst, later Field Marshal – commander LVI Motorised (later Panzer) Corps, later Eleventh Army, later Army Group Don

Martinek, Robert, General – commander XXXIX Panzer Corps

Meden, Karl-Friedrich von der, Oberst – commander eponymous cavalry group

Metz, Eduard, Generalleutnant – commander 5th Panzer Division

Meyer, Otto, Oberst – chief of combat engineers, Ninth Army

Model, Walter, General – commander Ninth Army

Pätzold, Hellmuth, Oberst – commander 2nd Luftwaffe Field Division

Paulus, Friedrich, Generalleutnant (later Field Marshal) – Quartermaster-General, later commander Sixth Army

Praun, Albert, Generalmajor – commander 129th Infantry Division and eponymous battlegroup

Reinhardt, Hans-Georg, General – commander Third Panzer Group

Richthofen, Wolfram von, General – commander *Fliegerkorps VIII*, later commander VI Corps

Romanov, Georgi Leonidovich – member of *Dienststelle Klatt*

Ruoff, Richard, General – commander V Corps, later commander Fourth Panzer Army

Scherer, Theodor, Generalleutnant – commander 83rd Infantry Division

Schmidt, Gustav, Oberst – commander 19th Panzer Division

Schmidt, Rudolf, Generaloberst – commander Second Army, later commander Second Panzer Army, later personal adjutant to Hitler

Stieber, Kurt, Major – panzergrenadier battalion commander, 5th Panzer Division

Strauss, Adolf, Generaloberst – commander Ninth Army

Trumpa, Kurt, Hauptmann – commander eponymous battlegroup, 1st Panzer Division

Turkul, Anton Vasilievich – member of the 'Max' spy network

Vietinghoff, Heinrich von, General – commander XLVI Panzer Corps

Warschauer, Horst, Leutnant – commander eponymous battlegroup, *Grossdeutschland*

Weiss, Walter, General – commander XXVII Corps

Wessel, Walter, Generalmajor – commander 12th Panzer Division

Wietersheim, Wend von, Oberst – commander eponymous battlegroup, 1st Panzer Division

Zeitzler, Kurt, General – chief of the general staff, *OKH*

SOVIET UNION

Andrusenko, Kornei Mikhailovich, Colonel – commander 329th Infantry Division

Arman, Paul Matisovich, Colonel – acting commander I Tank Corps

Baranov, Viktor Kirillovich, Major General – commander 1st Guards Cavalry Division

Belov, Pavel Alekseevich, Lieutenant General – commander I Guards Cavalry Corps

Bodnar, Aleksander Vasilevich, Lieutenant – tank commander

Bogatsky, Mikhail Moiseevich – paratrooper

Bogdanov, Ivan Aleksandrovich, Lieutenant Colonel – deputy commander Thirty-Ninth Army

Boldin, Ivan Vasilevich, Lieutenant General – commander Fiftieth Army

Dovator, Lev Mikhailovich, Major General – commander III Cavalry Corps, later renamed II Guards Cavalry Corps

Dremov, Ivan Fedorovich, Colonel – commander 47th Mechanised Brigade

Dübendorfer, Rachel – spy codenamed 'Sissy'

Efremov, Mikhail Grigorevich, Lieutenant General – commander Thirty-Third Army

Eremenko, Andrei Ivanovich, Colonel General – commander Bryansk Front

Galitsky, Kuzma Nikitovich, Lieutenant General – commander Third Shock Army

Getman, Andrei Lavrentiyevich, Major General – commander VI Tank Corps

Gluzdovsky, Vladimir Alekseevich, Major General – commander Thirty-First Army

Grishin, Petr Grigorevich, Brigade Commissar – commissar VI Tank Corps

Gorbachevsky, Boris Semenovich – soldier in the Red Army

Iushchuk, Ivan Ivanovich, Colonel – acting commander VI Tank Corps

Iushkevich, Vasilii Aleksandrovich, Major General – commander Twenty-Second Army

Katukov, Mikhail Efimovich, Major General – commander 1st Guards Brigade, later commander III Mechanised Corps

Kazankin, Aleksandr Fedorovich, Colonel – chief of staff IV Airborne Corps (and de facto commander)

Kazaryan, Ashot Vagarshakovich – junior tank officer

Khlebnikov, Nikolai Mikhailovich, Major General – commander of artillery, Kalinin Front

Khozin, Mikhail Semenovich, Lieutenant General – commander Twentieth Army

Kiriukhin, Nikolai Ivanovich, Major General – commander Twentieth Army

Kolpachki, Vladimir Iakovlevich, Lieutenant General – commander Thirtieth Army

Konev, Ivan Stepanovich, Colonel General, later General – commander Western Front, later Kalinin Front

Kononienko, Alexei, Major – intelligence officer, I Guards Cavalry Corps

Kovalev, Efim Maksimovich, Lieutenant Colonel – commander 28th Tank Brigade

Kreiser, Yakov Grigorievich, Major General – commander Second Guards Army

Kryukov, Vladimir Victorovich, Major General – commander II Guards Cavalry Corps

Kupryanov, Andrei Filiminovich, Major General – commander 215th Rifle Division

Kurkin, Alexei Vasilevich, Major General – commander of armoured and mechanised forces, Kalinin Front

Kurochkin, Pavel Alekseevich, Lieutenant General – commander Twentieth Army

Kursakov, Pavel Trofimovich, Colonel – commander 20th Cavalry Division

Lelyushenko, Dmitri Danilovich, General – commander Thirtieth Army

Lukinov, Mikhail Ivanovich – junior artillery officer, Kalinin Front

Lykov, Ivan Semenovich – tank crewman

Malakhov, Ksenofont Mikhailovich, Colonel – deputy commander Thirty-Ninth Army

Malygin, Konstantin Alekseevich, Lieutenant Colonel – commander 28th Tank Brigade, later commander armoured and mechanised forces, Third Shock Army

Managarov, Ivan Mefodevich, Major General – commander VII Cavalry Corps, later commander Forty-First Army

Maslennikov, Ivan Ivanovich, Lieutenant General – commander Thirty-Ninth Army

Oslikovsky, Nikolai Sergeevich, Colonel, later Major General – commander 2nd Guards Cavalry Division

Polyakov, Boris Petrovich, Lieutenant – signals officer, 17th Guards Rifle Division

Poplavsky, Stanislav Giliarovich, Major General – commander 220th Rifle Division

Popov, Iosif Ivanovich, Major General – deputy commander Forty-First Army

Povetkin, Stepan Ivanovich, Major General – commander VI 'Stalin Volunteer' Rifle Corps

Purkaev, Maksim Alekseevich, Lieutenant General – commander Third Shock Army, later Kalinin Front

Radó, Sandór – spy codenamed 'Dora'

Reyter, Maks Andreevich, Lieutenant General – commander Twentieth Army

Rodin, Georgii Semenovich, Major General – commander Second Tank Army

Rokossovsky, Konstantin Konstantinovich, General – commander Sixteenth Army

Romanenko, Prokofiy Logvinovich, Lieutenant General – commander Second Tank Army

Rössler, Rudolf – spy codenamed 'Lucy'

Rotmistrov, Pavel Alekseevich, Colonel – commander 8th Tank Brigade

Rybalko, Pavel Semenovich, Major General – commander Third Tank Army

Samokhin, Ivan Klimentinovich, Colonel – commander 215th Mixed Aviation Division

Sazonov, Kuzma Ivanovich, Colonel – commander 373rd Rifle Division

Seleznev, Dmitrii Mikhailovich, Major General – commander Twenty-Second Army

Semenchenko, Kuzma Aleksandrovich, Major General – commander V Tank Corps

Shaposhnikov, Boris Mikhailovich, Marshal – chief of the general staff

Shevchenko, Aleksander Iosifovich, Lieutenant Colonel – commander 65th Tank Brigade

Shvetsov, Vasilii Ivanovich, Major General – commander Twenty-Ninth Army

Sinitsky, Afanasy Grigorievich, Colonel – intelligence officer, Kalinin Front

Sokolov, Sergei Vladimirovich, Major General – commander XI Cavalry Corps

Sokolovsky, Vasily Danilovich, Colonel General – chief of staff, Western Front, later commander Western Front

Solomatin, Mikhail Dmitrievich, Major General – commander I Mechanised Corps

Starchak, Ivan Georgievich – junior officer, airborne forces

Sytnik, Vladimir Vladimirovich, Colonel – commander 24th Tank Brigade

Tarasov, German Fedorovich, Major General – commander Forty-First Army

Timoshenko, Semyon Konstantinovich, Marshal – commander Western Front, later commander Southwest Front/Southwest Direction

Vasilevsky, Alexander Mikhailovich, Marshal – chief of the general staff

Vlasov, Andrei Andreevich, Lieutenant General – commander Second Shock Army, later commander *Russische Befreiungsarmee*

Voloshin, Maxim Afanasevich, Colonel – chief of intelligence, Thirty-Ninth Army

Vostrukhov, Vladimir Ivanovich, Major General – commander Twenty-Second Army

Zakharov, Georgi Fedorovich, Major General – deputy commander Western Front

Zakharov, Matvei Vasilevich, Lieutenant General – chief of staff, Kalinin Front

Zhukov, Georgy Konstantinovich, General – commander Reserve Front, later Western Front/Western Direction

Zygin, Alexei Ivanovich, Major General – commander Thirty-Ninth Army

I Was Killed Near Rzhev

I was killed near Rzhev
In a nameless swamp,
In the 5th company, on the left
In a brutal raid.

I didn't hear the burst,
I didn't see that flash –
Just pitched into the abyss from the cliff –
And nothing above or below.

…

In the summer of a bitter year
I was killed. And of me –
No news, no reports
After that day.

…

I bequeath to you
To be happy in that life
And in your native land
To continue to serve with honour.

To grieve – with pride.
Without bowing your heads.
To rejoice – but without boasts
In the hour of victory itself.

And cherish its sanctity,
Brothers, your happiness –
In memory of your brother warrior
Who died for you.

Alexander Tvardovsky, 1946

INTRODUCTION

During the cold autumn of 1941, 19-year-old Boris Semenovich Gorbachevsky was living in the town of Kyshtym, close to the southern end of the Ural Mountains. In many respects, he was fortunate – his family were Jewish Ukrainians and had left Novograd Volynsk, a little to the west of Zhitomir, before the start of the war. Had they stayed in their old home, they would have shared the fate of millions of other Ukrainian Jews who were slaughtered before the winter of that same year.

As an apprentice lathe operator in a local metalwork company, the young Gorbachevsky was exempted from military service after the German invasion of the Soviet Union in June 1941, and was surprised when the local Communist Party officials dispatched him to a small village as an authorised representative of the Party. He found himself in a community that had changed little since the previous century:

> The village was called Babkino. There was no radio, no telephone, no newspapers, nor electricity – instead, we had kerosene lamps and candles … There were two broken tractors; the tractor driver would spend half a day trying to start one of them but despite his best efforts, he often didn't succeed. There were few men, with most serving in the army. There were many women, and the hungry way that they looked at me made me feel uncomfortable. As it grew colder, the cattle lived in the huts with their owners … The local shop seemed to have more mice than food. One building was the pride of the locals – a bathhouse with steam rooms in separate huts. It really seemed miraculous.
>
> The first tears of bereavement had already flowed, and many wives and mothers had attended funerals … [On days of mourning] nobody went to work. It troubled me but given the circumstances, I stayed silent and counted the days until I could leave the village. I felt awkward at these commemorations: alone and young – and not yet at the front. I couldn't explain to them that I was exempted since our factory produced military materiel.[1]

Like many men in many countries, Gorbachevsky wanted to serve in the military at the time of his nation's greatest need, and in December, as soon as he returned to Kyshtym from Babkino, he volunteered to join the army. The city of Chelyabinsk, about 49 miles (80km) to the southeast, was the home of the Chelyabinsk Tractor Plant, first built in 1933 and always intended for rapid switching to exclusively military output. As the German forces advanced and captured cities in the western parts of the USSR, Stalin authorised a massive transfer of industrial equipment to the east, and seven major industrial firms moved to Chelyabinsk, including the Kirov Plant from Moscow. The sprawling complex of factories producing tanks and other equipment became known as 'Tankograd', and by the end of the war had produced over 18,000 tanks.[2] Just days after the war with Germany began, the Red Army established a tank school in Chelyabinsk, and it was natural for Gorbachevsky to expect and hope that he would be assigned to the Soviet Union's armoured forces. Unfortunately, he was found to have red-green colour-blindness at his initial medical examination, which disqualified him from becoming a tank crewman. Instead, he was sent to the infantry school in Tyumen, 210 miles (338km) to the northeast of Chelyabinsk.

Meanwhile, the huge conflict between the Wehrmacht and the Red Army continued. Many of the Soviet formations that had started the war disappeared in the battles of the summer, smashed by the relentless German advance or caught up in great encirclements. Somehow, sufficient units managed to pull back to maintain a fragile front line, and the desperate need to restore these formations to a semblance of combat-worthy strength resulted in recruits like Gorbachevsky being rushed through abbreviated training programmes. Inevitably, these raw soldiers suffered the worst casualty rates when they were thrown into the fighting. It was the fate of Gorbachevsky and many hundreds of thousands of others to be caught up in one of the most brutal sectors of the entire war: the Rzhev Salient, where the interminable battles and massive loss of life earned the region the grim nickname among Red Army personnel of the 'meat grinder'.

Battles that drag on for long periods have a tendency to evolve far beyond their origins, in terms of scale and the objectives of the two sides. The Rzhev sector came under German control in the last thrusts towards Moscow, at a time when the Soviet capital seemed to be tantalisingly close; the subsequent Soviet counteroffensive tore huge holes in the German line, and when the front stabilised, the two exhausted armies warily faced each other on a front line that bent back on itself, creating a great salient that projected towards the north, just

70 miles (120km) to the west of Moscow. At first, the Red Army believed that the front line would quickly collapse and the momentum of the winter counteroffensive could be renewed, resulting in a rapid reconquest of the region; both sides were aware that the salient might serve as a springboard for a new German assault towards Moscow, and the elimination of the salient became a high priority for the Red Army, just as its retention became a similar priority for the Wehrmacht. As the fighting dragged on, the salient came to take on new meaning. The huge sacrifice of lives and materiel by the Red Army necessitated further attacks – the salient had to be destroyed to make any sense of the losses that had been suffered, and eliminating the salient became an obsession for senior Soviet commanders who saw its continued existence as a reminder of their earlier failures. For the Germans, retention of this bulwark to prevent rapid Soviet thrusts towards the west soon replaced any notions of a renewed offensive to capture Moscow. And ultimately, when enough blood had been spilled and the outcome of the war was decided in other sectors, the Germans quietly abandoned the territory that they had held for so long.

The legacy of the fighting around the salient is complex. Throughout the war, the Red Army continued to analyse its successes and failures and attempted to improve its performance. The bitter fighting around the salient undoubtedly contributed to the manner in which Soviet commanders planned *Bagration*, their massive summer offensive of 1944 that destroyed the German Army Group Centre, but although analysis of the repeated failures to overrun the salient was broadly correct, applying the lessons learned in a meaningful way often didn't follow that initial analysis. The determined German defence of the salient raised the profile of Walter Model, with Hitler demanding that other commanders show the same determination in defensive fighting. But when the history of the war on the Eastern Front was written, the battles for the salient were almost forgotten. The great sweeping advances and counterthrusts across Ukraine to the south, before and after Stalingrad, and the bitter struggle by the Red Army to break through to lift the siege of Leningrad far to the north, seemed to eclipse the long battles around Rzhev that resulted in few significant advances by either side. Soviet historiography struggled to deal with the terrible casualties suffered by the Red Army for so little gain around the salient, and it was safer just to downplay the entire sector. What mention was made of the battles was misleading: they were portrayed as a necessary adjunct to operations elsewhere, serving either to exhaust the Wehrmacht or to tie down its forces so that they couldn't be deployed in more important sectors. It wasn't until after the end of the Soviet era that the history of the Rzhev Salient was re-evaluated and the scale of the fighting became clear.

Battles are remembered for many reasons. Sometimes, they represent great turning points in history, or significant defeats or victories. In the west, we have become accustomed to remembering some battles, such as those of the First World War, purely to honour the memories of those who gave their lives. Even now, the memories of the battles around Rzhev are scarred by the need to justify the numbers who died, and are coloured by the historical legacy of commanders whose reputations were so great in the years that followed the war that questioning the conduct – or even the necessity – of the slaughter to the west of Moscow was unthinkable.

This is the complete story of the bloody history of the Rzhev Salient, from its formation to its final evacuation. It is also a testament to the terrible suffering of the soldiers of both sides, and the local civilians, who endured one of the most brutal and prolonged phases of the Second World War.

CHAPTER 1

BARBAROSSA AND *TAIFUN*

Barbarossa, the German invasion of the Soviet Union, began on 22 June 1941. The expectation in German circles was that just as the Wehrmacht had triumphed first over Poland and then in the west, it would repeat its success on a far larger scale. The Soviet Union would be destroyed, Bolshevism exterminated, and Germany would have sufficient resources and territory to establish an unassailable superiority over any conceivable enemies. At first, the rapid advance of the panzer groups seemed to suggest that the operation would unfold as planned, but gradually, reality began to diverge from the anticipated successes.

In many respects, Germany was not ready for war on the huge scale that developed in the Soviet Union. In every operation to date, there had been a large element of gambling in terms of resources. With almost no indigenous German oil production, fuel in particular was always in short supply, and the invasion of Poland and the thrust across Belgium and northern France to the English Channel consumed alarming amounts of stockpiled fuel. Those stockpiles were carefully rebuilt prior to *Barbarossa*, but a war on this scale had to be concluded rapidly; Germany lacked the industrial support and raw materials that would be required for sustained warfare across the vast spaces of the Soviet Union. Nor were industrial resources the only consideration. German industry was suffering from increasingly severe shortages of workers due to the numbers of men serving in uniform. A rapid victory was required so that significant numbers of men could be demobilised and made available for employment elsewhere. Any setback in the coming war with the Soviet Union, however small, threatened to exacerbate all of these problems.

To some extent, such setbacks had actually been predicted by German planners. Generalleutnant Friedrich Paulus, who would later play such a large role in the

German defeat at Stalingrad, was a staff officer serving in the German General Staff in the months leading up to the invasion of the Soviet Union and helped conduct a detailed wargame that simulated the coming attack. This demonstrated that German advances on Leningrad in the north, on Moscow in the centre, and into Ukraine in the south would proceed on diverging axes, creating significant gaps between the three thrusts. There would come a time, the wargame predicted, when army group commanders might seek to divert their mechanised units from the axes of advance in order to close these gaps. The wargamers advised that any such diversion would be detrimental to the operation – objectives had to be reached and secured before the onset of winter, and any delays on the main axes of advance had to be avoided. The implication of this conclusion showed just what a great gamble was being taken: the invasion could only succeed if open flanks were left exposed, and such risks were only justifiable if the Wehrmacht had accurate intelligence about the size and capability of its opponent.

During the preparations for *Barbarossa*, the task of gathering information on the Red Army was in the hands of *Fremde Heere Ost* ('Foreign Armies East' or *FHO*), a section of *Oberkommando des Heeres* ('Army High Command' or *OKH*). The head of this department from 1939 to 1941 was Oberst Eberhard Kinzel, and his qualifications for such an important task were limited. He served as an infantry officer in the First World War and remained in the army in the years that followed, designated as adjutant to an infantry training battalion. He was frequently detached from this unit and given brief assignments elsewhere, and was the official escort of a group of Soviet officers who visited Berlin in 1929. In 1933 he commenced a three-year assignment as assistant military attaché in Warsaw before returning to the infantry, but he had no formal training in intelligence issues and didn't speak Russian. Under his leadership, *FHO* was tasked specifically with obtaining information about the Soviet Union in July 1940 shortly after the defeat of France; at the time, Hitler believed that Britain would soon be forced to the negotiating table, and had already started to look to the east. But despite its mission to gather data on all potential enemies to the east, Kinzel's department had very little hard information. Some senior officers regarded the reports from *FHO* as adequate – Alfred Jodl, who served as the chief of operations staff in *Oberkommando der Wehrmacht* ('Armed Forces High Command' or *OKW*), later commented that he was generally satisfied with the intelligence produced by Kinzel.[1] Others were far more critical about the quality of both the raw data received by *FHO* and the briefings that it produced based on that data. Major Heinz Hiemenz, one of Kinzel's subordinates, felt that 'the bulk of intelligence reports that we received were just mist and fog.'[2]

These reports were based upon five main sources: radio intercepts; reports of German agents and travellers in the Baltic States; the reports of German military attachés; information from the intelligence services of Germany's allies; and from the interrogation of Soviet defectors and deserters. One of the most trusted sources of information was a network of agents known by the codename 'Max'. The network was led by Richard Kauder and included a number of White Russian émigrés, and was based in the Bulgarian capital Sofia, but after the war it was revealed that many of the agents working for 'Max' were in fact Soviet agents; while much of the data provided by the network was accurate, some of it was also very misleading.[3]

With no better sources of information, Germany's leaders worked with an estimated Red Army strength of 20 armies, fielding 150 rifle divisions, between 32 and 36 cavalry divisions, and 36 motorised or mechanised brigades. These were regarded as poorly led, and the entire Soviet Union was seen as a rotten edifice that would be unable to survive the first blows of the German invasion. The huge purges of Red Army officers in the 1930s had eliminated thousands of experienced leaders, and the performance of Soviet troops in the brief war with Finland in the winter of 1939–40 seemed to confirm that the Red Army would be incapable of standing up to the Wehrmacht. Although it was clear that steps were being taken to remedy the failures seen in the war against Finland, a report produced by Kinzel in January 1941 summarised the situation:

> The clumsiness, schematism, [and] avoidance of decisions and responsibility has not changed … The weaknesses of the Red Army reside in the clumsiness of officers of all ranks, the clinging to formulae, insufficient training according to modern standards, the aversion to responsibility, and the marked insufficiency of organisation in all aspects.[4]

A further report followed in May 1941, listing the forces available to the Red Army facing the planned German invasion as 130 rifle divisions, 21 cavalry divisions, five armoured divisions, and 36 motorised or mechanised brigades. There was no mention of Soviet forces deployed in the Soviet Far East, other than a statement that 'a substantial reinforcement [of the European theatre] from Asia is improbable on political grounds', though there was no explanation for why this would be the case. The report concluded that the Red Army would attempt to conduct its defence using the field fortifications along the existing frontier, to a depth of perhaps 18 miles (30km).[5] The clear implication was that once this frontier belt had been penetrated, the Red Army would be helpless and German victory would swiftly follow.

If the original timetable of *Barbarossa* was ambitious, it was made worse by a delayed start. The plans that were drawn up in early 1941 called for a start date in mid-May, but the diversion of German forces to occupy Yugoslavia forced a postponement. Even had the Yugoslav situation not necessitated the transfer of German units, Germany's main two allies in the coming invasion – Finland in the north and Romania in the south – would not be ready for a start date in May, and wet weather further hampered preparations.[6] Nonetheless, when it began, *Barbarossa* unfolded at a staggering pace. The German panzer groups seemed unstoppable and raced towards their distant objectives, meeting in great encirclement operations that resulted in the destruction of large numbers of Soviet divisions. But the gaps between the German army groups that had been predicted by the wargamers soon began to be felt, and on 19 July, less than a month after the invasion had commenced, Hitler issued Führer Directive 33. The two panzer groups operating with Army Group Centre were to stop their advance towards Moscow and priority was to be given to dealing with the flanks. In particular, there seemed to be a great opportunity in Ukraine; a rapid thrust by German mechanised forces might lead to the envelopment and destruction of several Soviet armies in and around Kiev.

The threats and opportunities on the flanks of the German advance were not the only reasons for Hitler calling a temporary halt to the drive towards Moscow. German infantry divisions were labouring to catch up with the panzer groups. General Gotthard Heinrici, commander of XLIII Corps, was assigned different infantry divisions during the early phases of *Barbarossa*. He wrote to his wife during the third week of the invasion about both the conditions in which his men were operating and the huge gaps that were opening up between the infantry and the mechanised units:

> Leaden sky, 40°C … impenetrable clouds of dust, deep sand … We have fallen far behind. We march 30 to 35km [18 to 21 miles] every day; we can hardly force the horses through the sand, but we need to go further … Our motorised forces fight 200km [120 miles] in front of us, on their own.[7]

The decision to pause while the infantry caught up resulted in furious arguments between the panzer commanders, who wished to continue their advance, and their superiors. Even as these debates about the rights and wrongs of Führer Directive 33 continued, the Red Army suddenly launched a series of powerful attacks on the German Army Group Centre near Smolensk. Ultimately, these attacks proved to be failures and resulted in another encirclement and the destruction of the Soviet Sixteenth and Nineteenth Armies; many of the encircled soldiers were now placed under the control of Lieutenant General Pavel Alekseevich Kurochkin, commander of Twentieth Army, and he successfully broke out to the east, but about 300,000 prisoners were taken.[8] Nonetheless, the battle inflicted substantial losses on the Germans and demonstrated that the Red Army was far from finished by its defeats in the frontier battles, as Kinzel had anticipated. The delay imposed on German preparations for an advance towards Moscow may have been crucial in the battles that were to follow.

It was clear to everyone that this war was different from any that had preceded it. The intention was to do far more than defeat an opposing nation: Hitler intended the utter destruction of the Soviet Union, its political culture, and even its people. There were longstanding proposals for an expansion of German hegemony and culture towards the east stretching back over several centuries, and the expansion of Germany played a large part in Hitler's plans; in *Mein Kampf*, he wrote:

> Germany must find the courage to gather our people and their strength for an advance along the road that will lead this people from its present restricted living space to new land and soil, and hence also free it from the danger of vanishing from the earth or of serving others as a slave nation.[9]

The overall plans for the subjugation of the conquered Soviet Union became known as *Generalplan Ost*. The precise details of this are not known, because most documents relating to the plan were deliberately destroyed in the closing months of the war. According to testimony given at the Nuremberg Trials, responsibility for drawing up the plan lay with Heinrich Himmler, head of the SS; Standartenführer Hans Ehlich told the tribunals that he had been responsible for drawing up and collating the plan.[10] Once the Wehrmacht had taken control of new territories, they would be handed over to civilian authorities and exploited ruthlessly. The Soviet urban population was estimated to have grown by about 25 million since the First World War, and the 'elimination' of these Soviet citizens would create substantial surpluses of food that could be transferred to the Reich.[11] Many, such as the Jews and Roma, would be exterminated or worked to death, while others, including most Slavs, would face a ban on medical care and reduced rations, which would ultimately result in death through starvation. Many would simply be expelled from former Soviet cities and driven east into Siberia to fend for themselves. Such policies were made explicit in a document known as the Hunger Plan, which was drawn up in March 1941.[12]

Even before the conquest of the new eastern territories was complete, Hitler intended the conduct of the war to be very different from that of the previous campaigns. He made this very clear to his subordinates, and General Franz Halder, chief of staff at *OKH*, summarised in his diary on 30 March 1941 a meeting between Hitler and senior figures in which the Führer spoke for over two hours:

> Clash of two ideologies. Crushing denunciation of Bolshevism, identified with a social criminality. Communism is an enormous danger for our future. We must forget the concept of comradeship between soldiers. A Communist is no comrade before or after the battle. This is a war of extermination. If we do not grasp this, we shall still beat the enemy, but thirty years later we shall again have to fight the Communist foe. We do not wage war to preserve the enemy ...
>
> War against Russia: Extermination of the Bolshevist commissars and of the Communist intelligentsia ... Formation of a new intellectual class must be prevented. A primitive Socialist intelligentsia is all that is needed ... This is no job for military courts. The individual troop commanders must know the issues at stake. They must be leaders in this fight ... Commissars and GPU* men are criminals and must be dealt with as such ...
>
> This war will be very different from the war in the west. In the east, harshness today means lenience in the future. Commanders must make the sacrifice of overcoming their personal scruples.[13]

This led to the Commissar Order of 6 June 1941, formally titled *Richtlinien für die Behandlung Politischer Kommissare* ('Guidelines for the treatment of political commissars'). Commissars were to be identified by the red stars on their uniforms and were to be separated from other prisoners immediately; they were to be executed without the need for any further legal process. Early drafts of this order included a paragraph intended to prevent excessive use of the order, but this clause was removed before the order was distributed.[14] There can be little doubt that this order was regarded as at least controversial, if not illegal – it was distributed only to senior officers, who were ordered to pass on instructions either verbally or to write their own versions of the order. Most senior officers showed little inclination to disobey this instruction. On the eve of the invasion,

---

Gosudarstvennoe Politischeskoe Upravlenie, 'State Political Directorate', the intelligence service and secret police – this designation was already obsolete by 1923.

Generaloberst Erich Hoepner, commander of Fourth Panzer Group, told his subordinates:

> [The coming conflict] is an essential part of the German people's struggle for existence ... The struggle must aim at the annihilation of today's Russia and must therefore be waged with unparalleled harshness ... [We are fighting for] the defence of European culture against Muscovite-Asiatic inundation and the repulse of Jewish Bolshevism ... No adherents of the present Russian-Bolshevik system are to be spared.[15]

After the war, many senior Wehrmacht figures attempted to claim that they had opposed the Commissar Order and other similar instructions, but in most cases these denials have been proved to be false; Erich von Manstein, who commanded armies and army groups with great distinction, was successfully prosecuted for passing on the Commissar Order to his subordinates. Many – perhaps most – German officers seem to have had little difficulty in accepting the nature of the war that Hitler intended. A variety of themes contributed to this: throughout the 19th and 20th centuries, anti-Semitism was widespread throughout Europe, even in Germany where the Jewish population was perhaps more assimilated than in many other regions; there was a widespread fear of Bolshevism among the officer class; and Slavs were generally regarded by Germans as inferior to themselves. The language used by men like Heinrici in their letters home is telling:

> We Germans particularly dislike the Russian's deceitful way of combat. He is rarely seen in the open country and if so, then only hidden in cornfields. Most of the time he crawls through the forest, through bushes and through the swamps. These people are glued to the unclear terrain like lice and one cannot get rid of them even by combing the area twice.[16]

At this stage of the war, there was little consideration about the manner in which brutal German policies were hardening Soviet resistance – the campaign was going well, and victory remained just a matter of time. But Heinrici's letters show a creeping sense of doubt beginning to emerge even in early August:

> We are amazed about how tough the Russian fights. His units are half destroyed, but he stuffs in new men and they attack again. I have not the slightest idea how the Russians do it ... Our swift advance has turned into a slow stumble. It is

unforeseeable how far into Russia we get this way, as long as resistance is as fierce as it has been so far. Maybe it will collapse one day. At the moment, however, it is all in limbo … We will have to spend the winter here being involved in positional warfare along an enormous front line. Nice prospects.[17]

After a lengthy delay in July and August, Army Group Centre's panzer forces carried out the attacks ordered by Hitler to secure the flanks. The encirclement at Kiev cost the Red Army a staggering 700,000 men killed, wounded or taken prisoner.[18] Despite these successes, many German soldiers were disquieted by the unexpected strength of their opponents. In particular, the appearance of increasing numbers of T-34 tanks was a particularly unwelcome development. Karl Volleth was a Gefreiter (corporal) in 4th Panzer Division:

It was 13 August 1941. At dawn we drove out, our platoon as spearhead and our vehicle as point. We had a sixth man on board as an interpreter. He made himself comfortable behind me on the machinery housing. The weather was bad and visibility was poor. With my hull machine-gun, I engaged a few Soviet infantrymen who formed a rearguard. There was no sign of tougher resistance. A large village came into sight.

After a short observation halt we drove into the place. In the centre of the village we signalled the spearhead platoon to follow us slowly. We soon heard the sounds of engines behind us. Our tank commander turned – and the blood drained from his face. Two heavy Soviet tanks, T-34s, were driving up to us as if they were on our side. We immediately turned around and drove up to them, stopping right in front of them and separated by no more than 5m. The Russian fired first but he hadn't brought his gun to bear on us and missed. We then fired a *Panzergranate-40*: a hit on the glacis plate! Sparks flew. But the T-34 calmly turned its turret and shot a second time and missed. But now I could see through the viewer that its turret was pointing right at us. The next shot would inevitably hit us if we didn't get him first. But that was unfortunately out of the question. Our gun loader tried in vain to eject the spent cartridge case from the gun. Misfortune seldom occurs in isolation, and it was totally jammed.

Our commander leaped out of the vehicle and tried to disable the colossus with a hand grenade. For the tenth time, the translator asked me what was happening. I hurriedly replied with a touch of gallows humour: 'You'll find out soon enough!' Then I let my machine-gun point upward, pulled up my legs and rolled myself up like a hedgehog. Then – a numbing crash and the entire vehicle seemed to fill with flames and the radio equipment lay at my feet. I shouted, 'Out! We're on fire!' Meanwhile, our translator had realised what was happening. He made a great leap through the loader's hatch into the open air without touching the track cover at all. I followed him ...

We carried our driver, who was badly wounded, to cover. He had managed to get himself out of the vehicle. I slipped through the houses behind us to seek out the armoured ambulance. I soon found it. Our staff doctor ran back with me as the armoured ambulance had shed a track.

When we got back, both T-34s were lying by the side of the road in flames. I climbed back into our tank and tried to move it a little to the side, but I couldn't because the direct hit had struck the gearbox.

The sounds of fighting slowly died down. Our troops pushed on. We remained by our tank, which although immobile was still able to fire, waiting for a towing vehicle. Once again we had a moment of terror. I was standing on the tank – and there was a huge blow. Shrapnel flew past my ears, and there was another roar, and still again. I immediately jumped away off the vehicle and crouched under it where I found my similarly dumbfounded comrades. Aircraft? Unlikely. Stalin organ [the German name for the *Katyusha* rocket system]? Another new weapon? No, it was something far less threatening. We had allowed ourselves to be frightened by something trivial. The ammunition in the burning T-34 was cooking off. It was a spectacular firework display.[19]

The evolution of anti-tank ammunition shows how German designers reacted to the realities of war. The *Panzergranate-40* was an armour-piercing round introduced in 1940 as a result of the first experiences of combat against heavy enemy tanks in the campaign in Belgium and France. Its predecessor, the *Panzergranate-39*, consisted of a ballistic hood and a soft iron cap; most of the body of the shell was made of steel, with an explosive core that was designed to detonate after penetration of the target. When they encountered heavy French and British tanks, German gunners were dismayed to find that these rounds often failed to penetrate their targets, hence the need for a new type of ammunition that would permit existing anti-tank guns to continue in service until newer and heavier guns were available. The new *Panzergranate-40* had no explosive content, and its core was made of tungsten or a tungsten-steel alloy that was less likely to break up on impact. Behind the ballistic cap was a soft steel element, designed to deform on impact against the side of the target, and the hardened core would then penetrate through the 'plug' that was formed – this reduced the risk of the round bouncing off sloped armour. The penetrative power of the newer round at short range was greater; the 50mm L/42 gun of the Panzer III variants in production in 1941 could penetrate 54mm of armour with the old *Panzergranate-39* at a range of 100m, whereas with the *Panzergranate-40* it could penetrate 96mm. This advantage fell off rapidly with range – at 500m, the respective penetrations were 46mm and 58mm, and at greater ranges the newer round became too inaccurate. As the war continued, tungsten shortages forced German industry to resort to a variety of steel alloys, and tank and gun crews increasingly complained of the rounds disintegrating on impact.

The thrust towards Moscow might be running behind schedule, but the destruction of the Red Army's divisions and armies suggested that the end of the campaign was in sight. The Red Army had resisted far beyond the original 18 miles (30km) depth anticipated by *FHO*, but its losses were close to the total estimated strength of the Red Army prior to the invasion. By this stage, it was clear that Kinzel's reports from *FHO* were inaccurate, but Soviet losses were so great that the Red Army had to be on its last legs. Undaunted by its past failures, *FHO* continued to produce optimistic reports – in August, it informed Hitler and *OKH*:

> The entire strength [of the Red Army] is inadequate either for a major offensive or for the creation of a continuous defensive front line ... The number of new formations has reached its maximum strength and virtually no additional new formations need be expected ... The available Soviet forces suffice only to retard the German advance against the bases essential for the survival of the army and the state, in the hope of prolonging the campaign to the period of bad weather, in order to gain a breathing spell in which to refurbish and enlarge the armed forces using British and American material assistance. Owing to the unbroken duration of the battles and the intercession of new, heavier casualties, the further diminution of the fighting morale of the Red Army is to be counted upon.[20]

Some had their doubts. Halder wrote in his diary:

> Our last reserves have been committed. Any regrouping now is merely a shifting of forces on the baseline within individual army group sectors ...
>
> The whole situation makes it increasingly plain that we have underestimated the Russian colossus, who consistently prepared for war with that utterly ruthless determination so characteristic of totalitarian states ... At the outset of the war, we reckoned with about 200 enemy divisions. Now we have already counted 360. These divisions indeed are not armed and equipped according to our standards,

and their tactical leadership is often poor. But there they are, and we smash a dozen of them, but the Russians simply put up another dozen. The time factor favours them, as they are near their own resources, while we are moving further and further away from ours. And so our troops, sprawled over an immense front line, without any depth, are subjected to the incessant attacks of the enemy. Sometimes these are successful, because too many gaps must be left open in these enormous spaces.[21]

Leaving aside the irony of Halder marvelling at how a 'totalitarian' state had prepared for war – and it should be mentioned that the equally totalitarian German state had failed to match Soviet preparations – it is remarkable that Halder could note this huge failure of intelligence, yet pass on without comment – there was no suggestion of any changes to *FHO* or any other steps to ensure that similar mistakes weren't made in future. Like almost everyone else in the German chain of command, Halder remained confident that final victory had to be close. It was, surely, impossible for any nation to suffer the losses that had been inflicted upon the Soviet Union and still survive.

Accordingly, the Wehrmacht prepared itself for one final offensive. Supply lines were fully stretched, and every unit was far from establishment strength; the men were exhausted, and despite detailed planning to convert the Soviet railways to the same gauge as those to the west, work was far behind schedule – not least due to manpower shortages – and the minimum numbers of trains required to provide food, fuel and munitions to front-line units rarely arrived. Everything would have to be committed to the offensive, codenamed *Taifun* ('Typhoon'). But this would be the last assault before final victory. There was no need to hold back reserves. One last effort was all that it would take.

The terrain over which the battle would be fought, and where hundreds of thousands of men would fight and die over the following 18 months, is generally flat, with small plateaus and a few lines of low hills, hardly any of which constitute a significant barrier. Only in the Kaluga region are there some relatively deep gullies and river valleys that might hinder troop movements. At the time, about a quarter of the region was forested, particularly in the centre and to the northeast; these forests were mainly in low-lying areas around rivers, lakes and swampy regions, and these formed a far more formidable barrier to troop movements than any high ground, particularly as few of the waterways had seen any significant attempt to stop them flooding or forming extended marshes. The region between the Volga River in the north and the Oka River to the south is sometimes referred to as the 'Smolensk gates' in Russian accounts and has been regarded as a traditional line of approach for armies threatening Moscow from the west – in the very centre of this area is Borodino, where Napoleon's troops fought a bloody engagement with the Russian Army in 1812. On that occasion, the invaders went on to occupy Moscow, but were forced to commence a disastrous retreat shortly after. In 1941, the ghosts of that campaign lurked in the minds of soldiers and officers on both sides.

The forces that gathered for the attack on Moscow under the overall control of Field Marshal Fedor von Bock's Army Group Centre were impressive. Three of the Wehrmacht's four panzer groups (renamed panzer armies at the end of 1941) were present, with three infantry armies. Air support would be provided by the Luftwaffe's *Luftflotte 2*, but like ground formations, its squadrons were badly depleted. Over 1,600 German aircraft had been lost during the fighting of the preceding months, and over 1,000 were awaiting repairs – many of these were victims of Germany's inadequate preparations for prolonged war, with critical shortages of spare parts hampering the abilities of the Luftwaffe's repair teams. Even at the start of the operation, some of the panzer formations reported that they had limited fuel supplies. Overall command of the German Army was, nominally at least, in the hands of Field Marshal Walther von Brauchitsch, but in reality he was little more than a messenger between Hitler and the army group commanders.

Opposing the Wehrmacht were the battered forces of the Red Army. The northern sector was defended by the forces of Lieutenant General Ivan Stepanovich Konev's Western Front, with eight armies; to the south was Bryansk Front, commanded by Lieutenant General Andrei Ivanovich Eremenko, with a further three armies. Between them, they collectively numbered about 1.25 million men supported by about 1,000 tanks and 7,600 guns. The total numbers of German troops facing the Red Army appeared greater on paper, numbering nearly 2 million men, but German formations had far larger rear area elements than their Soviet counterparts, and the number of combatants in the front line was probably fairly similar.[22]

Although the reports of *FHO* about the strength of the Red Army might have been wildly inaccurate, the Wehrmacht had good information about the damage that its opponent had suffered, both inflicted by Stalin before the war and the Wehrmacht since the summer. During the 1930s, the sweeping purges of its officers caused huge damage. Experienced men at all levels were executed or imprisoned, and those who replaced them were required to adhere rigidly to political orthodoxy. One of the early victims of the purges was Marshal Mikhail Nikolayevich Tukhachevsky, a leading theoretician in the Red Army. It remains unclear whether he invented the concept of deep operation or championed the ideas of others, but together with Georgii Samoilovich Isserson, he shaped the Red Army to conduct multi-echelon operations that would extend through the full depth of the enemy's position, with mechanised forces exploiting initial tactical breakthroughs made by shock armies.[23] Although the concept of deep battle remained in place after the purges, it was often regarded with suspicion, as it was associated with officers condemned and executed as traitors. Consequently, the new officer corps that took up posts throughout the military after the purges showed more allegiance to political theory and control from above than to the flexible thinking and independent decision-making required to make deep operations a success. The manner in which any independence of action had been eliminated from the Red Army contributed greatly to its inability to react quickly to the fast-moving German attacks, and by the beginning of *Taifun*, the high casualties of preceding months eliminated almost all of the officers who had survived the purges of the pre-war years. The soldiers of the Soviet Union remained tough and determined to resist the Germans, but the degree to which they would be able to do so was highly questionable. Heinrici's assessment in a letter to his family in mid-September was perhaps typical of the views of many Germans in the Soviet Union:

> The cities are almost completely deserted. In the villages only women, children and old people are left ... According to our prisoners, huddles of people crowd the railway stations and beg pieces of bread from soldiers. The casualties caused by the war among these uprooted people due to sickness and exhaustion are, in my opinion, as high as the bloody [battlefield] losses. Maybe this situation, together with the military defeat, will cause an opposition against the ruling system in Russia one day. However, as I mentioned before, there is no sign of it so far. The Soviets are greatly feared everywhere, their terror is without mercy, so that no one dares to protest. Besides, large parts of the youth are committed Communists who think that these measures are necessary to rule a primitive people like the Russians.[24]

Like many of his contemporaries, Heinrici showed no understanding for the realities of the changes that had swept the former Russian Empire during and after the Revolution. Undoubtedly, Stalin's imposition of his system upon a population that showed varying degrees of willingness to accept Communism was often brutal and resulted in huge numbers of dead as a result of deliberately exacerbated famines, and tens of thousands of others were executed after little or no legal process or dispatched to Siberia, where they died far from their homes; but at the same time, literacy in the Soviet Union increased far beyond the levels of 1914. The housing of workers might be primitive by the standards of other parts of Europe, but it too was a major improvement on what had existed before. Despite the unquestionable impact of patronage within the Soviet system, there were opportunities for able citizens from poor backgrounds to progress far further than they would have dreamed in the days of the tsars. In such circumstances, it is hardly surprising that so many younger people remained staunch supporters of a system under which they had personally benefited. Nor is there any recognition by Heinrici that the suffering and deaths due to people fleeing their cities would be far worse if Hitler's intentions to 'eliminate' 25 million urban Soviet citizens were fully implemented.

Many of the officers who would ultimately lead the Red Army to victory were beginning to emerge from the heat of battle. Konev had served as an artillery NCO in the First World War before joining the Bolsheviks and survived the purges of the 1930s unscathed. He became commander of Nineteenth Army when it was created at the beginning of the war and led it in the fighting near Smolensk in August 1941; when his forces were surrounded, he succeeded in gathering many of his men together and joined Kurochkin's breakout to the east. His army was brought back to combat strength by the addition of new divisions, and on 11 September Stalin assigned him to command of Western Front. Eremenko was another First World War veteran and commanded Sixteenth Army when hostilities with Germany broke out. The commander of Western Front at the beginning of the war, General Dmitri Grigorievich Pavlov, was blamed by Stalin for the disastrous defeats suffered by the Red Army close to the frontier and was arrested, charged with treason and executed; Eremenko took over command until the arrival of Marshal Semyon Konstantinovich Timoshenko a few days later. The two men alternated as commanders of Western Front for much of the summer, and Eremenko led the Front's armies in the fighting at Smolensk. He played a leading role in coordinating the escape of the encircled elements of his Front, and after the conclusion of the battle he was given command of the neighbouring Bryansk Front. He was an experienced officer with a long history of commanding cavalry and mechanised units, and was critical of the rigid thinking of many of his subordinates. Almost immediately on taking command, he issued instructions through his chief of staff to improve the training of men in combat against tanks and to take steps to ensure better cooperation between artillery and infantry. Recognition of these problems was important, but the implementation of such orders in the midst of intense fighting was a different matter.

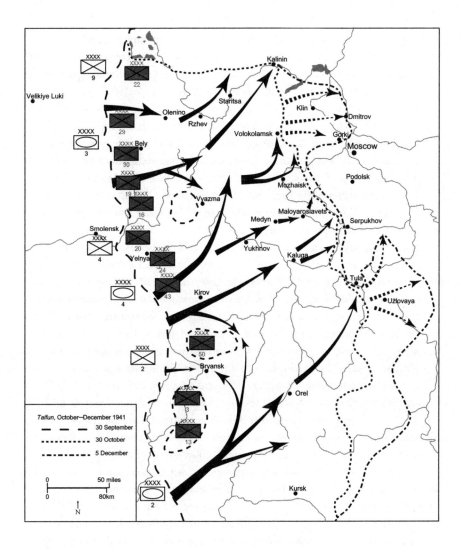

On 2 October, in what Halder described in his war diary – from East Prussia, several hundred miles from the battlefield – as 'sparkling fall weather', *Taifun* began. The Red Army knew that an offensive was coming, but preparations to oppose it were far from complete. With barely a sideways glance, the three German panzer groups burst through the Soviet defences. The central thrust by Fourth Panzer Group then diverged into attacks to the north and south, meeting with the two flanking panzer groups with the intention of creating two

encirclements, at Bryansk in the south and Vyazma in the north. Leading General Heinz Guderian's Second Panzer Group in the south was 4th Panzer Division, charging towards the city of Orel. Oberleutnant Arthur Vollschlaeger was the commander of its panzer regiment's 6th Company:

We approached Fominka, a small village a couple of hundred metres from a strip of woodland, behind which – according to my map – there should be a bridge. If there were any defences around Orel, this bridge would be garrisoned. Under the cover of bushes at the edge of the village, we took up a firing position. I ordered Jüppner to give me covering fire while we attempted to rush over the bridge. Suddenly all hell broke loose. There were eight anti-tank guns to the left and two to the right of the road that led to the bridge – two of them were heavy guns. Two of our tanks were shot up. But there was no turning back now. Jüppner and I charged at the anti-tank positions at full throttle. Right under their barrels we drove along the forest road and passed through another piece of woodland in which a Red Army camp was located and, now sheltered by the trees, found ourselves at the Orel garrison's training area. There were still plenty of men undergoing training there. Beyond we could see the airfield and planes taking off and landing. We stayed there under cover for a couple of hours, observing and sending back reports. There was no response from the Soviet side, just the planes flying over us constantly, almost close enough to touch.

Finally, our battalion reached us. They had overcome the anti-tank defences with motorcycle infantry and artillery. Orders for a further attack were issued. My crews weren't particularly pleased to find themselves at the point of the attack once more, as we had already lost two tanks and several good comrades were dead. In any case, we now had a combat strength of just four tanks.

The first attack objective was the road that led to a railway embankment enclosing the western edge of the city ... At top speed we raced towards our objective and quickly reached the town. According to my orders I was to halt here, but there was an old panzer expression – 'a stationary tank on the battlefield is a dead tank!' So we drove on. There was a railway underpass in front of us, leading to the city. There was only one thing for it – through and onwards! And so it went. And now there lay before us, wide and open, the main road through Orel. We drove on.

Life in the city was continuing as normal. As the citizens of Orel saw us, they fled in terror to their houses or into side streets. Rattling and swaying, ringing their bells in vain, tramcars were still trying to drive past. An explosive shell right before the leading carriage brought them to a halt ... The frenzied drive continued to a big railway bridge. We halted briefly to check the bridge for demolition charges – there weren't any. A tank stayed there on guard.[25]

It was a stunning success and seemed to be the forerunner of even greater victories. The 'sparkling' weather turned to snow on 7 October – the day that the German armoured pincers met to complete the Vyazma encirclement – but swiftly melted, turning the landscape into a muddy quagmire. The pincers closed around the Soviet armies in the two pockets, but fighting continued for several days, with Soviet troops slipping away to the east in groups ranging from just a few men to entire divisions – the southern German pincer was troubled more by these units marching east and clashing with the panzer formations than by resistance to the east and northeast. But despite these breakouts, the losses suffered by the Red Army seemed to justify the confidence in German circles that victory was close – about half a million Soviet soldiers were killed, wounded or taken prisoner.[26]

Just one day after the commencement of *Taifun*, Hitler gave a speech at the Sportpalast in Berlin: 'I can say that this enemy [the Soviet Union] is already broken and will never rise again.'[27] The German Propaganda Ministry announced on 9 October that the final destruction of the Soviet forces defending Moscow was 'imminent' and there seemed little reason to doubt this. Nonetheless, the battered Soviet armies that had been overwhelmed at the beginning of the month were now painfully regrouping. There were also changes at higher levels, and many of the senior officers who would dominate the Red Army for the rest of the war were summoned to Moscow. General Georgy Konstantinovich Zhukov was, like all his generation, a veteran of the First World War, having served as a cavalry NCO in the tsar's army before joining the Red Army in 1918. He became a cavalry officer during the Russian Civil War, distinguishing himself both in action against the White Russians and in the suppression of anti-Bolshevik peasant uprisings. In the purges of the 1930s, he was accused of failing to identify enemies of the people due to political shortsightedness, but he escaped punishment.[28] Rising steadily through the upper ranks of the Red Army, he commanded LVII Special Corps – soon to be renamed the First Army Group – on the Mongolian frontier in 1939 and showed characteristic ruthlessness in reorganising his units to improve their efficiency. His methods were often brutal – Pyotor Grigorievich Grigorenko, who was serving as a staff officer with Zhukov's immediate superior, later recalled that his headquarters received a regular series of reports of severe punishments:

At this time, there were already 17 men condemned to death. It wasn't just lawyers who were shocked by the details of the cases. In every case, there was either a report from the chief of staff, in which he wrote 'So-and-so received such-and-such an order and did not follow it' and a resolution on the report of 'Tribunal. Judge. To be shot' or a note from Zhukov: 'So-and-so received such-and-such an order from me personally and did not carry it out. Judgement: to be shot'. A verdict, nothing more. No interrogation protocols, no investigations, no examination. Nothing at all. Just a single piece of paper and a sentence.[29]

When the Japanese Army crossed the Khalkin Gol River in 1939, Zhukov's forces conducted an efficient defence in depth before transitioning smoothly to a counteroffensive, inflicting a major defeat on the Japanese – the battle is thought to be a major reason why Japan chose not to attack the Soviet Union in 1941. Zhukov was awarded the title of Hero of the Soviet Union and returned to Europe the following year, taking part in the Soviet occupation of Bessarabia and Bukovina before becoming chief of the general staff and Deputy People's Commissar for Defence. These roles covered a huge range of responsibilities, including the coordination with the Soviet Union's military industries in order to produce modern weaponry for the army. When war broke out, Zhukov was made commander of the Reserve Front before being sent to Leningrad to stabilise the situation in the north. He was now summoned back to Moscow to take control once more of the Reserve Front behind the Red Army's front line. As he took up his command, Zhukov found himself in familiar territory:

> As we passed through Protva, I remembered my childhood. I knew the whole of this area very well, as I had walked back and forth across it in my youth. Ten kilometres from Obninsky, where the headquarters of Reserve Front was located, was my home village of Strelkovka. My mother and my sister and her four children were there. How were they? What if we stopped by? No, it was impossible, there wasn't enough time. But what would happen to them if the Fascists came? What would they do with my loved ones if they found out they were related to a general of the Red Army? Surely they would be shot! At the first opportunity, they should be evacuated to Moscow.
>
> Two weeks later, German troops occupied the village of Strelkovka and the entire Ugodsko-Zavodskoy district. Fortunately, I managed to get my mother and my sister and her children to Moscow.[30]

On 13 October, Zhukov spoke to Stalin by telephone and learned that Stalin and *Stavka* – the Red Army high command – had decided to dissolve Reserve Front and allocate its forces to Western Front. Stalin wanted Zhukov to take command of the front, and Konev was moved to lead the forces defending Kalinin – at first as a subordinate of Zhukov, then as commander of the newly formed Kalinin Front. Zhukov immediately issued orders that his troops were to dig in and defend the 'Mozhaisk Defence Line', which ran from Kalinin in the north to Kaluga in the south. Some fortifications had been constructed in haste, despite being hampered by the weather, and positions of varying strength formed up to four distinct lines. But the recent losses suffered at the outset of the German attack had left the Red Army desperately short of men. Accordingly, Zhukov concentrated his forces to defend four key towns – Volokolamsk, Mozhaisk, Maloyaroslavets and Kaluga – while civilians were mobilised to construct extensive defences closer to Moscow.

On the same day, German infantry advanced to the railway line between Olenino in the west and Rzhev further east. By the end of the day, the Germans were just 15 miles (25km) from the centre of Rzhev. Spurred on by reports from aerial reconnaissance that Red Army units were attempting to withdraw over the Volga River via the bridges in Rzhev, the Germans resumed their advance during the night. The initial probe almost reached the outskirts before being driven back by energetic Soviet counterattacks, and fighting continued throughout 14 and 15 October in intermittent snow showers. The steady arrival of more German units tipped the balance in favour of the Wehrmacht, and the Red Army abandoned Rzhev late on 15 October. The city was home to about 54,000 people before the war; many had fled the approach of the Germans, and the remaining residents waited anxiously to see what the future held for them.

Among the armoured formations that had been concentrated for what was meant to be the final battle of the war against the Soviet Union was 19th Panzer Division, brought from Army Group North. It was held in the Smolensk area when the assault began – a welcome pause for the soldiers to undertake much-needed maintenance work on their vehicles. When it went into action on 8 October, it encountered only modest resistance and pushed forward to Yukhnov with few casualties. As it approached the town, it ran into the first line of defences that constituted the Red Army's Mozhaisk Defence Line, known to the Germans by a different name:

The division commander ... realised that the so-called Moscow Defensive Position was strongly fortified. It was made up in the main of concrete positions with tank turrets, anti-tank ditches, and countless mines and barbed wire entanglements behind the Vypranka River near Ilinskoye. In addition, the positions were mainly in woodland and were thus hard to spot. They were held by the personnel of the military and officer schools of Podolsk, i.e. with select troops.[31]

41

Despite the apparent strength of the defensive line, the Germans realised that there was a thinly held sector a little to the south and moved forward through woodland. After a careful build-up of strength, 19th Panzer Division attacked early on 15 October, pushing on towards Maloyaroslavets. Confused fighting continued for several days, with leading German units finding that the Red Army had recaptured the road behind them and threatened their supply lines, but after finally driving off the Soviet units in the area, the German division reached and captured Maloyaroslavets on 17 October. The road to Moscow seemed to be open.

Despite their successes, the Germans were struggling to move forward supplies and men. Many of Guderian's panzer units had reported fuel shortages even at the outset of the offensive, and matters were now even worse. Nonetheless, when the Wehrmacht attacked again in mid-October, the Red Army was once more driven back, with several formations enjoying the same degree of success as 19th Panzer Division in its thrust towards Maloyaroslavets. Kalinin in the north and Kaluga in the south were rapidly captured, and Guderian's southern group approached Tula. In the centre, too, the Germans pushed closer to Moscow, and after Mozhaisk fell on 18 October, Zhukov had no choice but to pull back further to prevent his forces from being encircled. But the combination of snow and rain that turned the landscape into a sea of mud, a worsening supply situation, and mounting casualties steadily slowed the German advance. Guderian's panzer formations clashed with the Soviet Fiftieth Army; reinforced by civilian fighters from the city's population, the Soviet soldiers fought off the German thrust, and a counterattack by I Guards Cavalry Corps prevented the Germans from encircling the city. Guderian had to screen the Red Army forces in Tula and bypass the city; it continued to be a drag on the advance of Second Panzer Group.

The sheer scale of the landscape meant that the Wehrmacht was unable to secure complete control of its rear areas or even the flanks of some of its front-line units, and even at this stage of the war there were sporadic attacks by partisans and Red Army stragglers. An officer from the German 6th Infantry Division had an unusual escape from one such attack:

> The deep, unprotected flank of 6th Infantry Division was covered only where absolutely necessary by 6th Reconnaissance Battalion. In one of the villages to the rear, elements of 58th *Panzerjäger* Company and their company commander, von der Kammer – he had lost both feet as a result of a landmine explosion and now had two prostheses – were ambushed by the Russians and only the company commander survived. A machine-gun bullet struck him in the hip. He lay as if

dead and was the only one who was not massacred by the Russians, as the odd appearance of his two prostheses – from the outside, they looked very unnatural – must have persuaded the Russians that he was dead. After dark he managed to reach us. We later found that all of the wounded men had been executed.[32]

To the north of Moscow, another future star of the Red Army made his first appearance in the battles for Moscow. Colonel Pavel Alekseevich Rotmistrov had led his 8th Tank Brigade, whose main fighting power was made up of 8th Tank Regiment, a battalion of motorised infantry, and an anti-aircraft battalion, in action against the German Army Group North. He was now ordered to move his unit – numbering just 49 tanks, of which seven were KV-1s and ten T-34s, the rest obsolescent models – from the city of Valdai, roughly midway between Leningrad and Moscow, to the capital. Almost immediately, Rotmistrov and his men found themselves in the thick of the action, and the brigade commander hurried to the front line and ordered his tanks to take up concealed positions:

> Not suspecting a trap, the Nazis approached the site of the ambush and when they were within 400m, our tanks and anti-tank guns struck ... the enemy became disordered, but everything depended on whether our tank battalions had time to strike simultaneously at the enemy's flanks. Every minute was precious, and I demanded that [Major Aleksandr Vasilevich] Egorov [commander of 8th Tank Regiment] speed up the advance of the battalions as much as possible.
>
> Finally, 2nd Tank Battalion crossed the Strenevo-Mednoe road and turned towards the northwest. We could already hear the guns of the T-34s as they moved towards the southern flank of the enemy ...
>
> Building on their success, 8th Tank Brigade pursued the enemy ... and broke through to Gorbaty Most on the western outskirts of Kalinin ...
>
> Heavy fighting continued for two days on the outskirts of Kalinin, but we failed to break the resistance of the Nazis. The enemy had a great advantage in numbers and support, especially in tanks, and was constantly supported by numerous aircraft, while we had no air cover ... our losses were heavy. More than half our tanks were seriously damaged. The motorised infantry also suffered significant losses.[33]

While Soviet units might have suffered major tank losses in this attack, the relative weakness of German infantry units in terms of anti-tank capability was increasingly obvious, particularly when the divisions were required to cover extended segments of the front line. When 6th Infantry Division cleared up a group of Soviet soldiers in their rear area, the soldiers were particularly pleased to capture four anti-tank guns and their ammunition – a valuable reinforcement for the division's depleted resources.[34]

The German advance ground to a halt at the end of the month through exhaustion and insuperable supply problems – for example, a supply column took six weeks to reach 6th Infantry Division from a depot 110 miles (183km) to the rear. With mechanised units reporting that they had barely one third of their vehicles still running and many infantry divisions below half their establishment strength, the Germans had to call a halt while supplies were brought forward. But despite these problems, the Germans were determined to make one more effort. Once the ground froze hard, the Wehrmacht would try once more – surely, after the losses of the Vyazma and Bryansk encirclements, the Red Army had to be close to collapse. The alternative would be to pull back into a defensive posture, and with victory apparently only just out of reach, there was no prospect of Hitler accepting such a policy. On the other side of the front line, Zhukov made an astute and accurate strategic assessment. The Germans might have won a major victory in the fighting at Bryansk and Vyazma, but there would now be a pause before the Wehrmacht could resume its assault towards Moscow. It was vital for the Red Army to use this precious time to maximum effect.

For the German commanders to the west of Moscow, the prospects of success looked far from straightforward. Halder glibly recorded in his diary on 4 November that 'there is no point in pushing operations onwards before we have, step by step, established a solid [logistic] foundation for them' – yet this was precisely what he and Hitler had been demanding throughout the autumn and winter.[35] Bock spoke to Halder on 11 November and advised the chief of the general staff that – provided all of the promised supplies arrived – his men might be able to press forward to Moscow and the Volga Canal. Time was running out, he warned, with deep snow likely to bring all operations to a halt. The coming attack would take the very last strength of Army Group Centre's exhausted men, but despite his misgivings, Bock remained cautiously confident he could reach Moscow.

The harsh treatment of Soviet civilians and the large numbers of Red Army stragglers, combined with soldiers and Communist Party officials who had deliberately stayed behind when the Red Army withdrew, resulted in a burgeoning partisan movement. Predictably, the reaction of the Germans was widespread reprisals and repression, with little or no recognition that this would only make matters worse. An officer in the headquarters of Heinrici's XLIII Corps, Leutnant Beutelbacher, was originally from Ukraine, and had lost several family members during the Russian Revolution. He showed great energy in anti-partisan operations, as Heinrici wrote in his diary on 6 November:

> Partisan actions ... are increasing. [Today] Beutelbacher catches sixty, among them forty Red Army soldiers; he convicts and finishes off twenty of them. One young man was hanged in the city centre ... This war is getting nastier and nastier. Everybody is impressed by the partisans' steadfastness. They all remain silent, do not reveal anything, and die.[36]

Just how many of those rounded up by people like Beutelbacher and condemned as partisans were either innocent civilians or people who, with varying degrees of willingness, had cooperated with the partisans, is unknown, but many innocent people were caught up in such punishment operations. The following day, Heinrici told Beutelbacher not to hang partisans closer than 100m to his window – while he clearly had little compunction about such executions, Heinrici clearly felt uncomfortable with having to see the consequences at first hand. As it advanced, Heinrici's corps found both of its flanks exposed, with only tenuous contact with neighbouring units. The weather grew steadily colder, adding to the struggle against both increasing Soviet resistance and the activity of partisans and Red Army stragglers:

> There are huge forests very close by. A stream of Red Army soldiers, who have remained behind in the wake of the battle for Vyazma and Bryansk, continuously rush across them towards Tula to get back to their front. In small groups of three to five men they walk along the train tracks avoiding the main roads. Usually they evade when we find them and fight only in self-defence. A division commander with 400 men ... passed our quarters at a distance of only 2km and not one of us noticed them in time ... Apart from them there are partisans up to mischief. Time and again they attack single cars or people whom they usually kill; they blow up rail tracks and cut telephone cables. We can only get these partisans with the help of the Russian people living here. They are happy to share information, because they themselves are terrorised and robbed of their food by these brigands. We are constantly fighting against this pest. But it is difficult to finish it because the terrain is too endlessly vast, the forest too huge and the hiding places too many. Our interpreter, Leutnant Beutelbacher ... fights vigorously against these partisans. Time and again he sets out together with some military police officers and supported by three devoted [former] Red Army soldiers, sons of peasants. He never comes back without having shot dead or hanged several brigands ... It is like the Thirty Years' War, the same habits and customs. Only those who have power have any rights.[37]

While commenting that the partisans terrorised the local civilians, Heinrici appears to have failed to see Beutelbacher's activities as an almost identical form of terrorism. Elsewhere, he writes about the necessity of stripping the countryside of food in the absence of adequate supplies, yet he is critical of the partisans and stragglers for behaving in the same manner. It seems highly likely that many civilians told whichever side they encountered that they were being oppressed by the other side – and in most cases, this was the truth.

The entire concept of the German invasion of the Soviet Union was based upon overly optimistic calculations: the size of the Red Army had been badly miscalculated; despite the presence of T-34 tanks in the fighting at Khalkin Gol in 1939, the Germans were unaware of their existence until the invasion began; and the massive logistic problems of mounting operations over such vast distances had not been taken into account adequately. The unit history of 6th Infantry Division recorded that supplies for the division would normally come to about 30 tons of food, fuel, ammunition, replacement equipment, etc. per day, but on the days that supplies arrived, they never amounted to more than 15 tons.[38] In the absence of adequate supplies from the rear, the division – like every other German unit in the front line – resorted to living off the land as best it could, but there was little to be had apart from abandoned Red Army cavalry horses. Many of these were slaughtered, and they formed the main source of meat for the division throughout November.

However, such a dislocation between intentions and what was actually possible existed on the other side of the front line too. Zhukov spoke to Stalin by telephone at the beginning of November. He warned Stalin that while German attacks had stopped for the moment, he believed that the Wehrmacht was gathering its strength for a final assault. Stalin replied that he and Marshal Boris Mikhailovich Shaposhnikov – who had replaced Zhukov as Deputy People's Commissar for Defence and was also chief of the general staff – thought that the best way of disrupting the German plans was to counterattack at Volokolamsk and Serpukhov. Zhukov was both surprised and alarmed:

'With what forces, Comrade Supreme Commander-in-Chief, are we going to deliver these counterattacks? Western Front has no forces to spare. Our strength is only enough for defence.'

[Stalin replied,] 'Use the right flank formations of Rokossovsky's [Sixteenth] Army, the [reserve] tank division, and Dovator's cavalry in the Volokolamsk area. At Serpukhov, use Belov's cavalry corps, Getman's tank division and parts of Forty-Ninth Army.'

46

'I think this shouldn't be done at this time. We cannot expend our last reserves in counterattacks when the prospects of success are doubtful. It will leave us nothing to reinforce the defences of our armies when the enemy goes over to the offensive with his strike forces.'

'Your Front has six armies. Isn't that enough?'

'The line of defence of Western Front is greatly extended and, taking account of its twisting nature, extends more than 600km [360 miles]. We have very few reserves in depth, especially in the centre of the front.'

'Consider the issue of counterattacks resolved,' snapped Stalin with displeasure. 'Let me have the plans tonight.'

I tried again to explain to Stalin that counterattacks were inexpedient and would consume our last reserves. But he hung up the telephone receiver and the conversation was over.[39]

Grimly, Zhukov ordered his subordinates to carry out the counterattacks that Stalin had insisted upon; he notes in his memoirs that they were made mainly by cavalry, perhaps implying that he managed to prevent his precious armoured reserves from being wasted. Major General Lev Mikhailovich Dovator's III Cavalry Corps had been encircled in the battles to the west of Moscow in October before fighting its way out to the east, and as a result was far from its establishment strength. One of those ordered to undertake the counterattacks was General Konstantin Konstantinovich Rokossovsky, commander of Sixteenth Army. During the purges of the 1930s, he was expelled from the Communist Party for 'loss of class vigilance' and was implicated in confessions extracted from other officers who had been arrested. In August 1937, he was also arrested and told that the evidence against him had been produced by an old associate, Adolf Yushkevich, that he and Yushkevich had had contacts with Polish and Japanese intelligence officers. Aware that Yushkevich had been dead for several years, Rokossovsky rejected the charges and was brutally interrogated but refused to 'confess' even after severe beatings. He lost several teeth and had his toes broken with a hammer, and on one occasion was led out into the prison yard and made to kneel while a pistol was levelled at his head. The gun was fired, but it was loaded with blank ammunition. In March 1940, he was released and restored to his previous army rank; he made a point of wearing stainless steel dentures, making no secret of how his teeth had been knocked out by his interrogators. Having distinguished himself in the Smolensk battles, he was one of the rising stars of the Red Army, and he was as unhappy with the counterattack order as Zhukov, but dutifully obeyed orders:

We were given one night to prepare for the operation. I must say that I was unable to fathom the commander's reasoning in issuing the order. Our strength was minimal, we were given practically no time for preparation, and the enemy himself was poised for the attack. My request at least to give us more time for preparation remained unheeded.

As expected, the partial counteroffensive launched on 16 November on orders from the Front command proved ineffectual. At first, having taken the enemy by surprise, we succeeded in penetrating some 3km into his positions. But then he launched an attack along the whole of our frontage, and our troops were forced to beat a hasty retreat. Most hard put was Lev Dovator's cavalry group, which was caught in an enemy pincer movement. It was only thanks to their mobility and the skill of their commander that they managed to escape.[40]

The Soviet General Staff study of the fighting in the months that followed made a number of criticisms of the attack:

As a result of the lack of time and the ceaseless fighting, the plan for the attack on Volokolamsk was drawn up by the army staff in the course of a single night while the questions of coordinating units and concentrating them in their jumping-off positions were not thought through; as a result of this the units reached their jumping-off points late …

The movement of the cavalry … was not exactly calculated (in accordance with their capabilities; the calculations were based on the units being in good condition, while the cavalry regiments had up to 50 per cent of their horses unshod, while the shod horses did not have studs) …

The army staff's communications with its units was poorly organised, telephone communications with [three] cavalry divisions had not been established, while radio communications worked intermittently; the location of a number of division staffs … was unknown to the army staff.

The cavalry divisions' rear services were still short of the jumping-off position at 0800 … [and] a number of them did not even know the exact location of their units.[41]

While this account is critical of Rokossovsky's staff, it misses a much more important criticism: in such circumstances, it was impossible to mount this operation at such short notice, as Zhukov and Rokossovsky knew. The responsibility for the failure surely lies with Stalin for insisting on proceeding with the attack. Even as Rokossovsky's troops were scrambling back to their positions, Bock's Army Group Centre attacked again. The drive towards Klin in the north made steady progress, not least because Zhukov had few reserves to send to the endangered sector. A soldier in 7th Panzer Division later wrote:

> The company was deployed against the heavily fortified Lama River sector and stormed one house after another with hand grenades in close-quarter fighting, excellently supported by tanks and assault guns. In a short time the entire village as far as the stream was in our hands. The enemy was still on the far bank. He defended with a bitter determination that only those who have experienced it can know and appreciate. The Red Army soldiers continued to shoot from burning houses, even when their clothes were alight! One after another, the daredevil NCOs who always led their men from the front were wounded. When Leutnant von Wickende and the NCOs Gothe, Roitsch and Seel fell, our platoon lost all its leaders. In order to establish a crossing over the Lama, Heilbronn's battalion attacked over the river shortly before dusk to seize a bridgehead. Our 1.Coy was once again leading, supported by the heavy machine-gun platoon, tanks, and heavy weapons. The motorcycle platoon and 2.Coy led by Feldwebel Friedrich surpassed themselves with their attacking spirit and took one bit of woodland after another and the intervening open fields in close-quarter fighting ... The attack continued the following morning without a pause.[42]

Despite the general tone of the piece, it cannot hide the reality that the Red Army was resisting with great determination, and the battle was forcing the Wehrmacht to pay a heavy price in experienced men.

In the southern pincer, 4th Panzer Division was once more leading 2nd Panzer Group's advance, this time towards the town of Uzlovaya, to the southeast of Tula. The front line in this sector had broken down into a series of almost isolated local battles, with both sides often unsure of the exact location of the enemy. The Germans were increasingly conscious of the inferiority of their tanks, as Oberfeldwebel Hermann Bix described:

> I was at point in my tank. Towards midday we reached the edge of the town. Ivan [a widely used nickname for Red Army soldiers in the Wehrmacht] didn't spot us. A truck loaded with infantry drove past me. The men waved in a friendly manner. I let them pass and then radioed back to Lekschat [in a tank following Bix] that he'd get a friendly welcome from the Russians.
>
> When we reached the marketplace, where the main road took a turn, I no longer knew which way to go as I hadn't had detailed maps for several days. The

[company] commander advised me to take the right turn. But Ivan was more watchful here. A truck full of soldiers stopped suddenly. The infantrymen took up covered positions. A second truck roared up. It was time to declare our colours. I fired an explosive round into the truck with fearful results. But however grim I felt, it was a stroke of luck as the truck was loaded with anti-tank rifles. I drove forward to make room for the advancing company behind me. Then I heard the first Russian tank. It sounded like a KV-1. This wasn't good news, as my gun could achieve nothing against such a steel colossus, whereas it could effortlessly fire on me from 1,000m.

Böckle radioed me that the KV-1 was firing at him and he outlined the Russian positions. I drove through a wooden fence with my tank. The great lump was about 30m away. I had a special round loaded, which might penetrate the turret at this close range. The first shot achieved nothing, nor the second or third. The fellow didn't react at all and continued to shoot calmly at Böckle. I radioed back that I couldn't penetrate with my gun. Böckle made a mischievous suggestion: 'Blow his gun off then, or you'll be knocked out!' I didn't take that seriously. But my gunner, who had overheard, suggested we try it at least once before we were blown to the devil.

We loaded an AP round and aimed at the barrel, right next to the gun mantle. We fired three times but I could see no effect through my scope because of the smoke. Then the Russian aimed at me. It was time to face our maker! His gun barrel struck a tree. He fired again at Böckle. I saw smoke burst out from the hatch. The commander tried to bale out but collapsed. We drove up and saw three shots had passed through the barrel. The crew was dead, as the last round had detonated in the breech …

[Two days later] We drove up to Venyov. We approached from behind through the back door where the Russians would least expect us. Again, I was point. After reaching the village square, I heard the approach of a heavy tank close by. The motor roared and I could hear it rattling closer. I positioned my vehicle behind a house so I could still see something if I leaned right out of the turret. A KV-1 drove blithely past. I tried to get back in the turret but my clothing was caught. Thank God Ivan didn't fire. But why not? Was he out of ammunition? He must have known that I could do nothing against him. That must have been well known by now.

The Russian roared on, sending the cobblestones flying. His brother headed towards me to ram me. I shouted into the microphone, 'Reverse!' But the driver couldn't hear me as I had pulled out the plug in the turret hatch. I leaped from the turret and stood before the driver's hatch and gestured. The driver immediately understood, selected a gear, and drove back, not a moment too soon. The big lump crunched past and struck the wall, half broke through and was left stuck there. The crew must have lost their senses. From 20m I fired two AP rounds at the monster's turret but without success. The Russian tank tried to push through the wall. It moved very slowly.

The company saw my duel and brought the KV-1 under fire. Shell after shell struck the turret but none penetrated. There was an unholy firework display just 10m from me, and Ivan was almost through the wall. Then I remembered Uzlovaja. 'Aim like Uzlovaja,' I roared. The gunner reacted like lightning. Three shells flew from the barrel at quick tempo. I asked the company to cease firing as the ricochets were dangerous to us. I could see that we had scored two hits. We fired a few more into the running gear and the Russians gave up. I saw them bale out of a side hatch and disappear into the houses.[43]

The time that the Germans had needed to gather their strength had been put to good use by the Red Army and its civilian auxiliaries, and German losses were heavy as the Soviet forces fell back in stages through the multiple lines of defensive positions. Halder and Bock discussed the fighting again, and despite reporting that some of his units had been reduced almost to nothing – one infantry division had suffered such heavy losses that one of its regiments was commanded by a first lieutenant and the battalions by second lieutenants – Bock speculated that the battle might ultimately be decided by the very last battalion that was thrown into the fighting. Accordingly, the assault was to continue. As they pushed towards Klin, the men of 7th Panzer Division encountered resistance in surprising forms:

In the morning attack, which our riflemen had to make at first without the support of tanks, anti-tank dogs were deployed by the Russians. The regiment commander had briefed the men about this before the attack and warned them – he himself had thought that the information about the use of dogs was another everyday 'latrine rumour', but told himself: 'Better safe than sorry. One can never know or suspect what bestiality the Russians still have in store.'

'It was like a hunting drive for hares; large numbers of dogs were gunned down,' one of those who took part in the attack reported. The radio operator in the regiment commander's half-track counted 42 shot dogs during the move forwards. During our attack, these dogs emerged from cover and ran up to our half-tracks and tanks. On either side and on their backs, they had explosive charges on a belt around their midriff, which as determined by our knowledgeable combat engineers was to penetrate the bottoms or sides of our advancing tanks, half-tracks etc. The Red Army dog handlers sat in their foxholes next to or a little back from the roads down which we were expected to advance and when ordered they sent their dogs out to rush towards the armoured vehicles. The dogs were meant to duck under the armoured vehicles when they got close. As they were released from the dog handlers' foxholes, the handlers pulled a line that pulled up a small rod about 12cm long on the back of the dogs and then functioned as a mechanical trigger …

'In our attack sector, I know of no case when this Red Army trick succeeded,' the regiment commander reported. 'We shot all the dogs.'[44]

This wretched weapon was hated by most of the soldiers in the Red Army too, with many dog handlers requesting other duties – they preferred to take their chances as ordinary infantrymen rather than send the dogs they had trained and got to know to such terrible deaths. Mansoor Giztulovich Abdullin, who witnessed the use of anti-tank dogs during the fighting in the Stalingrad encirclement a year later, was not alone in his sense of horror:

Like other men from the Siberian Taiga, I love dogs very much and when I learned about the suicide dogs I was very upset. What a thing to do to a loyal animal, the joy of childhood! A dog is a devoted friend. A dog trusts a man, yet the man deceives him and sends him to his death under a tank! I felt weak when I walked over to the dogs, waiting for their moment next to their dog-soldiers. Multi-coloured, shaggy, ears hanging or erect. And this one – one ear up, the other down – it was a mongrel – while a pack of explosives of 8kg was prepared. It looked at me, tilting its head from one side to the other, hoping for a treat.[45]

Klin fell on 23 November, and four days later 7th Panzer Division managed to cross the Volga Canal, just 22 miles (35km) from the Kremlin. Stalin had telephoned Zhukov shortly before to ask if he was confident that Moscow could be held; Zhukov replied in the affirmative but insisted that he needed further reinforcements of men and tanks. Stalin promised him two reserve armies but added that the tanks might take longer to be made available. These reserves arrived just in time to push back 7th Panzer Division. A further German attack directly to the west of Moscow broke through the Red Army's lines, but this too was unable to exploit the initial success and ground to a halt. Once more, Rokossovsky was ordered to launch a counterattack and Dovator's cavalrymen were sent forward; a number of villages changed hands, but the front line remained essentially unchanged.

Immediately to the northwest of Moscow, General Richard Ruoff's V Corps made its last attempt to reach Moscow. Flanked by 23rd Infantry Division to the north and 106th Infantry Division to the south, 2nd Panzer Division created battlegroups commanded by Oberstleutnants Karl Decker and Eberhard Rodt. Before the assault could begin, the panzer division had to beat off an attack by Soviet armour, which left the soldiers of the division's anti-tank battalion despondent about the efficacy of their weapons:

> During an enemy attack on Strelino, 1 and 2 platoons of 1 Company shot up several heavy enemy tanks and a light tank. Our panzer comrades from 3rd Panzer Regiment [the division's main armoured force] also disabled four enemy tanks. They were all English vehicles, constructed in September 1941. The 'milometer' of the 'Mark II' shot up by Gefreiter Vavra's gun showed it had driven just 40km [24 miles]. It was just newly imported from England!
>
> In these tank attacks, the faith of the gun crews in their 37mm anti-tank guns was badly shaken. These guns were now ironically known as *Heeres-Anklopf-Gerät* ['army door-knocking-equipment'] and no longer as effective anti-tank weapons.[46]

By the beginning of December, the leading elements of 2nd Panzer Division had reached the village of Gorki, a little to the north of the current location of Sheremetyevo Airport, but came under almost constant attack:

> At first light [on 3 December] we pulled back again to the secondary positions as there were just two machine-guns left on the southern edge [of Gorki]. The positions occupied during the night couldn't be held during the day as the enemy could dominate them from high ground. During the night we had beaten off three enemy attacks, not including scouting raids that repeatedly attempted to damage our tanks in groups of 30–40 men armed with 'Molotov cocktails'. During the morning, too, the enemy tried repeatedly to break into Gorki but was repulsed with heavy losses. At 1100 a Russian tank (18 tons, type unknown) managed to drive into the centre of the village along the main road. The crew of a 50mm anti-tank gun allowed it to come within 50m and then hit it with three shots. The tank was left ablaze.
>
> At midday we made our reports, including casualties. One platoon had no losses, but 2nd Platoon reported several dead and wounded and casualties from frostbite. Despite the constant attacks, all night and day we continued to work on our positions so that we had at least some protection against the constantly increasing artillery fire. The Russians attacked again at 1400, once more in vain ...

Roughly at midnight a 52-ton tank passed the eastern edge of the village just out of range. It turned across the snow-covered fields and from the direction of Ozeretskoye [just to the northwest of Gorki, i.e. in the rear of the German position] it trundled down the road towards Gorki. It made slow, difficult progress along the cratered and icy road. By shouted messages we and the other units, particularly 3rd Panzer Regiment, agreed we would try to destroy the enemy tank with mines. Passing just 10m from a 37mm gun at the platoon command post the colossus slipped into a snow-filled ditch. It was stranded. The gun commander, Unteroffizier Hantsch, had already armed himself with a Teller mine [a flat, plate-sized anti-tank mine] … The platoon commander and two other men covered him with machine-pistols. In three strides Hantsch was behind the 52-tonner and clambered onto it, placing the mine against the turret. At the same time, the NCO of a tank crew dragged over a petrol can, climbed onto the tank, poured half the can over the tank and jumped off. Hantsch triggered the Teller mine fuse and took cover. A few seconds later the turret was knocked sideways as if by a ghostly hand and at the same moment the tank began to burn.[47]

This account highlights the uncoordinated nature of Red Army attacks; had the heavy tank been accompanied by infantrymen – they would surely have been able to keep up with it, as it was forced to move so slowly on the damaged road – they might have prevented the Germans from attacking it at close quarters. Similarly, the repeated infantry attacks might have achieved more had they been accompanied by tanks.

The hard-pressed men of 2nd Panzer Division could see traffic within Moscow through their gun telescopes but could get no closer; Bock's attempt to force a final decisive victory with the last strength of his army group had foundered in the snow around Moscow – the 'last battalion' had been committed to no avail. To the south, Guderian's panzer group was unable to advance any further, the Soviet forces in Tula continuing to exert a major threat to his lines of communication. The German forces that had bypassed the southern edge of the city had then turned towards Moscow and had enveloped the defences along the eastern outskirts, but attempts by them to break through the Soviet defences to the northeast of Tula and to link up with Heinrici's men who were to attack at the same time from the west were unsuccessful. Both attacks managed to make some progress, but ultimately stopped a few kilometres short of each other. Heinrici's corps was still almost out of contact with flanking formations, and even if it had the strength to continue its advance, such a thrust carried the risk of exposing its flanks still further. Oberstleutnant – imminently to be promoted to Oberst – Heinrich Eberbach commanded 4th Panzer Division's 35th Panzer Regiment and later recalled the sense of frustration among his men, who were now enduring the consequences of the loss of vehicles and other equipment in the attempts to push forward before the ground froze hard:

> The troops had a feeling that nobody in the supreme command knew anything about the Russian muddy season and nobody there gave any thought to its effect. The loss of equipment was considerable. The city of Tula, which lay right on our route, couldn't be taken despite all efforts, as the artillery had too few guns up forward and insufficient ammunition reached the front line through the mud.[48]

The northern pincer of the German attack on Moscow reached a maximum penetration as far as the western edge of Dmitrov but could go no further. Immediately to the west of Moscow, Rokossovsky's Sixteenth Army held a paper-thin line perhaps 23 miles (37km) from the centre of Moscow. In their final attacks, the Germans managed to push through Sixteenth Army's positions north of Krasnaya Polyana, to the north of the city, but Zhukov scraped together a depleted tank brigade, a regiment of artillery, and four *Katyusha* rocket-launcher battalions to send to Rokossovsky; in combination with the few troops he could concentrate, this force drove back the German penetration. Heinrici, commander of the German XLIII Corps, could have been speaking for the entire Wehrmacht when he wrote:

> The army has not been able to achieve the desired success. And it did not help that the strength of the remaining units had dwindled to such a ridiculous level and that the men were mentally and physically extremely exhausted after five months of offensive warfare, while the Russian was sending more and more troops against us … We have nothing like that. Our victories have brought us to the end of our tether.[49]

Despite similar views from many officers in the front line, Bock, Halder and Hitler were not alone in believing that just as their own forces were exhausted and their reserves finished, the Red Army too had to be approaching the end of its strength. On 22 November, even while the final attacks to reach Moscow were staggering forward through the snow, Kinzel in *FHO* produced a report stating that most of the Soviet formations that had appeared as reinforcements had been transferred to Moscow from other sectors of the Eastern Front; this, Kinzel concluded, was proof that the Red Army probably had no further reserves that could be brought to Moscow from the Soviet Far East, and therefore a Soviet winter offensive was most unlikely.[50] The scale of the error was about to become clear. Even though Luftwaffe reconnaissance planes belatedly spotted the appearance of hundreds of railway wagons from the east, higher commands seemed to be oblivious to the danger, but many German soldiers on the ground had a grim foreboding of what was coming. One of them later wrote:

> The Moscow-Volga Canal lay before us and on the other side, masses of Russians were suddenly appearing. The sheer number of them left us speechless. There were endless marching columns, soldiers on skis, in white coats. And then there were tanks, artillery units and countless motor vehicles.[51]

In many respects, the outcome of the German attack seems to have been on a knife-edge, with Moscow remaining elusively just out of reach. Could the Wehrmacht have reached the city? Given the logistic constraints under which it was operating, the answer is surely a negative. Even if the Germans had been able to bring additional forces into the region, it was proving impossible to ensure adequate supplies for the forces already there – further units would have required yet more fuel, food and ammunition, and these supplies were not available. Furthermore, had the attacks succeeded in reaching Moscow, it is very likely that they would have been too weak to clear the city in costly urban warfare, and would have been badly exposed to a Soviet counterattack. As it was, they were still badly exposed, as they were about to discover.

The determination of the Red Army's defence of Moscow was epitomised in a statement attributed to a political officer in Major General Ivan Vasilievich Panfilov's 316th Rifle Division: 'Russia is big, but there's no place to fall back on. Moscow is behind us.'[52] The story of 'Panfilov's 28' – how a small group of men from the division fought a desperate battle against German armoured forces attacking them – became a legend almost immediately after the battle. An account in the newspaper *Izvestia* on 19 November 1941 first highlighted the battle, describing how the 'Panfilovites' destroyed nine German tanks and drove off many more.[53] By 26 November, an account in another newspaper, *Krasnaya Zvezda*, inflated the number of destroyed German tanks to 18.[54] In a movie made in 2016 about the battle, one of the survivors asked another how many tanks he thinks they destroyed. After a moment's thought, his comrade replied perhaps ten, and added that they would tell their children it was far more. While the newspaper accounts that gave rise to the legend are almost certainly largely works of fiction and the movie is truer to the legend than history, there can be no doubt that Panfilov's division put up desperate resistance. Nor can there be any doubt that this episode exemplifies the manner in which both sides inflated the deeds of their soldiers and the numbers of enemy tanks that were destroyed in the fighting.

The German attempt to reach and capture Moscow was over. With its waning strength expended in its last attacks, the Wehrmacht was stranded in the snow, its units in positions that might have made sense for an offensive operation but were inappropriate to face a Soviet counteroffensive. And that counteroffensive was about to be unleashed, as a consequence of which the front lines would assume the shape that they would hold through the following year.

CHAPTER 2

THE RED ARMY'S COUNTEROFFENSIVE, DECEMBER 1941

Stalin had urged counterattacks throughout November, which were largely ineffective, but planning for a more extensive counteroffensive began in earnest in the second half of the month. On 29 November, Zhukov spoke to Stalin by telephone and advised that it was time to start the offensive – the German assault on Moscow had ground to a halt, and it was important to strike before the Germans could consolidate their gains or bring fresh forces to the front. Zhukov's detailed plans for Western Front were discussed the following day, listing the planned objectives:

> Immediate task: to smash the main enemy grouping on the right wing [i.e. to the north of Moscow] with an attack on Klin and Solnechnogorsk and towards the Istra [River], and to smash the enemy on the left wing of Western Front [to the south of Moscow] with an attack on Uzlovaya and Bogoroditsk into the flank and rear of Guderian's group.
>
> In order to pin down the enemy forces on the rest of the front and to deprive him of the chance to redeploy troops, the Front's Fifth, Thirty-Third, Forty-Third, Forty-Ninth and Fiftieth Armies will commence offensives on 4–5 December with limited objectives.[1]

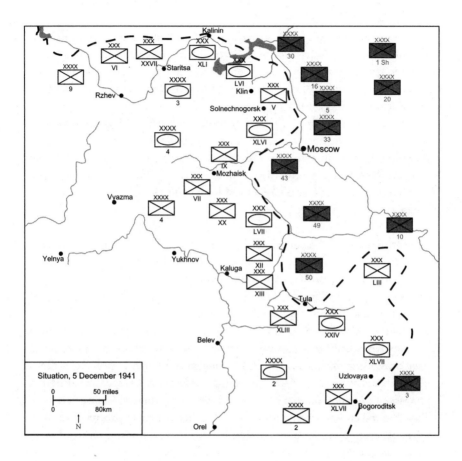

Situation, 5 December 1941

0 ___ 50 miles

0 ___ 80km

N

Soviet reserves had been gathering to the east of Moscow throughout November, and five armies were available to *Stavka*. Of these, two were directed to the south against Guderian's group while the other three would be used in the counteroffensive to the north and west of Moscow. In addition, Zhukov's neighbour to the north, Konev's Kalinin Front, was ordered to concentrate an assault group to strike into the rear of the German forces around Klin. The first Soviet attacks began on 5 December; it was standard Red Army practice to carry out an aggressive reconnaissance in force immediately before the main attack in order to secure the best start line for the offensive, and in some areas the initial attacks were so successful that the main forces were committed immediately. In other cases, for example with much of Rokossovsky's army, the counteroffensive merged seamlessly with the continuing heavy fighting.[2]

59

The weather had steadily worsened, and few German soldiers had been issued with winter clothing. What stocks of clothing were available to the Wehrmacht were often stranded far to the west; the very limited rail connections to the front line were prioritising the movement of ammunition, fuel and food. Many soldiers seized warm clothing from local civilians or dead or captured Soviet soldiers, while others simply endured as best they could. Heinrici's XLIII Corps had been part of the German Second Army until mid-October, when it became the northern wing of Guderian's Second Panzer Group, and on 3 December, just before the Soviet counteroffensive, Guderian visited Heinrici's headquarters. Heinrici took full advantage of the opportunity to describe the situation in which his men were fighting:

> I reported the increasing number of sick people due to a poor, entirely fat-free diet and completely insufficient winter clothing; I described the poor supply and transport situation. Between two armies and without any motorised vehicles – because they were all broken down except for the occasional one – we have to travel for many days just to get the necessary things to our position. Very often we do not get any provisions at all for half a week. We have got used to it now and help ourselves. But the area where we have been deployed for six weeks is empty and there is nothing more to find ... It cannot go on like this if we do not get at least fat and reasonable winter clothing this instant, and proper and regular provisions in future. Because right now we are getting shortened provisions for two days and then nothing for several days ... Other units also had better clothing than us, because the uniforms we were entitled to were sent to Second Army, which we left after being assigned [to Guderian's group].[3]

Having used all their strength to break through to Moscow, the German divisions were in a desperate situation – they were still in the positions they had seized in their last attacks, which were often not suited for defensive purposes. The experiences of the men of 7th Panzer Division were repeated at numerous points of the line:

> The defence against numerous Russian attacks south of Stepanovo and southwest of Yakhroma succeeded through the use of all our forces and the last of our fighting strength. At first, the defensive line was held on 6 December. On this day the Russians attacked three times in temperatures of -38 to -40°C. As before our troops were without winter clothing and our machine-guns froze increasingly frequently. 'Despite the bad weather, the enemy lay in the snow for four hours to try to catch

us off guard so they could commence their attack – it was quite incredible – you had to experience it and see it with your own eyes,' a rifleman wrote.[4]

Many of the Soviet units involved in the counteroffensive were relatively strong numerically, having been held in reserve through the battles before Moscow, but there were serious equipment shortages. On 1 December, the new First Shock Army – created from what had been Nineteenth Army – had a reported strength of just under 37,000 men. The number of NCOs was lower than the paper establishment (just 6,500), and the entire army had only 25,000 rifles and 1,400 machine-guns. There were also shortages of artillery and anti-aircraft weapons and the ability to move them, both in terms of trucks and horses.[5] The years of purges and the terrible losses of officers and NCOs in the opening months of the war had taken a huge toll. The men were inexperienced, the officers and NCOs lacked the training or experience for the level of improvisation and innovation that was essential for a successful attack, and coordination between tanks, artillery and infantry was poor. In many cases, the Soviet troops launched 'human wave' attacks on the German lines, suffering terrible casualties. The experiences of the past few years had resulted in an inflexible, rigid approach to issuing and following orders, and repeated assaults were made against German positions that had already beaten off attacks with heavy casualties. A German infantry officer wrote:

> We keep asking ourselves why the Russians make these pointless attacks repeatedly at the same positions around which we have now closed up, where nothing can slip past us any more. What are they trying to achieve? They may well capture a few villages – so what?[6]

Despite their heavy losses, the Soviet soldiers gained sufficient ground to make the German positions north of Moscow untenable, and the Germans began to withdraw. Much of their artillery and equipment, particularly in the infantry divisions, was horse-drawn, and losses of draught horses had been heavy throughout the campaign. In the increasingly difficult weather conditions of the past few weeks, the strain on the remaining animals – who were often poorly fed due to the difficulties in moving sufficient fodder to the front line – had greatly accelerated their loss rate, and local horses that had been commandeered by the Germans might have been wiry and tough, able to cope with the winter conditions, but they often lacked the physical strength of the German horses they replaced. The problem was exacerbated by decisions that had been made before the abandonment of *Taifun*; as the German advance slowed to a crawl, many divisions sent a large proportion of their horses a considerable distance to the rear, where it would be easier to supply them with feed and retained only a minimum number of horses in the front line, in the belief that any movement in what they expected to be a period of positional warfare would be minimal. It was now impossible to bring those horses back to the front line.[7] On 7 December, 2nd Panzer Division began its withdrawal from Gorki, immediately to the north of Moscow:

> The rearguard elements reached Solnechnogorsk on 10 December; they held off constant enemy activity and suffered losses, particularly from the bitter cold. Of the three anti-tank guns of the anti-tank platoon assigned to [the rearguard] only one was operational – the others had broken towing arms and defective recoil mechanisms …
>
> The fuel shortages gave rise to serious concerns; the increased consumption due to the cold and snow created problems that nobody had foreseen, but nonetheless the engines of the heavy vehicles had to be kept running continuously as they wouldn't restart in such cold weather. This meant that even without moving, the trucks consumed fuel normally sufficient for 100km of road travel in just 48 hours. Due to fuel shortages, many units had to abandon or destroy trucks and other equipment.
>
> It was particularly difficult to bring forward supplies – particularly fuel – along the single road, past the masses of vehicles heading west, if only because of the road and traffic situation. Supply elements and individual vehicles pushed on mindlessly to the west to reach safety from the threatened encirclement … There were constant pauses due to trucks knocked out by air attack and collapsed bridges, for which the sappers had almost no equipment or materiel for rapid repairs. The supply situation steadily worsened, as horse-drawn units also used the panzer group's withdrawal roads and slowed the movement of motorised units to the pace of horses …
>
> During these days, our Feldwebel Lehmeier coined the catchphrase: 'Forwards, comrades, we have to retreat!' He then turned his cap around so that the front of it continued to face the enemy during the withdrawal. Despite the serious situation, we had to laugh.[8]

As the German divisions began to pull back towards the west, they left behind them a trail of abandoned equipment – guns, supply wagons, ambulances, even wounded. The strength of many German units was evaporating at an alarming rate. On 6 December, 4th Panzer Division's Oberstleutnant Eberbach and his forces had to battle both the Red Army and the prevailing conditions, as Oberleutnant Hermann Voss, a signals officer, later recalled:

> At dawn the thermometer recorded -40°C. Gryslovo was in turmoil and nobody had time for reflection as they were concentrating on survival. Whatever was still mobile was made ready and everything else was completely destroyed. The signals truck was soon ablaze, the radio equipment and the personnel crowded into the command vehicle … Ice made it impossible to move through ravines. The first vehicle was already stranded on the slope behind the village, unable to climb up. The crew of an anti-aircraft gun tried to bring their gun up using a winch but the cable broke as if it were paper. The towing ring of a 105mm gun shattered like glass and the gun had to be destroyed. We drew a lesson from this: always stay on high ground and avoid every dip. Then the forward battalion withdrew from the main highway. It had been forced to leave a lot of equipment behind … In Nefedova three large Henschel trucks belonging to the sappers were burning. They had no snow chains and thus couldn't climb the slope … Finally we just couldn't move forwards and the losses of tanks became worse. As a last resort we threw our coats under the tracks and escaped from this awful spot to Fedyacheva. When we reached the high ground, it was dark. It had taken us that long to fight our way up the slope.
>
> Muzzle flashes blazed in the darkness. Oberst Eberbach had gathered together all that we still had available. 12th Rifle Regiment was fighting against the enemy who was advancing from the north, covering our flank but unable to break contact with the enemy. Eberbach dispatched the last tank in a thrust towards the north and our artillery fired its last rounds at the pursuing foe … The Russians pulled back from the tank and the riflemen were finally able to withdraw …
>
> The last tank in the regiment, commanded by Oberleutnant Wollschlaeger, also covered the retreat of the division on 7 December and the following days.[9]

In Germany, the Soviet offensive made little impression at first. Halder recorded in his diary that Guderian's over-extended forces south of Moscow were pulling back and that the Red Army had made a penetration in the German lines east of Kalinin, but the focus of attention was Ukraine, where Field Marshal Gerd von Rundstedt had been dismissed at the beginning of December for failing to hold the newly captured city of Rostov and had ordered a withdrawal to the line of the Mius River. At the daily evening conference, Hitler made light of Halder's report that the German divisions on the Eastern Front had lost, on average, 4,000 men each since the invasion of the Soviet Union. Total German losses, Hitler pointed out, were perhaps half a million men – the Red Army had lost up to 10 million. The number of captured guns meant that the Red Army's artillery had to be close to the 'zero point'; Halder recorded that immobility meant that the German artillery, too, was often effectively powerless.[10] Near Kalinin, the German 110th Infantry Division had to be redeployed hastily to cover Soviet attacks, and the neighbouring 6th Infantry Division was ordered to extend its front line to cover the sector previously held by its neighbour. This task was at first made easier by the news that as it redeployed, 110th Infantry Division left two battalions of artillery that could be used by 6th Infantry Division, but the reason that the guns had been left was because there were insufficient horses to move them. Not long after, 6th Infantry Division was forced to redeploy and was now expected to provide horses to pull these guns, even though it lacked sufficient horses for its own needs.[11]

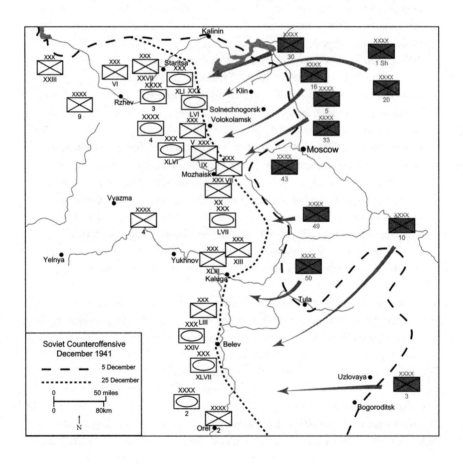

The counteroffensive against the northern armoured forces of the Wehrmacht was led by Thirtieth Army on the northern flank of Zhukov's Western Front. The commander of Thirtieth Army was General Dmitri Danilovich Lelyushenko, who had commanded Fifth Army earlier in the war but was wounded in October. He took command of Thirtieth Army in mid-November and immediately created a small mobile group that was given licence to operate in the rear of the advancing German troops. Inevitably, Lelyushenko claims in his memoirs that this unit performed remarkable feats and inflicted a great deal of damage, and when the general counteroffensive began in December, he was quick to repeat the operation, using elements of a motorised rifle division, a cavalry division and an independent tank battalion. Lelyushenko and many of his subordinates wanted to delay the start of the counteroffensive to allow more time to bring up reinforcements, particularly artillery and anti-aircraft weapons. On the eve of the offensive, men from the new mobile group ventured forth and captured several German soldiers – 'tongues', in the parlance of the Red Army – for interrogation:

> I interrogated the prisoners. They looked rather shabby but behaved arrogantly. But during the interrogation they revealed that the Nazis were frantically strengthening their defences, though they were unaware of preparations for our counteroffensive. The prisoners knew nothing about the approach of any [German] reinforcements.
>
> Consequently, it was inappropriate to postpone the counteroffensive for a few days. Even if not all the troops could be ready for the beginning of the offensive – perhaps just two regiments from each division on the first day [i.e. two thirds of their strength] – that was no longer alarming. In any case, it would be wrong to use all our forces at once. Surprise was vital, followed by a sustained strike.[12]

Despite having only 20 tanks available, half of which were lightweight T-26 tanks, and very little artillery, Lelyushenko ordered a night attack with little or no artillery preparation. The advance began before dawn and rapidly penetrated up to seven miles (12km) between the scattered German positions. As was the case elsewhere, Lelyushenko's men were then caught in German counterattacks that exposed the inexperience of the Red Army:

> I was informed that Major General [Fedor Vasilevich] Chernyshev's 371st Rifle Division attacked successfully but the advance then slowed. Serious trouble was brewing. The enemy had already counterattacked the division twice. Together

with my staff … we went to the division. We saw from afar that our tanks had pushed on a considerable distance. The enemy separated the infantry of Chernyshev's division from the tanks with machine-gun fire.[13]

Lelyushenko managed to get things moving again, but there was a limit to the ability of officers like Lelyushenko to intervene whenever problems arose.

On 7 December, as Japanese aircraft attacked Pearl Harbor and the war spread across the globe, the Soviet offensive continued. The seriousness of the situation north of Moscow became increasingly clear to *OKH*, but there was little that Brauchitsch, Halder or Hitler could do – they had no further troops that they could send to the east. The German front line near Klin had been breached, and General Hans-Georg Reinhardt, commander of Third Panzer Group to the north of Moscow, noted in his diary that his units were scrambling to send all available personnel to the front line; in one case, a regimental band was ordered to take up rifles and report for duty.[14] Bock was aware of the urgent need for reinforcements, but all that he could provide was a single understrength regiment from the neighbouring Fourth Panzer Group. There was great reluctance on the part of German commanders to release reserves that would be deployed elsewhere, and in an attempt to address this, Bock subordinated Reinhardt's panzer group to Hoepner's Fourth Panzer Group – now that Reinhardt's units were effectively under Hoepner's jurisdiction, perhaps Hoepner would be prepared to release more troops. In the meantime, Reinhardt reshuffled his forces and dispatched 1st Panzer Division to deal with the Klin penetration. Moving into position overnight, Generalmajor Walter Krüger's division counterattacked late in the morning, rapidly driving back two regiments of Soviet infantry. The entire episode was a pattern that would be repeated throughout the winter: the Red Army attacked and achieved local successes, often threatening to penetrate into the German rear areas, but timely German counterattacks caught the Soviet soldiers unprepared and often overwhelmed them. In other areas, the inexperience and rigidity of the Red Army's officers was lethally exposed. When initial attacks were beaten off by the German defences, the Soviet troops simply gathered their strength and attacked again, resulting in still more losses for little or no gain. Writing after the war, Rokossovsky blamed deep snow for the failure of the Red Army to sweep past the exposed flanks of German units and encircle them, but even if the weather had been less inclement, such operations were beyond the capabilities of Soviet units. The Moscow counteroffensive can perhaps be seen as the first painful step of learning how to conduct such operations, a process that would ultimately come to fruition in Operation *Bagration* in the summer of

1944, when Soviet units – in many cases, commanded by the men who were defending Moscow at the end of 1941 – overwhelmed the German Army Group Centre in a series of rapid encirclements.

Despite its inflexibility, the Red Army achieved considerable local successes, and such was the overstretched state of the German forces that it was inconceivable that the units of the panzer groups would be able to remain in their exposed positions. Bock spoke to Halder late on 8 December and informed him that in addition to the attacks against the panzer groups northwest of Moscow, the Red Army was also pressuring the southern flank of Generaloberst Günther von Kluge's Fourth Army, threatening to sever contact between this army and Guderian's Second Panzer Group. The peril of the entire German position was demonstrated when the Red Army attacked and captured the town of Mihailov, about 54 miles (90km) east of Tula, on 7 December. A withdrawal from the current positions was inevitable, but the same fuel and movement problems that had hindered the German advance now played a large factor in the retreat: if the German units pulled back too fast, they would have to abandon much of their equipment. The Red Army would surely follow and the Germans would then be forced – now without much of their artillery and other heavy weapons – to fight a new defensive battle. Third and Fourth Panzer Groups still held on to Klin but were doing whatever they could to withdraw to the west, and Second Panzer Group now began its own withdrawal from its high-water mark. A little to the southwest, the German Second Army – commanded by Generaloberst Rudolf Schmidt – was as overstretched as Guderian's formations, and a relatively weak Soviet attack, mounted by a single cavalry division supported by a handful of tanks, burst through its lines with ease.

Nonetheless, for the moment at least, there was little sense of panic. The German ability to mount counterattacks, combined with the Soviet tendency to throw repeated attacks against strong German positions, resulted in the Red Army paying a disproportionate price for the ground it gained. Nor was the Red Army the only group paying a price for the events of December. As they fell back, the Germans resorted to a ruthless 'scorched earth' policy, intending to create a dead zone in which the Red Army would find it difficult to survive. The result was that thousands of helpless women and children perished in the cold; any Russian men, particularly of military age, were rounded up by the Germans and marched off to prison camps. Among the villages destroyed was Strelkovka, where Zhukov had lived as a child.

Some German soldiers were regretful about this policy, and a few even took steps to protect civilians and their homes; while a few opposed the 'scorched earth' policy on humanitarian grounds, most of those who were opposed to it had rather more practical motives:

> Apparently on higher orders, VI Corps instructed that villages were to be set ablaze immediately before we withdrew. The division [6th Infantry Division] did not carry out this order as it regarded it as inexpedient and of no value. The Russians, equipped with thickly padded winter clothing, made themselves warm huts in every bit of woodland almost immediately. And the fires had a tactical consequence as the enemy could spot a withdrawal's location and timing immediately, much as we had discovered in the summer of 1915 during the Russian retreat.[15]

Regardless of such local decisions, it seems that most Germans regarded the destruction of villages a military necessity, and a few found it a welcome break from combat:

> Every day and every night there is skirmishing between us and the Russians. The burning of villages provides delightful relaxation.[16]

Ivan Semenovich Lykov was a soldier in a tank unit of Forty-Third Army, and as was the case for anyone witnessing destruction on their native soil, the sight of villages deliberately destroyed aroused strong feelings:

> The Nazis clung desperately to every strongpoint. When they left a village or town, they killed every living thing there, burned down peasant huts and buildings, and blew up stone buildings. It was often the case that we would advance to a settlement marked on a map, but in fact it wasn't there, only the smoking chimneys in the fierce December wind.
>
> I remember we drove the Nazis out of one of these villages. We fought for two days and on the third the Nazis couldn't take any more and ran. We entered the village and gaped in dismay: a few pipes protruded from the ground. And not a soul anywhere. Pelevin [one of his tank crew] and I stood near a mound of ashes that was still smoking and gathered the men and told them: 'Look around, remember what the enemy leaves behind.'
>
> And there was no need to say anything more. The ashes of destruction cried out for revenge.
>
> We had planned to leave the village in order to pursue the enemy further when Rukavishnikov, the battalion medic, came running and reported that

Sergeant Major Ryklin's crew had found a local resident hiding from the Nazis at the edge of the village ...

[The elderly man] told us that the Nazis drove almost all of the inhabitants from the village, including his daughter-in-law with two teenage sons. Some villagers managed to escape into the forest. Now they would return as the Red Army had driven the enemy away ...

I will never forget how in another village we liberated, in a burned shed, we found old people, women and children suffocated in the smoke. We didn't need to instil hatred for the enemy in our soldiers. It poured itself into their souls, making them stronger and more determined.[17]

The Russian civilians who returned to their devastated villages found little shelter, and many drifted east into larger towns, some of which had not been occupied by the Wehrmacht. Here, they found life very difficult; the civilian authorities had few resources for their usual residents and nothing to spare for refugees. Similarly, many of the civilians who were forcibly evacuated from their villages by the Germans and moved further west found that no provision had been made for them in the towns and cities where they were sent. The number of civilians who starved or froze to death in the winter is unknown.

To the west of Moscow, Soviet attacks drove the Germans back towards Volokolamsk. Gustav Schrodek was a tank commander in 11th Panzer Division, and experienced first-hand the plummeting morale of men who had believed just a few weeks before that they were close to winning the war:

The confidence of the troops in the high command rapidly diminished: morale collapsed. An order to retreat with the false implication of a well-constructed front line further back was widely exaggerated: every 'strongly fortified winter position' that we passed a few days later under constant threat from the Russians had no prepared machine-gun positions, and bunkers with 88mm guns were completely absent ...

We were to disinter our dead from their graves. Easier said than done. We limited ourselves to taking the crosses from the graves so that the Russians wouldn't know how heavy our losses had been, or the units to which the dead had belonged ...

The village of Novopetrovskoye, from which a road ran to the west, was burning brightly when we reached it. We drove through quickly towards Pokrovskoye. There we were able to get some rest. The fuel tanks were almost empty – and there was no fuel, at least officially. But I 'organised' two cans. I reckoned, better safe than sorry. But it's well known that a soldier shouldn't think, he should leave that to the horses, as they have bigger heads.

I realised the truth of this the following day, 18 December. 'Which vehicle is still able to drive back alone?' I reported back honestly and with a bit of malice. There was only one other tank in our company that wasn't short of fuel.

All other combat vehicles were destroyed – and the crews weren't at all sorry. They were secretly delighted as they were to march back to the rear positions immediately without getting caught up in the fighting. A few were even able to find horses and sleighs. We two company idiots had to stay in Pokrovskoye together with two tanks of another company.

But it got even worse. The infantry rearguard just beat off a Russian attack and called for tanks. It wasn't at all to our taste to go up against the Russians. But orders were orders and we drove off as we were urgently needed.

So: 'Clear for battle' and once more towards Novopetrovskoye. After two kilometres we turned to the left where we could see a village about 1,000m away. Our riflemen were meant to be there.

As we got closer to the village, the scene became increasingly odd. There wasn't a soul to be seen, which seemed very unlikely. We wouldn't have been sent to help a regiment that wasn't actually there.

Then we saw a German truck with a field kitchen, with smoke rising gently from its chimney. But where were the men? No guards or sentries, nothing. Unnatural, unlikely. Finally a couple of faces appeared. But good grief, they were Russians! After them!

But suddenly a few German riflemen also appeared and got involved. I drove further into the village in my vehicle to see what was happening. It was the same picture there.

But wait, not quite the same: there were heavily armed sentries outside the largest house – Russians. We moved closer cautiously. Even when we were barely 20m away and could hardly be overlooked, nobody took any notice of us. The Russians remained unbothered, walking back and forth – and when we turned off our engine we heard them laughing loudly and freely. It was too much. Did they think our vehicle was one of their tanks? If that was so, it must mean that there were Russian tanks close by. So we had to act quickly – and we did. A quick order to fire and a high explosive shell, and the Russian guards no longer had anything to laugh about.

Then German infantry moved towards the house. Unaware of the danger, they ran up to my tank and climbed onto the back, shook our hands in gratitude and even hugged us with joy ...

[Apparently,] The Russians had attacked so suddenly at 1100 that the riflemen were overrun. Constantly having to stand in the open in this bitter cold, short of food and sleep, they had no ability to resist or even be alert. Consequently, in a short time they were overwhelmed and taken prisoner. Liberating them made up for a lot. But now we felt responsible for them.

Russian tanks were close by, that was obvious. The icy wind brought the occasional droning of engines to our ears. We had to do something quickly to avoid a repetition of the morning's setbacks. But it was useless as we couldn't persuade the infantrymen's officer to evacuate the village, which could easily become a trap. They had been ordered to hold it until 1600 and intended to stick to this ...

It was 1400 when the inevitable occurred. The sounds of enemy tanks drew ever closer. We still couldn't see anything. Our teeth were chattering. I wanted to blame it on the cold. I looked out again. The infantry officers now seemed less certain about things. They ran up to us and asked us to move up against the Russian tanks. Nonsense! They still believed in fairy tales if they thought the appearance of our old wagons would scare the T-34s. And in the meantime they intended to abandon the village, they told us, as they felt it was impossible to stop the Russian attack ...

While we tank commanders were standing there trying to make our opinion of the facts clear to the infantrymen, there was a shout from my turret: 'Look out, they're coming!' We sprinted to our tanks and just as quickly the infantry officers set off to their men's positions.

As the gunner had climbed out to stand guard in my absence and was still sitting on the turret, I took his seat and as I clambered in I saw a T-34 approaching us at high speed. Unfortunately, it wasn't alone.

As I looked, it stopped suddenly and fired. My vehicle wasn't its target. I thanked him with a few well-aimed AP rounds. But as we had so often experienced, my sparrow-gun did nothing to him ...

I hadn't noticed that the other vehicle from my company was no longer operational and had dead aboard. Nor did I immediately notice that panic broke out amongst the riflemen and they abandoned their positions, trying to flee across the open snowfield, where many of them were gunned down. Something else I didn't see: a truck belonging to the infantry approaching me, trying to pass and reach the main road, and that a crowd of infantrymen were clinging to it.

While I was solely busy with firing round after round at the T-34, the monster rammed the truck at full speed and struck my barrel. The turret lurched sideways. Something had apparently broken and it could no longer be turned ...

'Away from here! Full throttle!' I roared to the driver and he knew exactly what was afoot. But there was no possibility of driving quickly as there were infantry standing on the road and wanting to be taken with us. With our combined strength we managed to turn the turret to the rear. Now for the first time I could see the entire drama. The riflemen were in wild flight across the entire line, pursued by Russian tanks. The other vehicle from my company had been shot up. We drove past another destroyed tank. We no longer were able to take aimed shots. There was no sign of the fourth tank. Only Russian tanks, which we couldn't oppose with our gun, were everywhere that we looked …

Eight riflemen were crouching on the front of my vehicle and bunches of them clung to the sides –and even more tried to cling to the back as we drove. Many of them had already been wounded by incoming fire …

Through the open gunner's hatch I saw how another rifleman tried to climb aboard but got caught in the tank's tracks. Quickly I leaned out, grabbed him and freed him from the tracks. At that moment, something flashed between us and struck him. He died in my hands. 'I'm sorry, comrade, but you'll have to stay here!' Slowly I opened my hands and let him slide back onto the snow.[18]

After a week of heavy losses, Zhukov was in a position to report cautiously that his Front had driven the German spearheads back from the Moscow approaches. On 12 and 13 December, Lelyushenko's mobile group, deliberately avoiding head-on clashes with German strongpoints, succeeded in cutting the German lines of retreat from Klin, where 1st Panzer Division found itself isolated, together with perhaps a thousand wounded men. The division staff concluded that although the best option for a breakout in terms of Red Army resistance was first to the southeast, and then to the west, this would involve the abandonment of a large proportion of the division's wheeled transport, which would mean that the wounded men would have to be abandoned. Instead, it was decided to break out along the main road to Nekrasino, i.e. directly to the west. By the end of 14 December, much of the division had reached the village of Golyady, just five miles from the centre of Klin, which was abandoned at the end of the day. Lelyushenko described how he created a second mobile group to prevent the Germans from carrying out a successful evacuation, but during the night the German column continued along the road, and by midday on 15 December, the division and the wounded men from Klin had reached the – temporary – safety of Nekrasino.[19] Rotmistrov described how his tank brigade fought a bitter battle for the small town of Vysokovsk, to the west of Klin, and how his men killed large numbers of Germans, but couldn't hide the fact that the Germans were able to break out.[20]

The episode demonstrated the limitations of Soviet successes. Their units might be able to penetrate the lines of the overstretched German forces and even, on occasion, achieve partial or complete encirclements, but the tactical superiority of the Germans when counterattacking allowed them to escape or to drive back the penetrations. It was part of a learning curve that would continue through the next two years; by 1944, the attacking Red Army units would be accompanied or closely followed by dedicated anti-tank battalions and brigades, and combat engineers also became increasingly integrated into army formations; dense minefields would be created in an astonishingly short time, making it difficult and often impossible for the Germans to conduct effective counterattacks. But in late 1941, almost every German counterthrust was successful. These sudden, surprisingly powerful attacks rapidly imposed a degree of caution on the Soviet units. Instead of continuing the momentum of their attacks and achieving maximum disruption, there was a growing tendency to proceed slowly in case a counterattack developed.[21] The painful slowness of the evolution of the Red Army in dealing with German counterattacks is perhaps a further example of the ongoing damage inflicted by the pre-war purges and the rigid political orthodoxy that was then imposed; German military manuals had always highlighted the importance of counterattacks to restore defensive positions, and such practice had been widespread even in the First World War, yet the Red Army had not made any specific preparations to deal with such counterattacks.

Soviet historiography treated the battles of December and January as a great victory that threw back the Wehrmacht from the approaches of Moscow, but it was impossible to hide the extraordinarily high cost paid by the Red Army for its successes, as Rokossovsky later wrote:

> The Nazi command had concentrated vast forces and were anticipating the triumphant entry of their hordes into the Soviet capital. Now they were compelled to flee ignominiously westward, thinking only of how to halt our advance.
>
> But it was hard going for us too. Sixteenth Army had suffered great casualties in the course of the protracted defensive fighting and subsequent counteroffensive. The divisions numbered no more than 1,200 to 1,500 men each, artillery and mortarmen, engineers, signallers and staffs included. The number of infantry effectives was small indeed, and our command and political personnel had also suffered serious losses in the fighting. The situation in the neighbouring armies was no better.[22]

The casualties included some notable figures. The 38-year-old Lev Dovator's cavalry corps had been in the thick of the fighting for months, and in November it was renamed II Guards Cavalry Corps in honour of its combat record. On 19 December, Dovator's two divisions were ordered to attack at Palashkino, due west of Moscow. An officer in the cavalry corps later described events:

> Dyakovo was burning to our right. There were flashes of explosions, enveloped in brownish clouds. Lines of dismounted cavalrymen could barely be seen. Squadrons of 103rd Cavalry Regiment emerged from the nearby forest and attacked Palashkino. No sooner had the horsemen reached the ice [of the frozen river] than the guns rumbled from the forest edge – the division's artillery, firing on the village.
>
> ... The dismounted cavalrymen advanced only 500m – heavy fire from the Nazis forced them to ground. After a while, three squadrons broke into Palashkino from the southeast but the enemy counterattacked with a battalion of infantry and seven tanks. Our squadrons pulled back and began to dig in.
>
> 'Tavliev, it's vital to get the men to attack!' shouted Dovator and ran down onto the ice, to the men of 22nd Cavalry Regiment. He was wearing a helmet and a grey Kuban coat, with a Mauser piston in his hand. The adjutant, Colonel Tavliev [commander of 20th Cavalry Division], Karasev (the political commissar of the headquarters squadron) and several officers and soldiers from the corps headquarters rushed after him.
>
> Dovator was already halfway to the lines of men lying on the ice. From the direction of Palashkino, a machine-gun fired a long burst. Dovator stopped, seemed to wilt, and fell heavily to the snow. The adjutant rushed to the general and tried to lift him but was cut down by the next burst. Tavliev also fell face down. Karasev rushed to Dovator but was killed before he could move a few steps.
>
> ... From the shore, we saw how Dovator fell and the men rushing to him were cut down. The Nazis continued to spray the area where the general lay with machine-guns. Finally, Senior Lieutenant Kulikov and Junior Lieutenant Sokirko managed to crawl to Dovator and carry him to our bank.[23]

An account of the defensive fighting by 2nd Panzer Division shows the problems of combat in such cold conditions, especially without the specialist lubricants necessary to keep machinery functioning:

> The enemy was able to penetrate into Plaksina ... The heavy machine-gun team, which was in position northwest of the 50mm anti-tank gun, fired

continuously until it jammed. Thereafter, the heavy machine-gun crew pulled out of their position. From this moment, the Russians attacked from here in strength into the village and moved against the anti-tank gun. The crew of the 50mm anti-tank gun defended themselves with their personal weapons and with an additional machine-gun that was close by. As they were outnumbered, the crew pulled back to my command post on the other side of the street. By now the enemy was already in control of most of the village. Wire communications were cut.

Now we saw how the enemy was working towards the anti-tank gun to the southeast. The crew defended themselves furiously but were put out of action by the Russians. Two men were killed, one was missing, but two were able to fight through to the machine-gun to their west and reach my command post. This machine-gun, whose crew had lost two men, was operated by Obergefreiter Schongott until it too jammed and he could do no more ... In the meantime a heavy machine-gun that was to the south of the 37mm anti-tank gun changed positions on my orders and covered the houses to the north where the threat from the enemy seemed most serious. Unfortunately this gun only fired a few shots and then, due to the cold, it too jammed and couldn't be fixed. At this point another heavy machine-gun was brought forward despite increasing enemy fire. Due to the cold, this gun couldn't fire at all ...

The MG-34 [the standard machine-gun of the Wehrmacht at the time] was frozen and despite every effort couldn't fire at all.[24]

The first two weeks of the Soviet counteroffensive effectively eliminated the two German salients – to the northwest and south of Moscow – where the Wehrmacht's panzer groups had stalled. On the German side of the line, on 18 December Hitler ordered his armies and divisions to hold their existing positions. This has sometimes been regarded as the moment when Hitler saved the Wehrmacht by preventing a stumbling retreat from becoming a rout, as Oberst Günther Blumentritt, who was serving as chief of staff in the German Fourth Army immediately to the west of Moscow, later wrote:

Hitler believed that he personally could ward off the catastrophe which was impending before Moscow. And it must be stated quite frankly that he did in fact succeed in doing so. His fanatical order that the troops must hold fast regardless in every position, and in the most impossible circumstances, was undoubtedly correct ... Hitler realised instinctively that any retreat across the snow and ice must, within a few days, lead to the dissolution of the front.[25]

The reality is more nuanced, as David Stahel has described in detail.[26] The order was not a comprehensive ban on any retreat, but required troops to hold their positions unless there was absolutely no choice, and to pull back only if fresh positions had been prepared. In practice, permission to conduct such withdrawals had to be secured by lengthy exchanges with *OKH*, resulting in avoidable casualties, and in other cases commanders at all levels in the front line simply ordered withdrawals anyway. Some, like Hoepner and Guderian, paid for this by being dismissed, but in many other cases these acts were either not detected or were ignored.

This order from Hitler shows the onset of a new factor in German calculations. As the war progressed, the 'will' to win, and to substitute 'fanatic' strength for material strength, played an increasing part in thinking at the highest levels of German leadership. The manner in which Blumentritt openly acknowledged and accepted that this would require troops to hold fast 'in the most impossible circumstances' demonstrates that such thinking was not confined to Hitler and his entourage, regardless of the attempts by German officers after the war to blame Hitler for such a mindset.

On the same day that Hitler issued this order, there were changes in command arrangements. Bock was replaced as commander of Army Group Centre by Kluge, who would command the army group throughout the coming battles around Rzhev. He in turn was replaced as commander of Fourth Army by General Ludwig Kübler, but the biggest changes occurred far from the front line. Brauchitsch's health had been poor throughout the autumn, and on 10 November, Halder recorded in his diary that he had been informed that Brauchitsch had suffered a heart attack and had been diagnosed with incurable heart disease. Increasingly sidelined, Brauchitsch clung on to his post in the hope that he would be able to crown his military career with the capture of Moscow, but the day after Hitler issued his 'stand fast' order, he was dismissed. Hitler announced that in future, he would take direct command of the army. As Bock departed, he met his headquarters staff to say farewell:

> I asked them to stay firm and confident, because I believe that the end of the present 'dirty period' is in sight. The Russians can scarcely have all that many forces left.[27]

Like all German estimates of the strength of the Red Army, this was a hopelessly optimistic assessment. The men in the front line had little doubt that they were facing a numerically superior foe, and the few withdrawals that were permitted were hugely hindered by the weather and shortages of horses. Motor vehicles were also often inadequate; 6th Infantry Division reported that the worn-out Krupp trucks that equipped its anti-tank battalion couldn't cope with either the snow or the cold:

> On the first change of positions, the [anti-tank battalion] needed a full 24 hours to get its vehicles moving. In addition to the engines, the gearboxes in particular were frozen so solid that the cogs could only be turned after prolonged warming over an open fire. Every single truck had to be towed. But despite this, we succeeded in saving most of our heavy equipment from capture by the enemy. Apart from the loss of the immobile heavy howitzer battery [four guns that had to be destroyed], only elements of 6th Artillery Regiment's II Battalion, supporting 37th Infantry Regiment, were lost after they became caught up in heavy close-quarter fighting when pulling back from the Staritsa position.[28]

The clumsiness of the Red Army notwithstanding, the Germans endured difficult days of fighting. On Christmas Day, 6th Infantry Division came under heavy attack and one of its battalions was briefly encircled. The remnants managed to fight their way out to link up with the rest of the regiment, but the Soviet attacks continued:

> At 0045 the Russians attacked Bukontovo in roughly regiment strength from the south and southwest. They slowly fought their way forward despite heavy casualties. The fighting swung back and forth, particularly around the church. The artillery horses had several losses. The regiment commander, fighting in the front line with a rifle, was wounded twice with head wounds but remained in combat. As the enemy had taken the eastern part of the village, Oberstleutnant Hirsch decided to make a counterattack with parts of I/37 [1st Battalion, 37th Infantry Regiment] towards the northeast while Oberleutnant Dunker conducted an active and careful defence against the enemy attacks at the church. Losses escalated. The Russians were too numerous. Finally they succeeded in pushing past the church and brought a small German group under fire from the church tower. The fight for Bukontovo was futile and consequently Dunker pulled back to the west and took up a new defensive line in front of the firing positions of 4th and 6th Companies of 6th Artillery Regiment. The Russians didn't spot their opportunity and didn't pursue …
>
> The troops, who had been marching and fighting in temperatures of -30 to -40°C for a week, began to stop holding firm in their usual manner – on 25 December five men from the reconnaissance battalion collapsed into unconsciousness. Utterly

exhausted, almost frozen stiff, receiving in the main only cold and inadequate rations, they stood without winter clothing in the most bitter – almost Siberian – weather in their tattered, flimsy uniforms, their footwear falling apart, wrapped in their thin coats, in icy, cutting snow showers, without trenches or accommodation, or defendable barriers against a numerically vastly superior enemy.[29]

The manner in which crises continued to develop along the entire front of Army Group Centre demonstrates that had the Red Army concentrated its forces in fewer areas, it might have achieved considerably greater success, instead of creating a wealth of opportunities that it then lacked the local strength to exploit. On the southern flank of the German Fourth Army, Heinrici's XLIII Corps lost contact with German forces further south and could do nothing to prevent Soviet units pushing on to Kaluga on 21 December. Heinrici's northern flank was also pushed back, and there was a serious risk of the entire corps being encircled. If this were to happen, an irreparable hole would be created in the German lines, and Kluge approved a short withdrawal. For the moment, disaster was averted, and further withdrawals – many after lengthy arguments with Hitler, some with little or no communication between Kluge and *OKH* – continued over the next few days. Heinrici's letters to his wife during these days showed his growing hopelessness, and the strain under which he and all other men in the front line were operating:

[20 December] It is becoming apparent that we are gradually being surrounded. We are forming a semicircle southeast of Kaluga and the enemy is encircling our flanks. We do not have any reserves to protect them. All pleas, all requests to our superiors have remained unanswered …

[22 December] Basically we are already encircled. Yesterday the situation was without any hope. We were anticipating our end in the encirclement. Then, at the very last minute, Kluge gave permission to evade again. That prolonged our existence a little bit longer …

The ups and downs are hardly bearable any more. For ten days I have seen the catastrophe coming, I have called, I have adjured. I get orders that are impossible to complete. Matters are on a razor's edge. Nothing I do makes my superiors see. The consequences are unforeseeable.

[24 December] We are going to our doom. And the highest authorities in Berlin do not want to see it … They do not want to admit failure. And this will end with the loss of their army before Moscow in four weeks' time, and afterwards with the loss of the war.[30]

However bitter and hopeless Heinrici felt, it was essential for his corps at least to delay the Soviet advance. Kluge issued repeated orders to Guderian, ordering him not to retreat any further, but it would have been suicidal for Second Panzer Group to remain in its exposed positions, and had Heinrici's corps either withdrawn or been overwhelmed, there was every prospect that the panzer group would face encirclement. Guderian famously travelled to Rastenburg to meet Hitler on 20 December, with growing awareness both at *OKH* and Army Group Centre that the panzer commander was simply turning a blind eye to most of the orders to stand fast. Guderian later gave his own account of the conversation with Hitler, in which the Führer criticised him for seeing events at too close a range and being too deeply impressed by the suffering of the soldiers in his command; Halder informed Kluge that Guderian seemed to have lost his nerve completely.[31]

Guderian's time as a front-line commander was rapidly approaching its end. Far from being persuaded to adhere to Hitler's 'stand fast' order after his trip to Rastenburg, Guderian continued to authorise his corps commanders to pull back. Regardless of the tactical exigencies that necessitated these withdrawals, to carry them out without coordination with Kluge's headquarters risked creating a dislocated front line. On 25 December, the two men had a further argument by telephone, resulting in Kluge contacting *OKH* and demanding Guderian's removal. Hitler gave his approval and Guderian was dismissed. His Second Panzer Group – imminently to be renamed Second Panzer Army – was placed under the control of Generaloberst Rudolf Schmidt, commander of Second Army, which was to the southwest of Guderian's former command; for the moment, Schmidt would control both formations. Guderian was a popular man with his subordinates, and – perhaps because Guderian made no secret of his views – there was a widespread recognition that he was paying the price for standing up to Hitler in the best interests of his troops. As if to reinforce this, Halder felt compelled to issue a new directive at the end of the year to all parts of the Wehrmacht:

> The soldier's duty to obey leaves no room for the sensibilities of subordinate commanders; rather it requires the most rapid and best possible execution of orders as desired by the authority issuing them. [We will overcome our difficulties] ... if a single will, the will of the Führer, prevails from the highest levels down to the soldier at the front.[32]

Guderian might have been the most flagrant breaker of Hitler's edict to stand firm and resort to 'fanatical' defence, but almost every senior commander quietly broke the rule when required. Kluge spent the entire winter conducting a delicate balancing act, giving his subordinates as much leeway as he could while negotiating with almost superhuman patience with Hitler to secure permission for withdrawals. This policy allowed him to authorise the slow withdrawal of Heinrici's XLIII Corps to Kaluga, but gaps remained on either side of the corps – to the south, there were no German troops for 48 miles (80km) before the first units of Second Panzer Army. Even though Hitler gave unequivocal orders that the retreat had to stop at Kaluga, there was little confidence in the front line that the position could be held. Eventually, Kluge secured permission from Hitler for a further withdrawal on 29 December. A tenuous connection to the lines to the north was restored, and the immediate risk of XLIII Corps being encircled was averted, but the huge gap to the south remained open.

To the north of Heinrici's corps, the situation of XII and XIII Corps was just as precarious, with substantial Soviet forces moving through gaps in the German line. Matters were exacerbated by the existence of only one good road for supplies, running from Yukhnov to Maloyaroslavets. The armoured reconnaissance battalion of 19th Panzer Division was ordered to ensure that the road remained open and that encirclement of the two corps was prevented. In difficult conditions, the battalion moved through dense woodland to take up positions for its attack. In doing so, it lost radio contact with the rest of the division, which attacked the Soviet penetration from the west. Unaware that much of the danger of encirclement had been eliminated, Major Hasso Booth, commander of the reconnaissance battalion, made a determined attack on 29 December. Partly because of the success of other elements of 19th Panzer Division, the Soviet units fought only long enough to inflict casualties on the attacking Germans before falling back; among those killed was Major Booth.[33] But there was no opportunity for the division to lick its wounds or mourn its dead, as news arrived that Soviet cavalry was advancing towards Medyn and Yukhnov, once more raising the threat that, at the very least, the German front line would be sundered between the northern flank of Heinrici's XLIII Corps and the southern flank of XIII Corps. To deal with this threat, 19th Panzer Division started to move its units back:

> On 30 December the division marched back along the main road with its main elements to Yukhnov, which it had captured in October with such great vigour. Where had all the hopes of capturing Moscow gone, and what remained of the

division? Many of the tanks and trucks were gone, and the losses of men and equipment were heavy ...

We drove through the battle positions at Cherkassovo, Ilinskoye, and Gusevo, where so many of our comrades were buried. We felt shame that we had to retreat when they had known only attack and success. When the division commander, leading the column, reached the command post of [Fourth] Army east of Yukhnov, he found great unrest there as the leading elements of the Russians had been spotted 200m to the south. All clerks etc. who had barely heard a shot fired in anger before were being deployed or were running around in panic. The division therefore arrived just in time. The ground crews of the airfields [around Yukhnov] were all deployed for defence of the airfields, which were under Russian fire. Supply by air was disrupted.[34]

Generalmajor Otto von Knobelsdorff, commander of 19th Panzer Division, was ordered to attack south from Yukhnov to eliminate the danger to the town, but much of his division was still struggling back down the road from Maloyaroslavets through deep snow. He gathered together what forces he could and took up positions, aware that it would take at least two days for the rest of his units to arrive.

Kluge's subordinates showed little sign of appreciating the delicate balancing act that the Army Group Centre commander had to pursue. The retreats that Heinrici and others demanded would have destabilised significant segments of the front line and would have resulted in the loss of much of the army's heavy weaponry; moreover, permission for each retreat had to be extracted from Hitler, or at least portrayed as absolutely unavoidable. At first, Heinrici greeted Hitler's assumption of command of the army as a positive development, but this was short-lived, and his letters to his wife continued to condemn everyone above him in the chain of command:

Everything has come true exactly as I told my superiors. They have declined all suggestions out of fear of the highest authority. If it is Kluge or Kübler, they are all afraid of the highest authority. And he himself leads according to platitudes such as 'no Napoleonic retreat' ... There would have been measures to turn things around, if they had decided to disengage three weeks ago, two weeks ago, even five or six days ago. We have made suggestions often enough. But the supreme high command refused them all, acting according to the objective not to give up 20 of the conquered 1,200km . And yet it is completely irrelevant where in Russia we are.[35]

The northern army in Kluge's command was Generaloberst Adolf Strauss' Ninth Army, and it too had slowly pulled back from its forward positions through December, under constant pressure from Konev's Kalinin Front. Both sides suffered heavy casualties in the battles that continued almost without a pause through the month, and Strauss was doubtful that he would be able to hold the line of the Staritsa River, where he was ordered to make a stand. Every request by Strauss and Kluge for a further withdrawal towards Rzhev was rejected by Hitler, who countered by producing evidence from the Luftwaffe's General Wolfram von Richthofen, commander of *Fliegerkorps VIII*, which provided air support to Army Group Centre. Richthofen rejected the claims of Strauss that the opposing Soviet forces outnumbered him, and said that his aerial reconnaissance could find no such Red Army concentrations. The commander of VI Corps, one of Strauss' subordinate units, was dismissed for failing to show the requisite determination to resist, and Kluge took advantage of this to exact a small degree of revenge on Richthofen: he asked Hitler to appoint the Luftwaffe general to take command of VI Corps. Probably to Kluge's surprise, Hitler agreed and Richthofen duly inherited a poisoned chalice that he had in part created. He remained in command for just a few days before he was replaced by General Bruno Bieler on 2 January, but his disparaging reports to Hitler ceased for the time being.

It had been a chastening month for Germany, for everyone from Hitler to the soldiers in the front line. Just four weeks before, it seemed as if the Wehrmacht was poised to capture Moscow; the Soviet counteroffensive exposed just how overstretched German resources were. There was now a desperate struggle for both sides: could the Germans find the means to shore up their line before it collapsed? And could the Red Army convert any of its local successes into something more tangible?

CHAPTER 3

FRUSTRATION, JANUARY 1942

The pressure on Ninth Army by the forces of Konev's Kalinin Front continued unabated through the winter. Despite terrible losses, the Soviet units constantly attacked and the danger of a complete collapse of the German line was never far away. Kluge argued bitterly with Halder on the last day of the year when he discovered that Halder had not even passed his reports on to Hitler, on the grounds that the Führer would reject any requests for a further retreat. Kluge finally spoke to Hitler personally late that night and was told once more that Strauss would not be permitted to retreat. Matters were further exacerbated by the manner in which German army commanders jealously guarded their assets – Reinhardt only released a small battlegroup of a single battalion with a small number of tanks in support to help Ninth Army after Kluge pointed out that if Ninth Army's positions along the Staritsa collapsed, Reinhardt's panzer army faced a severe threat to its supply lines. This danger materialised almost immediately.

The German VI Corps was slowly being forced back and in the last days of December had to withdraw over the Volga. Three 'ice bridges' had been prepared over the river – segments of ice that were carefully strengthened by combat engineers and where approaches were dug on either bank, at least as far as the frozen ground permitted. The exhausted men succeeded in bringing most of their remaining heavy equipment across the river, but the Red Army was close behind. Bitter fighting erupted around a small bridgehead established by Soviet soldiers in 6th Infantry Division's sector; the German battalions were reduced to the strength of barely a weak company each, while their opponents struggled to bring forward sufficient reinforcements to strengthen the bridgehead. Eventually, the German line had to be taken back further. More Soviet attacks developed on

1 January, with one group penetrating into the town of Staritsa and overrunning part of 6th Infantry Division's headquarters. Two battalions of the division were cut off but managed to fight their way to the west as the remnants of four German divisions staggered back along the road that led southwest towards Rzhev. Had the Red Army deployed a strong exploitation force in this area, it seems likely that the German line would have been unable to resist, but the dilution of effort across the entire front line meant that the only mobile unit pursuing the Germans was a cavalry battalion. It succeeded in reaching, and briefly capturing, a village astride the route being used by the Germans for their withdrawal before being driven off. Finally, around the village of Koledino, a little less than half the way from Staritsa to Rzhev, the Germans organised themselves once more into a coherent defensive line.[1]

This line was part of the *Königsberg-Stellung* or 'Königsberg line'. It had first been postulated by Bock on 9 December as a potential defensive line even before the full extent of the Soviet counteroffensive became clear, and the fact that it lay so far behind the front line at that time indicates that Bock, at least, appreciated just how overstretched his forces had become in their attempts to reach Moscow. The line commenced on the Volga to the north of Rzhev and then ran south through the city to Gzhatsk, Medyn, Orel and eventually to Kursk.[2] In places, it took advantage of geographical features that might favour a defensive position, but mostly it was an arbitrary line running between the major towns and cities of the region. Hitler repeatedly refused to countenance any wholesale withdrawal to this position for several reasons. Firstly, the line was no more than a proposed position rather than an existing line of fortifications. Secondly, most German formations lacked the mobility to reach the line in a single movement. In both respects, he was correct; when he learned that Strauss was threatening an early withdrawal to the Königsberg line, Reinhardt informed Kluge that 'If Third Panzer Group has to withdraw [rapidly, in order to retain contact with Strauss' Ninth Army], I'll come out with just carbines on our shoulders.'[3] Kluge was just as aware as Bock that Army Group Centre needed to pull back to a shorter line and that eventually this would involve a withdrawal to or near the Königsberg line, but he knew that this would have to be carried out in stages, both to extract permission from Hitler in incremental steps, and to stay within the mobility limitations of front-line units. Inevitably, rumours of a fortified line circulated widely among the retreating soldiers, who imagined that they would at least find sheltered positions where they might get some relief from the worst of the weather, but the reality of the new 'line' was an unpleasant surprise:

The 'Königsberg' winter line was occupied [by 6th Infantry Division] on 2 January between Kruptsovo and Nemtsovo, a segment about 17km [10 miles] long, and was a bitter disappointment. The only defensive positions were the few villages lying along the line. But in the open ground and in the woodland, which were often the preferred points of attack for the Russians, there was nothing. Once more, the soldiers stood in the snow without shelter in grim conditions of up to -40°C. As a result of their reduced combat strength – for example, III Battalion, 18th Infantry Regiment had one officer, four NCOs and 20 men – everything had to be deployed in the front line so that the position could be given the most basic protection. Units were created from the artillery, the signals battalion, the supply columns and other rear area formations and sent forward. In addition to their vital technical duties, the sappers too had to be deployed in the front line, and even 79th Construction Battalion, which had been assigned to the division.[4]

Just a day after they reached this line, the Germans came under renewed attack. A nine-mile (15km) gap was torn between the German VI and XXIII Corps, and Red Army forces threatened both the road back to Rzhev and potentially the city itself. Desperate counterattacks secured the road and sealed off the Soviet penetration, and defences were prepared, with the combat engineers using explosives to break up the frozen ground. Once more, the lack of fresh Red Army units to exploit the initial gains resulted in the Germans recovering their positions and restoring their wafer-thin line. On 10 January, 6th Infantry Division reported its first experience of coming under fire from *Katyusha* rockets and fought off almost daily attacks for several weeks. Had the Red Army paused for several days to gather its strength and make a concentrated, sustained effort, the consequences for the Germans might have been disastrous, but each attack was repulsed, often by the use of the very last reserves available. With a battlegroup made up of men from different units and supported by three assault guns, the Germans attempted to close the breach between VI and XXIII Corps; while this group attacked from the south, another unit was to attack from the west.

This second group was a cavalry brigade belonging to the SS, commanded by Standartenführer Hermann Fegelein. Once described by Albert Speer, who would end the war as Germany's armaments minister, as 'one of the most disgusting people in Hitler's circle', Fegelein was one of many prominent figures who rose to high rank in the SS despite having no formal military training. He was a keen equestrian and persuaded Heinrich Himmler, a personal friend, to allow him to establish a riding school for the SS. This was then transformed into a mounted regiment and took part in the invasion of Poland, where its main role seems to have been the extermination of Polish intelligentsia and clergy, including the slaughter of nearly 2,000 people in the Kampinos Forest in December 1939. Fegelein's personal conduct in Poland was perhaps an indication of the reason why Speer disliked him so much – he was implicated both in looting and in having sex with a Polish woman, but these investigations and several others were blocked by Himmler. The cavalry unit entered the Soviet Union with Army Group Centre and was used mainly in anti-partisan warfare, often involved in indiscriminate mass killings in order to increase the body count to a level that would impress Fegelein's superiors.[5] Neither Fegelein nor most of his men had any significant front-line experience, and it can have come as little surprise that the SS cavalry brigade failed to make any impression. Its attack was late, delayed by a snowstorm, and was easily fended off by the Red Army. Bitter fighting continued for several days, as the diary of 6th Infantry Division's 18th Infantry Regiment recorded on 13 January:

> During the night, firing centred on Gushchino broke the silence. At 0700 a Russian company appeared north of the main road … [The attack was] repulsed. At 0175 up to two companies attacked under cover of fog after heavy preparatory fire by light artillery, mortars and anti-tank guns on Gushchino. This was resumed at 1145 by up to three companies and repulsed …
>
> At about 1500 the attack on the left flank resumed, constantly supported by enemy reserves. This too was repulsed and at about 1900, after losing about 250 dead, the enemy retreated … The defence was mainly by infantry weapons as the artillery suffered greatly from a lack of ammunition … The loss of 45 men greatly weakened the combat strength of I Battalion.[6]

The failed attempt to restore the front line by counterattacks necessitated another short withdrawal to re-establish continuity. Thereafter, fighting continued at varying levels of intensity, but the front line would remain essentially unchanged until the summer, allowing the Germans an opportunity to construct the fortifications that many of them had expected to find when they first fell back towards the Königsberg line. Some of the encounters with Soviet forces were distinctly unorthodox, as the men of 6th Infantry Division noted:

> On 6 February, we captured a group of Russian spies who had been dispatched with very precise orders, including some pretty girls, attempting to cross our front line. Some of them gave themselves up willingly and informed us that they had been forced to take part.[7]

Further to the south, 19th Panzer Division was now assigned to XL Corps. Many of its panzer regiment personnel, deprived of tanks due to losses of equipment, were sent to the division's infantry battalions as reinforcements; in emulation of the old Prussian hussars, the panzer crews wore black uniforms, which were singularly inappropriate for combat in the snow, and the men rapidly acquired a mixture of overcoats. The division now had just six operational tanks, but even these were of limited use – a counterattack in early January failed because the turrets of most of the tanks were frozen in position and couldn't be turned.[8]

While the front line to the north of Rzhev was slowly stabilising, senior Soviet commanders increasingly turned their discussions to how they might develop the counteroffensive further. Zhukov was summoned to Moscow for a meeting on 5 January 1942:

> After Shaposhnikov's presentation about the situation on all fronts and his draft plans, Stalin said, 'The Germans are dismayed by their defeat near Moscow and are poorly prepared for the winter. Now is the best moment to begin a general offensive. The enemy is counting on us delaying our offensive until the spring – by then, having mustered his strength, he will once more resume offensive operations. He wants to buy time to recover.' None of those present, as I recall, raised any objections to this, and Stalin developed his thoughts further. 'Our task,' he mused, walking as usual around the conference room, 'is to not give the Germans this respite, to drive them to the west without a pause, to get them to commit their reserves before the spring.' He emphasised his last words, paused a little, and then continued. 'We have new reserves, and the Germans have none.'
>
> Having outlined his understanding of the possible options for offensives, the Supreme Commander proceeded to consider practical plans for each front. The *Stavka* plan was as follows. Considering the successful course of the counteroffensive by the troops of the Western Direction [i.e. the Fronts defending Moscow], the aim of the general offensive was to defeat the enemy on all fronts.
>
> The main blow was planned to be delivered against Army Group Centre and its defeat was to be carried out by the left wing of Northwest Front and Kalinin, Western, and Bryansk Fronts, which would conduct a double envelopment and subsequent encirclement and destruction of the main forces in the Rzhev–Vyazma–Smolensk region. The troops of Leningrad and Volkhov Fronts, the right wing of Northwest Front, and the Baltic Fleet were tasked with crushing Army Group North and breaking the Leningrad blockade. The troops of Southwest and Southern Fronts were to defeat Army Group South and liberate the Donbas region, while Caucasian Front and the Black Sea Fleet were to liberate

Crimea. The transition to a general offensive was supposed to be carried out in an extremely short time.

After outlining this plan, Stalin invited those present to speak.

'In the Western Direction,' I reported, 'where favourable conditions have been created and the enemy has not yet managed to restore the combat effectiveness of his units, we must continue the offensive. But for a successful outcome, we need to replenish our ranks with men and military equipment and reinforce them with reserves, particularly tank formations. Without this replenishment, our offensive cannot succeed. As for the offensive of our troops near Leningrad and towards the southwest, our troops face substantial enemy defences. Without powerful artillery, they will not be able to break through these defences. They will be exhausted and will suffer heavy, unjustifiable losses. I propose strengthening the Fronts of the Western Direction and conducting a more powerful offensive here.'

[Nikolai Alekseevich] Voznesensky [First Deputy Chairman of the Council of People's Commissars] supported me. 'We do not yet have the material resources sufficient for a simultaneous offensive on all Fronts.'

'I spoke to Timoshenko [who was now commander of Southwest Front and with overall control of the Southwest Direction],' said Stalin. 'He is in favour of action on the Southwest Direction. We must grind down the Germans faster so that they can't advance in the spring. Who else would like to speak?' There was no response. A proper discussion of his proposals never took place.

As we left the conference room, Shaposhnikov said to me, 'Your arguments were in vain. This issue was decided in advance by the Supreme Commander.'

'Then why did he ask our opinion?'

'I don't know, my dear fellow, I don't know!' replied Boris Mikhailovich, sighing heavily.[9]

Zhukov was aware that the successes of December had been won at a heavy price. His armies were badly depleted in men and equipment, and needed substantial reinforcements. Moreover, his belief that in order to win more decisive victories, a far greater concentration of resources would be needed was correct. Given the continuing threat to Moscow, with German units only 42 miles (70km) from the city, he felt that the resources available to the Red Army should be concentrated here rather than in other sectors. But just as Hitler, Halder and others had decided – from a considerable distance – that the Red Army was facing imminent collapse and the Wehrmacht could press forward to complete its triumph regardless of its own weakness, Stalin now made the same mistake, assuming that the Wehrmacht was facing catastrophe. Despite its losses and lack of expertise, the Red Army needed only to attack in order to destroy the invaders. On the face of it, he had grounds for his optimism: in the north, the Germans had been driven back from the town of Tikhvin, allowing Soviet forces to reach Lake Ladoga and thus to open a tenuous connection with the troops holding Leningrad via a road across the frozen lake; and in the south, the Germans had overreached themselves and had been driven back from Rostov, and were losing ground in Crimea.

Orders reached Western Front two days later, confirming Stalin's decision: on Zhukov's right flank, he was to attack with First Shock Army and Twentieth and Sixteenth Armies towards Sychevka and Rzhev, while Kalinin Front to his north drove towards Rzhev from Kalinin; the centre of Western Front was to advance on Mozhaisk and Gzhatsk with Fifth and Thirty-Third Armies; and further south, Forty-Third, Forty-Ninth and Fiftieth Armies would attack towards Vyazma. A reinforced cavalry corps would then exploit towards Vyazma, where it was expected the forces attacking further north would converge with the southern armies of the front, completing a great encirclement in which the German Army Group Centre would be destroyed. At the same time, there would be attacks to the north towards Velikiye Luki and to break the German siege perimeter around Leningrad, and in the south to capture Orel, Kursk and Kharkov, and then to press on to reach the Dnepr River at Dnepropetrovsk and Zaporozhye.

It was a hugely ambitious set of orders, requiring a level of penetration, command and control, and logistic support that was far from anything that the Red Army had ever achieved – even if all resources had been concentrated purely on Western Front, it is unlikely that the Red Army of early 1942 could have conducted such an operation. Recognising the weaknesses shown by Soviet formations in recent fighting, Stalin's orders included instructions for how the new offensives should be conducted. Each army was to avoid sending its divisions into action in a broad line, and was instead to concentrate its resources at a decisive point. Artillery coordination with attacking troops was also to be improved. Such improvements, though, would take many months, and there was little or no possibility of changes being made in time for the renewed offensive. Had the Soviet supreme commander heeded Zhukov's advice and concentrated his efforts against Army Group Centre – and equally crucially, had a more realistic set of objectives been set – a serious defeat might well have been inflicted upon the Wehrmacht. Instead, the preciously hoarded strength of the Red Army was frittered away in costly but ultimately pointless attacks.

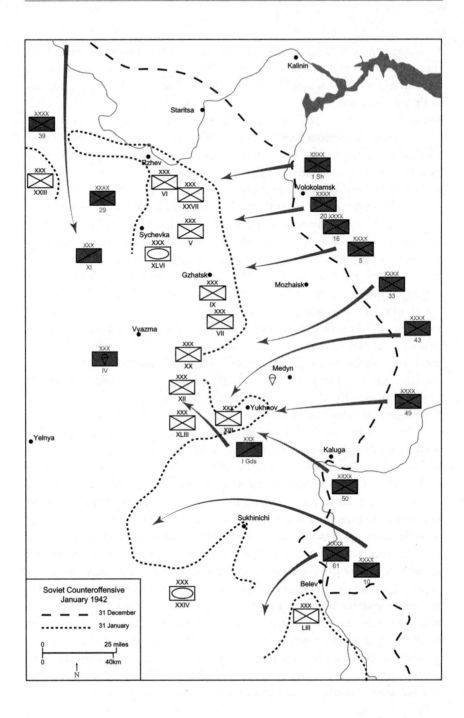

Kalinin

Staritsa

XXXX
39

Rzhev

XXX
XXIII

XXX
VI

XXX
XXVII

XXXX
29

Sychevka
XXX
XLVI

XXX
V

Volokolamsk

XXXX
1 Sh

XXXX
20

XXXX
16

XXXX
5

XXX
XI

Gzhatsk

XXX
IX

XXX
VII

Mozhaisk

XXXX
33

XXXX
43

Vyazma

XXX
IV

XXX
XX

Medyn

XXX
XII

XXX
XIII

Yukhnov

XXXX
49

XXX
XLIII

Yelnya

XXX
I Gds

Kaluga

XXXX
50

Sukhinichi

XXXX
61

XXXX
10

Belev

XXX
XXIV

XXX
LIII

Soviet Counteroffensive
January 1942

— — — 31 December
· · · · · · · 31 January

0   25 miles
0   40km
N

The December offensive by Western Front against the northern flank of Army Group Centre created some nervous moments for the Germans, but much of the German line was now in a stronger defensive posture, as the Soviet analysis of the battle later reported:

> The men and suppression weapons available in each [Soviet] army were insufficient to independently carry out an operational breakthrough and develop it into the depth ... [In January, the armies] encountered the enemy's timely organised and hard defence. Here new offensive methods were demanded. It was necessary to carefully prepare and skilfully organise a breakthrough, having concentrated large amounts of men and suppression materiel along a narrow front, so as to smash through the Germans' defence and then develop the breakthrough into the depth and along the flanks.
>
> However, evidently this was not immediately recognised. In all three of the right wing's armies at the end of December and the first ten days of January multiple attacks against the enemy's fortified positions were carried out, but they failed to yield any kind of significant successes as a result of the Germans' stubborn defence.[10]

The last paragraph is interesting in light of Zhukov's statement in his memoirs that he asked for greater concentration of forces. It is possible that he felt obliged to obey orders from *Stavka* for a general attack, but as with the memoirs of so many figures, his personal account undoubtedly includes a degree of hindsight.

To the north of Zhukov's Front, Konev threw his troops into assaults towards Rzhev. As was the case almost everywhere, these attacks resulted in disproportionately high losses for the Red Army, but the German line was ground back towards Rzhev. On 6 January, the road running west from Rzhev was cut and Konev ordered his men to press on to Sychyevka, to the south of the city; this would effectively encircle the German defenders. Generalleutnant Eccard von Gablenz, commander of XXVII Corps, informed Ninth Army headquarters that it was impossible for his men to hold their positions. When Strauss' chief of staff agreed with him but pointed out that Hitler was refusing permission for any retreats, Gablenz replied that he had no option other than to ignore the order if he was to save his units from destruction. The neighbouring formation, VI Corps, was now under the command of Richthofen, who had been so dismissive of the Wehrmacht's estimates of Red Army strength; just a short time in the front line had changed his opinion, and he too reported that he was pulling back. Kluge continued to try in vain to extract permission for his subordinates to continue their withdrawals, and when Gablenz continued to insist that he had to pull back, Kluge felt he had no choice but to dismiss him. He was replaced by General Joachim Witthöft. Richthofen was permitted to return to his Luftwaffe duties, and must have breathed a sigh of relief when General Bieler arrived to replace him. In an attempt to reshuffle the limited resources available, Hitler subordinated Reinhardt's Third Panzer Army to Strauss. To date, Reinhardt had hoarded his units and tried to obstruct Strauss' attempts to coordinate a wider defence; Kluge intervened, threatening Reinhardt with court martial and dismissal if he didn't cooperate. Grumpily, Reinhardt complied.

While threats against Kluge's Army Group Centre were developing from the north and northeast, a further crisis arose immediately to the east and southeast of Rzhev. Despite continuing to inflict heavy casualties on the attacking formations, the Germans were slowly driven back by the Soviet Twentieth Army. Major General Mikhail Efimovich Katukov, commander of 1st Guards Brigade, later suggested that the Germans had deployed SS troops in a second line to prevent soldiers from retreating. The reality is that the SS troops were there as a secondary line of defence rather than to enforce discipline, but the strength and depth of the German positions was beyond doubt:

> Perhaps this measure [the presence of the SS] played an important role in the fact that units of Twentieth Army 'gnawed' slowly into the enemy's defences, advancing 3–4km per day. But it seems to me that the main reason was that deep snow made it difficult to use mobile units, preventing the use of tactics such as bypassing and screening enemy strongholds.[11]

Despite the slow progress, this Soviet advance created a new series of potential encirclements. There was the prospect of Katukov's forces that were trying to advance into the area south of Rzhev linking up with Konev's units attacking from Kalinin Front in the north, thus creating a large encirclement to the east of the city. The southern flank of the German Fourth Army was still hanging in the air, disconnected from Second Panzer Army, and with Fourth Army's northern flank now being driven back, there was an additional danger that the Soviet forces might meet somewhere east of Vyazma. To make matters worse, a further break in the German lines developed near Medyn, shortly after 19th Panzer Division was withdrawn from that sector to try to prevent the fall of Yukhnov. Hitler responded by redrawing the northern boundary of Fourth Army, assigning the units north of this new breakthrough to Hoepner's Fourth Panzer Army, and repeatedly rejected Kluge's increasingly desperate requests for permission to withdraw Fourth Army before it was encircled. Kluge had already informed the commander of Fourth Army that if necessary, he would order a retreat even without Hitler's permission, but finally, late on 8 January, Hitler acquiesced. Meanwhile, Hoepner had taken it upon himself to start pulling back his units north of the new Soviet penetration, and when Kluge demanded that he cancel the withdrawal, he bluntly refused:

> Field Marshal, I have a duty that stands higher than my duty to you or my duty to the Führer. That is the duty entrusted to me by the troops.[12]

However much Kluge might privately have agreed, his entire strategy was based upon negotiating withdrawals with Hitler and only disobeying the 'stand fast' order when he had exhausted all other options – indeed, it was his willingness to enforce the order that bought him sufficient credit with Hitler to secure permission for withdrawals. On this occasion, he passed on a report to *OKH* that made clear Hoepner's refusal to obey the 'stand fast' order. Hitler's fury was unprecedented. Hoepner was dismissed and immediately expelled from the army with loss of pay and pension. Kluge tried in vain to change Hitler's mind – dismissing Hoepner was one thing, but these further sanctions were excessive. Even Kluge's threat to resign made no difference. The news of Hoepner's dismissal – Kluge chose to tell Hoepner of the further punishments later in a private conversation – was greeted at the headquarters of Fourth Panzer Army with shock. It was usual for the war diary to provide a dispassionate account of events, but on this occasion, the army diarist expressed an opinion that was widely held:

> One wonders who can oversee the situation better and more accurately, the commander of the troops here at the front or higher commands from a distance of 1,500km. How can a leader still take responsibility for his troops if he cannot use his initiative to make decisions after several hours in a demanding situation?[13]

Hoepner's replacement was Ruoff, formerly commander of V Corps. A few days after Hoepner's dismissal, Hitler agreed to Fourth Panzer Army withdrawing in some sectors exactly as Hoepner had intended – but with the proviso that Ruoff restore contact to the south with Fourth Army. A week later, the growing danger of collapse at numerous points forced Hitler's hand. Most of Kluge's recommendations for a withdrawal to a shorter line were agreed. Hoepner meanwhile returned to Germany, where he was able to overturn his dismissal from the army but was not given any new assignments. He was later implicated in the July 1944 plot to kill Hitler and was arrested and executed.

Despite the dilution of effort over the entire Eastern Front, the Red Army had created a potentially existential series of crises for Army Group Centre. The events that followed highlighted the doubts that Zhukov had raised at the conference at the beginning of January. Better concentration of resources would surely have permitted Western Front to complete at least one of the encirclements that seemed almost within reach; instead, momentum was slowly dissipated through a mixture of casualties, supply difficulties, and the inexperience of the Red Army's personnel at almost every level. After what must have seemed like an interminable wait for the Germans in the front line, reinforcements were finally appearing. Part of an infantry division was inserted into the gap to the south of Fourth Army and immediately became encircled in the town of Sukhinichi; just as the stubborn Soviet defence of Tula hampered Guderian's attempts to push on towards Moscow in December, this little garrison interfered with any Soviet attempt to exploit the gap in German lines. To the northeast of the town, 19th Panzer Division gathered its depleted strength and tried in vain to fight through to Sukhinichi, but was forced to divert forces to deal with an attempt by Soviet units to infiltrate past its western flank. Unable to stay in his post due to illness, Knobelsdorff was forced to leave for Germany, and command of the division passed to Oberst – soon to be Generalmajor – Gustav Schmidt. The division's strength was a shadow of its establishment – the infantry battalions had only 100 men each – but it remained one of the few mobile units available to Fourth Army and was forced to divert resources back towards Yukhnov when Soviet units threatened to break the German lines to the south of the city in an attack intended to bypass the southern defences and cut it off. Separated into two modest battlegroups, the men of 19th Panzer Division fought against Soviet penetrations both in the Yukhnov area and further to the southwest; the strain on the division's logistic and support services, stripped to the bone to provide more personnel for the front line, became almost unsustainable.[14]

There was a further change of command on the German side that would have major significance in the months ahead. As he attempted to pull his men back to the new, shorter front line, Strauss struggled to deal with Kalinin Front's penetration on his left wing. Here, the German XXIII Corps had been separated from the rest of Ninth Army, and Strauss wanted to concentrate the corps for a counterattack from the west. Instead, Kluge issued orders directly from Army Group Centre to XXIII Corps ordering it essentially to continue to hold its lengthy front line. Struggling with the stress of the recent fighting, Strauss protested at this interference with his command and requested sick leave. He was promptly removed from command.

The new commander of Ninth Army was General Walter Model, who would play a leading role in the battles around Rzhev in 1942. Unlike many of the men who rose to senior command in Hitler's Germany, Model was not the son of a military Prussian family with a long line of illustrious ancestors. His father was a schoolteacher, but the young Model joined the army before the First World War. With a reputation for ambition and hard work coupled with an abrasive habit of speaking his mind – something that left him with few personal friends – he served as a battalion and regimental adjutant in France; he was wounded twice and finished the war as a captain. He became part of the post-war Reichswehr, and although he avoided any personal involvement in politics, he showed no hesitation in following orders to use force to suppress left-wing uprisings and strikers. His work ethic earned him high praise, but his success also stimulated his impatience and forthright attitude to the point where many regarded it as arrogance. His appointment as chief of staff of IV Corps in 1938 resulted in widespread unhappiness in the corps, but his performance in the Polish and French campaigns was near flawless. When he took command of 3rd Panzer Division in late 1940, he was unpopular with many of the senior officers, but his blunt manner and willingness to lead from the front – and to share the hardships of his men – earned him the loyalty of the rank and file. In October 1941, he was appointed commander of XLI Panzer Corps, whereupon the entire corps staff requested new assignments, such was his reputation for abrasiveness. It was entirely characteristic of Model that when he was appointed to command of Ninth Army, he paid a brief visit to his new headquarters before departing for further meetings with Kluge and then at *OKH*, but pointedly didn't follow the normal etiquette of having a private conversation with his predecessor. After his visit to Hitler's headquarters, the Führer is alleged to have remarked:

> Did you see that eye? I trust that man to do it [restore the front line]. But I wouldn't want to serve under him.[15]

Model's chief of staff in his new post was also a new appointment, Oberst Hans Krebs, who would finish the war as chief of the general staff. He and Model knew each other well from before the war, and Krebs had a deserved reputation for diplomacy. This would be an important facet in his work, as he sometimes had to intervene when Model's abrasive personality caused friction both with subordinates and with Kluge at Army Group Centre; it was clear to everyone that there was little warmth in the relationship between Kluge and Model, though equally, it was clear that Kluge was well aware of the abilities of his subordinate and regarded him as a highly reliable army commander.

Kübler, who had replaced Kluge as commander of Fourth Army, was also dismissed. His repeated requests to pull back his army before it was encircled, together with his failure to restore contact with his neighbours to north and south – given that all of his troops were committed to preventing a complete collapse of the line, such counterattacks were impossible – resulted in him being summoned to Hitler's presence on 19 January. The following day, he was relieved of his command and replaced by Heinrici, who had spent the winter trying to save his XLIII Corps from destruction.

On the battlefield, matters were becoming ever more complicated for Kluge and his subordinates; early 1942 saw the appearance of a different part of the Red Army. As early as 1930, Soviet planners had experimented with airborne forces, with a steady increase in the number of men in these units. By the outbreak of war, the Red Army had five airborne corps available, but most were initially deployed as infantry. In the renewed offensive of January, Soviet airborne forces were dropped in battalion strength near Medyn, in the rear of the German XLIII Corps. A second operation unfolded a little to the southwest near Yukhnov involving a similar-sized airdrop, and achieved only modest success. One notable incident occurred when a group of paratroopers moved towards a railway line that they had been ordered to interdict:

> Where the forest came close to either side of the road, there was a train on the tracks. Anatoly counted three covered wagons and six flatcars with vehicles. The rest of the train was hidden around a bend.
>
> We sent scouts forward. When they returned they reported that there was about a platoon of troops with the train …
>
> 'How many wagons and flatcars are there?'
>
> 'Eighteen. And there are prisoners of war in the last three.'
>
> After a brief discussion, Balyakin and Avdeenkov decided to attack and wipe out the enemy. Balyakin's group was to engage the guards while Avdeenkov and his men circled around to blow up the line north of Myatlevo station. Vladimir Balyakin had only six men, and with such a force it was difficult to attack in daylight up a steep embankment. It took courage and speed. With their first shots, the paratroopers hit the sentry at the machine-gun on the rear flatcar and then shot up the carriages where the enemy soldiers were sheltering from the cold and wind. After killing the guards, they rushed to the wagons and pulled open the doors. 'Comrades! Come out!' shouted Balyakin.

Frostbitten, with swollen and festering wounds, covered in dirt, the freed men tumbled from the wagons …

[Later,] the rescued men told us that they had been surrounded in October 1941. They held out until December and then, exhausted and wounded, they were captured. They were sent to a labour gang and forced to clear an airfield near Kaluga. Many died from overwork, hunger and the cold, and others were shot.[16]

In mid-January, *Stavka* decided on a more ambitious airborne operation. The Soviet IV Airborne Corps – three airborne brigades collectively numbering about 10,000 men – would be dropped southwest of Vyazma. Starting from a position near Kaluga, the Soviet Fiftieth Army would drive west between Sukhinichi and Yukhnov before turning towards the northwest to link up with the paratroopers; at the same time, a cavalry corps from Konev's Kalinin Front would advance south and make contact. If the operation succeeded, four German armies – from north to south, Ninth Army, Third Panzer Army, Fourth Panzer Army, and Fourth Army – would be encircled. This, surely, would be the decisive culmination of the winter offensive and a war-winning victory.

From the outset, the airborne operation faced huge difficulties. The paratroopers were meant to assemble at airfields near Kaluga, but the devastation of roads and bridges by the retreating Germans, combined with winter conditions, caused delays. Even before they reached the front line, many of the soldiers had to ford rivers, and the transport aircraft tasked with carrying out the airdrops were also slow to assemble; only 61 planes could be made available, which meant that each aircraft would have to make three flights just for the initial drop – and that assumed that all of the planes remained available throughout. The operation was delayed until 27 January, and the first men began to descend that afternoon.

While the assets for the airborne operation were assembling, Zhukov urged his Front to attack and break through the German lines. Pavel Alekseevich Belov was the son of a factory worker and served in the Russian Army in the First World War as a private in a hussar regiment. He was undergoing training as a junior officer when the Russian Revolution broke out, and he returned home briefly before joining the Red Army, leading a number of cavalry units culminating as commander of a regiment. He held a variety of posts in the years after the war and escaped the purges of the Red Army, perhaps because he was closely associated with Budyonny, a close friend of Stalin. Belov was serving as chief of staff of V Cavalry Corps at the time of the advance of Soviet troops into Poland in September 1939. At the commencement of *Barbarossa*, he was commander of II Cavalry Corps in Ukraine, where he was awarded the Order of Lenin for his part in helping substantial Soviet forces to escape encirclement. Promoted to lieutenant general, he led his corps in the fighting around Moscow during the winter, in recognition of which the corps was renamed I Guards Cavalry Corps. Belov would be one of the most important commanders in the sector in the coming weeks.

The units of I Guards Cavalry Corps – five cavalry divisions and two rifle divisions, none of them remotely near their establishment strength – were in the front line between Tenth Army to the south and Fiftieth Army to the north. A relatively modest advance from this position would reach and cut the Varshavskoye highway, the main supply line for the German XIII Corps in Yukhnov, but Belov was doubtful that his men would prevail:

> We were opposed by four German divisions – 216th and 403rd Infantry Divisions [the latter was actually a security division], 10th Motorised Division, and 19th Panzer Division. But we captured many prisoners from units that were not part of these divisions. This meant that the Nazis were strengthening the troops defending the highway between Yukhnov and Minsk with regiments and battalions from other sectors. In terms of strength, we were roughly equal. But the Germans had about 60 tanks, whereas we had just eight. The Nazis dominated the air. From dawn until dusk, their planes bombed and fired at our combat elements, rear areas, and supply lines. The aviation regiment attached to us had only three serviceable fighters.[17]

At dawn on 18 January, a cavalry regiment reinforced with a battalion of infantry on skis attacked the German lines at the village of Trushkovo and caught the Germans by surprise, swiftly overrunning the village. Immediately, they came under heavy air attack, and a counterattack led by 19th Panzer Division swiftly recaptured the village. Doggedly, I Guards Cavalry Corps tried again and eventually secured the village, advancing to cross the vital highway. If his men were to secure the area, Belov would have to find a means of advancing without such costly battles for modest gains:

> Studying information about the enemy collected by intelligence officers and from prisoner interrogations, we were convinced that the Germans mainly defended settlements and paid little attention to forests. Therefore, we chose a narrow strip of woodland for our breakthrough on the eastern bank of the Popolta River close to the highway. There was also woodland beyond the highway.

In the fields and forests, the snow was at least 80cm [31 inches] deep. This meant that we couldn't take artillery, wagons or our few tanks with us. But it was the lesser of evils. It was important to get the main force of the cavalry divisions across the highway, and after the infantry had widened and secured the breakthrough, our artillery, wagons and support elements could follow us through the gap …

On the night of 26 January … [my troops] reached the highway. At dawn, the Nazis spotted our spearhead and tried to throw it back. A battle began in the forest east of the village of Podborezhye … The Nazis retreated, suffering very heavy losses.[18]

It was a risky undertaking, and further success would require the initial breach to be held so that Belov's less mobile elements could catch up with the leading cavalry division, commanded by Major General Nikolai Sergeevich Oslikovsky. Belov could see and hear German air attacks against his leading cavalry division but had no direct contact with Oslikovsky, as the first wave of cavalry had been unable to take a radio vehicle with them. At this point, he received an unwelcome visit:

I intended to lead my second echelon, which was preparing to enter the breakthrough, but the deputy commander of Western Front, [Major] General [Georgi Fedorovich] Zakharov, ordered me to stay in order to bring forward the trailing elements of 325th Rifle and 41st Cavalry Divisions.

General Zakharov arrived with an order to urge us to complete the task as soon as possible. His presence created an unpleasant atmosphere. He made a great many threats and warned of the most drastic measures. I disagreed strongly with such methods of leadership. The officers of my corps were experienced and conscientious. If there were failures, then as a rule these were not due to the failings of our commanders but because of the determined resistance of the enemy, who often outnumbered us in tanks, artillery and aviation.

Major [Alexei] Kononienko [I Guards Cavalry Corps' intelligence officer] was one of the first to encounter Zakharov. For no obvious reason, the general blamed him for the fact that the corps did not have good roads for the movement of vehicles. Kononienko could barely restrain himself and departed to try to join General Oslikovsky. Most of my other officers tried to avoid meeting Zakharov.[19]

Kononienko later wrote about his experiences but was unable to have his works published during the Soviet era, and they remained largely unknown until they were extensively reviewed in 2002. He wrote that requests from Belov's headquarters for supplies both for the men and for the horses were either ignored or brusquely dismissed; the few responses that I Guards Cavalry Corps received were often contradictory. On the one hand, Belov's staff were told not to concern themselves with rear area activities and to concentrate on front-line tasks; but on the other hand, they were told that if they found supply arrangements not to their liking, they should sort it out themselves without troubling Western Front headquarters. His account of Zakharov's visit includes a quote from what Zakharov said to Belov and his fellow officers:

> The task assigned by the Front is clear to you: you must break through the Varshavskoye highway into the rear of the enemy or die. And let me make it clear: either a brave death on the highway, as heroes behind enemy lines, or a shameful death here. I repeat, this is a task set by Zhukov, the Front, *Stavka*, and Stalin himself. I was sent here to force you to complete the task by any means possible and I swear I will make you complete it, I will drive you into the rear of the German lines even if I have to shoot half your corps to do this. You must break through to the rear of the enemy with the means that you now have. That is why here, in our discussions, we can only talk about how to complete the task, not about what is required to complete it.[20]

This account is largely in keeping with the recollections of others about Zakharov; Eremenko was not alone in his criticism when he later described him as 'very strong-willed, but too ill-tempered and sometimes rude'.[21] The degree to which Zhukov knew about Zakharov's behaviour is unknown, but given the brutal manner in which Zhukov had dealt with subordinates on the Mongolian frontier in 1939, it is unlikely that he would have disapproved.

Two days later, Belov moved forward to join Oslikovsky and Kononienko. Again, Zakharov tried to order him to remain so that he could ensure that 325th Rifle Division moved forward to secure the breach in the German lines, but Belov insisted on joining his leading elements, leaving the rifle division in Zakharov's control. It was, perhaps, a mistake. For reasons that are not clear, Zakharov made no attempt to move the division forward in support of the cavalry.

Meanwhile, German counterattacks to the west of Rzhev were transforming the situation. After inheriting Ninth Army, with one of his corps isolated to the west of Kalinin Front's drive towards the south, Model energetically organised his units to restore the situation. The troops either side of the breach were to attack towards each other, while a third group, starting from the town of Sychevka, 28 miles (47km) south of Rzhev, would thrust towards the northwest. The advancing units of Konev's Kalinin Front were close both to Rzhev and Vyazma, and, worried by the consequences of either city falling into the hands of the Red Army, Hitler ordered some of the units Model had intended to use for his operation to defend Vyazma. With characteristic refusal to accept interference, Model immediately drove to Vyazma and boarded a flight to Rastenburg, where he confronted Hitler with the words, '*Mein Führer*, who commands Ninth Army, you or me?' Startled, Hitler attempted to defend his position, but Model refused to accept the changes in his plans. Hitler eventually conceded, but with the clear warning that Model would have to answer for any mishaps that might result.[22]

When Model's counterattack began on 21 January, the two forces attempting to close the breach from east and west made slow but determined progress. The group starting from Sychevka, led by 1st Panzer Division, did rather better, catching the Red Army by surprise. The following day, the German attacks gained momentum, and on 23 January the front was restored. Substantial Soviet forces that had pushed south past Rzhev were now cut off. Further to the west, there was a development that would have far-reaching consequences for the shape of the front line and the battles that followed. Konev's neighbour, Northwest Front, found that it was almost unopposed and pushed forward quickly, scattering the few German units in its path towards the west and southwest. Despite the lack of opposition, the sheer scale of the landscape worked against Northwest Front, with its formations advancing on two diverging axes and thus dissipating their strength. In an attempt to coordinate with Kalinin Front, the units of Northwest Front closest to Konev were transferred to his command, but they were far too weak to go to the aid of the formations isolated by Model's counterattack. If the Germans could hold their new front line while eliminating the Soviet units that had been cut off, the threat of encirclement of significant parts of Army Group Centre would be reduced, though the general advance by Northwest Front resulted in the creation of a larger salient with its tip centred on Rzhev. In many respects, the planned Soviet airborne operation now became a last throw of the dice, a final chance to achieve victory in the winter fighting.

When the Soviet airdrop near Vyazma finally went ahead on 29 January, weather and other factors resulted in the paratroopers being dispersed over a wide area, and many struggled to reach the designated assembly points. Supplies that had been dropped were largely lost in the snowy terrain, and communications frequently failed. Rapidly becoming aware of the airborne operation, the

Germans reacted swiftly, bombing the airfields from which the paratroopers were embarking. By the evening of 29 January, only 12 of the original Soviet aircraft were still operational. Meanwhile, the men who had been dropped were gathered together by the few energetic officers who had been able to reach them and made a series of raids on villages, roads and railways west of Vyazma. Confused fighting continued in the area for over a month; Kluge's Army Group Centre was forced to divert considerable numbers of men to deal with the Soviet paratroopers and to escort any road convoys, but the Red Army's grand encirclement failed to materialise, largely because neither Western nor Kalinin Front was able to mount an attack that could reach the paratroopers and other isolated units. German counterattacks drove the Soviet XI Cavalry Corps back to the northwest, while the forces advancing from the east were themselves threatened with encirclement by German counterattacks in their rear. Meanwhile, just as Model had nipped off the penetration through his lines, the German Fourth Army mounted a local counterattack against the breakthrough achieved by Belov's cavalry corps. None of the units that Zakharov was meant to commit to hold open the breach was sent forward, and the Germans swiftly restored their front line. Belov and his cavalry were cut off. It was the beginning of one of the most prolonged and remarkable episodes of a large unit operating behind enemy lines.

Just as Hitler's hopes of achieving a war-winning victory at Moscow with his depleted and exhausted troops came to nothing in December, Stalin's equally false expectations were dashed a month later. Both leaders greatly overestimated what their forces could achieve. In the case of the Wehrmacht, Hitler made few if any allowances for supply difficulties, the fatigue of soldiers who had been in almost continuous action since 22 June, and the complete lack of preparation for winter fighting. In the case of the Red Army, Stalin made no allowances for the inexperience of his officers and men, or of the very limited capabilities of Soviet logistic services. Both sides greatly underestimated the strength of their opponents. Zhukov's summary written after the war might contain a large element of hindsight, but is nonetheless accurate:

> The actual development of events proved the erroneous decision of the Supreme Commander to go over to the offensive on all Fronts in January. It would have been more expedient to gather more forces on the Fronts of the western direction (Northwest, Kalinin, Western, and Bryansk Fronts) and inflict a crushing blow on Army Group Centre, defeat it and advance to the Staraya Russa–Velikiye Luki–Vitebsk–Smolensk–Bryansk line. After that, it would have been possible to gain a firm foothold and prepare the troops for the 1942 summer campaign.

> If the nine reserve armies held by *Stavka* had not been scattered on all fronts but had been brought to action on the western direction Fronts, the central grouping of Hitler's troops would have been defeated which, undoubtedly, would have influenced the further course of the war.[23]

As is discussed later, Zhukov was by no means blameless, and his preference for all the reserve armies to be allocated to his Front might have been as much due to a desire to have complete control of the great counteroffensive as to any actual recognition that Stalin's plan represented too much dilution of effort.

The Germans had been driven back a substantial distance from the outskirts of Moscow, but the cost was disproportionately high. Throughout the fighting, the tactical superiority of the German formations, particularly in rapidly improvised counterattacks, and the dilution of the Red Army's efforts, prevented any local Soviet successes from being turned into decisive advantages. The front line settled broadly into the shape that would last through the next year. There remained a substantial Soviet penetration to the southwest of Kaluga between Yukhnov in the north and Belev in the south, with a smaller German salient projecting northeast in the centre of this towards Suchinitschi; near Medyn, too, there was a small gap in the German front. From here, the line ran broadly towards the north before turning to the west a short distance north of Rzhev. West of Rzhev, the front line turned south again in a series of poorly connected positions stretching a considerable distance to the southwest. Between this region and the line running north from Medyn was the Rzhev Salient. From the perspective of both sides, it was an important position. Its eastern face was just 75 miles (121km) from the outskirts of Moscow – close enough to be a threatening presence. The Red Army would, inevitably, seek to eliminate the salient in the coming months to remove this threat, and conversely the Wehrmacht would try to retain its positions so close to the enemy capital.

Even after the humbling and disappointing results of the fighting in January, Stalin continued to believe that the Red Army might be strong enough – and the Wehrmacht weak enough – for a final round of attacks to achieve a decisive victory. Further setbacks would follow on the entire breadth of the Eastern Front while Stalin, his commanders, and the ordinary soldiers of the Red Army completed their painful and slow education in how to defeat their enemy.

CHAPTER 4

SNOW, MUD AND CONFUSION

At the start of February 1942, it seemed for the Germans that the winter crisis might not be over, but was easing, at least in some parts of the front line. The drive by Model's units to restore the front line in the north resulted in a large group of Soviet soldiers being cut off – the number isolated by this counterattack is difficult to determine with accuracy, but a reasonable estimate would be 60,000 men.[1] Supplies were dropped to them by air, often landing on German units, and confused fighting continued throughout the region, tying down substantial German forces on guard or escort duties. But the mixture of paratroopers and cavalry lacked the heavy weaponry and leadership to turn this confusion to their advantage. Ivan Georgievich Starchak was one of the airborne forces officers who struggled to carry out attacks on German convoys while trying to evade German patrols. Some of his men told him what happened on a mission:

> A group, including Sergeant Major Bedrin, Sergeant Panarin, and Private Erdeev, was tasked with blowing up a bridge on the Klin-Volokolamsk road. The paratroopers walked for a long time through the forest in impenetrable darkness. A bitter frost burned their faces and a blizzard began. It was difficult to navigate. They reached the objective before dawn. Fortunately, the bridge wasn't guarded. It was made of wood with two spans and steep ramps on either bank. Vehicles rumbled down the road. I had to wait for them to pass, and by then it was fully light. Finally, Bedrin, Panarin and Erdeev could get close to the bridge abutments. The paratroopers laid more than 20kg of explosives and quickly unrolled the fuse cord. Panarin and Erdeev crawled about 60–70m and took shelter under the bank but Bedrin

remained in the snowy hollow. He wanted to blow up the bridge at the moment when enemy vehicles were driving across. Soon they appeared, 12 three-axle trucks heading for the front line, carrying soldiers. When the leading truck passed a hillock and began to descend towards the bridge, Bedrin struck a match. His numb hands were clumsy with the cold and the strong wind extinguished the flame that appeared. The sergeant major hastily tried again and the second attempt also failed. The huge wheels of the first vehicle were already rumbling across the log deck. In just a short time the convoy would pass to the other side of the river. Seeing this, Bedrin decided to take extreme measures. He drew his knife, leaned forward, and hacked at the fuse cord almost next to the explosives. He applied a match head to the cut end and struck it with the matchbox. Pausing only to make sure that the fuse was safely burning down, he ran to the side. There were only a few seconds left and he had no hope of getting away, but still he tried. He had time to cover 15m before there was a terrible explosion behind him. Bedrin fell to the ground.

'So was he killed?' I interrupted the man telling me the story.

'We thought so at first,' replied Alexei Panarin. 'When the surviving Nazis ran away, we found him in a pit. He was unconscious. We shook him and rubbed his face with snow, and he awoke. He was just concussed.'

'So where is he now?'

'We left him in a village with someone we trust. He'll be fit to move in two or three days.'

A few days later the peasant let us know that Bedrin had recovered. Anatoly Levenets and another paratrooper went back to the village with him. When he returned to our camp, Bedrin said that the Germans had entered the hut where he was lying. They demanded a horse from the owner. 'They barely managed to hide me behind the stove. I was ready to shoot, but nothing happened and they left.'[2]

It is significant that the directives issued to Kalinin Front for its further operations by Stalin, via *Stavka*, spoke of completing the encirclement and destruction of German forces in the Rzhev area – the ambitions of the Soviet leadership remained undiminished despite the German counterattacks. The first attempts to break through the new German lines and to reach the isolated men further south came before the end of January, with a series of attacks against Model's new front line to the north and northwest of Rzhev. After the first assaults failed to make any headway, Konev gathered his strength and tried again on 30 January.

This attack was also in vain. But despite inflicting heavy losses on the attacking Soviet units, the German VI Corps was running out of men, with rifle companies reduced to the strength of platoons. The commitment of the last available reserves to a surprise counterattack restored the situation, and the German line continued to hold for the moment.

In an attempt to improve coordination across the Soviet Fronts involved in the fighting against the German Army Group Centre, *Stavka* appointed Zhukov as commander of the 'Western Direction' – in addition to Western Front, he now had Bryansk Front and Kalinin Front subordinated to him. However, despite their losses, the German defences grew steadily stronger. Construction supplies were at last reaching the front line, and the longer that men remained in one position, the more time they could spend on digging trenches and preparing bunkers. Reinforcements arrived in a steady stream, both as replacement drafts and as divisions sent to the east from France and other parts of Western Europe. In order to deal with the Soviet units roaming in the rear zones of Ninth Army, Model ordered General Heinrich von Vietinghoff and his XLVI Panzer Corps to attack towards the northwest from Sychevka – an earlier, more modest attack in this direction had formed part of Model's operation to close the breach in his lines. When the Red Army first broke through the German lines and motored south, 1st Panzer Division had been ordered to Sychevka and played a prominent role in preventing the Red Army from capturing the vital town, and in combination with elements of 5th Panzer Division and *SS-Das Reich* – at this stage of the war, the SS division, which would later become a panzer division, was organised as an infantry division – it now embarked on this new operation. The division encountered determined Soviet resistance but, inflicting heavy losses on the Red Army, the Germans advanced through heavy snow, reaching the railway line running west from Rzhev on 6 February. Here they linked up with other attacking German units, creating a loose encirclement around parts of the Soviet Twenty-Ninth Army about 24 miles (38km) from Rzhev.

North of Rzhev, the bitter fighting of December and January had been succeeded by intermittent periods of considerable pressure; for example, on 20 February, a powerful Soviet attack penetrated the lines of 6th Infantry Division, before a counterattack using an improvised battlegroup, including a group of freshly arrived replacements, restored the situation. Despite these attacks, the soldiers began to take steps to make their lives more comfortable. The construction of semi-permanent fortifications provided welcome shelter from the weather, and in mid-February, 6th Infantry Division commenced publication of a weekly newspaper under the direction of its chief intelligence officer, Oberleutnant Ahrens. The newspaper was entitled *Der Lückenbüsser* ('The Stopgap'), and provided the soldiers in the front line with news about events in the rest of the world – while the newspaper was heavily censored and reflected the point of view of Nazi Germany, it was greatly welcome in the absence of any other information. A small entertainment group began to tour the front-line divisions, and a cinema was created in a barn in the village of Maniulovo to the northeast of Rzhev; it was promptly nicknamed the *Kristallpalast* ('Crystal Palace') by the soldiers. Just as welcome was the creation of a *Lausoleum*, where the soldiers could treat both themselves and their clothing to try to get rid of the lice that were a constant presence.[3]

Within Rzhev, life for ordinary Russian civilians was grim. The Germans made repeated attempts through 1942 to remove the civilian population for a number of reasons. Some attempts were perhaps motivated by a wish to move them to safety, but greater importance was placed upon security. With the front line fairly close to the city, there was an abiding fear that civilians might report troop movements to partisans. Many civilians were taken away as forced labour and frequently forced to stay elsewhere. Even those who were relocated to other cities found that there was no provision for them in terms of food or accommodation – they were expected to fend for themselves. To a large extent, this was deliberate policy. The long-term German plans for the occupied parts of the Soviet Union envisaged the elimination of most of the population of urban areas and the transformation of the land into a rural economy run by, and for the benefit of, the Third Reich. These plans explicitly described the deaths of most of the 'surplus' urban population through starvation. Viktor Merkuryev was a young boy who lived in Rzhev, and his experience of life in the early weeks of the German occupation was fairly typical:

In January 1942, a German came and began to take my mother away for work. When she refused, the German began to strike her back with his rifle butt. With barely a gasp, my mother fell back. We wept, but quietly because the German was in our apartment. My mother became unwell and died a week later. We lived with our grandmother. A month later, my grandmother and I went to a village to look for provisions as we had absolutely nothing to eat. We got some rye and flax seeds. On the way back, a woman with a boy who was younger than me caught up with us and we continued together. She carried a bag of potatoes on her shoulder. German soldiers stopped us from entering the town and took away the woman's precious burden, which she had brought back for her children. They grabbed her bag and threw it onto the snow. Her boy ran to the bag and lay down on it, not wanting to give it to the German. The German struck the boy around the head with his fists. Then he turned his gun on the woman and killed her.[4]

Some German officers described in their memoirs after the war that much or even most of the population was friendly towards the occupying forces, and that cooperation between civilians and partisans was largely due to coercion and threats. This is impossible to square with the widespread indiscriminate killing of civilians who were suspected of being, or abetting, the growing partisan movement. Undoubtedly, there were many civilians in the Soviet Union who had no love of the Communist regime, particularly older people who remembered a time before Bolshevism, and many cooperated with the Germans out of a sense of self-preservation. But in the generally younger urban population, there were many adults who had known no other system than Communist rule. German policies towards the civilian population were hardly conducive to friendly relations. Another child in Rzhev later recalled:

My mum and I were at home when the Germans came and announced that we had to leave Rzhev. Mum dithered, not knowing what to take with her. We were a little slow to gather outside. So the Fritzes threw all our bundles in the corner of the room, took out whips and kicked us out of the apartment. We had to go from Sector 1 of Rzhev to Sector 2. And all the way the damned thugs beat us. Their lashes rained down on our heads. From that time on, I absolutely hated the Fritzes. The word 'German' was hated most of all.[5]

The German accounts often describe how new positions were built for defensive lines, but rarely mention the use of forced labour in their construction. The people in the occupied territories were often used for such tasks, and were also seen as an easy source of winter clothing to supplement the inadequate winter uniforms that had reached the German front line. Nina Solovieva was a teacher in the city:

After they occupied Rzhev, the Germans began to mistreat civilians. One day my sister and I were walking across the bridge when we saw five men who the Germans had shot lying on the edge. We recognised two of them, Medyusov and Drozhdov. Near them, the Germans had nailed a placard bearing the inscription: 'This is the punishment for disobeying the German rulers.'

The badly dressed thugs took boots and warm clothing from civilians. They took their boots from them on the road, forcing them to run barefoot through the snow. During the winter, people were forced to work, and anyone who refused was shot.

One day they took my sister, we had no idea where she had gone. Later we found her body behind the office of the commandant. They had shot her thinking she was a partisan.

The Germans were especially cruel when they heard of Red Army successes and they thought they might have to leave Rzhev. They often shot people who went to the Volga to get water. A passing German killed an old woman who couldn't get back up the riverbank.[6]

The combination of casual brutality, the seizure of clothing and other property without any regard for the needs of civilians, and the tendency to assume that people were partisans or assisting partisans unless they could prove otherwise, practically ensured that resistance to the German occupiers would grow. A teenage boy described the deaths of three men he knew:

I left the house early one morning. I don't remember why I crossed the Volga. The road ran past a garden near the Vladimir Ilyich Lenin memorial. As I came closer I saw that three men with tied hands had been brought to the garden. I recognised them – they were Bedyakov, Novozhevov and Teleshyev. They could barely stand. They had been kept in prison for a long time without food.

The Germans threw nooses around their neck. Other Nazis stood ready with their rifles. Some brought out a box and forced the partisans onto it. As soon as one of them did so, the Fascist pushed the box out from under his feet.

Each of the partisans who were killed made no attempt to plead for mercy but called to the people to mark how the Fascists behaved in our hometown of Rzhev. We all left vowing to take our revenge on the Fascists.[7]

A similar pattern of behaviour occurred throughout the occupied parts of Europe; indoctrinated to believe that they were superior to other nationalities, particularly Slavs, many – perhaps most – German soldiers showed little hesitation in resorting to brutal behaviour to suppress dissent, without any understanding that it would actually increase such dissent. It was the legacy of a century of social Darwinism and a belief that not only was it possible to assign characteristics to entire nationalities and ethnicities, but that such differences would inevitably lead to 'superior' nations ruling the 'inferior' people.

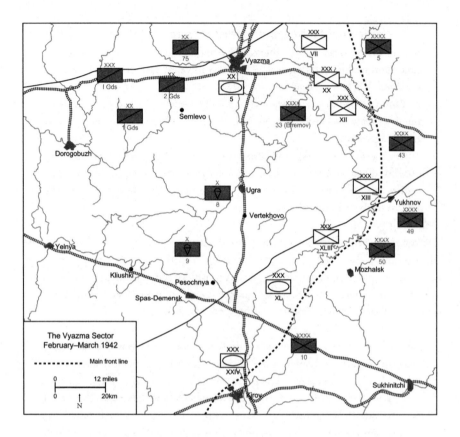

The Vyazma Sector
February–March 1942

- - - - - - - - - - Main front line

0   12 miles
|————————|
0   20km
    ↑
    N

Like many panzer divisions, 5th Panzer Division was struggling to prevent its precious armour being parcelled out to support infantry units. The officers of the panzer divisions believed – with considerable justification – that their units functioned best when the entire division was able to bring all its resources to bear. The problem for higher commands was that the anti-tank firepower of German infantry divisions was very limited, and without armoured support, the infantry units were frequently unable to hold back any Soviet attacks that were supported by tanks. This weakness persisted throughout the war; even though the anti-tank capabilities of infantry divisions improved, so too did the armoured forces of their opponents. Having been involved in repeated actions in the main east-facing line of Fourth Panzer Army, 5th Panzer Division was ordered to send an armoured battlegroup to Sychevka at the end of January to join XLI Panzer Corps' counterattack, and also to dispatch a motorised rifle battalion with tanks and anti-tank support to Vyazma in order to secure vital bridges to the west of the city from the large Soviet forces that continued to roam in the German rear area. At the same time, the division's orders required it to leave a panzer company in the front line near Gzhatsk; however, worsening news from Vyazma resulted in this company and any other units that had been left behind receiving new orders to proceed at full speed to join the counterattacks against the Soviet cavalry and paratroopers near Vyazma. Hindered by continuing heavy snowfall, Generalmajor Gustav Fehn's division (apart from the battlegroup that had been subordinated to 1st Panzer Division for the attack towards the northwest from Sychevka) laboured to its assembly positions immediately to the southwest of Vyazma. From here, the division fought along the roads to the west of the city, frequently encountering mixed groups of partisans, cavalry and paratroopers. A gunner in the division's 116th Artillery Regiment was part of a garrison in one of the villages along the main road when Soviet troops attacked one night:

I grabbed some bread, my webbing and some hand grenades – unfortunately I didn't take my camera with me – and rushed for the door. But even as I stuck my head out, bullets cracked past dangerously close to my ears and I quickly pulled back. But the brief glance sufficed to see what was going on outside. Despite it being dark – it was about 2230 – everything was lit up by brightly burning houses, flares, and muzzle flashes. I had spotted our anti-tank gun from the door, firing from the darkness. Two or three men from the gun crew were lying dead next to the gun. The commander was almost in tears with desperation and rage as he called for reinforcements. He peered left and right with his pistol drawn in a predatory manner while still trying to operate the gun. I rushed over to him. Two others came too and we pulled and pushed the anti-tank gun onto the village street, which was lined on both sides with burning cottages. From here we could at least guard about 150m of the road, at the end of which we could see some turmoil. Everything was obscured by smoke and flames. Screams, the clatter of gunfire and the dull thuds of hand grenades filled the night.

Perhaps one or two battalions of Russians had attacked from the northwest. They advanced in a broad line from the woodland about 100m away and pushed into about a third of the village with their first rush. Unfortunately, one of the quad guns fell into their hands and was promptly turned on us. As I joined the fight I realised that their right flank had already passed us and was trying to sweep past us across an open snowfield. We could barely see them but we could tell what was happening by the noise. This attack was brought to a standstill. But the Russians then tried with all their strength to push along the road. Bitter

111

nightfighting developed with spades, pickaxes, iron bars, farm implements and other tools ... It was almost impossible to fire as there was the danger of hitting our own side in the darkness.

Bit by bit, I worked my way forward through the melee from the cover of a tree. The others joined me. We kept close to the houses burning on either side so as not to block the anti-tank gun's field of fire. A few of our comrades who had been wounded were caught in the blazing buildings ... Behind a tree, an NCO tried to find a target with his rifle. He suddenly fell and then asked me to help him back onto his feet. But even as I did that, his head dropped and realising that he'd been fatally wounded, I lowered him to the snow. A wild fight had developed 50m away around our other quad anti-aircraft gun, its driver slumped over the steering wheel with a head wound. The gun-aimer swung the mount with his feet in circles to hold off the Russians who had encircled him while an NCO fired at them with his pistol while also loading the quad gun. Despite desperate attempts we couldn't reach the quad gun. Finally we were pushed back. Even when we could no longer see the quad, we could hear it still firing.[8]

Villages changed hands regularly as Belov's cavalry, the leading divisions of Thirty-Third Army, and Soviet paratroopers – all cooperating with each other and with partisan formations when they could – moved through the area. The clashes with the partisans resulted in widespread mass punishments, usually in the form of burning down villages that were suspected of having given succour to the partisans, often accompanied by mass executions. Some officers, like Heinrici at XLIII Corps, may have turned a blind eye to the excesses of their subordinates and may have made little distinction between proved partisans and those merely suspected of helping them, but Model seems at least to have tried to set a different tone in Ninth Army's area. He informed his corps commanders that mass punishments simply created new recruits for the partisans. The degree to which he succeeded in limiting such mass punishments is open to question, as villages continued to be burned throughout the region, and he showed little inclination to rein in the activities of SS units in their wide-ranging sweeps against partisans, Jews, Communists and others.

In the southern sector of Army Group Centre, both Second Army and Second Panzer Army appeared to have weathered the worst of the Red Army's assaults. Snowfall in the last few days of January was particularly heavy, greatly impeding the ability of both sides to mount mobile operations, and while this hindered the German units trying to mount sharp counterattacks, it greatly limited Soviet options for further major advances. Nonetheless, Heinrici's Fourth Army remained in a perilous position on both flanks, particularly with Hitler still greatly restricting the freedom of action of both Kluge and his subordinates. The Soviet Thirty-Third Army had been fighting for possession of the town of Vereya when it received orders from Zhukov to move west immediately in order to attack just to the north of Yukhnov and to break through to Vyazma. It seems that Zhukov believed all German resistance in the Vereya area had been overcome, but in reality General Rudolf von Roman's XX Corps was still fighting hard with four infantry divisions, slowly falling back towards the west. As a result, Lieutenant General Mikhail Grigorevich Efremov's army moved to its new forming-up area in stages, often clashing with German units along the line of march. Led personally by the army commander, the leading four divisions brushed aside the German defences north of Yukhnov and pressed on towards their objective at Vyazma, but much of the army's strength – and almost all of its rear area services – were still lagging many miles behind. There could be no question of waiting for the rest of the army to arrive; Western Front headquarters continued to urge Efremov to advance towards Vyazma without delay, and there was no mention of how the lines of communication would be protected. To make matters worse, there was little attempt by Forty-Third Army, immediately to the south of Efremov's advance, to widen the breach in the German lines, and in addition to trying to reach Vyazma, Efremov's Thirty-Third Army was still responsible for an extensive section of front line to the north of the axis of advance. Consequently, as had been the case with Belov's cavalry corps, the Soviet penetration was highly vulnerable to a German counterattack against its base.

Such a counterattack developed on 4 February when the German forces either side of Efremov's breakthrough advanced from north and south. The main attack came from the north, where 20th Panzer Division was deployed as part of XX Corps. Roman had gathered the much-diminished strength of the panzer division behind his exposed southwest flank, and – reinforced by an additional two panzer companies from 5th Panzer Division – this force rapidly advanced over the six miles (10km) that separated its start line from the German positions northwest of Yukhnov. The main forces on the southern aide of the breach were elements of XIII Corps, in particular 4th SS Infantry Regiment. This unit had been raised the previous year and spent much of 1941 involved in 'anti-partisan' warfare in the Baltic States; in reality, such deployment involved everything from combating armed civilians and Red Army stragglers to mass killings of civilians suspected of harbouring or supplying genuine partisans. In December 1941, the remnants of the regiment – its losses in the north suggest that at least some of its actions were genuinely against armed partisans – gathered in occupied Poland where they were replenished and reorganised as a motorised regiment. As the Soviet counteroffensive of December 1941 unfolded, the regiment's personnel were dispatched to the Eastern Front by air transport, where they were subordinated to 19th Panzer Division and took part in its local counterattacks to defend the main supply route through Yukhnov. As 20th Panzer Division attacked from the north, this motorised regiment advanced a short distance from its positions in the south. When the two German pincers met late on 5 February, they cut the tenuous lines of communication between Zhukov's Western Front and Efremov's four divisions that were still advancing towards Vyazma. Zhukov is almost silent about these battles in his memoirs, but other sources describe his rage at the German counterattack, and orders issued by him that the local commanders who had been unable to stop the German counterattack were to be arrested, tried and executed without delay, regardless of how many were identified.[9] In the case of the failure to hold open Belov's penetration, the person most at fault was Zhukov's deputy, Zakharov; in the case of Thirty-Third Army, blame must rest with Zhukov himself.

The Red Army continued to learn, both about how to conduct warfare and about the capabilities and limitations of its equipment. Most tank brigades had a mixture of vehicles, and it was commonplace for the T-34s to move ahead of the slower, heavier KV-1s. As a result, the T-34s often suffered substantial losses before the heavy tanks arrived; in any case, the two tanks had the same gun, and the only advantage of the KV-1 lay in its better armour. This came at a price, and the tanks were often unpopular with their crews; the gear levers frequently jammed, and drivers sometimes improvised by carrying a heavy hammer and applying brute force when required. Another area of improvisation was the use of informal code in radio communication. Ivan Semyonovich Lykov was a commissar in a tank battalion in Forty-Third Army and found himself in a stranded tank that was being used as an observation post. He later recalled some of his radio transmissions:

For example, the battalion commander and I once reported to the brigade command post: 'The picture is unenviable. Thunderstorms over the beautiful Grunya. Strong granite. The artists gave five concert performances. The audience wants more. Ash is in place. Seryozha is sad and weeps. We will try to console him. There is enough water. Cucumbers are growing. The groats are not quite right.'

Translated into ordinary language, this meant: 'The situation is complex. We are attacking Krasnaya Gorka. The Germans have a lot of artillery. Our mortars fired five volleys to good effect, but more artillery support is needed as the enemy is still in his positions. We have taken losses and damage and are trying to repair it. There is sufficient fuel and shells [for the main tank guns]. We are short of cartridges [for machine-guns].[10]

It isn't clear whether such a code was effective; it seems likely that the Germans listening to Soviet transmissions would have had little difficulty in understanding it.

Most German units were operating ad hoc combat groups, often with large numbers of men who would normally have been performing specialist roles but were now serving as infantry. A signaller in 2nd Panzer Division later recalled:

At that time, I was deployed with my radio troop with 1st Company in Pustoy Vtornik. We were keeping radio silence and constantly helped construct positions and bunkers. But 3 February would be a memorable day for us. 'Prepare to move out' – with these words, Oberleutnant Naumann entered our bunker as we were hunched over our mess-tins, spooning our daily stew. In a few moments we were ready for action and we set off. The situation: an enemy raiding party had succeeded in breaking through a weakly occupied position on the front line and had penetrated as far as an artillery battery position.

Our task: to destroy or capture the enemy.

We were a right mixed bunch as we climbed onto the anti-aircraft gunners' vehicles and later trudged through the woodland. Officers, NCOs and 30 men from three different units, mainly radiomen, clerks, and *Küchenbullen* ['kitchen bulls']. Despite hardly ever working like this, everyone was determined to do their best. It was a wonderful winter afternoon. Deep blue sky arched over the wintry splendour of the forest. The snow glittered like crystal where the sunlight shone through the branches. Up ahead, the commander strode forward in an overcoat, his machine-pistol ready. His face too showed the pleasure of working on such a beautiful winter's day.

For a good hour we moved forward, avoiding making a noise, along the small paths through the woodland. Suddenly, from up ahead, the message: 'Halt, take cover!' About 20–30m from us an enemy group of similar strength was moving through the woodland, in the same direction as us. They clearly felt completely safe.

A quick discussion. Our group divided to encircle the enemy. But this proved impossible as we couldn't move faster than the Russians through knee-deep snow. We tried to follow the Russians and get as close to them as possible.

Suddenly the noise of the commander's machine-pistol tore through the unnatural silence: it was the signal for us to open fire. In a moment there was wild fighting. The enemy came under fire from all our barrels. They were all blown away as we stormed forwards – orders were shouted – nobody took any more notice of the deep snow – we didn't let the enemy out of our sight. They were taken completely by surprise. While just a few tried to defend themselves, the rest tried to flee.

I don't know how long the fight lasted, before most of the enemy lay dead in the snow. Then came the order to regroup. It was pointless to pursue the few Russians who had fled into the scrub because of the deep snow.[11]

Bitter fighting continued in the rear area around Vyazma. A soldier in 5th Panzer Division's combat engineer battalion was involved in fighting for a small village:

At daybreak we suddenly realised that there were figures leaving the edge of the woodland and crossing the open ground before us. In no time everyone was in position to deal with the enemy as soon as he was close enough. At first we estimated the enemy strength as 50 to 60 men, but we later discovered just how wrong we were. We opened fire when the Russians were 80m away with good effect. But more and more enemy appeared out of the wood and their fire grew stronger. The snow gave protection against being seen but not against bullets. Our losses increased. Leutnant Wegner, a squad leader and our machine-gunners were killed. The enemy tried to bypass us on both sides. It was clear that we couldn't hold our position. Meanwhile, Hadamczik's platoon had arrived to guard our flank and under constant enemy fire we had to pull back more than 100m across the snow. Many comrades were hit by enemy fire …

After the risk of encirclement had passed, we took up new positions to await the further approach of the Russians. Oberleutnant Lattemann estimated the strength of his company at 14 rifles and three machine-pistols, a poor total against 200 to 300 Russians.

At midday the forward artillery observer made contact with his battery and as the Russians commenced a new attack, they were hit by a bombardment. We cheered like children when the shells had an excellent effect and we added the fire of our guns. The enemy began to withdraw.

Reinforcements of 40 men arrived and took up positions, but the expected replacement by the rifle regiment didn't take place, so as evening fell we were still there. Our fatigue was overwhelming. Comrades had to shake their neighbours awake during the night to prevent them freezing to death in their sleep. Thus passed a night of immense strain until our replacements finally arrived at dawn.[12]

The Soviet forces that had been cut off around Vyazma were from I Guards Cavalry Corps, 8th Airborne Brigade – the only part of IV Airborne Corps that was actually dropped before aircraft shortages forced the planned full deployment to be abandoned – and the four rifle divisions from Thirty-Third Army. The various units continued to bump into each other from time to time, not always intentionally; one notable moment of success for the Soviet soldiers came on 10 February when a group of paratroopers came across the headquarters of 5th Panzer Division. The startled German officers and men were able to escape, but the paratroopers recorded with delight that the German division commander's jacket was one of the items of loot that they captured.[13]

On 4 February, Zhukov issued orders to Belov's I Guards Cavalry Corps and Efremov's four divisions from Thirty-Third Army. They were to launch a simultaneous attack, from the south and east respectively, to capture Vyazma. During the late summer and autumn of 1941, the Red Army had built extensive fortifications around the city and these were now occupied by German troops. As Belov later wrote, the interlocking fields of fire from these positions made it almost impossible to infiltrate between them, and both his cavalry and Efremov's infantry lacked the artillery that was needed to suppress the bunkers. Just as many German commanders in the front line were exasperated by orders from above that revealed a complete lack of appreciation of the reality on the ground, Belov and Efremov too had to cope with interference from distant superiors:

Every success we gained, even the smallest, was won at a high price. Only the heroism and selfless courage of the soldiers and commanders gave us a chance to move forward, albeit slowly, forcing back the superior enemy forces. But our offensive effort soon dissipated. Many unit commanders were killed in the fighting. The commander of 96th Cavalry Regiment, Lieutenant Colonel Danilin, was evacuated [by air] after being wounded. The commander of 2nd Guards Cavalry Division, [Colonel Nikolai Sergeevich] Oslikovsky, was also wounded. After ten days we had almost completely exhausted our ammunition. The command of Western Front promised to resupply us with shells and bullets through General Efremov's Thirty-Third Army, but it was simply impossible to keep this promise. The troops of Thirty-Third Army were in the same position as us.

General Efremov and I exchanged information on the radio regularly and we believed that it would be expedient for us to create a continuous front line, thus protecting our inner flanks. This would then allow us to manoeuvre more freely with our limited forces. But we were not permitted to do this. Front headquarters sent me a strange order: 'You don't need to be shoulder to shoulder with the infantry.' However, I believe that it would have been worth uniting our forces all the same ...

Our reconnaissance reported the appearance of new enemy units in the front line. On 10 February, the enemy struck at 75th Cavalry Division and surrounded it. To free the division from encirclement we had to withdraw forces from other sectors. The Germans took advantage of this and launched attacks where we had weakened our defences. After a stubborn battle, 75th Cavalry Division escaped from the enemy ring. We saved our comrades but the group as a whole was thrown back 12–15km from Vyazma. There was no longer any thought of attacking the city.[14]

Zhukov's order is difficult to comprehend. If he genuinely argued with Stalin against diluting the Red Army's forces over the entire Eastern Front, then the same logic should have applied both to his Front's plans for offensive operations and for the elements that were isolated near Vyazma. It is possible that he believed these units could control a greater stretch of ground if they didn't concentrate and unite, but unless he could break through to them, this was irrelevant.

In addition to the units of Western Front near Vyazma, elements of Twenty-Ninth Army from Kalinin Front were still fighting further to the northwest, cut off by Model's successful counterattacks, and Konev ordered these formations to try to break out to the north. For Model's troops, depleted by their successful defence against the Soviet attacks from the north, there was now the added problem of Soviet soldiers attempting to move through their positions from the south and there was widespread confused fighting. As it became increasingly clear that the trapped Soviet units lacked the strength to escape to the north, Konev ordered them instead to try to move southwest to attempt to make contact with Thirty-Ninth Army, one of the units from Northwest Front that had pushed towards Smolensk earlier in the winter. After an arduous march and continual skirmishes with German units, the first parts of Twenty-Ninth Army reached safety, with more groups trickling in over the next few days. Almost all of the survivors were wounded or frostbitten; a nurse in a medical battalion later recalled that there wasn't a single healthy man among them.[15]

Denied permission to cooperate more closely with Efremov's infantry, Belov could at least coordinate his men with elements of the airborne forces in the area. Much of 8th Airborne Brigade was encircled by the Germans near the town of Semlevo, in the rear of I Guards Cavalry Corps. Belov decided to try to link up with these men and also to try to capture Semlevo, 17 miles (27km) southwest of Vyazma – although it was strongly garrisoned, there were reports that the Germans had stockpiled considerable supplies there:

The 1st Guards Cavalry Division and 114th Ski Battalion advanced on Semlevo but due to deep snow, they failed to make a swift surprise attack. The dismounted squadrons moved forward very slowly. The enemy had a lot of weaponry, especially mortars. Under heavy fire, the guards were driven to ground and then began to crawl forward. The artillery and 107mm mortars of the cavalry division couldn't provide effective fire support to their troops due to ammunition shortages. After several hours of intense combat, two cavalry regiments captured the southeast outskirts of the village but couldn't advance further. They were stopped by the fire of numerous machine-guns and artillery, and counterattacks by Fascist tanks.

[At the same time,] 11th and 131st Cavalry Regiments approached the eastern outskirts of Semlevo. On their left, 75th Light Cavalry Division moved forward. Overcoming strong enemy resistance, the soldiers moved forward slowly. Meanwhile, my corps headquarters' radio operators intercepted several radio messages from Major Steinbock, the garrison commander in Semlevo. The major reported that he was surrounded by 'Cossacks and partisans' and urgently asked for help.

To reinforce the besieged garrison, the Nazis transferred two battalions and some tanks from Vyazma … German planes appeared over our battle formations from time to time. The bombing didn't stop at night, when the Nazis dropped flares to seek out targets.

The battle for Semlevo reached its climax on 15 February. The Germans continued to receive reinforcements, increasing their strength. Our men had to repel frequent counterattacks by Hitlerite tanks and infantry, supported by strong artillery and mortar fire …

On this day, 8th Airborne Brigade broke out of its encirclement and joined the main forces of my group. The brigade commander, Lieutenant Colonel Anufriev, and Commissar Raspopov reported to me that only 380 men remained in the brigade.

'Let me cheer you up,' I said. 'My cavalry gathered about 200 paratroopers who were scattered during their drops. Take them under your command.' …

We had to stop the assault on Semlovo without capturing it.[16]

Despite the weakened and depleted state of his units, Zhukov had to make a further effort to reach the encircled units near Vyazma; if he could mount a successful attack, there was still a possibility that the situation would swing greatly in favour of the Red Army, with German units once more being threatened with encirclement. The new plan called for Lieutenant General Ivan Vasilevich Boldin's Fiftieth Army to drive west along the main Moscow–Warsaw highway, while the rest of IV Airborne Corps would be dropped in an arc to the west of Yukhnov and would attack the town, linking up with Boldin's advancing men. This time, rather more aircraft had been gathered, but the total was still fewer than 70. This would necessitate a series of drops to bring all of the paratroopers into action.

The first battalion was dropped before dawn on 18 February, and as had been the case with previous airdrops, the men were scattered over a considerable area. Operations continued over the next few days, with a little over 7,300 men parachuting into the area by 23 February. Nearly a third of these men failed to reach their assembly points, though most of the stragglers eventually linked up either with partisans or the various ground units that had been cut off in the area.[17] One such group reached Belov's command, and he assigned them to 8th Airborne Brigade. Numerically at least, the brigade was once more at a reasonable strength, though it remained short of ammunition and lacked heavy weapons. Although German fighter aircraft were operating in the area, they made little impression on the airdrop, but scored an important success on the last day of the drops when they damaged the Soviet aircraft carrying the commander of IV Airborne Corps, Major General Aleksei Fedorovich Levashev. Although the plane was not shot down, Levashev was killed and several of his senior officers wounded. His chief of staff, Colonel Aleksandr Fedorovich Kazankin, took command of the troops on the ground.[18] Meanwhile, Belov moved his men further west and succeeded in cutting the Smolensk–Vyazma highway. Even if his units were weak, they could still cause huge inconvenience to the Germans.

At the same time as this renewed attack by Zhukov's Front, Kalinin Front was to capture Olenino and Bely, to the west and southwest of Rzhev. When these new attacks began, they made almost no progress. After receiving reinforcements to refill its depleted ranks, Major General Vladimir Ivanovich Vostrukhov and his Twenty-Second Army managed to fight their way into Bely, but the Soviet forces were unable to dislodge the German defenders. Nor were the attacks by the neighbouring Thirtieth, Thirty-Ninth, and Thirty-First Armies any more successful. Much of Major General Sergei Vladimirovich Sokolov's XI Cavalry Corps was still operating behind German lines, and it was ordered to link up with Belov's men advancing from the east. At one point, the two groups were barely two or three miles apart, but even though a battalion of paratroopers succeeded in reaching the villages where Sokolov's men were meant to meet them, the Germans were able to drive XI Cavalry Corps to the north before contact could be made and then turned to face Belov's men, repulsing their attack with heavy losses.

Western Front began its offensive in a somewhat chaotic manner, with little apparent coordination between neighbouring armies. The attack by Fiftieth

Army to break through the German lines further east made little progress, as Kazankin learned when he managed to make contact with higher commands. Aware of the presence of the various Soviet units that were cut off in the general area around Vyazma, the German rear area and security units scattered throughout the region had fortified their positions and organised plans for mutual fire support in the event of coming under attack. They were of course aware of the new Soviet airdrops but could do little to react. Early on 24 February, Kazankin attacked towards the south; at first, his men achieved surprise and overwhelmed a small German party at Vertekhovo, but the paratroopers lacked the heavy weapons to storm prepared German positions. Nonetheless, Kazankin's men advanced about 12 miles (20km) and captured valuable supplies when they overran a German train near Ugra. From here, they pushed on further south to try to capture Pesochnya and Klyushki. The latter town came under heavy attack by the Soviet 9th Airborne Brigade, and despite air support, the Germans were unable to beat off the assault.

The airborne forces were now tantalisingly close to the battlefield where Fiftieth Army was still trying to break through the German lines, but this began to work against them. The Germans were able to divert troops from their main front line to face the paratroopers, and their artillery could also be directed to provide fire support, whereas Kazankin and his men were running out of supplies. At the end of February, the paratroopers pulled back to the Klyushki area, lacking the strength to force their way through to Fiftieth Army. In total, the airborne forces, cavalry and other Red Army units that were operating behind German lines now numbered about 29,000 men, supported by an unknown number of partisans, but they were short of munitions, food and heavy weapons.

Meanwhile, Belov continued to receive contradictory orders. He had been denied permission to concentrate his men alongside Efremov's divisions in the failed attack on Vyazma and was then directed west to cut the Vyazma–Smolensk highway. But in the first week of March, he was startled to receive a signal from Zhukov, which stated:

> Why did you, contrary to the orders of [Front] headquarters and the Front Military Council, move away from Vyazma? Who gave you the right to choose your task? Your mission is determined by my order. You seem to have forgotten the consequences of failure to comply with an order.[19]

Throughout the operation, Belov was repeatedly frustrated by Zhukov's often contradictory micromanagement of his command. On this occasion, Belov's intelligence officer noted that the corps commander wearily muttered, 'What a cruel and soulless man.'[20] In response to the signal, Belov replied with a detailed list of the instructions that he had received to move west in his attempt to link up with Sokolov's cavalry corps. Zhukov grudgingly conceded the point.

At the beginning of March, the Germans organised an attack against IV Airborne Corps with a battalion of infantry supported by artillery and tanks. As had been the case when the Soviet troops attacked the Germans, the defending side had the advantage, especially when the fighting moved away from the one good road in the area – the Moscow–Vyazma–Smolensk–Warsaw highway – and entered the wooded and swampy terrain to the north. After a few days of fighting, the Germans paused for breath, not least because Soviet attacks on Yukhnov finally forced the Wehrmacht to abandon the town. The German XLIII Corps had started the winter under Heinrici's command, but when he was assigned to lead Fourth Army, he was replaced temporarily by Generalleutnant Gerhard Berthold. His tenure lasted just 11 days, filling in until the arrival of General Karl Brennecke. The corps controlled 31st and 131st Infantry Divisions and was required to hold its sector of the front line as well as providing security along the Moscow–Warsaw highway and mounting raids against the mixed paratroopers, cavalry and partisans operating north of the road. Despite his comments in his memoirs that the plans of Stalin were overly ambitious, it seems that Zhukov made little effort to dissuade *Stavka* about its over-optimistic assessment of the situation as the Germans withdrew. He passed on the instructions he received from above: Boldin was ordered to renew his attacks with Fiftieth Army, while Kazankin was to gather together as much strength as he could and cut the roads and rail links running from Yukhnov to Vyazma. Again, Konev was to throw his forces at Olenino and Bely, but was also required to capture Rzhev.

Inevitably, these new attacks had almost no effect on the front line. The Germans had continued to improve their defences, whereas the Soviet units were almost completely exhausted, despite their reinforcements. Kazankin's paratroopers launched an uncoordinated attack from their stronghold around Klyushki and were driven back in disarray. With Zhukov's renewed attacks achieving little, the Germans were able to divert more resources to deal with the Soviet units operating in their rear, and most of 131st Infantry Division was tasked with attacking Kazankin's men. The Soviet attacks failed partly because of inadequate reconnaissance, and the Germans by contrast carried out extensive reconnaissance before launching their assault; nevertheless, the first German attack was repulsed on 11 March. Two days later, reinforced by detachments from two other German divisions, a second attack was also beaten off. A series of bitterly contested battles followed with heavy losses on both sides, but the advantage lay with the Germans. With their supplies almost exhausted, the airborne forces were driven into an ever-smaller area.

Efremov and his four badly depleted divisions were still functioning as a coherent whole. On 3 April, the Germans dropped leaflets calling on Efremov and his men to surrender. As was usually the case on both sides, the ultimatum included assurances of good treatment, but Efremov ignored them.[21] There was now clearly no possibility of Zhukov's troops breaking through to link up with the encircled men, and Efremov was ordered to conduct a breakout; he was to move south towards the town of Kirov, relying on partisans to help him. At the same time, Belov received a new order from Zhukov urging him to cooperate with Efremov's men. One of Efremov's units, the 329th Rifle Division, was cut off from the rest of Thirty-Third Army and was closer to Belov's group than the rest of Efremov's men. The division was subordinated to I Guards Cavalry Corps, and Belov sent scouts to make contact with the division; when he learned from these scouts that Colonel Kornei Mikhailovich Andrusenko, the division commander, was planning to try to break out to the east to link up with the rest of Thirty-Third Army, Belov ordered him instead to head south in order to link up with the cavalry corps. Andrusenko and about 250 men succeeded in fighting their way through the encircling Germans and reached Belov's lines; about 400 other men from the division broke out to the east in small groups and rejoined the rest of Thirty-Third Army. The rest of the division was wiped out, and its wounded men who had been left behind fell into the hands of the Germans.

On the orders of Western Front, Andrusenko was placed under arrest a week later for allowing his division to disintegrate. Officers of Belov's headquarters tried Andrusenko and Sizov, his political commissar, on the instructions of Western Front headquarters. Belov mentions this only in passing; the court martial found both men guilty of dereliction of duty and sentenced them to death. Their sentences were commuted and Sizov remained in the front line; he was killed in action in the summer of 1943. Andrusenko was demoted to major and sentenced to 'ten years' imprisonment on active service with the army' and commanded an infantry brigade in Stalingrad in the second half of 1942. Once more, he found himself encircled and after ten days of fighting succeeded in breaking out with just 300 of his men. He was once more court martialled, this time for retreating without permission. He was further demoted, but given command of an infantry regiment. He led his men with distinction in the battles that followed and was restored to his previous rank of colonel, ultimately being awarded the title of Hero of the Soviet Union for his leadership in an assault crossing over the Dnepr River in 1943. He ultimately ended the war as a division commander.

Efremov's designated escape route to the south would involve a long march, probably under constant German attack, and Efremov contacted *Stavka* by radio to request permission to use an alternative, shorter route. A telephone conversation between Zhukov and Stalin followed. The Front commander wanted Efremov to adhere to his original orders, but Stalin overruled him. When the breakout attempt began in the second week of April, it quickly disintegrated under almost constant German attack. A plane was sent to evacuate Efremov and his staff, but the army commander decided to stay with his men, and his staff officers similarly chose to stay with him. Small groups of men continued to try to escape to the east, but Efremov was wounded three times. Rather than surrender, he shot himself. The German units operating in the area were under the command of V Corps, and Major General Arthur Schmidt, who would serve as Paulus' chief of staff in Stalingrad, was the corps' chief of staff. He later wrote that he arranged for captured Soviet soldiers to carry their dead general to the village of Slobodka, where he was buried, and arranged for a plaque in both German and Russian to be erected on the site.[22]

After the war, Efremov was reinterred in a new grave. Examination of his remains revealed that his fatal wound was a bullet to the left temple, but Efremov was known to be right-handed, and it was not obvious from his remains that his right hand had been injured sufficiently to prevent him from using it in his apparent suicide.[23] This has led to speculation that he had been betrayed and perhaps murdered. It was alleged that substantial German reinforcements were moved to the area of Efremov's planned breakout to block the move, and this was due to the Germans being tipped off, but equally it can be argued that Efremov deliberately chose the most direct route for his attempt, and it was entirely logical that the Germans would reinforce this area.[24] An officer in I Guards Cavalry Corps later asserted that a soldier called Bocharov was captured by the Germans immediately before the operation and either voluntarily revealed the breakout plan, or the Germans extracted details during interrogation.[25] The true details will probably never be known with certainty.

Even as Efremov's men were being overwhelmed, the rest of the paratroopers of Kazankin's airborne corps joined forces with what was left of Belov's cavalry. The Germans continued to compress the perimeter of the area held by this group, and on 10 April Belov requested permission to fight his way towards Fiftieth Army. This would require a march of 15 miles (25km), but the area was strongly held by the Germans. When the attempt began late on 13 April, the paratroopers seem to have surprised the German defences and secured several small villages.

At the same time, Fiftieth Army succeeded in capturing a small ridge, and it seemed possible that the breakout would succeed. Contrary to Belov's request, Zhukov had insisted that he leave his best unit, 1st Guards Cavalry Division, to hold Dorogobuzh, 43 miles (69km) southwest of Vyazma – even at this stage, it seems that Zhukov had hopes that by linking up with the encircled Soviet units, he would still be able to achieve an envelopment of German forces around Vyazma. As German resistance to the breakout stiffened, Belov found himself desperately short of reserves, and the situation worsened for the Soviet forces when the Germans mounted an energetic counterattack and pushed Fiftieth Army back to its start line.[26] After regrouping and beating off powerful German attacks, Belov made one last attempt to break out on 23 April. This too failed, and Zhukov ordered an end to the operation. Belov and Kazankin would have to continue operating behind German lines with their men.

There were recriminations following the death of Efremov. Zhukov largely blamed Efremov for allowing himself to be cut off, but later acknowledged that he had underestimated the strength of German forces in the area. A report produced later in 1942 by Colonel Konstantin Fedorovich Vasilchenko, a staff officer at *Stavka*, suggested that the primary responsibility lay with the Front commander:

> The operational plan for the swift capture of Vyazma ... did not correspond to the forces present and the resources allocated for this mission by Western Front. [There were] incorrect assessments of the enemy and his combat effectiveness after his serious defeats in earlier battles. Incorrect timing and ignorance of the conditions in which our troops were operating led to errors, as a result of which the planned operation failed ...
>
> Western Front pursued excessively ambitious objectives, wanting simultaneously to defeat [numerous] enemy groups ... without having sufficient forces or means for this. The actions of Western Front can be likened to a hand with its fingers spread. Each army had its own strike force, which operated on its own axis without close coordination with its neighbours ... Accustomed to acting independently, the armies remained true to their old habits.
>
> As the operation unfolded, when the shock group of one army advanced, another stood still, and then the roles were reversed. The command of Western Front continued to observe how shock groups of different armies were fighting without coordination and did not intervene ...
>
> Western Front did not create a concentration in the form of a large, powerful grouping of all combat arms on a decisive axis ... The forces and resources were almost evenly distributed along the entire front. Strident orders from the

commander of Western Front were impracticable ... [and] did not reflect the actual position of the troops ... The haste shown by the command of Western Front was transferred to the troops, resulting in great harm.

Operations were poorly prepared without close interaction of different combat arms, units were brought into action piecemeal, preventing any surprise ...

The control of troops ... was weak. This was particularly marked by the absence of sufficient reserves in the key sectors.[27]

Zhukov would perhaps have argued that he was merely attempting to implement the orders he had received from *Stavka*.

Slowly, German units were recovering their strength. In the southern sector of Army Group Centre's area, 4th Panzer Division was able to report by mid-April that it could field up to 30 tanks, largely due to the efforts of its repair teams. As the Red Army's assaults on German positions ebbed away, warfare took other forms:

Ageing biplanes bumbled over night after night from Tula and gave us no rest. From sunset until first light, these nerve-fraying machines ruled the Russian skies. They scattered shrapnel bombs across the entire area. The soldiers had a whole litany of names for these ghostly flyers: night owls, sewing machines, *Unteroffizer vom Dienst* ['duty NCO'], Natasha, and nerve saw. These nightly troublemakers flew so slowly that it seemed as if they were hanging in the air from rubber bands. Shortly before their bombing run they switched off their engines and flew almost silently to their targets, just a few hundred metres above us. At the same time, they called out battle slogans over loudspeakers, or hurled insults at us. Our anti-aircraft guns didn't take them seriously and did little against them. It was only at the Dumtchino railway station that an anti-aircraft battery was set up after they blew up a munitions train.[28]

These raids were carried out mainly by squadrons flying the venerable Polykarpov Po-2; a version of this known as the U-2 was modified to carry a number of small bombs, with a total payload of just 350kg.[29] The material damage carried out by their attacks was minimal, but by operating from small airfields immediately behind the front line, pilots could fly several missions in a single night, and their effectiveness in depriving the Germans of sleep was considerable. Their silent approach made it difficult for anti-aircraft guns to engage them effectively, and their normal cruising speed was less than the stalling speed of German fighters, making aerial interception very difficult. The efficacy of these planes ultimately led to the Luftwaffe creating similar units with its obsolete open-cockpit aircraft.

126

The Soviet offensive operations that ran from the second week of January until the spring thaw and exhaustion brought all operations to a halt in April are collectively termed the Rzhev–Vyazma Operation in Soviet accounts, with the different phases sometimes given separate names, sometimes in terms of location and sometimes based upon when they took place. As a result, some Soviet-era books refer to the Sychevka–Vyazma Operation, covering Western Front's attacks from 8 January until 20 April, the Toropets–Kholm Operation by Kalinin Front between 9 January and early February, and the Vyazma Airborne Operation from 18 January to 28 February. It would be incorrect to describe these as completely separate operations; they were interlinked at the tactical and operational levels, and generally flowed from one to the next with considerable temporal overlap. By the time that they came to an end, the Red Army had lost over 770,000 men killed, wounded or taken prisoner.[30] The losses of Kluge's Army Group Centre in the same period amounted to a little over 330,000.[31] The two sides compiled their figures in different ways, and the Soviet system does not include a full accounting of men disabled by injury or illness; the discrepancy between the losses suffered is therefore probably greater. The territorial gains for the Red Army were minimal and utterly disproportionate to the casualties. The only significant result was that Belov's cavalry corps and Kazankin's paratroopers were left in the rear of the German front line, and would continue to operate there for several weeks more.

The material losses in terms of men and equipment suffered by the Wehrmacht were severe, but there was an additional effect on the morale and self-confidence of soldiers at every level. Prior to being permitted a month of home leave in June, Heinrici's letters to his wife showed his continuing sense of pessimism:

> The winter was an incredible trial for all who were there. Only very few troops are left who started with us on 22 June. But this campaign also had an impact on the higher ranks. Many of them, like me, have been part of it from the beginning until now, have experienced the continuous battle without ceasing, without relief, without leave, without rest ...
>
> I feel miserable and exhausted ... I am at the end of my tether, so discontented and frustrated, shattered, demoralised and worn out by the imbalance between expectations from above and the reality of war.[32]

In terms of skill and efficacy, the Red Army still had a long way to go in order to put right the damage done by the pre-war purges; like almost every army in the Second World War, it also needed to re-evaluate its pre-war plans and training. The process of carefully examining operations and attempting to learn from them began almost immediately. Shaposhnikov oversaw these assessments, particularly after worsening health forced his retirement from the general staff in the summer of 1942. While the general conclusions of the study of the fighting around Moscow are accurate, the document is notable for what it doesn't say – there is no attempt to discuss who was responsible for errors of over-ambition, dilution of effort and underestimation of enemy strength. To a large extent, it can be argued that such considerations weren't necessary, and it was sufficient to highlight the errors that had been made, but there was also probably a large element of caution on the part of the authors. The memories of the recent purges were still fresh, and it is understandable that nobody wished to point fingers of blame at the powerful figures at the summit of Soviet power.

Soviet post-war historiography created distortions in the historical narrative that remain problematic. The memoirs of many of the senior figures try to portray the Rzhev-Vyazma Operation as a continuation of the December counteroffensive and therefore include the gains of that earlier counteroffensive in the overall assessment of the 'success' of the Red Army's winter offensive. Although many accounts acknowledge the over-ambitious plans of Stalin and *Stavka*, there is little recognition of the roles played by Front commanders like Zhukov in the setting of operational objectives that were far beyond the resources and capabilities of the troops. Zhukov later wrote:

In general, the resources of our nation at that time were very limited. The needs of the troops could not yet be met as required by their missions and the general situation. We reached the point that every time we were summoned to [Stalin's] headquarters, we literally begged the commander-in-chief for anti-tank rifles, PPSh submachine-guns, anti-tank guns, and the minimum numbers of shells and mines that we needed. Everything that could be obtained in this manner was promptly loaded onto trucks and sent to the most needy armies.

The supply of ammunition was especially poor. For example, the provision of ammunition for the first ten days of January for our Western Front [compared to the actual requirement] was: 82mm mortar rounds – one percent; and artillery ammunition – 20–30 percent ... The February planned delivery was also not implemented. None of the 316 railway wagons planned for the first ten days arrived. Due to the lack of ammunition for rocket artillery, some of it had to be withdrawn to the rear.

It seems hard to believe now that we had to set a consumption rate of just one or two rounds of ammunition per gun per day. And this, it should be noted, was during an offensive! The report of Western Front to the commander-in-chief on 14 February said: 'As combat experience has demonstrated, the shortage of shells makes it impossible to carry out offensive artillery strikes. As a result, the enemy's fire system is not disrupted and our units, attacking the enemy's weakly suppressed defences, incur heavy losses without achieving any success.'[33]

Given such catastrophic ammunition shortages, it is all the more extraordinary that Zhukov continued to demand aggressive offensive operations from his army commanders.

Kononienko, who served as an intelligence officer with Belov's I Guards Cavalry Corps, was very critical of Zhukov in his unpublished memoirs, and any analysis of the fighting would be incomplete without considering the points that he made. He drew attention to the high losses suffered by Western Front:

> *Stavka* replenished Western Front two or three times as much as other fronts, but these reinforcements were lost unacceptably quickly due to the unit commanders' negligent attitude towards preserving lives and the health of their troops. The attitude towards avoiding casualties in Fiftieth and Tenth Armies was particularly bad, due to unacceptably poor and irresponsible preparation for battle, an inability to organise proper support services ... *Stavka* and the Military Council of the Front [a political body run by the Communist Party] received numerous letters from soldiers, officers and political workers, testifying to the criminally negligent attitude of command at all levels to preserving the lives of Red Army infantry. Hundreds of examples were given in letters and reports of unit commanders killing hundreds or thousands of Red Army men in ill-prepared attacks on intact enemy defences.[34]

Kononienko went on to assert that the orders given to I Guards Cavalry Corps by Zhukov were often contradictory; for example, he felt that at the end of 1941, Belov's corps could have captured Yukhnov and cut the supply lines of the German Fourth Army, but had to abandon its planned attack when Zhukov ordered Belov instead to move west and cut the roads running from Smolensk to Vyazma. Soviet doctrine for breakthrough operations and deep exploitation required troops in a second echelon to move forward quickly in order to secure the 'shoulders' of a breakthrough, while exploitation forces pressed into the depth of the enemy position. Belov followed the orders that Zakharov had imposed upon him and exploited towards Vyazma, but as described above, both in the case of Belov's corps and Thirty-Third Army, it seems that there were almost no troops designated for the role of keeping the flanks of the breakthrough secure, and the few units that were available were not committed in time.

In response to Zhukov's demands after the Germans repaired their front line, a team of military lawyers was sent to the front line. One of them flew to Belov's group and sent a report from behind German lines to Major General Aleksei Semenovich Rumiantsev, the senior legal officer in Western Front, in mid-March. This report described plainly that Belov's I Guards Cavalry Corps suffered heavy losses in forcing its way through heavily fortified German lines and then, without any reinforcements, was ordered to proceed towards Vyazma:

> It should be noted that almost all [the corps'] heavy equipment, including many automatic weapons, were left in the city of Mozhaisk due to a lack of adequate roads. The corps thus embarked on the raid inadequately equipped or armed and without reinforcements of either men or horses. The airborne units, in cooperation with which I Guards Cavalry Corps was supposed to act, were dropped in disarray and took several days to concentrate, and some groups descended directly onto enemy units and were destroyed by them. It is beyond question that given the strength of the enemy, the corps could not fulfil its mission to capture Vyazma, as it was pointless to attack a heavily fortified enemy equipped with artillery, mortars and tanks ... The corps has suffered major losses of men and horses ... the divisions are so degraded that they do not have the strength of a single regiment ... Moreover, there is an acute shortage of fodder and food in the corps' area of operations. The personnel are exhausted by constant fighting and sleepless nights and require rest.[35]

The report concluded with the recommendation that Belov's corps be pulled out as quickly as possible. The response from Zhukov's headquarters, signed by the Front commander, arrived the following morning. Musabeev, the author of the report, and Brigade-Commissar Aleksei Varfolomeevich Shchelakovsky, the commissar of I Guards Cavalry Corps, were ordered to suppress such 'decadent sentiments' among senior officers. Musabeev was told bluntly not to send reports of an operational or tactical nature and to restrict himself to the orders he had been given. A second message to Musabeev criticised him for failing to understand the importance of Belov's raid in stimulating the partisan movement behind German lines. While this was undoubtedly a benefit of the raid, it was entirely unanticipated and played no part in the original orders given to Belov.

It is unsurprising that Kononienko was unable to secure permission for his memoirs to be published, given how damning they were of Zhukov and others.

Even before the war was over, a 'cult of infallibility' grew up around Stalin, and all of his decisions were regarded as showing almost superhuman insight and cunning; after his death, the memoirs of senior Red Army officers like Zhukov, Vasilevsky, Eremenko and Konev began to appear, but while they often placed the blame for the over-ambition that cost the Red Army such heavy losses on Stalin, they showed no insight whatever into any role that they might have played in such errors themselves. The following winter, the Red Army would make the same mistake again, assuming that after its defeat at Stalingrad the power of the Wehrmacht was irrevocably broken, and would push forward too far, too fast, exposing itself to a deadly counteroffensive by Manstein in March 1943; on that occasion, Nikolai Fedorovich Vatutin, commander of Southwest Front, was widely blamed for being too impetuous, with no recognition that the orders to push forward so energetically originated in *Stavka*. It is perhaps worth noting that Vatutin died of wounds inflicted by nationalist Ukrainian partisans before the end of the war – he was therefore unable to give his version of events and was a convenient figure for everyone else to blame. Similarly, after Stalin's death and particularly after Khrushchev's condemnation of the wartime leader, it was easy to assign all responsibility for the errors of 1941–42 to Stalin.

Zhukov was not the only Front commander who attempted to blame all mishaps on his subordinates. Konev expressed his anger at the failure of Twenty-Ninth and Thirty-Ninth Armies to complete their designated missions, telling Corps-Commissar Dmitrii Sergeevich Leonov, a member of his Front's military council:

> Warn [Major General Vasilii Ivanovich] Shvetsov [commander of Twenty-Ninth Army] that he will be put on trial for failing to carry out the task to seize Rzhev … Give [Lieutenant General Ivan Ivanovich] Maslennikov [commander of Thirty-Ninth Army] a threatening warning that for the indecision of his actions, overestimation of the enemy, and susceptibility to all sorts of rumours, he will be removed from his post as army commander.[36]

Shvetsov was removed from command of Twenty-Ninth Army and became deputy commanding officer of Fourth Shock Army. Maslennikov, who had a long history of service for the NKVD* behind him, survived unscathed.

Narodny Komissariat Vnutrennikh Del or 'People's Commissariat for Internal Affairs', the Soviet Union's internal security force and forerunner of the KGB.

The winter fighting saw Hitler increasingly imposing his personal will upon the Wehrmacht, and the concept of the 'will' became an increasingly significant factor in German assessments. Hitler, his immediate entourage, and even senior figures in the Wehrmacht seem to have regarded this intangible 'will' as an adequate substitute for men, munitions and equipment. Such attitudes are indistinguishable from the manner in which Zhukov, Zakharov and others bullied their subordinates. Zakharov was a ruthless man who clearly understood the power of Stalin, and perhaps during the 1930s he learned the importance of avoiding Stalin's suspicion and disapproval by complying with every instruction from above. Zhukov, too, showed little flexibility, and perhaps such attitudes were essential if these men were to ensure their personal survival. It seems that regardless of their personal views at the time, all senior figures chose at the time to blame the failure of the Rzhev–Vyazma Operation on their subordinates. Ultimately, responsibility for the need to be seen to be adhering to Stalin's orders must lie with Stalin himself for creating the climate of fear that prevailed among his senior officers. But the price for their rigidity, and for the increasing rigidity on the German side of the line, was paid by the million or more soldiers – and an unknown number of civilians – whose frozen bodies littered the battlefields as the spring thaw set in.

CHAPTER 5

HANNOVER

Twice a year – in the autumn and then in the spring – the landscape of the Soviet Union became muddy and often impassable, particularly where there were few good roads. The constant military traffic degraded these roads, reducing mobility still further, and the few vehicles that could move over the rutted terrain suffered increased wear and tear, resulting in constant breakdowns. Consequently, both periods of *Rasputitsa* – the 'muddy season' – became natural pauses in military operations, allowing the opposing armies a chance to regroup and make plans for the future.

There was a significant change in the personnel at the very summit of the Red Army. Shaposhnikov, who was both chief of the general staff and Deputy People's Commissar for Defence (a post that would be known as deputy defence minister in other nations), had been suffering from ill health for some considerable time and was unable to continue in both of these roles. He became chief of the Military Academy of the General Staff and retained his position as Deputy People's Commissar for Defence, but was replaced as chief of the general staff by his deputy, whom he had been preparing for this role for some considerable time.

Alexander Mikhailovich Vasilevsky was one of eight children. His father was a Russian Orthodox priest, and he was sent to a theological school but was expelled from a seminary in 1909 for joining a students' strike. He volunteered to join the Russian Army in 1915, taking part in the Brusilov Offensive of 1916; as a result of heavy casualties among officers, he rapidly rose to command a battalion. He took advantage of the October Revolution in 1917 to return home and worked as a teacher, turning down a request by the soldiers of his regiment who had asked him to return to take command. In 1919 he was drafted into the Red Army, fighting against anti-Bolshevik forces and being involved in the war with Poland.

He survived the purges of the 1930s without being arrested, at least partly due to Shaposhnikov playing a role as his mentor, and he became deputy chief of the Operations Directorate of the general staff in 1939. When the war with Germany commenced in 1941, Shaposhnikov arranged for Vasilevsky to become his deputy, and he was now a natural candidate to replace his former boss.

Vasilevsky's memoirs are unusual in that they contain very little of the self-aggrandisement that features in the works of so many of his contemporaries, both in the Red Army and in the Wehrmacht. His accounts of the men with whom he worked are almost always generous and tolerant, and even during the war many senior Red Army figures regarded him as too weak and reticent, particularly in his dealings with Stalin. It is rather more likely that he was a good diplomat and knew that confrontational arguments with Stalin were unlikely to achieve anything. Stalin appears to have held genuine affection for him, urging him to mend a longstanding rift with his father, and perhaps the Soviet leader recognised a very capable staff officer who lacked personal political ambition and was therefore not a threat to his own position. In the pantheon of great Soviet commanders of the Second World War, Vasilevsky has rarely received the recognition that is due to him, largely because he made little effort to praise himself.

For both sides, an essential part of planning for the coming months was an assessment of the enemy's intentions. Stalin and *Stavka* remained strongly focused on the Moscow region, and in particular the German salient around Rzhev. This was effectively the start line from which the Germans had launched *Taifun* – in many places, the front line was actually closer to Moscow than it had been prior to the German assault of 2 October 1941. It was perhaps natural for senior Soviet figures to believe that once the ground had become firm enough for major operations, the Germans would try once more to capture the Soviet capital. Detailed analysis of the winter fighting also began, and although much of this would take time before it was published and circulated, there were clear lessons that could be learned in the short term. Vasilevsky later recalled the discussions that took place in April:

> None of us had any doubt that the enemy would once more take serious actions no later than the summer so as to retrieve the initiative and defeat us …
>
> On completing the winter campaign, our armed forces were still inferior to the enemy numerically and especially in materiel; at that time we had no ready reserves and big material resources. *Stavka* and the general staff reckoned that a temporary strategic defence had to be the main immediate task … Its aim would be to wear down the enemy assault groupings on deliberate defences, and both to

halt the summer offensive which the Fascists were preparing and to sap their energy so that we might prepare favourable conditions for the Red Army to go on to the offensive decisively with the least loss of men. The main emphasis of the plan was naturally on the central direction …

The enemy had been thrown back from Moscow, but he still threatened the city. The biggest enemy grouping (over 70 divisions) was located on the Moscow approaches. This gave *Stavka* and general staff grounds for believing that the enemy would try to make a decisive attack on the central direction with the start of the summer season. This opinion … was shared by the command on most fronts.

Stalin did not think it feasible to start big offensive operations in early summer and therefore favoured an energetic strategic defence, like the rest of us. However, at the same time he thought it sensible to launch local offensive operations in the Crimea, in the Kharkov area, in the Lvov–Kursk and Smolensk directions and in the Leningrad and Demyansk areas. Shaposhnikov was against large-scale counter-offensive actions before the summer. Zhukov basically supported Shaposhnikov but felt it vitally necessary at the same time to destroy the Rzhev–Vyazma enemy grouping at the beginning of summer …

We did not take account of the information from our intelligence on the enemy's preparations for a major thrust in the south. The southwest direction was allotted fewer forces than the western …

We considered that the most likely danger to Moscow came from the Orel–Tula direction … with the subsequent development of an enemy advance by a wide sweep around Moscow from the southeast.[1]

It is human nature to place greater value on evidence that confirms pre-existing beliefs than evidence that contradicts them. Having decided that the German Army Group Centre would renew its offensive, Stalin, Vasilevsky and others downplayed the reports of increasing German strength in Ukraine. The Germans were aware of continuing Soviet concerns about a threat to Moscow – aerial reconnaissance couldn't fail to spot extensive defensive preparations to the west of the city – and deliberately fostered this belief. On 5 April, Hitler issued a new directive to the Wehrmacht:

The winter battle in Russia is nearing its end …

The enemy has suffered severe losses in men and materiel. We must seize the initiative again, and through the superiority of German leadership and the German soldier force our will upon the enemy.

Our aim is to wipe out the entire defence potential remaining to the Soviets, and to cut them off, as far as possible, from the most important centres of war industry ...

In pursuit of the original plan for the Eastern campaign, the armies of the central sector will stand fast, those in the north will capture Leningrad and link up with the Finns, while those on the southern flank will break through to the Caucasus.[2]

However, in order to improve the prospects for German forces advancing in the south, the Germans exploited the Soviet leadership's suspicions about a renewed attack on Moscow. Under the codename of *Kremlin*, detailed planning was carried out by Army Group Centre about an operation to encircle Moscow and secure substantial territory beyond the city. Street maps of the city were distributed down to regiment and battalion level, and there was widespread signals traffic to simulate preparations. Stalin and others took these signs as confirmation of their own beliefs, and as Soviet reserves began to build up once more, they were concentrated largely in the central region.

The Wehrmacht might have survived the winter counteroffensives with its lines intact, but there was no doubt that it had suffered heavy losses of personnel and equipment. On 21 April, Halder presented data to Hitler summarising the state of the armies on the Eastern Front. Since the beginning of January, the Wehrmacht had suffered about 900,000 'losses', including from illness, while replacements had come to only half this figure, and he added that this demand for manpower was having a serious detrimental impact on German industry. Only ten per cent of the 74,000 wheeled vehicles that were lost had been replaced, but the situation with tracked vehicles was rather better – losses came to a little over 2,300, while replacements numbered about 1,800. Given that many of the tanks that had been lost were in any case obsolete models, the shortfall probably had little impact on fighting power. Significantly, the army had also lost nearly 180,000 horses, while replacements numbered only 20,000. In many cases, front-line units were able to round up cavalry ponies abandoned by Red Army formations, but these were physically smaller than the packhorses used by the Wehrmacht to pull much of its artillery, wagons, etc. Halder noted that the eastern armies had a collective shortfall of about 625,000 men. This was particularly pronounced in infantry formations; in order to build up the strength of Army Group South for the campaign planned for 1942, the infantry divisions of Army Group Centre and Army Group North would be left badly depleted. Importantly, Halder added that motorised units in both of these sectors, which would be considered secondary theatres for 1942, had 'insufficient mobility for extensive operations'.[3] Such mobility would be essential if they were to compensate for the weakness of infantry units by mounting counterattacks.

Despite what seemed unanimous agreement, the Soviet plan to adopt an active strategic defensive posture was not followed as rigorously as might have been expected. Marshal Timoshenko, a Civil War comrade of Stalin and currently commander of Southwest Front, was permitted to launch an offensive aimed at the recapture of Kharkov; this resulted in a disastrous defeat and in many respects paved the way for the German advance across the valley of the Donets River towards the Don and ultimately to Stalingrad and the Caucasus. Zhukov's wish to eliminate the German forces in the Rzhev–Vyazma region was also contrary to the overall strategic plan, but nonetheless Zhukov issued detailed orders to the various Fronts under his overall control for renewed offensive operations that were to commence at the end of the spring thaw. On this occasion at least, Zhukov had better grounds for launching an offensive than Timoshenko or commanders on other sectors: Belov and his men remained at large behind German lines, in control of a substantial amount of territory.

Zhukov's new plans for an offensive were as ambitious as his plans in the winter, and the configuration of the front line as shown in the accompanying map provides some justification for this. Once again, both Western Front and Kalinin Front would be involved in another pincer operation to pinch off the German salient around Rzhev. The attacking forces would seek to link up with Belov's cavalry corps and the paratroopers still in the region, as well as with partisan units. As part of preparations, Zhukov ordered his chief of operations, Major General Vladimir Sergeevich Golushkevich, to fly to Belov's group in order to discuss arrangements. Belov had submitted proposals of his own at the end of April; a new I Guards Cavalry Corps was being created behind the front line, and Belov suggested that, suitably reinforced with this corps and other units, Fiftieth Army could break through the German lines – and, crucially, hold open the breach – enabling a link-up with the encircled troops. Thereafter, it might be possible to drive further west along the highway towards Smolensk and ultimately to meet troops from Kalinin Front. This was as ambitious as every other planned Soviet offensive in the area, and Belov cannot have been surprised when it was rejected.

Somewhat in contradiction of the decision by *Stavka* to concentrate on a strategic defensive posture, Stalin authorised the transfer of seven rifle divisions and eight artillery regiments from strategic reserves to Western Front in preparation for this new offensive. Further reinforcements of tanks and air assets

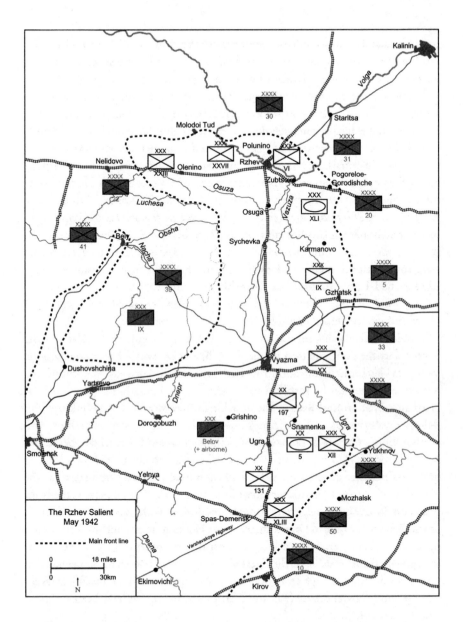

The Rzhev Salient
May 1942

- - - - - - Main front line

0   18 miles
0   30km
↑
N

were to join Zhukov's units, and the supply of equipment, fuel, food and ammunition to Belov was to be increased. The plans also called for an additional 9,000 men to be flown into Belov's area.[4] The plans proposed a start date for the new offensive of early June, with Twentieth and Forty-Third Armies advancing to capture Vyazma in the middle of the month. At the same time, Thirtieth, Twenty-Ninth and Thirty-First Armies, on the eastern flank of Konev's Kalinin Front, would attack to the west of Rzhev before turning towards the city itself. But the preparations failed to proceed as planned, particularly the airlift to Belov's troops. By the end of May, perhaps 20 percent of the personnel and equipment intended to reach Belov had actually been delivered. Other preparations were also repeatedly delayed, and the doubtful prospects for success steadily worsened.

Far from the front line, young men from the Soviet Union underwent training in preparation for being sent to the divisions fighting against the Wehrmacht, in order to bolster the reserves that Stalin and his subordinates were planning to use in the coming year. Boris Gorbachevsky, whose hopes of becoming a tank crewman were dashed by his colour-blindness, was now in the infantry school in Tyumen, about 215 miles (346km) northeast of his home town of Kyshtym, undergoing training as an officer cadet. Conditions in the school were as tough as those endured by recruits in any nation:

> We had an accelerated training programme. From the very first day, we were worked to the point of exhaustion. I was supposed to become commander of a mortar platoon after six months. Drill was carried out daily. Shooting – twice weekly. We [learned about] communications, tactics, small arms (pistol, rifle, carbine, machine-gun), mortars. We were also taught hand-to-hand combat. Once a week – skis: marches for short or long distances, up to 30km [18 miles], with reconnaissance of the terrain and setting up outposts. Additionally, we were alerted many times and made nightly marches of 15km [nine miles] with full equipment.[5]

The sheer scale of the Red Army, the losses suffered in the first year, and the urgent need to get men to the front line meant that there weren't enough instructors with experiences of the reality of modern warfare. Training often fell far short of what even a new recruit might regard as appropriate:

> We were taught how to fight and defeat the enemy, but I couldn't understand how this could be done if we hadn't read a single military textbook. All of our studies were based mainly on the principle of 'do as I do'. If you showed any initiative, the response you heard was: 'Don't try to be clever! Follow your orders!'[6]

It was therefore unsurprising that the new units that fought in the winter campaigns were so rigid and inflexible in their tactics. Occasionally, the recruits encountered an instructor who rose above the rather mediocre average. One such was Gorbachevsky's political commissar, who impressed upon them the importance of the bond between a soldier and his commander:

> 'For a soldier, his commander is the main, lasting representative of the Motherland,' said the commissar. 'The person closest to him in front line life – in the days of victory, defeat, and perhaps in the hour of his death. The commander is obliged by his own example to teach the soldier to love the Motherland, and this is the main guarantee of our victory. In turn, the commander is responsible to the Motherland for the fate of the people entrusted to him, for their development and training, for ensuring their physical and spiritual needs ... At the front, the main concern of the commander is his soldiers! Field Marshal Suvorov [a Russian general of the 18th century], going around the sleeping camp at night, encountered some sentries and asked them to sing and talk more quietly. "Let my Russian knights sleep peacefully." Of course, the songs of the sentries couldn't really disturb the sleeping army. But the next day the entire camp knew that the commander himself spoke in a whisper so as not to disturb the sleeping soldiers. This is how camaraderie is born. This is what you should strive for.'[7]

At the beginning of May 1942, after just four months of training, Gorbachevsky and his comrades were on their way to the front. Although he was meant to be training as a mortar platoon commander, he left basic training without ever having fired a mortar round. It took two weeks for their train to reach Moscow, where they were assigned to the newly created 215th Rifle Division, part of Kalinin Front's Thirtieth Army. Gorbachevsky was fortunate to have a veteran company commander, who became known to all the soldiers as 'Uncle Kuzya'. He taught the recruits the realities of front-line life: how to use their sapper shovels and bayonets when digging in; how to light a fire in difficult weather; the use of terrain as cover; how to pack away their equipment most efficiently; in short, the hard lessons learned by soldiers of every army in the front line. The recruits were also taught about their enemy. Gorbachevsky chatted about this with Yurka Davydov, an old school friend and a fellow recruit, who replied:

> '[As we were told in training,] "The Germans are Fascists, murderers, marauders, rapists, Hitler's thugs." He was a political instructor, he knows these things.'
>
> 'But Yurka, not all Germans are Fascists, they had the largest Communist Party in Europe! Where have all their Communists gone?'
>
> 'As far as I'm concerned,' replied Yurka, 'all their Communists went over to Hitler, the bastards! Some were cowards, some did it for personal gain, others

believed their Führer. I have no doubt that in the very first battle you and I will shoot at former Communists.'[8]

The pause in major operations proved to be a valuable interval for men like Gorbachevsky to continue their training. Despite his original designation as a future mortar platoon commander, he was assigned to the crew of a 45mm anti-tank gun.

While he waited for Western Front to formulate its own plans, Belov did what he could to improve the fighting strength of his formations. Careful searches of woodland revealed significant quantities of equipment and ammunition abandoned by the Red Army at the end of 1941 during its retreat towards Moscow, and by using this, Belov improvised a mortar battalion and two batteries of 152mm howitzers; his men even found shells for the guns but lacked fuses, and Belov arranged for these to be flown into the encirclement. A solitary long-range gun was found complete with a small stock of ammunition and was deployed in a well-camouflaged position near Grishino. From here, it fired occasionally at the railway station in Vyazma. The damage inflicted would have been modest, but the harassment value of such shelling was considerable. A small number of tanks was also found, and ultimately several were returned to service, though their operational usefulness must have been severely curtailed by fuel shortages.[9]

In addition to the regular Red Army units operating behind German lines, there were large numbers of partisans. The precise number is difficult to determine; Belov later wrote that in the area controlled by his troops there were about 3,000 active partisans, and that as more recruits joined the partisan movement, he sent them to reinforce groups in neighbouring areas, or added many of them to the ranks of his own units. There were several Red Army officers and NCOs in the area, men who had been cut off during the retreats of 1941, and they helped turn the partisan groups into organised formations. Increasingly, the Wehrmacht was forced to use large numbers of troops to escort supply columns and trains, or in anti-partisan sweeps through the area. These sweeps regularly killed dozens of civilians with little or no connection to the partisans, something that only increased the number of recruits. By late March, the partisans felt confident enough to try to capture the town of Yelnya. A three-day battle ensued, and ultimately the Germans prevailed after bringing in further reinforcements. Despite the failure to capture the town, the operation forced yet more German strength to be diverted from the front line. This was unsustainable in the longer term, and a better solution to the 'partisan problem' was clearly needed.

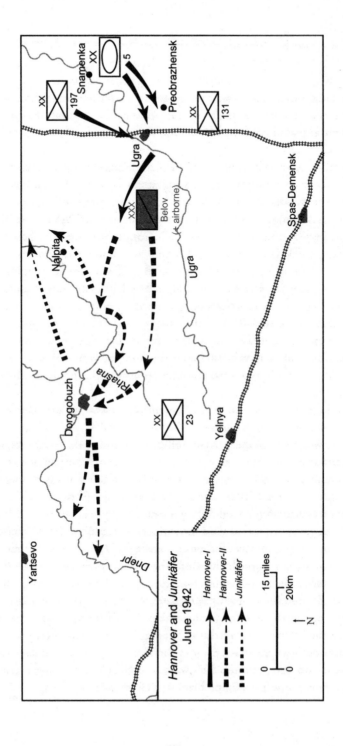

Hannover and Junikäfer
June 1942

Hannover-I
Hannover-II
Junikäfer

15 miles
20km

N

In order to reduce disruption in their rear zones, the Germans planned an extensive operation against both Belov and the partisan formations. A substantial force was to be deployed – elements of no fewer than seven divisions from Fourth Army would be involved, including most of 5th Panzer Division, which had been operating against Belov's units for several weeks. The operation was codenamed *Hannover* and would come in two phases. *Hannover-I* would involve 23rd and 197th Infantry Divisions advancing towards the west from a start line north of the Ugra River near Snamenka, while 5th Panzer Division operated to the south of the river, advancing towards the southwest. At the same time, 131st Infantry Division would form a line to the south, against which 5th Panzer Division would drive the Soviet units in its path. In anticipation of Belov attempting to escape to safety by breaking out to rejoin the rest of the Red Army, the attack was to be delivered from the east, in order to drive Belov's men further from the forces of Western Front. The operation got off to a poor start; it was scheduled to begin on 24 May, but the preceding day, a group of paratroopers from Belov's group had an unexpected encounter with a group of men:

The platoon leader [of the paratroopers] decided that they must be partisans. Leaving his men in some woodland, he went forward to investigate. He was taken to an elderly man who identified himself as Colonel Rogozhin. The platoon leader introduced himself and asked what the colonel's detachment was doing there. Rogozhin replied that he was carrying out a special mission for General Belov.

During the conversation, the platoon leader looked closely at the men who were resting in the clearing. There were about 300 of them. It was odd that they were all dressed smartly in new uniforms. All were wearing cadet insignia with stiff collars and shiny buttons, helmets on their heads, and many had backpacks. Neither the cavalrymen, nor the paratroopers, nor the partisans had such uniforms. Our soldiers were wearing worn-out clothes. 'They probably only arrived recently,' the platoon commander thought as he returned to his paratroopers.

The paratroopers moved further along a narrow forest path. But they had not gone 500m when a breathless man wearing a soldier's jacket appeared from the bushes. He waved to the platoon leader. 'Do you know who you were talking to in the meadow? He's a White Guard colonel [an expression used at the time to describe almost any anti-Bolshevik Russians],' he said in a quick whisper. 'The colonel is leading a special forces squad. Tomorrow the Germans will begin their offensive and this detachment is meant to capture Belov and destroy his headquarters. Let's approach the clearing from the other side. You have a light machine-gun and other automatic weapons. As soon as you open fire, everyone will scatter. They were recruited in prisoner of war camps and joined Rogozhin to escape starvation. And they won't fight their own people. I was one of them.'

At first, the platoon leader feared a trap. Rogozhin's group was far larger than his. But the man's sincere tone gave the platoon commander confidence. After sending a report to the brigade commander with a request for reinforcements, he decided to attack. The paratroopers quietly took up firing positions at the edge of the clearing. The man [who had defected to them] indicated the most important targets: the colonel himself, two German officers in Soviet uniform, and other senior figures. On command, the paratroopers opened fire. The startled traitors scattered through the forest. The paratroopers pursued them.

Two companies sent by Lieutenant Colonel Anufriev, the brigade commander, soon arrived. They began to comb through the forest. Almost all the saboteurs were caught and those who resisted were killed.[10]

According to Belov's account, interrogation of those who fell into the hands of the paratroopers provided details of the forthcoming *Hannover-I*, particularly the important information that it was to begin the following day, 24 May. The story is interesting, but it is difficult to know how accurate it is. At this stage of the war, the Wehrmacht was using significant numbers of former prisoners of war as helpers, or *Hilfswillige* – auxiliary volunteers, usually abbreviated to *Hiwi*. These men often opted to help the Wehrmacht as drivers, stretcher-bearers, cooks etc. in order to escape the appallingly harsh conditions of prisoner of war camps, where hunger and exposure resulted in tens of thousands of deaths; some may have volunteered out of a genuine desire to help defeat the Bolshevik regime. Even in the first winter of the war on the Eastern Front, there were cases of these men being armed and being involved in fighting against the Red Army, as will be described shortly, but the practice was far less widespread than would be the case in subsequent years.

The treatment of prisoners of war was harsh on both sides of the front line. The Soviet Union was not a signatory to the Hague Conventions and was therefore not legally bound to abide by their terms; although Germany was a signatory, Hitler had declared the war against the Soviet Union as being a *Rassenkrieg* ('racial war') and had exempted the military from having to face charges for any alleged war crimes. A young Russian girl who was living in Rzhev witnessed the manner in which prisoners of war were treated:

In 1941, the Germans invaded Rzhev. Not long after, prisoners of war were driven through Rzhev. At different times of the day I saw how brutally the Germans treated our prisoners. They were starved and forced to do hard labour. Many couldn't walk because of exhaustion and were shot. Here's one example. Early one day I went to fetch water. At that moment they were driving prisoners past. Hungry men grabbed at rotten scraps, for which they were beaten with rifle butts. I had some cake in my pocket. I gave it to a soldier. A German struck him with his rifle and the soldier fell to the ground. I rushed away, horrified.

On another occasion, prisoners of war were carrying food for the Germans. The starving men ate two jars of jam. They were taken to the military headquarters and interrogated. After interrogation they went to the yard where they were beaten with belts. They made a gallows on the side of an old house. The prisoners were taken there and ordered to stand on a bench. Nooses were put around their necks and the bench was kicked away. The bodies of the Russian soldiers were left hanging in the air. For two jars of jam, our soldiers paid with their lives.[11]

At a later stage of the war, the Germans would attempt to raise large-scale formations which collectively became known as the *Russische Befreiungsarmee* ('Russian Liberation Army') or more commonly as the 'Vlasov Army', named after Lieutenant General Andrei Andreevich Vlasov. During the winter fighting around Moscow, Vlasov commanded Twentieth Army and was awarded the Order of the Red Banner for leading his men in the recapture of Solnechnogorsk and Volokolamsk in the Soviet counteroffensive, and even earned high praise from Stalin and Zhukov. In March 1942, he was appointed deputy commander of Volkhov Front in the north, and then became commander of Second Shock Army when the previous commander became unwell. When the Red Army launched a major assault to try to lift the siege of Leningrad, Second Shock Army became dangerously isolated when the armies on its flanks failed to advance and was then cut off completely. Several attempts to break out of the encirclement failed and Vlasov rejected an offer to be flown out of the pocket, choosing to stay with his men. In July, he was captured and Vlasov subsequently agreed to fight against Stalin. His motives for this are not clear; he may have been bitter at the manner in which the other Red Army units failed to support him in his advance to try to break through to Leningrad, and it is also possible that he helped to create the Vlasov Army in an attempt to save both his own life and the lives of thousands of other prisoners. Ultimately, he was captured by the Red Army in May 1945 – he was offered political asylum in Spain and a flight to safety, and also safe conduct into American-held territory, but characteristically refused on both occasions, choosing to stay with his men – and was executed in 1946.

Additional Soviet airborne troops were dropped into the area in an attempt to reinforce Belov's group. Mikhail Moiseevich Bogatsky had been waiting to go into action with his platoon of sappers for several weeks:

We were first put on alert [for a parachute operation] in March and moved to the airfield at Lyubertsy, where we waited for two days for the order to board the planes. But the drop was cancelled. In April, we were again transferred to an airfield and the bustle of preparation before a landing began, but again it was postponed. Only on the third occasion, at the end of May, were we parachuted into the German rear, and then only part of the brigade was dropped.

All of this moving around from one airfield to another and the cancellation of landings didn't have a good effect on the morale of the paratroopers, but nonetheless it calmed our anxiety and we began to regard a drop in the German rear zone as an everyday inevitability that would happen soon.

When we were finally ordered to board the planes, many were very calm outwardly, only their fussy movements and slight trembling betraying them. We checked the packing of our parachutes for the last time – combat jumps were made without a reserve parachute – and loaded our backpacks to the maximum. For example, I took an extra 360 rounds of machine-gun ammunition, stuffed my PDMM [*Parashyutnyy Desantnyy Myagkiy Meshok* or 'parachute landing soft bag', dropped with the paratrooper and containing additional supplies] and tied a bag of grenades to my belt with rope. I had no maps, compass, binoculars, or anything else that would show me to be an officer.

We were told that we would be parachuted into the 'Landing Republic' where Belov's cavalry and the paratroopers of IV Airborne Corps had been holding a section of territory captured in the German rear zone several months ago. What was really going on behind the front line in the territory of this 'republic' – we didn't have the slightest idea. Moreover, as a simple platoon commander, I wasn't supposed to know … Only 12 of my paratroopers boarded the plane allocated for our platoon, and we dragged several extra PDMMs in. Paratroopers from other units in the brigade were also with us. When the plane taxied to the runway in the middle of the night, all conversation stopped, and there were only occasional remarks during the entire flight. Internal emotions churned around … I didn't even think that immediately after landing we might find ourselves in a German ambush.[12]

On the morning of 24 May, Belov and his staff heard German artillery fire as the operation began. When they moved forward, the two battlegroups of 5th Panzer Division swiftly cut through the opposing forces, losing more vehicles to landmines than Soviet gunfire. Although the presence of minefields was at least suspected, if not confirmed, the division's combat engineers struggled to clear safe lanes – the thaw in April softened the ground, and many mines sank deeper into the earth, where it was no longer possible for magnetic mine detectors to locate them. As the day progressed, heavy rain set in, further impacting upon German progress. Nevertheless, all of the first day's objectives were achieved. Two partisan regiments were largely destroyed, and the units of IV Airborne Corps together with 8th Guards Cavalry Regiment found themselves in danger of being encircled and isolated from the rest of Belov's command.

The second day of *Hannover-I* saw the Germans make better progress, though the overall rate of advance remained modest – in difficult, wooded and swampy terrain, 5th Panzer Division's battlegroups had pushed forward a total of no more than ten miles (16km) by the middle of the day. The partisan regiments fighting alongside the Soviet paratroopers were largely destroyed, but the regular Red Army units put up tougher resistance. Heavy fighting raged around the small village of Preobrazhensk near Ugra for two days before the Germans could complete their drive towards the south in order to link up with 131st Infantry Division. During this fighting, 5th Panzer Division made use of a company-sized group of former Red Army personnel, *Freiwilligen Kompanie von Rentelen*, to clear woodland along its southern flank.[13]

Belov ordered the preparation of two further defensive lines to which his men could retreat if required. Most of the airborne units that had been cut off by *Hannover-I* were able to infiltrate to and across the Ugra River, rejoining I Guards Cavalry Corps in the last days of May; to aid their escape, Belov threw his modest reserves – 6th Guards Cavalry Regiment assisted by two repaired T-26 tanks – into a counterattack to hold off the German pursuit.[14] Not all the Soviet troops succeeded in escaping the German net; at least one company of paratroopers was annihilated when it was encircled in a small village. Despite these setbacks, Belov remained calm. He had established a more or less continuous front line facing east against the German forces. If help arrived from the east, Belov believed, the overall situation was still favourable:

> All our plans during these days were made in the firm belief that in the first days of June, and in any case no later than 5 June, a large offensive operation by the troops of Western Front would begin. The timing was very encouraging for us. The main forces of the German XII and XLIII Corps were advancing against us, turning their front to the west and northwest. The planned assault by Fiftieth Army would have struck the flank and rear of the two Nazi corps. At the same time, we would have

tied them down with a frontal attack. For this purpose, we planned to use significant forces: all of 1st Guards Cavalry Division, which had 4,500 men, five airborne brigades with about 6,000 men, and part of a partisan division.

The Germans could hardly have withstood a simultaneous attack from the front and rear and two of their army corps would have been destroyed. The troops of Western Front would have entered the territory we had already liberated and perhaps would have been able to complete the task that they had been trying to accomplish throughout the winter: the capture of Vyazma and the encirclement of the two Fascist armies to the east of the city.[15]

Bogatsky and the other paratroopers who had been dropped to reinforce Belov's group were destined to have a difficult time:

We were told that we would be dropped in the 'bridgehead' in the German rear zone, but in fact we were dropped about 40km [24 miles] from the encircled brigades … It was bloody chaos, and for a whole month the Germans pursued us through the forests, as if driving wild animals on a hunting expedition. We jumped at dawn from a height of 1,500m. Several other transports flew alongside our Douglas … When I landed, there were paratroopers from other planes nearby, but I saw only two of my sappers. We started to gather. We didn't even have time to roll up the parachutes before machine-guns opened fire on us from one side and the paratrooper next to me was hit and fell down. We dropped our parachutes and rushed into the nearby forest, and at this time mortar bombs began to fall on our drop zone. There were only 30 of us in the forest, and the most senior, a lieutenant, took command. We tried to locate the PDMMs but we didn't find a single bag anywhere. The assault force and the PDMMs had been dropped over too large an area, and not where it was intended. We went deeper into the forest and new groups of paratroopers joined us until there were about 200, including a major with a map and compass. He indicated the direction we should follow, but we had walked only about 500m before we were ambushed and came under gunfire and mortar bombardment, with a machine-gun firing from just 100m away. We returned fire and took losses before retreating into the forest.

This continued for several days, constant skirmishes wherever we went – there were frequent ambushes and we were pursued through the forest with firing from all directions. We were already low on ammunition and our food ran out, and we were becoming desperate. But then we encountered General Kazanin's paratroopers from IV Airborne Corps and Belov's cavalrymen in the forest … It was painful to look at the cavalry horses, emaciated and reduced to just skeletons covered with skin. We were all starving and the paratroopers were gathered in groups, no longer into precise battalions, and the Germans pursued us methodically to finish us off. We broke through in one direction or another, scattered groups wandered and merged once more into larger groups before scattering again after the next battle in the forest, a chaotic and bloody mess moving now east, then north.[16]

Belov contacted Zhukov's headquarters by radio, asking if Fiftieth Army's attack could be brought forward, but received no response. Zhukov had been waiting for the arrival of armoured formations before committing his troops to their offensive, but the Red Army suffered a disastrous setback in Ukraine, where Timoshenko's attack towards Kharkov ground to a halt after just three days in the face of tough German resistance and powerful air attacks. On 17 May, the Wehrmacht commenced a counteroffensive codenamed *Fridericus* that swiftly encircled three Soviet armies. Consequently, the tank units that Zhukov had expected were diverted to the south, and in their absence there was no prospect of a successful assault.

Hannover-I was an unquestionable success for the Wehrmacht, but Belov estimated that he still had 17,000 men under arms. However, his men were forced back to their first reserve defensive line and in doing so lost one of the few airfields under their control. Unless help arrived soon, the pocket faced destruction, particularly as improving weather allowed the Luftwaffe to operate more freely. In order to complete the clearance of the region, the Germans now progressed to *Hannover-II*, intended to break up the remaining area under Soviet control and to capture the large town of Dorogobuzh, which had been under the control of the 'Landing Republic' for several weeks. For this phase, the Germans moved 5th Panzer Division north of the Ugra; from its start line it would drive first west, then northwest to Dorogobuzh and then further west in conjunction with 23rd Infantry Division operating on its southern flank. This operation was to commence early on 4 June.

As had been the case with *Hannover-I*, 5th Panzer Division encountered considerable problems with minefields laid by Belov's men. Throughout the first day of *Hannover-II*, the Soviet troops put up tough resistance but couldn't hold back their opponents. On the evening of 4 June, Belov sent an urgent radio signal to Zhukov:

> It is time to seek your advice. My assessment of the situation is that three enemy divisions, with an overwhelming superiority of tanks and aviation, are successfully

advancing, overcoming the heroic resistance of the group's troops and bringing up further reserves, disregarding their own heavy losses.

After 12 days of heavy fighting, the enemy has captured more than half the area previously held by the group. Another day of fighting could see the enemy break through into the centre of our group, perhaps splitting our forces. Further fighting in this encirclement threatens the destruction of my units' manpower. In order to preserve men and their high combat quality, we ask permission to break out of the encirclement …

I propose to break through to the east of Yelnya in the zone held by 5th Partisan Rifle Regiment. Beyond that, we will break through towards Kirov to link up with the troops of [Western] Front.

We ask for your urgent help and advice.[17]

The following day, Zhukov sent his reply. He offered Belov two options – either to try to head north in order to break out to the lines held by Kalinin Front west of Rzhev, or to march directly east towards Mozhaisk. Belov disliked both of these suggestions. The route to the east via Mozhaisk had such obvious flaws that it is remarkable Western Front even suggested it: such an escape march would involve Belov fighting his way through the very units that were crushing his pocket. A march north to try to reach Kalinin Front was, at first glance, a much more inviting option. There were substantial areas under the control of partisans little more than 30 miles (50km) north of Dorogobuzh, and beyond these partisans were the units of the Soviet Thirty-Ninth Army and XI Cavalry Corps, but Belov regarded the prospects of success as poor. A march in that direction would pass through difficult terrain, including crossing the flooded valley of the Dnepr River. The Germans had already positioned substantial forces to the north of Dorogobuzh precisely to stop the Red Army units and partisans in their rear areas from combining their forces and had fortified the line of the highway running west from Vyazma to Yartsevo. Belov had limited information about the exact location and strength of the partisans operating to the north of this road, and even if he was able to reach them, joining up with Kalinin Front's troops further to the north would require a further prolonged march through forests and swamps.

Belov convened a meeting of his corps' military council to discuss what they should do. The weakest side of the encirclement was to the west, and Lieutenant Colonel Petr Semenovich Vashurin, his head of operations, suggested that they should head in this unexpected direction and make contact with the burgeoning partisan movement in Belarus. This wouldn't result in an immediate escape from the encirclement but would allow them to continue fighting behind German lines. Belov vetoed this, as he felt that it would effectively turn his command into a partisan formation, and he wanted to preserve its conventional fighting power – once the corps was replenished with men and equipment, the experience gained in recent fighting would help turn it into a formidable force. He proposed once more that they should head south towards Yelnya, where partisan units were active in the countryside; they would then be able to proceed towards Kirov and a link-up with the Soviet Tenth Army. This was the plan that was adopted.

On the battlefield, 5th Panzer Division was now to the southeast of Dorogobuzh and fought its way forward to the line of the Rhasna River, just seven miles (12km) from the town centre. The bridges across the river had all been destroyed by the retreating Soviet units and no fords could be located, forcing the division's armour to a standstill. The weather had deteriorated, and torrential rain made movement of support services almost impossible. This would delay the arrival of any bridging equipment, and even the division's artillery struggled to move forward to support the advance. Men and equipment laboured to reach the river overnight, and early on 7 June an assault was launched directly towards Dorogobuzh, advancing out of two small bridgeheads over the Rhasna that had been established towards the end of the previous day. By midday, the leading elements of 5th Panzer Division were in the town and the area immediately to the south. They didn't know that they were very close to Belov's headquarters; with his planned escape route decided, Belov dispersed his senior officers to his units in preparation for the hazardous escape attempt, even as German tanks started firing on the village where he was based. One of the biggest problems that I Guards Cavalry Corps faced was the presence of about 2,000 wounded men. Some could not be taken on the breakout attempt due to the severity of their wounds, and Belov ordered that these men should be moved to improvised hospitals that had been created in partisan-controlled forests. Each formation was ordered to collect its wounded personnel and to organise them into an ad hoc unit. The medical staff gathered what wagons were available and loaded as many men as they could aboard. Belov accepted that the presence of so many wounded would inevitably hinder movement, but to leave the men behind was unthinkable.[18]

One of the men with Belov was Colonel Ivan Klimentinovich Samokhin, commander of 215th Mixed Aviation Division, which had been providing air support for the cavalry corps. Belov ordered him to fly out of the pocket in order to coordinate the escape attempt with Western Front. A Polykarpov Po-2 biplane was waiting nearby:

The colonel and the radio operator accompanying him rode to the plane on horseback. Leaving the horses with another man, Samokhin tried to start the engine but it stubbornly remained silent. For ten minutes, it refused to start. Germans had already appeared from the direction of the [nearby] village and, noticing the plane, moved towards it. Anyone other than Samokhin would have abandoned the plane and run to the undergrowth where the paratroopers were fighting nearby. But the colonel was both brave and stubborn. He continued to tinker with the motor.

Bullets from Fascist submachine-gunners were whistling around when the engine finally started. Normally, it was necessary to warm the engine prior to take-off, but there was no time: a German tank appeared from the village. The plane took off and began to gain height over the heads of the Germans, and suddenly the cold engine stalled. Undaunted, Samokhin landed behind some bushes about 700m from where he took off. He quickly examined the plane. There were several bullet holes in the fuselage but no serious damage. The propeller was undamaged.

The sounds of battle were very close although nothing could be seen through the bushes. Samokhin sent the radio operator to stand guard while he tried to restart the engine. This time, it fired up easily. The radio operator found a clearing nearby and with his knife he cut down the thickest bushes that blocked the path to the clearing. Samokhin taxied through the bushes to the clearing, risking damage to the propeller, and took off. He managed to reach an airfield near Kaluga safely. From there he tried in every possible way to help us.[19]

Indeed, Belov and his men would require all the help that Samokhin and others could provide if they were to escape the encirclement.

CHAPTER 6

BELOV'S ESCAPE AND *SEYDLITZ*

Having secured Dorogobuzh, 5th Panzer Division attempted to push on towards the west but ran into heavy fire in woodland just outside the town. Belov's units were now actively trying to disengage in order to commence their breakout attempt, and 5th Panzer Division reported that its units lacked the strength to tie them down and destroy them – the Soviet units simply slipped away into the woodland and then reappeared behind the advancing Germans and harassed their supply lines.[1] While these raids were problematic for the Germans, they rapidly faded away over the next day as the Soviet soldiers began to move south. As *Hannover-II* began to wind down in the second week of June, the officers of 5th Panzer Division felt largely dissatisfied. Compared with *Hannover-I*, the operation had been less effective, and there was plentiful evidence that the area remained far from secure. Although Belov had been given permission to commence his breakout attempt, he had been ordered to leave behind all of the partisan formations that had been subordinated to him and these mounted repeated hit-and-run attacks, forcing 5th Panzer Division to mount a new thrust. Until now, its efforts had been directed towards Dorogobuzh and on to the west, but it now sent troops back to Dorogobuzh from where they were to conduct a sweep to the northeast to eliminate the troublesome partisan groups. While this operation, codenamed *Junikäfer* ('June bug') might clear the rear area, it diverted forces away from any pursuit of I Guards Cavalry Corps.

Time was running out for 5th Panzer Division to complete its task of destroying Belov's group. The great German-held salient that had Rzhev at its northern tip contained a Soviet-held salient impinging on it from the northwest, the remnant of the advance by units of Northwest Front during the winter. The German front line ran from east to west to the north of Rzhev and then turned sharply south about 50 miles (81km) to the west of the city. Thereafter, it turned east again towards Rzhev and curved around a large 'sack' before circling back around the town of Bely before it continued to the southwest. The German garrison in Bely, connected to the German lines further southwest by a tenuous corridor, was only about 18 miles (30km) from the German lines to the west of Rzhev. The neck of the sack, sometimes called the 'Nelidovo Corridor', was held by infantry from the Soviet Twenty-Second Army facing north and Forty-First Army facing Bely in the south, with Maslennikov's Thirty-Ninth Army and Sokolov's XI Cavalry Corps and large groups of partisans within the sack itself. The total strength of Soviet forces is difficult to calculate with certainty, as figures for the two armies at the neck of the sack include units that held portions of front line outside the sack itself, and assessing the fighting strength of the partisan formations accurately is almost impossible. However, the combined strength of Twenty-Second, Forty-First, and Thirty-Ninth Armies, and of XI Cavalry Corps, is estimated to be nearly 190,000 men.[2] A German estimate of the fighting strength of the Soviet forces within the sack itself suggested that if the Nelidovo Corridor could be closed, about 60,000 Red Army soldiers would be trapped.[3] Maslennikov's army had eight rifle divisions and a small number of independent battalions, while XI Cavalry Corps had four cavalry divisions; this suggests that each division averaged fewer than 5,000 men, which is not unreasonable given how badly depleted so many of the units on both sides were.

The southern limit of this sack was close enough to threaten the railway line running to Vyazma from the west, and just as *Hannover-I* and *Hannover-II* had been intended to eliminate the Soviet forces that threatened this line of communication from the south, so a new operation, codenamed *Seydlitz*, was to eliminate the forces of Kalinin Front that lurked to the north. While these Soviet forces remained in position, there was always a threat – however small – that the Red Army might be able to break through to them either from the north with Kalinin Front or from the east with Western Front, or conceivably from both directions, in which case a significant part of the German Army Group Centre would be isolated. The reality was that the roads in the area were very poor, and there were no major roads or any railways that Konev could use to reinforce Maslennikov's army. Far from trying to strengthen the forces in the sack, Konev was actively transferring units out of both Thirty-Ninth Army and XI Cavalry Corps, despite the protests of their commanders. But regardless of these protests, it was almost impossible to move sufficient supplies into the area to keep Sokolov's and Maslennikov's troops adequately supplied. At the end of June, Sokolov

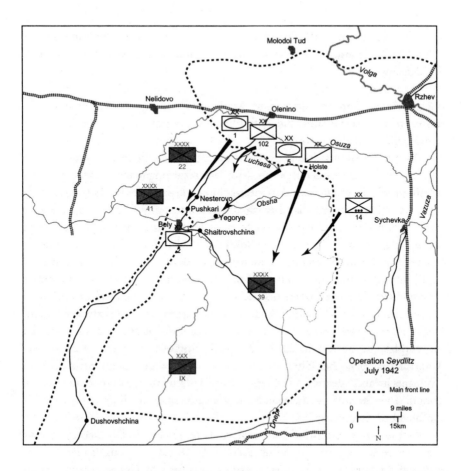

reported that his units had enough rifle ammunition to last just one day. His artillery would run out of ammunition in less than a morning of fighting and his mortars had almost no ammunition at all; even food was in short supply, with barely enough to last four days. Thirty-Ninth Army was in little better shape, with ammunition shortages in particular causing concern to Maslennikov. Although some parts of the sack were fortified, these positions were largely improvised, as it had been impossible to move forward barbed wire, cement, and landmines. Nonetheless, provided he received more ammunition and food, Maslennikov felt that he could hold the sack:

> I am prepared to fight on in a most disadvantageous situation, that is to say, combat within an encirclement, if I don't have permission to withdraw the

army. For this, only ammunition and food are necessary. By taking advantage of the fortified positions that are available, the army can conduct a prolonged defensive action.[4]

Given Konev's strong criticism of Maslennikov in the winter battles, it is unsurprising that the commander of Thirty-Ninth Army was prepared to promise a prolonged defensive action.

Prior to the latest fighting, the Germans suffered a serious setback on 23 May when Model, commander of Ninth Army, was returning to his headquarters after visiting 2nd Panzer Division. His Fieseler Storch aircraft was flying at an altitude of barely 50m over woodland when it came under fire from a machine-gun, probably operated by partisans. The burst of gunfire struck the plane's cabin and wounded both its occupants – the pilot, Feldwebel Wilhelm Haist, was struck in the leg, while Model sustained a chest wound. Both injuries could have proved fatal, but Haist remained conscious and was able to turn back to 2nd Panzer Division's headquarters, where he landed safely. The bullet that had struck Model resulted in considerable loss of blood, necessitating an immediate field transfusion. This almost certainly saved his life, and it was a few days before he was deemed fit enough to be evacuated to the main military hospital in Smolensk. Characteristically, when Blumentritt, now serving as Chief Quartermaster of the Wehrmacht and effectively Halder's deputy, visited Model a few days later, he found Model in uniform, determined to continue running Ninth Army from his hospital bed if necessary.

Despite his protests, Model was ordered to return to Germany on convalescent leave for several months. In his absence, Ninth Army was commanded first by General Albrecht Schubert, then – during *Seydlitz* – by General Heinrich von Vietinghoff. Even during his convalescence, Model remained active, visiting Berlin for talks with other senior figures. During one such visit, he met Oberst Gisbert Cascorbi, a relative of his wife's family. Cascorbi was hostile to the Nazi regime and allegedly put out feelers to test Model's views, telling him that 'the German people look more to some of their senior generals than to others'. Cascorbi recalled that Model responded simply: 'I am a soldier' and refused to discuss the matter further.[5]

Junikäfer degenerated into a slow push through swampy terrain, worsened by recent heavy rain; the remaining Soviet regular units and partisan groups simply slipped away from the advancing Germans and reappeared in their rear, and disruption of German rail and road movements continued, albeit at a reduced level. But further anti-partisan operations would have to be left to other units, and 5th Panzer Division began to move north towards Rzhev. Here, it would come under the control of XXIII Corps for the forthcoming operation. The plan called for the division to attack southwest towards Bely from the German positions to the west of Rzhev. Once a link-up with the German garrison in Bely was achieved, much of the Soviet Thirty-Ninth Army and XI Cavalry Corps would be encircled. At that stage, 5th Panzer Division would switch its axis of advance towards the southeast, directly into the encirclement, in order to break it into two or more fragments.

While the Germans prepared for *Seydlitz*, Belov and his men began their attempt to escape encirclement. Belov wrote that the attack would be led by IV Airborne Corps and his two guards cavalry divisions, followed by the wagons of wounded men, with the remnants of 329th Rifle Division bringing up the rear, but after several weeks behind German lines and particularly after the recent fighting, many units consisted of men from differing formations – they were distinguished purely by who was commanding each unit. In order to try to mislead the Germans, a partisan division made a feint attack against Yelnya and then pulled back towards Dorogobuzh with the intention of luring German troops after it, dispersing into the forests and swamps to escape capture. Belov describes how his men broke through the lines of the German 137th and 221st Infantry Divisions to escape the encirclement, but most of the former was still in the front line facing east. The second was actually a security division and was unable to stop the Soviet group as it moved south to the east of Yelnya and made contact with partisans operating in the area. The initial phase of Belov's plan had succeeded, with the partisan attack on Yelnya successfully luring much of 221st Security Division to the north.[6]

Time was now of the essence as the Germans were certain to realise a breakout was underway. In an attempt to evade German air attacks and reconnaissance flights, Belov's men tried to restrict their march as much as possible to night-time, but the summer nights were short, and the Luftwaffe made extensive use of parachute flares to light up the landscape. The Soviet soldiers slowly approached the Varshavskoye highway, which they had crossed with such high hopes in their initial advance. The final approach to the road was through a forested, swampy region using a temporary road of felled trees that had been built by the Red Army during the fighting of the autumn of 1941; able-bodied men could seek shelter in the trees during air attacks, but the wounded in wagons were helpless and many were killed. Nonetheless, most of the group reached the highway late on 15 June. To their relief, Soviet fighters – dispatched to provide air cover by the intrepid Samokhin – managed to give temporary protection from further

Luftwaffe attacks. However, there was no question that the Germans were aware of the breakout attempt, and the highway provided an easy means for the Germans to intercept the Soviet group – even as darkness fell, the outposts of the leading paratroopers reported that a German infantry regiment supported by a small number of armoured vehicles was patrolling the highway. Accordingly, even though some of his men were still struggling forward through the forest and everyone was exhausted by the long march, Belov decided to cross the road immediately.

In order to force their way through the German units along the highway – there were now reports that German artillery was also deploying in the area – Belov deployed the paratroopers on his western flank, organised with three brigades in the first wave and two in the second, and four cavalry regiments – two in the first wave, two in the second – to the east. The remnants of 329th Rifle Division and a weakened cavalry division were held in reserve. Belov had been able to bring few heavy weapons with him, and in any case there was a shortage of ammunition; the attack would rely on surprise. The cavalrymen in the first wave attacked on foot, leaving their horses with other men:

> The regiments in the first echelon pushed back the enemy infantry and crossed the highway. The troops had to make a dash across the road, but the Germans brought up tanks and armoured cars on our left flank [i.e. from the east] and began firing along the road with cannons and machine-guns. Long lines of tracer bullets cut through the darkness, and shell explosions flared up.
>
> The men from the first echelon regiments who were holding the horses, and the second echelon cavalry, all hesitated, not daring to throw themselves forward under fire. The Nazis increased their pressure on our flank, trying to cut off the units that had crossed the highway. In the meantime, dawn was approaching. The decisive moment was at hand. And suddenly, above the roar of explosions and the crackle of gunfire, the hoarse, powerful voice of [Major General Viktor Kirillovich] Baranov [commander of 1st Guards Cavalry Division] rang out: 'Forward, Guards! Follow me, men! Urra!'
>
> On horseback, with his headquarters staff, he rushed onto the highway. The nearest squadrons hurried to Baranov, drawing with them the neighbouring squadrons and the men with the first echelon's horses. Despite the uneven ground and undergrowth, the cavalrymen moved at a trot, some even at a gallop. The soldiers of the airborne corps rose up alongside the guardsmen and attacked. More than three thousand horsemen and several thousand paratroopers rolled across the highway in an unstoppable avalanche, sweeping away the enemy's

screen. A mighty 'Urra!' rolled from flank to flank. When people are seized with such an impulse, it is impossible to stop them.

During the attack, our mortars and a few guns fired at enemy gun emplacements and suppressed some of them, but nonetheless the enemy fire remained heavy. Dozens of soldiers fell on the highway. A Fascist bullet struck the commander of 6th Guards Cavalry Regiment, Lieutenant Colonel Knyazev. His comrades carried him out of the battle to an old pine tree not far from the highway and dug a grave.[7]

More German tanks appeared from the east, driving along the highway, and Belov was forced to order the men still on the north side of the road to pull back into the forest. As he took stock, he found that about half of the paratroopers, 2nd Guards Cavalry Division, and 329th Rifle Division – together with most of the wounded – had been unable to cross the road. After establishing a defensive position in the forest, he succeeded in contacting Baranov by radio and ordered him to proceed towards Kirov. Baranov and his force succeeded in reaching the lines of Tenth Army with little incident, but Belov and his men were now cut off as the Germans reinforced their units along the Varshavskoye highway. On 17 June, he and his headquarters staff were involved in a skirmish as German troops closed in on his temporary headquarters but managed to slip away through the surrounding woodland.

The paratrooper Bogatsky endured a difficult time before reaching the Varshavskoye highway. It seems that at least some of the Soviet units received little or no help from contact with partisans:

> We had constant battles, large and small, with the Germans – endless bombing and shelling of the forests where we were hiding. I ran out of ammunition for the machine-gun at an early stage and picked up a rifle on the battlefield, but didn't abandon my PPSh [*Pistolet-Pulemyot Shpagina*, a cheap submachine-gun widely used by the Red Army] because I worried that if we managed to break out, I might be shot for loss of my personal weapon. All the time I was behind enemy lines, I didn't have to do any sapper work, I fought not in my special role but as a simple commander of an airborne platoon. We were dead tired, constantly thinking about food. There were only burned villages around us and nowhere to get provisions. If we killed a German, ten people immediately rushed to the corpse, even under fire, looking for any food in his backpack.
>
> Our group was lucky and we killed a dying horse – we roasted the meat over a fire and everyone had some, but we had no salt. And as soon as we had our fire

going the Germans spotted us and commenced accurate shelling. We ran, tearing raw horseflesh with our teeth …

The worst thing was that we could do nothing to help our seriously wounded comrades, and there was nowhere to leave them and no treatment available for them, and we couldn't carry them with us. Perhaps it's better to keep silent about this, but we surviving paratroopers had to live on with this heavy burden on our souls.

Some time in June, we reached the Varshavskoye highway in the forest where the remnants of the original air landing had concentrated – we were told that about 2,500 men had gathered there. The Germans noticed us and began to bomb the forest, there was endless shooting from all sides … And then a command: 'Run! Forward for a breakthrough!' And like madmen, we rushed to attack.

Shots were fired at us from all sides, we fired at the Germans at point-blank range with our last rounds and stabbed them with bayonets, there were shouts and curses all around. A comrade ran next to me and a bullet struck him in the chest – he just managed to say 'Mother!' and fell dead on the ground. And we pressed on, not stopping, not picking up the seriously wounded. Everyone was shouting or cursing, and some carried on shooting until we realised that we had broken through.[8]

Despite being driven back from the highway with many of his men, Belov was determined to try again. After the success of his previous attempt to draw German troops away from his intended line of march, he drew up orders for a redeployment some distance to the west, followed by a march south towards Roslavl. These orders were placed in the saddlebag of a rider who ventured into no-man's land in front of a position held by Belov's cavalry; when he came under fire, the man's horse was shot – according to Belov, by a Soviet sniper – and the rider then escaped back into the forest. When the Germans moved forward to investigate, they discovered the set of orders in the saddlebag. Belov wrote that the Germans fell for this ruse and moved significant forces west, aiding his continuing operations.

The actual plan was to move only a little to the west, but to return to the highway shortly after crossing the Desna River. At the river, many of the cavalry were forced to leave their horses behind as the stream was swollen by the recent heavy rain, and the surrounding ground was generally too swampy even for the horses to approach the banks. In order to improve the chances of slipping past German positions, the Soviet soldiers divided into groups of about 200 men as they turned south once more to reach the Varshavskoye highway near the village of Ekimovichi, about 15 miles (25km) west of the previous attempt to cross to the south. Late on 19 June, they slipped across the road in small groups without detection. After making contact with local partisans, Belov and his headquarters group moved towards the southeast and the Desna River, which they crossed late on 22 June in small boats provided by the partisans. It was even possible to use a radio set owned by the partisans to make contact with Tenth Army. Via this link, Belov was informed that a flight of about 15 Po-2 planes would reach the partisans by night and were to be used to evacuate the senior staff in the encirclement. Belov left by plane on the night of 24–25 June; the improvised airstrip was overrun by German troops shortly after his departure.

The rest of the Soviet troops, now commanded by Belov's intelligence officer, Kononienko, had a difficult time. Kazankin was still with his remaining paratroopers and managed to evacuate many of their wounded by air; the paratroopers then fought their way through the front line to make contact with Tenth Army just to the north of Kirov.[9] Shortly after, the rest of the cavalry corps together with some paratroopers and what remained of 329th Rifle Division made their attempt to break through to Tenth Army. Kononienko and his men made an arduous and tricky march, infiltrating past several German positions, including at one time crossing a railway line periodically patrolled by an armoured train. Exhausted and short of all supplies, the cavalry tried to find shelter during the day and moved mainly at night; when they finally reached the front line, three days after Belov had been flown to safety, they charged across en masse, and it seems that they took the Germans by surprise. Many of the wounded were still with them, loaded in a few carts, and Belov was particularly proud that many of the cavalrymen had managed to bring their horses out of the encirclement. Kononienko was wounded in the leg during the final moments of the breakout. The total number of men who escaped the encirclement is difficult to determine, as many of those who were left behind, including a large proportion of the wounded, joined the partisans. The Germans were largely disappointed with their haul of prisoners and the numbers of dead that they found, suggesting that most of the paratroopers and cavalry either reached safety or continued fighting in the partisan bands.

Although Belov had been ordered to leave the partisan formations to continue operating behind German lines, many of the partisans – in some cases, accompanied by their families – joined Kazankin's paratroopers during their breakout. German forces were now combing through the area, and they disrupted and dispersed many of the groups that had helped Belov and his men escape.

Alexei Nikolayevich Galyuga, commander of one of the partisan detachments, continued to operate in the area, but in early 1943 he was captured when a Po-2 in which he was travelling crash-landed in German-held territory. The Germans produced a leaflet with his signature calling on other partisans to surrender and dropped it over a wide area.

The escape of Belov, Kazankin and many of their troops marked the end of an extraordinary operation that had seen large numbers of Soviet regular troops, working with partisans, operate behind German lines for several months. During this period, they often controlled large areas and hundreds of villages, as well as the substantial town of Dorogobuzh, and frequently disrupted German supply movements. Ultimately, *Hannover-I* and *Hannover-II*, which brought the episode to an end, tied down seven German divisions for a considerable time, and although many of the partisan units were wiped out, sporadic attacks on German supply lines continued throughout the war. Despite this, the Germans did not regard the Soviet operation as a particularly effective one:

> However unpleasant it was for the Germans to have this danger to their rear and although it especially affected systematic supply of the front, at no time was there a direct, strategic effect. The chief of staff of the German Fourth Army stated in this connection that 'Although the whole matter was very annoying, it had no strategic consequence.'[10]

This is perhaps an understatement of the impact of the 'Landing Republic' – after all, its elimination required the diversion of substantial German forces, including 5th Panzer Division. The 'annoyance' caused by Belov, Kazankin and their men, together with the grudging respect that they earned from their opponents, was further remarked on after the war by Blumentritt, who had been chief of staff with the German Fourth Army until mid-January:

> How [Belov] managed to obtain supplies was a mystery to us … Only Russians and Russian horses can exist on absolutely 'nothing'. Nobody was able to catch him. German forces in the rear areas were too weak and not suited for that type of Indian warfare in the wintry forests … [The escape of Belov and his men] caused many humorous remarks at the time and the motorised troops that had taken part in the operation became the butt of these jokes. I admired General Belov as a soldier and I was secretly glad that he had escaped.[11]

Blumentritt wasn't the only senior officer to hold such an opinion. On 17 June, Halder noted in his diary that Belov was 'quite a man, that we have to send no less than seven divisions after him'.[12]

While the cavalry and airborne 'raid' may not have accomplished any strategic gain, it had a considerable disruptive effect. Engineers in Belov's group were able to improvise a landmine factory in a small station – with farming collectivised, the Soviet Union instigated the creation of machine and vehicle stations for servicing and repairing farm equipment for all the collective farms in a given area – and used it to manufacture both mines for use against German troops and demolition charges. These were used to good effect against railway lines, sometimes destroying locomotives and tracks and disrupting rail traffic for several days; given the vital nature of rail transport for German supply lines, any such disruption was more than just a passing nuisance.

Nonetheless, it cannot be denied that the presence of almost 30,000 armed troops behind German lines did not result in a major operational success. Could more have been achieved? The answer is surely that opportunities were missed. At the height of the operation, several different formations were operating independently: I Guards Cavalry Corps; IV Airborne Corps (which was further broken into different formations given disparate missions); and the isolated divisions of Efremov's Thirty-Third Army. Zhukov made little attempt to order these units to unite and coordinate their efforts until it was too late to maximise their efficacy. The attempts to link up with the isolated units were poorly handled and were largely defeated with ease by the main German defensive line, and Zhukov could and should have concentrated his forces better, particularly as he had lamented a lack of concentration of resources by Stalin, and the failures of January had amply demonstrated the consequences of dispersing effort over too many objectives and too wide an area. While the grand encirclement that he repeatedly hoped for might have been beyond the resources of the Red Army, establishing proper contact with the isolated units would have created considerable difficulties for the German position, putting their lines of communication within easy range of Soviet artillery.

Bogatsky was with one of the groups that reached safety. About 1,300 men from his brigade had been parachuted into the encirclement in May and perhaps 300 survived. Even several decades later, he had no doubt about the factors that resulted in them enduring and ultimately escaping:

The brigades in the German rear zone survived all their ordeals due to just one factor: we were selected men, young patriots, with many Komsomol members [the title given to young adults who joined the youth wing of the Communist Party], brave and healthy guys who were recruited as paratroopers. If a regular rifle division had been in our place, it would have broken in such conditions in a week. Even among the paratroopers, some were demoralised at times and there were cases when commanders were told to 'go fuck themselves' and their orders ... But we continued to fight, sometimes with just our bare hands although almost all of the paratroopers, including me, thought we would never get out alive.[13]

For Bogatsky and his fellow survivors, there was little respite. They were re-formed as part of 118th Guards Rifle Regiment, and after just a few weeks of rest near Moscow, they were transferred south to Stalingrad.

While Belov and his men were making their way to safety, the Germans proceeded with *Seydlitz* in the north. Through much of the winter and spring, a small battlegroup from 2nd Panzer Division had held the town of Bely, and German reconnaissance reported the continuing presence of Soviet troops from Thirty-Ninth Army and XI Cavalry Corps to the east of the town. Bely was at the end of a long, thin salient projecting north from the German positions nearer Smolensk, and the road on which the Bely garrison depended was subjected to repeated attacks by partisans as well as the units of Kalinin Front. Mines were frequently laid during the night, and travel on the road was only possible in convoys protected by armoured vehicles. Despite intermittent clashes, 2nd Panzer Division slowly began to recover its strength after the losses of the winter. After the absorption of parts of Czechoslovakia in 1938, Germany had benefited from the armaments produced by firms such as Skoda, and several of the panzer divisions that entered the Soviet Union in the summer of 1941 were equipped at least partly with the Pz.38(t), a Skoda-manufactured tank. Armed with a 37mm main gun and with armour only 25mm thick – a later version produced from October 1941 had this increased in some areas to 50mm – this tank was totally outclassed by the T-34 on the Eastern Front, and Hitler issued orders for the chassis to be used in future for assault gun manufacture. In an attempt to remedy the poor firepower of anti-tank formations, several hundred chassis were fitted with captured Soviet 76.2mm anti-tank guns from April 1942, creating the vehicle known as the Marder. The gun was mounted in an open housing and had fairly limited lateral traverse, but it provided a welcome boost to the penetrative firepower of German anti-tank formations. The first company equipped with these vehicles belonged to 2nd Panzer Division. The improvement in firepower was greatly welcomed, but fuel shortages persisted, hindering training efforts to bring the new company to full combat-readiness.

With *Hannover* and *Junikäfer* completed, Model's Ninth Army was now ready to move against the forces of Kalinin Front that occupied the area to the east of Bely. Much as Belov's men had attempted to restrict their movements to the hours of darkness to avoid detection, the Germans too tried to carry out most of their build-up at night, which inevitably delayed full deployment, particularly as many roads and bridges were in poor condition and needed repair before vehicle traffic could use them.

The plan called for the German XXIII Corps to form two groups. One in the west was built around 1st Panzer Division, supported by two infantry divisions; the eastern group was largely made up of 5th Panzer Division, supported by a unit that demonstrated Model's ability to improvise. While the Red Army continued to use cavalry formations throughout the war, the Germans withdrew their only cavalry division from the front line at the end of 1941 for conversion into 24th Panzer Division. Horse-mounted troops repeatedly demonstrated their usefulness on the Eastern Front, being able to move through terrain that was often impassable for wheeled or tracked vehicles, and while their lack of heavy equipment might limit their efficacy against organised enemy defences, they were of considerable value in operations against irregular or less well-organised opponents. In early 1942, German army corps had a reconnaissance battalion made up of horsemen, and Model grouped together the battalions from three corps and combined them with smaller cavalry platoons from other units into a special cavalry formation of three regiments, each with five squadrons – two cavalry squadrons, two bicycle squadrons, and a heavy weapons squadron. This new *Kavallerie Kommando* was placed under the command of Oberst Rudolf Holste, who was replaced shortly before the commencement of *Seydlitz* by Oberst Karl-Friedrich von der Meden; he and his men deployed in support of 5th Panzer Division for the coming operation.

At the same time as the thrusts by XXIII Corps, 2nd Panzer Division was to try to advance from Bely towards the approaching columns. The force in Bely was led by the division commander, Generalmajor Hans-Carl Freiherr von Esebeck, and now consisted of much of the division. Esebeck divided it into two battlegroups, each centred on one of his infantry regiments; the division's panzer regiment should have had two battalions of tanks, but after the transfer of one battalion to another regiment in early 1942, it remained far from its normal strength. When 7th Panzer Division was transferred to France to recuperate at the end of the winter fighting, it handed over its few remaining tanks to 2nd Panzer Division – mainly obsolete Pz.38(t) models – and the equipment of the battalion in July was a mixture of these old tanks and a handful of Pz.III and Pz.IV; this modest force would have to suffice for Esebeck's attack.

As the winter fighting around the northern part of the Rzhev Salient died down, the Germans took the opportunity to extract some of their units for some much-needed rest. One such unit was 6th Infantry Division, which withdrew from the trenches to the northeast of Rzhev and moved to the area west of Sychevka. Most of the villages in the region had been partly or totally destroyed in previous fighting and proper accommodation was scarce, and on numerous occasions the division's personnel were required to take part in anti-partisan operations. Inevitably, the division – now commanded by Generalmajor Horst Grossmann – was required to provide units for *Seydlitz*; with some elements of his division still en route from their previous front-line positions – mobility remained greatly restricted due to the shortage of trucks and horses – Grossmann had to release the first units that had arrived in the rear area. The dismay of the soldiers, who had been looking forward to a prolonged period of rest, can be imagined.

After the rain that had hindered operations during *Hannover-I* and *Hannover-II*, the commencement of *Seydlitz* was postponed when troops were slow to assemble, and further rain degraded roads still further. When the operation began on 2 July, the morning was foggy, but clear weather was expected later in the day. German air attacks began at first light, accompanied by the artillery fire of the German divisions that stood ready to attack, but when 1st Panzer Division moved forward it struggled to penetrate the first line of Soviet defences. The initial advance was towards the west in this sector, down the Luchesa River, while the neighbouring 102nd Infantry Division secured the high ground overlooking the river from the south, but both attacks faltered in the face of heavy defensive fire. To make matters worse, the weather turned rainy again at midday; the approach roads that the German armour had used were already softened by the rain of preceding weeks and downgraded by the passage of the German tanks and other vehicles, and supply columns now struggled to move anything forward to the front line. Suffering substantial losses, the soldiers of 102nd Infantry Division gradually moved up the slope to the south, and its attack gained a little momentum towards the end of the day, pushing forward about two miles, but the dismounted infantry from 1st Panzer Division made almost no progress; one battalion reported that by the end of the day, two company commanders and almost all the platoon commanders of the leading battalion were casualties.[14]

To the east, 5th Panzer Division fared no better than 1st Panzer Division. The ground here hadn't dried out from the rain of the preceding days, and even the division's Pz.III tanks repeatedly became stuck. The rain steadily grew heavier, and by the end of the day 5th Panzer Division had moved forward only two miles; the only positive development was the capture of a prominent hill that had overlooked the German units as they attempted to advance. If the Germans were expecting better weather the following day, they were disappointed – the rain was even heavier, and low cloud prevented the Luftwaffe from providing any support. Both panzer divisions struggled to bring forward any supplies and made little progress, and despite the shortages of equipment that Maslennikov had reported, his men had laid extensive minefields, further restricting German movement. On 4 July the weather remained poor, but 1st Panzer Division finally began to make headway, and its leading elements drove back the opposing Soviet units; however, breakdowns, enemy action and minefields took a heavy toll on its tanks and guns, with most companies reporting just three or four vehicles still operational. In an attempt to improve progress on the main axis of the attack – i.e. the attempt to link up with the garrison at Bely – Ninth Army ordered 5th Panzer Division to switch its advance towards the southwest.

The southern part of the German operation, advancing from Bely, also faced considerable difficulties due to the weather. Both of Esebeck's battlegroups attempted to attack northwards in the area east of Bely. Several groups of Soviet tanks clashed with the Germans, who managed to clear some of the area around Bely, but fuel shortages limited the ability of 2nd Panzer Division to function effectively. It was far from the swift advances enjoyed by panzer divisions in the past; through difficult terrain, the battlegroups reached and secured the village of Shaitrovshchina.

Even though they were delayed by the weather, terrain and Soviet resistance, the German units were slowly gaining the upper hand. On 5 July, 1st Panzer Division made tenuous contact with the German units near Bely in the village of Pushkari, cutting the supply lines to Maslennikov's and Sokolov's forces. A battle against Red Army armour flared around Pushkari for much of the day before the surviving Soviet tanks pulled back.[15] Despite his assertions that he would be able to conduct a prolonged defence, Maslennikov had already started pulling back the perimeter of his army in anticipation of this moment, particularly from the northeast corner of the sack closest to Rzhev. Further south, Sokolov's cavalry also began a withdrawal towards the northwest, destroying the few bridges in the area as they pulled out. The redirection of 5th Panzer Division resulted in a rapid advance on 6 July, with its leading battlegroup moving forward about 15 miles (25km); in its previous sector, the cavalry group that Model had created continued to encounter tough resistance but, supported by parts of 14th Motorised Infantry Division, it was able to take advantage of the withdrawals by elements of Thirty-Ninth Army and moved south.

With 1st Panzer Division taking up positions facing both east and west in order to prevent any withdrawal by Thirty-Ninth Army and any relief operation from Kalinin Front, 5th Panzer Division began to accelerate its drive down the valley of the Obsha River towards Bely. The Soviet units in the northern part of the encirclement were labouring to concentrate their resources for an attempt to break through the positions held by 1st Panzer Division and thus to escape to the northwest, and this allowed 5th Panzer Division to push forward with a battlegroup consisting largely of the division's motorcycle battalion supported by a tank company. This force reached the village of Yegorye, about six miles (10km) northeast of Bely, but the area to its rear was only weakly held, with substantial Soviet formations moving freely across towards the northwest. The small roads in the region remained muddy and almost impassable, and it took another two days for the Germans to concentrate enough strength at Yegorye to complete a link-up with the units of 1st and 2nd Panzer Divisions, which were moving east and northeast from the area around Bely.

The encirclement was now effectively broken in two. While the wheeled and tracked elements of the Wehrmacht floundered in the heavy mud, the improvised cavalry group demonstrated its value, moving swiftly through dense woodland on 5th Panzer Division's eastern flank. For the Germans, the main objective now was to overwhelm the encircled Soviet troops as swiftly as possible, and some Red Army soldiers later described encountering small groups of Germans accompanied by former Red Army personnel, all wearing Red Army uniforms, moving through the woodland and seeking either to locate and kill Soviet officers and headquarters groups or spreading rumours that most of the encircled men had already surrendered.[16]

As had been the case with Belov's men further south, the local population helped the Soviet soldiers in the area near Bely throughout 1942. Boris Petrovich Polyakov was a signals officer with 17th Guards Rifle Division, which was holding the area where the German armour attacked to create the encirclement, and he later recalled that he and his men were always welcomed by villagers, though he added that he was never certain whether this reflected genuine enthusiasm for their arrival or an attempt to avoid being suspected of having collaborated with the Germans.[17] On many occasions though, the villagers showed the soldiers where weapons and supplies had been hidden by the Red Army during its retreat in 1941; while these finds were useful, they were poor compensation for the widespread shortages of food, ammunition and medical supplies. As the German noose tightened, Polyakov managed to slip through Yegorye before the arrival of 5th Panzer Division's motorcycle battalion:

July 5 and 6 were the last days of organised resistance for the division. I will remember the smallest detail for the rest of my life. On 5 July, we set off at 0200. The short summer night gave us no more than three hours. Walking between the carts [carrying the division's equipment and wounded], I found myself next to the most popular person in the regiment – the postmaster, Makarikhin. He told me that the road was 'plugged'. He had tried to reach Nesterovo the previous day to collect mail but returned empty-handed as there were Germans everywhere. Nesterovo was on the Bely–Olenino road; if this road had been cut, the only way that remained to escape was to go across country through the swampy forest. The tail of the column was still 500m from the forest edge when the first rays of the rising sun appeared. As the last carts disappeared under the canopy of the trees, planes appeared overhead ... The regiment settled down for the day.[18]

Polyakov was ordered to take a message to his regiment's headquarters, and he made his way through the forest on horseback, following a signal cable. At his destination, he learned that a close friend had been killed in the fighting, and he set off on his return journey with a heavy heart and reached a road near which his men had set up camp:

The road was now completely different. Previously deserted, it was filled with carts and vehicles, mainly ambulances, moving towards me. Near the lake, a logjam of vehicles had accumulated. There were also tanks and guns. The sight of such disarray filled me with anxiety and dismay. The clearing was visible from above. The unopposed superiority of German aviation was absolute and they took no notice of red crosses. I quickly decided to leave this dangerous area. Further to the rear [of his regiment] I found frantic activity, with men destroying all unnecessary equipment in order to lighten the carts, and burning documents to prevent them falling into enemy hands. I immediately joined the work. As I put another stack of papers into the fire, I noticed one was a German leaflet with a proclamation to the soldiers and commanders of several of our armies, saying: 'Your position is hopeless, and you are surrounded on all sides.' This was unsurprising for me ... Soon, above the canopy of fir trees, we heard the roar of planes flying past followed by the explosions of bombs, merging into one continuous roar. I had no doubt that the road I had just passed was being bombed. At 1800 we received orders to move out. I left with the last carts at 2000. The road I had passed twice before was a terrible sight. I didn't see a more terrible scene in the entire war. Large craters were already full of water. The road was littered with wrecked carts, motor vehicles, dead horses, and the corpses of people.

A particularly dense jumble of wrecked vehicles and weapons surrounded the small lake. From the woodland to the sides, I could hear the groaning of wounded men. A desperate voice seared into my memory: 'Medic! Medic!' It was the voice of a doomed man … Near the village of Solidovo I saw one of our '34's. The tank moved towards us along a deserted street, its turret facing backwards and firing repeatedly … Solidovo had been abandoned by our infantry. The tank served as a rearguard, covering our retreat. No sooner had we entered the forest than German submachine-gunners occupied the village. That was why there had been such haste moving through the preceding forest strip. Any delay of even five minutes, and it would have been too late and the path to safety would have been cut.[19]

Polyakov and his comrades still had some distance to go before they were safe. He returned to regimental headquarters to ask what they should do next and found most of the remaining staff overcome by apathy, fatigue and in some cases alcohol. When he rode back to the column he had left near Solidovo he found that it was under heavy mortar and machine-gun fire:

It was obvious that the division, as an organised combat unit, no longer existed. The reality of the situation was no longer in doubt. I could rely only on myself to get out of the encirclement as quickly as possible … After considering my options, I headed deeper into the forest … It soon became quite light. German planes appeared overhead once more. I heard their sirens for the first time – the pilots switched them on for psychological impact. The thicket was pathless. Swampy low areas alternated with dry elevated ridges. At about 1000 I encountered a tank captain. He showed me where we were on a map. According to him, the German tanks captured the last section of the Bely–Olenino road the preceding afternoon at 1400, between the villages of Pushkari and Nesterovo. But the Nelidovsky highway, further to the west, was still in the hands of our troops. He added that we should leave the encirclement in ones and twos, not in large groups … After wandering for a time, I met a group of soldiers from our division. One of them was the postmaster Makarikhin. I told them the situation and suggested we proceed together towards the Nesterovo road. They agreed and we moved slowly and carefully. Occasionally, we heard bursts of machine-gun fire ahead, and planes howled past above us. When we judged by the sounds of firing that the road was about 1.5km away, we decided to stop … We slept for an hour or two. Gunfire from the road continued and sometimes stray bullets struck nearby trees with a soft sound. After a short march we encountered a group of 50 men. Among them I recognised the division's chief of staff, Zvanduto

… although he was the senior person present, it seemed he was behaving as just another soldier in the group. We tried to move silently in a compact mass but the forest began to thin out … Everyone gathered and began to discuss what to do next. Some suggested waiting until dark, but most were in favour of crossing the road immediately. We approached with great care, hiding behind bushes or crawling across open ground. Ahead and to the sides, machine-gun fire was continuous. Suddenly, almost unexpectedly, a grey strip of road appeared a few metres ahead. For a few seconds everyone froze, and then silently rushed forward as if on command. Jumping over the roadside ditch, I glanced quickly to the sides. The road was deserted. There were fresh caterpillar tracks underfoot. Apparently, quite by chance, we had reached an unguarded section of road, and it was obscured by a sharp bend. The whole group successfully passed through this dangerous spot without a single shot fired.[20]

Polyakov and his group were fortunate, as were other small bodies of men. Sealing the encirclement in such difficult terrain was almost impossible, and men filtered through for several days. Major General Aleksander Dmitrievich Berezin was commander of Polyakov's division but on the eve of the encirclement was appointed deputy commanding officer of Twenty-Second Army; he entered the encirclement on foot twice to try to round up stragglers of his former command and bring them to safety. He disappeared during his second attempt; his remains were identified in a mass grave in 1969.

Mopping up work continued for several days. The battlegroups of 1st Panzer Division in particular were often hard-pressed to beat off attacks from both within the pocket and from the northwest. A little further south, 2nd Panzer Division was alerted on 7 July by Luftwaffe reconnaissance flights that a group of about 20 tanks followed by up to 300 vehicles had been spotted approaching from the east. Believing that this represented an attempt by the encircled Soviet units to break out, the division prepared its defences, but moments later fresh reports arrived: the column was made up of German units approaching from the eastern side of the encirclement. When they linked up with 2nd Panzer Division later in the day, the Red Army units within the pocket were further fragmented.[21]

On 7 July, the Red Army managed to gain control of a section of the main 'highway' running north from Bely – in reality, it was little more than a very muddy country road, and a swift German counterattack retook the road. Finally, a week later, 1st Panzer Division was able to report that the situation was 'quiet'.[22] A little further to the west, 5th Panzer Division was withdrawn from the operation and moved to a rear area. Similarly, 2nd Panzer Division was permitted to withdraw from Bely to Smolensk for a period of rest and recovery. Learning from its experiences in the previous winter, the division rounded up a number of captured horses and wagons in preparation for the difficult movement conditions that could be expected later in the year. It would prove to be a sensible preparatory step.

Konev's Kalinin Front recorded that contact with the headquarters of Thirty-Ninth Army and XI Cavalry Corps was lost late on 8 July. Although the area became much quieter, it was impossible for the Wehrmacht to achieve complete control of the region. Partisans continued to operate in the dense woodland, often reinforced by bodies of stragglers from the encircled Red Army formations. Substantial groups continued to escape to rejoin Kalinin Front; one such group numbered about 8,000 men, and included Maslennikov, commander of Thirty-Ninth Army. Maslennikov was wounded in the leg and was evacuated by air on 18 July; his deputy commander, Lieutenant General Ivan Aleksandrovich Bogdanov, chose to stay with the encircled men.[23] Together with perhaps 5,000 men, including many wounded, Bogdanov attempted to break out while Twenty-Second Army attacked from outside the pocket. In large and small groups, most of Bogdanov's men managed to reach safety. Bogdanov was wounded in the fighting and taken to Kalinin, where he died of his wounds.

Mikhail Ivanovich Lukinov was a junior artillery officer in the encirclement who remembered how discipline broke down and his regiment disintegrated. He was captured by German soldiers as he and a small group of men tried to find their way through the forests:

> I was separated from my fellow soldiers – they were taken away in another direction and I never saw them again ...
>
> The soldiers took me – or rather, dragged me – into a tent, probably part of a headquarters, where there was a large table and benches. They took my greatcoat and equipment and turned out all the contents of my pockets onto the table. Some German officers came and carefully reviewed all the things taken from me – documents and photographs. Fortunately, my [Communist Party] membership card and certificate were hidden in the lining of my boot and weren't found. Then one of the officers began to interrogate me in bad Russian, often switching to German. First they asked me if I was a commissar. To confirm my denial, they carefully examined the sleeves of my tunic where the political staff wore stars. Had there been stars there before, and had I removed them? Then they asked if I was a Communist Party

member, whether I was a career officer or reservist, what nationality, whether I was purely Russian, and where the division commander was …

After the interrogation they took me to a barbed wire compound with some pitiful huts made from boxwood and rusty iron. Russian prisoners of war who worked for this German unit lived there. They gave me a warm welcome. They went to a kitchen and they brought me a pot of *kasha* and a piece of bread. Later they warned me to be careful – there was a German here who looked for Jews or even anyone looking like a Jew amongst the prisoners, then took them into the forest and killed them. The other Germans didn't like him but didn't interfere with his executions. It turned out he had already asked the prisoners about me because my dark hair seemed suspicious to him.[24]

Soviet prisoners of war received slightly better treatment in 1942 than during the preceding year – aware that the war was likely to last a considerable time, the Germans attempted to alleviate the crippling shortages of manpower within the Reich by using prisoners. Nonetheless, conditions remained very poor, and Jews were still systematically singled out:

If the situation for most of the prisoners was terrible, then for those of a Jewish nationality it was even worse. They were doomed in advance to certain death. In the camp near Sychevka, Jews were subjected to all kinds of bad treatment … When some were taken from the camp, they were stripped to their underwear and their clothes were thrown into the crowd of other prisoners, who shamefully scuffled and fought for them. Through the wire, I saw how these poor people were taken away barefoot. At the front were two young girls, probably medics, tightly holding onto each other. The executioners may have been too ashamed to strip them. Or maybe some of the German officers had troubled consciences and gave orders for the girls not to be undressed.[25]

Lukinov was eventually sent to Germany where he survived the war as a labourer. After he was released, he had to locate his former unit in order to secure documentation that confirmed his identity and previous good record. Despite managing to do this, he was then put in a camp near Frankfurt-an-der-Oder, where, together with other officers who had been prisoners, he was rigorously interrogated by security officers:

We were sent to one interview commission after another, filling out countless questionnaires, personal accounts, and explanatory notes with links to witnesses

… Strange as it may seem, the prisoners of Jewish nationality who miraculously survived in captivity were subjected to the most intensive interrogations. 'How did you manage to stay alive?' They seemed to suspect that these people saved themselves at the cost of some kind of betrayal. But every family has its black sheep. In our group a few traitors – Vlasovites – were identified. They were isolated and taken away …

Sometimes the camp commissar, a fat man with a prosperous air, talked to us. He said several times: 'All of you should have died in 1941. But others died for you, and their blood is on your hands.' Nobody dared ask him in what year he should have died – after all, the fate of each of us depended on him, to be rehabilitated and sent home or to be sent to 'distant places'.[26]

After six months in the camp, Lukinov and some of the others were told that a new order had been issued, restoring their rank and authorising their demobilisation. Finally, they were permitted to board trains for home, but even then the taint of having been prisoners remained. Lukinov worked after the war in factory construction and was apparently destined for a post as chief engineer in a department responsible for factory constructions in the Urals, but his appointment was then blocked as he had been a prisoner.

As was the case with Belov's men further south, it is almost impossible to determine how many of the encircled Soviet troops succeeded in escaping; the upper estimate is about 18,000. The Germans reported that they had taken nearly 50,000 men prisoner, and this correlates well with the total of Red Army soldiers recorded as missing in action. *Hannover-I* and *Hannover-II* were only partly successful – they eliminated Belov's cavalry and the paratroopers operating around Dorogobuzh, and inflicted considerable damage on the local partisan groups, but a very large proportion of the cavalry and paratroopers managed to evade the Germans and reached safety. *Seydlitz*, by contrast, was a major success. Regardless of the plans of *Stavka* for a strategic defensive posture, even with local offensive operations, the loss of most of Thirty-Ninth Army and XI Cavalry Corps was a serious blow for the Red Army, particularly as German losses in the operation, while substantial, were far lower. The diary of 5th Panzer Division reported that the battle cost 132 dead and 522 wounded, but at the end of the operation a replacement battalion of 53 NCOs and 857 men arrived from Germany.[27] It is interesting that Halder noted in his diary on 9 July that the operation was costing the Wehrmacht 'very heavy casualties', suggesting that other units involved suffered higher losses than 5th Panzer Division.

The first men from 2nd Panzer Division to be permitted to return home on leave during 1942 left for Germany at the end of *Seydlitz*, and ordinary soldiers reacted with the grim humour of combatants in all armies. A leaflet began to circulate, stressing the importance of not behaving as if they were still in the occupied territories of the Soviet Union:

> Low-level white porcelain bowls of a singular nature, which are installed in designated rooms in German houses, are for a particular function that can best be explained by the housewife. After completion of this specific function, pull the chain that is to one side. (Don't be alarmed, the noise is harmless.) These porcelain bowls are impractical for washing your hair or shaving …
>
> The existence of anti-tank dogs is exclusively limited to the Soviet Union. German dogs will at worst bite, but they don't explode. The normal practice in this country of shooting every dog will result in unpleasant consequences in Germany and is therefore to be avoided …
>
> Men on leave! Be careful in the homeland with your descriptions of the paradisiacal circumstances in the Soviet Union, or everyone will wish to come here and our idyllic situation here will come to an end.[28]

Could the Red Army have made better use of the presence of so many Soviet troops in threatening positions close to the German lines of communication? Inevitably, in a period dominated by the memoirs of men like Konev and Zhukov, Soviet historiography made little attempt to consider this. It is important to consider that the two Soviet groups – Belov's men in the south and the soldiers of Kalinin Front in the north – were in rather different situations. Belov was potentially within reach of Western Front, and it is certainly arguable that the numerous attempts to link up with his men frittered away resources for little gain – had Zhukov concentrated his troops for one decisive attack, there might have been a greater probability of success. Belov showed considerable resourcefulness in improvising weaponry and cooperating closely with partisan groups, and his energy in handling the final breakout contributed to the survival of many of his men. By contrast, Maslennikov and Sokolov in the north were in terrain where there were few good roads, and even though their units were still connected to Kalinin Front via a small corridor north of Bely prior to the onset of *Seydlitz*, there were no roads remotely of the scale of the main Moscow–Warsaw highway that played a part in Belov's operations. Even before the Germans moved to cut off Thirty-Ninth Army, it was impossible to move sufficient supplies to Maslennikov. Consequently, their ability to resist when *Seydlitz* began was limited. However, Maslennikov showed little of the initiative and improvisation that Belov demonstrated, and both he and Konev seem to have been remarkably passive in the weeks prior to the German attack. Given that it was almost impossible to support Thirty-Ninth Army and XI Cavalry Corps in the positions they had reached by the end of the winter fighting, serious consideration should have been given to a timely withdrawal. Had this taken place, tens of thousands of Red Army soldiers could have been saved. Instead, Konev and Maslennikov simply left their units in a position where they were almost encircled and desperately short of supplies, effectively inviting the Germans to complete the encirclement and then to destroy the trapped formations.

Writing after the war, Konev attempted to defend the retention of dangerously exposed salients that practically invited German counterattacks:

> We were convinced of the importance of the salients ... The Germans didn't undertake any active operations here in the course of all of 1942, and in particular this was because of the threat that was hanging over them all the time ... In the complex overall situation of the summer and autumn of 1942, when fighting was continuing at Stalingrad, the configuration of our front lines tied down large enemy forces.[29]

How much of this is retrospective rationalisation? There is no record of Konev advocating the defence of exposed salients at the time. The argument that operations against Army Group Centre in general, and the Rzhev Salient in particular, tied down valuable German forces and prevented their deployment in the critical battles in and around Stalingrad recurs throughout the history of the salient, but for this thesis to carry weight, there would have to be evidence that the Germans intended to transfer divisions from Army Group Centre to the forces fighting further to the south. When the Soviet counteroffensive of November created a crisis at Stalingrad, troops were moved from other sectors to the region, but prior to November there seemed little intention for such movements, not least because Hitler and many around him believed that the war was as good as won. It is therefore difficult to justify Konev's view that by holding exposed salients, the Red Army tied down large numbers of German divisions. Given Halder's report of April in which he emphasised the weakness in terms of mobility and infantry strength of units in Army Group Centre and Army Group North, and the clear declaration by Hitler that there was no intention – at least in the short term – for major operations in the central and northern theatres, it seems that German inaction was more due to a combination of lack of mobility caused by the loss of so many horses, and units that were far from their establishment strength. Moreover, the German operations that carried the Wehrmacht to the Don valley, into Stalingrad and to the approaches of the Caucasus were often hindered by fuel shortages, and even this was only possible by effectively starving other theatres of fuel supplies. Any major operations by Army Group Centre would have required far more fuel than the Germans had available, and even if divisions had been shifted to the southern sector, consuming considerable fuel resources in the process, they would still have required more fuel and ammunition than Germany could produce if they were to contribute to the battles in and around Stalingrad. In that context, the loss of such large numbers of Soviet troops in *Seydlitz* suggests that any impact on German plans was at a very high price.

The passivity of Konev's Kalinin Front contributed considerably to the destruction of Thirty-Ninth Army. Even if Konev was against withdrawing Maslennikov's troops from the salient, and local road conditions prevented him from keeping them supplied adequately, he could have taken steps to alleviate this. The German garrison in Bely was badly exposed and was at the tip of a very thin German salient projecting north. It should have been possible to concentrate sufficient strength to the west of this salient to threaten it, forcing the Germans either to risk the destruction of the Bely garrison or to withdraw to the south. In far less favourable weather, the Red Army succeeded in advancing through the terrain to the south of Bely just a few months later. Had this happened in July, the encirclement achieved in *Seydlitz* would have become almost impossible.

In some respects, *Seydlitz* would have an impact on military thinking in the months that followed. The Germans had succeeded in mounting a major operation in difficult terrain and had destroyed a substantial Soviet concentration; the Red Army therefore began to consider that it too could mount such operations with the expectation of success. But this failed to take account of the circumstances of *Seydlitz*. Maslennikov's army was poorly supplied, and although it had laid considerable minefields, it had done little to construct the multi-tiered defences that were such a feature of the preparations that Model's forces had made around the salient. Konev too was at fault for not ensuring that Twenty-Second and Forty-First Armies, holding the neck of the 'sack' in which Thirty-Ninth Army and IX Cavalry Corps were in danger of being trapped, didn't take greater precautions to counter an almost inevitable German attack. These failures to match the promises to hold the salient with practical measures were major factors in the German success in *Seydlitz*, and there was little or no indication that the Germans would be equally negligent.

Despite being criticised by Konev in the winter fighting and having presided over the destruction of his army, Maslennikov escaped dismissal; he was a close associate of Lavrentiy Beria, head of the NKVD, and it is likely that Beria shielded him from punishment. After recovering from the wounds he received in the breakout, Maslennikov was assigned commander of the Red Army's Northern Group of forces before being sent to the Caucasus. He continued to hold senior posts throughout the war, but ultimately his close association with Beria proved fatal. When Beria was suspected of plotting to seize power in 1954, Maslennikov committed suicide, fearing that he faced imminent arrest.

CHAPTER 7

THE FIRST RZHEV–SYCHEVKA OPERATION

Zhukov's plans for a renewal of offensive operations to pinch off the Rzhev Salient were derailed by the disastrous outcome of Timoshenko's attempt to recapture Kharkov in the south; this necessitated the diversion of substantial armoured reinforcements that Zhukov had intended to use for his forthcoming operation. Despite this development and the escape of Belov's cavalry and Kazankin's paratroopers, Zhukov continued to develop his plans. The salient remained a constant presence and a threat to Moscow, one that Zhukov was determined to destroy. While his determination was a great asset to the Red Army, it often overflowed into stubbornness and blind persistence. The Red Army was about to pay a severe price for this.

The arrangement that had been established in the winter, with Zhukov having overall control of both his Front and the neighbouring Fronts, had since been abandoned. In July, as *Seydlitz* was coming to a conclusion, Zhukov received a telephone call:

> Stalin phoned me and asked if I knew that German troops had broken through the defences of Kalinin Front and had cut off the forces of Thirty-Ninth Army. I replied that I knew of the situation from the reports of the general staff.
>
> 'We must take measures so that Thirty-Ninth Army doesn't find itself in a difficult situation,' Stalin said. I replied that Kalinin Front was not subordinate to me, but was directly subordinate to *Stavka*. Stalin didn't answer, apparently having forgotten that the Western Direction overall command had been abolished by his own directive. Then he continued, 'Call Konev. I will give him instructions.'

Stalin then asked if I could organise an offensive by my Front's forces in order to divert the enemy's attention from the southwest [i.e. the developing German offensive towards the Don and Stalingrad], where we faced a difficult situation.

I replied that such an offensive would be useful and could be prepared quickly. One [thrust] on the left wing of the Front from the Kirov–Volkhov area; the other on the right wing in the Pogoreloe Gorodishche area, which it would be best to conduct in cooperation with Kalinin Front.[1]

The proposals that Zhukov had drawn up were codenamed *Sverdlovsk* and called for the new operation to commence at the beginning of August. A formal directive from *Stavka* followed on 16 July, ordering the neighbouring wings of Kalinin and Western Fronts to cooperate and drive the Germans back, retaking Rzhev and Zubtsov. This was markedly different from Zhukov's initial proposal and was directed at the tip of the salient rather than mounting another attempt

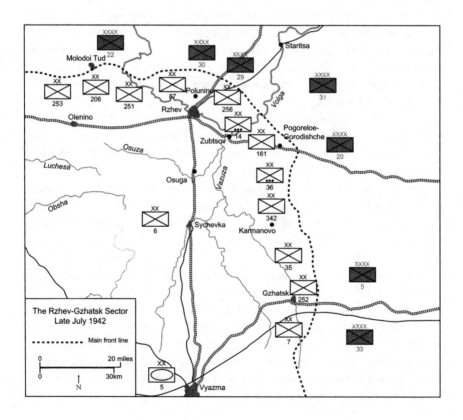

to cut it off at its base, and called for the entire operation to be completed in just a week, commencing on 28 July.[2] Despite this, Zhukov continued to develop plans for an operation further south near Gzhatsk, using Fifth and Thirty-Third Armies. The intention was for this attack to commence a few days after the expected end of the *Stavka*-directed operation at the tip of the salient, and Zhukov anticipated being able to divert considerable artillery and air assets from the assault on Rzhev to the south.

As was so often the case, the *Stavka* directive was ambitious in terms of timescale. Rzhev was expected to be captured on the second day of the assault. Kalinin Front would make the initial attack on 28 July, with the forces of Western Front attacking three days later, by which time it was expected that Kalinin Front would have tied down German reserves. *Stavka* had some justification for expecting success. Reinforcements had continued to arrive for all the armies in the sector throughout the summer, and the combined strength of the two Fronts was estimated at 43 rifle divisions and 21 tank brigades, with two guards rifle corps available as reserves. Between them, these units fielded over 1,700 tanks – surely such a force would suffice for an operation that involved an advance of less than 30 miles (50km).[3] However, this took little account of the fact that the Germans were occupying positions that they had held for many months. If the admittedly disorganised attacks of the winter had failed to dislodge them, the task would be far harder now, given the time that the Wehrmacht had undoubtedly used to improve its defensive fortifications. Nevertheless, the Soviet armies enjoyed manpower, artillery and tank superiority of between 3:1 and 7:1.

Soviet-era historiography repeatedly emphasised the ability of the Red Army to hide its preparations from the Germans and to mislead them about their intentions – such countermeasures came to be known as *Maskirovka*. The reality was that the Germans repeatedly spotted Soviet troop movements throughout June and July and correctly interpreted them as preparations for new attacks. Any possibility of surprise was effectively lost when Soviet radio stations broadcast repeated messages warning of a coming offensive. The rationale for these announcements is almost impossible to understand. Many civilians acted on this to leave Rzhev in order not to be caught up in the expected fighting, but even if the broadcasts were a clumsy double-bluff, they confirmed what the Germans already suspected: an attack was imminent.

Throughout this period, fighting continued at varying levels of intensity. Ashot Vagarshakovich Kazaryan was a junior officer from Armenia, serving in a tank brigade that formed part of the assembled forces. His cousin had been killed outside Rzhev in June and he was anxious to avenge him, but he had mixed feelings about the coming operation, not least because he and his men were unfamiliar with their equipment:

> I confess that I was in no hurry to climb into the commander's seat in the vehicle. The fact was that this English Valentine tank – one of those that the Allies supplied to the USSR under Lend-Lease – was something of a mystery to me. We had mastered driving tanks in our training in a T-34 and in field exercises we used old T-28 and BT-7 vehicles, and only in recent days had we learned anything about the Allies' tanks from diagrams and drawings ...
>
> The next three days turned out to be relatively quiet and it was possible to study the Valentine thoroughly. I wasn't particularly impressed by it – the armour was weak, probably easily penetrated by German shells; the engine lacked power, just 130 BHP. This meant that the vehicle lacked speed or manoeuvrability.[4]

Despite the misgivings of Kazaryan, the Valentine proved to be a popular tank in the Red Army. It may have been underpowered, but its compact size proved to be an asset, particularly as heavier tanks were prone to damaging roads and bridges, and its armour was actually quite effective – indeed, the Soviet Union requested that it remain in production for the duration of the war. When Kazaryan's unit went into action in early July, the tanks came under heavy air attack, and a near miss damaged the track and running gear of his tank. After dark, the vehicle was recovered and repaired, and was soon back in the front line. In readiness for the coming offensive, the tank brigade was ordered to attack again in an attempt to secure favourable positions for the main attack. As they moved forward, the Valentines encountered a group of German tanks:

> The enemy tanks approached within range – the black crosses on their sides always reminded me of the bull's-eye of a target – and I gave the order to fire. Yakovlev's shot was accurate and the leading German tank stopped suddenly, as if it had hit an invisible obstacle, and a few seconds later thick smoke was rising. 'Well done, Nikolai!' I praised the corporal, without taking my eyes off the other enemy vehicles. It seemed that the Nazis didn't understand what was happening and the other tanks didn't slow down.
>
> But we had been spotted. There was a crash and the turret of our tank shook. Fragments flew from the inside of the armour. The gunner reported a wound in his arm and I took his place. The German tanks had already moved forward considerably. We had to change position, break contact. And if we moved parallel

to them, we could engage them from the flank. No sooner decided than done – and how well it worked out! But unfortunately, my shot wasn't as well aimed as Yakovlev's. I fired five times at two tanks ...

I knew that the game wouldn't last long. Any second, the Germans would turn their guns and shoot at our Valentine from point-blank range. But they had no time to do so. The enemy tanks seemed to hit a wall of explosions. As we learned later, Senior Lieutenant Moiseev led our T-34s forward to meet the Fascists' thrust. Under accurate fire, the enemy battle formation broke down and their tanks turned back.

'Pursue the enemy!' ordered the company commander.

The excitement of the battle, which seemed to be turning in our favour, seized all the crew. The fuel pedal was pressed to the floor. The Valentine's weak engine began to cough and misfire, on the edge of stalling. We had to slow down, and as a result we struggled to keep up with our platoon. With difficulty, the tanks crawled through the sticky mud to the outskirts of the village. Here, on harder ground, they picked up speed again, crushing a mortar and its crew, and then, noticing a German tank lurking amidst the ruins, approached it from the side and set it ablaze with two shots. Shells exploded all round but, excited by what was happening, I seemed to forget our vulnerability, and repeatedly commanded: 'Forward! Forward!'

Grey smoke spread through the village, making it difficult to see ... Suddenly the tank shook violently and shrapnel rattled against the armour. A German gun was firing from somewhere. We had to find it – but we didn't have time. A shell pierced the left side of the Valentine with an incredible crash. Lance Corporal Dylnik was killed and flames filled the compartment. For a moment it seemed to me that we were all ablaze – flames licked at our overalls and the upper hatch was jammed. 'The escape hatch!' I shouted to Yakovlev and Kozhevnikov. But the emergency hatch was difficult to reach and refused to open. 'You're the commander, you are responsible for your men and you must find a way out,' I told myself, my head pounding. Leaning towards Kozhevnikov, I croaked, 'Help me with the top hatch.' Supporting his wounded arm, Yakovlev joined us. The flames raged all round. Our overalls were burning, the fire scorched our hands and faces and the smoke made our eyes stream. The air was so hot it felt like we were swallowing boiling water. But straining with our utmost strength, we pushed at the hatch.

Finally, it began to move. Another push – and the hatch swung open with a bang. The fire burst out like a torch. Helping each other, we climbed out and fell to the ground, rolling on it to extinguish the flames on our overalls.

The pain from the burns, the shock we had experienced, all deadened our senses and we didn't immediately hear the bullets whistling overhead – German machine-gunners had crept closer to the wrecked tank and were firing. Realising the new danger, we took cover behind the tank and prepared to fight to the last. We had one submachine-gun for the entire crew, held by Corporal Yakovlev, and the rest had pistols and grenades.

The Nazis lay down when we opened fire, and we took advantage of the poor visibility and dashed to the forest.[5]

Kazaryan and the other two crewmen managed to reach safety. When he had recovered from his burns, he was delighted to be assigned to a unit equipped with T-34s.

Throughout the winter, Soviet attacks hurled soldiers at intact German defences, resulting in huge losses for little gain. On this occasion, Konev's armies were better prepared. Major General Nikolai Mikhailovich Khlebnikov had been the commander of Twenty-Seventh Army's artillery assets and was now given the same role for all of Kalinin Front. Konev informed him of the coming attack in mid-July, and Khlebnikov and his staff immediately set to work:

Large numbers of batteries and individual guns were allocated for direct support of the infantry. Many guns, including those of large calibres, were deployed for direct fire at enemy firing points and bunkers in the front line. Artillery support groups for the infantry were created, with separate long-range groups to combat enemy artillery and long-range targets.

When the plan had been worked out, we presented it to the Front commander. 'Two hours of artillery preparation is a lot,' he said, 'the enemy will have time to regroup reserves in the depths of his defences.' Ivan Stepanovich [Konev] gave several examples from his experience when this had happened. In the end, it was decided to limit the duration of the artillery bombardment to one hour, but at the same time firstly we increased the firing rate accordingly, and secondly we placed even more guns in direct fire positions …

At the same time, the Front artillery headquarters and the artillery headquarters of Thirtieth and Twenty-Ninth Armies continued their daily, painstaking, and very difficult work to identify the enemy's defensive system, from its forward edge into the depth of the defence of up to 15km [nine miles].[6]

At the beginning of the First World War, German officers were often surprised by the technical skill of Russian artillery, and this expertise was carried through to the

Second World War. Together with his reconnaissance and intelligence officers, Khlebnikov and his staff carefully analysed aerial reconnaissance photographs, looking for signs that apparent artillery positions were genuine or just simulations. The calibre of many German guns was identified, allowing for their effective range to be calculated and priorities for artillery suppression to be decided. As intelligence accumulated, it was clear to Khlebnikov that he lacked the guns and ammunition to destroy all of the identified targets. Nonetheless, he set his gunners the task of destroying 90 bunkers and 120 other field fortifications, and suppressing 53 artillery batteries, 47 mortar positions, and dozens of individual German field guns, anti-tank guns and mortars. The difference between the coming attack and previous attempts in the winter was starkly demonstrated by the density of Soviet artillery – Thirtieth Army was expected to attack on a front of six miles (10km) and had over 1,400 guns, mortars and rocket launchers in support, while Twenty-Ninth Army, attacking on a slightly narrower front, was backed by over 900 guns and mortars. In keeping with common practice at the time, tanks waiting in reserve to exploit a breakthrough would fire their guns in support of the artillery, though this was soon abandoned as it contributed little to the value of the bombardment. But as was so often the case with artillery, one factor dominated Khlebnikov's concerns:

> Throughout those days I was concerned about the shortage of ammunition. It was held in stockpiles at various levels but delivering it to the troops involved enormous difficulties. Three days before the onset [of the attack], there was heavy rain. It lasted for several days without interruption. Low-lying wetlands immediately became impassable. The dirt roads disintegrated and both horses and caterpillar-tracked vehicles got stuck in the bottomless mud. We literally delivered ammunition by hand. With great difficulty, we accumulated two complete sets of shells for the troops, amounting to about 14,000 tons.
>
> I never saw such impassable terrain during the entire war. US Vice President [Wendell] Willkie [who was actually functioning as an envoy of President Roosevelt rather than as vice-president], who visited our Front at that time, just gasped and shook his head, marvelling at the endurance and courage of our soldiers.[7]

The delays occasioned by the weather resulted in the planned start date of the operation slipping. Khlebnikov and Konev visited the front line on 29 July and came away with concerns about the flexibility of artillery support – Khlebnikov ordered the local commander to shell some trees among the German lines, but communications between forward observers and the gun batteries proved to be unreliable, and the wrong target was shelled. Konev departed with the warning that there was almost no time left to resolve such issues; the reality was that they would have to proceed with what they had.

On 30 July, the massed guns of Kalinin Front began their bombardment. Khlebnikov was gratified to find that German counter-bombardment rapidly ceased as the Red Army's gunners silenced German batteries. The entire front line was churned up by the shelling, and in many places the first wave of Soviet infantry encountered almost no resistance when they moved forward. The German defences in this sector were manned by VI Corps, part of Ninth Army; with Model still recovering from his chest wound, the army remained under Vietinghoff's command. One of the units of the corps, 6th Infantry Division, which had been pulled out of line and sent to a rear area for a chance to rest and recuperate, was now ordered back to the front line even as its last elements were arriving in Sychevka. As a result of the recent rain, the 'rest area' to the west of Sychevka was little more than a swamp, with many small bridges over the numerous rivers and streams damaged or swept away entirely. Leaving behind its vehicles, the first battalion of the division set off for Sychevka with just the weapons that the men could carry. After an exhausting night march, the men reached Sychevka early on 31 July, where they boarded trains that took them north to Rzhev.

The arrival of German reserves via the road and rail corridor running to Rzhev from the south was an entirely predictable development, but although there were frequent Soviet air attacks on the railway station in Sychevka, Kalinin Front made little provision to interdict the route with its considerable air assets; it seems that the Soviet assessment was that either the reinforcements would be modest and inconsequential, or that with the capture of Rzhev timetabled for very early in the operation, the use of this route for German reinforcements would become irrelevant within days. It proved to be a serious miscalculation.[8]

To the north and northwest of Rzhev, the German 87th and 256th Infantry Divisions were driven back on the entire frontage of the attack, conceding three or four miles of ground. Several German artillery batteries were overrun – a legacy of the loss of irreplaceable draft horses made it impossible to withdraw the guns in a timely fashion. The units of 6th Infantry Division were ordered into line between the two divisions that had fallen back.

As had been the case for the German units involved in *Hannover* and *Seydlitz*, the weather proved to be at least as big an enemy as the opposing troops. Khlebnikov later recalled:

> Those who attacked in the lowlands and swamps near Rzhev will never forget those days. Water poured down from the heavens in torrents and welled up from

186

below, instantly filling freshly dug trenches. The infantry moved forward in mist and damp. Their feet were bogged down so firmly in the black liquid mess that it felt as if claws were gripping their boots. The gunners harnessed a dozen horses to pull a single light 76mm gun free, but to no avail. The horses sank up to their bellies in the mud and had to be hauled out with ropes.

The mud was our main enemy, and cost us a lot of time to gain every kilometre.[9]

The swamps and forests might have interfered greatly with the ability of both sides to manoeuvre their forces, but there were occasionally unexpected benefits, as Mikhail Petrovich Bogopolsky, a gunner in the Red Army later remembered:

We fired from isolated positions, up to 3km from the main battery position. We had several such locations, and fired from each one for no more than 15 minutes, because the Germans could detect the location of our guns by the sound of their shots and would then give the coordinates of our locations to their gunners tasked with counter-battery fire, and they didn't hesitate to bombard us. Moreover, unlike us the Germans didn't seem to be short of shells and fired hundreds of rounds. A favourite position for isolated firing was in a swamp. The gun was placed on metal plates on swampy ground and we fired calmly until the Germans spotted us. But when they plotted our locations on maps and saw that the fire was coming from a swamp, they probably thought they had made a mistake and didn't attempt suppression fire against our guns. But after the third or fourth time they decided to carry out powerful shelling. We were saved by the fact that their shells fell into the swamp around the gun and went deep into the boggy ground – their explosive power wasn't enough to blow away the mud over them. But some of the shells did explode on impact, making us 'plough the ground with our noses' and causing us some unpleasant moments.[10]

The second day of the operation saw the Red Army make almost no gains. In conditions in which the infantry could barely move, it was impossible to bring forward the supporting artillery and the ammunition that Khlebnikov had so carefully built up. Tanks became stuck in the mud, and as they returned to Rzhev, the first elements of the German 6th Infantry Division were ordered to make an immediate counterattack towards the north. One battalion of the division's 58th Infantry Regiment deployed just to the north of Rzhev for a counterattack, which was to be supported by two assault guns. When the counterattack began, the assault guns were nowhere to be seen, but an energetic attack drove the leading Red Army elements out of the village of Polunino, just four miles (6.5km) from the centre of Rzhev. A key position on the former boundary between the German 256th and 87th Infantry Divisions became known as 'Strongpoint Emma'; despite being outflanked, its small garrison beat off repeated Soviet attacks and helped act as a breakwater in the path of the Red Army, and it was only on 10 August that the position was finally abandoned. A modest hill near Polunino, marked on maps as Hill 200, also became a critical position. The counterattack by 58th Infantry Regiment resulted in the front line running across the northern edge of the low hill, and there were frequent Soviet attacks throughout the first few days of August; all were repulsed by the defenders, though an artillery bombardment on the headquarters of the battalion from 6th Infantry Division disrupted command arrangements and left several men dead.

Despite having plenty of warning that a Soviet attack was imminent, the German Ninth Army had few reserves available. A motorcycle battalion from 14th Motorised Infantry Division was almost the only mobile asset that Vietinghoff had, and he had no choice but to order it into action on the left flank of 256th Infantry Division, alongside the regiment from 6th Infantry Division. For the moment the line was holding, but all would depend on the next few days – with no further reserves available, Vietinghoff feared that his divisions would collapse if the Red Army could mount another attack of the same magnitude.

Kalinin Front's Twenty-Ninth Army attacked at the same time as Thirtieth Army, but here the German front line held firm. A report from Shvetsov, the commander of the army, described the same conditions as those later remembered by Khlebnikov:

> As the ground was heavily saturated after the downpours, the tanks became mired and the infantry was pinned down ... After an hour, the division commander [leading the first wave] continued the assault without tanks. The infantry had regrouped and advanced again, running into enemy positions that opened up a withering fire; consequently, the infantry suffered heavy losses and once more was driven to ground in a zone covered by enemy artillery and mortar fire. The offensive staggered to a halt.[11]

It seems that here, at least, the Soviet artillery was far less effective than in Thirtieth Army's sector. Vasily Romanovich Boyko was political commissar of Twenty-Ninth Army's 183rd Rifle Division, and he later recalled the attack:

> The enemy put up stubborn resistance and we didn't have enough ammunition to suppress his artillery and mortars. Admittedly, in comparison with the winter

battles, we were beginning to receive more shells and mortar bombs. But at the same time, more had to be held in reserve for each gun or howitzer. For example, the commander of an artillery regiment did not have the right, without the permission of the division commander, to release an extra 122mm round if there was no immediate threat to the gun.

We captured the first enemy position and liberated the village of Deshevka. But we couldn't advance any further, moreover we were forced to abandon the village – the Nazis threw in reserves, and we had none to oppose them. The division assumed a defensive posture.

And yet, even in these battles, our commanders and soldiers showed increased expertise. The height that dominated the terrain, captured from the enemy during the battles for Deshevka, significantly improved our position. All regiments in the division's sector were firmly entrenched on the captured line.[12]

The Soviet infantry made repeated attempts to try to reach Rzhev, but as had been the case in the winter, their attacks degenerated into repeated frontal assaults on German positions that resulted in escalating casualties for almost no gain. Khlebnikov advised Konev to call a halt while his guns were laboriously brought forward, as further attacks without adequate fire support were pointless. On the German side, there was now just enough time to restore the situation. The rest of 6th Infantry Division arrived and was inserted into line between 256th and 87th Infantry Divisions, and the immediate threat of complete collapse seemed to have passed.

Having recovered sufficiently from their burns to return to front-line service, Ashot Kazaryan and his two surviving crewmembers were involved in the renewed attacks on 6 August. As a platoon commander, he was fortunate enough to be in a tank with a radio, and waited nervously as it began to grow light. His third foray in the front line proved little more successful than his previous two, despite now being in a T-34:

The silence was broken by the roar of artillery preparation. It lasted only 20 minutes but it seemed very effective. In any case, it was clearly visible through binoculars that the shells landed close together and blew several enemy firing points into the air.

'Forward! Move through the gaps at top speed!' The voice of the company commander Vasily Moiseyev sounded in my headphones. Our three platoons – Senior Lieutenants Alexander Prokhorov, Konstantin Kazantsev and mine – formed a line and moved to attack simultaneously. A third of the distance passed.

Half. And then the tank shook for the first time, shrapnel drummed on the armour – the German artillery was firing. Near misses were nothing, only a direct hit would matter. Faster!

We passed through the first, heavily damaged enemy trench. Well done to our artillerymen, their work was superb! But the enemy's anti-tank guns seemed to have survived. Clearly it was so – the tanks that were moving up ahead were manoeuvring under accurate fire. How long would their luck last? Perhaps it would be better to rush forward at full speed and crush the enemy battery.

In the firm hands of Tekuchev [the new driver who replaced Kazaryan's previous crewman, killed in the earlier action], the tank quickly climbed a sandy embankment, turned sharply – and everything happened in a matter of seconds. The vehicle seemed to hang in the air before plunging down with a crash. I hit my head so hard on the hatch cover that, despite the tank helmet, my vision darkened. The rest of the crew were also injured. What had happened?

I cautiously raised the hatch and looked around. It was a discouraging sight: it turned out that the T-34 had fallen into a dilapidated dugout, right up to its turret. Even as I looked around I checked to see if the turret could still rotate – it worked! The gun seemed to be intact too. So we were still capable of combat.

Prokhorov hurried over to help. Under fire, he drove his vehicle to ours and tried to attach a towing cable. But it soon became clear that the only way to get the heavy machine out of the hole was with lifting equipment. Where were we going to get that in a battle?

So unexpectedly and absurdly, we found ourselves in a difficult situation, which became worse when we realised that the attack had failed and the other vehicles were retreating. I reported the incident to Major Onishchenko [the battalion commander] by radio. He paused and then asked what our field of view was.

'It's good. I can see right into the enemy's defences,' I replied, and then had a sudden thought. 'We can spot enemy firing points, artillery positions, and report them to you.'

The battalion commander approved this plan and the tank, stuck in no-man's land, became a kind of observation post. The Nazis fired at it for some time; shells exploded all around and twice rattled against the tower. We remained silent and didn't return fire, confident in the toughness of the T-34, hoping the enemy would think the tank was knocked out and the crew dead. Indeed, the shelling soon stopped and calmly, as if during training, I began to transmit my reports.[13]

Kazaryan managed to direct Soviet artillery fire onto a couple of German positions before German infantry, supported by an anti-tank gun, tried to move closer to the stranded T-34. Despite this, a signaller managed to reach the tank with a field telephone and cable – vital, as without a functioning engine the tank's battery was running down – and the valuable work of spotting German positions continued. Soviet gunners managed to break up a German counterattacking group that was assembling within sight of Kazaryan, and after a few days his tank battalion managed to push forward far enough for Kazaryan and his comrades to be moved to safety.

Struggling with personal losses – his brother, a colonel in the Red Army, had died in the fighting in Sevastopol in June, and he now received news that his father had died – Khlebnikov reorganised his artillery in preparation for a new assault. Meanwhile, Zhukov's Western Front was completing its preparation. As had been the case with Konev's armies, the formations under Zhukov's control needed additional time to bring forward supplies and equipment on the muddy roads, with the result that the start date slipped to 4 August. The assault was preceded by the almost inevitable fierce artillery bombardment, and once again, a large proportion of the German defences were either damaged or completely demolished. On this occasion, the Red Army used a new tactic. At the end of the main artillery bombardment, aircraft laid a smokescreen, and this was followed by a final brief rocket bombardment of the German positions, in the hope that the defenders would have resumed their positions in anticipation of the Red Army attacking as soon as the smokescreen was in place.[14] The first thrusts either side of Pogoreloe Gorodishche made good progress and rapidly isolated the village. After further artillery preparation, a mixed infantry and tank assault overran the defenders during the afternoon. The neighbouring sector to the north was held by 161st Infantry Division, and here too the attacking Soviet troops enjoyed early success. By the end of the day, Zhukov's units had pushed up to five miles (eight km) into the German line on a broad front. It was an encouraging start.

On 5 August, Stalin once more appointed Zhukov as overall commander of both Western and Kalinin Fronts, with Konev subordinated to him in an attempt to improve cooperation between the neighbouring Fronts. Zhukov reiterated the orders that were already in effect: Thirtieth Army, part of Kalinin Front, was to renew its attacks on Rzhev from the north, while Thirty-First Army was to attack towards the city from the east. Rzhev was to be taken no later than 9 August, while a little to the south, Twentieth Army was to exploit the capture of Pogoreloe Gorodishche and push the Germans back to and through Sychevka. If this town could be captured, it would be almost impossible for the Wehrmacht to remain in Rzhev, as the critical supply lines for the German Ninth Army would be cut.

The considerable successes of Zhukov's initial attack required swift deployment of mobile exploitation forces if they were to be converted into a major victory. Conversely, if Kluge's Army Group Centre was going to salvage the situation, it needed to reinforce the front line and repair the damage that had been inflicted. Much would now depend on which side could move its pieces into position fastest. The terrible unseasonal rain that had plagued the operations of both sides showed no signs of letting up, and Western Front's 'mobile' units laboured forward through thick mud, with even tanks becoming bogged down and needing assistance to move forward. Organised into three groups, some of Western Front's tanks were just nine miles (15km) from Sychevka on 5 August, while other units to the north were within striking range of Zubtsov. But the Germans had put their prolonged tenure of the region to good use. Secondary lines of defence had been prepared, and the retreating infantry divisions that had been driven back on the first day were able to delay the Soviet advance. The intensive efforts of the Luftwaffe also greatly hindered the Soviet attempts to exploit their success, and the narrow nature of Zhukov's initial penetration resulted in second echelon units becoming compressed as they attempted to move forward, making the task of German bombers far easier.

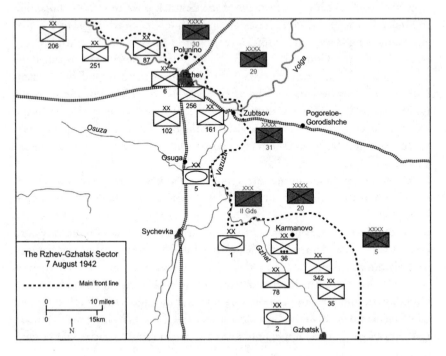

Meanwhile, help was on the way for the hard-pressed German units. Heinrici's Fourth Army had planned a local offensive of its own aimed at eliminating the Soviet-held salient that had Kirov at its tip. Plans for the operation, codenamed *Wirbelwind* ('Whirlwind'), had been drawn up in mid-July with the intention of mounting attacks in early August; once the front had been straightened by this attack, it would be possible for the sectors held by individual divisions to be reduced, and for units to be pulled out of line to create both local and operational reserves. The units that had been earmarked for the operation, including 1st Panzer Division, which had been sent south at the end of *Seydlitz*, were therefore available for use against Zhukov's attack. Kluge immediately ordered Heinrici to reduce the scale of the planned attack and to release the forces for use by Ninth Army. Largely by chance, the support elements of 1st Panzer Division were still to complete their move south and were immediately south of Zhukov's penetration; consequently, the panzer division's supplies and engineering workshops were perfectly positioned to give it support in a counterattack. However, merely getting to the new sector was a considerable undertaking as the division set off late on 4 August:

> Great cloudbursts of rain through the night made road conditions worse minute by minute. Conditions were particularly bad for wheeled vehicles. It was only through the greatest exertions and by the constant use of tractors towing trucks through the worst spots that the division's leading elements managed to reach the main Smolensk–Moscow highway. From here onwards, the deployment proceeded more easily.[15]

In addition to 1st Panzer Division, 2nd and 5th Panzer Divisions had also been ordered to deploy in preparation for *Wirbelwind*, and Army Group Centre thus had a considerable force available for a counterattack. Much of 5th Panzer Division was still in or near Vyazma, and the division commander, Gustav Fehn – newly promoted to Generalleutnant – arrived in Sychevka with his headquarters on 5 August. The town was the location of the headquarters of Ninth Army, and Vietinghoff, who had commanded 5th Panzer Division in the heady days of September 1939 during the invasion of Poland, must have been glad to have his old unit available in this moment of crisis.

As *Seydlitz* was coming to an end, the panzer divisions of the Wehrmacht were given a modified nomenclature. Their original force structure consisted of a panzer brigade and a rifle brigade; each brigade had two regiments, and each regiment had two battalions. The panzer brigades had already ceased to have a total of four battalions, not least due to irreplaceable losses, and the infantry component had lost its brigade headquarters. The latest step was to rename the rifle regiments as panzergrenadier regiments. The intention was for these troops to function as 'armoured infantry' mounted in half-tracks, but the reality was that there were insufficient armoured vehicles for this. At best, panzer divisions had two of their four battalions of infantry equipped with half-tracks, sometimes just a single battalion, and as the new name was meant to reflect their armoured status, the troops adopted a nickname for the battalions that were still dependent upon wheeled trucks with rubber tyres for transport – these became known as the *Gummigrenadiere* ('rubber grenadiers'). It was standard practice since the beginning of the war for panzer divisions to organise their resources into separate battlegroups, concentrating their half-track infantry, their armoured artillery (again, only a proportion of each division's artillery regiment was equipped with tracked, self-propelled artillery), their best-equipped panzer battalion, and perhaps some of their anti-tank battalion into a *Gepanzerte Kampfgruppe* ('armoured battlegroup'), often given the name of its commander; this battlegroup would form the division's main strike force, with the other wheeled battlegroups acting as support or secondary groups. Given the opportunity, battlegroups would continue to be organised in this manner throughout the war, but in the current crisis, troops were often committed to the battlefield as they arrived, such was the urgency to intercept the advancing Soviet units.

The first combat element of 5th Panzer Division – two battalions of panzergrenadiers supported by an artillery battalion and a company of tank destroyers – was already in action on 5 August, holding the line of the Vazuza River to the northeast of Sychevka. With other German armoured forces now beginning to arrive and the deployment of Zhukov's mobile groups hindered by the weather, perhaps the best opportunity for a major success for the Red Army had already slipped away. The outcome of the operation would now depend on which side's armour performed best, and despite the setbacks they had suffered, the Germans must have started to feel a little more confident. In almost every battle, their panzer formations had demonstrated tactical superiority over the Red Army, and even if Zhukov's forces could field tanks in greater numbers than the German divisions – and it should be remembered that at this stage of the war, most of the tanks in the panzer divisions lacked the firepower to engage Soviet T-34s on equal terms – there were good reasons to expect an improvement in the overall situation.

In addition to 5th Panzer Division, the regiments and battalions of 2nd Panzer Division were ordered to move from their rest area near Smolensk to

Vyazma – as was usual for panzer divisions, the wheeled elements of the division moved by road, while tracked elements were loaded onto railway flatcars. The initial warning order for the division specified that it would deploy near Yukhnov, but instead it was now ordered to intervene near Gzhatsk. The first units reached Gzhatsk and Karmanovo on 5 August, aware that a division equipped with obsolete Pz.38(t) and Pz.III tanks was of limited efficacy, and in a six-hour battle the division's panzer battalion lost seven tanks and was reduced to just two companies.[16]

But moving units to the area of crisis was hard enough; tactical deployment within the area continued to be hindered by the disintegrating roads. Under what must have seemed like endless rain, a battalion of 5th Panzer Division's panzergrenadiers was dispatched towards the east in order to cross the Vazuza and move up to make contact with the division's elements already defending the river line, but struggled to make any headway along muddy tracks that were congested with other traffic. Reluctantly, Fehn – who was struggling with illness and was about to step down from command temporarily – abandoned his original intention to reinforce this battalion with further elements of the division, and in the coming days the battalion came under the control of the neighbouring 2nd Panzer Division. In almost constant combat against Soviet armoured units, it lost all of its heavy weapons, and when it rejoined 5th Panzer Division at the end of August, it had been reduced to just 30 men.[17]

A flavour of the fighting is given in an account by a combat report from a battalion of 5th Panzer Division's panzer regiment:

The battalion was to stand ready for an attack from Gorchkovo towards Zubtsov either side of the main road ... The battalion prepared for an attack with Wenske's company forward and the rest in and south of Gorchkovo. During these preparations, a Russian artillery bombardment struck the northern end of Gorchkovo. Just before the advance had properly begun came the call: 'Enemy tanks up ahead!' Two T-34s drove into the village from the north. The first was disabled by two Pz.IIIs of Wenske's company while the other continued to the southern edge of the village and was shot up at point-blank range by the staff Pz.III ... The commander of the battalion, Major Seidensticker, arrived from the south. He ordered Wenske's company to thrust north along the road to help *Kampfgruppe Kurz*, which was under heavy Russian tank attack, to occupy the village of Bukontovo [a little to the northwest], and to secure the area. Wetstein's company was ordered to thrust through Kulshevo to Koslovo, and to hold these villages to protect the right flank of *Kampfgruppe Kurz*. Besch's company was tasked with the security of Gorchkovo.

Wenske's company quickly moved up to Bukontovo and there it was ordered by Oberst Kurz, commander of 14th Panzergrenadier Regiment, to continue north along the road. The company deployed either side of the road and immediately set off. Shortly before reaching the edge of the woodland northeast of Bukontovo the company came under heavy fire from T-34s and anti-tank guns amongst the trees. Several of our tanks were shot up. At the same time the enemy counterattacked against either flank of the company and a swift thrust managed to get into the rear of the company. Under heavy fire, the panzergrenadiers had to pull back and Hauptmann Wenske decided to withdraw to Bukontovo in order to engage the enemy counterattack more effectively. In these actions the company lost eight tanks shot up but destroyed three Russian T-34s and an anti-tank gun. Company casualties came to two dead, 14 wounded and four missing.[18]

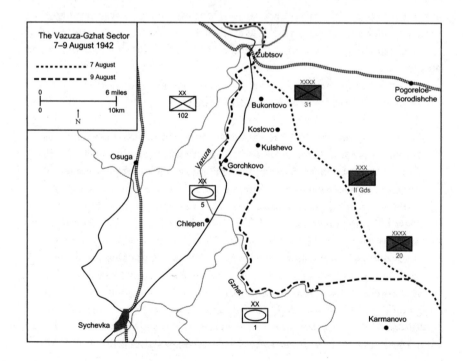

By the end of the year, the Pz.III tank would be widely regarded as no longer able to contest the battlefield with its opponents. Even in mid-1942, the tank that was the mainstay of the panzer divisions was able to engage T-34s only at close range; although successive versions had thicker armour, even the latest models had frontal armour of just 50mm, and the long-barrelled 50mm gun had little chance of penetrating the frontal armour of its opponent at ranges greater than about 400m.[19] By contrast, the T-34 had similar thickness of armour, but the 60-degree slope made it far more resistant. Its 76mm gun could penetrate the armour of a Pz.III at more than twice the effective range of the German tank, and it also benefited from far better mobility. Tanks of both sides were often lost or disabled by terrain difficulties, and the withdrawing German tanks had some nervous moments when two of them slipped off the road through a village and had to be towed to safety; a T-34 appeared but was destroyed by the intervention of a Pz.IV from the battalion's 'heavy' company. The Soviet armour, too, was struggling with ditches:

> A short time later a messenger from a panzergrenadier company reached the panzer company with a request for help in destroying two T-34s that had broken into the village of Kulskhevo and were stuck in a ditch. The company commander, Oberleutnant Wetstein, drove back in a Pz.IV and destroyed one of the stranded T-34s and killed the crew of the other. A renewed attack by several T-34s was broken up by the company's fire during the afternoon … Late in the afternoon another 15 T-34s broke through and rushed up to Gorchkovo at high speed. The range was too great for the company. After a while about ten T-34s pulled back and disappeared into dense woodland …
>
> Four succeeded in breaking into Gorchkovo before they were shot up by Besch's company. The attacking T-34s were carrying a crowd of Russian infantry who dismounted in the village. A wild close-quarter battle developed but after a short time the place was firmly in our hands.[20]

The German reports indicate that communications were limited to radio messages, as it was impossible for signallers to lay telegraph wires. Here, the Germans enjoyed a substantial advantage over their opponents. At the start of the war, most Soviet tanks did not have radios – only the command vehicle was equipped, and communication from this vehicle to subordinate tanks was meant to be via a system of waving flags from the hatch. In reality, this was almost impossible to do in battle, and equally impossible for subordinates to see and interpret correctly, and Soviet armoured attacks were usually carried out with strict adherence to the orders that were issued before the attack began, with little ability to change plans once the engagement began. Had the numerous groups of tanks thrown at the dwindling battalion of 5th Panzer Division been concentrated into a single force, there can be little doubt that the Germans would have been driven back or destroyed, but they were able – with difficulty – to beat off each attack as it came. But if the attempts by Zhukov's forces to push south towards Sychevka had been repulsed, the German intention to push north with 5th Panzer Division also failed. A small bridgehead over the Vazuza River came under fierce attack during the night of 6–7 August; the German force was composed of a group of anti-tank guns from 5th Panzer Division and a few *Alarmeinheiten* ('alarm units') hastily organised from rear area troops, and despite the appearance of numerous Soviet tanks, all the assaults were beaten off. Unfortunately for the German force, the bridge over the river was blown during the confusion, and throughout the following day the small group came under attack and was forced to give ground. Just in time, as ammunition was running out, the bridge was restored late on 7 August. The division report that evening claimed that since the fighting near Sychevka had begun, it had destroyed 54 T-34s. Given that some of these were apparently 'destroyed' at a distance, it is impossible to know whether they were permanently destroyed or merely disabled and subsequently recovered by the Red Army. But in this field, the Germans continued to enjoy a substantial advantage. Unlike Soviet tank formations of the day, the panzer divisions had integral engineering workshops and recovery vehicles, and many tanks that had been put out of action were often repaired or at least patched up without much delay. By contrast, the equivalent engineering teams in the Red Army were often far to the rear, and it wasn't until well into 1943 that engineering assets were increased and routinely went forward immediately behind the advancing tanks, in order to recover and repair vehicles as quickly as possible.

Having recovered from its losses in the winter fighting, the Soviet II Guards Cavalry Corps was one of the 'exploitation groups' of Zhukov's Western Front. It made a long approach march to the battlefields, held up by roads choked with traffic, and the cavalrymen gathered in the forest near Pogoreloe Gorodishche before entering the battle. From here, they moved up to the Gzhat River on 7 August:

It was already quite light when the vanguard reached the Gzhat. The rain had stopped but the air still felt damp. A thin fog hung over the river and the lowlands. The river was normally low at this time of year but the rain had turned it into a wide, turbulent stream up to 3–4m deep. The vanguard had no means of crossing. There were no boats, rafts, or even wooden planks along the shore.

They began to cross by swimming. Heavy machine-guns and several field guns, which had accompanied the cavalry on the march, took up firing positions. The leading detachments reached the opposite bank, deployed, and moved forward. About 1km from the river, the [leading] squadrons ... came under fire. The cavalry dismounted and attacked from the line of march. Our field guns fired from across the river. The line of soldiers moved up to the entrenched enemy and drove the Nazis out in a fierce battle.

By 0800 on 7 August the vanguard was across on the western bank, dug in, and had moved the horses to shelter. Sappers transported heavy machine-guns, anti-tank guns, and mortars on rafts. The clumsy rafts, made of rough logs, floated deep in the water and were often carried away by the strong current. There were no oars or ropes. Instead, they used shovels, reins tied together, and wooden boards picked up along the way ...

Two Messerschmitts swept over the crossing, descended, circled, and fired several machine-gun bursts before heading west. 'Just wait for the other guests to show up,' said the experienced soldiers, who were well acquainted with the enemy's habits. They were right, they had gone to alert the Stukas. At about noon, there was a growing rumble. Aircraft appeared in the sky. Bombs howled down, explosions echoed. Huge columns of water and mud rose from the Gzhat. The ferrying of materiel had to be suspended. The anti-aircraft batteries had not yet arrived and the attack was answered only by small-arms fire. The Stukas dropped their bombs and left.[21]

Unable to advance further, the cavalry dug in to hold their small bridgehead. Aleksander Borisovich Stepenskiy was another soldier in II Guards Cavalry Corps:

We moved up to [Pogoreloe Gorodishche] – we were on high ground overlooking it, in the forest, and then the Germans flew over and bombed the trains and the railway station. We left our horses in the forest, and I never saw them again. We walked through the forest and moved to the Vazuza [River] as part of the second echelon. The entire bank was dug up with trenches to protect against bombing. German planes arrived every morning between 0700 and 0800. Junkers – we just called them 'bastards'. Their intelligence had apparently alerted them that our echelon was moving up and they bombed us every day. And we asked ourselves, where are Stalin's falcons? We never saw them. Two ground attack aircraft appeared one time and one was shot down by the Germans and crashed near us, the pilot was probably killed.

Then we attacked and took a village. We had to go further and were concentrated in a ravine, waiting for the command to attack. Then – forward! And the Germans had already aimed their guns at the ground ahead of us and as soon as we jumped out they began to bombard us with mortars. If it hadn't been for my helmet, I would have died, as a splinter pierced the helmet and got stuck in my temple. I fell and the orderlies dragged me back into the ravine and bandaged me. They took us – me and another soldier – to the medical battalion. On the way I saw two *Katyusha* launchers, standing in a ravine. They fired a volley, maybe at the village we were attacking. But after firing their volley they immediately turned around and left because the Germans had good radio intelligence and quickly spotted where they were shooting from and would shell this spot. And as we passed, the *Katyushas* left and the Germans began their shelling. We found a hollow and dropped into it and waited.[22]

Many Soviet veterans recalled the bitter fighting as they tried to push forward. Lieutenant Aron Semenovich Gorodinskiy was serving in a mortar battalion and saw the terrible losses suffered by the Red Army at first hand:

The infantry suffered losses that can't be described in any way other than 'savage'. I simply couldn't believe that I would come out alive from all this slaughter. It was just a conveyor belt of death ... before the war, I was afraid of seeing dead people, but in a couple of days here we got used to being surrounded by corpses ...

The Germans attacked the observation post I occupied with two soldiers. They apparently noticed the stereoscopic periscope and decided to try to capture everyone in the OP. We shot back but the Germans were already closing in. I reported to Lukomsky [the battalion commander] in the command post that they were closing in from all sides and he said, 'Olezhka, I will now fire on your OP – get down in the trench when you hear the first salvo.' We did so, which is how we got out alive. But this was distorted and glorified in the army newspaper, which said that 'Despising death, Lieutenant Gorodinskiy called down fire on himself' and so on. But that wasn't true. As [Mikhail] Bulgakov [a writer of the era who was constantly censored by the authorities] said, 'Don't read Soviet newspapers' ...

Our regiment lost about 50 per cent of its personnel in the attack. Most were from enemy aircraft attacks.[23]

Early on 8 August, one of Zhukov's mobile groups, moving south to widen the initial breach in the German lines, managed to penetrate the German defences to the east of Sychevka, but the first formations of 2nd Panzer Division were now arriving and were able to intervene on the eastern flank of 1st Panzer Division. These new arrivals linked up with the single battalion of 5th Panzer Division that had been sent in that direction, and alongside 1st Panzer Division these forces fought a series of actions through the day, breaking up one Soviet tank group after another. As had been the case with the tank units that clashed with 5th Panzer Division over the preceding days, lack of coordination cost the Red Army dearly, and further exploitation of the initially successful attack proved impossible.

One of the biggest developments of the day came away from the front line. Hastening back before he had fully recovered from his chest wound, Model resumed command of Ninth Army. With his characteristic acerbic style, he rapidly asserted himself upon the situation, demanding absolute clarity from his subordinates in their reports. The embattled bridgehead on the east bank of the Vazuza was abandoned, and a flurry of orders reached front-line units, resulting in numerous minor withdrawals; by doing so, the units were able to release desperately needed reserves with which to oppose the constant Soviet attacks. During the winter fighting, Model had been very energetic in organising ad hoc *Alarmeinheiten* from rear area units, something that was greeted with great approval by front-line soldiers who, like their equivalents in almost every army in history, had a generally low opinion of those who were serving in the comparative safety of the rear areas, and there was little need for Model to reiterate orders for such measures: every division in his army was now accustomed to this practice, and all available men were already in action. However, Model identified some battalions of labourers from the *Reichsarbeitsdienst* ('Reich Works Department', often abbreviated to *RAD*) and ordered them to be sent into the front line. The men were armed with personal weapons, mainly for protection against Soviet partisans, and their efficacy and survivability in the front line was doubtful. Nonetheless, the situation was desperate enough that every man counted. Heavy fighting continued throughout, with the air assets of both sides intervening from time to time. In places, the Red Army succeeded in forcing the line of the Vazuza, but further exploitation proved almost impossible. When vehicles attempted to make use of a ford across the river, they found that the unseasonal rains had rendered it almost impassable. Sappers succeeded in erecting a bridge, but after just a handful of tanks had crossed, it collapsed and was washed away. The frustrated commanders demanded that pontoon bridges were erected as quickly as possible, but the columns of vehicles and horses carrying the equipment needed for this were stuck in the huge traffic jams on the muddy roads stretching to the east.

Despite these difficulties, the Soviet troops that had crossed the river were steadily reinforced. On 9 August, they succeeded in expanding their bridgehead to a depth of perhaps a mile, but at a great cost. Any intention to concentrate armoured assets in order to achieve a decisive local success failed in the face of the terrible conditions of roads and the general terrain, and the guns of the German 1st, 2nd and 5th Panzer Divisions were able to deal with any Soviet tanks that succeeded in advancing. For the first time since the battle had begun, the sky was clear of clouds, permitting increased air activity, and German bombers struck repeatedly at the tangled concentration of Red Army units struggling to reach and cross the Vazuza. The main cause of concern for the German defenders was a gap between the eastern flank of 1st Panzer Division and the western flank of 2nd Panzer Division, and both formations organised battlegroups for convergent attacks to close the hole. On 10 August, as these two battlegroups commenced their attack, further Soviet units attempted to push south between them. A battalion of German soldiers from 78th Infantry Division had been holding a series of positions across the gap and, having suffered heavy losses in the preceding days, now began to give way as Soviet tanks approached. While officers from both the infantry battalion and the advancing 1st Panzer Division attempted to rally the retreating men, the two German armoured attacks struck into the flanks of the Soviet troops. Several tanks were left ablaze, and the moment of crisis passed.[24] But if the Germans were able to stop Zhukov's forces from advancing, they too found it difficult to advance. Supplies of all kinds were running short as trucks remained stranded in the mud, and an attempt by 1st Panzer Division to attack towards the northeast ran into an array of anti-tank guns and suffered heavy losses for no gain.

This small encounter was an example of the continuing evolution of the Red Army. During the preceding year, the Germans had reassessed their use of anti-tank guns and had concluded that deploying them individually or in small platoon-sized groups was of limited value. Consequently, the concept of the *Pakfront* was developed, with larger groups of guns under the command of a single officer. This person would designate targets to each of the guns, which would then open fire together; as a result, several enemy tanks could be knocked out in the first exchange of fire. The Red Army observed the fighting in the west in 1939 and 1940, and even before the conflict with Germany, there were moves to improve both the quantity and the quality of anti-tank units. A new structure for anti-tank brigades was drawn up and then modified repeatedly, especially in the light of combat experiences after the beginning of hostilities. In particular, the Red Army hadn't anticipated the density of armour used by the Wehrmacht, and the anti-tank brigades were often overwhelmed. In order to improve the strength of these units, they were upgraded to full regiments in late 1941; as both British and German troops had discovered, weapons like the 85mm anti-aircraft gun of the Red Army, with a high muzzle velocity, long range and good accuracy, proved to be highly effective in an anti-armour role, but as dedicated anti-tank guns became more available, many of these weapons were withdrawn from anti-tank formations and redeployed in their original role; their usefulness as anti-tank guns on the battlefield was also limited by their size, making them difficult to deploy quickly, and in any case they were desperately needed to defend against German air attacks. Weaponry of the Soviet anti-tank formations varied from old anti-tank rifles – relatively small-bore weapons with limited penetrating power, but capable of disabling tanks by breaking their tracks and very effective if used in built-up areas, where they could fire down onto the relatively thin deck armour of tanks – to 45mm and 76mm anti-tank guns.[25]

In an attempt to improve the performance of anti-tank troops, Stalin authorised higher rates of pay and cash bonuses for gun crews for each enemy tank that they destroyed. The evolution of anti-tank brigades, regiments and even divisions was still ongoing in the summer of 1942, but the use of these weapons en masse in conscious emulation of the German *Pakfront* was proving to be an increasing problem for the Germans. The Red Army went a step further than the Germans, adding combat engineers to these dedicated anti-tank units – as they deployed, these men would rapidly lay minefields to channel the German armour into selected areas where the massed fire of their *Pakfront* would be most effective. It was commonplace for panzer commanders to go into action with their head and shoulders exposed from the commander's cupola, as it was felt that the increased vulnerability was justified in terms of the greatly improved field of vision, but even if anti-tank rifles were unable to penetrate the hull or turret armour of German tanks, the accuracy of these weapons made them useful in forcing German tank commanders to drop down into their tanks. Forced to rely on their periscopes and viewing slits, they were far less able to respond quickly to developments on the battlefield. Reports of casualties in panzer units often mention officers being killed by head wounds or even by decapitation, and on this occasion it is noteworthy that the leading panzer company lost two officers out of a total of 14 dead and over 30 wounded.[26]

Given the lack of progress by either side, it might have been prudent to call a halt to attacks. For the Red Army, there was no prospect of achieving the advances that had been expected at the outset of the operation, especially now that German armour was operating in the area; conversely, further German counterattacks were equally unlikely to recover the ground that had been lost to Zhukov's initial attack. But Zhukov's stubborn desire to achieve his objectives at all costs dominated his thinking, and he remained determined to throw his formations into action. For the Germans, counterattacks to recover lost positions were a longstanding part of their mode of operation, and they too showed little sign of accepting the new front line. The result would be several more weeks of slaughter in the almost impassable mud.

CHAPTER 8

GRINDING THROUGH SUMMER

On 10 August, the Germans made a new attack to try to improve contact between the panzer divisions by driving back the Soviet forces that had attempted repeatedly to break through towards the south. This time, they launched a more organised and deliberate attack, preceded by 'exemplary' artillery support, but the Red Army had also reinforced its units. By the end of the day, 1st Panzer Division had succeeded in seizing two key hills, though at considerable loss. Fighting continued for the next few days with repeated Soviet attacks, which were all repulsed – as had been the case since the battles around Moscow, the inexperience and lack of initiative of Soviet officers resulted in frontal attacks which, even when supported by artillery bombardments, were unlikely to succeed. While the Soviet units had rather more by way of artillery than during the winter, ammunition remained in short supply for the few guns that had been able to move forward through the mud, and poor reconnaissance resulted in their modest bombardments achieving little. A few days later, the small Soviet bridgehead over the Gzhat River held by II Guards Cavalry Corps also came under concentrated attack. Anti-tank guns brought the small number of German tanks in the attack to a halt, and accurate mortar fire drove the accompanying infantry to ground. After a Stuka bombardment, the German infantry tried again, this time turning the flanks of the cavalry position and threatening to encircle it. The Soviet defenders claimed an improbable 46 German tanks destroyed and five aircraft shot down, but regardless of the true numbers, the shrunken bridgehead managed to beat off the German attacks. Later that day, the cavalry units were extracted and replaced by a rifle division.

On the southern flank of the Soviet assault, the German 2nd Panzer Division was under constant pressure. The most effective tanks serving in the panzer battalion were actually T-34s, captured in the closing days of *Seydlitz*, and when the last T-34 was lost on 9 August it represented a substantial setback. Just two days later, the division suffered another blow when the division commander, Esebeck, was wounded during an air attack. The arrival of five new Pz.IV tanks armed with long-barrelled 75mm guns on 12 August was a huge boost to the panzer battalion's fighting strength, and they were used almost immediately in a counterattack to restore the front line.

Zhukov had held back his tanks with the intention of unleashing them as an exploitation force, with just small groups of tanks accompanying the initial infantry attacks. During both these attacks and subsequent assaults as the exploitation forces attempted to force their way through the German lines, the lack of experience of both tank crews and infantrymen on close cooperation was clear to see. An after-action report criticised the command and control of the mobile groups. The groups rarely took proper steps to concentrate their resources before attacking, and they often received contradictory orders – one group received four completely incompatible sets of instructions within just nine hours, another lost contact with higher commands for two days, and a third was unable to give accurate information on its precise position and floundered around in the muddy terrain to the east of the Vazuza without getting into combat for several days – to make matters worse, its repeated to-and-fro movements choked the roads and degraded them still further.[1]

By the end of 10 August, Zhukov's timetable for a swift capture of his main objectives was in complete disarray and he reconsidered the overall situation. He later speculated on what might have been achieved if he had been given more resources:

> If we had one or two more armies at our disposal, it would have been possible, in cooperation with Kalinin Front, not only to defeat the Rzhev grouping but also the entire Rzhev–Vyazma group of German troops and significantly improve the operational position in the entire western strategic direction. Unfortunately, this real opportunity was missed by the supreme command.
>
> I should add that the supreme commander realised that the unfavourable situation that developed in the summer of 1942 was the result of his personal mistake, made when approving the plan of action for our troops in the summer campaign of this year. And he did not seek to apportion blame to other senior figures in *Stavka* or the general staff.[2]

This assessment is questionable. It presupposes that a further 'one or two armies' could have been made available – while this is possible, it would have been at the expense of other theatres, or by drawing upon the reserves that were being built up with great diligence and which would be used with such decisive effect at Stalingrad. There is also the question of how Zhukov might have used these additional troops, as the road and weather conditions made it almost impossible to use his existing forces effectively. Moreover, it is absurd to blame Stalin for the 'unfavourable situation', which Zhukov states arose because Stalin approved Zhukov's plans for a new offensive. And lastly, Zhukov was guilty of having squandered resources in the past in profligate and wasteful frontal assaults. Just as he blamed Stalin for dispersing the Red Army's resources over too wide an area, he too failed to concentrate the forces of Western Front for a single thrust for most of the year.

In any event, the main objectives of the operation – Rzhev and Sychevka – remained frustratingly out of reach. Losses among Zhukov's tank formations were climbing alarmingly, and although many of these losses were recoverable – tanks that had either been damaged or were stranded due to breakdowns or mud – his forces no longer had the strength to force their way through to Sychevka and Rzhev from the east. The original German front line had been pushed back on a breadth of about 27 miles (45km) and now ran from north to south, before turning sharply to the east. Zhukov turned his attention to this latter part of the line; behind the new north-facing German positions was the small town of Karmanovo, and if this could be captured, it would reduce the risk of further German attacks from the south into the flank of the newly gained territory. An attack in this area also had the benefit of involving relatively fresh units to the south. For the moment, the attempts to bludgeon the German lines defending the eastern approaches to Rzhev and Sychevka were to halt. The front-line trenches near Polunino were barely 300m apart, and no-man's land was strewn with the corpses of dead Soviet soldiers and the wrecks of burned-out tanks. While the German armoured groups were battling with Zhukov's forces to the south, Kalinin Front tried once more to take Hill 200 and break through to Polunino on 10 August. There was bitter fighting all through 10 August, with the German defenders counting an additional 25 tanks destroyed. Stuka dive-bombers intervened with devastating effect on the Red Army troops massing for an attack, but German losses too were heavy.

At the headquarters of Ninth Army, Model too was reviewing the overall situation. The steadily rising casualties of Ninth Army were causing Model and Kluge serious concern. Late on 14 August, the commander of Army Group

Centre spoke to Halder by telephone and painted a grave picture. Halder promised to do what he could to help and phoned back a few hours later: four battlegroups from various formations were being sent to Kluge's embattled armies, together with 72nd Infantry Division from Army Group North. One of the Wehrmacht's premier units, *Grossdeutschland* – currently configured as an infantry division – was already en route from the south.[3]

The intervention of 5th Panzer Division seemed to have stabilised the situation to the east of the Rzhev–Sychevka road, and the deployment of 1st and 2nd Panzer Divisions further south had stopped further Soviet attacks in that direction, even if the German attempts to push back the Red Army had achieved little other than casualties. From the German perspective, there was no sign of Soviet attacks slackening, and Model knew from aerial reconnaissance that a good proportion of the forces opposing him were still trying to get into action through the mud and congested roads. Reconnaissance reports and prisoner interrogations gave an estimate of the Soviet forces facing Ninth Army as being made up of 47 rifle divisions, five cavalry divisions, 18 independent rifle brigades, and 37 tank brigades. Even if all of these units were below establishment strength, they still represented a daunting total. The German infantry divisions that had been driven back by the initial assaults of both Kalinin Front and Western Front had now stopped their retreat and were fighting hard, but even though the constant Soviet attacks were not gaining any ground, the losses of infantry units meant that some sectors were under severe strain. Every German infantry unit had mobilised improvised *Alarmeinheiten* from rear area troops, and this source of emergency reinforcements, increasingly used by the Wehrmacht during the war, was for the moment exhausted. The consequence of redeploying so many rear area personnel into the front line was that their previous tasks – logistics and support – were far harder to carry out, placing still more pressure on the front line. Most of the local reserves that Model had improvised by tactical withdrawals were committed to counterattacks in the days that followed, and by the middle of August, Ninth Army's resources looked dangerously close to being exhausted. From the moment that the crisis began, Model had been asking for reinforcements, and Kluge had done what he could – the reduced scale of *Wirbelwind* had permitted the redeployment of panzer forces, which had proved critical in stopping Zhukov's offensive. But with his infantry units fading away, Model now demanded more help. On 16 August, he sent a signal to Army Group Centre:

Ninth Army is at the end of its strength and must receive three or four more [infantry] divisions. If these cannot be provided, then Army Group [Centre] will have to take responsibility for future developments and must provide detailed instructions as to how the battle is to be continued.[4]

During the winter fighting, army commanders had frequently demanded reinforcements, threatening either disaster or unauthorised retreats unless their requests were met. In many cases this resulted in their dismissal, but Model was high in Hitler's esteem for the manner in which he had stabilised the lines of Ninth Army earlier in 1942, and perhaps he could afford to make such demands with less fear of repercussions. In any event, the diminution of *Wirbelwind* had freed some resources in addition to the panzer divisions, and Kluge was able to send them north. Even if they didn't amount to the three or four divisions that Model had said were vital, they were sufficient to prevent any immediate collapse. Generaloberst Hans-Jürgen von Arnim's XXXIX Panzer Corps headquarters was transferred from Fourth Army to Ninth Army to take command of the units defending the Vazuza. The forces facing the southern flank of Zhukov's attack were under the command of XLVI Panzer Corps, and it received the main body of fresh troops in the shape of 78th Infantry Division, which had been resting behind the front line in Fourth Army's sector. Model was also able to rearrange the divisions already at his disposal. To the northwest of Rzhev, the front line remained relatively quiet, and 206th Infantry Division was transferred from XXVII Corps to the embattled VI Corps around Rzhev itself.

The fighting was becoming a terrible struggle for minimal territory. When the armies on Zhukov's southern flank attacked, the Germans were expecting them, having detected their preparations. The fresh troops of 78th Infantry Division found their lines were put under immediate pressure, and over four days the division reported that it came under attack by two rifle divisions and two tank brigades. Had these attacks been coordinated and made en masse, they might have achieved something; instead, they were defeated in turn. But the German defensive successes came at a price both in terms of casualties and the manner in which units were deployed. From late 1941 until the end of the war, commanders of panzer formations complained bitterly about the manner in which their armoured resources were parcelled out to support infantry units, and this was just such an occasion. On 18 August, the German line facing Zhukov's attempts to reach Karmanovo consisted, from west to east, of 1st Panzer Division, 2nd Panzer Division, 36th Infantry Division, 78th Infantry Division, and 342nd Infantry Division; 1st Panzer Division was forced to loan three tanks to 36th Infantry Division, and another seven tanks in three separate groups to 78th Infantry Division. Many of 1st Panzer Division's remaining tanks were showing signs of battle damage; a period out of the front line was desperately needed to allow for essential maintenance, and such a pause would also allow for vehicles currently in the workshops to be returned to the front line, but for the moment the pressure remained relentless.[5]

While Zhukov's troops ground forward towards Karmanovo, Konev's Kalinin Front gathered its strength to make a new attempt to reach Rzhev. Here, too, logic would surely have dictated that the German defences that had repulsed the first assaults were highly unlikely to crack in the face of renewed attacks, but directed by Zhukov, Konev ordered his army commanders to try once again – Rzhev seemed tantalisingly just out of reach. Lelyushenko's Thirtieth Army regrouped so that it concentrated its forces on its eastern wing; for the renewed assault, six rifle divisions would be supported by three independent rifle brigades and two tank brigades. A further two tank brigades were held as a second echelon to exploit any breakthrough, but an indication of the losses suffered to date can be gained by the strength of one of these brigades – when the assault was renewed, it had just five heavy KV tanks, 12 T-34s and five light T-60s.

Supported by tanks from 143rd Tank Brigade, a regiment of 375th Rifle Division penetrated into a village to the north of Rzhev on 14 August and two days later attempted to push on towards Rzhev itself. They made no headway at all: the Germans had turned every building into a miniature fortress. The neighbouring 243rd Rifle Division seized the ruins of a small village but immediately came under heavy counterattack, and the shattered buildings changed hands eight times over the next few days in a series of increasingly senseless clashes that left the terrain littered with the dead of both sides.

Anatoly Petrovich Schvebig was a tank commander who was tasked with supporting an infantry attack towards the ruins of Rzhev. He later recalled the struggle to keep the tank brigade at anything approaching combat strength:

> Our attack couldn't be sudden – the tanks regularly got stuck in the mud and had to pull each other free. There was no other place where we could attack as the terrain was swampy and the Dobry River, filled with rainwater, became impassable ...
>
> By the end of 15 August, when it seemed that victory was close and only one last push was needed to get us to the eastern outskirts of Rzhev, we had just three light T-60 tanks left in the brigade. Colonel Malygin [the brigade commander] summoned me to his location. 'Anatoly Petrovich,' he said quietly, 'you know how things are. What do you suggest we do?'
>
> 'We could advance to the eastern edge of Rzhev and capture the airfield.'

The brigade commander raised his tired eyes to look at me. 'Only if the repairmen can help us.'

About two hours later, three KV-1 tanks, five T34s, two T-70s and four T-60s were operational. During the fighting from 20 July to 23 August, the specialists in the technical support company returned to service ten KV-1s, 28 T-34s and several light tanks.[6]

While the technical support company struggled to repair damaged tanks, the men of the brigade also did what they could to improvise improvements:

> The Germans laid a lot of minefields and we had to improvise homemade mine trawls. We took KV road wheels and welded metal tongs onto them, and then made something like a sledge and attached it to the front of a T-34 with bars. The spiked wheels detonated mines – the rollers were tough enough to withstand several mines. Other tanks could then follow.
>
> We also had to convert T-34s into flamethrower tanks. Five sets of equipment came from Moscow for our brigade and we installed everything ourselves. The tanks could throw a fiery jet about 100m through a barrel that replaced the normal gun. This weapon burned the Germans out of their bunkers.[7]

Flamethrower tanks were feared by both sides and were high-priority targets for defending anti-tank guns. The tank carrying fuel for the flamethrower was of course easily set ablaze, and the loss rate of these vehicles was often disproportionately high.

Lelyushenko's neighbour to the east was Twenty-Ninth Army, and this too failed to reach its objectives, the attack stalling on the banks of the Volga outside Rzhev. With an average width of about 70m, the river was a substantial barrier, particularly as it was swollen by the recent heavy rain. The village of Polunino, which had been the high-water mark for the initial advance of Kalinin Front, remained a bitterly contested spot, with the Soviet 16th Guards Rifle Division ordered to overcome the German defences. Here, elements of the German 6th Infantry Division clung to the ruins of the village and to the summit of Hill 200, and this account describes both the structure of the German defensive system and the repeated, unimaginative assaults that were thrown at the defences:

> The Russian bombers suddenly attacked Polunino in unprecedented numbers. Tremendous detonations shook the foxholes and the village was set ablaze, with thick clouds of smoke swirling over the positions, which were battered by a hail

of artillery and mortar shells. Then ten, twenty, thirty Russian tanks – T-34s and
KV-1s – moved up and drove over the positions, and the attacks of the Soviet
infantry continued ceaselessly often up to seven times a day. But the German
infantrymen, crouching in the earth as best as the wet terrain would allow, their
uniforms, hands and faces plastered with mud, held out in their foxholes and
separated the Russian infantry from their tanks. The artillery gave staunch
support, firing all the ammunition that could be brought forward. The gunners
frequently smashed the Russian infantry attacks and without this it wouldn't have
been possible to hold the positions. Behind our infantry were the anti-tank and
anti-aircraft guns, and assault guns moved up too to help destroy the Russian
tanks … The Russian losses were very heavy, and the groaning of the wounded in
front of the positions continued all night. Scouting parties that were sent forward
found extraordinary heaps of dead. A foul stench of putrefaction from the dead
Russians lay over the entire terrain.[8]

The weeks prior to the Soviet attack had been put to good use by the defenders,
with carefully devised fire plans that allowed them to concentrate their artillery
fire on advancing Soviet formations; some officers found them reminiscent of the
manner in which defences had been organised in the First World War. In addition
to the defensive efforts of the soldiers on the ground, swift attacks by Stuka
squadrons provided valuable support – operating from airfields close to the front
line, the German bombers were able to intervene repeatedly, and their short
flight times to and from the battlefield reduced their vulnerability to fighter
attack. Indeed, like the ground troops, the Soviet fighter arm was slowly learning
how to fight effectively, and compared to the air cover routinely provided by
western air forces, Soviet control of the battlefield airspace remained relatively
poor until the closing months of the war.

Despite these defensive arrangements and their effectiveness, German losses
continued to climb. By the last week of August, several infantry companies in 6th
Infantry Division were commanded by NCOs. A counterattack to eliminate a
Soviet penetration on the right flank of the division on 13 August failed despite
the supporting fire of the division's artillery and air support – the terrain was
forested and, faced with rising casualties for no gain, the Germans were forced to
make a small tactical withdrawal of their defensive line. The neighbouring 256th
Infantry Division was also forced to concede ground, and the front line inched a
little closer to Rzhev.

A few days later, one company from 6th Infantry Division had to be pulled
out of line due to the losses it had suffered:

The remnants of 58th Infantry Regiment's 2nd Company withdrew from the front line. There were just 15 survivors. They were all shell-shocked, utterly exhausted, filthy, and looked terrible. That evening [late on 16 August] there were barely 1,000 exhausted soldiers left in the trenches manned by the division, and two battalions had just 150 men each. No more than 20 anti-tank guns survived in the division's positions.[9]

Despite this, the grim defence continued to hold, and Grossmann reshuffled his battered battalions to try to prevent collapse of his lines. When reports reached Kalinin Front headquarters that the attacks on Polunino had failed because of poor artillery support – on one occasion, a Red Army infantry battalion was hit by a heavy burst of 'friendly fire' and almost wiped out – Khlebnikov went to Thirtieth Army to investigate. From Lelyushenko's command post, he attempted to contact 16th Guards Rifle Division, but learned that the signal cable seemed to have been cut. He then discovered first-hand the difficulties of mounting large-scale operations in the swampy, heavily forested terrain:

It was already night and it was still raining. Neither horses nor even all-terrain vehicles could travel to the division through these swamps … I went out with a signaller. It was pitch-black, broken from time to time by flashes of lightning, and nothing at all visible in between. We moved forward holding the telephone wire, sometimes in woodland, sometimes in swamps. We fell waist-deep into clay pits and shell craters full of water, and stumbled through bushes. After the first few steps we discarded our raincoats – they were soaked through and solid with mud and just impeded us.

It wasn't easy for us to move 2–3km until we came to a break in the wire. Ahead, we could see flashlights. It was a group of signallers from 16th Guards Rifle Division. They too were looking for the break. We found and spliced the cable. Together with them, at 2am, I reached the division command post.

Colonel [Sergei Alekseevich] Knyazkov, the division commander, was seriously ill but hoped that he would recover enough to continue. He was a good combat commander and would soon become deputy commander of Third Shock Army, but at that moment his health meant he simply couldn't lead the division's assault … [After discussion with Lelyushenko] the artillery commander of the division, Colonel [Petr Grigorevich] Shafranov, was immediately appointed commander of the division and Knyazkov was sent to the rear.[10]

The western side of Polunino was protected by an area of swamp, marked on Soviet maps as impassable, and consequently every attack had been made from the north across ground that was covered by German artillery, mortars and machine-guns. But Shafranov's scouts discovered that there were usable routes through the swamp. The details of the battle that follow are not clear. In Khlebnikov's account, the critical attack took place on 21 August, as part of a general resumption of attacks, whereas the war diary of the German 6th Infantry Division gave a very different account of the fighting. According to Khlebnikov, 16th Guards Rifle Division made a renewed attempt to take the village. While a tank brigade and a rifle regiment simulated another attack from the north, two other regiments moved through the swamp and struck the German defenders from the west. After days of heavy losses, the Soviet soldiers rapidly overwhelmed the startled defenders. This was clearly a relief for the men who had struggled in vain through the mud and machine-gun fire for so many futile attacks, but it raises serious questions about the competence of Knyazkov and his failure to carry out adequate reconnaissance. When he had recovered from his illness, Knyazkov was once more given front-line command, this time with 28th Rifle Division; this was followed by higher posts, as deputy commander of armies or as commander of rifle corps. One can only hope, for the sake of the men under his command, that he learned from his errors at Polunino.

By contrast, the German account describes repeated Soviet attacks being smashed before 6th Infantry Division withdrew in a more or less planned redeployment to a new line codenamed the *Neu-Kolberg Stellung* and makes no mention of a successful Soviet attack on Polunino; the final withdrawal was apparently made on the night of 24–25 August, and the Germans left a desolate landscape behind them:

> The entire field of battle presented an especially terrible picture of death and destruction. The terrain was continuously cratered, pitted by countless explosions. There wasn't a single intact building in any of the villages, and Fedorkovo, Berdikhino, Polunino, Galakhovo and Timofeeva no longer existed. The bitterly contested ground around Polunino was strewn everywhere with spent cartridges, boxes and cans, abandoned and broken weapons, scraps of bandages and equipment, shattered logs and other ragged debris. Over 150 wrecked and burned-out Soviet tanks, clustered here and there in groups or standing in isolation, resulted in the Germans naming the fields the *Panzerfriedhof* [the 'tank graveyard']. And along the gullies and between them, thousands of corpses of dead soldiers were scattered across the trenches and dugouts that had been smashed by tanks and explosions. Many of the corpses were torn apart by explosions or crushed by caterpillar tracks. Unexploded bombs, shells, and grenades were everywhere.[11]

This new defensive line was right on the edge of Rzhev, and the exhausted defenders faced the challenge of constructing new defensive positions while under constant Soviet bombardment. Casualties continued to rise; at one stage, an Obergefreiter ('senior lance-corporal') commanded an artillery company, ultimately directing the fire of three artillery batteries to fight off a Soviet attack and earning himself the Knight's Cross in the process.[12]

Both sides took increasingly tough measures to ensure discipline. As early as 1935, Hitler authorised the creation of *Sonderabteilungen* ('special battalions') for men who were regarded as 'disruptive'; the soldiers were subjected to a regime of harsh discipline, indoctrination lectures, and severely restricted home leave, and those who didn't show the required improvement faced transfer to a concentration camp. After the start of the Second World War, these units were replaced by battalions under the jurisdiction of the military police closer to the front line, and at the end of 1940 a new formation was created, *Bewährungsbataillon 500* ('500th Probation Battalion'). The number of such formations increased, and soldiers convicted of a variety of offences were assigned to them; the battalions were often used in particularly dangerous tasks, and soldiers who distinguished themselves were then permitted to rejoin their original units. One account by an officer in Thirtieth Army wrote about the character of the bitter fighting north of Rzhev, and encounters with men of the penal battalions:

> The fighting went on for every hill, crossroads, isolated building, shed, and fold in the ground. The Germans had adapted all of these for a lengthy defence and points of resistance ... There were cases when after seizing enemy bunkers, German soldiers were found who had been chained to the machine-guns – penal suicide fighters.[13]

This seems an extreme example; usually, the men in penal units were deployed as a group rather than as individuals.

The Red Army was also taking measures to stiffen the resolve of its soldiers. On 28 July 1942, Stalin issued Order 227, which became known as *Na Shagu Nazad* ('not one step back'):

> The enemy throws new forces to the front without regard to heavy losses and penetrates deep into the Soviet Union, seizing new regions, destroying our cities and villages, and violating, plundering and killing the Soviet population ...
>
> The population of our country, who love and respect the Red Army, start to be discouraged in her and lose faith ...

Each commander, Red Army soldier and political commissar should understand that our means are not limitless. The territory of the Soviet state is not a desert, but people ... After the loss of Ukraine, Belarus, the Baltic republics, Donetsk, and other areas we have much less territory, much fewer people, bread, metal, plants and factories ...[14]

The order required each Front to take steps to suppress talk of further retreats and to dismiss and court-martial any officers who permitted unauthorised withdrawals. Each front was to establish *Shtrafnoy Batalyon* ('penal battalions', often abbreviated to *Shtrafbat*) where those who were guilty of breaches of discipline or cowardice would be given an opportunity to redeem themselves. In addition, each army was to use NKVD personnel to create *Zagraditelny Otryad* ('blocking detachments', often abbreviated to *Zagradotryad*), which were to intercept anyone attempting to flee from the front line. These units were authorised to use force, and a report to Beria, the head of the NKVD, stated that in the three months following Order 227, these units had intercepted over 650,000 men. Of these, nearly 26,000 were arrested – the rest were presumably ordered back to the front line or were able to demonstrate that they were moving in accordance with official orders – and a little over 10,000 of those arrested were executed after court martial. In addition, over 1,000 were shot and killed when they refused to stop.[15] Those who were not executed were assigned to a *Shtrafbat* and often used in feint attacks to draw the fire of German defenders while regular troops mounted the real attack. On many occasions, the men were sent into action with only a few of them armed with rifles – the rest were ordered to wait until a rifle-carrying soldier was killed, and then to take up the weapon. The blocking detachments were unpopular with many front-line soldiers – some regarded them with contempt, as their personnel escaped front-line service but enforced it on others, and many soldiers going to the rear area on verbal orders from their officers to request reinforcements, ammunition etc. found themselves caught by the NKVD. By late 1942, the blocking detachments were largely disbanded.

Anatoly Anreevich Solodov was a mortar crewman who found himself sentenced to serve in a penal battalion:

There was a sentry near the bread store, a friend from Kostroma. We couldn't resist climbing in. We found some crumbs of bread and some raisins sprinkled with sugar. He ate them, and in the morning the storekeeper found traces of someone having been there. They asked who had been on guard ... We were both given two years' sentence, him for stealing and me for not stopping him ...

There were many men in the battalion like me, there for all sorts of nonsense ...

I wasn't particularly upset. Why should I be? We all expected to die anyway. Whether it was here or there, it made no difference. Only here, we had men behind us with machine-guns ... We were usually armed with a rifle ... I was there for about a month. At first we were in reserve, but then we went into an attack. I was hit by shrapnel in my knee. I spent about a month in the medical battalion and was then given a certificate; 'I atoned for my guilt with my blood.'[16]

A cavalryman later recalled the punishment that awaited men who had deserted but were then recaptured:

One morning the entire brigade was led into a forest clearing and lined up. We had been brought there to witness the execution of some deserters. They brought two men in undershirts and stood them near a pit that had already been dug. Our platoon was close to them. They lined up a squad of soldiers with rifles and read out the verdict. It seemed to me that the condemned stood there indifferent to their fate. After a volley, they were gone. We were immediately ordered to march past the corpses. The impression was unpleasant, although I had seen many deaths before. I remember that the deserters were from the nearby regions of Ukraine and Belarus. There was dense forest, lush greenery, warm summer weather – perhaps this lured them towards freedom.[17]

Waiting to go into action for the first time in the forests to the north of Rzhev, Boris Gorbachevsky remembered when the order was read to the soldiers:

Listening to the terrible words of the order, everyone seemed turned to stone – I saw how the faces of those in the ranks turned pale ...

I believe that the publication of this order was a timely step, forced by necessity. The order was not intended as reprisals against individual commanders or soldiers, it only threatened those who would allow themselves or others to retreat without orders – be they the highest military commanders or private soldiers. Tough measures were required for the soldiers and commanders to understand their personal responsibility for the fate of the country.

In the evening, everyone in our tent talked about Stalin's order. Some praised it, others cursed ...

[Later in the war] I myself witnessed how the penal units were the first to make frantic assaults on the German defences near Minsk. How many penal companies and battalions did the commander of 1st Belarusian Front, Marshal Rokossovsky, have at his disposal for this purpose? Almost all of them were killed. But it was they who helped break through the strong, echeloned enemy defences – seven rows of trenches – and opened the way for the tank armies. But it should be added that in many cases the NKVD, which controlled the penal units, showed complete arbitrariness.[18]

It wasn't just Soviet soldiers on the ground who were suspected of attempting to avoid hazardous service. The air units assigned to provide support for the attacks towards Rzhev and Sychevka had 400 fighter aircraft at the beginning of the operation, but this number declined rapidly. A total of 51 were lost due to combat, and 89 were reported to be unavailable due to mechanical problems. An internal report in *Stavka* interpreted this in an ominous manner:

This is a sign of plain sabotage, of saving one's own skin on the part of some of the air force staff, who are striving to avoid combat.[19]

There were suggestions that, as was the case with ground soldiers, a penal battalion of aviators should be created. In reality, spare parts were in very short supply, and the number of aircraft reported as available at the beginning of the operation was probably exaggerated – commanders were fearful of being held responsible for lack of preparation, even when this was completely out of their hands, but their over-optimistic reports about spare parts and other supplies were then used against them when their units suffered from shortages.

On 23 August, Zhukov's Western Front's Twentieth Army threw its last reserves into the battle for Karmanovo. Lieutenant General Maks Andreevich Reyter, the army commander, issued dire threats to his division and regiment commanders, telling them that they would pay personally if they failed to achieve success. Nikolai Avraamovich Guzhva was a senior NCO in a rifle regiment, and his experience was replicated thousands of times by men on both sides of the front line:

As we got closer to Karmanovo the forest came to an end – there was a meadow, an open field with a small rivulet, and then Karmanovo on some high ground. They had fortified the place, though just a few machine-guns would have been sufficient to cut us down. All the buildings in Karmanovo were made of brick and were like bunkers. We attacked, maybe a thousand of us charging together. I was seriously wounded in the thigh, just above the knee. I shouted to Nazarenko (the commander of 1st or 2nd Company, I can't remember which), 'Leave me, carry on.' It didn't hurt so I tried to move a little, and screamed – the bone was broken.

I managed to crawl into a trench. I lay there all day under machine-gun fire. Terrible machine-gun fire, shredding the bushes above me. I was very afraid of being wounded again by the Germans. An ambulance came up from the rear and picked me up, and drove me 5km to a field hospital. There was the most terrible bombing ... The doctors and a nurse worked 24 hours a day, not less ... They brought in a boy with curly blond hair and blue eyes and put him next to me. He was moaning, but in the morning he was gone ... A train arrived and we travelled for two hours. There were terrible numbers of wounded ... I asked, 'Did we take Karmanovo?' 'Which Karmanovo?' [replied someone.] 'Nobody knows anything, there's only death there! The villages are all burned to the ground.'[20]

Supported by the neighbouring Fifth Army, VIII Guards Rifle Corps and VIII Tank Corps finally secured control of the ruins. The Germans had already prepared their positions for such an event and fell back to a new, straighter defensive line. To the north, the Soviet Thirty-First Army captured Zubtsov, an objective that it had been expected to seize in the first couple of days of the operation. Here too, the German forces had prepared a new line and fell back in good order and there was no possibility of a breakthrough.

Western Front's armies were approaching exhaustion, but Konev's Kalinin Front was still prepared to make one last attempt to take Rzhev – the capture of Polunino might have created a small opportunity for success, and after all the casualties for so little gain, one final attempt seemed to be justified. After his original training as a mortarman and then assignment to an anti-tank gun crew, Boris Gorbachevsky found himself serving as an ordinary infantryman when the time came for his baptism of fire. He reflected on this with the grim humour of soldiers in the armies of every nation throughout history:

'A clever man is in the artillery, a dandy is in the cavalry, a drunkard is in the navy, and a fool – in the infantry.' Well, so I was in the infantry.[21]

On 24 August, Gorbachevsky's division moved forward and took up positions in trenches and foxholes. As they handed over their greatcoat bundles, they were issued with helmets, but there weren't sufficient helmets for all the men. As it grew light, the assault began:

High above us, with a whistle and a roar, the fiery arrows of Katyusha rockets flew past. The noise increased as our bombers and attack aircraft got down to business and struck the enemy's trenches. It looked great, just as it should be! It was all going to plan. Huge columns of black smoke and red flames rose from the villages that we were about to take – what a heartening sight! Tanks with soldiers riding on their backs were moving out of the forest, and I quickly counted at least 30. Two columns swept past the trench line and moved forward rapidly …

A green flare shot up. The commander's voice echoed in my head: 'Follow me! Forward! Into battle!'

How difficult it was to get off the ground. It seemed as if we were half-buried and couldn't move our arms or legs … Time stretched strangely and moved in fits and starts, and I glanced up at the bright sky, the wonderful field – and gritting my teeth, already not thinking about anything, almost unconscious, I rose from my foxhole, my obedience to duty pushing me out and forward, and suddenly I was running with everyone else, head bowed, protected by my helmet as we had been taught – bent low, my rifle pushed forward with fixed bayonet. I hurried to keep up with those running nearby and like everyone else I screamed in a daze, cold sweat on my forehead under the helmet. I strained my lungs and shouted 'Urrah!' – and this cry gave us some new strength, muffled our fear. We attacked head-on, in the second wave – in front of us, others were hurrying forward, and others behind us – if we could, we all tried to follow the tanks, hoping for their protection … Forward, up a hill for 300m, we had already come more than halfway! And then the German trenches opened fire. A destructive fire that increased every minute struck the attackers with machine-gun bursts. The hoarse sound of mortars joined the machine-guns. Artillery thundered. Huge fountains of earth shot up high, bearing aloft the living and the dead. Thousands of shell fragments tore into us like poisonous scorpions, tearing at our flesh and the earth …

Ahead, the tanks with mounted infantry passed through the minefields successfully and approached the enemy line, firing at the bunkers while moving. Now they would put everything right, they would break into the German fortifications and shell them, they would clear the trenches. Suddenly, bombers appeared over the battlefield from the direction of Rzhev. Confidently they set to work on the tanks. One, then another, a third – they burst into flames from direct hits, enveloped in black and red; but the rest dispersed quickly and continued to move forward. The bombers flew in waves. The first activated its siren and dived, dropped its bomb on its target and soared away. Behind him came a second, third, fourth – even a tenth, circling over the tanks that had dispersed … After that terrible day, I couldn't bear the wild, bestial scream of the dive-bombers. Their howl tore your head to pieces, chilled your soul, plunged you into paralysed confusion. Even after the war, I never dared go to the zoo: it seemed to me that if I heard an animal roar, I would collapse.[22]

Under heavy fire, Gorbachevsky and his comrades were forced to take cover. The first task of the German defenders, to separate the attacking infantry from their tanks, had succeeded. Further waves of Soviet infantry moved forward and were cut down by defensive fire. Gorbachevsky was hit by a shell fragment and briefly lost consciousness. When he awoke, the attack was effectively over. The tanks that had survived the Stuka attack had disappeared, and the field was covered with mounds of dead and wounded. In just a few brief hours, Gorbachevsky's division, which had been completing its assembly and training for the past three months, lost nearly a third of its personnel for no gain. He later learned the full scale of the casualties while waiting to be evacuated to a field hospital:

> Our 1st Rifle Company ... no longer existed. Of the 136 men, just eight riflemen remained in the ranks. The rest were killed or wounded. Our commander, Senior Lieutenant Sukhomirov, was killed. The commissar was seriously wounded by shrapnel and sent to a field hospital. Of the three platoon commanders, two were killed. The fate of the 45mm gun battery in which I served for such a short time was also tragic. The gunners rolled their guns forward with the infantry. The Stukas bombed both the men and the guns. Many died ... Osip Osipovich, the commander of the artillery battery, was wounded by shrapnel in the buttock and somehow got out of the battle. He now lay on his stomach, groaning pitifully, waiting to be sent to the hospital.
>
> Someone said that our cook waited for a long time for the return of the company and several times he reheated a good lunch for our commander. A long time passed but nobody came back and the cook, realising what happened, wept and didn't touch the food ...
>
> Years later, I learned that after two months of fighting, only 200 men out of the original 3,000 officers and men of 711st Rifle Regiment remained in the ranks.[23]

Gorbachevsky's account of his division's attack highlights several factors that were continuing problems for the Red Army. The initial artillery bombardment might have looked impressive, but the heavy defensive fire from the German positions showed how ineffective it had been. When Soviet tanks moved forward, they had a few soldiers riding on their hulls, but they made little attempt to coordinate their movement and attack with the infantry of Gorbachevsky's division; without proper infantry support, the tanks that survived the Stuka attack disappeared into the depths of the German lines where they were destroyed piecemeal, while the infantry following them was held up by defensive fire and failed to overcome the German defences without tank support. The heavy artillery fire from German guns that descended upon the attacking division shows that, just as the initial bombardment failed to suppress the German front-line positions, it also failed to silence German guns further to the rear. The intervention of the Luftwaffe with Stuka dive-bombers highlighted the failure of Soviet aviation to contest the airspace over the front line – these same dive-bombers had been greatly outclassed in combat against British fighters in the west, but continued to serve on the Eastern Front throughout the war, and ground units lacked anti-aircraft weapons that might have driven them off. The criticism of units not exploiting their initial successes in previous attacks now resulted in successive waves being pushed forward in dense formations, which were slaughtered by German fire. The reports about the shortcomings of previous attacks might have identified several failures, but it would take time for those lessons to be learned, and in the meantime, the Red Army's front-line troops continued to pay a heavy price.

In accounts written during the Soviet era, the 'First Rzhev–Sychevka Operation' was deemed to come to an end on either 23 or 24 August. In reality, no clear orders were issued for Kalinin and Western Fronts to cease assaults, and as is described below, the attacks continued almost without a pause. The battlegroups of 1st Panzer Division described occasional reductions in the intensity of Soviet attacks, but no cessation of such assaults – on 26 August, the division reported that the situation was once more 'critical', with the strength of its panzergrenadier battalions badly depleted, and it was only through the intervention of Stukas that the line was held. One battalion lost all its officers apart from the commander and one Leutnant.[24] Further attacks the following day resulted in the outskirts of one village being seized by the Red Army, and 1st Panzer Division lacked the strength to drive the attackers back – a measure of how the battle had degenerated into fighting for the ruins of a few huts on the edge of a village, with little to show for the casualties that continued to mount on both sides. The losses of Grossmann's 6th Infantry Division on the northern edge of Rzhev were so heavy that it had to be withdrawn from the front line and replaced by 253rd Infantry Division, which had been holding a far quieter sector of front line, but implementing this redeployment proved difficult. The first battalion of 6th Infantry Division was extracted on 30 August, but the staff of the parent regiment suffered casualties when attempting to pull out; the officers were travelling in a truck loaded with munitions when it was hit by Soviet artillery. Elements of the exhausted division remained in Rzhev for much of September. Locations marked on maps as factories or other buildings were little more than a few ruins still standing in an almost continuous field of craters.

Casualties to date were huge for both sides. By 17 August, Model's Ninth Army had lost over 20,000 men killed, wounded or missing, and losses were more than double that figure by the end of the month. The Red Army's casualties were far higher. Direct comparisons are difficult because the reporting periods for the two sides did not coincide, but by early September the combined losses of Kalinin and Western Fronts were at least 192,000, and according to some accounts exceeded 300,000 men.[25] The gain for Zhukov and Konev for this appalling cost was minimal – the front line had moved to the outskirts of Rzhev, and the Germans had been driven back on a fairly broad front to the east of the city, but the key objectives of the operation – Rzhev and Sychevka – remained in German hands. Slowly, the fighting died down through utter exhaustion. Characteristically, Model spent much of the battle visiting his divisions, sometimes joining the troops in their front-line positions; by contrast, there is no record of Konev or Zhukov ever travelling further forward than the headquarters of their armies and divisions.

Despite their clumsy nature, the Soviet attacks often resulted in 'tank fear', with German infantry refusing to hold their positions in the face of armoured attacks unless they too were supported by tanks or at least anti-tank guns. Fehn, the commander of 5th Panzer Division, had in the past suggested that in such cases, infantrymen should allow the Soviet armour to pass through (or over) their positions and should then resume combat to separate Soviet infantry from the advancing tanks, which could then be destroyed further to the rear by his division. In response, infantry commanders protested that they were under standing orders to prevent any Soviet penetration of their lines. Such orders were perhaps easier to issue than to follow, particularly for the exhausted infantrymen whose ranks grew ever thinner, and who had to face repeated waves of Soviet attacks. Even when German tanks were present, the infantry often showed an unwillingness to face the intensity of battle, as a reinforced panzer company from 5th Panzer Division found when it attempted to mount a counterattack with elements of 87th Infantry Division at the end of August:

The attack was from Snamenskoye towards the northeast and rapidly reached the bank of the Volga. However, the terrain was singularly unsuited for a tank attack. The opposite bank was higher and from there the enemy could oppose our attack from three sides. A long-barrelled Pz.III was shot up during this attack. The tanks halted about 400m from the Volga and waited for the infantry to move up, but 90 minutes later they still hadn't appeared. Zobel's company drove back to bring them forward, and then moved up again. By now, most of the tanks were taking hits from the opposite bank. As the infantry still hadn't appeared, the remaining mobile tanks pulled back to the northeast edge of Snamenskoye and spent the night in defensive positions. Late on 28 August 87th Infantry Division ordered a new attack for the following morning at 0330. Major Seidensticker argued with all his strength against the renewed deployment of tanks in terrain that was so unsuitable for them. But the attack and its support by tanks was ordered from the army headquarters and it was only due to Oberst Decker (later our division commander and at that time the panzer liaison officer at Ninth Army headquarters) that all of Wenske's company … wasn't also deployed.

The attack started at the ordained time and proceeded just as on the preceding day. A long-barrelled Pz.III took a direct hit from artillery and burned out and another was knocked out by enemy anti-tank fire. In total seven tanks were completely destroyed, five of them set ablaze. Another eight tanks had severe damage. In the two days, two of the battalion's NCOs were killed and 28 personnel wounded.[26]

A significant change occurred on the Soviet side of the line on 26 August. Stalin appointed Zhukov Deputy Supreme Commander, a role that would see him move to whichever sector was deemed to be the most critical. At that time, in spite of the intensity of the battles around Rzhev, the real point of crisis was far to the south at Stalingrad, and Zhukov departed to oversee operations in that sector. Konev was moved from Kalinin Front to Western Front. In his place, Lieutenant General Maksim Alekseevich Purkaev, formerly commander of Third Shock Army, inherited command of Kalinin Front. In an attempt to improve coordination between neighbouring units, Twenty-Ninth and Thirtieth Armies were transferred from the control of Kalinin Front to Western Front on 29 August, but Konev seems to have had growing doubts about continuing the bloody assaults. As soon as he took command of Western Front, he ordered his southern flank units to cease their attacks and to take up a defensive posture, but this was only a temporary measure. On 4 September, the Soviet Fifth Army tried once more to attack near Gzhatsk; fighting continued for two or three days, with no significant change in the front line.

Konev called for a brief pause in operations along his entire front on 5 September, in an attempt to allow ammunition stockpiles to be restored and for the battered front-line units to regroup. However, he clearly felt that there was still a possibility that Rzhev could be captured, and he requested additional artillery and air assets for a renewed assault. On 9 September, the fighting began again with renewed artillery bombardments, and the Red Army battered its way into the edge of Rzhev. Counterattacks followed, with further heavy losses on both sides. The struggle for control of the devastated streets was as pointless as the similar fighting for the ruins of Stalingrad, but neither side was able to disengage. Outside the city, there were repeated attempts by the Red Army to eliminate a German foothold on the northern bank of the Volga. Nikolai Petrovich Vershinin was a tank crewman who, like Ashot Kazaryan, was in a formation equipped with Lend-Lease tanks:

As luck would have it, the brigade was equipped with American tanks – they gave us 20 four-man M3 'Stuart' tanks and a similar number of seven-man M3 'Lee' tanks. I got the first model. A tank brigade armed with British tanks was nearby. I must say that none of us were taught anything, we were just assigned to a tank, and that was it. We took them from the railway and formed up in our units a few hours later. We were given shells and ammunition for the machine-gun and an entrenching tool, but there was no time to get to grips with the tank. The driver tried to figure out the instruments instinctively, but couldn't understand them all. Although the Stuart was a four-man tank, we had no commander, because we had three men per crew for light tanks [i.e. the gunner and vehicle commander roles were combined].

We attacked along the left [north] bank of the Volga, with the Germans on the far bank. The M3 light tank was just an iron box with poor visibility. I couldn't get comfortable with the periscope at all and the driver was struggling with the steering levers. There were several small villages in the area and for some reason or other our command demanded the immediate liberation of one of them. We couldn't really see any important reason for this. We approached the start line and I still couldn't see anything, and gave instructions to the driver instinctively. We moved into an entrenched position and stayed there for three days while the terrain and enemy positions were reconnoitred. Then the vehicle commanders were taken forward for familiarisation. The scouts told us that we could use some trees and bushes in front of the village for cover and would not come under artillery fire. We paid dearly for their mistake when this proved to be inaccurate.

After this reconnaissance we returned to the tanks, lined up in formation and advanced. As soon as we reached the bushes, the formation began to break down – after all, we hadn't mastered the American tanks. Artillery bombardment of the German positions began and the wooden houses still standing in the village caught fire, their smoke interfering with our field of vision. And then we were ordered to attack. As soon as we moved along the bushes, we came under concentrated anti-tank artillery fire. Most of the light Stuarts were quickly shot up. Our tank was lucky – we weren't hit and entered the village. The Germans chose not to engage in close-quarter combat and retreated.[27]

The light Stuart tank was intended for reconnaissance rather than this form of attack, and even by the summer of 1942 was regarded as too underpowered. Its use in a formal attack such as this was certain to result in heavy losses. While many Soviet veterans were disparaging about the tanks sent to the Soviet Union from Britain and America, they were also critical of some of their own vehicles. Aleksander Vasilevich Bodnar recalled the variable quality of replacement tanks:

[Replacement] T-34s arrived, but unfortunately they came from the Stalingrad factory and their road wheels had no tyres. They rattled terribly. I fought in just such a machine. A lot of T-60s came from Gorky. There were very few KV-1s because Leningrad had stopped producing them and the Chelyabinsk factories weren't fully operational yet. So our KV-1s were old tanks that had been repaired.[28]

When his tank battalion went into action, Bodnar saw first-hand how clumsy the Soviet attacks were:

I remember we were maybe 1.5km behind the [infantry] battle formation and suddenly we were in a field strewn with our dead and wounded. Young guys with Guards badges, in new uniforms. A German machine-gunner was in a bunker and mowing down our men. We advanced across no-man's land awkwardly. The ordinary soldiers were ready for anything but their commanders didn't know how to attack correctly. It was obvious that they needed to bring up mortars, any kind of artillery, to suppress this machine-gun. But no, the commanders continued to urge the men, 'Forward! Forward!' It was a hot day. I remember a nurse running around the field shouting, 'Oh, good people, help me! Help me move them into the shade!' I helped her move some of the wounded. Most were in a state of shock, unconscious, and it was difficult to see who was wounded and who was already dead. It left a lasting impression. What losses we were suffering and how the war was developing! In later years I never saw such inept leadership, that a whole clearing full of people died from the fire of just one machine-gun ... We really didn't know how to fight back then ...

[Near the village of Krivtsy] three tanks remained in the battalion: two T-34s and one T-60, the rest had been destroyed ... The battalion commander called me and said, 'Son, I have nothing left to command. You're to press on. Take the two T-34s and the T-60 ... and try to break into Krivtsy at night and stay there. The infantry will move up in the morning.' That was our mission. In front of the village was a small river with a bridge. As a rule, the Germans mined these bridges. The river was so swampy that if we went through it we would get bogged down and wouldn't be able to complete our mission. I decided to take a risk and 'sacrifice' the T-60 – if it passed over the bridge, that meant it wasn't mined. We crossed the river … We approached the village and came under machine-gun fire. We started firing back with our machine-guns. I wanted to fire the main gun but had to stick my head out of the hatch to check … I could see Dolgushin's tank was burning and thought, 'Why aren't you bailing out?' As I looked, someone leaped out and I thought, 'Thank God!' I didn't really think about myself. I was left with one T-60 and one T-34 on the outskirts of the village. In the early morning while it was still cool, maybe at about 0600, the Germans launched a counterattack. I saw a dense line of Germans walking forward, dressed in overcoats with machine-guns and carbines. I mowed them down with a machine-gun and shreds of greatcoats flew into the air … I held out. We shot up five tanks. They couldn't do anything because they were Pz.III and Pz.IV tanks and I was in a T-34. They couldn't penetrate the frontal armour of my tank …

In the afternoon there was a knocking on the hull of the tank and a soldier told me, 'Lieutenant Bodnar, here's a note from the battalion commander.' I told him to pass it through the hatch. It said, 'Son, the *Katyushas* will play at 1700. As they fire, try to break through with the infantry to the opposite side of Krivtsy.' …

And so we attacked. I could see sunlight on the opposite edge and all I wanted to do was get there, to the open ground … And as soon as I thought that, I saw in the viewer – a German tank gun turning towards me! We were hit in the side by a shell. The driver shouted, 'Commander! Radio operator Tarasov's been killed!' I bent over Tarasov – he was blackened, the shell had torn through him. Another blow! The tank stalled and burst into flames. We had to save ourselves from the fire. I threw open the hatch and shouted to the crew: 'Bale out!' Three of us got out. The dead man remained in the tank.[29]

Bodnar was wounded in his leg, and he and the other two surviving crewmen lay in a potato field next to their tank. When he saw that the fire had gone out, Bodnar ordered his driver back to the tank – abandoning a functional tank might have resulted in all of them being sent to a penal battalion. He told the driver to restart the tank and drive over to them so that they could try to get in through the escape hatch under the vehicle, but instead the driver turned tail and drove off. Bodnar and Slepov, the other surviving crewman, found an old dugout where they took shelter. A civilian Russian woman helped Bodnar crawl back to the Soviet lines.

Finally, fatigue and casualties brought the attacks to an end. The front line had moved closer to Rzhev and the northern edge of the city was now a bitterly contested battleground. The attempts to cut the long German lines of communication running up to the city from the south were all defeated, but here too the Red Army had gained ground. Nevertheless, the price paid for this gain was huge. On the German side, losses were also heavy, though not as bad. The exhausted men of 2nd Panzer Division reported that they had lost 26 tanks during the fighting, mainly the old Pz.38(t)s and Pz.IIIs, and claimed the destruction of 88 Soviet tanks. A steady stream of replacement vehicles had allowed the division to remain operational; a total of 14 Pz.IVs with long-barrelled 75mm guns and 18 with the less penetrative short-barrelled 75mm gun arrived during the fighting. In addition, replacement Pz.IIIs also arrived; although their 50mm guns were less effective, the experienced tank crews were able to put them to good use at close range in woodland. Nonetheless, the rising toll of experienced officers and men represented a huge loss and the fresh troops from Germany were inadequate replacements, as men in the division's anti-tank battalion noted:

> The replacement drafts from the *Ersatzheer* ['Replacement Army'] were relatively poorly trained. *Panzerjäger-Ersatz-* and *Ausbildungsabteilung 17*, which was responsible for our battalion, suffered badly from a shortage of weapons and training equipment, particularly in terms of trucks. All the young soldiers were therefore gathered together in the division's newly established *Feldersatzbataillon-82* in Melechovno ...
>
> In addition to general basic training, which covered all types of weapons – infantry training including with machine-guns – the main training was with the 37mm anti-tank gun. Training was to a small extent based upon experiences in the Polish and French campaigns, but was inadequate for the circumstances encountered later in Russia as it took too little account of battlefield conditions ... The 50mm anti-tank gun was only available in small numbers and was therefore regarded as something of a *Wunderwaffe* ['wonder weapon'] ... No value was placed at that time on training for night and woodland fighting.[30]

The significance of the terrible fighting of August has been subject to numerous interpretations. In purely tactical terms, the battles were undoubtedly a success for the Wehrmacht, as the territory gained by the Red Army came at a disproportionate price, and none of the Soviet gains could be regarded as of more than local value. The impact of the fighting on the overall situation on the Eastern Front is harder to assess. The diversion of several divisions from their planned deployment in *Wirbelwind* undoubtedly reduced the scope of the planned German operation, which was ultimately abandoned in late August without having achieved its objectives, but the real controversy centres on whether this phase of the fighting for Rzhev had a critical impact further afield. There could be little doubt by August that the key theatre for 1942 was in the south, with the German drive towards Stalingrad and the Caucasus. Did Zhukov's pressure on Model's Ninth Army divert German resources from that sector? Zhukov and others certainly took this view in their memoirs, and this became part of accepted Soviet historiography.

But any such assessment requires consideration of how the Germans might have used additional resources in the south. Throughout the summer, Halder's diary entries repeatedly mentioned the impact of logistic problems on Wehrmacht operations in the push towards Stalingrad and the Caucasus – the impression is that fuel shortages in particular constrained German plans at least as much as enemy action. At the time, all of the supplies for the German advance had to be channelled across a single railway bridge over the Dnepr River in Ukraine, and the lines to and from this bridge were often running at full capacity. Had even more German troops been deployed in the south, the difficulties of keeping them supplied adequately would have been even greater. And the resources that the Red Army devoted to the battles around Rzhev would also have been available for redeployment in the south to oppose the Germans.

The failure of the Red Army to advance a relatively short distance is striking, and several factors contributed. The German defences benefited from having been in place for several months; positions had been prepared in depth, with extensive minefields and barbed wire entanglements. Careful fire plans had been drawn up for German artillery, allowing gunners to bring advancing Soviet units under heavy fire after they had been channelled into deadly killing zones by the minefields and wire obstacles. Nonetheless, the losses suffered by Ninth Army escalated steadily through the fighting, and Model, Kluge and Halder were all concerned that the strength of the defenders might run out, allowing the Red Army to make a key breakthrough – in such a situation, with no further reserves available, the entire position of Army Group Centre might have begun to unravel.

The terrain and weather also played a major role in the outcome of the battles. There were few good roads on the axes selected for the Soviet attack, and in terrain that was dominated by forests and swampy ground, this was a huge constraint; in particular, it repeatedly hindered the ability of the Red Army to move forward its artillery and exploitation groups. The unexpectedly rainy weather had a major impact, making all movement far harder. While the weather was largely an unpredictable factor, the failure of Zhukov and Konev to take proper account of the poor road network was a major oversight.

The performance of Red Army officers at middle and lower levels was also far from what was required. The initial attacks, prepared over several weeks, were often successful, but the ability of army, division and regiment headquarters to improvise further plans, particularly in the face of setbacks, was still very poor. As Khlebnikov's account described, even officers widely regarded as good leaders showed little initiative in conducting proper reconnaissance and instead threw their men forward in wave after wave. The soldiers of their units paid for their lack of expertise with their blood.

CHAPTER 9

1942, PREPARING FOR OPERATION *MARS*

The pause in the fighting around Rzhev that was brought by exhaustion and catastrophic casualties didn't last long. Even as the last remnants of the shattered armies of Kalinin and Western Fronts made their final attempts to capture a few more metres of ground, plans were being made for a major new offensive.

The closing weeks of 1942 would be dominated by the development of two major Red Army operations against the German forces in and around Stalingrad – Operation *Uranus*, the great counteroffensive that resulted in the encirclement of the German Sixth Army in the city, and Operation *Saturn*, the intended exploitation of this breakthrough, subsequently reduced in scale to *Malyi Saturn* ('Little Saturn'). However, there were other operations that were also named after planets. In the third week of September, *Stavka* gave approval for Thirty-Ninth Army, part of Kalinin Front, to attack the area west of Rzhev with the intention of destroying the German 87th Infantry Division. One account of this operation assigns it the codename *Venus*; when the attack began it drove back the German infantry and eliminated a bridgehead on the northern bank of the Volga, but as had been the case throughout the year, the amount of territory gained was small compared to the cost.[1]

Venus may have been the first Soviet operation named after a planet – though few sources give the attack by Thirty-Ninth Army this designation – but a far larger operation in the central sector would follow. The initial planning of Operation *Mars* remains the subject of debate and controversy, and even 80 years after the event, many of the official records, particularly relating to the plans of Kalinin Front, have not been released. The reasons for this are not clear, but probably relate to the manner in which Soviet historiography attempted to portray what followed. Was *Mars* a great, if costly, contribution to the Red Army's successes in and around Stalingrad, by tying down so many German divisions in Army Group Centre? Or was it a disastrous defeat, costing the Red Army tens of thousands of casualties for no significant gain?

The intentions of the Red Army in *Mars* are not the only point of controversy. The date at which the operation was first conceived remains unclear. In September, Zhukov returned to Moscow several times from the Stalingrad sector for one of a series of conferences held by Stalin and *Stavka* to discuss the overall situation and to draw up plans for the future. It was at this stage that planning began in earnest for the counteroffensive that would encircle Stalingrad, and Zhukov later described how a meeting on 12 September led to the plans for what would become *Uranus*:

> The terrain on the sector of Stalingrad Front was extremely unfavourable for our troops to mount an offensive: it was open and cut by deep ravines, where the enemy could shelter from artillery fire. The enemy had occupied a number of commanding heights and had long-range artillery surveillance, allowing him to direct fire in all directions ...
>
> 'What does Stalingrad Front need to eliminate the enemy's line of communication and connect with Southeast Front?' asked Stalin.
>
> 'At least one more full-strength army, a tank corps, three tank brigades and at least 400 howitzers. In addition, for the duration of the operation, it will be necessary to concentrate at least one additional air army.' Vasilevsky fully supported my estimate.
>
> The supreme commander took out his map with the location of the *Stavka* reserves and examined it for a long time. Aleksander Mikhailovich [Vasilevsky] and I moved away from the table to one side and spoke very quietly about the fact that, apparently, it was necessary to seek some other solution.
>
> 'And what is this "other" solution?' asked Stalin, suddenly raising his head. I had never known Stalin had such acute hearing. We returned to the table. 'This is what we'll do,' he continued, 'go to the general staff and think carefully about what needs to be done in the Stalingrad area – where and what troops can be transferred to strengthen the Stalingrad grouping and at the same time think about the Caucasian Front ...'
>
> The next day, Vasilevsky and I worked with the general staff. All our energy was focussed on the possibility of conducting a large-scale operation, rather than using the reserves available on local operations ... Having looked through all the

possible options, we decided to offer Stalin the following plan of action: first, continue to wear down the enemy with active defence; and then, to start preparing for a counteroffensive ...

As for the specific plan of the counteroffensive, naturally we couldn't prepare details in one day, but it was clear to us that the main blows should be delivered on the flanks of the Stalingrad grouping, covered by the Romanian troops.[2]

Despite the costly failure to eliminate the Rzhev Salient during the summer, Zhukov in particular continued to believe that the Germans had suffered heavy losses and must be close to breaking. Another major effort in this sector would surely result in a substantial victory. With the German Army Group Centre broken and forced to retreat, the German lines to the north and south would be exposed – and, of course, the Red Army would finally capture Rzhev and eliminate any lingering possibility of the Wehrmacht attacking towards Moscow. Although Zhukov makes no mention of it in his account of the discussion on 12 September, a resumption of operations against the Rzhev Salient must have been considered at this time. Kuzma Nikitovich Galitsky, who at the time was commander of Kalinin Front's Third Shock Army, later recalled receiving orders for a wide-ranging operation in the central sector codenamed *Mars* during October, and preparations throughout the region for renewed attacks took place throughout the autumn. Zhukov's memoirs suggest that discussions about *Mars* occurred much later, on 13 November – he describes how Vasilevsky was appointed to oversee *Uranus*, while he was to coordinate the renewed attack at Rzhev.

The destruction of the Rzhev Salient had become almost an obsession for the Soviet high command in general, and – it seems – Zhukov in particular. The German forces in the region had made no attempt to advance towards Moscow since the previous winter, and given the changes that had occurred in the intervening months, it seems highly unlikely that there was any serious prospect of Kluge's Army Group Centre driving back the Red Army units opposing it and once more threatening the Soviet capital. Yet it seems that the possibility of such an assault continued to trouble Stalin and his immediate subordinates. The huge investment that the Red Army had made in terms of its losses in the area may also have played a part in the ongoing planning. Simply to leave the sector intact would be acceptance that the terrible losses of the summer and autumn were being written off and had achieved nothing. If the salient could finally be overrun, it would be possible to claim that these casualties had been a necessary, if heavy, price that had to be paid as preparation for the definitive defeat of the Germans.

The events of the preceding winter almost certainly played a part in the thinking of Stalin and Zhukov. Both the Wehrmacht in November 1941 and the Red Army the following month had made rapid advances through this sector, so in principle at least it should have been possible to repeat that achievement. There were several important considerations that were ignored or not recognised. The Wehrmacht had benefited from a weak Soviet defensive line in November, and the Red Army had benefited from an even weaker German defensive line in December. Once both sides had been able to establish proper defences – the Red Army in early December and the Germans at the end of the year – it became almost impossible to achieve similar advances. Moreover, both the Wehrmacht and Red Army were ultimately brought to a halt by logistic difficulties as much as enemy resistance – the terrain and importantly the road network were not conducive to rapid advances.

Having recovered from the wounds he received in his baptism of fire, Boris Gorbachevsky returned to the front line in October. He had been promoted to 'cadet sergeant' and was assigned to 220th Rifle Division, a different formation from the one with which he had attempted to attack towards Rzhev earlier in the year. Despite his minimal front-line experience, he was appointed platoon commander and ordered to join his men on the northeast outskirts of the city, where the Red Army's units were still hugely depleted after their recent battles:

> You couldn't imagine worse weather – cold, penetrating autumn rains driven by a sharp wind. I walked close to no-man's land. Here, near the forest, there had been a road from Tver for centuries; now it was smashed, cratered and pitted, overgrown with weeds, and all along my route – in ditches and craters – corpses were strewn around in various poses, both ours and Germans, not cleared since the summer when there was heavy fighting here. It seemed that the cold clay earth preserved the corpses from decay. And when I entered the forest, all smashed by shelling, there was the terrible evidence of real carnage – in the gloom were the vague shapes of fallen trees, huge roots torn from the ground, the crumpled skeletons of burned-up tanks.
>
> I reached the battalion in complete darkness and introduced myself to Senior Lieutenant Malyshev [the company commander]. He took a drink and greeted me cordially. He had already been notified by regiment headquarters about me and our meeting was short. 'Cadet sergeant, then?' he asked.
>
> 'Yes, sir.'
>
> 'So you've already been in battle and been wounded?'
>
> 'Yes, sir.'

'Fine, we can talk later. Go to the trenches and take over your platoon. But what a platoon, it's almost all of my command! When we broke into Rzhev, there were 300 [in the battalion], and after the dreadful night of 2 October, there were just 62 and me. The most important thing, platoon commander, is to keep in touch with me and your neighbours. The rest doesn't matter. It's a difficult situation. If anything happens, hold on to the last man, don't hope for reinforcements, there aren't any.'[3]

The previous platoon commander, Pavel Ivanov, became Gorbachevsky's deputy. He had far more experience than Gorbachevsky, but – perhaps as a result of that experience – he was prone to periods of low mood and often stuttered, and had lost the confidence of his superiors. Gorbachevsky did what he could to improve the positions held by his platoon. He organised work parties to collect timber to reinforce the walls of the trenches and bunkers, and false positions were constructed to mislead German attackers. A new reserve line was constructed, but perhaps the biggest boost to morale came with the appearance of replacement boots. Many of them were bloodstained, and Gorbachevsky was astonished to learn that two of his men had taken it upon themselves to crawl out of their trenches at night in order to collect boots from the corpses of dead Germans. When a small vodka ration was issued, the grateful men of his platoon ensured that the boot collectors received double rations. At a later stage of the autumn, one of Gorbachevsky's soldiers arranged for a horse's saddle to 'disappear' and used it to manufacture additional pairs of boots.

But even though the brutal battles of preceding weeks were over, low-level fighting continued with frequent exchanges of fire. One of the most popular men in Gorbachevsky's platoon was a Ukrainian, Vasil Badulya. Before the war, he had briefly been a singer in the Kiev Opera, but when his fiancée demanded he return to their village he turned his back on his singing career. He sang to his comrades every day, and Gorbachevsky suggested to his battalion commander that Badulya should be transferred out of the front line and perhaps assigned to the regiment's headquarters, from where he would be able to provide entertainment to a larger number of men. It seems that even the Germans in the trenches facing Gorbachevsky's platoon appreciated Badulya's singing – whenever he sang, the desultory fire died down, and when Badulya was briefly too ill to sing, the Germans called out to ask where he had gone. They even left a harmonica in no-man's land so that Gorbachevsky's men could collect it to accompany their singer, but nonetheless, a sniper killed Badulya shortly afterwards.[4]

The preparations for the winter battles around Rzhev provide interesting insights into the gathering of military intelligence by both sides. The standard sources of information available to intelligence officers on both sides had changed slightly since the onset of hostilities. Of the five original sources of intelligence, four – aerial photographs, the interception of radio traffic, prisoner interrogations, and reports from intelligence agents – continued to be available, but military attachés were no longer of any use. However, these had been replaced by intelligence provided by allied nations. There were considerable differences in the capabilities of the two sides in almost every respect.

The aerial reconnaissance resources of the Soviet Union were limited, with a variety of aircraft available. The Kharkiv KhAI-5, often known as the R-10, was designed in the mid-1930s and was a two-man plane that was outdated by the beginning of the conflict with Germany; its relatively low maximum speed of 240mph (387km/h) made it vulnerable to fighters, and its development effectively came to an end in 1938 when its designer, Iosif Grigorevich Nyeman, was arrested on charges of deliberate sabotage and imprisoned after a crash that killed a senior test pilot. In its early days, the R-10 was thought to have a good top speed and its manoeuvrability was highly regarded, but during its development it increased substantially in weight to the detriment of its performance. Its engine was prone to overheating to the extent that it couldn't be flown on hot days.[5] In addition to the Po-2 biplane, the Polykarpov design bureau also produced a larger, similar aircraft designated the P-5 or R-5. Like the Po-2, this was a biplane and was produced in large numbers, but its vulnerability in daytime greatly limited its value after 1941 and it was used mainly as a night bomber and liaison aircraft, as was the revised version that was designated the R-Z.[6]

By contrast, the aerial reconnaissance assets of the Luftwaffe were rather more modern. One of the most numerous aircraft, which entered service in August 1941, was the Focke-Wulf Fw189, often known to its aircrew as the *Uhu* ('eagle owl') and to German ground forces as the *Fliegende Auge* ('flying eye'). It was a twin-engine twin-boom plane, and this unique structure resulted in Soviet soldiers giving it the nickname *Rama* ('frame'). It had a relatively low top speed of 214mph (317km/h) but was very agile and could out-turn most Soviet fighters.[7] Soviet soldiers grew to detest the appearance of the *Rama* overhead, as it was often followed by German ground attack aircraft; the liaison between aerial reconnaissance and bomber units and ground artillery was consistently better than that achieved on the Soviet side.

Radio intercepts were widely used by both sides. In the first two years of the war, Soviet radio discipline was often very poor, with messages being sent uncoded, but this improved as the war developed; nonetheless, the Wehrmacht continued to deploy considerable resources for signals intelligence, numbering about 12,000 men and women by the end of the war.[8] Prior to hostilities, German signals intelligence concentrated on long-range radio transmissions, but its usefulness was limited by the sheer scale of the Soviet Union, and it wasn't always possible to intercept messages to or from the Soviet east. In addition, a great deal of Soviet military communication during peacetime was via landlines, making interception impossible. Despite this, the Germans successfully cracked several Soviet codes prior to *Barbarossa*, resulting in little difficulty in deciphering messages once hostilities began. Dedicated intercept companies accompanied the Wehrmacht into the Soviet Union, rapidly refining their operating procedures in the light of experience. For example, the Germans became aware of a tendency for Soviet radio operators to send brief signals to check communications after they had deployed, and this frequently alerted the Germans to a new deployment or concentration. Tank units in particular tended to send such signals to their higher commands immediately before an attack, a practice that continued well into 1942. As the Wehrmacht advanced, the capture of equipment and documentation proved valuable both in determining the frequencies used by the Red Army as well as its standard operating procedures and ciphers. At first, most of the German interception was centred on communication between higher commands and subordinate headquarters, but this changed as *Barbarossa* unfolded. Every division had a signals battalion, and these units started routinely monitoring local Soviet radio traffic, both for use within the division and to be passed to higher commands. In response, many Soviet operations were marked by orders for strict radio silence during the preparation phase, but these instructions were often ignored by troops on the ground. Artillery and rocket units seem to have been particularly lax, and the appearance of increasing radio traffic from such units soon became a clear sign for German listeners that an attack was being prepared.

The indiscipline of Soviet radio traffic resulted in major successes for the Germans. During *Seydlitz*, the elimination of Kalinin Front's penetration to the west of Rzhev, the signals battalion of 2nd Panzer Division intercepted an uncoded transmission from the Soviet 82nd Tank Brigade, one of the units that had been encircled by the German operation. The signal reported the intention of the brigade to attempt to break out, listing its planned route. The anti-tank battalion of 2nd Panzer Division was swiftly deployed, destroying several tanks and driving the rest back into the encirclement. When signals were intercepted reporting the locations of numerous Soviet tanks that were stranded in the forest and requesting towing equipment, German infantry was deployed to eliminate the vehicles, and attempts by the Soviet brigade headquarters to concentrate the surviving elements at various locations – again, transmitted uncoded – allowed the Germans to bring these locations under heavy artillery fire.

Both sides attempted to use signals traffic as a means of misleading their opponents, with varying degrees of success. In January 1942, *OKH* ordered the signals interception companies attached to each army group to commence extensive transmissions to try to deceive Soviet listeners, but there is little evidence that this had much effect. Similarly, attempts were made by the German Sixth Army when it was encircled in Stalingrad to simulate preparations for a breakout, in the hope that this would tie down significant Soviet forces and reduce the resistance to the relief column attempting to reach the encirclement, but the deception attempt had no impact. By contrast, the Red Army used deceptive messages regularly in the preparation of major operations to try to persuade the Germans that major tank formations were deployed in different locations, and this achieved some success in 1944. However, Soviet signals interception proved to be of limited value. Radio discipline was generally better on the German side, and the Red Army had few dedicated interception units.

Prisoner interrogations were a common source of information; as has already been described, the Red Army routinely conducted patrols purely to capture 'tongues' who were then interrogated to identify the name and state of opposing units. In addition, deserters from both sides often provided useful information, but interpreting this was more difficult, as there was always the possibility that the deserter was deliberately giving incorrect information. On occasion, prisoner interrogation overlapped with radio intelligence. When the Soviet Twelfth Army was destroyed in Ukraine in 1941, its signals officer, Colonel Karmin, was taken prisoner, and he proved willing to help the Germans interpret radio intercepts from preceding weeks. This provided considerable insight for the Germans about Soviet radio procedures, improving their ability to intercept and understand messages. But in April 1942, it was the Soviet side that benefited. The Red Army started to use a new set of ciphers, disrupting German attempts to monitor transmissions, and this was probably due to a German signaller who deserted to the Soviet side and revealed details of German monitoring practice.

Writing his memoirs after the end of the Soviet Union, Gorbachevsky was able to be more honest about defectors than would have been possible during the Soviet era:

It was widely believed that our people didn't lose faith in victory from the first day of the war. This isn't true. In fact, confidence in victory over the enemy only appeared in 1943 – after Stalingrad and the Battle of Kursk. Constant heavy defeats of the Red Army in 1941–1942 and huge losses led some of the great mass of soldiers to lose faith in our success. As in 1941, desertions during 1942 were still large-scale. Many deserters didn't consider their actions to be treason; for them, the pre-war reality didn't serve as an ideal for which they would die and they saw in escape the only way to escape the Stalinist system of slavery, naively believing that having defeated the Soviet Union, the Germans would destroy the Stalinist regime and grant them freedom …

Even at the end of 1942, soldiers in the front line of our army lived in poor conditions with far worse clothing than the Germans. Generally, their uniforms were worn out: an old tunic, a battered and shapeless garrison cap, boots with foot bindings [widely used in the Red Army in place of socks], tattered and windblown overcoats. In winter we were given quilted jackets with washed-out bloodstains to protect us from the frost. The food was bad. There wasn't even a mention of leave or the opportunity to meet women. The weapons, especially automatic firearms, didn't compare to German ones. Ammunition, especially shells and mortar bombs, was in short supply. German aircraft still dominated the sky. Discipline was maintained in the units under the watchful eye of political personnel …

Commanders sometimes took the most desperate measures to prevent mass desertion. Possible exits from the forward positions were mined. Officers at lower levels were severely punished if their subordinates deserted. Companies and even entire battalions were reorganised and transferred to new sectors of the front. Artillery fire was sometimes brought down on the fugitives … [Company] commanders, senior sergeants and sergeants could be demoted to the ranks for a single desertion from their unit. If a group deserted, there would be a tribunal and a term of five or ten years in a camp. The camp sentence was soon replaced by penal battalions …

[From our positions on the Volga during the winter] a deserter had to climb over the parapet of the trench and go down the icy slope to the river, run across the uneven ice to the opposite bank, make the difficult climb up the slippery slope, and then, even worse, crawl through a minefield to reach the German trenches. All this had to be done unnoticed by his own side and at the same time trying to let the Germans know his intentions.[9]

If a deserter reached the safety of the opposing trenches, he was often taken to a bunker from where he could send a message back via loudspeakers to tell his former comrades that he was alive, and exhortations to others to emulate him followed. In many cases, Gorbachevsky and his comrades listened to the speeches read out to them by deserters and concluded from the words and sentences that they had been written by German officers, and that the deserters were merely reading prepared speeches that they had been given, but the sincerity of others was beyond doubt. Aware that many men deserted because their homes were in German-controlled territory, Gorbachevsky divided his men into twos and threes, ensuring that only one man in each group had family in the occupied zone and that there was, if possible, a Komsomol member in each group. As the numbers of German prisoners of war increased in the second half of the war, the Soviet side too used prisoners and deserters in a similar manner, and in a rather more systematic manner with the creation of the *Bund Deutscher Offiziere* ('League of German Officers' or *BDO*) from captured Wehrmacht officers. This group transmitted messages to the German lines, and individual members of the *BDO* wrote personal letters to old acquaintances; these were then dropped on the relevant positions to encourage further desertions.[10]

There were many reasons why men deserted. Gorbachevsky may be correct in his statement that many doubted the ability of the Red Army to defeat the Wehrmacht in the opening 18 months of the war, and undoubtedly there were large numbers of men who had seen first-hand the repressions and famines that Soviet rule had brought to parts of Ukraine and elsewhere, but it would be an exaggeration to suggest that this was a majority view. Most Soviet soldiers were young enough to have no real experience of life under any other regime and were recruited from the urban centres of the Soviet Union, where Bolshevik support had always been strongest. Nonetheless, desertions continued right to the very end of the war, when the outcome was no longer in doubt. Many of those who tried to cross the front line in either direction were attempting to avoid involvement in imminent fighting, and the information that these men brought about plans for such fighting were invaluable sources of intelligence.

The espionage source for much of German intelligence on the coming operation came via the 'Max' network, which was run by Richard Kauder, and the details of this operation shed fascinating light on the workings of German and Soviet intelligence services. Originally from Vienna, Kauder was a member of the German *Abwehr*, Germany's military intelligence service. His department was known as *Dienststelle Klatt* ('Department Klatt'), and in addition to the 'Max' network, it was also responsible for the 'Moritz' network, which attempted to obtain intelligence about British forces in the Middle East. As the war

German general Walter Model (in vehicle holding map) led Ninth Army from January 1942 until September 1943. He would play a leading role in the battles around Rzhev. (Nik Cornish at www.Stavka.org.uk)

Generalmajor Walter Hörnlein commanded Panzergrenadier Regiment *Grossdeutschland*. In 1943, he was awarded the German Cross in Gold and the Knight's Cross with Oak Leaves. (Photo by ullstein bild/ullstein bild via Getty Images)

Overall command of the German Army was in the hands of Field Marshal Walther von Brauchitsch (seen here with Romania's leader Marshal Ion Antonescu to his right). In reality, however, he was little more than a messenger between Hitler and the army group commanders. (Nik Cornish at www.Stavka.org.uk)

Generals K. K. Rokossovsky and
G. K. Zhukov had both fought in dragoon
regiments during the First World War.
(Courtesy of the Central Museum of the
Armed Forces, Moscow via Stavka)

Lieutenant General P. A. Belov's I Guards
Cavalry Corps operated behind enemy lines
in one of the most prolonged and remarkable
such episodes of the war. (Photo by: Sovfoto/
Universal Images Group via Getty Images)

Politically astute Marshal A. M. Vasilevsky
rose to be Deputy Defence Minister in
October 1942 but has rarely received the
recognition that is due to him. (Courtesy of
the Central Museum of the Armed Forces,
Moscow via Stavka)

Lieutenant General A. A. Vlasov
commanded Second Shock Army during
the siege of Leningrad. He was captured in
July 1942, and agreed to fight against Stalin
as commander of the *Russische
Befreiungsarmee*.
(Nik Cornish at www.Stavka.org.uk)

The muddy conditions on both sides of the front line created an environment that would have been familiar to older combatants or their fathers during the First World War. (Nik Cornish at www.Stavka.org.uk)

Beautifully posed, a Soviet unit advances through deep snow. From this image it is clear how well the camouflage suits blend in. (Courtesy of the Central Museum of the Armed Forces, Moscow via Stavka)

A Soviet river crossing by pontoon is completed by horse power. Often, unseasonable rains made rivers almost impassable. (From the fonds of the RGAKFD in Krasnogorsk via Stavka)

Bread for the Soviet front-line troops being delivered by sledge. By the time it arrived it would be frozen solid. (Courtesy of the Central Museum of the Armed Forces, Moscow via Stavka)

A German supply column made up of commandeered local farm carts that proved more efficient when drawn by hardy local horses than the much heavier horses and wagons issued by the *Heer*. (Nik Cornish at www.Stavka.org.uk)

A company runner delivers a message to his HQ. Such men were obvious targets for
Soviet snipers and suffered accordingly. (Nik Cornish at www.Stavka.org.uk)

A German NCO peers cautiously over
the lip of a trench while the cameraman
nestles under cover.
(Nik Cornish at www.Stavka.org.uk)

A German flamethrower team advances
cautiously through heavily wooded terrain.
When identified, the operator became a
priority target for any enemy infantrymen.
(Nik Cornish at www.Stavka.org.uk)

A Soviet sub-machine-gun unit advances towards the enemy. They are wearing waist
length, quilted *telogreika* jackets, felt *valenki* boots and the *ushanka* imitation fur cap.
(Courtesy of the Central Museum of the Armed Forces, Moscow via Stavka)

A German machine-gun team keeps a careful watch, with a mix of grenades close at hand. (Nik Cornish at www.Stavka.org.uk)

Soviet infantrymen moving up to the lines. A farmer's cart has been pressed into service for transport duties. (Courtesy of the Central Museum of the Armed Forces, Moscow via Stavka)

Troopers of the I Guards Cavalry Corps charge into action. The Red Army raised a large number of cavalry units during the Second World War, many of which fought with distinction in a theatre where there were few continuous lines and mobility was vital. (Courtesy of the Central Museum of the Armed Forces, Moscow via Stavka)

A Ju 87 awaits maintenance. The intensive efforts of the Luftwaffe greatly
hindered the Soviet's attempts to exploit their successful attacks in August 1942.
(Nik Cornish at www.Stavka.org.uk)

An unidentified radio team checks in. The efficiency of German communications was vital
to their defensive operations. (Nik Cornish at www.Stavka.org.uk)

Panzerbefehlswagen III Ausf. H command tanks such as this one carried extra wireless equipment that replaced the main armament.
(Nik Cornish at www.Stavka.org.uk)

Heavy artillery was Stalin's 'god of war'. This is a 152mm M1935 (Br-2), which had a rate of fire of one shot every two minutes. (Courtesy of the Central Museum of the Armed Forces, Moscow via Stavka)

The iconic Russian-made Maxim M1910/30 heavy machine-gun in a support role. Used in both world wars, it remains in service today. (Courtesy of the Central Museum of the Armed Forces, Moscow via Stavka)

Minefields caused substantial losses on both sides. Here a Soviet operator uses a VIM-203 mine detector, attached to his Mosin rifle. (Nik Cornish at www.Stavka.org.uk)

A Soviet partisan scout, high in the trees. Clashes with partisans often resulted in widespread punishments by the Germans – such as the burning of villages and mass executions. (Courtesy of the Central Museum of the Armed Forces, Moscow via Stavka)

A lonely and dangerous duty: German sentries were frequently taken by Soviet patrols for interrogation. Victims were known as 'tongues' to their captors. (Nik Cornish at www.Stavka.org.uk)

Soviet intelligence officers interview a captured German 'tongue' in this picture. However, the position of the POW's Iron Cross seems a little odd. (Courtesy of the Central Museum of the Armed Forces, Moscow via Stavka)

A Red Army man moves from his foxhole as supporting artillery fire bursts on enemy lines. Hedgehog anti-tank defences are visible in the distance. (Courtesy of the Central Museum of the Armed Forces, Moscow via Stavka)

The dreadful muddy conditions caused massive transport problems not just for the Germans, as seen here, but for both sides during the more clement days of winter. (Nik Cornish at www.Stavka.org.uk)

A Panzer IV crew keeps up with the never-ending maintenance regime. One consolation is that their main armament is short barrelled. (Nik Cornish at www.Stavka.org.uk)

A T-34 with 76mm gun on fire. Most tank brigades had a mix of vehicles, and the T-34s often suffered substantial losses before the heavier KV-1s arrived. (Nik Cornish at www.Stavka.org.uk)

A Soviet gun crew firing a captured German 75mm Pak 40. Ammunition and spares shortages limited the value of such 'trophy' weapons, however. (From the fonds of the RGAKFD in Krasnogorsk via Stavka)

A wounded German is supported by his fellow soldiers. Soldiers on both sides at Rzhev endured one of the most brutal and prolonged phases of the Second World War. (Nik Cornish at www.Stavka.org.uk)

Civilians also suffered terribly during the Rzhev fighting. (Courtesy of the Central Museum of the Armed Forces, Moscow via Stavka)

Red Army men advance towards a church in this atmospheric shot. The winter camouflage overall was such a treasured item of clothing that injured men would apologise for their bloodstains. (From the fonds of the RGAKFD in Krasnogorsk via Stavka)

Two exhausted German infantrymen catch a few moments' rest during the intense fighting. (Nik Cornish at www.Stavka.org.uk)

Eternal rest in no man's land. (Nik Cornish at www.Stavka.org.uk)

continued, the accuracy of the information from 'Moritz' was increasingly questioned, but the Germans continued to regard 'Max' as a reliable source. The network apparently obtained its reports from a network of White Russians and their sympathisers; one was a former Tsarist, Anton Vasilievich Turkul, who was based in Rome, and another was Ira Fedorovich Longin, who lived in Sofia. Both Turkul and Longin were in Anglo-American custody after the war and were interrogated at length. The British and US intelligence officers felt that their attempts to discover the truth about Kauder's networks were 'protracted, inconclusive, and wholly disappointing', but nonetheless, they discovered many interesting details.

Kauder was the son of Austrian Jews, though he was baptised and professed himself to be Roman Catholic. He became a member of the Austrian intelligence service in 1932 but fled to Budapest in 1938 after Austria was absorbed by Germany, and shortly after he was approached by *Abwehr* officers who attempted to recruit him. He declined their approaches and was arrested by the Hungarian police, presumably acting on a German request, and handed over to the Gestapo, but shortly after the *Abwehr* made another approach. On this occasion, he agreed to work for the Germans in return for his mother being protected from racial persecution, and was issued with new identity documents in the name of Richard Klatt.

Returning to Budapest, Kauder encountered Longin, who would later tell his British and American interrogators that he was a Catholic Russian who had fought against the Red Army in the Russian Civil War and had been imprisoned for a short time before leaving Russia for Istanbul. He claimed that he first met the White Russian Turkul, who was attempting to establish a 'Russian liberation' movement, in Berlin. Turkul had served in the Imperial Russian Army in the First World War, rising from the ranks to become a captain at the time of the Russian Revolution. He then volunteered to join the pro-White Russian forces of General Mikhail Gordeevich Drozdovsky. During the Civil War he was further promoted and became commander of an infantry division, before fleeing in August 1921 when the victory of the Bolsheviks became inevitable. After living in comparative poverty for many years and holding a series of poorly paid jobs, he became markedly more prosperous in the mid-1930s; he later claimed that this was due to a combination of income from a book he had written about his service in the Russian Civil War and payments from Japanese sources for training anti-Bolshevik volunteers.

On the basis of an introduction by a mutual acquaintance, Turkul asked Longin, who was living in Budapest at the time, to become head of the Hungarian branch of his new anti-Bolshevik organisation. Longin agreed and returned to his home in Budapest, while Turkul appears to have fallen out with members of the *Abwehr*; he had been in intermittent contact with Oberstleutnant Heinz Piekenbrock, a senior officer in the *Abwehr*, but Piekenbrock soon broke off contact and issued strict instructions that *Abwehr* officers were not to contact Turkul. Meanwhile, Longin returned to Budapest, where he was arrested by the Hungarian police in December 1939 for distributing pan-Slavist material. It was during this period under arrest that he first met Kauder.

When the two men met again in the summer of 1940, Kauder obtained permission from his German superiors to recruit Longin as an intelligence agent. Longin replied that he would have to seek the approval of Turkul, and after obtaining this he helped establish the 'Max' network. He apparently remained under suspicion from the Hungarian authorities and was arrested again in the summer of 1941, and released only after the intervention of the *Abwehr*.

'Max' started producing data from the summer of 1941. The volume of information grew steadily, with reports often appearing several times a day. The data was held in high regard, and by late 1941 there were regular requests from *OKW* for reports on specific subjects. In most cases, Kauder and Longin were able to obtain answers to these questions within a few days. *Dienststelle Klatt* grew into a considerable bureaucratic empire, with stations in Vienna, Istanbul, Sofia and Bratislava, and had contacts with numerous foreign officials, including Turkish, Japanese and Spanish diplomats. The conclusions of Kauder's post-war interrogators were that this elaborate department was created primarily as a justification for a large expense account funded by the *Abwehr* and secondly to disguise the fact that almost all of the information obtained by 'Max' actually came through just one source: Longin. A number of agents operating for Longin were named, but getting accurate identification of these persons after the war proved to be almost impossible.

Not all Germans seem to have regarded the reports of *Dienststelle Klatt* as above suspicion. There was an investigation within the *Abwehr* into Kauder's operation, at least partly motivated by some figures within the *Abwehr* becoming aware of his Jewish ancestry and resenting his high standing within the organisation. Complaints were made to Admiral Wilhelm Canaris, head of the *Abwehr*, about the number of black marketers and other 'dubious' figures associated with *Dienststelle Klatt*; the response was an order forbidding any investigation of Kauder's organisation. Although Canaris had expressed enthusiastic support for many of Hitler's policies before the war – the use of yellow 'star of David' badges for Jews is thought to have originated with Canaris – he became increasingly opposed to the Nazi regime and was horrified by the reality of German atrocities against Jews, Poles and others.[11] A Polish spy named Halina Szymanska became his lover, and through her, Canaris passed information to the Polish government in exile in London about the start date of *Barbarossa*.[12] Canaris was in contact with British agents via Spain throughout 1942, and his intervention in the Kauder case may reflect personal suspicion or knowledge that the entire operation was actually run by the Soviet Union.

Despite Canaris' order, unofficial investigations into *Dienststelle Klatt* continued. Otto Wagner, an *Abwehr* officer, was suspicious of the information provided by *Dienststelle Klatt*, particularly because on the one hand, there was the sheer volume of reports and their rapid response to any questions asked by *OKW*, and on the other hand, Kauder's organisation in German-controlled parts of Eastern Europe appeared to have no radio receivers in Eastern Europe that could have received this information from intelligence sources. When Wagner challenged Kauder about this, Kauder replied that there were radio receivers in Samsun, on the northern coast of Turkey – these received the transmissions from the Soviet Union, and the reports were then telephoned to Istanbul. Couriers took the reports on to Sofia. This did little to satisfy Wagner, as his investigations revealed that telephone contact between Samsun and Istanbul was poor and very unreliable. The route allegedly used by the couriers between Istanbul and Sofia would have had to use a road bridge in Greece, which had been washed away by floods. Wagner had no doubt that the entire operation was being managed by the enemies of Germany – he speculated that it might be a British operation, planting information that alternately prejudiced the operations of both the Red Army and the Wehrmacht, in an attempt to weaken both sides, but rejected this in favour of 'Max' being an entirely Soviet operation. However, when he presented his findings to Canaris, the head of the *Abwehr* merely repeated his previous injunction against any investigation into *Dienststelle Klatt*.

The details of precisely how Kauder obtained the information for his reports remain obscure. He was in close contact with Colonel Otto Hatz, the Hungarian military attaché in Sofia and later in Istanbul; Hatz was arrested in 1944 under suspicion of working for the Soviet Union, and the amount of information being produced by 'Max' immediately diminished. Hatz was released shortly after and immediately deserted to the Soviet side, and briefly formed part of the pro-Soviet Hungarian government after the war. The full role of Longin also remains unclear. When he was interrogated by the British after the war, Wagner complained that 'One could never get a clear picture' of Longin. To complicate matters further, much of the information produced by 'Max' was both accurate and of high quality, which suggests that it wasn't simply an attempt to plant misinformation. Rather, it is likely that the network operated as a two-way process, passing information back to the Soviet Union as well as to Germany. The questions from *OKW* would have been very valuable, as they would indicate areas of German ignorance and interest. Kauder later admitted that the information he had given Wagner about the location of radio receivers was false, and that he had no clear idea of the route by which Longin was obtaining the data that was then passed to the *Abwehr*.

There can be little doubt that Longin was working for the Soviet Union; it is likely, but perhaps less certain, that Turkul was also a Soviet agent. A letter written by Sir Percy Sillitoe, head of MI5, in 1950 concluded:

> We were unable to prove that Turkul was a Soviet agent and reluctantly came to the conclusion that he was the head of a scattered number of bona fide White Russians, who were originally anxious to overthrow the Soviet regime, but who were later prepared to aid the Germans in their fight against Bolshevism. It must eventually have become obvious to Turkul that his organisation was being used by the Soviets; and under interrogation he did finally admit that his organisation had actually penetrated pro-German White Russian organisations over Axis controlled Europe. He has maintained that this went on either without his knowledge or, when he did know, without his approval.[13]

The post-war interrogation – more an interview, as it took place on Swiss territory – of a man named Georgi Leonidovich Romanov by a British intelligence officer sheds further light on Longin. Romanov was from Tiflis, in the Caucasus, and fought for the White Russian cause in the Russian Civil War before fleeing to Paris in 1923. He became a member of Kauder's organisation in 1943 while living in Belgrade, and after the war took holy orders and became a Russian Orthodox priest. He performed numerous tasks for *Dienststelle Klatt* but always felt that he was kept away from the details about the original sources of information that Kauder was passing to the Germans. He spent three weeks in Sofia in 1942, staying in Longin's apartment, and commented that although Longin possessed a radio receiver, he almost never used it. Nor were documents ever delivered to Longin; instead, Longin met a woman known as 'Tanya', from whom he received the information that he then passed on to Kauder. Romanov stressed that these visits to 'Tanya' – identified tentatively elsewhere as Natalya Balkanova – were relatively brief; there was insufficient time for them to have been deciphered before being passed on. In other words, 'Tanya' must have been receiving deciphered documents, or perhaps was deciphering them herself, even though she was not part of *Dienststelle Klatt*. Romanov was of the opinion that Longin was a habitual liar and was almost certainly a Soviet agent, with 'Tanya' as a conduit for the information that he passed to Kauder.[14]

In January 1946, Kauder was living in Salzburg, and Soviet agents attempted unsuccessfully to abduct him; the motivation for this is unclear but suggests that Kauder was not a direct employee of the Soviet Union, at least at that time, or was in possession of information that the Soviet authorities wished to keep secret.

This was the main source of the information that the Germans used in their intelligence assessments of Soviet intentions. As had consistently been the case, the efforts of the German *FHO* to discern Soviet intentions remained vague and imprecise. Kinzel was no longer head of the department and had been replaced by Oberst Reinhardt Gehlen, a staff officer who had been involved in transport planning during the opening months of *Barbarossa*. He had no intelligence experience, nor did he speak any foreign languages, yet he now found himself responsible for intelligence about the Red Army, the military forces of Sweden, and even the development of the USAAF. Perhaps in an attempt to address his personal shortcomings and expertise, he rapidly reorganised *FHO* and created a staff of linguists, geographers and other experts. It is all the more remarkable that his predecessor Kinzel had attempted to function without such a staff. Perhaps inevitably, given the nature of the regime in Nazi Germany, the experts appointed by Gehlen included anthropologists who were to give advice based on the perceived racial characteristics of Germany's enemies.[15] On 29 August, Gehlen produced a report assessing Soviet intentions for the coming winter. All through the summer, Hitler had maintained that the Red Army was approaching the end of its strength; at first, Halder appeared to agree with him, but changed his opinion as the fighting continued. Gehlen's report, which correctly assessed that the Red Army retained considerable reserves capable of major offensive operations, further reinforced Halder's view, but Hitler remained unconvinced. Conferences at Hitler's headquarters featured increasingly frequent outbursts by the Führer against the apparent inability of German commanders, particularly in the southern sector, to overcome what Hitler regarded as the last dregs of Soviet resistance. Halder noted in his diary on 29 August that Hitler was 'very peevish about the conduct of operations by Army Group A', and the following day there were further complaints:

> Today's conferences with [the] Führer were again the occasion of abusive reproaches against the military leadership abilities of the highest commands. He

charges them with intellectual conceit, mental nonadaptability, and utter failure to grasp essentials.[16]

Gehlen's report, therefore, was a further source of friction, with Hitler minded to reject it while Halder took it as evidence that the Red Army was far from finished. But while Gehlen and his staff correctly identified the capability of the Red Army, they continued to regard the central region as the main theatre for future Soviet operations:

> [We can expect attacks] against Army Group Centre, to eliminate any threat to Moscow and to secure a success where the arrangement of the front line will not stretch the tactical capabilities of subordinate commanders.[17]

This is a clear reference to the exposed nature of the Rzhev Salient, but fails to recognise the far greater opportunity provided by the larger German salient stretching to Stalingrad. Moreover, the terrain over which any attack on Rzhev would take place was greatly favourable for defensive warfare, whereas the open landscape between the Don and Volga was much more suited for mobile operations. Perhaps in recognition of this, Gehlen issued a revised report two weeks later. He now regarded Soviet attacks in the southern sector as more likely than further offensives against Army Group Centre. However, Gehlen rapidly acquired a reputation for ambiguous reports that seemed to cover his options widely, and just two days later, *FHO* warned of increasing Soviet rail traffic in the Rzhev sector, which might presage a renewed attack. The reports continued to give confusing information – on the one hand, Soviet forces facing Rzhev seemed to be making defensive preparations for the winter, but on the other hand, there were signs of reinforcements for the Soviet units on either side of the base of the Rzhev Salient.

On 6 November, Gehlen produced a report based upon information received from 'Max'. There had been a conference in Moscow two days before, presided over by Stalin, with a dozen senior commanders present. Among other topics, there was mention of planned offensive operations at several locations. In the south, Red Army units were to advance out of the Caucasus Mountains, and there was to be a major attack across the Don near Voronezh; in the north, there were to be renewed attempts to break the siege of Leningrad; and there would be further attacks against Rzhev.[18] Soviet records provide no corroboration of this meeting, with both Zhukov and Vasilevsky away from Moscow visiting units in preparation for the coming offensives, but such a conference did take place in the last week of October. If 'Max' was run entirely by Soviet intelligence services as part of a grand deception plan, this was remarkably accurate information to pass to the Germans.

In addition to its extensive infiltration of German and other intelligence services – it should be remembered that during this period, much of the work of British intelligence services was known to the Soviet Union as a result of the 'Cambridge' spy network, the leading member of which was Kim Philby – Soviet intelligence officers received extensive information via a number of spy networks. One such group, under the loose overall direction of Rudolf Rössler, a German refugee living in Switzerland where he ran a small publishing company, was operated by the *Glavno Razvedyvelno Upravlenie* ('Main Intelligence Directorate', a branch of Soviet military intelligence, usually abbreviated to GRU). Rössler, codenamed 'Lucy', was given an Enigma coding machine and short-wave radio by two old acquaintances, Generalleutnant Fritz Thiele and Oberst Rudolph von Gersdorff, who were serving in the *Abwehr* and were part of the group of anti-Hitler conspirators who ultimately attempted to assassinate the Führer. Thiele, who was deputy head of communications at *OKW*, then transmitted encrypted messages that Rössler could decipher and pass on to contacts, who in turn would relay the information to GRU officers. The carefully compartmentalised system for encrypting and transmitting messages in Berlin worked in favour of the spies; the staff who transmitted the messages had no idea what they contained, as they had already been encrypted, and those responsible for the encryption had no idea of the intended recipients.[19] In addition to the information that he could obtain personally, Thiele had several other contacts within the German military, and the full details of the personalities involved remain unclear. Almost certainly, they included Thiele's superior in *OKW*, General Erich Fellgiebel, and Generalmajor Hans Oster, Canaris' chief of staff.

The series of steps by which 'Lucy' passed information to the GRU was intricate. At first, in 1939, Rössler gave Thiele's reports to Xavier Schnieper, an old friend of Rössler; he then passed them to Roger Masson, head of Swiss Military Intelligence, and from there they were sent to London for use by the British. Rössler was dissatisfied with this, as he felt his valuable information disappeared without any apparent impact. Purely by chance, one of Rössler's employees in his publishing company was Christian Schneider, who was already an active agent under the codename 'Taylor' for a completely different GRU operation. The two men were on very friendly terms, and in early 1941, when Rössler confided in Schneider that he was receiving intelligence from Germany and passing it to London via Switzerland, Schneider offered to send it to Moscow instead. He began to pass Rössler's reports to his superior in the spy network, Rachel Dübendorfer, codenamed 'Sissy'; she in turn gave the information to Sandór Radó, a Hungarian who had been recruited by the GRU in the mid-1930s and was now living in Lausanne, operating under the codename 'Dora'.

The information provided by 'Lucy' was both detailed and accurate. Late on 17 June 1941, just three days before the onset of *Barbarossa*, a message was sent to the GRU about the imminent attack:

> About 100 infantry divisions are now positioned on the German–Soviet frontier. One third are motorised. Of the remainder, at least ten divisions are panzer. In Romania German troops are concentrated at Galatz. Elite divisions with a special mission have been mobilised.[20]

Two days later, just hours before the attack began, 'Lucy' sent a further message upgrading German strength to 148 divisions. Details of the overall operational plan of *Barbarossa* were also included, but Radó was suspicious about the information. 'Sissy' had refused to identify Rössler, and Radó believed that the reports were either deliberate German disinformation or that the military activity on the Soviet border was a form of posturing intended to pressure the Soviet Union to agree better terms for trade. This scepticism was replicated in Moscow; right up to the onset of *Barbarossa*, Stalin continued to believe that the Germans wouldn't attack. He suspected the British of plotting to start a war between Germany and the Soviet Union, and interpreted the reports from 'Dora' – which were corroborated by intelligence from numerous other sources, such as Richard Sorge, a German journalist in Japan who worked for the GRU from 1929 – as further misinformation. It was only after the German invasion commenced that 'Dora' was informed that reports from 'Lucy' were to be reclassified as 'VYRDO', i.e. urgent and of the greatest importance. The data provided by 'Lucy' was both copious and detailed, with almost daily updates of the German order of battle. Allan Foote, a British man who transmitted messages from 'Dora' to Moscow, later wrote:

> 'Lucy' provided Moscow with an up-to-date and day-to-day order of battle of the German forces in the east. This information could only come from *OKW* itself. In no other offices in the whole of Germany was there available the information that 'Lucy' provided daily. Not only did he provide information on the troop dispositions ... but he also produced equally good information emanating from the headquarters of the Luftwaffe ...

One would normally think that a source producing information of this quality would take time to obtain it. No such delay occurred in the receipt of information. On most occasions it was received within 24 hours of its being known at the appropriate headquarters in Berlin – in fact, barely enough time to encipher and decipher the messages concerned.[21]

Despite the classification of the 'Lucy' reports as VYRDO, many in the Soviet Union, especially Stalin, remained doubtful about the information, and its impact on Soviet thinking is a controversial subject. Deeply suspicious by nature, Stalin repeatedly feared that the information that reached him was deliberately planted to mislead him, and the attempts by Soviet agents to mislead the Germans may have led the Soviet leader to assume that his enemies would behave in a similar manner. In the spring of 1942, 'Lucy' informed Moscow about the planned German offensive towards Stalingrad and the Caucasus – the entire ten-page strategic overview in Hitler's original directive was sent by Thiele to Rössler, and thence to Moscow. This was further corroborated on 19 June when the plane carrying Major Reichel, the operations officer of 23rd Panzer Division, was shot down and crashed in Soviet-controlled territory.[22] Reichel was carrying a full set of plans for the forthcoming operation giving full details of the campaign, but Stalin remained convinced that the main German effort in 1942 would be directed against Moscow, and that both the information from 'Lucy' and the documents captured from Reichel's crash were deliberate misinformation. Even with excellent sources of intelligence, interpretation of that intelligence is ultimately the decisive factor.

Just as so many figures in *FHO* had little or no intelligence experience, many of the men working in intelligence posts at army group or army level also had no formal training in this field. Oberst Georg Buntrock was head of Ninth Army's intelligence branch. His later comments about his role are revealing about his initial ignorance of intelligence matters:

I saw ... only the heavy responsible toil, the queer resigned work far from troop life and battle, in the midst of which I had been [prior to assuming this role] ... I was surprised to observe and experience how this branch succeeded in unveiling the hidden image of the enemy situation ... It took some time before the nature of [intelligence work] opened up to me in all its ramifications and possibilities. But then it enthralled me.[23]

Relying mainly on local information obtained from subordinate formations, Buntrock soon identified the transfer of Soviet artillery elements from their previous positions facing Rzhev to the eastern side of the salient. Increased Soviet raiding activity against the German units defending the base of the salient was further evidence of Soviet preparations. As the autumn muddy season commenced, Soviet activity appeared to slacken, and deserters and prisoners reported that – as expected – many of the roads behind the Soviet front line were impassable until the advent of the hard winter frosts, but other reports continued to arrive of Red Army preparations. 'Max' revealed that large new artillery concentrations were forming around the eastern side of the base of the Rzhev Salient facing 102nd Infantry Division. The intelligence officer of this division, Hauptmann Friedrich Lange, astutely calculated that the number of guns facing his division were far in excess of what could be expected for the Soviet rifle divisions known to be in this sector: this could mean that the infantry of other rifle divisions were being held further back to mislead the Germans about the build-up of forces.

In the front line, the Red Army continued its well-rehearsed policy of raiding German positions to capture 'tongues'. Gorbachevsky was ordered to mount such a raid shortly after he took command of his platoon; his commander also informed Gorbachevsky that he was promoted to junior lieutenant. Gorbachevsky's men had identified an isolated German dugout where it seemed that security was lax and where there was good cover to hide the raiding party. A small party of sappers went out to clear barbed wire as soon as it grew dark, and the raiding party then set off. There were occasional bursts of gunfire and a few German flares rose into the sky, but the small group slipped into the trenches undetected. In seconds, they grabbed a sleeping German soldier and killed two others. As the raiding party began to withdraw, the Germans found the corpses of their comrades and opened fire with machine-guns and mortars, and two of the raiders were killed, including a man who Gorbachevsky had first met during his basic training. They sent their prisoner back to headquarters, where he was doubtless interrogated and the information obtained passed to higher commands.[24]

Despite the terrible casualties of the year, the Red Army had considerable reserves at its disposal. In the central sector alone, Soviet formations comprised about a third of the entire fighting strength of the nation. Even allowing for the planned counterstrike in the Stalingrad sector, there were surely sufficient resources available for two major operations to be carried out at the same time. Even though they were separated by a considerable geographical distance, the operations near Stalingrad and Rzhev would be mutually supporting, preventing the Germans from diverting resources from one sector to another.

It seems that Stalin shared Zhukov's sense of frustration at the failure of the Red Army to eliminate the Rzhev Salient and was willing to make a further effort. Konev's Western Front issued an order specifically using the codename *Mars* to Thirty-First and Twentieth Armies early on 1 October, with operations commencing on 12 October – the very tight timetable for preparations is a further indicator that even if this was the first formal order, there must have been some form of 'warning order' prior to this. After the German lines had been penetrated, a mobile exploitation group – II Guards Cavalry Corps, reinforced by VI Tank Corps – would penetrate deeper in order to link up with units of Kalinin Front, which were to attack in the Bely region.[25]

October was not an auspicious month for a major offensive operation. The weather was likely to be poor but not yet cold enough for the ground to freeze. Given the huge problems experienced with movement during the summer months, conditions would probably be far worse, particularly as all approach roads were already degraded by the preceding campaign. Based upon their previous experiences, both Konev and Zhukov were perfectly aware that even if the weather didn't interfere with preparations and the unfolding of the operation, the constraints of inadequate roads, terrain that favoured defence, and the strength of German defences would make the success of any attack almost impossible to achieve, yet they both proceeded as if such considerations were irrelevant. It should of course be remembered that both men would have seen reports from the front line describing the terrible conditions of the summer and can have had no doubts about the unsuitability of this sector for such an operation. The only change that developed in the plan was that attention was concentrated on the region to the southeast of Rzhev; it was here that the main effort would now be made, with the intention of first cutting off Rzhev from the south and then capturing it once it was isolated.

One of the major criticisms of Red Army offensive operations throughout 1942 was the dilution of effort on too many axes, and the planning for the coming offensive showed that, yet again, this lesson had not been learned. Kalinin Front received orders to attack into the Rzhev Salient from the west towards Bely, in order to link up with the advancing forces of Western Front, but it was also ordered to mount an attack with Galitsky's Third Shock Army to capture the city of Velikiye Luki, 145 miles (233km) to the west. The city formed a bridgehead over the Lovat River and was a tempting target for the Red Army. The main rail and road connections between the German Army Group Centre and Army Group North ran north from Vitebsk through Novosokolniki, some distance to the west of Velikiye Luki, and while the capture of the city on the Lovat would move the Red Army closer to this railway line, it would still require a further Soviet advance to sever the link. Although this sector didn't contain a substantial body of German troops that had to be tied down to prevent them being transferred elsewhere, the capture of the town would nonetheless improve logistics for the Red Army. An important railway line ran from the northeast to Velikiye Luki, and if the city was captured it would be possible to use this line to move more trains onto the rail line running east, towards Nelidovo, Olenino and Rzhev. Khlebnikov, the artillery commander of Kalinin Front, later justified the attack on Velikiye Luki:

> The enemy turned the city of Velikiye Luki into a strong node of resistance. It became a kind of springboard hanging over the right flank of Kalinin Front. The operational significance of this bridgehead also lay in the fact that it blocked our line of approach to the large railway junction at Novosokolniki and for further operations towards the Baltic. Therefore, in order to improve future prospects for fighting by the Front, we had to defeat the enemy's Velikiye Luki grouping as soon as possible.[26]

This is a debatable point of view. The German presence in Velikiye Luki was only a threat to Kalinin Front's right flank if it was possible for the Germans to mount offensive operations from there, and the terrain was only marginally more suitable for this than it was around Rzhev – the German advance during *Taifun* was highly dependent upon the single good road and rail link between Velikiye Luki and Olenino, and by mid-1942 the Red Army was surely capable of setting up robust defences on such a narrow front. Nor did the Germans have any significant forces capable of such an operation in the area; Khlebnikov's memoirs describe the German forces in and around the city as being made up of elements of LIX Corps, specifically 83rd Infantry Division reinforced by artillery and assault gun formations – hardly a major threat to the flank of Kalinin Front. However, it is certainly the case that *Stavka* believed that the Germans would be able to assemble a threatening force in Velikiye Luki, and that alone made an operation against the city necessary. But in order to support this attack, valuable artillery resources were allocated to Third Shock Army, reducing the number of guns, mortars and rocket launchers that might support the attack on the Rzhev Salient. Ultimately, the operation was a victory for the Red Army, but nonetheless, given that it was intended as a subsidiary or local attack, it diverted resources from *Mars*, which was seen as part of a much larger overall scheme.

The terrain over which the forthcoming battle would be fought was well known to the Soviet commanders, as large parts of it had been captured by the Red Army the preceding winter before the Germans recovered the region as a result of *Seydlitz*. Afanasy Grigorievich Sinitsky was an intelligence officer in the headquarters of Kalinin Front, and he attended a planning meeting being held by Lieutenant General Matvei Vasilevich Zakharov, the chief of staff of Kalinin Front:

> For a while, the Front commander silently studied the map. Then came a stream of questions. They concerned not only the location of the enemy's troops, their combat strength, and weaponry. Purkaev was interested in the state of the roads in the enemy's rear, the presence and serviceability of bridges across the numerous rivers and streams, and how passable the swamps were at different times of year.
>
> 'It's good that you know a lot about the enemy's troops,' he summed up finally, 'but that isn't enough now. Please be aware that the hour will come for us to advance. We don't know yet when that will be. Our business is to prepare. And to prepare so that not a single extra drop of blood is spilled.'[27]

While such alleged concern about keeping losses as low as possible may reflect the author's desire to adhere to orthodox Soviet historiography, the incident nonetheless makes clear that the state of roads and bridges was an important part of Soviet planning. Such considerations should have made clear to all concerned that undertaking a major offensive in this region was certain to be a formidable task.

Inevitably, the weather imposed delays on the ambitious timetable for *Mars*. It was impossible for Western Front to get its forces into position for the planned start date, and revised orders were issued on 10 October, putting back the start date to the end of the month. The overall plan stayed the same, and there were clearly intentions to develop the success further. After they had captured Rzhev, the armies of Western Front, moving forward with the mobile exploitation group, would link up with Kalinin Front's Forty-First Army, which was to capture Bely, and thereafter it was envisaged that further operations would see the Red Army capturing Vyazma. This would effectively move the front line back west roughly to where it had been before the Germans launched Operation *Taifun* the previous year. Some accounts give this deeper exploitation of *Mars* a different designation; just as *Saturn* was intended to follow *Uranus* at Stalingrad, so *Jupiter* would follow *Mars* in the central sector. However, the exact status of *Jupiter* remains controversial. No published Soviet material from that era specifically mentions the codeword *Jupiter*.

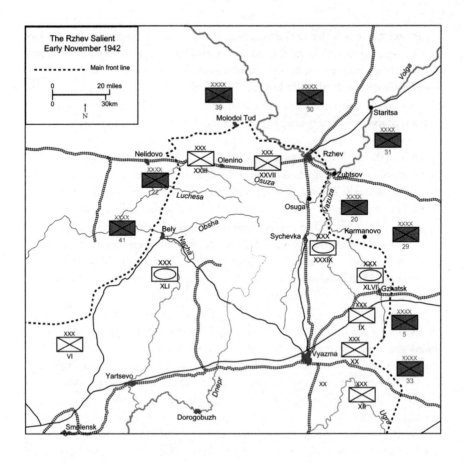

The scale of Soviet forces allocated for the coming offensive was impressive. Many studies suggest that the Red Army allocated more men and tanks to *Mars* than it did to *Uranus* – Kalinin and Western Fronts had over 700,000 men and 1,700 tanks at their disposal, compared with about 670,000 men and 1,300 tanks in the Fronts around Stalingrad.[28] Admittedly, this figure includes significant Soviet forces that would play no part in the coming battle, but nonetheless, Kalinin and Western Fronts had major resources at their disposal. There were also signs that some of the painful lessons of the summer were being learned. Konev had acted swiftly to stop some of the divergent and uncoordinated attacks of Western Front as soon as he took command in late August and then concentrated on bringing his armoured and mobile forces back to some semblance of strength. Steps were also taken to improve command and control, and to avoid the problems of lack of coordination between infantry, artillery and armour that had featured persistently in the previous attacks. The command of the main exploitation force, II Guards Cavalry Corps, was in the hands of Major General Vladimir Victorovich Kryukov, who served under Zhukov in the mid-1930s. He started the war commanding a mechanised division in the north facing the Finnish Army. He had been in the central sector for most of 1942 and was regarded by his superiors as a capable commander; in addition to his cavalry, he had VI Tank Corps subordinated to him.

Zhukov visited both Western and Kalinin Fronts several times during the prelude to *Mars* in order to ensure that preparations were proceeding properly. The main obstacle seemed to be the weather, with almost constant rain reducing the landscape to a muddy morass in the second half of October. The planned commencement of operations on 28 October was now impossible, and a further postponement was agreed by Stalin and Zhukov the following day. *Uranus* was planned to commence on 19 November, and Zhukov now suggested that *Mars* should begin five days later. By this time of the year, it was hoped that the numerous rivers in the Rzhev sector would be frozen and would thus be lesser obstacles; the ground would also be far firmer. In any case, there was no possibility of commencing the operation sooner, given the strength of German defences. The forces that were to carry out the attacks had to be given sufficient time to complete their preparations. But the reasons for these delays were either well known when the plan was first conceived, or in the case of the weather, they could have been predicted given the season. None of this appears to have played much of a part in Soviet planning.

The further delay was agreed and orders to Western and Kalinin Fronts amended accordingly. At the same time, Vasilevsky presented his final plans for *Uranus*, the coming counteroffensive near Stalingrad. It was agreed that Southwest Front would attack the Romanian Third Army along the Don to the west of Stalingrad on 19 November, and Stalingrad Front would attack the Romanian Fourth Army to the south of the city the following day. If the operation unfolded as planned and the Germans were encircled in Stalingrad, follow-on operations – tentatively codenamed *Saturn* – would commence in the second week of December, aimed at reaching Rostov and isolating the German forces operating in the Caucasus. While it was now impossible for *Mars* to begin at the same time as *Uranus*, this might prove to be advantageous; if Vasilevsky's operation succeeded, it was likely that the Germans would start moving reserves south, and this would make the task of Western and Kalinin Fronts far easier. Indeed, Zhukov was so confident that his plans would succeed that he made further alterations. Originally, Forty-First Army had been allocated two mechanised corps for its attack towards Sychevka from the west, but Zhukov now informed Stalin and the other commanders that he intended to move one of these two corps to reinforce Third Shock Army's attack on Velikiye Luki. The terrain in the Bely–Sychevka region, he informed the conference, was not suited to two mechanised corps operating side by side, and the German forces in the region would not be able to resist the attack of a single corps, particularly as he intended to reinforce it with two independent mechanised brigades.

Zhukov's memoirs give the misleading impression that this conference was the occasion that a renewed attack in the Rzhev sector was first discussed:

> Vasilevsky and I drew the attention of the Supreme Commander to the fact that as soon as a difficult situation arose in the Stalingrad and north Caucasus regions, the German high command would be forced to transfer some of its troops from other regions, in particular from the Vyazma region, to help the southern group. To prevent this from happening, it was urgently necessary to prepare and conduct an offensive operation in the area north of Vyazma to defeat the Germans in the region of the Rzhev Salient. For this operation, we proposed to use the troops of Kalinin and Western Fronts.
>
> 'That would be good,' said Stalin. 'But which of you will take up this business?'
>
> [Vasilevsky] and I had previously agreed our proposals in this regard, so I replied, 'The Stalingrad operation has already been prepared in most respects. Vasilevsky can take over the coordination of the troops in the Stalingrad area and I can take over the preparation of the offensive of the Kalinin and Western Fronts.'
>
> … On 17 November, I was summoned to *Stavka* to develop an operation for the troops of Kalinin and Western Fronts.[29]

This is hugely disingenuous, as preparations had been underway for several weeks under Zhukov's supervision.

On 19 November, several hours before it grew light, the ground to the west of Stalingrad began to shake as the massed artillery of Southwest Front began its preparatory bombardment for *Uranus*. Zhukov was in Moscow, and he and other officers in *Stavka* waited impatiently for news of the great counteroffensive in the south. As reports began to arrive, the anxious expressions were replaced with more confident smiles. Despite mist obscuring accurate direction of artillery fire, the Romanian positions had been hit by such a massive bombardment that the Red Army's ground troops were making good progress. In the early afternoon, the armoured exploitation forces were unleashed. In just a few hours, Southwest

Front gained more ground than the Soviet forces in the central sector had managed to secure in their entire summer offensive at Rzhev. As he returned to his headquarters to finish overseeing preparations for *Mars*, Zhukov must have felt a growing sense of confidence. If the gunners of Western and Kalinin Fronts could reproduce the successes achieved in the south, there was every reason to believe that here, too, a major success was possible.

The first snow of the season had fallen on Rzhev on 15 November. The German soldiers in the front line were hugely relieved that there was no repetition of the failure of 1941 to provide winter clothing, with supplies arriving on 20 November. The pause in fighting had been put to good use; the combat engineers of 6th Infantry Division reported that in the month preceding the renewed Soviet assault its personnel erected over 1,700 anti-tank obstacles and laid nearly 1,000 mines. Numerous bunkers and gun positions were constructed, and extensive barbed wire entanglements created. The limited replacement drafts were incorporated into the greatly thinned ranks of the front-line battalions, and, wherever possible, the veterans of the summer fighting did what they could to teach the new arrivals the realities of front-line warfare. Any renewed Soviet attack in the entire Rzhev sector would face serious challenges in storming the German positions.

The Red Army's preparations for a new offensive were increasingly clear to the Germans. From 18 November there were sporadic bombardments as artillery units zeroed their guns, and the following day there was what seemed a reconnaissance in force against the northern flank of 5th Panzer Division. As was almost routine, the Germans reacted with a counterattack to restore their front line, but the initial attempt was beaten off and it took until 20 November for the former positions to be recovered.

A further Soviet attack on 20 November was correctly interpreted as a reconnaissance probe in advance of a major assault. Some of these attacks were more effective than others, and they were not popular with soldiers in the front line. North of Rzhev, Gorbachevsky was told to prepare for such an operation:

An order from Glukhov, the regiment commander, arrived: reconnaissance in force! The operation was entrusted to our battalion.

How many tragic stories I have heard about reconnaissance in force! How the generals believed in it and valued it highly, and with what horror the soldiers spoke those words – few survived them and it was considered good fortune if they were wounded and dragged back from the battlefield by their comrades ...

... Even then I understood that 'reconnaissance in force' was an invention of the Supreme Commander and his generals. Depending on the task, a platoon, company, or battalion was sent on a mission, but the numbers made no difference – the fact was that men were driven to slaughter, to certain death. The staff officers believed that the main purpose of the operation was to scare the enemy as much as possible so that he thought a large-scale attack had begun and thus opened fire from all points; our clever observers would then spot them and bring down suppressing fire. In practice, this was often not the case.

In fact, reconnaissance in force was pure deception. The most it could do was clarify the position of the leading edge. With defence in depth and the constant movement of firing points, even this couldn't be achieved. Counting on the complete suppression of the enemy's firing points during an attack was just stupidity: like us, the Germans quickly figured out such tricks. Like a monster, reconnaissance in force devoured lives and when the attack took place, the enemy's weapons usually opened fire and the infantry bled to death when they reached the enemy's positions.[30]

To Gorbachevsky's great relief, the operation was cancelled at the last moment. While he might have had a low opinion of reconnaissance in force, others saw it as very valuable. Colonel Maxim Afanasevich Voloshin was chief of intelligence in Thirty-Ninth Army, facing the Germans at the northern tip of the Rzhev Salient:

Reconnaissance in force, generally speaking, is active action aimed at fully discovering the enemy's fire system, and clarifying the characteristics of his defences. Could this data be obtained through everyday observation? It was possible, but was often incomplete. The fact was, the defending side strove not to reveal its secrets until necessary. Therefore, part of the firepower in a fixed defensive line was 'frozen'. This meant that they were prohibited from firing at small groups or single soldiers. They only became effective at the beginning of a major attack. And then, carefully camouflaged machine-guns, field guns, and mortars would suddenly come to life.

What could be done to counteract this ploy? The answer: an imitation of an offensive. The task was to force the enemy to believe that it was really an offensive operation, making them use all their firepower and perhaps to bring forward reserves. Having done this, the unit conducting the reconnaissance in force withdrew to its previously occupied positions.

... On the eve of our reconnaissance in force, we decided to carry out special training. Some in the selected regiment shrugged their shoulders in bewilderment. What sort of training were we intending? War was war, there was no need for any rehearsal. After all, you couldn't predict in advance what would happen in a real battle. Nevertheless, the regiment commander insisted, and as it turned out, he did the right thing.

At some distance from the front line, in the rear of the regiment, we chose terrain that largely resembled the area where we were to operate. We marked a start line and deployed the men. The groups moved forward on our signal. Everything seemed to proceed according to plan, but neither Major Tomin [commander of the rifle regiment] nor I were satisfied with the actions of the soldiers and their officers. They advanced sluggishly and uncertainly. Moreover, the first and second groups merged and didn't cover their flanks, and contrary to our plan, attempted to attack the bunker before them. After a short discussion of the exercise, the groups returned to their original position. We did it again and again. The training continued until it was possible to move quickly, with clear interaction of all the subunits of the detachment ...

The next day, at precisely the appointed hour, the regimental field gun fired its first shot at the enemy bunkers. This was the signal to start. Artillery and mortars began to fire ... Some of the shells were smoke rounds. It seemed that we were inflicting a powerful blow with all the means at our disposal. The Nazis came to the conclusion that the regiment was advancing across the entire sector.

After one or two minutes, the flank groups broke into the [German] trench. Hand-to-hand fighting ensued ... The soldiers seized a machine-gun, ammunition, and documents from dead men; all other ammunition, personal effects and equipment were set ablaze with bottles of fuel. Meanwhile, dozens of observers in our trenches recorded firing points and the direction from which the Nazis' artillery was firing. More and more marks appeared on our maps. I remember that the reconnaissance in force lasted just 17 minutes, but we managed to discover their full system of fire and to a large extent clarify the positions of the Fascists' front line.[31]

Given the manner in which the Red Army repeatedly found that the German defences had not been suppressed by the initial bombardment and were firing from previously unsuspected positions, it seems that Gorbachevsky's assessment of the value of reconnaissance in force is perhaps closer to the truth than Voloshin's memoirs suggest.

Astonishingly, the German signals interception service picked up a transmission to a Soviet commissar operating with partisans, informing the partisan group that the offensive would commence on 25 November at 0600.[32] Other than alerting units in the front line and issuing warning orders to the few that were held in reserve, there was little for Model to do. His main army-level reserves were 1st Panzer Division and the *Grossdeutschland* motorised division. The panzer division was pulled out of the front line in early November after the arrival of 337th Infantry Division from France; it had been in almost continuous action since the onset of *Barbarossa*, and its men were relieved that they were finally getting a much-needed opportunity to recover their strength, and the warning order about a possible new Soviet offensive was therefore particularly unwelcome.

Grossdeutschland grew out of a unit that had been stationed in Berlin during the years after the First World War. The Reichswehr – the 100,000-strong army that Germany was permitted under the terms of the Treaty of Versailles – was regional in its structure, with each regiment drawing its recruits from specific areas of Germany. These units sent companies to Berlin in rotation to provide troops for a largely ceremonial unit, and ultimately this developed into *Wachtruppe Berlin* ('Guard Troop Berlin'). In 1936, this was further reorganised as *Wachregiment Berlin*, with officers and NCOs serving in annual rotations while lower ranks were rotated every six months. In 1939, the unit became the *Grossdeutschland* Infantry Regiment; while the other formations of the Wehrmacht remained largely regional, *Grossdeutschland* was intended to have volunteer personnel from all parts of Germany. It played no part in the invasion of Poland but participated in the campaign in the west in May 1940. At the onset of *Barbarossa*, the regiment joined Second Panzer Group as a reinforced motorised infantry regiment and took part in the attempts to capture Tula before pulling back to the line of the Oka River. In April 1942, the regiment was brought back to Germany and expanded into a motorised infantry division. Unlike other infantry divisions, the new unit received a panzer battalion of 30 tanks and a battalion of 21 assault guns, making it far stronger than other such motorised infantry divisions.[33] Once assembly was complete, the new division was ordered back to the Eastern Front and advanced from the area northwest of Kursk during the summer offensive towards Voronezh. By August, *Grossdeutschland* was immediately north of the lower Don, where most of its personnel enjoyed a period of rest and recuperation. There were widespread rumours that the division was to be transferred to France – a favourite posting for Wehrmacht personnel – and when orders were issued on 13 August for the division to board troop trains, it seemed that the rumoured move to France was about to happen. Instead, the division was dispatched to the north, with its leading elements reaching Smolensk on 17 August.

Grossdeutschland was technically subordinated directly to Kluge at Army Group Centre, but it was Kluge's intention to use the division in support of Model's Ninth Army. At the end of August, its troops were sent forward to the front line and took part in a local attack on 10 September. For men used to the wide open spaces of the Don steppe, their new theatre of deployment came as an unpleasant surprise:

> The way to the front led over terrible paths and log roads, which had been built by our soldiers. We passed through several destroyed villages where soldiers from other units sat in bunkers and billets among the ruins watching us approach ...
>
> [The division staff] had just arrived with the first of the headquarters personnel and begun to dig foxholes in a small area overgrown with bushes when a pair of armoured Soviet Il-2 ground attack aircraft carried out an attack on the position. Bombs fell all around the foxholes, a field policeman was blown to bits, wounded screamed and others trembled in fear. It was a small foretaste of what was to come.[34]

Later in September, *Grossdeutschland* was deployed in counterattacks to improve the German positions around Rzhev. In two weeks of fighting, it lost nearly 1,400 men killed or wounded. As it was pulled out of line and placed in reserve, its two infantry regiments were renamed the Grenadier Regiment and Fusilier Regiment. With winter approaching, men from the mountainous regions of Germany who were serving in the division were grouped together in a new ski battalion, a measure inspired by the use of ski troops by the Red Army the previous winter. As intelligence about a new Soviet attack continued to accumulate, Oberst Erich Kassnitz – the commander of the Fusilier Regiment – was ordered to form a battlegroup with his regiment, the assault gun battalion, the reconnaissance battalion, an artillery battalion and anti-aircraft and anti-tank companies, and move to the Bely area where it would form a local mobile reserve.

A little further back, Kluge's Army Group Centre had 12th Panzer Division near Bely, 19th Panzer Division to the south in Orel, and 20th Panzer Division in Dukhovshchina, to the southwest of the base of the salient. None were remotely near full strength, and Kluge and Model were both aware that they might be required to intervene in emergencies along the entire breadth of Army Group Centre's sector; consequently, Model could not automatically rely on them should his men come under attack once more.

The tremors from the steppe around Stalingrad were spreading as the scale of the Red Army's assault became increasingly clear. As Soviet tank units rolled almost unopposed towards each other on either flank of the German Sixth Army, *OKH* anxiously contacted Army Groups North and Centre to ask what reserves they might be able to release for intervention in the south. Kluge replied that he could spare nothing. His army group had barely survived the Soviet onslaught of the summer, and there was every sign that a new offensive was coming. However, it wasn't clear precisely where the blow would fall. Given the previous efforts by the Red Army to batter its way into the ruins of Rzhev, it was plausible that there would be a resumption of attacks here, and in order to encourage the Germans to believe this, Konev's Western Front ordered the armies facing the city to make preparations for an offensive. However, this attack was to start only after the main blow, directed further south at the base of the salient, had reached its first objectives. In the meantime, the preparations of Twenty-Ninth and Thirtieth Armies would serve to distract German attention from the main point of attack.

Facing the German line in front of Sychevka was Major General Nikolai Ivanovich Kiriukhin's Twentieth Army. The artillery assets that had been concentrated in this sector were immense – no fewer than 53 regiments of howitzers, mortars and rocket launchers. Behind the front line waited the main exploitation group, consisting of II Guards Cavalry Corps and VI Tank Corps. Numerically, the exploitation force was imposing, with a combined strength of over 21,000 men and 170 tanks. This was in addition to about 350 tanks in other formations of Twentieth Army. Surely this time, the sheer weight of artillery would reduce German defences to ruins, and the exploitation forces would be able to move forward quickly. The failures of the summer had been discussed at length, and the attack plans included careful and detailed preparations for the movements of all units in an attempt to ensure that reserves, artillery and supplies reached the advancing front, thus ensuring that momentum was sustained.[35] But drawing up such plans was one thing; getting troops to adhere to them was quite another.

At the same time, Kalinin Front's Forty-First Army, commanded by Major General German Fedorovich Tarasov, would attack from the west. It too had impressive assets, with over 400 tanks and about 105,000 men, and it would attack the German lines immediately south of Bely. Once the rifle divisions had overcome the German defences, Tarasov intended to insert his main exploitation force, I Mechanised Corps. The commander of the corps was Major General Mikhail Dmitrievich Solomatin. Like so many senior commanders on both sides, he had served in the First World War, rising to the rank of sergeant major prior to the revolutions of 1917, when he was elected to his battalion's committee of soldiers' representatives by his comrades. He returned to his home near Perm in the Ural Mountains and fought with the Red Guards against the Orenburg Cossack Army, one of many groups that opposed the October Revolution. In the months that followed, he was wounded twice in actions against the opponents of the Bolsheviks, ending the Civil War as a regiment commander. He was an early adherent of mechanised warfare, but in 1938 he was caught up in Stalin's purges and dismissed from the Red Army and arrested. Unlike so many others, he was released after the charges against him were not substantiated and he was reinstated. The onset of *Barbarossa* found him commanding a tank division near Kiev, and after a series of battles that cost his division almost all of his tanks, he and his surviving men – now fighting as infantry – were surrounded near Uman. He led about 300 men out of the encirclement in late August but was then caught in a second encirclement, escaping alone in civilian clothing. He commanded a tank brigade in the Battle of Moscow before being assigned to command of VIII Tank Corps during the summer of 1942, when he was heavily involved in the costly attacks against the Rzhev Salient. In September, he took command of I Mechanised Corps.

Solomatin was therefore familiar with the sort of terrain over which his corps would be expected to advance. He later wrote about some of the preparations that he described as almost routine for mechanised forces in the Red Army:

> Much time and effort had to be spent on improving roads and tracks for the corps troops to advance from their forming up areas. With almost continuous forests of swamps, the lack of good roads created great difficulties. In overcoming this, corps and brigade commanders followed a good tradition that existed in our armoured and mechanised formations even before the Great Patriotic War. Its essence was that wherever they were located, subunits studied up to 100km [60 miles] of routes of possible advance without direct instructions from their superiors, and found and eliminated any problems they located. Following this practice, the subunits of the corps were always ready for action in the appropriate direction.[36]

The degree to which this was a 'tradition' is questionable, given the repeated problems experienced by mechanised units when they were ordered to move forward; in any event, even if the commanders of the brigades of a mechanised corps took the initiative to take such steps, it is unlikely that they considered the intentions of other unrelated units to use the same roads.

I Mechanised Corps was to be committed to the attack in order to exploit the initial successes of Tarasov's Forty-First Army and would drive east. As one of the two mechanised corps originally assigned to Forty-First Army was en route for Velikiye Luki, the exploitation force was weaker than originally planned, despite the addition of independent armoured formations. Solomatin had little doubt that his men faced a tough challenge:

> In the corps' impending area of operations the enemy had strong defensive positions with bunkers and well-constructed trenches with barbed wire and minefields. This area had very numerous rivers and streams with steep and often swampy banks. There were very few roads, and even these were only country tracks.
>
> As it was to be inserted to develop the initial breakthrough made by the first operational echelon of the army, it was especially important for the corps command to have detailed information on the location of the enemy's reserves and about defensive lines in the depths of his positions.
>
> According to intelligence, the corps headquarters staff established that on the banks of the Vena River in the forests to the southeast of the town of Bely, the enemy had created strongpoints with heavy weapons and elements of 1st Panzer Division, which was considered one of the best in the Hitlerite army, and further south in Sementsevo, there were elements of 12th Panzer Division. It was known that ... a breakthrough was quite possible, but immediately after it entered the breakthrough, the mechanised corps would encounter the enemy's panzer divisions. This required appropriate organisation of the corps' battle formations.[37]

This account is probably coloured by knowledge acquired after the battles; at the time, 12th Panzer Division was not in this area. Nonetheless, Solomatin had little doubt that exploitation of any breakthrough would not be straightforward. He therefore proposed two alternatives. The first was that in the event of a rapid breakthrough, he would commit his mechanised corps in two echelons, with three brigades leading and tank brigades held behind each flank to exploit further successes. The second plan, to be followed if I Mechanised Corps needed to assist in the initial breakthrough, had two tank brigades and a mechanised brigade in the first echelon.

As final preparations were made, there were disagreements between Solomatin and Tarasov: the former wanted to have the independent mechanised units of Forty-First Army assigned to his command, whereas Tarasov insisted on holding them back in reserve. Perhaps assuming that the brigades would be released to him once the attack began, Solomatin planned for their early deployment alongside his corps and therefore intended to deploy his own brigades on diverging axes – the independent brigades, he assumed, would be available to ensure that none of his units was overwhelmed in isolation.

On the northern flank of Forty-First Army was Major General Vasilii Aleksandrovich Iushkevich's Twenty-Second Army. Although it had been assigned a largely supporting role in *Mars*, it possessed the relatively new III Mechanised Corps, now commanded by the redoubtable Katukov. He had spent much of the summer in battles near Bryansk and in mid-September had been summoned to a meeting with Stalin, where the two men discussed the strengths and weaknesses of Soviet tanks in a manner that showed how Stalin was beginning to trust his front-line commanders, even as Hitler was moving in the opposite direction. But the conversation also shows that, just like Hitler, Stalin was inclined to get involved in minutiae that were perhaps inappropriate for a supreme commander:

[Stalin asked] 'Do you think our tanks are good or not? Give me your honest opinion.'

I replied that the T-34s had fully proved their worth in battle and we had high hopes for them. But the heavy KV tanks and the T-60s and T-70s were not popular in the army.

Stalin raised a questioning eyebrow. 'Why?'

'The KV is very heavy and clumsy and not very manoeuvrable. They overcome obstacles with difficulty, while the T-34s have no such problems. In addition, the KV often damages bridges and generally causes a lot of avoidable difficulty. The gun on the KV is the same 76mm gun as on the T-34. So the question is, what combat advantages does the heavier tank give us? If the KV had a more powerful gun with a larger calibre, it would be a different matter. Perhaps we could put up with its problems and design flaws.' I also criticised the T-60 light tank. Its gun was self-loading but only 20mm calibre. It couldn't be used in serious combat against enemy armoured forces. It also had low ground clearance and to try to advance and attack through snow and mud often left it stranded. In the battles near Moscow, we often had to tow these tanks. The light T-70 had better armour and was armed with a 45mm gun, and had two engines, but it had only just entered service and so far had not demonstrated any special capabilities.

The supreme commander listened attentively without interrupting. But after I had outlined my opinions about the tanks in our army he tried to persuade me with unexpected sharpness that my criticisms of the KV, T-60 and T-70 were incorrect and that perhaps we tankers just underestimated them.

Of course, I was worried as I listened to Stalin but I stuck to my guns. I gave a number of examples that showed that the KV, T-60 and T-70 hadn't performed well on the battlefield. He then suggested to me: 'If we arm the tanks – at least the heavy ones – with a more powerful gun, they will be more useful to us.'

… I also told the supreme commander about the lack of radios in the tank forces. At the beginning of the war, only the command vehicles had radios while the other vehicles didn't, making control of the battle difficult. The situation remained almost unchanged in 1942. I also complained about shortages of signal cable for field telephones …

He asked me: 'Do our tanks shoot while moving?' I replied that they didn't. 'Why?' he looked at me intently.

'Accuracy is poor while moving and we can't waste the shells,' I replied. 'After all, our requests for ammunition aren't being met.'

Stalin stopped and looked at me closely, speaking each word clearly. 'Tell me, Comrade Katukov, do you need to hit the Germans every time during an attack? And who do you need to hit first of all? Our tanks are hindered by enemy guns moving forward. Even if your shells don't hit them, but explode nearby, how can the Germans operate in such an environment?'

'Of course, their accuracy will decrease,' I conceded.

'This is what we need,' Stalin said. 'Shoot on the move, and we will give you more shells, now that we have them.'[38]

At the end of the meeting, Stalin offered Katukov the command of III Mechanised Corps. Katukov even had the choice of which brigades he would have in his new command – he pointedly didn't select a brigade equipped with heavy KV-1 tanks, on the grounds that they would struggle in the swampy terrain.

It was a wise choice, as the region in which Kalinin Front made its preparations was far from ideal. As the Red Army had discovered in the previous 12 months, there were few decent roads in the region, and the almost endless swamps and forests made the task of a defending force far easier. The rivers in the area were likely to be frozen hard but they often had steep banks, which would greatly impede motorised units trying to advance – this was the very region in which the Soviet units encircled during *Seydlitz* had struggled to escape and had been crushed by the Wehrmacht. The distance from the eastern side of the Rzhev Salient to the western side was about 65 miles (105km). The leading forces of Southwest Front had advanced nearly 30 miles (50km) on just the first day of their counteroffensive; a replication of that success in the central sector by the two attacking Fronts would leave them within touching distance. The Soviet plan actually expected a slower advance, given the more difficult terrain, but in any event, Zhukov and his Front commanders were confident that their units would be able to achieve the advances expected of them.

In order to tie down German forces to prevent their use against the attacking groups, Kalinin Front also planned to strike against the northern tip of the salient. Here, the last operations of the spring had concentrated on clearing German bridgeheads on the line of the Volga and nearby rivers. While preparing for one such operation, Major General Alexei Ivanovich Zygin, commander of the reconstituted Thirty-Ninth Army, surprised Lieutenant Colonel Konstantin Alekseevich Malygin, commander of 28th Tank Brigade, with an unwelcome order that he was to release his motorised infantry battalion to a different formation on the eve of the operation. When Malygin protested, he found himself summoned to Thirty-Ninth Army's military council:

Half an hour later I stood in front of the members of the military council of the army in a small bunker, illuminated by a kerosene lamp. Among those present I saw my old colleague Colonel [Ksenofont Mikhailovich] Malakhov [deputy commander of Thirty-Ninth Army]. He was the only one who supported me. The others sharply criticised my protests, terming them as arrogant and intolerant of orders from a superior.

'The brigade's motorised infantry,' I explained, 'is inseparable from the tanks. We have experience of attacks on Usovo, when we lost 11 vehicles without achieving success because we had no infantry with us. This happened because the brigade didn't have its own motorised battalion, and the infantry of the rifle division to which we were attached did not follow the tanks that had pushed on ahead. We took this into account and now each motorised platoon is responsible for the vehicle with which it operates. They are always linked to the tank crew and appropriate signalling measures have been developed and studied to that end. Motorised riflemen fill the gap between the tanks and the advancing infantry of the [rifle] division. When the tank stops on the battlefield and the crew need to get out to fix a malfunction, the motorised infantry can protect it. If the tank crew are then endangered, the only ones who can warn them are the motorised infantry platoon assigned to them.

'Everyone knows that visibility is limited from a tank. If it moves ahead and the infantry lags behind, the crew may not notice. Who can protect them in those circumstances? If there is no enemy fire, the motorised infantry sits on the tank and they can advance quickly to an important objective. The tank isn't alone. I could list many cases of cooperation between a tank and a motorised infantry platoon. And also, they are friends and know each other's habits, abilities, and personalities. This is an entire organism and I think it's unacceptable to tear it apart just before battle.'

Zygin pondered this. 'Fine,' he said, 'as soon as a penetration is achieved, the battalion will be at your disposal again.'[39]

It seems that at least some commanders were now aware of the need for greater improvement in infantry–armour cooperation, but this dispute was about the use of mechanised infantry after a penetration had been achieved. Malygin still expected infantry divisions to provide the initial breakthrough, and to cooperate closely with his tanks until this had been achieved.

Despite the losses suffered in the recent fighting and the enormous strain that they had been under, it seems that morale was generally good among the men of the German Ninth Army. They were aware that they had fought a battle of great intensity and had inflicted huge losses on their opponents; while the German line had been driven back in many locations, the key positions of the salient – the road running from Sychevka to the north, and of course Rzhev itself – remained firmly in German hands. Their belief in their army commander was high, and while the terrain was the same area where Soviet troops had burst through the previous winter, the situation was now very different, with German forces occupying prepared defences and with armoured forces standing ready behind the front line.

The German unit that would bear the brunt of Western Front's new offensive was XXXIX Panzer Corps, still commanded by Arnim, though he would be replaced by General Robert Martinek on 1 December. His divisions faced the Red Army over the battlefields of the late summer and autumn, the shallow, muddy valleys of the Osuga and Vazuza Rivers; from right to left, 337th, 78th and 102nd Infantry Divisions licked their wounds and continued their attempts to build fortifications in the swampy landscape. Much of 1st and 5th Panzer Divisions remained in the front line, with elements scattered among the infantry divisions to provide them with vital anti-tank support, greatly to the dissatisfaction of the panzer division commanders, while 9th Panzer Division and part of 337th Infantry Division were held near Sychevka in readiness to intervene if required. Just on the eve of the Soviet assault, 78th Infantry Division took over much of the sector held by 5th Panzer Division, allowing it to concentrate behind the front line. Further north, the sector up to Rzhev was under the control of XXVII Corps. On paper, the corps – commanded by General Walter Weiss since the beginning of July – looked formidable, with 95th, 72nd, 256th, 129th, 87th and 251st Infantry Divisions in the front line and 14th Motorised Division standing in reserve, but none of these divisions were remotely near full strength – regiments were barely at the strength of a single battalion, and in many cases units remained under the command of junior officers or even NCOs as a result of the summer casualties. The units of 6th Infantry Division, which had been involved in some of the bitterest fighting to the north of Rzhev, were now under the control of 129th Infantry Division, while the headquarters of 6th Infantry Division withdrew into Rzhev itself and was assigned as the main control point for the entire Rzhev bridgehead.

Next in line was General Carl Hilpert's XXIII Corps with 206th, 253rd and 110th Infantry Divisions holding a line that ran from east to west to the north of Olenino before curving sharply back towards the south. Beyond XXIII Corps was Model's left flank formation, XLI Panzer Corps around Bely under the command of General Josef Harpe. Two of its formations – 246th and 86th Infantry Divisions – were in much the same state as their neighbours in Ninth Army, but the third division in XLI Panzer Corps was a new innovation on the Eastern Front.

With the German infantry divisions on the Eastern Front all far below their establishment strength, there were discussions at the top of the German command structure about transferring manpower to replenish their ranks. The obvious source was the Luftwaffe, which was lavishly manned and had large numbers of men in relatively quiet rear area posts; this was exacerbated by the aircraft losses the Luftwaffe had suffered, resulting in many of its support services being effectively redundant. On 12 September 1942, Hitler issued orders for a remarkable 200,000 men to be transferred to the army. These men were to be used to bring the infantry divisions back to something approaching full strength. Although the Luftwaffe personnel had only basic training in the use of small arms and no experience whatever of fighting as infantry, it was felt that by using them as replacement drafts who would be deployed alongside the veterans in the front line, they would perform no worse than the new recruits being sent to the infantry divisions.

Almost inevitably, the plan fell foul of the constant rivalry and empire-building that prevailed in the Third Reich. Hermann Goering, the commander of the Luftwaffe, had no intention of permitting such large numbers of men to be taken from his command, and he made an alternative proposal to Hitler. Instead of transferring the men to the army, he suggested, they should be used to create Luftwaffe field divisions. There was a precedent for this; *Luftwaffen-Division Meindl* was created in Army Group North in February 1942 from surplus Luftwaffe personnel; it had up to six Luftwaffe field regiments in its ranks, which were assigned to support different front-line formations in the German Sixteenth Army rather than fighting as a single entity. In this role, they performed adequately, not least because many of their personnel were from paratrooper units – unlike the forces of Britain and the United States, airborne forces in Germany came under the control of the Luftwaffe rather than the army. The division commander, Generalmajor Eugen Meindl, had started the war as an artillery officer, seeing action in the occupation of Norway, before transferring to the Luftwaffe. Here, he commanded glider-borne air-landing infantry during the invasion of Crete in May 1941, during which he was seriously wounded before taking command of a group of former paratroopers and air-landing infantry on the Eastern Front in early 1942. He was therefore an experienced front-line soldier with extensive knowledge of fighting in a ground role; the same was not remotely true of the great majority of Luftwaffe officers.

Rather than relinquish control of so many men, Goering wished to create unified divisions that would be deployed as complete units rather than being parcelled out as had been the case with *Luftwaffen-Division Meindl*. One of the arguments that might have played a big part in what followed was his assertion that the Luftwaffe's personnel were more politically attuned to National Socialism than the regular army. The winter fighting outside Moscow in late 1941 and early 1942 had reinforced Hitler's belief that the conservative officers of the army would never fully embrace his political views. This is perhaps a further indication of the trend that first surfaced during the winter fighting outside Moscow, when the intangible and unmeasurable 'fanatical will to fight' became as much a factor in the thinking of Hitler and his entourage as more practical concerns such as numerical strength and manpower. The alleged greater commitment to National Socialism of the Luftwaffe was regarded as adequate compensation for the obvious and huge disadvantages of deploying these new units as exclusively Luftwaffe formations rather than using their personnel to provide much-needed reinforcements for the 'less politically reliable' regular army formations.

Much to the irritation of the army, Hitler agreed with Goering's proposal, and five days after Hitler's order for the transfer of personnel to the army, a new set of instructions was issued. The Luftwaffe personnel were now to be used to create 20 Luftwaffe field divisions, which would function under the overall command of the Luftwaffe. Officers for these divisions were meant to volunteer, while lower ranks would be re-assigned from existing Luftwaffe posts. Anti-aircraft artillery in the German armed forces had always been part of the Luftwaffe, and these units were expected to provide the personnel for the artillery components of the new divisions.[40] Many senior officers in the army were convinced that this decision was complete folly. Manstein, who commanded panzer corps, armies and army groups through much of the war on the Eastern Front, argued at length with Hitler about the plans, and later wrote:

> Considering what a wide choice had been open to the Luftwaffe in making its selections for these divisions, they were doubtless composed of first-class soldiers. Had they been drafted into army divisions as replacements in autumn 1941 to maintain the latter at their full fighting strength, the German Army might well have been saved from most of the emergencies of the winter of 1941–42. But to form these excellent troops into divisions within the framework of the Luftwaffe was sheer lunacy. Where were they to get the necessary close-combat training and practice in working with other formations? Where were they to get the battle experience so vital in the east? And where was the Luftwaffe to find divisional, regimental and battalion commanders?
>
> I covered all these aspects in detail during that talk with Hitler and a little later set them out in a memorandum I drafted for his attention. He listened to my arguments attentively enough, but insisted that he had already given the matter his fullest consideration and must stick to his decision.[41]

It was recognised from the outset that these new divisions would lack any front-line experience. Goering issued orders that the officers were to undergo short courses in which they would learn about tactics and the technical management of infantry divisions, while lower ranks would be expected to learn the new skills essential for ground fighting after they arrived behind the front line. Goering insisted that these divisions should then be assigned to quiet sectors of the front line, where they would have time to bring themselves up to the standard required.

Unfortunately for the personnel of these new divisions, there were few sectors of the Eastern Front that could really be regarded as 'quiet', and from the outset, the new divisions were deployed right in the front line. Numerically, they were far weaker than their army equivalents, with two *Luftwaffen-Jäger* regiments, each with three battalions, a separate *Luftwaffen-Füsilier* battalion, an artillery regiment, a battalion of combat engineers, and a *Luftwaffen-Panzerjäger* battalion. In many cases, these supporting units – particularly the vital *Panzerjäger* battalions – were far weaker than their army counterparts. By contrast, regular divisions had – at least on paper – three infantry regiments, each with three battalions. One of these new Luftwaffe units, 2nd Luftwaffe Field Division, formed the extreme left wing of XLI Panzer Corps. Its personnel began to arrive in Ninth Army's sector in early November and were immediately ordered to take up positions in the front line. Its commander was Oberst Hellmuth Pätzold, who had no experience whatever of commanding ground-based combat formations; nor had the great majority of his subordinate officers. The time between the arrival of the personnel of 2nd Luftwaffe Field Division and the beginning of the new Soviet offensive was too brief for any meaningful training to take place, and far short of the time required to bring the division up to the standard required for serious ground combat. Pätzold and his men were about to learn the realities of life on the Eastern Front in the most brutal manner.

CHAPTER 10

THE COMMENCEMENT OF *MARS*: WESTERN FRONT, 25–30 NOVEMBER

In any attack during wartime, surprise is a most desirable element, even if it isn't absolutely essential. Surprise can come in many forms. The timing of an attack, its location and strength, the scale of overall intentions, the illusion of an attack at a different location – all can contribute considerably to improving the chances of success. In the case of *Mars*, the Germans knew almost exactly when and where the attack would fall and were as prepared as they could be to receive it. The omens for the new Soviet operation were not good; when one takes into account the failure of the Red Army to break through to Rzhev and Sychevka earlier in 1942, the odds against success were daunting at best, yet Zhukov and his subordinates do not appear to have placed any value on such considerations before they commenced another attempt to crush the salient that had already been the scene of so much bloodshed.

On the German side of the front line, Model and Kluge had no doubt that an attack was coming, but there was little clear indication of the scale of the new assault. Gehlen's reports from *FHO* continued to be ambiguous, particularly regarding the capabilities of the Red Army – did the Soviet Union possess sufficient resources for a major offensive in the central sector at the same time as the operations unfolding around Stalingrad? Kluge issued a warning order on 23 November that a Soviet attack would probably occur early on 25 or 26 November, and the following day, Model's army began artillery bombardments of suspected Red Army movement routes and forming-up areas.

Mars involved no fewer than four major assaults on the Rzhev Salient: Western Front's attack from the east; and three separate attacks by the armies of Kalinin Front. These unfolded simultaneously, with the result that Model and his corps commanders had to use their limited reserves with the utmost care.

Shortly before 0800 on 25 November, the massed guns of the Red Army began their bombardment. While the weight of the shelling was impressive, the German fortifications and bunkers facing Konev's Western Front protected most of the defenders from the hail of shrapnel and explosions. In earlier months, the screech of *Katyusha* rockets – known to the German soldiers as 'Stalin organs' – was a terrifying sound, but the hardened veterans of Ninth Army had learned during the summer and autumn that these weapons were relatively inaccurate and that they always represented the end of the Red Army's bombardment. As the shrieks of the rockets died away, the German infantry took up their positions in preparation.

The weather had changed slightly overnight, with the advent of fog. As a consequence of this, there was little scope for the Soviet gunners to correct their aim, but at this stage of the war the initial bombardment almost always proceeded according to plans drawn up in preceding days. After 90 minutes of shelling, the Red Army commenced its ground attack. The first obstacles were barbed wire entanglements, minefields, and the frozen Vazuza River. As the leading attackers climbed the riverbank away from the ice and the following waves of infantry moved forward, the defenders opened fire in earnest.

Despite taking heavy casualties, the Soviet rifle divisions of Twentieth Army in the first assault managed to press forward perhaps a mile or so into the German lines. Nonetheless, the area that had been secured remained under almost constant German artillery fire, making it difficult to move forward reinforcements. Crucially, the advance had failed to secure the route that Kiriukhin had intended to use as a forward forming-up area for his exploitation group of cavalry and tanks. As a result, these units would have to be committed in the small space that had been gained at such heavy cost. Their forward movement was certain to add to the congestion and would provide the Germans with an irresistible target for air and artillery attack.

In addition to Kiriukhin's Twentieth Army, the neighbouring Thirty-First Army attacked a little to the north. In its path were the lines of the German 102nd Infantry Division, and the lethal defensive fire shredded the attacking units. Almost no impression was made by the attack, which left many battalions and regiments reduced to half their starting strength. Immediately to the south of 102nd Infantry Division, elements of 5th Panzer Division were still in the

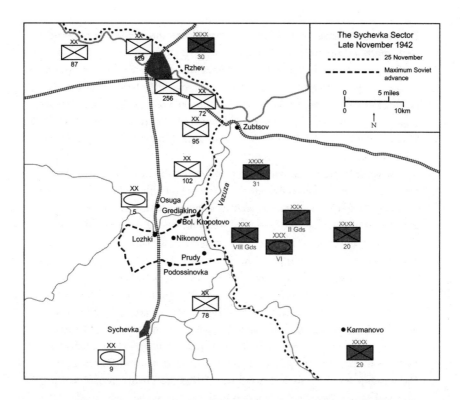

front line. The Soviet bombardment had destroyed almost all telephone cables running back from the trenches, but the division's experienced subunit commanders needed no directions from above. An NCO in the division's panzer regiment wrote an account shortly after:

Drumfire began at 0530 [the Germans operated on Berlin time, regardless of where they were deployed], far exceeding anything previously experienced during this war. Immediately we climbed into our tanks and drove into positions that had been prepared for a daytime attack. I took command of the platoon. While our position shuddered under the hail of fire, 30–40 Russian tanks, including ten T-34s, rolled towards our position from the forest. Masses of infantry in winter clothing followed.

The first attack collapsed under the heavy fire of our artillery. We brought the tanks that had advanced within effective range under fire. Within three minutes I shot up four American-built tanks. Oberleutnant Kettner shot up two more.

The rest of the enemy pulled back into the forest. The infantry were brought under machine-gun fire and driven off.

Every hour, the Russians launched infantry attacks against our position supported by heavy artillery fire. Icy snowstorms helped them advance and significantly reduced our field of vision and we could only see them through our gunsights. Despite this, the enemy didn't succeed in reaching our positions. Machine-gun fire and HE rounds from the tank guns were lethal, raising the morale of our men.

The Russians made a second tank attack at 0930. Eight T-34s advanced from Timonino Wood in a line and fired at us. I took a hit on the right track, reducing my mobility and leaving me stranded in a rather unsatisfactory position. We remained in the vehicle, firing with all weapons. The tanks approaching from Timonino grew more numerous. In a short time 43 tanks, including heavy models, moved towards our position. When they were 500m away they turned towards Gredyakino. We bitterly rued the lack of long-barrelled guns, but continued to fire at the steel lumps. As I was no longer mobile and the Russians had noticed this, I came under fire from a T-34. A shot passed through the vehicle and a few seconds later the commander's cupola was blown away. We baled out, everyone was uninjured apart from a few scrapes. I immediately formed a 'tank destruction troop' armed with hand grenades, cans of fuel, and smoke grenades. The Russians broke through between our village and Gredyakino with strong armoured forces. We could only watch in frustration as the enemy tanks rolled towards Boblevo and Nokonovo.[1]

During the afternoon, Kiriukhin reorganised his forces to try to exploit the gains made in the initial attack. The full weight of his army struck the centre of the German XXXIX Panzer Corps and pushed the Germans back further, though at a terrible cost. During the evening, the Germans moved their modest local reserves into the front line in an attempt to shore up the defences. Model authorised the release of 9th Panzer Division to XXXIX Panzer Corps, as both he and Arnim anticipated that the Red Army would attempt to commit its armoured exploitation force in this sector, where they had enjoyed the most success.

The modest gains made by the Red Army were a disappointment for Konev, but the full weight of his forces was yet to be deployed. Interrogation of prisoners captured during the day revealed that, in many cases, the positions that Soviet scouts had identified as the main German battle line were in reality no more than strong outposts, with the main line further back; consequently, much of the preparatory artillery bombardment did little to suppress the German defensive fire plan. There was little time for extensive reconnaissance before the attack was renewed, and the Soviet commanders could only hope that their artillery would do better the following day. Kiriukhin and Konev discussed the situation and concluded that the cavalry and armour could move forward. Originally, it had been intended to commit these formations together, but insufficient ground had been secured to the west of the Vazuza for both corps to form up for battle; consequently, VI Tank Corps was to move forward first and support the infantry in their ongoing attempts to widen their penetration. The cavalry corps would then follow, and a third group, consisting of a motorised rifle division and a tank brigade, would follow the cavalry. This would permit the leading tanks and horsemen to bypass isolated German units and push on into the depths of the German defences, while the motorised infantry and tanks then mopped up the Germans left in their wake.

One of the big factors in the Red Army's failures of the summer and autumn was the poor road network of the region. There were no major all-weather roads running in the direction of the Soviet thrust, and the poor-quality roads and tracks that the ground forces had to use had been badly degraded by the combination of large-scale troop movements, the inclement weather and artillery fire. The painful lessons of the previous attacks had been learned, but the adopted solutions proved to be ineffective. In order to try to avoid the problems experienced with advancing units being left without supplies and reinforcements, columns of transports and horse-drawn carts had been assembled with orders to follow the advancing units as closely as possible, but in the absence of adequate roads and tracks these arrangements merely added to the congestion. Throughout the night, columns of men and vehicles struggled forward through the forests. The German artillery units were of course well aware of the routes that advancing Soviet units would have to take and fired constantly through the night, adding to the chaos – every time a vehicle was hit and disabled, movement came to a halt until it was pushed to one side. Although a few crossing points across the Vazuza had been reinforced, there were still considerable bottlenecks at the river, and none of the units intended for the second day's attacks were in position by dawn. An officer with II Guards Cavalry Corps reported about the struggle to move forward:

> The small area was packed with troops, wagons, trucks, ammunition, artillery, cavalry and other units. In places the terrain was open and there were no trees. Consequently the combat units, supply and transport columns, artillery, and cavalry became muddled and crowded together … The enemy is sweeping our

combat units with artillery and mortars from left to right and through the full depth of their positions and attacking from the air. Our units have no cover and are packed together in low ground and in the open, and suffer huge losses of men, horses and equipment. In some places the gullies are packed with thousands of corpses and dead horses. Some regiments are almost unfit for combat due to the heavy losses of men and horses. As far as I can see there is no unified command over the units in this sector.[2]

When they reached the Vazuza, the tanks of VI Tank Corps found that the river ice was up to 20cm thick but could support the weight of only wheeled vehicles – tanks would simply break through and sink. The few bridges that the Red Army's combat engineers had constructed became the focus of columns of traffic trying to move east. German shelling of the area continued throughout the night, adding to the chaos and confusion.

Before dawn on 26 November, fighting flared up again. The Soviet armoured forces were still struggling to move into position, and the renewed attacks were made largely with the rifle regiments that had suffered heavy losses the previous day; at the same time, the German forces attempted to restore their lines. The columns of VI Tank Corps struggled into position and finally attacked in the early afternoon after another artillery bombardment. Inevitably, many tanks didn't reach the start line, stranded in the rear either by breakdowns or the tangle of traffic, but three brigades moved forward against the German defences. The tank corps had been ordered to reach the road and railway line running north from Sychevka to Rzhev, and despite intense defensive fire it pushed through the German positions, literally crushing some while bypassing others, much as the Soviet planners had intended. Despite local successes though, a decisive breakthrough eluded the Soviet units. The right flank tank brigade lost half of its tanks trying in vain to overcome the fortified villages where the Germans repeatedly fought back tenaciously. Only a single tank battalion from the brigade managed to break through and reach the critical road. The other two tank brigades of VI Tank Corps enjoyed greater success, and by the end of the day they had reached positions just to the east of the Sychevka–Rzhev road, but most of the tanks were unaccompanied by infantry. Numerous German strongpoints remained in their rear, hindering the forward movement of reinforcements and, critically, supplies. The tank corps had had barely half its tanks still running at the end of the day, and the surviving vehicles were short of fuel and ammunition. Without infantry and logistic support, they would be very vulnerable. To make matters worse for the Soviet troops at the tip of the advance, 9th Panzer Division was now arriving in strength and making its presence felt as it deployed along the Sychevka–Rzhev road.[3]

A little further north, the men of 5th Panzer Division came under renewed attack; the survivors of the previous day's fighting had taken up positions that they held despite repeated attacks by tanks and infantry, and a major counterattack was made with two battlegroups, one from the north and one from the south. The northern group enjoyed considerable success, but the southern group made almost no progress. This allowed the Soviet units to switch their forces to oppose the northern group, preventing any further German advance. The village of Prudy, at the southern edge of the penetration in 5th Panzer Division's sector, was in Soviet hands by mid-morning. Having started the battle with few long-barrelled Pz.IVs that could engage T-34s on equal terms, 5th Panzer Division was now down to just one such tank and in danger of being broken up by the numerically stronger Soviet units opposing it, but help was on its way. A small group from 1st Panzer Division was ordered to move up and provide support, but far greater help would come from 9th Panzer Division, which was ordered to dispatch a group of about 40 tanks to the endangered sector. Generalleutnant Eduard Metz, commander of 5th Panzer Division, wanted to concentrate all available forces on the northern flank of the Soviet penetration and then strike towards the southeast; he argued that he knew the terrain well and that this would be the best direction of attack, but he was overruled, not least because delays in refuelling held up the arrival of 9th Panzer Division's tanks. Finally, as the day drew to an end, the reinforcements arrived and attacked the Soviet forces directly from the west. The attack made very little progress before it came to a halt.[4]

The front line was badly disrupted. Everywhere, there were small pockets of German troops that had been bypassed by the advancing Soviet units – subsequent echelons were meant to be mopping up these isolated groups, but the traffic chaos in the immediate rear of Western Front's units remained a huge problem. The German counterattacks might have made little progress, but they had isolated several of the leading Red Army units. Both sides desperately needed to bring forward supplies, establish or repair communications, and reorganise battered or muddled formations. Konev and Kiriukhin met that evening and were joined by Zhukov. It was an unhappy meeting, and Zhukov demanded greater success. The men and horses of II Guards Cavalry Corps were now moving forward, but found the approaches to the crossings were choked with men and equipment struggling to reach their parent units with supplies and reinforcements. The commander of 20th Cavalry Division, Colonel Pavel Trofimovich Kursakov, could do little but wait impotently, but his scouts discovered that there was a ferry towards the south that was barely being used. Immediately, Kursakov ordered his 103rd Cavalry Regiment to use this to cross. The horsemen moved forward to Novo-Grinevka, which they discovered was still in German hands. A first attack was beaten off by the Germans, but supported by mortars and artillery, the dismounted cavalrymen attacked again. Despite suffering serious losses, including most of their officers, they succeeded in overrunning the village by dawn.[5]

The plans for the following day for Western Front remained broadly unchanged. The cavalry corps was to join VI Tank Corps and cut the Sychevka–Rzhev road, while infantry would clear the area where isolated German groups continued to hold out. The huge congestion on the roads and at the river crossings meant that most of Western Front's powerful artillery assets remained stranded in their original positions and it would thus be impossible for them to support the leading units, but delays in continuing the operation were unacceptable to Zhukov and Konev – the Germans would have sufficient time to bring up reinforcements and reorganise.

The third day of the offensive commenced with a bitter argument between Kiriukhin at Twentieth Army headquarters and Colonel Paul Matisovich Arman, the acting commander of VI Tank Corps. The experienced Major General Andrei Lavrentiyevich Getman had been unable to command the corps at the outset of the operation, and Arman radioed Kiriukhin to protest that without resupply, his tanks were unable to advance further to take control of the Sychevka–Bely rail and road link. Several villages to his rear were still in German hands, either because they had been bypassed or because German soldiers had moved back into them after the Soviet armour had moved on – the failure of the Red Army's infantry to keep pace with the advancing tanks was once more exposed. Kiriukhin reluctantly withdrew his demands that the tank corps continue its advance and agreed that, for the moment, Arman was to take up a defensive position and await reinforcements and supplies.[6] With the cavalry corps moving forward, Kiriukhin had good reason to hope that this delay would be temporary.

Unfortunately for Kiriukhin, the men of II Guards Cavalry Corps were not making the progress that had been expected of them. Far from being inserted into a gap in the German defences, the cavalry found itself having to create the breach, a task for which it lacked the firepower. Lev Markovich Plonskiy witnessed the cavalry attack:

> Our losses were wild. I will never forget one incident. Many of our troops were gathered together on open ground. The cavalry corps, which was intended to

break through into the German rear, was brought up to the forward positions. There was nowhere to take cover. Shells ricocheted and struck everything. It was as if death passed through the ranks of the cavalry with a scythe. But nobody gave the order for the squadrons to pull back to the nearest woodland where they could shelter from the deadly fire. The whole field was littered with the corpses of men and horses. The offensive was a failure but we were stubbornly driven into the slaughter. When we approached the forward observation post, my radio operator was seriously wounded by a mine explosion. The cavalry medics couldn't save him and he died in their arms.

The infantry manned small ditches and trenches right under the noses of the Germans. There were heaps of corpses everywhere. They couldn't be removed because of heavy mortar and machine-gun fire. We covered the trenches with the corpses of our dead comrades. The only advantage in being in the outpost was that the German artillery struck the front line less frequently than the immediate rear zone. Some of the infantry began to waver. There were two infantrymen next to me in a nearby trench. In turn, they raised an arm from the trench until they were shot, and then bandaged their wounds and crawled to the rear. But in those days, any arm wound was considered 'suspicious'. Some infantrymen later told me that these two 'jokers' were shot by the NKVD detachment in full view of everyone else …

It's impossible to describe in words what happened near Rzhev and Sychevka in those days. You just can't find words that would fully reflect this terrible tragedy. You can't talk about it … After the war, for a long time I tried to forget all those terrible and monstrous things I saw. I carried a bitter burden of guilt about my dead comrades – why did I stay alive when they were all killed?[7]

With grim determination, the leading formations of the cavalry corps – 20th Cavalry Division and 3rd Guards Cavalry Division – succeeded in overrunning several villages and pushed into the positions of the German 78th Infantry Division and 5th Panzer Division.[8] Two batteries of the panzer division's artillery regiment were overrun, and a counterattack by a battlegroup from 9th Panzer Division failed to restore the situation – although the German force reported the destruction of 18 T-34s, it lost eight of its own tanks and several more were unable to take part in the attack due to mechanical problems. The village of Nikonovo – more accurately, the fortified ruins of the village – became a key position, held by Oberst Gustav Freiherr von Bodenhausen, the commander of 5th Panzer Division's panzer regiment. As the Soviet cavalry attempted to slip past the southern flank of his positions, Bodenhausen gathered a handful of tanks and launched a stinging counterattack into the flank of the horsemen, inflicting substantial losses and driving them back. As the day wore on, there was welcome news of reinforcements. A regiment of 129th Infantry Division was being withdrawn from the Rzhev defences, and its two battalions would be deployed on the seam between 5th Panzer Division and 78th Infantry Division, with one battalion supporting each division. Less welcome was the news that the battalion that was assigned to support 5th Panzer Division was to be held in reserve and could only be committed with the explicit consent of the corps commander.[9] Late in the day, a fresh Soviet attack on Nikonovo was beaten off with further heavy losses for the attackers.

From the German point of view, the situation remained serious but not desperate. The front line continued to hold, and minimal reserves were available to shore up the defences; moreover, ammunition remained plentiful, allowing German artillery to continue its heavy fire. In some cases, this was poorly directed, but as signallers laboured in the face of constant snowstorms and fire from Western Front's artillery to restore communications with front-line units, forward observers were able to start directing the fire of the guns to the rear with greater accuracy. Losses on the German side were substantial but not catastrophic. Provided there were no further serious developments, Arnim was confident that his XXXIX Panzer Corps would continue to hold out.

The third day of fighting had been hugely frustrating for Kiriukhin and Konev. A small group of tanks with modest quantities of fuel and ammunition succeeded in reaching Arman's isolated group close to the Sychevka–Rzhev link, but VI Tank Corps remained without adequate infantry support and was unable to do more than defend its position. However, Arman reported that by distributing the supplies brought by the small group that had reached him, he hoped to be able to resume the advance on 28 November. The troops of II Guards Cavalry Corps remained stuck in the front line; the two leading divisions had made little or no progress, and the third division came under constant German artillery fire and – whenever the snowstorms permitted – air attack. Losses were heavy even before the division could go into action. A rifle division moved forward to replace the cavalry in the few positions that they had managed to capture during the day's struggles.

Aware that a decisive success was no closer, Konev and Zhukov considered their limited options. Logically, the solution seemed straightforward. If II Guards Cavalry Corps could reach VI Tank Corps, the combined force would then surely be sufficient to break through and permanently sever the Sychevka–Rzhev link. In the meantime, the battered remnants of Twentieth Army's rifle divisions had to suppress the German strongpoints that continued to hold out – unless these were destroyed, it would continue to be almost impossible to move forward sufficient supplies and reinforcements for the operation to succeed. But this overall assessment of the situation ignored the reality on the ground. The two approach roads leading to the Vazuza crossings remained choked with traffic, and the crossings were still comfortably within range of German artillery. Having lost most of their supporting tanks in the first three days of action, the rifle divisions lacked the firepower to crush the German strongpoints, and coordination between the infantry and the substantial artillery resources of Twentieth Army remained poor. Moreover, attempts to move forward several of the artillery batteries resulted in the guns becoming caught up in the huge traffic jams leading to the Vazuza crossings, reducing the number of guns that could be made available.

Konev demanded greater energy from the cavalry corps and insisted that it reach VI Tank Corps at all costs. Kryukov, the corps commander, summoned his division commanders for a conference and tersely told them the situation. All of those present were aware that large bodies of mounted men would make easy targets for German artillery and machine-guns, but they also knew that the orders given to their units were uncompromising. The best that they could do was to try to move as quickly as possible between the German-held strongpoints.

On 28 November, the frustration of Konev and Kiriukhin continued to mount. Despite all of their attempts with reconnaissance, radio intercepts, and the capture of 'tongues', the Red Army's units only identified the precise seam between 78th Infantry Division and 5th Panzer Division after the offensive began – such a seam was a favourite point of attack for the Red Army but had not been exploited on this occasion. For 28 November, both senior Soviet commanders demanded a major assault to break open this seam, while the tanks and cavalry of the exploitation group were to push on and cut the Sychevka–Rzhev link. Once the road was reached, Arman and his tank corps were to turn south to roll up the German line by capturing Sychevka, while the cavalry exploited further to the west.[10]

The weather remained unfavourable for major operations, with further heavy snowfall. Arman's remaining tanks dutifully set off before first light in the hope that II Guards Cavalry Corps was approaching from the east and advanced towards the road and rail links upon which the German defence of Rzhev depended. Tanks fell by the wayside, stranded in snow-filled ditches, but the leading battalion reached and occupied the small village of Lozhki, astride the vital railway line. The Osuga River was immediately north of the village, and the rail bridge was defended by a battalion of German combat engineers; without infantry support, Arman could do little to dislodge them and ordered his tanks to proceed to the west to try to find a different crossing, from which they could then outflank the defenders of the bridge. As his columns moved on, the Germans moved back into Lozhki and effectively blocked his supply line.

The result of this struggle was that Arman's tank corps was now deviating towards the northwest, rather than striking first west and then south towards Sychevka. To make matters worse, 100th Tank Brigade failed to keep up with the rest of the tank corps and was brought to a standstill by German defenders on the Sychevka–Rzhev railway. The combination of tank losses through breakdown, fuel shortages and German action, and the arrival of further German reinforcements, was shifting the balance of the battle in favour of the Wehrmacht, but the intervention of II Guards Cavalry Corps might still give Kiriukhin and Konev the victory they were desperate to achieve.

The cavalry divisions had been ordered to press forward as fast as they could, avoiding German strongpoints, and to link up with VI Tank Corps. The advance of 20th Cavalry Division was led by its 103rd Cavalry Regiment, setting out before dawn. They moved forward at a trot – the long approach march and the struggle through deep snow meant that the horses were already tired before the thrust began:

> The eastern horizon was beginning to grow light when the horsemen approached the railway line. The leading group was met by fire, dismounted, and began to respond. Senior Lieutenant Paschchenko deployed the squadron and hurried the men forward. The first squadron galloped up on the right and engulfed the enemy from the north. Still further to the right, reserve squadrons from 22nd and 124th Regiments rushed forward as fast as they could. The light field guns fired at the small railway station. After a short skirmish, the German company was destroyed. The squadrons remounted and as dawn broke, they crossed the railway line that ran between Rzhev and Vyazma.[11]

The passage through the bitterly contested villages between the Vazuza valley and the railway line resulted in substantial losses for the cavalry; the Germans could hear the horsemen moving forward and saw them clearly by the light of parachute flares, and called in heavy artillery fire. Nonetheless, after the frustrations of the previous day, this represented an encouraging start for the cavalry corps, and the men of 20th Cavalry Division pressed on to overrun a battery of German howitzers that was moving forward. But as it grew light on 28 November, further German reinforcements began to arrive. The third cavalry regiment of 20th Cavalry Division suffered heavy losses as it attempted to slip past the German-held villages and was forced to take up defensive positions in open ground. By mid-morning, it became clear that the cavalry regiment was effectively surrounded, unable to move forward or pull back. The regiment commander was killed, and the survivors of the regiment managed to break out to the village of Asestovo. A small group of men were left behind, fighting until they were overwhelmed.

The neighbouring 3rd Guards Cavalry Division fared no better. Due to delays in orders reaching the start line, it set off several hours later than 20th Cavalry Division; consequently, the Germans were now fully alert and it was beginning to grow fully light. Under constant artillery, mortar and machine-gun fire, the cavalry tried desperately to work their way through to the west. One regiment succeeded in reaching its objective more or less intact, but two others were badly hit. Far from making the most of an initial breakthrough, the exploitation group had been forced to engage in costly fighting to achieve the breakthrough, and there was little strength left for any exploitation. Some of the cavalrymen were wounded before their units even reached the front line, as German aircraft took advantage of small breaks in the weather to intervene. Georgy Platonov was commander of a cavalry troop:

> I was appointed commander of thirty men and junior commanders ... German aviation struck us before we could move up. I was wounded in both legs and a piece of shrapnel struck me on the head. We were taken to the hospital in Tula. While I was undergoing treatment, my regiment ceased to exist. Our squadrons were preparing for a deep raid and were advancing when the Germans attacked again from the air. Almost everyone died.[12]

While the cavalrymen attempted to reach the ever-shrinking number of tanks operating further to the west, the fighting continued in their rear as the Red Army tried repeatedly to suppress the stubborn German strongpoints that continued to prevent a definitive breakthrough. Early on 28 November, a battlegroup from 5th Panzer Division, made up of the remnants of numerous units supported by three assault guns and two 88mm anti-aircraft guns, continued to hold on in Maloe Kropotovo on the southern flank of the division's sector, midway between Nikonovo and the critical Sychevka–Rzhev link. Before dawn, Oberst Walter Cetto, the battlegroup commander, reported that Soviet armour and accompanying infantry was bypassing his northern flank, and that the heavy snowstorms prevented his anti-tank weaponry from intervening. The panzer division's artillery immediately responded with a sharp bombardment, but Cetto sent a further signal that the Soviet column was advancing almost unopposed. As the sky began to lighten, this Soviet column turned south and attacked Cetto's battlegroup from the north and northwest. At almost the same moment came more welcome news: 430th Grenadier Regiment, part of 129th Infantry Division, had been ordered to the sector as reinforcements, and its leading battalion was now arriving in Podossinovka, to the south of *Kampfgruppe Cetto*. A small group of tanks from 9th Panzer Division was already in Podossinovka, and the combined force of tanks and newly arrived infantry was ordered to counterattack towards the northwest in order to reduce pressure upon 5th Panzer Division's southern flank. But before the counterattack could begin, another group of Soviet tanks and infantry appeared out of the snowstorms and struck Podossinovka from the east, tying down the German force.

From their headquarters to the north of Cetto's beleaguered troops, the officers at the headquarters of 5th Panzer Division could see more Soviet cavalry attempting to move west:

It slowly grew lighter and as the snowstorms eased, from the division headquarters we could see about 3km to the south there were masses of horsemen, towed guns and vehicles. Podossinovka was ablaze at numerous points and a counterthrust from there couldn't be expected. With improving sight, our artillery, rocket launchers and 20mm anti-aircraft guns in Bolshoye Kropotovo and Maloye Kropotovo now fired on the massed enemy. The result was devastating.

General Metz, whose birthday it was, was in a half-track of the combat engineers with the rocket launchers. The preparations of the rocket batteries were too slow for him. He argued about the delay with the rocket battery commander, an NCO. When the rockets fired and everything was wreathed with their black smoke, General Metz muttered to the NCO with his thick Bavarian accent, 'You dumb ox, you've fired too short, can't you see the mass of horses that are still moving forward?' 'Of course, Herr General,' came the reply, 'but the horses no longer have any riders!' General Metz confirmed this with a quick look through his binoculars. He asked his messenger to give the NCO and his crew a bottle of Cognac from his 'special purposes' stock.[13]

In the circumstances, it was difficult for either side to be sure of the precise situation. Neither the cavalry officers nor Arman knew each other's location, and Arman's radio contact with Kiriukhin at Twentieth Army's headquarters was tenuous. But the presence of numerous Soviet groups near or across the railway and road links between Sychevka and Rzhev had a disruptive effect on German calculations. Another battalion of 430th Grenadier Regiment had arrived, but instead of being deployed in the hard-pressed front line, it was ordered to take up positions to ensure that the railway bridge near Ossuga remained in German hands. Heavy fighting continued to flare around 5th Panzer Division's scattered battlegroups, but as the day drew to an end, there was a sense that a critical day had passed – none of the small fortresses had fallen, and while the division suffered substantial casualties, these were far exceeded by the Red Army's losses.

The Germans tried to reorganise their forces towards the end of the day, with 9th Panzer Division's headquarters tasked with gathering together stragglers, rear area personnel and those returning to the front from leave or convalescence into a reserve force; 9th Panzer Division's combatant units were, for the moment, subordinated to 5th Panzer Division. The officers of 5th Panzer Division might have lamented the manner in which one of their units suffered when it was subordinated to 2nd Panzer Division earlier in the year, but they were delighted to have control of these additional forces in the current circumstances. On the other side of the front line, the senior Soviet commanders once more reviewed the situation. Very little of Western Front's massive artillery resources had been able to cross the Vazuza, which meant that even when he had reliable radio contact, Arman couldn't get any artillery support further to the west. Zhukov demanded that the artillery move forward, despite the protests of Kiriukhin and Konev that with German strongpoints still holding out close to the Vazuza, German artillery was able to subject the entire area to heavy bombardments. The strongpoints had to be destroyed as soon as possible; in the meantime, the remnants of II Guards Cavalry Corps that were still caught up on the Vazuza were to proceed west as fast as possible. The cavalry would then link up with Arman's VI Tank Corps and the entire group would resume their advance towards the west. The Germans had to be running out of reserves, and if the exploitation group could gather its strength, it might be able to make a decisive contribution, regardless of its losses.

Throughout the day, the badly depleted rifle divisions of Kiriukhin's army had struggled in vain to defeat the German positions that continued to hold out; another consequence of Zhukov's demands that the artillery regiments move forward was that fewer guns were available to support the infantry attacks. An infantryman whose unit was involved in the bloody assaults on the main German positions later described one of the aftermaths of the advance of the cavalry corps:

> The Germans were waiting for them and apparently their scouts spotted their advance, and the poor cavalry caught a lot of fire and fewer than half of them managed to retreat back to our lines. The front line froze in place and all winter we dug the carcasses of dead horses from under the snow, boiled the horsemeat, and thus avoided hunger.

And if it hadn't been for the horsemeat, some of us would have had our last days there, because we were sometimes told that our rations had been stopped because of transportation problems, or often we were given no reason at all. The food situation was bad for the Germans too. I remember how the village of Poliki was in no-man's land, and the two warring sides secretly divided it into two zones. Both the Germans and we went to this village at night and looked for potatoes in the cellars, while nobody shot at each other.[14]

In the early hours of 29 November, the front line ran through the ruins of deserted villages and across heavily pitted and cratered fields, forests and frozen swamps. Kiriukhin and Konev had issued fresh orders reiterating Zhukov's demands for II Guards Cavalry Corps and VI Tank Corps to drive on towards the west, but Zhukov issued fresh instructions overnight, belatedly recognising the impossibility of his previous orders. The tank corps was almost cut off, and it needed to regroup and receive reinforcements before it could mount a serious advance. Accordingly, he ordered Arman to break out immediately to the east so that it could be pulled out of line for a brief period. The depleted divisions of II Guards Cavalry Corps were ordered to assist this withdrawal.

By the time the order reached Arman, his command of fewer than 50 remaining tanks had just a couple of hours before dawn to attempt their withdrawal. The motorised rifle brigade that had accompanied his tanks was just as badly degraded as the tank battalions, and it was tasked with organising a rearguard to the west of the Sychevka–Rzhev road. A few groups of cavalrymen had succeeded in reaching the tank corps, and these, too, were assigned to flank and rear protection during the withdrawal. Most of the units of II Guards Cavalry Corps – 3rd and 20th Cavalry Divisions – were a short distance to the south of VI Tank Corps, and they, too, attempted to move back to the east.

The ground over which the Soviet exploitation force had advanced was once more in German hands. As had consistently been the case, German units of varying sizes had moved into the area during the preceding night and reoccupied the ruins that had formed such stubborn strongpoints in the path of the Soviet attack. Without artillery support – the guns of Western Front were too far to the east to be of help – Arman's tanks lacked the firepower to overcome these German nodes of resistance. Early on 29 November, the commissar of VI Tank Corps, Brigade Commissar Petr Grigorevich Grishin, sent a signal to Kiriukhin and Konev:

On the night of 28–29 November, it was not possible to withdraw to the rear. Tanks moved on their own through the forest southwest of Lozhki. The men are out of food, and fuel and ammunition is running out. Please expedite the clearing of the passage to the rear or provide supplies by air.[15]

It was Kiriukhin's intention that II Guards Cavalry Corps would provide the necessary help to rescue the isolated tank corps, and Kryukov, the corps commander, tried to gather his weakened divisions to make a decisive effort. At least a third of his cavalrymen were dead or wounded, and the cavalry corps lacked the heavy weapons to subdue the German strongpoints. After a terse discussion with Kiriukhin, a plan of action was agreed. The rifle divisions of Twentieth Army would assault the strongpoints once more, backed by the weight of Kiriukhin's artillery. At the same time, the cavalry would attempt to advance between the German strongpoints and link up with VI Tank Corps.

The initial artillery bombardment lasted less than half an hour – there was insufficient ammunition for the lengthy preparation of previous days. The infantry and cavalry then moved forward through mist and fog, to be greeted by a storm of German fire. The attacks were across the same ground that had been repeatedly contested for several days, and German artillery added to the slaughter. As the morning progressed, the mist slowly cleared, allowing the Germans to bring more accurate fire to bear. Aerial reconnaissance confirmed that the Red Army was using the same forming-up areas as it had done on previous days, and these too were subjected to fierce bombardment. By mid-afternoon, Kiriukhin's men were exhausted. Almost no ground had been gained in a day of brutal losses – the fresh 1st Guards Motorised Rifle Division was reduced from 9,000 men to 3,500, and the horsemen of II Guards Cavalry Corps fared no better. A further attempt by VI Tank Corps and the elements of 20th Cavalry Division that had joined it succeeded in capturing Lozhki, astride the Sychevka–Rzhev road, but a German counterattack retook the village and drove the Soviet troops back into their encirclement west of the road.

Inevitably, the fighting took a heavy toll on German strength too. The experience of a battalion of 5th Panzer Division's 14th Panzergrenadier Regiment in the village of Grediakino on the Vazuza, at the very northern end of the Soviet attack, was typical. Despite Soviet attacks, often several per day, the Germans held the village resolutely, even when advancing Soviet infantry bypassed their flanks, slowly enveloping the village. Oberleutnant Eduard Kraus, commander of one of the panzergrenadier companies, and his men endured days of almost constant fighting:

An enemy tank stood on top of the [company] command post bunker, a second about 20m to the left, and a third drove towards the battalion command post.

Unteroffizier Funke was able to disable the tank on the bunker with a demolition charge. I was covering the tank that was further to the left. To my surprise, the turret opened and a Russian climbed out and came towards me. I fired at him with my machine-pistol and he collapsed. I was able to fire a rifle grenade into the turret, and it exploded inside the tank.

But what was happening in the main trench? With Funke and a couple of messengers, I crawled to the front line along the almost flattened communication trench and came across Feldwebel Dannenbring and the remnant of his platoon in a large crater. Dannenbring had also disabled a tank with a demolition charge and had taken prisoner a Russian who had baled out. We launched an immediate counterattack and were able to drive the Russians back. It was no longer possible to clear up the entire penetration. Unteroffizier Funke was killed by a headshot. The left third of the trench remained in Russian hands.

Russian tanks, accompanied by infantry when it was dark, rolled forward between our position and Cholm-Beresuisky [immediately to the northwest]. We held our position but we were now cut off. As a result of an icy snowstorm, our automatic weapons repeatedly froze. The bunkers could only be warmed at night … Supplies of food and ammunition began to run out. An expected counterattack by 9th Panzer Division failed to develop. Amazingly, the men held on despite the cold.[16]

Despite their determined stand, the strength of the battalion was almost exhausted. Major Kurt Stieber, the battalion commander, signalled division headquarters with increasing desperation during the fighting of 29 November. The times of these signals are, like all Wehrmacht communications, 'Berlin time', approximately two hours behind 'Moscow time':

0445: Russian attack on Kraus with powerful forces. Heavy barrage on Kopper on the left. Strong enemy probe from [Hill] 77 against the anti-tank ditch repulsed.

0535: Our artillery fires in support of our blocking position.

1325: Requested supply by air as from now fuel shortage means there is no other possibility of resupply. Drop zone in anti-tank ditch. The following supplies arrived: food for one day and 60 litres of fuel for tanks. Fuel stock and ammunition almost completely exhausted. Proper support must be provided.

1425: Most of the men are listless, exhausted, ill or fought out. Request urgent support.

1545: Russian infantry attacks entire sector with [shouts of] 'Urrah'.

1830: Company strength Russian attack repulsed. Company torn apart.

1900: Request reply about supply requests. What help [is] available?

1910: [Message] from regiment: supplies, ammunition and [winter] clothing [will be brought] to Brüning's position.

1940: Does regiment [headquarters] understand that there is no possibility of [us] reaching [position] 49?

2240: [Message] from regiment: a tank [is] bringing supplies from 49.[17]

Short of all supplies and running out of strength, Stieber continued to hold his positions, hoping desperately either for reinforcements and resupply or permission to withdraw. Increasingly, commanders at every level were aware that if the Red Army continued its pressure, such withdrawals would become necessary or the units that continued to hold the front line would simply cease to exist. Harpe and the other German commanders were of course aware of the huge losses they had inflicted upon Konev's attacking formations, but the Soviet resources seemed endless.

On the eastern side of the salient, after continuous combat since early on 25 November, and with almost no opportunities for sleep or rest, Major Stieber and the remnants of his panzergrenadier battalion endured more Soviet attacks before dawn on 30 November. The promised supplies failed to materialise, and as it grew light, Stieber requested urgent resupply and combat support by air, followed by a stream of increasingly desperate requests for help or for clear orders. Finally, instructions arrived just before midday. He was to attempt a breakout to the west. For the moment the opposing Red Army units appeared to be too exhausted to repeat their assaults of the previous day, which was most fortunate for Stieber. As darkness fell, German artillery fired a brief bombardment of the Soviet positions, and under cover of this Stieber and his men withdrew. Many of them were wounded or frostbitten, and only eight officers, 24 NCOs and 87 men remained. They brought three tanks back with them.

After its failed attempt on 29 November to break out of encirclement and escape to the east, Arman's VI Tank Corps tried again the following day. Moving out before dawn, the tanks managed to bypass the German strongpoint in Lozhki, and then ran into strong German defences in woodland near Bolshoye Kropotovo:

Exhausted by many days of unequal combat but united by a single impulse, their unyielding determination to break through the enemy ring, our soldiers struck unexpectedly towards the northeast. At the same time, units of 100th Tank Brigade with infantry were advancing towards them from Bolshoye Kropotovo.

A fierce battle broke out in the darkness. The superiority of forces was with the enemy. In addition, the troops attempting the breakout were down to the dregs of their ammunition. Dozens of our soldiers died in heavy fighting, including the commanders of 200th Tank Brigade and 6th Motorised Rifle Brigade.[18]

Anatoly Mikhailovich Barash was with VI Tank Corps in the encirclement and was assigned a special mission by his company commander, and his experience showed that tanks operating on their own had a chance of escaping:

Company commander Fomin ordered me to load a seriously wounded battalion commander and a few more wounded tankers onto my tank and break out on my own, as the battalion commander would bleed out unless he was evacuated. We passed through the Germans at speed like a knife through butter. We unloaded the wounded at a medical unit and I drove to the brigade headquarters [some command elements had remained in the rear when the rest of the corps moved forward]. I was ordered to take a senior lieutenant who was a stranger to me with me back through the minefield to the brigade commander, who was wounded and needed urgent evacuation.

The senior lieutenant turned out to be a new trainee and the nephew of the corps commander. Our quartermaster ran up and threw additional rations for the officers into the tank. I told the gunner to stay at the headquarters and took his place while the senior lieutenant took my seat as the tank commander. We drove through the minefield, the anti-tank mines visible through the snow. And then I noticed a German gun on a hillock to our right. I only had time to shout 'A gun, to the right!' before a round pierced our armour. The senior lieutenant, who was sitting in my seat, was torn in two, and his blood and body fragments splashed over me. The round smashed the gun's breech and it swung around, shattering Pavlik's leg. A small piece of armour struck my leg, but I was able to pull it out. Konkin was hit in the shoulder. But the tank was still mobile and using just one hand on the controls, Konkin drove the T-34 onward. We crawled out of the minefield and then saw a T-34 stuck in a narrow ravine. It was Fuchs' crew. We pulled them clear and then returned to brigade headquarters ...

The medical orderlies took Konkin and Pavlik away and then pulled what remained of the trainee officer from the tank. I was left to wash off the blood and fragments of other people with snow and water.[19]

The remnants of VI Tank Corps pulled back across the Vazuza to be replenished. Within two weeks, its tank strength increased to seven KV-1s, 64 T-34s, 12 T-70s and 17 T-60s, but irreplaceable tank crews had been lost in the failed operation. The motorised rifle brigade was reduced to just 170 combatants, but the men had little rest before they were sent back into action.

Near to the route used by VI Tank Corps to escape to the east was the village of Maloye Kropotovo, and this became the scene of a desperate attack by elements of II Guards Cavalry Corps. The German defenders managed barely to hold on, inflicting terrible losses on the attacking Soviet formations. Not far away, 20th Cavalry Division was ordered to attack Lozhki, but this was then countermanded with instructions to support the breakout of VI Tank Corps. The initial attack cleared the Germans from two positions on the Sychevka–Rzhev road, but a German battlegroup consisting of a regiment from 6th Infantry Division reinforced with other units was dispatched to restore the situation. The battlegroup had already been heavily involved in the fighting for Lozhki and now fought against the cavalry. Aided by an armoured train that was moving north from Sychevka, the German infantry inflicted heavy losses on 20th Cavalry Division and forced it back to the west.

Reduced to fewer than 1,000 men, the cavalry division abandoned its breakout:

Unit commanders and political officers were summoned to the command post – such was the name given to a small hut made of pine branches and roofed with a raincoat. It was cramped, with the vapour from men's breath mingling with tobacco smoke. The casing of a small-calibre round, flattened at the top with a wick inserted into it, filled with gasoline, sputtered irregularly …

'I received a radio message from the Front commander,' Kursakov [commander of 20th Cavalry Division] began quietly, clearing his throat. 'The cavalry under my command is to head deep into the rear of the enemy to conduct partisan operations towards the Rzhev–Velikiye Luki railway and the highway between Sychevka and Kholm-Zhirkovsky. We will break through in two echelons. Tonight, 12th Guards and 124th Cavalry Regiments with the divisional artillery form the first echelon. Tomorrow night, 103rd Cavalry Regiment forms the second. Destroy unneeded equipment. Transfer anti-aircraft gunners to reinforce the artillery battalion and regimental guns. Do not get involved in protracted battles during the breakout. The first assembly area is the Pochinkovsky swamp. You will receive further instructions there.'[20]

Earlier in the year, Belov and his cavalrymen had found themselves forced to operate in the German rear area for several months, and given the strength of

German positions blocking their line of retreat to the east, an attempt to repeat Belov's adventure was now the only alternative to surrender or destruction.

As darkness fell at the end of the day, Konev and Kiriukhin had to face the reality of failure. Their exploitation force was either destroyed, back across the Vazuza, or reduced to little more than a partisan support group far from the front line. The German positions had been dented but hadn't been breached as expected, and the losses suffered were appalling. German reports from 78th Infantry Division and 5th Panzer Division estimated that they had killed over 70,000 Soviet soldiers and destroyed over 350 tanks.[21] But German casualties had also been heavy, with most of the divisions facing Konev's Western Front losing nearly half their strength.

As November drew to a close, Zhukov was faced with the bitter reality that Western Front had failed to produce as spectacular a success as Vasilevsky had achieved with *Uranus*, far to the south. The German units defending the eastern side of the Rzhev Salient had been battered and stretched to breaking point – but they had held out, and the Red Army's losses were nothing short of catastrophic. This might have been the moment to switch strategies and maintain sufficient pressure to prevent the Germans from moving any of their units, particularly the panzer divisions, to intervene in the growing crisis on the Don River. But Zhukov wasn't ready to stop. It seems he believed that a further effort was justified, even though none of the attacks on the salient looked like achieving anything approaching a decisive success.

CHAPTER 11

THE COMMENCEMENT OF *MARS*: KALININ FRONT, 25–30 NOVEMBER

Konev's attack towards the Rzhev–Sychevka supply link was only part of *Mars*. At the same time, Kalinin Front was required to make no fewer than three attacks against the western and northern sides of the salient. One of the slightly unusual aspects of *Mars* was that, unlike other operations such as *Uranus*, all the Soviet attacks commenced on the same day.

The Soviet 3rd Mechanised Brigade, commanded by Colonel Amasp Khachaturovich Babadzhanian, was part of Katukov's III Mechanised Corps. At the last minute, Iushkevich, commander of Twenty-Second Army, asked Katukov whether it was possible to bring forward the start time of the attack along the Luchesa valley, the middle component of Kalinin Front's attacks. If the leading elements of the mechanised corps could move forward late in the afternoon of 24 November rather than early the following morning, they might take the Germans by surprise. It was an unorthodox start time for a major assault, and the onset of darkness might hinder the inevitable German counterattacks. Katukov makes no mention of this in his memoirs, but it seems that he agreed with Iushkevich, and fresh orders were sent to Babadzhanian, whose brigade was about 18 miles (30km) behind the front line. Babadzhanian later recalled the moment:

A liaison officer from the commander of Twenty-Second Army arrived at my command post and handed me an order – to start the offensive today at 1600 and not tomorrow, as envisaged in the corps commander's orders.

I looked at my watch and showed it to the liaison officer. 'The order is impracticable, not only because you're giving it just two hours after the appointed time. It will take another two hours for the brigade to reach the front line. Neither my commanders nor I have any idea about the enemy's defensive system, our artillery cannot fire without knowing their targets, and tanks can't attack at night.'

The liaison officer replied that it was his duty to give me the orders. I took the orders from him and signed a receipt, but added the time of receipt. He just shrugged. 'You're not an automaton,' I exploded, 'Promise at least to give my opinion to the [army] commander.' He agreed.

By midnight, the brigade's units had barely managed to reach their forming up areas in the darkness and deploy for the offensive. This was only possible because we had sent out officers to these areas before dusk to guide them. Busy with dispersing my subunits and giving orders for tomorrow morning, I didn't notice a tracked vehicle stopping nearby and three officers accompanied by submachine-gunners approaching me. 'Are you Colonel Babadzhanian?'

'Yes.'

'I am the head of the Special Department of Twenty-Second Army, these are the prosecutor and chairman of the military tribunal. You are under arrest for not obeying a combat order in wartime. Surrender your weapon.'

The submachine-gunners surrounded me. I unfastened my pistol and handed it to the prosecutor. 'Perhaps you'd like to tie my hands, otherwise with only six of you against me, it might be dangerous for you.'[1]

Babadzhanian was taken to the headquarters of Twenty-Second Army, where Iushkevich asked him why he hadn't obeyed his orders. Babadzhanian explained that the result would have been an attack after dark, in which his entire brigade would probably have been wiped out. His men were now at the start line, and given a further three hours of preparation after dawn, he was confident that he could break through. Iushkevich agreed and ordered the three arresting officers to return Babadzhanian's pistol and to apologise to him.

Kalinin Front's main thrust would be by Tarasov's Forty-First Army immediately south of Bely. A little to the north, Twenty-Second Army would attempt to drive east along the Luchesa valley, while Thirty-Ninth Army made a pinning attack from the north against the very tip of the salient. While the number of attacks would stretch the German reserves, the three thrusts were too far apart to provide direct support for each other, though it was hoped that the three armies might be able to cooperate as the offensive developed. In any event, it would have been difficult to organise the attacks closer to each other – there weren't adequate roads for such a concentration of forces.

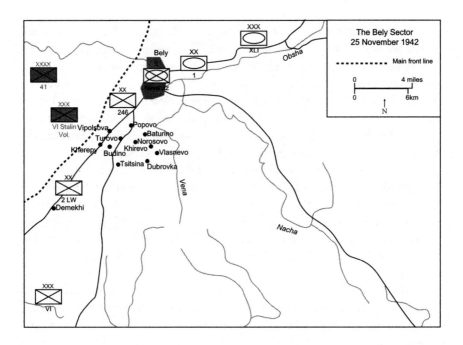

The leading unit in the main thrust to the south of Bely was VI 'Stalin Volunteer' Rifle Corps. This formation was reported in Soviet newspapers as being made up of men from Siberia who had volunteered for front-line service; what was less well known was that many of its personnel were men from prison camps who had 'volunteered' to escape from the harsh conditions of their imprisonment. Even before they reached the front line, it seemed as if the misfortune that had sent the men to Siberia continued to dog them. The lack of adequate railway lines to the immediate rear of Kalinin Front's positions resulted in the troops detraining about 115 miles (170km) from the front line. The soldiers then had to march along muddy tracks and roads to reach their assembly area, but as nobody had expected them to be detrained so far to the rear, no rations had been organised for them. Subsisting mainly on inadequate quantities of bread that their officers managed to obtain from other units, the soldiers staggered forward for 30 days; several died en route from exhaustion and malnutrition, and the rest were in no state to commence a major operation. Hastily, 'rest homes' were created where they received additional food to restore their strength.[2]

When the assault began, the 'volunteers' still faced a difficult situation. Although most of the men had at least partly recovered their strength, they were now sent into action with inadequate equipment. Due to shortages of rifles, some were unarmed and were ordered to pick up weapons from fallen comrades. There were insufficient white winter uniforms available, leaving many soldiers exposed to the bitter cold; moreover, their brown uniforms made them easy to spot against the snow. Their attack sector was a shallow valley extending into the German positions, but the defenders were dug in on the high ground on either side of the valley and had dominating fields of fire.

Immediately to the south of Bely were numerous villages. A road ran to the southwest from Bely – this was the tenuous supply line by which a battlegroup had been sustained in the town prior to *Seydlitz* – through Popovo, Vipolsova and Kherepy; the last of these was soon in Soviet hands. To the east of the road were Turovo, Baturino, Budino, Norosovo, Khirevo, Vasnevo, Dubrovka and, a little further south, Tsitsina. Some had already been fortified by the Germans and the rest were hastily strengthened with whatever materials were available. In the coming days, these villages would be fiercely contested as the Red Army attempted to edge north to Bely and the Germans strove to press down from the north and eliminate the penetration achieved by Kalinin Front.

Tarasov had identified the presence of 2nd Luftwaffe Field Division in the German front line, and he and his officers correctly assessed it as a weak unit. As was the case with Konev's Western Front, the initial heavy artillery bombardment was concluded with salvoes of *Katyusha* rockets before the ground troops moved forward. But unlike the preliminary bombardment in the east, Kalinin Front's artillery did a far more effective job of suppressing the German defences. In some sectors there was little resistance as the infantry moved forward, at first cautiously but then with greater confidence, particularly opposite Tsitsina. This was one of the villages that the Germans had prepared for all-round defence and a fierce firefight developed. After an hour, the village was in the hands of the Red Army, and the surviving German units pulled back into the neighbouring forests. Elsewhere, the attacking units enjoyed less success. The 'Stalin Volunteers' were cut to pieces by defensive fire, and attacks against the German lines to the north of Bely made only minimal progress at a disproportionate cost.

Pätzold's Luftwaffe soldiers proved to be as fragile as the Red Army had hoped and the Germans had feared. Wherever they came into contact with the advancing Soviet forces they were driven back in disarray; only around the village of Demekhi did they succeed in holding their positions, but most of the division ceased to function as a coherent unit. From this position, the German lines to the north had been broken over a breadth of perhaps seven miles (12km); just to the southwest of Bely, the remains of one of 246th Infantry Division's regiments held a blocking position on the northern shoulder of the penetration. However, it too had suffered heavy losses during the day, and its ability to stop the Red Army from pushing it back to and perhaps through Bely was doubtful. Model flew to the sector and met both Harpe, commander of XLI Panzer Corps, and Krüger, commander of 1st Panzer Division; he briefed his subordinates about the Soviet attacks on either side of the salient.

The German policy of launching counterattacks was so widespread and such a part of standard Wehrmacht procedure that it had become almost proverbial, and the fighting to the south of Bely on the first day of the battle was no exception. A battlegroup was assembled around a panzergrenadier regiment supported by an artillery battalion, both from 1st Panzer Division, under the command of Oberst Wend von Wietersheim, and ordered into action alongside *Kampfgruppe Kassnitz* from *Grossdeutschland*. Both were to counterattack against the northern flank of the Soviet penetration. The precise positions of the advancing Red Army units were unknown; it was likely that some had turned to the northeast and north after their initial successes, in which case it was vital to stop them in order for a defensive line to be established. Without waiting for the rest of the battlegroup to form up, Wietersheim immediately dispatched a single battalion supported by a few light tanks to probe towards the southeast from Bely towards Baturino, if only to determine the precise positions of the enemy.

The counterattack by *Kampfgruppe Kassnitz* had to pass through the villages of Knychnikova and Sharki and was typical of the stubborn, confused fighting that would continue in this sector over the following days:

> In spite of the deep snow, 2nd and 3rd Companies were able to reach the village of Knychnikova before dark. The enemy defended desperately and the fighting went on far into the night; the village had to be taken house by house ... 1st Company got to within 1,000m of Sharki but then had to call off its attack in the face of heavy enemy fire.[3]

Model had already released 9th Panzer Division to support his forces defending the eastern side of the salient, and he now approved reinforcements for the western side. In an attempt to shore up the broken flank of 2nd Luftwaffe Field Division, he ordered the SS cavalry to deploy alongside Pätzold's surviving units.

At the same time, with the approval of Kluge at Army Group Centre, 12th, 19th and 20th Panzer Divisions were ordered to move forward and prepare to operate against the southern flank of the Soviet penetration. These forces would take several days to assemble, and in the meantime, Model and Harpe had to hope that their defences could hold out.

To the north of Tarasov's attack, Iushkevich's Twenty-Second Army also attacked the German lines on 25 November, attempting to advance east along the line of the Luchesa River. The units of III Mechanised Corps, commanded by Katukov, had struggled forward through deep snow and dense forests, along roads and tracks that were entirely unsuited for offensive operations with mechanised forces, and only a single brigade had reached the start line. The attack would have to follow the Luchesa eastwards for at least 12 miles (20km) before reaching the road from Olenino to Bely; until then, the freedom for manoeuvre of Twenty-Second Army would be severely constrained. This, of course, made the task of the defenders far easier.

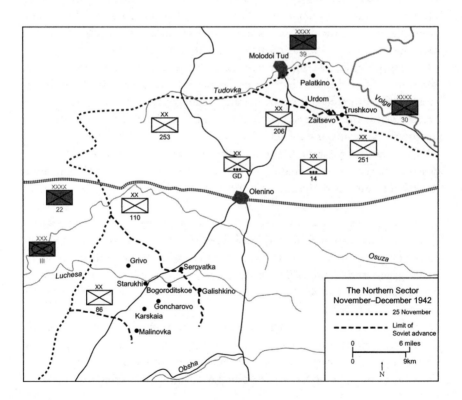

The effect of the initial Soviet bombardment was patchy. As a result, the surviving German defences held up some of the attacking groups, resulting in the Red Army's advance becoming uncoordinated and piecemeal. There was modest progress south of the Luchesa, but little headway further north. The open ground to the east remained beyond reach; in the meantime, Katukov and his staff officers struggled to organise resupply for the battalions of tanks that they had committed in support of the initial attack. It had been difficult for Twenty-Second Army to get its units into their start positions for the offensive, and moving supplies and – critically – artillery forward in support of the modest gains proved almost impossible.

Once again, the Soviet attack was directed at a seam in the German lines, between Harpe's XLI Panzer Corps to the south and Hilpert's XXIII Corps to the north. Only a single battalion of panzergrenadiers from *Grossdeutschland* was immediately available as reinforcements. It was committed in an immediate counterattack, recapturing a small village, but without further reinforcements there was little it could do. The dispersal of *Grossdeutschland* and the subordination of its units to other commands left the division commander, Generalmajor Walter Hörnlein, with just a mixture of rear area elements and fragments of other divisions under his personal command; more significantly, many of the battlegroups now had complex supply problems, with many of the units in their areas suddenly expected to provide fuel, food and ammunition for the *Grossdeutschland* battlegroups.

To make matters worse for Hilpert, the northern flank of his corps also came under attack. At the very northern tip of the Rzhev Salient, around the small town of Urdom, the Germans held a curved sector of front line roughly along the line of the Tudovka valley to the confluence of the Tudovka River and the Volga; the Soviet forces to the north, from Zygin's Thirty-Ninth Army, had been ordered to attack to tie down local German forces and prevent their transfer to the more important sectors further south.

The forces available to Zygin were substantial – he intended to attack in the centre with three rifle divisions and two tank brigades, with subsidiary attacks on either flank – but he lacked the massed artillery of his neighbours. Nonetheless, the guns of Thirty-Ninth Army subjected the German 206th Infantry Division to a lengthy bombardment. When they advanced, the Soviet infantrymen discovered that the German line, composed of strongpoints with interlocking fields of fire, was still largely intact. The first waves of infantry crossed the frozen Yudovka and pressed into the dense woodland on the southern bank, but were then cut to pieces by defensive fire and driven back to the river. The tanks of

Malygin's 28th Tank Brigade moved forward and reached the southern bank, smashing through the ice at a few fords that had previously been identified:

> Our mine-clearing tanks went first and made two sweeps through the minefield. The heavy tanks moved to one lane, the medium tanks to the other ... but the infantry lagged behind them and were driven to ground by the fire of the Hitlerite machine-guns. Despite the fact that our tanks were already in the enemy's rear, he resisted desperately. The Nazis crouched in their bunkers, enduring the impact of 152mm artillery shells and fired back furiously.
>
> I ordered my tankers to return to the infantry, but they still wouldn't move forward. Our neighbours to the left, 135th Rifle Division and 81st Armoured Brigade, were in no better a position. General Zygin was anxious, but couldn't do anything to help. Having learned of our serious losses, he ordered the tanks to pull back from the front line; the attack would be repeated on 26 November.[4]

Writing several years after the war, Voloshin – the intelligence chief of Thirty-Ninth Army – commented that it hadn't been possible to identify the reason for the failure of the offensive to progress more rapidly. It seems that despite his enthusiastic appraisal, the reconnaissance in force that he had ordered immediately before the attack was far less effective than he portrayed.

In addition to this frontal assault on the positions of 206th Infantry Division, Zygin's army attempted to strike at both flanks of the German position. The attack on the western flank enjoyed greater success than the main assault. The German defences were weaker, and the first Soviet attack succeeded in advancing two miles into the forest. The objective of the Soviet force was a road running from Olenino to Molodoi Tud – if this road was cut, the German defenders that had stopped the main attack of Thirty-Ninth Army would lose their main supply line. Once more, the Soviet attack fell on the junction of two German units, 253rd Infantry Division to the west and 206th Infantry Division to the east, and there was a serious risk that the two divisions would be forced apart. To make matters worse for Generalmajor Alfons Hitter's 206th Infantry Division, its eastern flank was also under pressure. Here, the eastern wing of Zygin's Thirty-Ninth Army succeeded in reaching the village of Trushkovo, where the attackers were halted by the appearance of almost all of the reserves available to Hitter. Without further reinforcements, his positions were now fully stretched.

The only such reinforcements immediately available consisted of a single motorcycle battalion from *Grossdeutschland*, and the arrival of this group halted the withdrawal of 253rd Infantry Division. Further elements of *Grossdeutschland* arrived as darkness fell and were immediately pitched into counterattacks. A small amount of ground was gained, though at a heavy cost. From the German perspective, it was vital that this Soviet penetration be driven back the following day if their orthodox policy of restoring the front line to its previous position was to be followed; for Zygin, it was equally vital that reinforcements were sent to the area and that the advance should continue, in order to unhinge the stubborn German defences facing the centre of his army. However, his request to make such a transfer was rejected by Purkaev at Kalinin Front headquarters. The main mission of Thirty-Ninth Army was to tie down German units in this sector, and in Purkaev's opinion this would be best achieved by continuing the frontal assaults.

With the various elements of *Grossdeutschland* being dispersed to the crises erupting all along the front line of XXIII Corps, the last significant reserve available to Hilpert was 14th Motorised Infantry Division. This unit had been designated for conversion to a full panzergrenadier division – had this taken place, it would have received a panzer battalion in addition to its existing three grenadier regiments – and was currently in reserve near Rzhev. For the moment, Hilpert was reluctant to commit this division fully to the fighting in 206th Infantry Division's sector – if the Red Army resumed its attacks on Rzhev, he would find himself with no reserves at all. Already, he had been forced to deploy much of the division's artillery, and by the end of the day he had little choice but to deploy more assets. A regiment from 14th Motorised Division was sent to 206th Infantry Division as reinforcements. German resources were being stretched to the limit.

While the fighting on the eastern side of the salient was characterised by bitter struggles for small amounts of territory and huge congestion behind the Soviet front line, the overall picture on Kalinin Front's sector was very different. During the night of 25–26 November, Soviet troops moved forward to reinforce their success. In order to assist the infantry to break the German defences, Solomatin had been forced to adopt his second plan, and 219th Tank Brigade moved forward in support of the Siberian infantrymen:

> The tanks attacked in close cooperation with infantry from the army's first echelon. Where it was not possible for the tanks to attack positions due to local terrain (forests and ravines) and the surviving enemy anti-tank defences, they used their firepower to destroy the enemy and at the same time, under cover of this fire, our infantry infiltrated into the enemy trenches and destroyed the Fascist invaders with grenades and bayonets, clearing the way for the tanks. Where the

terrain allowed the tanks to operate freely, they attacked boldly, destroying the Nazis with fire and their caterpillar tracks, moving forward rapidly, and exploiting their success the infantry developed the offensive at a faster pace.[5]

At this stage of the war, such successful close cooperation between tanks and infantry was relatively unusual in the Red Army, especially when the tanks and infantry were from different corps, but it shows that at least in this instance the Soviet troops were learning from their previous mistakes. The first unit of Solomatin's echelon that had been held back to exploit the success, 35th Mechanised Brigade, moved forward to take up the advance. A tank battalion had been detached to help the Soviet infantry trying to push back the German line at Budino to the south of Bely, where the battered German groups continued to fight off every Soviet attack, but the rest of the mechanised corps moved east in two waves. The first priority was to secure crossings over the frozen Nacha River; immediately to the east of the river was an important road running from the southeast to Bely, and cutting this road would greatly worsen the situation of the German units in Bely itself.

As Tarasov had hoped, the two German divisions – subordinated to different corps – that took the brunt of his attack to the south of Bely retreated on diverging axes once they were separated. The result was that I Mechanised Corps was now advancing into open space, and its progress was every bit as rapid as Tarasov and Purkaev might have hoped. The first physical obstacle in its path was the line of the Vena River, and it seems that the Soviet armour took the Germans by surprise, capturing an intact bridge across the small river. A tank brigade from Solomatin's corps turned south and drove off a detachment of SS cavalry while other units turned north along the Vena. The key to the battle, though, wasn't here at the tip of the Soviet advance, but at the shoulders of the initial penetration. The stubborn resistance of the German defences to the south of Bely continued to repulse every attempt by the Red Army to break through to the town, and as units of 1st Panzer Division and *Grossdeutschland* arrived, energetic counterattacks, often supported by German tanks, added to the problems of the Soviet 150th Rifle Division.

Solomatin was forced to detach a second tank battalion from his corps to support the attacks on Dubrovka. His corps' second echelon was 19th Mechanised Brigade, and he now ordered this to turn north against the German defences south of Baturino rather than proceed to the east in support of the leading tanks. In bitter fighting, the Soviet forces managed to edge their way closer to Bely, but at a terrible price; both the infantry of 150th Rifle Division and the supporting tank battalions from Solomatin's corps lost about half their strength. They had reached Baturino but could go no further. Vasnevo, to the south of Bely, was now the focus of attention. If Kalinin Front's troops could capture it, they would bypass the fortified villages that were blocking attempts to advance on Bely from the south and southwest, and 1st Panzer Division hastily dispatched what forces it could spare to set up a blocking position.

Despite the heavy fighting near Bely, the commanders of Kalinin Front and Forty-First Army remained confident that they had made a good start to their assault. The leading units of Solomatin's corps seemed to be close to achieving a decisive breakthrough; if they reached the Nacha valley on the third day of the attack, they would be able to bring the German supply line to Bely under fire and perhaps cut it entirely. Solomatin was concerned that he had been forced to divert so much of his strength to the fighting near Bely and asked Tarasov to assign him the two independent mechanised brigades that had been given to Forty-First Army when one of its mechanised corps was withdrawn and sent to Velikiye Luki, but Tarasov declined to do so. Concluding that the leading elements of I Mechanised Corps were strong enough to reach the Nacha and the supply road beyond, he instead ordered infantry – mainly in the form of the depleted Siberian formations – to move forward to help Solomatin secure his positions. In the meantime, the mechanised corps was ordered to press on at full speed. The independent mechanised brigades would for the moment be held back and used to take advantage of opportunities on the flanks of Solomatin's advance.[6]

More units of 1st Panzer Division reached the Bely sector during the day, and the division was assigned the sector of the defensive perimeter that faced southeast. Krüger had already dispatched *Kampfgruppe von Wietersheim* and the first units of the Fusilier Regiment of *Grossdeutschland* in an attack to secure his open eastern flank. He intended for the attack to continue towards the south, but heavy Soviet artillery and rocket fire made any early advance impossible. For the moment, the German defences on the northern shoulder of the Soviet penetration were holding firm – even though they had suffered serious casualties, the defenders had prevented the Red Army from advancing towards Bely. Their attempts to counterattack towards the south had failed, but further German reinforcements were en route, and Model could hope that these would swing the battle in his favour. He now turned his attention to the southern flank.

The SS cavalry had functioned poorly under the command of Fegelein earlier in the year but had been extensively reorganised. The addition of further units converted the pre-existing cavalry brigade into 8th SS Cavalry Division, largely by the addition of ethnic German recruits from Romania. Although Model might have regarded punitive measures against the local civilian population as counter-productive, he appears to have been content for the SS division to be used in an operation codenamed *Spätlese* ('Late harvest') during the autumn, directed against Red Army stragglers and partisans behind German lines. As was consistently the case with such operations, civilians who were suspected of having aided partisans were killed indiscriminately. As commander of Ninth Army, Model was well aware of the utter uselessness of Fegelein as a field commander, but also knew that Himmler would protect Fegelein from any criticism. Consequently, Model resorted to another method of removing him: he submitted glowing reports recommending him for immediate assignment to higher roles.[7] This strategy rapidly bore fruit, and Fegelein was awarded the Knight's Cross and transferred to the headquarters of the *Reichssicherheitshauptamt* ('Reich Main Security Office' or *RSHA*). The cavalry division was now under the command of Brigadeführer Wilhelm Bittrich, who – unlike his predecessor Fegelein – had served in the First World War both as an infantry lieutenant and latterly as a pilot. He was transferred from the Reichswehr to the SS in 1934 in a deliberate attempt to improve the experience and expertise of SS command structures. His men were now deployed in support of the open flank of 2nd Luftwaffe Field Division, and overall control of this sector was now assigned to XXX Corps. The headquarters of this corps, commanded by General Maximilian Fretter-Pico, was transferred from Army Group North and was to take control of the remnants of the Luftwaffe division and Bittrich's cavalry division, as well as the units of 19th Panzer Division as they arrived.

After regrouping during the night, Iushkevich's men tried again on 26 November to advance down the Luchesa valley, to the north of Bely. An initial attack across the frozen river cleared some of the stubborn German defences to the north but foundered in the face of determined resistance around the village of Grivo. Katukov's tanks managed to help the forces south of the river reach the village of Starukhi, but a trickle of German reinforcements allowed the defenders to hold firm. The overall advance during the day was less than a mile, at a high cost.

Zygin's Thirty-Ninth Army spent the night of 25–26 November trying to reorganise. Intelligence from a reconnaissance unit that had slipped into the rear of the positions of the German 206th Infantry Division reported the arrival of the regiment of 14th Motorised Division that Hilpert had dispatched to the region. It also tentatively reported the presence of elements of 5th Panzer Division. In reality, almost all of 5th Panzer Division was fully committed against the attack by Western Front, but Zygin was deeply worried by these developments, as his intelligence officer Voloshin recalled:

> When I reported the information to the army commander, he gave me such a look that I felt uneasy.
>
> 'Where did these units come from? Why are they not on my map?'
>
> How could I explain? Should I say that these divisions had been held a relatively large distance from the front line, in areas where our scouts couldn't reach? These explanations wouldn't satisfy anyone. After all, it was I, as chief of intelligence of the army, who was obliged to foresee such developments. And not only to foresee them purely theoretically, but also practically to take effective measures to obtain comprehensive information from these rear areas. All I could do was remain silent.
>
> Frowning, the commander bent over the map again, then began to pace back and forth with his hands behind his back. Finally, he turned abruptly to the chief of staff and ordered, 'Contact the division commanders. Warn them about possible ...' he was silent for a moment – 'no, about imminent enemy counterattacks. Tell them to prepare to repulse them. And not a single step back! In the morning, perhaps before dawn, the Nazis will try to restore the situation in our sector.'[8]

Whatever gloss Voloshin attempted to put on events, his failure to identify the presence of 14th Motorised Division was a serious shortcoming. The division had been in this sector of the front line throughout the year. Far from being deep within German-held territory, most of its units were in the immediate area of Rzhev. At the very least, Voloshin should have been aware of its approximate location. The soldiers of Thirty-Ninth Army began to prepare to face the expected German counterattack, as well as resuming their own attempts to advance.

Unlike the first day of the battle, the weather was relatively clear early on 26 November in the northern sector. Using information gathered during the aborted assault the previous day, Thirty-Ninth Army's artillery was able to do far more damage to the German defensive positions, and when they advanced, the Soviet troops enjoyed greater success. The line of the Tudovka River was cleared in heavy fighting – one of Malygin's tank brigade commanders was killed when his vehicle took a direct hit from a German anti-tank gun – but the German defensive fire was far more disjointed, permitting infantry to move forward with the tanks. A battery of German anti-tank guns briefly stopped the advance near the ruins of the village of Palatkino, but the improving weather permitted Soviet aircraft to intervene. The air strike silenced some of the guns and Malygin's armour finished off the rest. Fending off persistent German counterattacks, the exhausted soldiers of Thirty-Ninth Army succeeded in moving forward perhaps a mile from their start line.

On the eastern flank of Thirty-Ninth Army, the first day had seen the Soviet attack reach the village of Trushkovo. Despite orders to concentrate on the main frontal assault, Zygin had dispatched a rifle brigade and a mechanised brigade to this sector, but as was the case for units on both sides, their move to the front line was slow and repeatedly delayed. In the meantime, the attempts by the Soviet infantry to push on repeatedly failed in the face of tough German defences that had been set up overnight by the regiment of 14th Motorised Division just outside Trushkovo. The main road running west from Rzhev passed through the village of Zaitsevo, tantalisingly just out of reach of the attackers, and German units continued to use this road – one of the few good roads in the area – to shuffle their fast-disappearing reserves. Due to the pressure on the western side of the salient, Hilpert was anxious to dispatch the elements of *Grossdeutschland* operating in support of 206th Infantry Division to deal with the Soviet penetrations either side of Bely, but the pinning attack by Zygin in the north was succeeding in tying down German resources. Like all German commanders, Hilpert knew that Hitler remained hugely reluctant to consider any withdrawals, but he had to shorten his line if he was to release sufficient forces to deal with the pressure on his corps. His men still held a small bridgehead on the north bank of the Molodoi Tud, and he now ordered its evacuation – as was frequently the case, he covered himself from criticism from above by specifying that this could only take place if the bridgehead came under heavy attack.

The successful penetration that Zygin's men had achieved on the western flank of the German position was the target of a substantial German counterattack. The few reinforcements that Zygin had been able to dispatch to the sector despite being overruled by his Front commander weren't enough to replace the losses suffered the first day, and the infantrymen who had advanced so successfully on the first day of the offensive now found themselves in danger of encirclement as a mixed force of German infantry and armour attempted to cut the base of the small salient that had been created. The commitment of a fresh rifle battalion briefly stabilised the situation, but the balance of power remained with the Germans. By the end of the short day, encirclement seemed almost inevitable.

For Purkaev and Kalinin Front, there was growing frustration at the inability of the attacking forces to overcome the stubborn line of German defences to the south of Bely. To date, every assault had been beaten off with heavy losses, and like their equivalents in Western Front, the rifle divisions tasked with capturing Bely were badly depleted. In an attempt to link up with the German forces assembling to the south of the Soviet penetration, the German attempt to mount an attack of their own from the north finally got underway:

II Battalion [Panzer Fusilier Regiment, *Grossdeutschland*] had scarcely left its blocking positions and moved into the open when it was struck by a firestorm. Within 20 minutes the battalion had been shattered by artillery fire whose intensity was unlike anything we had imagined before. The very leading elements of II Battalion did succeed in reaching the first bunkers in Simonovka, but they were met there by Soviet infantry and badly shot up. Only a few of the men made it back to their starting position. The commanding officer, adjutant and all of the company commanders and company officers were killed or wounded. The battalion executive officer was the only officer to return unhurt. Losses in men and NCOs were correspondingly high.

Things went better for I Battalion which attacked from further back on the right. It was able to take the first part of the old main line of resistance fairly quickly but the attack then bogged down as a result of the extremely heavy Soviet artillery fire. Moreover, the enemy infantry had settled into the bunkers and trenches and were defending tenaciously.[9]

Two villages were captured in the counterattack. However, further progress proved impossible, and the Red Army was able to regain both of the villages later on 27 November. For the moment, neither side was able to prevail. Solomatin continued to request that the two independent mechanised brigades be released to him so that he could continue his drive in strength, but Tarasov was unwilling to relinquish his last powerful reserve. Perhaps in an attempt to satisfy Solomatin while retaining control of the two brigades, Tarasov informed the mechanised corps commander that the two brigades would move forward into the rear of Solomatin's corps, and that Tarasov would release them at an appropriate moment. For the moment, all that Solomatin could do was press on with the forces at hand.

Before dawn on 27 November, the advance of I Mechanised Corps was being led by small armoured reconnaissance units, while the bulk of the force spent the hours of darkness refuelling and rearming. The diversion of parts of the mechanised corps to the fighting around Bely was having a serious disruptive effect on Solomatin's plans, which originally called for his tank brigades to lead the advance and the mechanised brigades to follow as exploitation forces. As his men prepared to force their way to and over the Nacha River, Solomatin found himself forced to commit almost all of his remaining forces in a single echelon – hence his constant requests for the two independent brigades, which he could then use as an exploitation force. Unfortunately for Solomatin, Tarasov had decided to use the two brigades for a different purpose – he wanted them to attack between Bely and I Mechanised Corps and strike towards the northwest. This, he hoped, would outflank the German forces around Bely and force them to abandon their positions.

The terrain through which Solomatin's men were advancing was far from ideal for mechanised formations, as he later described:

> There were no roads for our transport columns to use with any freedom. The enemy destroyed all the bridges as he withdrew and the deep snow and poor visibility in fresh snow showers greatly restricted movement. The corps had no specialist vehicles to clear snowdrifts or for road construction and we had to use T-34s for that purpose. They moved in column, one after another, in order to create a trail for infantry vehicles and towed guns. In some cases the motorised infantry had to dismount and follow the tanks on foot, tiring them and further limiting the ability to manoeuvre ...
>
> The leading tank units often ran into each other and advancing formations frequently found themselves in the path of their neighbours, making it difficult to coordinate forces and slowing the rate of advance even more.[10]

Despite the terrain difficulties, Solomatin's units continued to advance, not least because there were almost no German forces in their path. The only significant group was a reinforced company from 1st Panzer Division's reconnaissance battalion, and it was rapidly brushed aside. At the end of the day, the leading units of I Mechanised Corps reached the Nacha; a village on the west side of the river was held by a small improvised group of German soldiers, and while elements of the leading 65th Tank Brigade, commanded by Lieutenant Colonel Aleksander Iosifovich Shevchenko, attempted to drive off the little garrison, a battalion of tanks moved up to the Nacha. Combat engineers rapidly improvised a small wooden bridge, and several tanks crossed to the east bank, from where they thrust forward to cut the vital road running to Bely. The obvious satisfaction that the objective had been reached was tempered by the sudden appearance of German mechanised units on the road. These were from the leading elements of 12th Panzer Division, hurrying up from the south, and Meden's battlegroup from 1st Panzer Division. Briefly, the Soviet tanks managed to capture the village of Bossino, but Meden's panzergrenadiers counterattacked after nightfall. Operating without infantry support, the Soviet armour pulled back to the riverbank, from where they were still able to interdict the road with gunfire. Shevchenko's brigade had entered the operation with its full complement of five KV-1 tanks, 24 T-34s and 20 T-70 light tanks; several of these had either broken down or been knocked out during the advance, but sufficient numbers remained to form a serious threat to the vital supply road.

To the north of Bely in the Luchesa valley, there was a brief moment of success for Iushkevich as the leading tanks of 49th Tank Brigade finally managed to reach open country. A breach had opened in the German lines, and although Hilpert was able to hold the northern shoulder of the Soviet penetration, he lacked the troops to restore contact with Harpe's XLI Panzer Corps to the south. Two battalions arrived in time to set up a temporary defensive line, but Iushkevich ordered Katukov to switch his main thrust to the south to take advantage of the penetration that had been achieved. In almost impossible terrain, the tank crews struggled through deep snow towards the breakthrough, along inadequate tracks that were choked with columns trying to move forward supplies while the wounded were taken in the opposite direction.

The perilous position of the Soviet infantry on the western flank of Zygin's Thirty-Ninth Army was fully exposed on 27 November, when two battalions from *Grossdeutschland* resumed their counterattacks. By the end of the day, the Soviet penetration that had been achieved on the first day of the offensive was completely eliminated and the former front line restored. Immediately, one of the two *Grossdeutschland* battalions was ordered to hurry to the Luchesa valley. On the other flank of the northern battle, 14th Motorised Division's regiment drove the Soviet infantry out of their positions to the west of Trushkovo, but in the centre the German line pulled back further. To a large extent, this was because Hitter took advantage of Hilpert's orders that retreats could be carried out if absolutely necessary; deeming that the current positions were impossible to hold, Hitter ordered the regiments of his 206th Infantry Division to pull back to a shorter line. The small town of Molodoi Tud was abandoned and the bridgehead north of the river of the same name evacuated. Zygin took this as a sign that his frontal attacks were finally achieving results – even if the first day's successes on the western flank had been reversed, his central units were now close to the Olenino–Rzhev road.

Throughout the night to 28 November, Solomatin continued to request reinforcements from Tarasov. The leading elements of I Mechanised Brigade might have reached the vital road to the east of the Nacha River, but he sensed the growing strength of German motorised formations on the road. In addition, his long southern flank was poorly protected. To date the Germans had made no attempt to exploit this, but it was surely only a matter of time before a counterattack from that direction. With most of his reserves committed, there was little that Tarasov could do. If his units could envelop the Germans on the northern flank of the penetration and roll them back to Bely – and perhaps through the town – this would release sufficient resources to shore up the southern flank of the penetration as well as permit several infantry units to move further east in support of Solomatin's formations. In keeping with the decision he had made the previous day, he ordered one of his reserve units, 47th Mechanised Brigade, to strike northeast between the battlefields near Bely and Solomatin's men to the east. For the moment, the second reserve mechanised brigade would be held back to provide cover for the southern flank of the penetration. The transfer of a mechanised corps to Velikiye Luki was having a serious effect on Forty-First Army's ability to continue its advance.

The battle to the south of Bely flared once more early on 28 November. The village of Ananino, to the southeast of Bely, was overrun by Soviet infantry, and immediately the Soviet 47th Mechanised Brigade advanced through the breach that had been created. Confused fighting continued all morning, with groups of Soviet tanks appearing and disappearing through the frequent snowstorms, but during the afternoon the mechanised brigade reached and crossed the road to Bely from Vladimirskoye at Shaitrovshchina. The infantry that had created the gap exploited by 47th Mechanised Brigade now turned west to try to roll up the Bely defences. Tarasov attempted to exploit this success by moving armoured units from the bitter stalemate south of Bely; they were ordered to move into the new breach and join the attack towards Bely from the east. Meanwhile, attack followed counterattack in the ruins of the villages that were scattered in the woodland and narrow valleys south of Bely. In an attempt to shore up their defences in the face of the new threat along the Vladimirskoye road, the Germans made small withdrawals and sent the troops that were thus released to create a new group, together with whatever rear area personnel still remained outside the front line. Lacking heavy weapons, this group had limited strength in the face of the forces being sent against them by Tarasov.

Meanwhile, Solomatin was attempting to continue his advance towards the east. He later wrote that prisoners taken on this day revealed the recent arrival of 12th and 20th Panzer Divisions, somewhat undermining Solomatin's previous comments that elements of 12th Panzer Division had been detected in his area of operations before the offensive began. On his southern flank, his units fought a brief battle for the village of Nikitinka, destroying several German tanks. More importantly, they cut the railway line running through the town, a key route by which the Germans were moving heavy equipment up to the Nacha valley. The central sector became a struggle to see which side would be able to reinforce its units the fastest, and the village of Bossino became the focus of the fighting. Accompanied by a few handfuls of infantry, Shevchenko's tank brigade clung to the village despite every German counterattack, but without reinforcements it was questionable whether the Soviet group would be able to remain in the village, let alone advance further. In an attempt to prevent his dwindling strength from being dissipated too widely, Solomatin ordered the group that had penetrated to and beyond Nikitinka on his southern flank to dispatch forces northwards. The troops available were modest, just a single platoon of tanks accompanied by a company of infantry and an artillery battery, but it was all that could be spared; nonetheless, if it surprised the Germans by appearing in their rear, this group might permit Solomatin's central units to resume their advance.

For the Germans, the situation remained serious. The Soviet penetration to the southeast and east of Bely might represent a decisive shift in the battle, but Harpe remained determined to hold on to Bely. The penetration of Solomatin's mechanised corps to Nikitinka was a setback, but for the moment Meden's battlegroup could afford to ignore it on the assumption that elements of 12th Panzer Division were expected in the region, moving up from the south. In any case, there were no units to spare to deal with this emergency. Everything hinged on holding Bely.

Towards the end of the day, the frustrated and angry Zhukov travelled from Western Front to Kalinin Front for a further meeting. The advance from the west had gone far better than the attack from the east, and he urged Tarasov and Purkaev to make greater efforts – if they advanced further, they would start to threaten the rear of the German XXXIX Panzer Corps, which would in turn make the task of Western Front easier. At the end of the conference, he spoke to Stalin by telephone. The details of the conversation aren't clear, but it seems that he stressed the stubbornness of German defences and requested that *Stavka* release several rifle divisions to bring his attacking groups up to strength. Stalin was reluctant to do so, and replied that the offensive had to show better progress – and therefore better chances of success – before he would commit any further troops. Of course, Zhukov could assert that without fresh reinforcements, such a success was harder to achieve, but Stalin refused to listen to such arguments.

Zhukov still had V Tank Corps in reserve, with over 130 tanks, but like Stalin he was reluctant to commit reserves to the battle until there was a good chance of success.

Katukov's mechanised corps struggled to reach its start line for Twenty-Second Army's renewed attack in the Luchesa valley on 28 November. After lengthy delays, the assault finally began at about midday and immediately achieved local success. The terrain was heavily wooded, and the armour had little choice but to follow the few tracks in the area. When the advancing infantry and tanks reached the village of Goncharovo, they ran into another group of panzergrenadiers from *Grossdeutschland* and once more their advance came to an abrupt halt. Attacks north of the Luchesa were also frustrated by German defences, and Iushkevich decided that he had to reinforce his attacks. He ordered his reserves – a single rifle brigade and a tank regiment with 30 tanks – to move forward. The Germans, too, were sending their last reserves into the battle. *Kampfgruppe Köhler*, consisting of two battalions of panzergrenadiers from *Grossdeutschland* under the command of the regiment commander, Oberst Otto Köhler, were sent into action. One of these battalions was freshly arrived from the fighting against the Soviet Thirty-Ninth Army in the north, and while the counterattack in that sector had been successful, the German battalion still suffered substantial casualties and was far from full strength. Nevertheless, by the end of 28 November, the two *Grossdeutschland* battalions had gathered for what Hilpert hoped would be a decisive counterattack that would seal off the Soviet penetration and restore contact with Harpe's XLI Panzer Corps to the south.

The fighting in the northern sector was degenerating into a slugging match as Zygin tried to push forward with his centre. If he had hoped that the German withdrawals of 27 November were signs that resistance was weakening, he was disappointed. True to form, the Germans launched repeated counterattacks and, combined with the dense forests and ongoing snowfall, this made further progress for the attacking Soviet units almost impossible. An attempt by Malygin to unhinge the German defences by outflanking a German defensive line ended in disaster when the tank battalion carrying out the manoeuvre ran into strong German anti-tank defences and was driven back with heavy losses. With his 28th Tank Brigade rapidly running out of vehicles – many had been knocked out by German defences and many more were disabled by mechanical problems or stranded in the difficult terrain – Malygin could do little more. His tanks were accompanied by the infantry of Colonel Kuzma Ivanovich Sazonov's 373rd Rifle Division, and the two men met to discuss the next step. All they could do was bring forward further supplies and what few reinforcements were available and try to resume the attack the following day.[11]

Near Bely, the crisis in the German lines was no less severe, and Tarasov was confident as 29 November dawned that his men were close to a decisive success. Despite the difficulties imposed by the unfavourable terrain, his units had torn a large gap in the German lines and the steady outflanking of the German position near Bely looked as if it would result in the fall of the town. Colonel Ivan Fedorovich Dremov's 47th Mechanised Brigade was now advancing northeast and encountering only minimal resistance. A further attack on the German lines south of Bely resulted in a small advance, triggering yet another German counterattack, but there were reports of German rear area units attempting to escape from Dremov's advancing units by moving west towards Bely. A further rifle brigade and mechanised brigade were meant to be following Dremov's forces towards the northeast, but concluding that German forces were at the end of their strength, Tarasov ordered them to turn towards the west and attack Bely. As they advanced, the Soviet infantry ran into heavy German fire and were brought to a halt – unknown to them, most of the artillery assets of 1st Panzer Division and five battalions of corps-level artillery had been deployed in their path to support the ad hoc line of infantry that had been assembled the previous day. Backed by this formidable firepower, the few German infantrymen defending the eastern approaches of Bely were able to bring this latest Soviet threat to a halt immediately to the east of the Vena River, barely two miles from the edge of Bely.

Deprived of the reinforcements he had been expecting, Dremov was left in a precarious position with both his flanks in the air. Without support, he couldn't advance without inviting German mobile forces to turn one or both flanks. Had Tarasov allowed the two supporting brigades to join 47th Mechanised Brigade, the envelopment of Bely would have been completed and the forces in the town would have been left without supplies. Alternatively, had the entire force turned west to strike into Bely, the paper-thin German line hastily deployed along the Vena, despite its substantial artillery support, would have been overwhelmed. Instead, another bloody stalemate developed along the Vena River while Dremov's troops sat nervously in an exposed position to the east. On the other side of the front line, 1st Panzer Division, with what remained of 246th Infantry Division subordinated to it, shuffled its diminishing strength. A few strongpoints to the south of Bely were abandoned to release men to defend the Vena line. The only reserves available to Krüger consisted of four half-tracks with their panzergrenadiers and five Pz.II tanks. These tanks were of little use in battle conditions, with maximal armour thickness of just 35mm and a 20mm gun, but the little group was rushed to shore up the defences to the southeast of Bely. In case there had ever been any doubt about the matter, Model sent orders to Harpe that Bely had to be held at all costs. In any event, withdrawal was now impossible, with the main roads from the town cut. Even if an order had been given for a breakout, there was insufficient fuel. The exhausted men of 1st Panzer Division, 246th Infantry Division, and Kassnitz's battlegroup from *Grossdeutschland* would either hold the town until relieved, or die in the attempt.

To date, the most spectacular success achieved by Tarasov's forces – indeed, by all of the armies involved in *Mars* – was Solomatin's advance. Tarasov continued to urge his subordinate to press on towards the east, but Solomatin was increasingly worried about the strength of resistance in his path. With the bulk of one of his mechanised brigades guarding his southern flank, he sent a second mechanised brigade supported by a tank regiment against a small German bridgehead on the west side of the Nacha. The assault was successful, forcing the Germans back across the river, but when the Soviet group tried to cross and create a bridgehead of their own, they encountered tougher resistance. The road that followed the valley was the main axis along which German reinforcements were arriving from the south, and these units struck repeatedly in an attempt to drive the Red Army units back to the west. As darkness fell, Solomatin's men remained in control of a small segment of the road, but the cost had been high, with both the infantry and tanks losing half their strength in bitter fighting. The Soviet bridgehead across the Nacha a little to the north was also the scene of bitter fighting. The armoured reconnaissance battalion of 1st Panzer Division had been a prominent part of the German force attempting to screen off Solomatin's breakthrough, and its motorcycle battalion was almost completely destroyed in the day's fighting; the battalion commander, Hauptmann Harro Freiherr von Frydag, was killed leading a desperate counterattack. A panzergrenadier battalion commanded by Hauptmann Helmut Huppert was effectively trapped between the two Soviet bridgeheads across the Nacha but repulsed every Soviet attack; however, by the end of the day, Huppert was running out of men and ammunition and contemplating the complete destruction of his small garrison.

Given the swift advances achieved in the preceding days, this slow grind across the Nacha was a source of frustration both for Solomatin and Tarasov, but without further reinforcements, there was little that Solomatin could do. Further elements of Generalmajor Walter Wessel's 12th Panzer Division were beginning to arrive, but they were not yet in action. The waning strength of *Kampfgruppe von der*

Meden had been enough to hold back Solomatin's troops, but it would have to continue to do so for at least another day before Wessel's forces could intervene.

In the Luchesa valley, 29 November saw both sides launching major attacks. For Iushkevich, this was meant to be the day that his forces achieved a decisive victory – even though his Front was a secondary component of the overall Red Army plan of operations, a breakthrough here would undoubtedly facilitate the success of Kalinin Front's main effort to the south of Bely, even if only by tying down further German forces. On the German side of the front line, most of the limited forces available to Hilpert for a counterattack were now in position. Much would depend on whether Katukov could exploit the minor breakthrough achieved the previous day.

On the northern flank of Twenty-Second Army, there was heavy fighting around the ruins of Starukhi. *Kampfgruppe Warschauer*, the German force holding the village, consisted of a battalion from *Grossdeutschland* reinforced by two combat engineer companies, and they had to deal with the full weight of the Red Army's assault, with up to 40 tanks supported by motorised infantry. In the nick of time, elements of *Kampfgruppe Köhler* arrived as reinforcements and helped drive off the first Soviet attack, but the signals unit with the German force immediately intercepted Red Army messages suggesting that another attack was imminent. Despite Katukov's reservations about the heavy KV-1 tanks, they proved invaluable when the advancing armour encountered a group of German 50mm anti-tank guns. Against such heavily armoured vehicles, these guns were of very limited value; the frontal armour of the KV-1 was 90mm thick, with side armour only marginally thinner at 70mm. The 50mm guns of the German anti-tank units could achieve a maximum penetration of 130mm, but only at ranges of less than 100m and using the more potent *Panzergranate 40* – even this round would fail against the frontal armour of a KV-1 at longer range, and the older *Panzergranate 39* lacked the power even to penetrate the side armour of a KV-1 at any range. The Soviet tanks literally crushed the German *Pakfront* and pushed on, but were halted when they encountered a battery of far more potent 88mm guns. Several tanks were destroyed and the attack came to a halt. The overall Soviet advance was a mere seven miles (12km), a little over half the distance to the Olenino–Bely road, and casualties had been high. But equally, German losses were substantial, and although Iushkevich wanted to pause to regroup, Zhukov insisted that he press on – the remaining strength of Twenty-Second Army would be sufficient to brush aside what remained of the German units in his path.

In any event, the German position in Starukhi was untenable, as it had been outflanked to the east. Under heavy pressure, *Gruppe Warschauer* began to fall back. The commander of a company of combat engineers was killed in a desperate counterattack, and as the fighting continued all of his subordinate officers and NCOs became casualties. As they gathered around the Luchesa bridge, the soldiers of the panzergrenadier battalion that had formed the main combat strength of the German battlegroup amounted to little more than a reinforced platoon, with fewer than 50 men available for combat, but half of the Soviet tanks were left burning or stranded on the battlefield. A sense of the fighting and the difficult withdrawal can be gained from the account of a *Grossdeutschland* artillery officer who was in a forward observation post, trying to direct the fire of guns further to the rear in the face of constant snowfall and difficult terrain:

At about 0900 the first [Soviet tank] crossed our lines, and rammed our anti-tank guns; one rolled straight over our trench. Unfortunately, we had no hand grenades or demolition charges at hand. When it cleared for a moment we could see our infantry crawling about and heard the 'Urrah!' of the Bolsheviks. I tried every means to range in the guns but when I actually did see an impact, by the time the next shot was fired there was such a thick wall of snow in front of us that we could see nothing more.

Suddenly, at about 1000, ten more T-34s appeared in front of us and rolled over our foxholes. A hundred paces behind them followed the Russian infantry. We wondered why our grenadiers weren't firing and then saw them pulling back in a group behind us. What to do? If we pulled back too the Russians would soon be on our hill and would simply shoot us down as we climbed down into the gully. So we decided to try to hold.

We collected all the machine-guns and submachine-guns. Hauptmann Fromm, who had come forward a short time before, took command of the last defenders – about 45 men – including two anti-tank gun crews, several grenadiers, and our radio operator. We allowed the Bolsheviks to approach to about 80m and then we opened fire with our limited supply of ammunition. But there always seemed to be more, charging at us with horrible cries of 'Urrah!' There was nothing else to do – we would have to make a run for it. Fromm ordered an orderly withdrawal along the road, but there wasn't much chance of that …

The last hope for escape lay in flight across the snow-covered field to the left. One man after another toppled over into the snow, fatally hit. Fromm was hit in the groin but was able to keep going with my help. Then there was a cry behind me: Wachtmeister Budecke had been hit in the head.

I was able to drag myself slowly through the snow. I had already lost my boots … There were splashes in the snow all around me; I don't remember anything else, except that once, when I turned around, I saw a number of dark forms standing behind me shooting at me.

The snow became deeper and deeper. I wasn't going to get much further, I was all in. About 40m ahead was a small bush and I trudged towards it. A deep snowdrift lay before me. I couldn't get through standing up. I tried to crawl through on all fours, tried to roll over – my strength was simply at an end. I had to leave Fromm. He had apparently been hit again and the only sign of life from him was a soft moan.

Was I now to fall into the hands of the Bolsheviks, stuck in the snow? For the first time in my life I called for help. I saw another form close by. It was a Leutnant of an anti-tank gun crew coming to my aid. Summoning the last of my strength I grasped at this straw and stood up. Now I was in cover and at least the Bolsheviks could no longer see me. The Leutnant and I were the only survivors.[12]

The thrust by Zygin's Thirty-Ninth Army against the northern tip of the Rzhev Salient had reached the town of Urdom, which had been the original objective in Zygin's orders, but despite repeated attacks the Red Army failed to take the town on 29 November. As was the case in the Luchesa valley, a heavy KV-1 proved to be almost invulnerable to German fire and succeeded in silencing a bunker that was holding up the advance, but Soviet losses continued to climb. More than half of Malygin's tanks were now out of action and 373rd Rifle Division had also lost half its men. The minimal ground that had been gained during the day had to be abandoned as darkness fell, and the badly depleted Soviet formations attempted to reorganise for another attack the following day.

As 30 November dawned, Tarasov remained confident in the headquarters of Forty-First Army that the German lines would collapse at any moment. Once again, his forces attempted to break through to Bely, and despite heavy casualties from German artillery fire, the thrust from the east succeeded in taking the ruins of Golovenka. It is a measure of the degree to which 1st Panzer Division was stretching its resources that its headquarters was now just 400m from the front line and being defended by groups of rear area troops. An improvised battlegroup built around the division's military police detachment and signals battalion, commanded by Hauptmann Kurt Trumpa, finally brought the Soviet assault to a standstill and even succeeded in recovering the lost positions in Golovenka.[13] The southern perimeter was also the scene of bitter fighting. Motshalniki fell to the attacking Soviet infantry at midday but was recaptured before dark by the inevitable German counterattack.

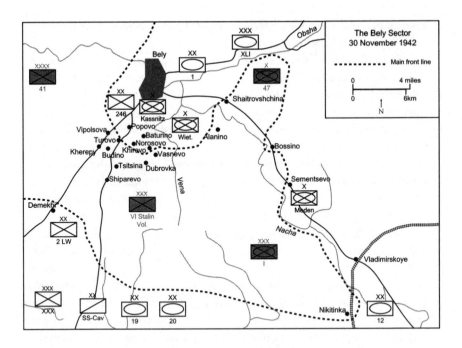

To the east, Dremov's 47th Mechanised Brigade spent most of the morning perched on the Obscha River. The only force that the Germans could send to push Dremov back and thus reopen the road to Bely was a single motorcycle battalion from *Grossdeutschland*, and this unit launched an energetic attack at midday. With much of his infantry still protecting his lines of communication, Dremov lacked the strength for a protracted battle and withdrew a little to the southwest. The amount of ground that changed hands was modest but of vital importance to the Germans: the road to Bely was once more open. Immediately, a column of trucks carrying desperately needed ammunition motored through the snow to the town.

The various elements of *Kampfgruppe von der Meden* were approaching the end of their strength, unable to fight in a coordinated manner. The panzergrenadier battalion isolated between the two Soviet bridgeheads came under renewed attack but, remarkably, repelled every attempt by Solomatin's troops to break through. The key development in this part of the battle came on the southern side of the Soviet bridgehead over the Nacha. Here, 35th Mechanised Brigade was attempting to push further to the southeast along the supply road, but made almost no progress against determined German defences near Sementsevo. In the second half of the day, there were alarming reports: German forces were bypassing the open eastern flank of 35th Mechanised Brigade and moving north. It was the reconnaissance battalion of 12th Panzer Division, which was finally close enough to intervene. As darkness fell, the leading company of 12th Panzer Division's 29th Panzer Regiment linked up with the isolated panzergrenadier battalion, ending its long siege. Shortly after, the first panzergrenadier companies from 12th Panzer Division also arrived, allowing the exhausted battalion that had defied the Red Army to withdraw.

A single panzer company attempted to halt a Soviet tank attack on Bossino with a counterthrust, in the centre of Meden's sector. When it was first deployed, it had 11 tanks, but by this stage of the battle it had a single operational Pz.IV and a few damaged Pz.IIIs. The latter were deployed for static defence around Bossino, while the long-barrelled Pz.IV attempted to mount a more active battle. Its commander claimed to have destroyed ten T-34s in the preceding days, and, accompanied by a 75mm anti-tank gun mounted on a tracked chassis, he moved forward against the advancing Soviet tanks. The two vehicles added another 14 T-34s and two KV-1s to their score before the Pz.IV was hit. With several of its crew wounded, the tank retreated to Bossino, where a repair team was trying to patch up the damaged Pz.IIIs; the damage to the Pz.IV was fixed and the tank returned to action with a new commander, who claimed a further four T-34s. While it is perfectly feasible that a total of 18 T-34s and two KV-1s were hit, it is unlikely that all were destroyed. Nevertheless, the number of tanks still available for Solomatin's subordinates to continue operations was unquestionably declining rapidly.

As darkness fell, Solomatin issued orders for his formations to cease their attempts to advance towards the east. Instead, they were to pull back to defend the bridgehead they had established across the Nacha. Even holding this position would require reinforcements, as Solomatin informed Tarasov by radio. The problem for Tarasov was that the fighting around Bely had sucked in all of his reserves, and unless the town could finally be taken, he had no men to spare to strengthen the positions along and across the Nacha.

The battle in the Luchesa valley would be, in the memories of German survivors, one of the greatest trials suffered by *Grossdeutschland* in the war to date. Leutnant Horst Warschauer, the commander of the battered battlegroup facing the northern flank of the Soviet Twenty-Second Army, found his positions under heavy attack once more after a night of repeated Soviet artillery and rocket attacks. The battalion of panzergrenadiers – little more than a platoon in strength – was surrounded and forced to fight its way out to safety. Until now, the Germans had still been able to bring Starukhi under fire, even if they were no longer in physical possession of its ruins, but now they had to pull back. The Red Army attempted to follow up its success and took the next village in its path – Bogoroditskoe – only to lose it to a desperate counterattack by Warschauer's combat engineers. The main thrust by Katukov's mechanised corps drove further east, and there was little that the depleted ranks of Köhler's infantry could do to stop them. The gap between the southern flank of this depleted battlegroup and the next German unit – 86th Infantry Division – was now about seven miles (12km), and the only reason that this had not proved fatal to the overall German position was the terrain: the gap ran through thick forests and swamps, and there were no straightforward options for the Red Army to send an exploitation force through the gap, even if they had been aware of it. Hilpert spoke to Model late on 30 November and described the seriousness of the situation in the Luchesa valley. Without further reinforcements, his lines would surely collapse and the continuing defiance around Bely would be irrelevant. With the approval of Model, he ordered 110th and 253rd Infantry Divisions to release at least one battalion each so that these units could be sent to the Luchesa valley. As had been the case in the past, an order was issued demanding that rear area units release personnel for combat duties.

At the end of the day, Zhukov had reason to feel justified in insisting that Iushkevich continue his assault. The German lines were surely close to breaking, and Twenty-Second Army still had a rifle brigade and a tank regiment in reserve. Iushkevich probably had far greater reservations; his army had lost nearly half of its tanks and about half its infantry, and had advanced just nine miles (16km). The terrain had been almost as big an obstacle as the defending German forces, and despite his intact reserves, the losses of the units that had fought their way forward were so great that exploiting any final breakthrough was questionable.

Meanwhile, Zygin's Thirty-Ninth Army continued its struggle to capture its preliminary objective, the town of Urdom. Perhaps aware of the growing setbacks elsewhere, Zhukov and Purkaev urged Zygin to seize the town without delay. With grim determination, Zygin obeyed, throwing two rifle divisions in a frontal assault at Urdom, while two tank brigades attempted to push forward on each flank. Unknown to Zygin, the Germans had already concluded that Urdom couldn't be held. After a brief battle, which nonetheless cost the attackers heavy casualties and nearly half their tanks, the German infantry pulled back to a new defensive line immediately south of the town. Among the mixture of units that abandoned Urdom was the improvised ski battalion from *Grossdeutschland*. In just a week of fighting, over half its personnel had been lost, but Zygin's units were exhausted. Further attacks on the same scale as the preceding days were impossible.

Just as Western Front had failed to deliver the expected results, Zhukov had to face the fact that the assaults by Kalinin Front – with the exception of Solomatin's mechanised corps – had also failed to gain much ground. Further futile attacks would merely add to the butcher's bill; sufficient damage had been inflicted on the German divisions to make their transfer to other sectors almost irrelevant, even if they could be released from the Rzhev sector. But as is so often the case in war, the battle had assumed a momentum of its own, and for the moment, Zhukov showed no inclination to call it off.

CHAPTER 12

DECEMBER: THE VAZUZA VALLEY AND THE BELY SECTOR

The slaughter on the eastern side of the salient died down in the first days of December as exhaustion and huge losses enforced a halt on Konev's operations. By any standard, the attacks had been little short of disastrous. Every division and brigade involved in the operation had suffered crippling losses, with almost nothing to show for the sacrifice. The German lines had been bent and battered in places, and German losses were substantial, but the price paid for these modest gains was terrible.

Far to the south, the German Sixth Army was encircled in Stalingrad, and preparations were proceeding for new Soviet operations along the Don. *Stavka* was aware that the Germans would mount a relief attempt to reach Paulus' divisions trapped on the Volga, but they were confident that they could beat off such an attack; in any case, the new attacks against the Italian and Hungarian armies holding the Don front would force the Germans to divert resources to shore up their lines, reducing the forces available to lift the siege of Stalingrad. There was a mood of cautious but growing optimism, and as the man who had largely overseen the successful operation, Vasilevsky was held in increasingly high regard. By contrast, Zhukov's attempts to break into the Rzhev Salient had been a bloodstained disaster. Zhukov's memoirs suggest that he was still intimately involved in the operations in the south, but his main focus was the continuing struggle against Model's Ninth Army. He needed to salvage some sort of success from the disappointments and setbacks of late November, if only to save face.

The exhausted and bled-out units of Kiriukhin's Twentieth Army were hastily reinforced. Just as Model and his corps commanders ordered rear area units to be

324

'combed out' and the 'surplus' men to be sent to the front line, the Soviet formations were ordered to reduce their support sections to the bare minimum. As was the case in the Wehrmacht, this resulted in a numerical increase in the front-line units, but contributed little in terms of their combat power. Many of the men in the rear area formations were not fit for front-line service as a consequence of previous injuries, illness or age. Most lacked the experience that was essential for survival in the brutal conditions that prevailed around the Rzhev Salient. Moreover, compared with their German equivalents, the Soviet units were comparatively light in terms of their support services, a problem that had deep roots in the Red Army, actually preceding its creation.

When the Russian Army of Tsar Nicholas mobilised in 1914, the main priority was to fill the ranks of the combat formations. The complex mobilisation plans also specified the creation of logistic formations, including many dedicated to ensuring the smooth running of Russia's railways, without which armies of that era were almost completely immobile, and logically these units should have been mobilised first. The failure to ensure that essential transport personnel were in place before front-line troops began to be mobilised resulted in repeated setbacks in the formation of Russia's armies, delaying operations against Germany; this was critical, as the entire basis of Russia's alliance with France was a swift attack by Russia on Germany before the German Army could overwhelm France.

In the years preceding the First World War, the generals of the tsar behaved as if logistics were an irrelevance. Field and paper exercises were conducted as if supplies of all kinds were infinite, and there was no consideration even as to how ammunition and food would be moved forward to keep pace with Russia's field armies. This lack of priority for the humble rear area units persisted after the Russian Revolution. When the Soviet Union moved its troops into the eastern parts of Poland in 1939, there were constant shortages of fuel and food for the Red Army columns as they advanced. Throughout the Second World War, the failure of rear area support was a constant factor in Soviet operations, and repeated attempts were made to improve matters, particularly in the armoured formations; the ability of organic repair teams to fix disabled tanks was an important factor in the functioning of Germany's panzer divisions, and the Red Army steadily increased its own provision of such services, rightly identifying this as an essential means of keeping front-line tank strength as high as possible. But in late 1942, the support services at all levels remained a neglected part of the Red Army, often badly below their already inadequate establishment strength and filled with men of limited value. These men were now sent into the front line, where they would achieve little other than add to the already terrible casualty lists, and at the same time, the already weak support for front-line units became even poorer.

Zhukov was clearly frustrated by the failure of Konev's Western Front to achieve a breakthrough. Someone had to be blamed for the setback, and Zhukov was not long in finding the first target for his wrath. Kiriukhin was dismissed from command of Twentieth Army on 4 December. In the opening months of the war, such a dismissal might have resulted in serious consequences, including summary execution, but Kiriukhin survived. He was a veteran Communist, having been imprisoned as a 17-year-old on the eve of the First World War for membership of a socialist organisation, and had participated in the February Revolution in Petrograd in 1918; he had served in the Red Army from its inception. With extensive service both as a front-line commander and as a political commissar, he survived Stalin's purges of the 1930s unscathed, and was now deemed to be sufficiently politically reliable that serious punishment for his 'failure' was thought unnecessary. He was given a new role as deputy commander of Kalinin Front's Twenty-Ninth Army, and in February 1943 given command of XXIV Rifle Corps. He led his corps with distinction in the Battle of Kursk and the subsequent advance to and across the Dnieper, and ended the war as deputy commander of Thirty-Eighth Army. He died in 1953.

Kiriukhin's replacement was Lieutenant General Mikhail Semenovich Khozin, who had something of a chequered past record. He was sent to Leningrad in September 1941 as chief of staff of Leningrad Front before taking command of Fifty-Fourth Army. During the first winter of the war, he held a complex series of simultaneous commands and oversaw the operation to try to lift the siege of Leningrad in the late spring of 1942. This resulted in the encirclement and destruction of the Soviet Second Shock Army, and Khozin was dismissed as commander of Leningrad Front:

> [Dismissed] for failure to comply with the orders of *Stavka* regarding the timely and prompt withdrawal of Second Shock Army, for overly bureaucratic methods of command and control, and for permitting the divergence of units with the result that the enemy cut the lines of communication of Second Shock Army and the latter was put in an extremely difficult situation.[1]

In October, Khozin was appointed as Konev's deputy at Western Front headquarters but again failed to impress; his dismissal was recommended due to 'inactivity and a frivolous attitude'.[2] It is perhaps a sign of the limited resources available to the Red Army that, despite this, he was now assigned command of Twentieth Army.

Kiriukhin wasn't the only man to lose his post as a result of the failures of November. Arman, who had been acting commander of VI Tank Corps during its attempt to break into the salient, was also dismissed. His replacement was Colonel Ivan Ivanovich Iushchuk, who had been deputy commander of Western Front before he was wounded early in 1942 and replaced by Khozin. Further changes of command would follow as December unfolded.

While Western Front licked its wounds and reorganised its forces for a final attempt to break through from the east, Tarasov continued his increasingly desperate attempts to turn his initial success into a major victory. With so much of his strength tied down in fighting around the Bely perimeter, he had little choice but to order his men to continue their attempts to overwhelm the German lines. Throughout the first three days of December, Soviet artillery hammered at the defenders, and Tarasov's infantry tried in vain to move forward. Grimly, the Germans endured the onslaught:

The strength of our troops declined steadily. In addition to the high losses, particularly from mortar and rocket fire, there were also large numbers of cold weather injuries. These were particularly severe amongst the artillerymen and rear area personnel deployed on the southeast perimeter. Their weaponry consisted almost exclusively of rifles and hand grenades with just a few isolated machine-guns. The leadership of these troop elements was also insufficiently experienced and the soldiers were unaccustomed to battle. Therefore, the southeast front, which was clearly the key point of the defensive line, had to be reinforced. [1st Panzer] Division deployed further elements of a half-track company behind these positions and at the same time sent forward the *Grossdeutschland* rocket launcher battery, which had effectively exhausted its ammunition, in an infantry role. The last soldiers of 1st Panzer Division's staff – a few messengers, radio operators, clerks and supply men – were assembled as a 'security platoon'. Together with the elements of 37th Armoured Signals Battalion that could be spared as infantry, they formed the division's last reserves.

Unfortunately, the weather hindered attacks by our aircraft during these days. The Russians, however, made constant attacks against the almost defenceless positions of the division at an altitude of just 50m with their armoured Il-2 aircraft. The few available 20mm guns could hardly be used for air defence as they constantly had to be deployed in ground fighting on the front line.[3]

Despite a week of fighting in appalling weather conditions with almost no shelter, the German defenders stubbornly repulsed every attack. They watched helplessly as Red Army vehicles moved around in the rear areas of the Soviet front line with their headlamps blazing – artillery ammunition was running short for the Germans, and interdicting these traffic movements was a low priority compared with providing fire support for the hard-pressed front line.

A little to the east, the balance of power was shifting decisively against Solomatin and his I Mechanised Corps. Further elements of 12th Panzer Division arrived to reinforce *Gruppe von der Meden*, and there were repeated attacks against the bridgehead held by Solomatin's men on the east bank of the Nacha. Tarasov rejected every suggestion by Solomatin that it might be prudent for the exposed bridgehead to be abandoned, followed by a withdrawal to a shorter line of defence further west. The first attacks by the Germans to reduce the bridgehead made slow progress through the wooded terrain, but a new threat developed at the southeast tip of Solomatin's penetration. Oberst Rudolf Holste, commanding elements of 1st Panzer Division's artillery regiment and combat engineers, began to drive back the isolated groups of Soviet soldiers. There was no possibility of Solomatin sending reinforcements, as reports from his reconnaissance elements, backed by messages from partisan groups, indicated the appearance of substantial German forces to the south of Forty-First Army's penetration. For the moment these German units were unidentified, but Solomatin decided to take no chances. With no prospect of a resumed drive towards the east and growing pressure all along his Front, he had no intention of leaving his men tied down while a new threat erupted behind his southern flank. The only way that he could put up any sort of defensive screen to cover the appearance of these new German forces was to order withdrawals along the Nacha front. Late on 3 December, he outlined the situation to Tarasov in a signal and added that he had already issued orders for the necessary withdrawals.

The new forces appearing to the south were the first elements of Generalmajor Heinrich Freiherr von Lüttwitz's 20th Panzer Division, which had been part of Army Group Centre's reserve before the onset of *Mars*. As was the case throughout the region, the roads over which the division moved towards battle were terrible, and there were repeated delays while vehicles that had broken down or become stranded in the deep snow were moved aside. Nonetheless, the appearance of this unit effectively brought the crisis on the southern flank of Harpe's XLI Panzer Corps to an end. To the west, 2nd Luftwaffe Field Division had managed to reorder its battered ranks, and the SS cavalry had deployed immediately to its east. Lüttwitz now completed the new front line by filling the gap between the SS unit and 12th Panzer Division. To make matters even worse for the Red Army, 19th Panzer Division was also beginning to concentrate to the rear of 20th

Panzer Division. Partisans soon reported its presence and did what they could to interfere with German preparations, but there could be no doubt that a major German counterattack would take place in the coming days. Belatedly, Tarasov had to admit defeat. Bely remained unconquered, and the growing strength of German units being deployed against Solomatin finished off any lingering possibility of a breakthrough. The shoulders of his army's penetration into the German positions were separated by just six miles (10km), and there was now a growing danger of the Germans attacking this narrow neck.

Khlebnikov, the chief of artillery in Kalinin Front, had been supervising the efforts of the Red Army at Velikiye Luki, where Third Shock Army had attacked the German positions at the same time that *Mars* commenced. Unlike the brutal struggles around the Rzhev Salient for minimal gains, the Red Army's units enjoyed better fortunes, encircling the German garrison after three days of fighting. Attempts to drive further west and capture the key railway junction at Novosokolniki failed, but Purkaev and Khlebnikov were largely satisfied that they had encircled a substantial German force, and the artillery chief now returned to the Rzhev Salient. Purkaev immediately sent him to Tarasov's headquarters:

> [Tarasov] told me that he feared for the flanks of the wedge that his men had driven into the enemy's defences. According to intelligence, the Nazis were constantly bringing up fresh forces. General Solomatin, the commander of I Mechanised Corps, gave a similar report to General Kurkin, the Front headquarters representative of armoured and mechanised troops. According to Solomatin, a real threat of encirclement hung over his units. He had already ordered some vehicles to withdraw to the rear. Only tanks, gun tractors, ammunition carriers and ambulances remained with his combat formations.
>
> It was urgently necessary to regroup the artillery on the flanks, which I decided was a priority.[4]

To date, the Red Army had been dictating the course of events, but the arrival of German reserves was about to change that. Would Khlebnikov have sufficient time to reorganise his artillery assets?

To the south of Bely, events were rapidly slipping out of Tarasov's control. The infantry units facing Bely were down to barely a third of their establishment strength, and despite Khlebnikov's efforts, improved artillery support could not substitute for their losses. Dremov's 47th Mechanised Brigade, dispatched by Tarasov in a thrust towards the northeast, was still in position, but its tank strength declined steadily. The brigade commander was increasingly aware of

German forces concentrating near Shaitrovshchina, and he attempted to disrupt German preparations by launching tank raids but was soon forced to abandon these. His men prepared anti-tank defences and awaited the inevitable assault, and a battalion from 1st Panzer Division's 1st Panzergrenadier Regiment, reinforced by a mixture of tanks and assault guns, attacked on 4 December. Caught by fierce flanking fire and lacking heavy weapons, the battalion was forced to halt its first attack. It had lost all but three of its officers and its companies could field no more than 30 men each. Nonetheless, a renewed effort was made the following day, as a German account described:

> The enemy infantry had taken up strong positions in and around Shaitrovshchina. They occupied old positions of the Bely Defences from the summer of 1941. The strung-out village, which the enemy tried to hold at all costs, could only be taken in close-quarter fighting, according to the report from Hauptmann Olze [commander of the panzergrenadier battalion]. The battalion lacked the manpower to do this. On the other hand, ten T-34s with mounted infantry soon attacked along the main road from Shaitrovshchina towards Shamilovo in the southeast ... In hard tank combat that ebbed and flowed, 2nd Company, 1st Panzer Regiment shot up seven T-34s and tank destruction troops from 1st Battalion, 1st Panzergrenadier Regiment accounted for another. During the evening, a counterthrust by 1st Battalion finally managed to penetrate into the southern part of the village.[5]

The panzergrenadier battalion had fewer than 100 men left, but the attack on Shaitrovshchina continued the following day, largely led by reinforcements from 246th Infantry Division. By the end of the day, Dremov's surviving units had been forced out of the village. Much of 47th Mechanised Brigade was cut off by the German attack, and an attempt was made on 7 December to break out to the south. The remnants of the German panzergrenadier battalion destroyed a further seven T-34s, and together with the battalions from 246th Infantry Division broke up the Soviet group. By the end of the day, Dremov's brigade had ceased to exist, with a few survivors escaping either to join local partisan groups or infiltrating their way south.

Throughout the unfolding of *Uranus* on the steppe to the west of Stalingrad and *Mars* around the Rzhev Salient, Major General Yakov Grigorievich Kreiser's Second Guards Army and Major General Pavel Semenovich Rybalko's Third Tank Army had been held in central reserve. There had been a degree of rivalry between the two operations about the further use of these powerful groups, and

Zhukov had already pleaded – successfully – with Stalin for both armies to remain in the Moscow area; once *Mars* achieved its initial objectives, he had wanted to commit them for a deeper attack against the German Army Group Centre. The success of *Uranus* led to calls for both armies to be sent south, ideally to participate in further attacks to complete the destruction of the southern wing of the entire German front line; in addition, it was now increasingly clear to *Stavka* that the encirclement of Stalingrad had resulted in far more German troops being trapped than they had anticipated, and the need to maintain a tight siege perimeter left the Fronts in the region with few resources for further offensive operations, or to deal with the growing danger of a German relief attack towards Stalingrad. The only way that sufficient resources could be found both to maintain the siege of the German Sixth Army in Stalingrad and to exploit the great success that had already been achieved was to send the two armies south.

The commitment of these valuable reserve formations was now the focus of Zhukov's attention. On 7 December, he travelled to Moscow again for meetings to discuss ongoing operations. Although there had been little success in the attacks on the Rzhev Salient to date, Zhukov presented a strong case that the Germans were exhausted and at the end of their strength. The brigades of VI Tank Corps were being rearmed, and V Tank Corps had not yet been committed to the battle. Fresh rifle divisions were also arriving, and in combination with the new attack planned for close to Rzhev, the collapse of the salient was imminent. At the end of the conference, Stalin gave qualified approval for *Mars* to continue. However, if there was no significant success within two days, the operation would be called off. As if to emphasise the point, Stalin showed Zhukov orders that had been drafted for Rybalko's Third Tank Army to be sent south – if *Mars* failed to yield results, the orders would be issued.

Accordingly, new instructions were sent out by *Stavka* that evening. Western Front was ordered to renew its attacks and capture Sychevka with Twentieth Army 'no later than 15 December'; at the same time, Kalinin Front's Forty-First Army was to capture Bely 'no later than 20 December' and link up with Western Front's advancing units, completing the isolation of the salient. Immediately to the north of Twentieth Army, Thirtieth Army was to cut the Sychevka–Rzhev railway and main road before turning north with the intention of capturing Rzhev 'no later than 23 December'.[6] Even if the armies of Western and Kalinin Fronts had been at full strength, these orders were ambitious; given the weakened state of the front-line units, they were wildly optimistic and could only be achieved if the German lines were to collapse as Zhukov had repeatedly predicted.

The new directives would have been difficult enough to accomplish, even if the Germans had sat passively and awaited a resumption of Soviet attacks. But Model now had substantial forces arriving as reinforcements, in the shape of 12th Panzer Division along the Nacha front and 19th and 20th Panzer Divisions directly south of the Soviet penetration. The destruction of Dremov's 47th Mechanised Brigade to the east of Bely allowed the resumption of supplies to the German forces in and around Bely, restoring their firepower in a remarkably short time. The geometry of the front line practically invited a German attack from the south with the fresh panzer divisions and from the north with the forces in Bely; this would leave Solomatin's I Mechanised Corps isolated and stranded far to the west and would effectively eliminate the gains that Tarasov had been able to make.

In accordance with the new orders that had been received from *Stavka*, Konev ordered Khozin to resume attacks with Twentieth Army. The losses of the preceding days had been appalling, but Khozin received substantial reinforcements. V Tank Corps had been held in reserve throughout the opening phase of *Mars* and was now assigned to Khozin, together with six rifle divisions; four of these were transferred from neighbouring armies, while two had previously been in action on the Vazuza front but had been withdrawn to regroup and receive fresh drafts. An additional two fresh rifle divisions were allocated as a reserve, to be sent into action once Twentieth Army had broken through to Sychevka. VI Tank Corps had received replacement vehicles, many of them recently repaired in workshops in Moscow, but if tanks could be found relatively easily, the same was not true of the personnel required to operate them. The new crews were barely trained, with some having less than five weeks separating them from their first day in the army. Nonetheless, between them, V and VI Tank Corps fielded about 230 tanks. Given the losses that the Germans had suffered, this – together with the replenished infantry units – would, Konev believed, be sufficient to achieve at least some of the ambitious objectives that had been set.[7]

The plan for a renewed offensive by Western Front was little different from what had preceded it. Four rifle divisions would launch a frontal attack on the German defences, and the two tank corps – VI Tank Corps in the north, V Tank Corps in the south – would then exploit any early gains. The attack was to commence on 11 December, which would leave just four days for Twentieth Army to break the German defences that had defeated every attack in November and then advance 11 miles (19km) to Sychevka.

On the German side of the front line, 5th Panzer Division was pulled out of its positions; it was replaced by parts of 78th Infantry Division and 9th Panzer

Division. Model intended to hold the division in reserve behind the front line until it could be swapped with the fresher 2nd Panzer Division further south. With debatable accuracy, 5th Panzer Division claimed that it had faced attacks by no fewer than 44,000 men and 550 tanks; it also claimed to have destroyed 183 Soviet tanks and killed 42,000 Soviet soldiers. It seems inconceivable that only 2,000 of the soldiers deployed by the Red Army against 5th Panzer Division survived – one or other number has to be inaccurate. What was beyond question was the price that the division had paid for holding its positions – 66 officers and 1,574 other ranks were killed, wounded or missing. The losses of tanks were remarkably light. Only 18 tanks were reported as destroyed, with a further 12 awaiting repairs. This was standard practice for panzer divisions, and if some of the tanks awaiting repairs were later written off, those 'losses' never appeared in the total of destroyed tanks. But regardless of the accuracy of the estimates of Red Army losses, there could be no doubt that the fighting on the northern flank of Konev's assault had resulted in disproportionately heavy losses for almost no gain.

As his division withdrew wearily from the front line, Metz drafted a report on the recent fighting. The purpose of this was to try to share his division's experiences so that lessons could be learned by others, but there is no evidence that the report was circulated to other units. He stressed some of the shortcomings of his subordinates as well as those of the enemy, and his assessment sheds an interesting light on the manner in which the battle unfolded. He was critical of some of his juniors for discounting signs of Soviet preparations, and the manner in which they persistently underestimated the mobility of Soviet T-34s – most of his officers were of the opinion that the Ossuga River was impassable for tanks, yet throughout the battle T-34s crossed the frozen river without any difficulty.

> Counterattacks proved to be effective if made *immediately* after Russian penetrations. It was sufficient to advance against the Russian infantry with a few men shouting loudly. The Russian infantry withdrew immediately without firing back despite considerable numerical superiority ...
>
> By our standards, the Russians made poor use of artillery fire prior to their attacks. Above all they didn't concentrate their entire bombardment on the designated points of attack. They believed that they also needed to suppress 'neighbouring' positions. As a result our losses of personnel and equipment were limited to the point that we had sufficient defensive strength when the Russian tanks and infantry attacked ...
>
> Russian preparations for attack are more for morale than material purposes. They wish to make as much noise as possible ... The fragmentation of field gun

and mortar shells is strikingly poor. Their artillery ammunition has lacked the efficacy of our shells for some time. There were no ricochets. By contrast, our shells bounced off the hard-frozen ground with outstanding results [the rounds then exploded in the air, scattering shrapnel over a larger area] …

Russian anti-tank shells are also of little value. They often result in very little shrapnel [after penetration] … Fighting enemy tanks is largely a test of nerves. Men who realised this formed energetic close-combat anti-tank squads …

The Russians were also predictable in the timings of whatever they attempted. Scouting parties were deployed mainly between 2000 and 2300. After midnight they ceased activity. Their attempts to break through with cavalry took place between 0500 and 0700. The cavalry division vanguard that broke through between Podossinovka and Maloe Kropotovo succeeded in crossing our lines almost undisturbed during the hours of darkness …

At first, the Russians began their attacks between 0830 and 0900. However, the end of the artillery bombardment and the advance of tanks never coincided. As long as anti-tank weapons hadn't been knocked out, there was sufficient time to prepare them for defence against the attacking tanks.

The Russian T-34 has little value when fighting entrenched or well-positioned infantry. Only when it has been able to move through the infantry positions unhindered for a period of time is it able to knock out one foxhole after another with single shots. Rapidly deployed anti-tank weapons must be used to prevent this. Close-quarter anti-tank weaponry needs to be improved. A tank demolition charge that one can throw 5–6m at a tank should be devised. The Teller-mines are too heavy for this …

A Russian breakthrough was prevented at the last moment because of my artillery commander, Oberstleutnant Cetto, who during one night took firm and effective control of batteries from three separate divisions. This experience demonstrated that artillery is a valuable and essential tool for defence, particularly when that defence is improvised and patchy.

Our ammunition consumption was very high. By far the greatest proportion of our ammunition – I estimate about 90 per cent – was consumed in harassing fire largely to settle our nerves. Where we succeeded in getting our soldiers to fire only on 'clear' targets and to use only the most minimal ammunition on 'assumed' targets, we were more economical and reduced the demands on our supply lines and fuel consumption … I personally saw how the bulk of the Russian cavalry attempting a breakthrough were smashed by two shots from heavy howitzers and the entire breakthrough was thus brought to a halt. A Russian infantry attack on Maloe Kropotovo was halted by six shells from the howitzers.[8]

Throughout the last days of November, Tarasov had been aware of the threat to his southern flank but took little action to deal with it. Firstly, the protracted battle for Bely tied down a disproportionate number of infantry formations, leaving him with few resources to send to the south. Secondly, the near-rout of 2nd Luftwaffe Field Division left him confident – or at least hopeful – that it would be a considerable time before the Germans could rally and mount a threat from the south, and by that time he intended to have achieved a decisive breakthrough to the west. Thirdly, the terrain along his southern flank was, to say the least, difficult for mobile operations. His troops found it difficult to move into defensive positions, and he could reasonably expect that German units sent to the region would also struggle to manoeuvre. Unfortunately for Tarasov, the roads immediately to the south were rather better than those running through the area that his men had secured. While movement wouldn't be easy for the German units, it was less difficult than the conditions that faced the soldiers of Forty-First Army.

Even while Zhukov argued with Stalin and other officers about the continuation of *Mars* and the deployment of Third Tank Army and Second Guards Army, the German counterattack against the penetration south of Bely was commencing. Despite their modest reinforcements and fresh supplies, *Kampfgruppe Kassnitz* and *Kampfgruppe von Wietersheim* in Bely were hardly powerful units, and accordingly the northern part of the German operation was assigned a relatively modest set of objectives; most of the ground that needed to be covered to encircle Solomatin's corps would be taken by the units attacking from the south. Fretter-Pico and the staff of XXX Corps headquarters had been present in the area for several days, helping reorganise 2nd Luftwaffe Field Division while the SS Cavalry Division, supported by 20th Infantry Division, began to cover the southern side of the Soviet penetration. As the units of 19th Panzer Division arrived, Fretter-Pico reported that he had sufficient forces to overcome the relatively weak Red Army units before him, even before the arrival of all of 20th Panzer Division. He informed Model that he had taken careful measures to disguise the scale of his forces and planned to make the initial attack with minimal artillery preparation.

As has already been described, partisans and Red Army scouting units had correctly identified the arrival of German mechanised forces but had been unable to identify them with confidence. Even if he had been inclined to take precautions, Tarasov had no reserves available, and on 7 December his troops renewed their attacks on the Bely perimeter, while to the east of the town the isolated remnants of Dremov's 47th Mechanised Brigade tried in vain to fight their way back to the southwest. The plight of Dremov's troops was Tarasov's overriding concern; the renewed attacks on Bely were at the instigation of Purkaev, and given the greatly weakened state of the Soviet infantry units involved, there was little or no prospect of any success. He scraped together what forces he could spare and sent them to the region southeast of Bely, in the hope that they would be able to link up with Dremov's men.

Fretter-Pico's attack from the south began shortly after it grew light on 7 December. The panzer regiments of 19th and 20th Panzer Divisions collectively fielded about 70 tanks for the thrust, which was supported by 19th Panzer Division's 74th Panzergrenadier Regiment. With little difficulty, the group broke through the thin Soviet line and moved north, with the SS Cavalry Division covering the western flank. On the eastern flank, progress was slower due to the terrain being more difficult, but there was little threat from the few Red Army units in the area.

By mid-afternoon, the thrust was gaining pace. As reports reached Tarasov, he issued orders for the infantry units that had been deployed on the southern flank to counter the German advance, but they had started the day in a weakened state and had been further depleted as their sub-formations were either overwhelmed by Fretter-Pico's attack or were dispersed. The only force with the firepower to stand any chance of stopping the Germans was the unit that was most threatened: Solomatin's I Mechanised Corps, still facing the Germans along the Nacha front. With some desperation, Tarasov ordered Solomatin to release two tank brigades and send them west to Tsitsina. They were to reach this area by the evening, and would thus be directly between the German units in Bely to the north and the new attack from the south. Solomatin's two mechanised brigades were to spread their forces to cover the gaps created by the withdrawal of the tank brigades. Solomatin knew that the German units facing him had been growing steadily in strength with the arrival of 12th Panzer Division, and his worst fears were realised as he began the ordered redeployment. Parts of 19th Mechanised Brigade were still holding a small bridgehead across the Nacha, and this now came under heavy attack – not only did *Kampfgruppe von der Meden* succeed in eliminating the bridgehead, but it also succeeded in crossing the river and securing a bridgehead of its own. The two tank brigades struggled west along the inadequate roads; they were ordered to concentrate in Shevnino but were dismayed to find that the Germans had already captured the village. An attempt to drive the Germans back that evening failed to make any impression.

Tarasov was increasingly frantic to save his army from disaster. Solomatin had repeatedly warned him of the threat of encirclement, and it now seemed almost inevitable. Shortly before midnight on 7 December – even as *Stavka* was drawing up the fresh orders that arose from the conference attended by Stalin and Zhukov – Khlebnikov was in Solomatin's headquarters with Kurkin, the Front's head of armoured and mechanised forces:

> The situation was very unclear: should we continue to defend ourselves on the lines we held and wait for help from the remaining formations of Forty-First Army? Or should we break out of the encirclement? Solomatin asked Kurkin and me to return to the army's headquarters while the ring of enemy troops was not yet concrete in order to clarify these issues. We agreed and with the help of some tanks we managed to escape from the encirclement under fire in a car.[9]

When he reached Tarasov's headquarters in the village of Klemyatin, Khlebnikov was relieved to find that Zhukov was also present:

> His fortitude in this difficult situation was astonishing. Undoubtedly, both the army commander Tarasov and the army's artillery commander [Major] General [Emilii Vilgemovich] Toikka made a major mistake by failing to strengthen the flanks of the strike group in a timely manner. The result was that the strike group was now surrounded. Listening to their explanations, asking questions to clarify various details, Zhukov was stern and tough but never raised his voice. There were no unnecessary emotional outbursts in this conversation, only the matters at hand. After all, as representative of *Stavka* on the Kalinin Front, he was aware of his responsibility for the difficult situation that had arisen in Forty-First Army.
>
> Having clarified everything in the smallest detail and after asking the opinion of everyone present, he dealt with matters briefly and with precision. The encircled troops were to remain in place. General Solomatin was ordered by radio to take command of all four mechanised brigades and the two rifle brigades that were in the encirclement. These measures were taken so that the bridgehead occupied by Solomatin's tankers and Povetkin's Siberian riflemen in the depths of the enemy defence could be held, so that they could later continue the offensive.[10]

This account gives an interesting insight into Zhukov's thoughts. He had returned to the front line aware that Stalin demanded quick success, only to find that the few gains that had been made were evaporating in the face of the German counterattack. The situation was rapidly becoming critical: with strong German forces facing him in the east, Solomatin faced an almost impossible task to pull back to the valley of the Vena, where he was now ordered to take up defensive positions with both his mechanised corps and the remnants of Major General Stepan Ivanovich Povetkin's VI 'Stalin Volunteer' Rifle Corps. An immediate breakout was just as difficult an undertaking, and while it might have been wildly optimistic to talk of continuing the offensive at a later stage, there were few good options left. Until the full strength of the German counterattack became clear and Forty-First Army was reorganised, Solomatin would simply have to hold out.

Zhukov's account of these days in his memoirs is massively misleading. He describes the *Stavka* directive that was agreed on 7 December but makes little or no mention of the bitter fighting that took place in the preceding two weeks. The implication in his account is that the advance and encirclement of Solomatin's mechanised corps took place as a consequence of Forty-First Army's attempts to carry out the instructions that it received in the second week of December. There is no mention of the manner in which Zhukov repeatedly urged the armies of both Western and Kalinin Fronts to persist in their bloody attacks in the preceding days.

For Tarasov, the German counterattack was effectively a mortal blow to his tenure of command of Forty-First Army. He remained in post for several days before he was formally removed, but Zhukov effectively took over the functioning of his army, giving Tarasov very precise instructions on how he was to deploy his units. Having extensive service in the NKVD in the years before the war, Tarasov was well placed to escape punishment for his failures, and was assigned to command the Separate Army of the NKVD, which was being created in the city of Sverdlovsk in the Ural Mountains. This army was then renamed Seventieth Army and deployed as part of Central Front, where it took part in a failed attempt to recapture Orel. Rokossovsky, the Front commander, had Tarasov dismissed, but while Seventieth Army performed badly during the operation, it did no worse than the other units involved, and it is possible that the stigma of Forty-First Army's failures near Bely still tainted Tarasov. He held a number of other posts and was deputy commander of Fifty-Third Army from January 1944. In October, he was killed in a German air raid near the city of Kisújszállás in Hungary.

Tarasov's replacement as commander of Forty-First Army was Major General Ivan Mefodevich Managarov, the commander of VII Cavalry Corps. This unit had been in reserve for several months, and Managarov had spent much of the second part of 1942 overseeing the construction of defensive positions in Bryansk Front. He had served with Zhukov in the Far East before the war, and Zhukov regarded him as a man more likely to deliver success than the unfortunate Tarasov.

Fretter-Pico's units paused during the night to regroup and bring forward supplies before continuing their thrust on 8 December. At midday, the two German battlegroups in Bely made an attack of their own and reached the northern edge of the village of Dubrovka; the leading panzergrenadiers of 19th Panzer Division were within firing range of the southern edge of the village, with the battlegroups that had been defending Bely just a short distance to the north. An attempt by *Kampfgruppe von Wietersheim* to take the village failed in the face of a powerful Soviet counterattack; the steps that Khlebnikov had taken to reorganise Forty-First Army's artillery were beginning to bear fruit, and a fierce bombardment forced Wietersheim to make a small withdrawal. Nevertheless, 19th Panzer Division reported that it had edged further forward from the south, and its guns commanded the small gap that remained between its forces and the German units to the north. Solomatin was effectively encircled.

As Solomatin's troops pulled back from the Nacha, the Germans moved forward in pursuit. In addition to *Kampfgruppe von der Meden*, most of 12th Panzer Division was now in the area, and there was little that Solomatin could do to stop their advance. Outside the encirclement, Tarasov struggled to assemble a meaningful relief force. He had just one tank brigade that had not been committed to the earlier fighting and had received a fresh rifle division that he was meant to have used in the pursuance of the latest *Stavka* directive. The following day, the German units attacking south from the Bely perimeter tried again:

> An attack group of six assault guns and a company of the Fusilier Regiment *Grossdeutschland* (strength: one officer, 15 men) managed to thrust through to Dubrovka. From here, the group commander reported that 19th Panzer Division was actually halted at the southern edge of Kherepy, not actually in Dubrovka. After enemy counterattacks began, during which the group commander became a casualty, [1st Panzer] Division had to conclude that lacking adequate infantry fighting strength and as a result of heavy losses, it wasn't able to push forward to make firm contact with 19th Panzer Division. For the moment, it was only through the repeated support of 73rd Panzer Artillery Regiment that the attack group in Dubrovka could be helped, particularly by blocking bombardments to the west of the village.[11]

Within the incomplete encirclement, Solomatin found that the instructions that he had been given to take command of all units in the area were being contradicted by others. From the headquarters of Forty-First Army, Major General Iosif Ivanovich Popov, Tarasov's deputy commander, sent orders directly to infantry regiments that were now technically under Solomatin's control. The result was almost disastrous, with a section of the front line left completely undefended. The pursuing German units swiftly identified the gap and moved forward to take advantage of it, and it took a costly counterattack for Solomatin to restore the situation. Scraping together a reserve group of two battalions – one of armoured cars, one of motorcycle infantry – Solomatin decided to ignore the orders he had received to hold his positions and made an immediate attempt to break out to the west. The key was the village of Tsitsina, and it had been his intention to dispatch troops to hold the village at an earlier stage, but when his armoured column reached the area it found that 19th Panzer Division had got there first. The breakout attempt was led by 37th Mechanised Brigade and immediately ran into tough German resistance; Schmidt, commander of 19th Panzer Division, had anticipated such a move, and a defensive line of panzergrenadiers supported by the division's anti-tank battalion brought the Soviet attack to an abrupt halt. The commander and commissar of 37th Mechanised Brigade were both killed, and the remnants of the breakout group pulled back into nearby forest to regroup.

Kampfgruppe Kassnitz, made up largely of the Panzer Fusilier Regiment *Grossdeutschland*, attacked on the western flank of the northern pincer. As it moved forward, often under heavy artillery fire, the German group recaptured a position formerly held by the German 246th Infantry Division before Tarasov's successful attack of 25 November, and discovered a battery of German howitzers that had fallen into Soviet hands. Perhaps more useful was the recapture of a series of German bunkers, which permitted the German infantrymen to take shelter from Soviet artillery. There was still considerable resistance from Soviet infantry in and around Dubrovka, and an attempt by Kassnitz to storm the Soviet positions in a surprise attack resulted in the near-complete destruction of one of his companies; reduced to just one officer and five men, it was withdrawn from action. Nevertheless, late on 9 December, a patrol from *Kampfgruppe Kassnitz* established contact with 19th Panzer Division. The tenuous gap between the two German pincers was closed.[12]

Even before the Soviet commanders had begun to implement all of the new instructions sent out by *Stavka*, the overall situation was at best a mixed picture. Western Front was yet to attack, and the renewed thrust in the Luchesa valley was still awaited, but Forty-First Army had gone in an astonishingly short time from being the most successful part of the operation to having most of its mechanised forces encircled and threatened with destruction; almost all of the ground gained in the first days of *Mars* had been lost. In the north, Zygin might have made modest gains, and there was some evidence that the Germans were running out of reserves, but conducting a successful operation through such difficult terrain would have been a struggle with fresh forces, let alone the depleted divisions and brigades available to Thirty-Ninth and Thirtieth Armies. It must have been clear to Zhukov that, regardless of what he had discussed with Stalin, he no longer had the strength to force a success, with most of the initiative now in German control. Model, by contrast, was feeling increasingly confident. Regardless of the manner in which his divisions had been repeatedly stretched, they had largely held out, and he now had powerful armoured assets available. Once the Soviet penetration south of Bely was eliminated, he would have 1st, 12th, 19th and 20th Panzer Divisions available to restore the situation in the Luchesa valley. Provided that there were no further setbacks elsewhere, he could anticipate a successful conclusion to the fighting.

Such a success was badly needed. Hitler had deliberately compartmentalised the sharing of information in the Wehrmacht, following a disaster earlier in 1942 when the complete plans for the forthcoming drive to the Don and Volga fell into Soviet hands when a liaison officer's plane crash-landed on the wrong side of the front line. Despite this, officers at the level of Model and his corps commanders were aware of the crisis that had developed in the south. Many already feared that it would be impossible to save Sixth Army in Stalingrad; by the second week of December, the failure of the Luftwaffe to deliver on the assurances given to Hitler by Goering that it would be possible to supply Sixth Army by air were increasingly apparent. Every day, the fighting strength of the encircled German forces decreased, and everything would depend on the relief attempt about to be launched by Fourth Panzer Army. The forces for this attempt had been slow to assemble, and even as the operation – codenamed *Wintergewitter* ('Winter storm') – commenced, a new Soviet offensive overwhelmed the Italian Eighth Army on the Don.[13] It was highly likely that units would have to be released by Kluge's Army Group Centre in order to try to fill the huge holes being torn in the German lines further south, and a rapid resolution of the fighting around Rzhev was therefore essential.

One of the main problems facing the German units operating against Solomatin was a recurring one. Ever since the beginning of *Barbarossa*, the Wehrmacht's panzer divisions repeatedly encircled large groups of Red Army units, but the panzer divisions lacked the infantry strength to make these encirclements secure, and the infantry divisions that followed in the wake of the panzer formations couldn't move quickly enough to keep up; consequently, Soviet units, either in a fragmentary manner or en masse, often succeeded in escaping to safety before they could be overwhelmed. The thrust by Fretter-Pico's XXX Corps had linked up with the German forces around Bely, but the corridor that was established was only about two miles in width, and there were too few infantry units available to secure both the front line facing Forty-First Army in the west and Solomatin in the east – on this occasion, it wasn't so much a matter of infantry not keeping pace with the panzers as there being no infantry available. Throughout 10 December, the German units pursuing Solomatin's men from the east struggled forward through deep snow and established contact with the battlegroups moving out of Bely towards the southeast and with 20th Panzer Division to the south of the encirclement. Krüger was now ordered to take control of all German forces securing the northern part of the encirclement.

Solomatin attempted to organise his diminished units for the ordeal that awaited them. As a precaution, he ordered rations to be reduced as early as 8 December. His men benefited from the dense woodland to inflict substantial losses on the German units attempting to compress his perimeter, but such defence rapidly depleted his diminishing stocks of ammunition. He later described the privations faced by his men, and the pressure – not always by way of attacks – that the Germans attempted to apply to them:

> Weakened from their earlier battles and experiencing severe shortages of ammunition and food, I Mechanised Corps and the rifle brigades subordinated to it clung to their positions heroically while completely encircled. Great concentrations of enemy tank and infantry divisions, supported by artillery and aircraft, attacked several times a day, but each attack was beaten off.
>
> After they failed to achieve success in open battle, the Fascist generals resorted to low tricks. Every morning, the Hitlerites announced loudly through powerful loudspeakers that the command group of the corps had flown out to the rear, leaving their forces to their fate, and suggested that rather than giving up their lives for nothing, the men should cease their resistance and surrender. Absolutely nobody believed these provocative broadcasts. In response, Soviet soldiers threw leaflets with the text of a message from the defenders of Zaporozhye to the Turkish sultan into the enemy's trenches.[14]

The incident to which Solomatin alludes is one from the Russian–Turkish War of 1672–81. The Sultan of Turkey allegedly sent a demand to the Cossacks of the Dnepr region that they submit to his rule. The Cossacks replied with a rude message:

You are the Turkish Satan, brother and comrade of the damned devil, and assistant to Lucifer himself! What sort of knight are you, when you can't kill a hedgehog with your bare behind? Your damned face is a mess. You son of a dog, you will not have the sons of Christians under your rule, we are not afraid of your troops and will fight you with earth and water, we will destroy your mother.

You are a Babylonian cook, a Macedonian charioteer, a Jerusalem brewer, an Alexandrian goatherd, a pig herder of Egypt, an Armenian thief, a Tatar bandit … you pork-faced mare's anus …

That is how the Cossacks answer you, ragged one.[15]

It is likely that the story of the Cossack reply to the Sultan's emissary is at least exaggerated, and may have been entirely invented about a hundred years later. Nonetheless, one wonders what the Germans made of such a response.

Throughout this time, the encircled group attempted sharp probes to the west to try to establish contact with Forty-First Army. Every probe was repulsed, and the entire encirclement was within range of German artillery, resulting in steadily worsening casualties. Khlebnikov described how events unfolded:

I was in constant radio contact with the commander of artillery in the mechanised corps, Colonel Trakhtenberg. He reported on the activity of his artillery, giving targets for bombardment by the army's artillery group. It was thus possible to coordinate our actions with the encircled troops. Delivery of ammunition and food to them by aircraft was extremely difficult due to the weather preventing flights. Constant low clouds and strong snowstorms reduced visibility and made navigation difficult, resulting in much of the cargo that was dropped from the air not falling on the location of our troops. Fighting off the growing enemy attacks, they were forced to count every shell and machine-gun belt. Repeated attempts to break through to them from outside the encirclement were also unsuccessful.

At this time, General Zhukov was almost continuously with us, at the headquarters of Forty-First Army or its forward command post. When it was clear that it was not possible to break through to Solomatin's encircled group and that its situation was becoming very difficult, Georgy Konstantinovich ordered the group to break out from the encirclement.

General Solomatin reported his plans for a breakout by radio. The location and timing were coordinated with us. Together with General Toikka, the commander of the army's artillery, we prepared artillery support for the breakout and assigned the task to Colonel Trakhtenberg. We planned a 20-minute bombardment along the enemy's front line on the outer front of the encirclement [i.e. the troops facing Forty-First Army in the west]. This would divert the attention of the Germans from the encircled troops and would allow General Solomatin to deliver an unexpected blow from within the ring. Our artillery would then conduct blocking fire on the flanks of the breakout zone, creating as it were a corridor with walls of gun and mortar fire. The units of VI Siberian Rifle Corps and I Mechanised Corps would then leave the encirclement along this corridor. As the breakthrough would take place at night, large bonfires were to be made to help guide the breakout troops towards the village of Klemyatin.

On the night of 15–16 December, our artillery thundered. The troops moved through the fire corridor to break out. General Solomatin did an excellent job. He prepared his attack with secrecy and it took the enemy by surprise, disorganising his defences. Our units suffered only minor losses and left the encirclement, taking their wounded with them.

The troops who attacked the enemy from the external front played an important role in the successful completion of this operation. Colonel Artamonov's 154th Independent Tank Brigade, transferred to this sector from Fourth Shock Army, performed with particular distinction.[16]

Solomatin's account of the breakout describes the options open to him:

If we didn't have wounded men and didn't have to take our heavy equipment, the easiest route for breakout would have been towards Shesnino and Demekhi. There were continuous forests and swamps in this direction, which were completely frozen and could be passed on foot. The enemy units here turned out to be significantly weaker than in other sectors of the encircling ring. However, moving military equipment and evacuating the wounded was impossible in this direction. Therefore the command decided on a troop withdrawal along a difficult but shorter route with a breakthrough via the more solid enemy defences at Dubrovka and Shiparevo ...

To conduct the breakthrough, a first echelon was created with 74th Rifle Brigade and 19th and 37th Mechanised Brigades ... All tanks, artillery and anti-aircraft guns were assigned to these brigades. The second echelon of 91st Rifle Brigade and 35th and 48th Mechanised Brigades were to hold the encirclement ring until the breakthrough of the enemy's defences. The withdrawal of these brigades would be covered by 32nd Independent Tank Battalion, commanded by Captain Vlaskov, and 57th Independent Motorcycle Battalion led by Major Ledyuk. The brigades in the first echelon were to open fire with all weapons on the order of the corps commander and promptly attack the enemy. Kalinin Front approved of the plan.

Preparations to break through the enemy's defences and the withdrawal of troops were carried out covertly. The remaining brigades on the previous defensive line were ordered to conduct active combat reconnaissance on their fronts and maintain the previous level of fighting. The brigades that took up positions for the breakthrough were instructed to show no activity in order to avoid drawing the premature attention of the enemy to themselves.

At 2240 on 15 December artillery of Forty-First Army opened fire on the enemy's location in the Shiparevo–Dubrovka sector. This immediately drew the enemy's attention to the outer front of the encirclement, which was what the corps command wished. At 2300 a signal was given to the first echelon brigades to open fire and commence their attack. The enemy had no inkling of an assault from this side. When the brigades opened fire and without a pause moved on to attack, the Nazis began to scatter in panic discarding their tanks, artillery, machine-guns and other weapons. Our soldiers mercilessly destroyed the Fascist conquerors with gunfire and bayonets.

The brigades in the first echelon opened a gap with their bold attack and, in accordance with the previously developed plan, the withdrawal of all our troops from the enemy's rear began.

Unexpected developments like this often occur in combat conditions. Previously, Forty-First Army's command had launched several attempts to break through from outside the encirclement ring with a relatively large force but every time they were unsuccessful. Now, a much smaller force managed to mislead and defeat the enemy by surprise and achieved success. With almost no losses, the brigades of I Mechanised Corps and VI Rifle Corps left the enemy's rear zone in an organised manner by dawn on 16 December, and tanks, vehicles and heavy weapons that were immobile or disabled were destroyed on the spot.[17]

The accounts of Solomatin and Khlebnikov are less than completely accurate. The first group succeeded in overcoming the German defences in its path and passed through the corridor created by Khlebnikov's artillery, but the second group struggled to reach the forming up area before the operation commenced, delayed by German bombardments and heavy snowfall. When it attempted to follow the first group, it found that the Germans had guessed what was happening and were subjecting the corridor to a bombardment of their own. Consequently, the breakout resulted in further losses of nearly 5,000 men killed or wounded, including Trakhtenberg, the artillery commander of I Mechanised Corps, and barely 4,000 men from the corps reached safety, leaving behind all their remaining heavy weapons.

As the fighting died down, the survivors of 1st Panzer Division could take pride in their accomplishment; without the determination of their battlegroups – reinforced by elements of *Grossdeutschland* – to hold Bely, the outcome of the battle might have been very different. In its after-action report, 1st Panzer Division estimated that it had destroyed 121 enemy tanks and 17 armoured cars. It is noteworthy that the haul of prisoners was just 488, far fewer than in many other battles of similar magnitude.[18] This reflects partly the escape of much of Solomatin's group from encirclement, but also perhaps that the Soviet soldiers were less inclined to surrender, and that the Germans were less inclined to take prisoners – the elimination of Dremov's 47th Mechanised Brigade, for example, would have been expected to yield a substantial haul of captives.

The breakout effectively brought combat operations in the Bely sector to an end. The German units in the area – particularly the defenders of Bely – had suffered heavy losses and endured difficult moments, but they had held out until help arrived. Even as Solomatin and his surviving men escaped, the events far to the south began to have an effect on the Germans. Fretter-Pico was ordered to move his XXX Corps headquarters south to take command of the disparate units being cobbled together to repair the shattered front line along the Don, and a substantial part of 19th Panzer Division was also withdrawn. They left behind them a devastated region, strewn with the dead of the past few weeks. For the German armoured forces that remained, there was little rest. They would be needed to restore the front line in the Luchesa sector.

There was desultory fighting along the front line of Western Front in the first few days of December, but 11 December began with a new heavy Soviet artillery bombardment. When the replenished units of Twentieth Army moved forward to attack, German gunners laid down their own heavy bombardment. Despite improved cooperation between Soviet infantry and tanks, there was almost no progress. Losses mounted steadily as German defenders poured fire into the attacking ranks from positions that had survived the Red Army's preparatory bombardment almost unscathed. Where the Soviet soldiers succeeded in gaining a little ground at enormous cost, German counterattacks promptly drove them back.

Khozin continued to throw his units forward. The ruined village of Podosinovka became a microcosm of the futile slaughter throughout the year:

[Podosinovka] changed hands three times. Not a single intact house or building remained in it. It was only after numerous attacks that our tankers and riflemen took possession of Podosinovka. But at the end of the day, the enemy managed to bring forward reserves – 46 tanks and self-propelled guns and 30 vehicles carrying infantry. After an artillery bombardment, he launched a counterattack. This time it was supported by aircraft: as soon as one group of planes flew away over the smoky horizon after dropping their bombs, the next began its bombing run.

Suddenly, enemy tanks appeared on the left flank of 1st Motorised Rifle Battalion. The battalion commander, Major Ognevoy, swiftly assessed the situation and ordered the men to lie down and repel the enemy attack.

Grenades and Molotov cocktails were thrown at the tanks. Three were set ablaze. The rest began to turn and withdraw from the battle. The Hitlerites accompanying them rushed back, and then Ognevoy ordered his men to attack.

The commander of 1st Motorised Rifle Company, Captain Yushkov, suddenly shouted: 'The battalion commander is wounded! We will avenge him!' He led the attackers into the trenches of the Nazis. Hand-to-hand fighting ensued. The riflemen of 3rd Motorised Rifle Battalion, led by Major Zyrenkov, came to their aid. The battalion had been in reserve in a gully and it attacked the enemy on the orders of the brigade commander, Lieutenant Colonel Skripka. The battle flared even hotter. The deputy brigade commissar, Lieutenant Colonel Nikolaev, his Komsomol assistant Strygin and commissar Kolotov appeared in the attacking line of riflemen. They carried the men forward with their personal example. An enemy bullet cut down the brave Kolotov. The battalion commissar, Lieutenant Kutyrkin, was also killed. The brigade commander, Lieutenant Colonel Skripka, was wounded. He was replaced by the brigade chief of staff, Major Khailenko ...

An artillery battery led by Captain Ochkasov moved its guns out for direct fire. The battery commander was soon killed and replaced by Lieutenant Kovalev. The ranks of the gunners were melting away by the minute. Only one gun, led by Komsomol Sergeant Abramov, remained in action. The crew fired rapidly. Two enemy tanks were already alight ... Shells exploded in the gunners' position. Almost all the crew were wounded.[19]

This account is characteristic of many written during the Soviet era, but despite the heroics that it describes, it cannot hide the reality that the Red Army failed to make any real progress. Infantry and tank strength diminished at a terrifying rate. On some occasions, German artillery fire was so heavy and accurate that attacks were broken up before a single man had left the Soviet trenches. Many of the recruits being sent to the front line had received truncated training and were in no way adequately prepared for the brutal slaughter that lay ahead – one battalion failed to take proper measures to use cover while moving up to the front line and lost over 40 per cent of its strength before it even attacked. The efficacy of German infantry working as tank destruction squads made some Soviet tank crews nervous and on at least one occasion resulted in three tanks firing indiscriminately at infantry who approached them, unaware that they were Soviet soldiers moving up in support.[20] Both tank corps lost most of their vehicles in just a few days, together with more of their irreplaceable experienced crews.

Many of the German accounts almost make light of the renewed attacks, describing them as purely a sign that the Red Army hadn't quite given up its hopes of a breakthrough and was making one last effort. But in some cases, the intensity of the attacks put the German line under pressure once more. Although Metz may have concluded that defending infantry positions against tank attacks required strong nerves above all else, some soldiers – perhaps newer arrivals on the Eastern Front – were still overcome by fear when Soviet armour moved against them, as one soldier recorded in his diary:

> In the morning, an unimaginable firing of artillery, Stalin organs, and of tanks began at our positions … It seemed as if the world was coming to an end. We were sitting in our trenches, hoping that a direct hit wouldn't blow us all away. This hell continued for a full hour. When the artillery preparation ended, I wanted to climb out but had to take cover again as tanks were advancing against us. From my fighting position I counted up to 40 heavy tanks. Two of them were heading directly toward my position, one behind the other. It was enough to drive one mad. We thought that we would perish, but we were saved by a long-barrelled assault gun. I will never forget this day.[21]

As casualties mounted, the fighting took on an increasingly implacable character on both sides. After beating off a German counterattack, V Tank Corps captured about 60 Germans. The corps diary recorded their fate:

> In light of the extraordinary stress of heavy fighting and intense enemy artillery fire, they couldn't be sent to the rear. Documents were taken from the officers, and they were all shot.[22]

Colonel Vladimir Vladimirovich Sytnik was commander of 24th Tank Brigade, which was temporarily assigned to V Tank Corps. He led his brigade into action on the second day of the renewed offensive aboard a KV-1, and as his tanks crunched through the German trenches, artillery and machine-gun fire drove their accompanying infantry to take cover. The Soviet tanks then came under fire from German anti-tank guns, assault guns and tanks that were waiting for them, but the thick armour of the KV-1 proved its worth:

> The KV was hit by the anti-tank guns of the enemy battery. The gunner was wounded and Colonel Sytnik took his place at the sights. He patted Sergeant Peregudov, the driver, on the shoulder: 'Come on, foot to the floor!' And the heavy tank, its engine roaring, rushed forward towards the positions from which the enemy gunners were firing. Only a few metres short of them, a shell hit the turret, jamming the mechanism. In the next moment a round pierced the left armour and damaged the clutch. The brigade saw a dim muzzle flash of the enemy gun through the whirlwind of snow. 'There!' It didn't fire again; Peregudov crushed it with the multi-ton weight of the KV. But then the tank shuddered, shook, and as if overwhelmed by an impossible burden, the engine stalled.
>
> Seeing that the tank was helpless, the Nazis began to fire at it at close range. The brigade commander once more looked through the sight. The gun was damaged, but he told the loader to prepare the shells. 'How many of them do we have?'
>
> The loader quickly counted. 'Ten, Comrade Colonel.'
>
> 'Not many.' The brigade commander glanced at his communications chief, Captain Neupokoev. 'Sergei Alekseevich, give our location to headquarters. We can call in artillery fire on ourselves.'
>
> The close-range Nazi fire smashed into the tank, cutting the external radio antenna with shrapnel. Resourcefully, the crew used an ordinary wire as an antenna, passing it through the machine-gun port in the turret. Having adjusted the radio, Neupokoev restored radio contact with brigade headquarters, but it didn't last long. Climbing onto the KV, the Nazis cut the wire.[23]

The tank crew drove off a German tank destruction squad with hand grenades, and Sytnik then decided it was time to try to escape, but the tank had slipped into the position occupied by the crushed German anti-tank gun, and the belly escape hatch couldn't be opened. When the soldiers tried to exit through the turret and driver's hatches, they came under fire from German soldiers close by. Not long after the onset of darkness, a group of Soviet infantrymen reached the tank and helped the crew to escape. As they made their way back, they fought off a German tank using an anti-tank rifle and Molotov cocktails.

The last reserves of V Tank Corps consisted of its 70th Tank Brigade. Perhaps in an attempt to achieve some sort of success, which might justify the appalling losses suffered to date, the corps commander, Major General Kuzma

Aleksandrovich Semenchenko, threw it into the battle. An account by a journalist who was accompanying V Tank Corps reveals in passing how ill-prepared the Red Army was for this attack, with an astonishing failure to carry out proper reconnaissance and assessment of the German defences, despite the bloody experiences of preceding weeks and months:

> [The tank brigade] had to break through the enemy's defences in conditions of difficult and moreover poorly reconnoitred terrain. The fact was that in this situation, the brigade did not have the means or the time to carry out its own reconnaissance. Only at the very last moment was a single T-34, commanded by Lieutenant Colonel Fyodor Yakovlevich Degtev, sent forward for this purpose. In addition to him, the brigade operational department's head, Captain Stekh, the driver Popov, and the gunner Krupa were in the tank. At high speed, it burst into the enemy's position and advanced 1.5km towards the railway [from Sychevka to Rzhev]. 'As we moved along the front line,' recalled Degtev, 'we found carefully camouflaged dugouts and bunkers. In addition, armoured trains moving along the nearby railway were firing at our advancing units.'
>
> During the first attack, the tankers, working closely with the motorised riflemen, suffered considerable losses. The brigade commander, Lieutenant Colonel Konstantin Nikolaevich Abramov, was seriously wounded. He had opened his hatch to look around and was hit in the chest by a sniper's bullet. Fortunately, it didn't hit his heart. The commander fell back into the tank, breathing heavily, and ordered Lieutenant Colonel Degtev, his deputy: 'Take command of the brigade.'[24]

Degtev led the rapidly diminishing group of tanks forward towards the railway where they came under fire from a German armoured train. Degtev's tank was hit and he suffered broken legs; when he was undergoing emergency surgery in a field station, the location was bombed and the surgeon killed in mid-operation.

Even Zhukov had to admit defeat. The reinforcements that had been rushed to Twentieth Army had evaporated in the face of intense defensive fire. The two armies that he had repeatedly sought to detain in the Moscow area for use in a future exploitation were dispatched to the southern sector of the front, where they played important parts in the Red Army's successes to the west of Stalingrad. So effective was the German defence against Western Front's failed second assault that at no point was there any suggestion of bringing further German units up to the front line as reinforcements. A report from Model's headquarters dated 15 December highlights the failure of the renewed offensive by Western Front:

Disappointed by failure in all sectors of the front and using almost unlimited resources, the enemy wanted once again to try to find a weakness on the eastern front [of Ninth Army] and force a decision. This attack was led by an even greater concentrated deployment of tanks ... However, in such a short period of time and on such a narrow frontage, this resulted in enemy tank losses that exceeded those of the heavy armoured battles at Rzhev during the summer. In just 48 hours, 300 tanks were shot up in a sector of just 4km width.[25]

Losses for the Red Army's formations in the Vazuza sector were staggering. Twentieth Army lost over 58,000 men. VI Tank Corps effectively lost almost all its tank strength in its initial penetration, was re-equipped, and was then almost wiped out a second time. Despite the heroics attributed to the officers and men of V Tank Corps, the reality was that this unit lost almost all of its tanks in three days of brutal attrition for almost no gain.

About 900 men of 20th Cavalry Division had been left behind German lines after the failed attacks of November. When they succeeded in a few minor operations to attack road convoys or destroy bridges, they received a congratulatory signal from Konev:

Bravo, cavalry! Ruthlessly smash the enemy's rear units. Hold high the heroic traditions of the First Cavalry Army.[26]

This is a reference to a formation of the Russian Civil War. The First Cavalry Army was created in 1919 and commanded by a former NCO, Semyon Mikhailovich Budyonny. He later claimed that he and Stalin led the creation of the army, but it seems that the initiative actually came from Boris Mokeevich Dumenko, who was Budyonny's commander in the early days of the Red Army, Filip Kuzmich Mironov, a Cossack, and Alexander Ilyich Egorov, a former officer in the tsar's forces who became commander of the Tenth Army. Despite considerable initial successes, the First Cavalry Army performed badly in the Russo–Polish War, becoming bogged down in fighting for Lviv rather than supporting the southern flank of the main Bolshevik advance. Discipline in the army was poor, and Budyonny's men acquired a bad reputation for looting and violence towards civilians, particularly towards the large numbers of Jews living in the southeast part of Poland. Soviet historiography portrayed the First Cavalry Army as an invincible striking force of the Bolsheviks, and Budyonny was able to use his personal friendship, together with the undeserved reputation he gained as a great cavalry commander, to good effect. Other close confederates of Stalin, such as Kliment Efremovich Voroshilov and Semen Konstantinovich Timoshenko, similarly constructed their reputations on a mixture of truths, half-truths and invention. Budyonny remained convinced that large cavalry formations would play a major part in future wars, and he was sent to Ukraine by Stalin in July 1941 to take command of Southwest Front. Here, he was hopelessly out of his depth and allowed most of his forces to be encircled in Kiev, resulting in the loss of over 700,000 men.[27] Budyonny escaped from the encirclement, and Stalin assigned him to a number of roles that kept him away from the front line for the rest of the war.

Even if the example of the First Cavalry Army had been one worth following, it was impossible for the men of 20th Cavalry Division who were operating to the west of the Sychevka–Rzhev road to emulate. Many of the cavalrymen had been wounded in the attempts first to break through the German lines, and then to escape to the east. They were now cut off from their comrades, in an area that the Germans had attempted to denude of resources in attempts to reduce partisan activity:

> The living conditions of the horsemen behind enemy lines were extremely difficult. It was a harsh winter, often with temperatures 25 degrees below freezing. The men lived in huts made from pine branches and warmed themselves by fires, and even then only during the day. They had no opportunity to undress or wash themselves properly. The main food ration was horsemeat, together with some food concentrates and biscuits delivered by air. It was especially bad for the horses. At first, foraging parties brought in swamp hay mixed with sedge and straw from the roofs of farms and villages in the forest, but soon this ceased. There was no food and the horses began to die.[28]

It was possible to create small airstrips, and Polykarpov biplanes delivered equipment, food and medical supplies in small quantities, and flew some of the wounded to the east. A radio set reached the cavalrymen shortly after they were cut off, and news of the German setbacks in and around Stalingrad did much to improve morale. It was clear to the cavalrymen that the Germans were looking for them; whenever the skies cleared, they spotted Luftwaffe reconnaissance flights attempting to find them, and some of the units of 5th Panzer Division were organised into ad hoc groups to hunt for the Soviet soldiers, but they were largely able to escape detection in the dense forests. However, their limited supply of ammunition and shortage of food, particularly for their horses, prevented them from carrying out any significant attacks on German positions or lines of communication. It is also noteworthy that unlike the previous cavalry penetration by Belov and his men, the memoirs of men in this cavalry group make little or no mention of contact with partisans. It seems that the German anti-partisan operations that swept the area repeatedly in 1942 had reduced activity significantly. Probably as a result of those sweeps, there were also far fewer civilians in the area from whom the cavalrymen might seek help. Nor was there any possibility of the small group receiving the sort of aid that Belov received from airborne reinforcements.

Finally, their numbers badly depleted and with almost no ammunition or other supplies remaining, the surviving cavalrymen were ordered to try to make their way to safety. Escape to the east through the dense defences of the German positions that faced Western Front was impossible, and instead a decision was made to try to move west to link up with Kalinin Front:

> On the night of 24 December, the cavalry group set out from the Pochinkovsky marshes. They walked through forests on roads that were covered with snow. The men, completely exhausted, trampled a path in the deep snow in order to make it easier for the horses, stumbling with fatigue. The marches took place only at night. At the head of the column, following the vanguard, sometimes swearing, sometimes laughing, encouraging the tired men and walking with the aid of a stick, was the stout elderly soldier [and division commander], Pavel Trofimovich Kursakov, whose breathing was often laboured because of a Finnish bullet that was lodged there since 1941.
>
> For several days the horsemen groped for weak points in the enemy's defences. Ski reconnaissance groups, covering tens of kilometres through the forest, reached a highway and started a firefight to distract the enemy's attention …
>
> Making its way further off the roads, in almost continuous battles with pursuing enemy units, the cavalry group broke through the enemy's lines on 6 January 1943 and joined the forces of Kalinin Front.[29]

The 'stout elderly' Kursakov was actually just 44 years old. The first elements of 20th Cavalry Division to reach safety actually linked up with scouts from Kalinin Front in late January. Thereafter, Kursakov led a group of men in a successful breakout, and a raid by tanks from III Mechanised Corps opened a corridor in the German lines for the rest to escape. Of the approximately 900 men who had broken through the German lines on the Vazuza front with Kursakov, 527 escaped the encirclement. The Soviet accounts claimed that the Germans diverted all of 87th Infantry Division and several independent battalions from the front line to pursue the cavalry group, but this is patently untrue. Kursakov remained in command of his division as it was rebuilt while being held in the Red Army's central reserves; when it returned to action, he led it with distinction once more, and it was renamed 17th Guards Cavalry Division in recognition of its contribution to Soviet successes in the second half of 1943. It is a measure of how long the Soviet armed forces continued to value the role of cavalry that Kursakov ended his military service in 1948 as head of 2nd Stavropolsk Military Horse Stud Farm.

CHAPTER 13

DECEMBER: EXHAUSTION IN THE LUCHESA AND NORTHERN SECTORS

For much of December, the subsidiary sectors – the Luchesa valley and the northern tip of the Rzhev Salient – remained the scenes of heavy fighting.

To the north of Bely, the scattered elements of *Grossdeutschland* continued to frustrate every attempt by the Red Army to advance down the Luchesa valley in the first days of December, but the cost of resistance continued to rise. In response to the increasingly urgent requests from the German battlegroups for reinforcements, Hilpert's XXIII Corps could send just one battalion of 473rd Grenadier Regiment – with a strength of five officers and 127 other ranks, this unit was effectively no more than a rifle company.[1] There was growing friction between Walter Hörnlein at the headquarters of *Grossdeutschland* and Hilpert; the former felt that his corps commander wasn't taking the threat in the Luchesa seriously enough, but the reality was that Hilpert had nothing that he could send to help Hörnlein's hard-pressed men.

The Soviet forces that opposed *Kampfgruppe Köhler* had been driving it north slowly since the first battles around Osinovka on 29 November. Late on 1 December, a further group of T-34s attacked near Serovatka. A single 88mm gun was present to provide the defenders with anti-tank firepower, but it was knocked out after it destroyed the leading Soviet tank. After crushing the local German positions, the T-34s moved on against the next German bunker, where Oberst Otto Köhler and a mixture of survivors of his battlegroup were attempting to renew their defensive efforts. The small group held their bunker until the last moment and then attempted to withdraw. Köhler was one of the last men to leave, at the very moment that the area was struck by a brief mortar bombardment. The battlegroup commander and several of his men were killed. He had been with *Grossdeutschland* throughout the history of the unit from when it was first formed as a regiment, and his loss was a severe blow to the men with whom he had served.[2]

Kampfgruppe Köhler had effectively ceased to exist. Hörnlein sent whatever rear area personnel still remained as reinforcements to the scattered remnants of the battalion from Panzergrenadier Regiment *Grossdeutschland*. In place of Köhler, Major Karl Lorenz, former commander of the division's combat engineer battalion, took command, and order was restored through the night. The new *Kampfgruppe Lorenz* was perhaps the strength of two rifle companies and lacked heavy weapons; many of its personnel were exhausted from days of combat in the bitterly cold conditions and numbed by the loss of so many of their comrades. At first, the best that Lorenz could do was deploy his men in a series of relatively isolated 'strongpoints' and hope that the difficult terrain would be a sufficient barrier to prevent the Red Army from infiltrating through his positions; matters improved later in the day with the arrival of four assault guns.

There seems to have been growing criticism of the performance of *Grossdeutschland* during the fighting of November and early December. On paper, the division was one of the strongest in the Wehrmacht, but seen from the distance of Hitler's headquarters, it seemed as if it had failed to achieve any significant successes. Hörnlein and Major Cord von Hobe, his senior staff officer, protested in vain that the division was widely dispersed and unable to function as a coherent whole. A message from Hitler, received in early December, was particularly galling:

> The Führer expects that the fully equipped Division *Grossdeutschland* will clear up the situation in the Luchesa valley.[3]

This resulted in a detailed signal from the headquarters of *Grossdeutschland* describing the state of the division and the manner in which it had been widely dispersed. The response was an order that Hobe was to be replaced, ostensibly because he needed more experience in panzer formations, and was to move to a staff post at corps level. Hörnlein attempted to have the order rescinded, sending his adjutant to East Prussia to raise the matter with the high command, and Generalmajor Rudolf Schmundt, Hitler's personal adjutant, travelled to the headquarters of *Grossdeutschland*. The removal of Hobe was confirmed, but

Hörnlein took the opportunity to make clear the circumstances in which his division was operating. Hobe's replacement was Oberstleutnant Oldwig von Natzmer, who had been serving as senior staff officer with 26th Panzer Division.

Despite the near collapse of *Kampfgruppe Köhler*, the German line somehow remained intact. The losses suffered by the opposing Red Army units were heavy, making any exploitation of the day's gains almost impossible. On 2 December, there was further tough fighting. At one point, the leading Soviet units were just a mile from the open ground through which ran the vital road that was their objective, but a definitive breakthrough was impossible. Just in time, the few *Grossdeutschland* assault guns that had been operating in the Bely area and had arrived as reinforcements during the night were used in a counterattack by Lorenz. The Soviet advance had succeeded in cutting the road that ran southwest from Olenino to Bely, but the main route ran due south from Olenino to the Obsha valley, from where it followed the river to Bely, and this remained in German hands. Increasingly desperate to reach this second road and thus achieve his objective, Iushkevich urged Katukov and his other subordinates to continue their assaults, but his army was finished. Although there was further heavy fighting on 3 and 4 December, the crisis had passed for *Grossdeutschland* and its scattered units. Iushkevich started the operation with about 270 tanks; he now had fewer than 100 still undamaged, and more than half his infantry had been lost. Moreover, many of the remaining tanks were partially damaged, and given the terrain and weather, it was all but impossible to concentrate them adequately to achieve a breakthrough. But although the commander of Twenty-Second Army could see that his men were at the end of their strength, Purkaev continued to demand one last effort. The Germans also had to be equally exhausted, and Iushkevich ruthlessly stripped units from all along his Front and dispatched them to the east. The earliest that this final attempt to overcome the German defences could begin was on 7 December.

At the northern end of the salient, Zygin's Thirty-Ninth Army was effectively exhausted after the capture of Urdom, but Zhukov was unwilling to cease operations. Originally, this had been intended as little more than a 'fixing attack' to pin the Germans in their defences, preventing their withdrawal or transfer to other sectors, but the lack of success elsewhere made the modest gains of Thirty-Ninth Army seem disproportionately significant. The eastern flank of Thirty-Ninth Army had enjoyed success in the early phases of the battle, and Zhukov now demanded an attack by the adjacent flanks of Kalinin and Western Fronts, closer to Rzhev. The new assault would fall on German defences that had been untouched in the recent fighting and would be opposed by relatively fresh

German units – some personnel might have been transferred elsewhere during the crises of late November, but the front line around Rzhev remained a formidable multi-tiered complex of defensive positions. It seems that given the modest attritional success achieved by Zygin in the last days of November, and the diversion of German reserves to other sectors, Zhukov hoped that the defensive line immediately to the west of Rzhev might break apart in the face of a renewed assault. There was, perhaps, some reason for such optimism. If the Germans were running out of men, a new attack here might crack the stubborn defences of Ninth Army. At the same time, the renewed efforts by Kiriukhin on the eastern side of the salient and Iushkevich in the Luchesa valley might be aided by the need for the Germans to reinforce their front line around Rzhev. But the reality was surely that this was an increasingly desperate move by Zhukov to salvage a few crumbs of success from what had to date been a costly failure. He had to achieve some form of victory, if only to justify the slaughter of the preceding fortnight.

Grimly, local Soviet army commanders began the laborious task of regrouping their units, once more struggling with inadequate roads and unsuitable terrain. In the meantime, a series of local attacks developed in Thirty-Ninth Army's sector, with each attack sequentially a little further to the east. On 7 December, the Soviet infantrymen who had captured Urdom attacked again and drove forward about two miles, but every attempt in the following days to exploit this resulted in escalating casualties and no further gains.

New orders were drawn up and issued to the two active sectors in the north and northwest areas of the salient. Iushkevich's renewed attack towards the west was confirmed; a day later, the northern attack would attempt to break the German lines immediately west of Rzhev. The two thrusts would then combine their strength and collapse the salient from the north. In the circumstances, with all of the hindrances of roads, terrain, weather and earlier losses, Iushkevich's Twenty-Second Army managed both to plan its new operation and move troops into position with considerable efficiency. But even as the Red Army gathered its strength, the Germans were also moving troops into position. A battalion of the independent 18th Grenadier Regiment under the command of Oberst Carl Becker had been fighting on the Vazuza front and had been ordered to the Luchesa; in recognition of the performance of the regiment in the late summer battles on the eastern side of the salient, Becker had been awarded the Knight's Cross, and despite losses in the bitter fighting along the Vazuza, morale in the battalion was high. The battalion was just one part of a substantial group of German units that were assembling for a counterattack to eliminate the threat from the Soviet Twenty-Second Army. A motorcycle battalion from 2nd Panzer Division and a handful of tanks and assault guns accompanied Becker's men, and additionally two battalions from 110th Infantry Division's 252nd Grenadier Regiment were made available. Artillery support was provided by a battalion from *Grossdeutschland*, and the entire group was under the command of Generalmajor Albert Praun, the commander of 129th Infantry Division, which held a sector of front line immediately to the northwest of Rzhev. It is perhaps an indication of the degree to which the Germans were improvising their defences that this new group was composed of elements drawn from so many different formations and commanded by a man whose own division provided none of the group's components.

Hilpert knew that this group, effectively at the strength of a reinforced regiment, was fairly modest, and he ordered Praun to maximise surprise by attacking with no artillery preparation. To Praun's chagrin, Soviet units detected the assembly of his men and subjected their forming up area to a mortar bombardment. When German radio operators intercepted a Red Army signal reporting the new German concentration, Praun and Hilpert were relieved that the report clearly underestimated the strength of the new battlegroup.

As *Kampfgruppe Köhler* was driven north to and across the Luchesa, the pursuing Soviet units were left with their eastern flank exposed. To exploit this, Praun ordered his motorcycle battalion to swing around the east wing of the Red Army units and attack the exposed flank early on 6 December. Once this attack was underway, he intended to throw the rest of his battlegroup at the Soviet positions with the intention of driving them back west along the Luchesa. Immediately, the plan fell foul of the terrain, and the motorcycle battalion was repeatedly delayed as it attempted to move into position. As precious hours slipped away, Praun decided he couldn't wait any longer and ordered the frontal assault to begin. It is a measure of the losses suffered by the German units in the Rzhev Salient that the leading battalion was commanded by a senior lieutenant, who was killed by mortar fire as the attack began. In heavy fighting, the ruins of the village of Galishkino were overrun but at a heavy price, with all but one of the tanks and assault guns that accompanied the German attack being knocked out. Deciding that the position in Galishkino was too exposed to be held, the Germans pulled back to the adjacent forest, claiming the destruction of 19 Soviet tanks. While the battle was a relatively minor one, it had a major impact on Iushkevich's preparations, forcing the commitment of precious reserves to restore the line and disrupting preparations for his own attack.[4]

In addition to renewing attacks at all four previous locations – the Vazuza in the east, the Bely sector in the west, the Luchesa valley in the northwest and at Urdom in the north – Zhukov had also ordered Thirtieth Army to attack between Zygin's Thirty-Ninth Army in the Urdom sector and Rzhev. The first attack came on 7 December, striking the seam of 251st Infantry Division and 14th Motorised Infantry Division. The soldiers of Generalmajor Karl Burdach's 251st Infantry Division were in well-prepared defences; they sat out the initial Red Army bombardment and then met the attacking infantry with heavy fire. Rather than accumulate senseless losses, the Soviet officers rapidly gave up their assault. The neighbouring 14th Motorised Infantry Division didn't fare so well, and its positions, weaker than those of its neighbour, were overrun. The commitment of an independent battalion – the only local reserves – and a couple of assault guns briefly restored the situation, but Soviet pressure continued the following day. In order to prevent the two German divisions being forced apart, 14th Motorised Infantry Division was subordinated to Burdach, who scraped together what men could be spared and launched energetic counterattacks on 9 December. These continued through the day and into the next, recovering much of the lost ground. For the moment, the line was held, but at the price of exhausting the available reserves. On the eastern wing of 251st Infantry Division, closer to Rzhev, a motley battlegroup under the command of Oberstleutnant Rudolf Freiherr von Recum – the sapper battalions of both 251st and 87th Infantry Divisions, collectively amounting to perhaps two or three companies, a ski battalion from 87th Infantry Division, a motorcycle battalion from 72nd Infantry Division, and a company from 129th Infantry Division – defeated every attempt to force it from its positions, launching repeated counterattacks whenever the attackers gained any ground.

It seemed for the moment that Zhukov's assessment of the weakness of the German positions might be correct. Without any further reserves, the German lines to the west of Rzhev were in danger of collapse, not least because the multiplicity of assaults around the Rzhev Salient in preceding weeks had drained away all the available reserves. Malygin, who had commanded 28th Tank Brigade in the initial attacks by Zygin, received a new appointment at the beginning of December, assuming the role of commander of armoured and mechanised forces of Third Shock Army.[5] His replacement was Lieutenant Colonel Efim Maksimovich Kovalev, who led the brigade into action on 11 December. The tanks swiftly overran the German defences and advanced southwest, slowed more by the forests and snow than German resistance. The village of Gonchuki was captured, and if the German defensive line was to be restored, it was essential to recapture it. With no other options available, Hilpert ordered Becker, whose troops had inflicted a stinging check on the Soviet forces in the Luchesa valley, to intervene. Radio intercepts had tentatively identified the commander of the Soviet group as a man named 'Nikitin', who was in constant contact with 'Doroshenko'; it isn't clear who these persons were, but their almost unrestricted use of radio communications provided the Germans with valuable information about his location and intentions.

With characteristic energy, Becker took control of the situation. By the evening of 11 December, he had effectively sealed off the Soviet penetration, but in this new sector, the German infantrymen were forced to endure repeated bombardments and attacks in relatively exposed positions. The ground was too hard for trenches and bunkers to be constructed, and soldiers occupying improvised positions in woodland had the added peril of Soviet mortars exploding in the branches above them, showering them with shrapnel. But the German counterattack had effectively isolated the tanks of 28th Tank Brigade, and when Zhukov once more urged Zygin to renew his efforts, in the increasingly desperate hope that further pressure in the north might force the Germans to divert units from the Vazuza front and thus finally permit Twentieth Army to move forward, Zygin responded by pointing out that his infantry formations were too weak and he could do no more without reinforcements. Zhukov immediately ordered the neighbouring Thirtieth Army to release a rifle division for Zygin's use. This effectively undermined the plan for Thirtieth Army to attack closer to Rzhev, and the addition of a single division, which was significantly below establishment strength, was unlikely to have a major impact on Zygin's attack.

After a further pause, Zygin's troops tried once more to move forward to link up with 'Nikitin' and his tanks. Artillery ammunition had been stockpiled for several days, and the gunners of Thirty-Ninth Army hammered the German positions for four hours before the ground assault began, but the Germans had been hard at work trying to improve their positions:

The troops tried hard to dig in. They lacked entrenching tools, but 57th Construction Battalion happily provided them. Chevaux-de-frise [iron anti-tank obstacles] were diligently constructed. Mines were laid along the main expected axis of attack. Its exposed nature permitted the enemy to prepare for an attack almost in front of our lines.

On 13 December the expected Russian assault began. Enemy artillery began firing at 0945. At first the fire was weak but steadily strengthened and by 1320 had reached monstrous strength. The battle raged and the earth trembled as it was swept by a whirlwind of fiery iron. Under the command of 'Doroshenko', the Russians attacked [Leutnant] Volperding's battalion [a mixture of men from 206th Infantry Division and 14th Motorised Infantry Division] and I/18 [1st Battalion, 18th Infantry Regiment from 6th Infantry Division]. There were repeated attacks. The defenders fired back with everything they had and the enemy attempted to break through. While the staunch German soldiers fought against the enemy attacking their front, the soldiers of 'Nikitin' suddenly appeared from behind the command post of I/18. In fierce fighting, the headquarters staff delayed the enemy for a considerable time. When tanks attacked from the outside and a tank group tried to break out simultaneously from the rear, the hard-pressed I/18 was split in two.

A battlegroup from 18th Regiment and 2nd Motorcycle Battalion, 2nd Panzer Division came to the rescue at 1930, and with the remaining 59 men of I/18, once more captured the old defensive line. The boil was lanced and there was a great sense of relief. But 'Nikitin' intended to break out and he duly succeeded. It was fortunate that in combination with the enemy who had penetrated from the outside, he didn't roll up our positions.[6]

There was further heavy fighting on 14 December. Once again, Zygin's gunners did their best to support the assault, and the tattered remnants of Volperding's battalion and its neighbouring units spent a hellish day fighting off repeated attacks and launching bloody counterattacks of their own to recover lost positions. Becker was now in overall command of the threatened sector, and as the day drew to a close, the front line had barely changed. Further attacks continued over the next few days, with diminishing intensity. Zygin's last effort to break through from the north was as much a failure as the Red Army's attacks elsewhere. The price that the Germans paid to defeat these assaults was high. When it returned to 6th Infantry Division, 18th Infantry Regiment reported the loss of 440 men in just a week.[7]

The attack by the neighbouring Thirtieth Army, weakened by the transfer of a rifle division to Zygin's Thirty-Ninth Army, began on 13 December. Despite being accompanied by tanks, the attacks failed to make any impression. As was consistently the case in the fighting around the Rzhev Salient, German machine-gun and artillery fire forced the attacking infantry to take cover, and when the Soviet tanks attempted to advance alone, they were rapidly picked off by anti-tank guns and tank destruction squads.

Kazaryan and his comrades were among the tank units that the Red Army gathered for this renewed attack:

From the morning of 13 December, we sat ready in our vehicles for half the day waiting for the signal to attack. The front line from Koshkino to Burgovo ran in a zigzag. To our left, fighting had already been raging since the previous evening with assault groups, supported by artillery, trying to break into the first line of enemy trenches. This would open a route for them to bypass Rzhev …

It was relatively quiet at first. Two tank battalions took cover behind the reverse slope of a hill covered with dense spruce. The enemy was up ahead of us, on the same hill. In between us was a wide hollow, dotted with clumps of trees, boulders, and barbed wire entanglements. A narrow passage had been made through a minefield – under cover of snowstorms the preceding night, our sappers had done excellent work.

The enemy hillock suddenly came to life. Judging from the direction of their fire, they were trying to support their neighbours to the left where it seemed that our infantry was attacking the second defensive line. Only now did we realise that the defences in front of us weren't just a hill with a few trenches, but rather a powerful stronghold with numerous heavy weapons. Perhaps right now, while the enemy focussed on helping their neighbours, the time had come for a tank attack.

'Forwards!' As if guessing my thoughts, Major Onishchenko issued the order. At the same moment that the battalion commander gave his order, the ground trembled to the thunder of artillery – our guns were bombarding the hillock. Engines roared. The tanks picked up speed and moved through the hollow in wedge formation.

It was often difficult to keep up the pace. Tanks pitched and tilted sharply from side to side and skidded. Only the most experienced drivers like our Tekuchev were able to cope with a vehicle moving off-road at speed. Some of the other crews were less fortunate; a few tanks ended up outside the passage made through the minefield and were disabled by mines or fell into pit traps.

Despite this, speed and surprise proved important and the main group of tanks managed to slip through the open space before the German batteries switched to direct fire. After bypassing the hillock we turned and fired at the Germans from the rear, confusing them …

We spent the night in our tanks. When we moved forward to the [Volga] ford, it was completely dark. At dawn we slipped over the thick ice of the ford, turned right, and camouflaged ourselves in the forest not far from the road. [Later] we moved back to the Volga. We found a bridge and having overcome the defenders screening it we took up a perimeter defence. With difficulty, we managed to get in touch with brigade headquarters. 'Wait for the infantry!' ordered Dukhovny, the brigade commander. But the infantry couldn't reach us.

Half an hour later, the Germans threw us back with a powerful tank attack. We were back at our start line.

This was repeatedly the case during that winter offensive. For ten days, from 13 to 23 December, the troops of our Thirtieth Army stubbornly attacked the German defences, trying to cross the Volga and cut the railway in the Chertolino–Rzhev sector, but managed to advance only a few kilometres. We had neither the strength nor the firepower to achieve more.[8]

On the perimeter of Rzhev itself, Gorbachevsky and his comrades were spared the ordeal of having to attack, but even in the absence of another senseless charge against the German positions, Gorbachevsky had to contend with other losses that were equally senseless. He had been assigned to a new company and was anxious to implement the measures that he had used to prevent desertions. Unfortunately, just one day after he took command and before he could make the necessary changes, he was woken by his junior lieutenant: two men, an older soldier and a new arrival, had deserted.

I was awake in an instant. We rushed to the trench. On the parapet, their rifles and a Komsomol card had been placed neatly, covered by a thick layer of snow. I thought I had seen them the previous night but couldn't recall their names – they had greeted me warmly. Where were they from, who were they, how and where had they seen action? I knew nothing about them. An old soldier, and he had persuaded a new recruit, a Komsomol member ... I looked at the abandoned rifles and felt a moment of unease. Such desertion meant a penal battalion for me, and a penal battalion was a death sentence.

An hour later, the battalion commander arrived in a rush, accompanied by a 'special officer'. I explained the situation, giving them the report I had prepared. I had written, in my defence, that I had come to the company just the previous night and hadn't had time to get to know my men or introduce my system [to prevent desertions].

Korostylev, the battalion commander, didn't read the report or listen to me, but glared around angrily and launched into savage abuse and obscenities. Suddenly he drew his pistol and struck me on the head with the handle. 'You bastard!' he hissed through his teeth. 'You're all scoundrels and will have to face the tribunal.'

Next to me was Junior Lieutenant Belenky. He was trembling, biting his lip – he seemed about to burst into tears. Gorbunov [who had commanded the company before Gorbachevsky's arrival] intervened. 'Why are you raging like that, Battalion Commander? The company commander had nothing to do with it. Both the deserters were from my platoon. I take full responsibility.'

... As he left, the battalion commander spat out, 'Mark my words, Comrades, you weren't sent here on holiday. If you don't put things in order, if you permit more desertions, you won't get away with it. Don't expect any mercy!' The 'special officer' was silent throughout, but we had the impression that all the loud words and insults of Korostylev were not just a part of his character, he showed excessive zeal in front of the 'special officer'. In four months, I never saw the battalion commander in a combat situation: he tried to hide away whenever he could. Such people were known in the army as 'dogs' tails', wagging back and forth in the rear.[9]

Gorbunov was a veteran and had already served one spell in a penal battalion. He had started the war as a crewman in an assault gun before being deployed as an infantryman after his vehicle was destroyed. He was ordered to make an attack on a German-held village during the great counteroffensive outside Moscow in late 1941 and made some injudicious remarks to his battalion commander about the failure of promised support to be deployed. One of his comments – that the battalion commander should pass on the greetings of the 18 men killed in the futile attack to the supreme commander – resulted in him being charged with insulting Stalin and he was sent to a penal battalion. He took part in the summer attacks on Rzhev and was wounded when he attacked a German bunker; he destroyed the bunker with hand grenades and was judged to have redeemed himself and returned to a regular unit. He told Gorbachevsky that he had voluntarily taken responsibility for these latest desertions because, having served in a penal battalion before, he would now be sent to a labour camp. Two NKVD officers then appeared and took Gorbunov away. There were other repercussions; a sergeant was demoted to the ranks and a junior lieutenant reprimanded and informed that he might face further punishment. Faced with this threat, the 19-year-old junior lieutenant shot himself the following night.[10]

In the Luchesa valley, Iushkevich ordered his troops to carry out their planned attack on 7 December, even though they had suffered losses from Becker's sudden attack the previous day. Despite his attempts to gather the greatly diminished strength of his units for a final effort, the attack degenerated into small groups of infantry and tanks attempting to dislodge the German defenders from their trenches and bunkers. As had consistently been the case, losses among the attackers were high, and given the reduced strength of Twenty-Second Army's units at the beginning of the attack, it was inevitable that these attacks would fail.

Iushkevich wanted to abandon the offensive, but his requests to do so were rejected both by Purkaev at Kalinin Front headquarters and Zhukov, who still hoped desperately that this attack might allow him to snatch victory from the jaws of defeat. Perhaps because of his repeated requests, Iushkevich became a further casualty in Zhukov's attempts to blame his subordinates for the failed offensive. On 11 December, he was dismissed from command of Twenty-Second Army. His replacement was Major General Dmitrii Mikhailovich Seleznev, who had been deputy commander of Forty-Third Army. Purkaev ordered him to continue the offensive, but the fighting had degenerated to little more than local exchanges of fire. A day later, he was ordered to cease attacks. Soon, German reconnaissance aircraft reported that columns of Red Army tanks were withdrawing from the front line – it was what remained of Katukov's III Mechanised Corps, pulled out to regroup and rearm.

Seleznev remained in post until March 1943, when he was transferred to become deputy commander – later the commanding officer – of Fourth Shock Army. When he left Twenty-Second Army, his replacement was Iushkevich, who had spent the intervening months in reserve; it was, perhaps, belated recognition that the failures of the Luchesa valley attacks were not entirely due to any shortcomings on his part.

Any lingering doubts that *Mars* had failed completely were about to be extinguished. With the fighting south of Rzhev dying down, the Germans began to concentrate their attention and strength in the Luchesa valley. It took several days for the Wehrmacht's units to assemble due to a number of factors. There was deep snow on the few roads in the area, and Red Army troops and partisans had mined many of the roads – every time a vehicle struck a mine or slipped into a ditch, the column would be forced to halt until the obstruction could be removed. Scattered sharpshooters – again, both regular troops and partisans – sniped at the Germans, and there was also the need to mop up isolated Soviet formations. The remnants of Dremov's 47th Mechanised Brigade were destroyed in a series of scattered actions to the east of Bely, and it wasn't until 20 December that the leading elements of *Kampfgruppe von der Meden* began to engage Seleznev's men. With no reserves available to bolster his lines, Seleznev had no option but to permit a withdrawal, but only to the village of Malinovka.

The battlegroups being directed to the Luchesa valley were from a variety of units, reflecting the degree to which the German defence had improvised in preceding weeks, cobbling together combat formations with whatever was available. In addition to Meden's group, 1st Panzer Division provided a battalion of panzergrenadiers reinforced by a company from the division's panzer regiment. Other troops came from *Grossdeutschland*, 129th Infantry Division, 12th Panzer Division and *Kampfgruppe Praun*. The combined force was subordinated to Generalmajor Hellmuth Weidling, commander of 86th Infantry Division. The bulk of Weidling's division was still holding the front facing west between Bely and the Luchesa, and would provide only limited artillery and logistic support to the operation to eliminate the Soviet penetration.[11]

The key position was the village of Malinovka, at the southern edge of the Red Army's penetration into German lines in late November. The bulk of the defending force was made up of 238th and 155th Rifle Divisions, both of which were far from full strength as a result of the bitter fighting of recent days. When all of the troops allocated to Weidling for the counterattack had gathered, he launched an assault on 21 December. The first obstacle was a belt of mines; after this was cleared, the Germans struggled forward through the dense woodland – just like their opponents, they found it difficult to advance through such terrain. Casualties rose steadily, but a series of Red Army trenches were overrun, and by midday the assault group was close to the edge of Malinovka. The price was a heavy one – the commander of a panzergrenadier company was badly wounded, and the NCO who took command in his absence was then also wounded. The panzer company accompanying the attack started with two Pz.IVs, three Pz.IIIs and two Pz.38s, and lost all three Pz.IIIs to the fire of anti-tank rifles at close range.

The following day, the Germans renewed their attacks. A further four tanks were hit and disabled, but Malinovka was taken. From here, the advance was meant to continue towards Karskaia, but the casualties suffered by the attack group were too high to permit a further advance, and orders arrived from Hilpert for the troops to dig in and cease their attacks. However, this attack was only part of the German operation. The rest of the units dispatched to deal with the Luchesa penetration attempted to move around to attack from the east and northeast, but these attacks also foundered in the face of determined Soviet resistance and the almost impossible terrain. Fighting continued for several days in this sector, with repeated attempts by the Germans to eliminate the small salient held by Seleznev's Twenty-Second Army; all attempts were defeated with heavy losses.

Eventually, on 23 December, fighting on the battlefields near Rzhev and to the west dwindled to a desultory, intermittent exchange of artillery fire; snipers from both sides kept watch for the unwary. The Germans reorganised their forces; 6th Infantry Division was pulled out of Rzhev, handing over its sector to 129th Infantry Division and taking up new positions along the Volga. Far to the south, on the bank of the same river, other German soldiers huddled in the ruins of Stalingrad as the attempt to reach them foundered in the face of heavy resistance – just when a small possibility of success seemed to beckon for the panzer divisions struggling to force their way through to the encirclement, the Soviet Second Guards Army, finally released from reserve, began to make its presence felt and effectively ended the diminishing hopes of salvaging the trapped army. As they marched out of Rzhev, the men of 6th Infantry Division gazed on the ruins of the city, as the division commander's whimsical account recorded:

We went through the streets one more time. The sun was on the horizon, and its blood-red rays swept over the shattered ruins of houses. The front remained active. From the direction of Polunino, one could hear the clatter of machine-guns. The shells of our artillery howled overhead. A few seconds later they flashed down on the enemy. Young boys in ragged clothes emerged from the nearby houses and asked for bread. The litter of shrapnel overflowed down the roads, over stone walls and ruins. Rzhev! This was the city now, of which the entire world had spoken for months. Was it the last time we would see it? It felt difficult to say goodbye, yet we should actually have been happy to get out of there and never see it again. The last rays of the sun played upon the dark red, glittering snow. It grew dark ...

During the winter of the preceding year, we had learned to fear and hate the cold as it suited the enemy more than us. But now that we knew how to deal with it, we could see it as a benign transformer of the landscape. How much beauty there was in the magic of every hour, as the glowing sun sank in the far west. Gold-red rays ran over the snow and the ice crystals turned purple in their light. Even if friendly faces didn't appear at the doors of the desolate Russian huts, didn't the dirty villages of the spring and summer seem so much cleaner in this weather? Or when one went into the forest in the morning, when the hoarfrost had changed the trees into a silvered picture of wonder? The birches by the roads, the bushes in front of the bunker, even the sheds, everything that one saw bore a delicate blanket of fresh whiteness.

At night the moon swept the endless expanse with soft light and from the solitude and silence left us with memories like bright, vivid pictures. Memories of a happier, untroubled time.[12]

Astonishingly, there were still civilians alive in Rzhev. A young girl described events that suggest that many Germans took a rather less picturesque and friendly attitude to Rzhev and its residents:

I lived under German rule for 17 months. We experienced many terrible things during this time. On 25 December 1942 the Germans took us to a village. There, I saw how the Germans killed a woman because she refused to give them her cow. It was in the morning. I went out onto the street and heard screams. A woman lay in the barn, covered in blood … When the Germans came for her cow, she refused to hand it over. So one German brutally shoved her and began to beat her with his fists, and then began kicking her. She soon stopped screaming and was unconscious. The Germans thought she was dead and left. She died a few days later from the beating. In the same village, the Germans beat a 14-year-old boy because he refused to work clearing snow. They ordered everyone to gather in a barn and dragged the boy in, and beat him with an iron bar and kicked him. He howled. His mother was there. She cried, screamed, and ran to her boy. The Germans who were surrounding us stood there grinning. The monsters felt no pity for the boy. They continued to smile like animals through the boy's screams as he was beaten to unconsciousness.[13]

The battle was over. All that the Red Army had to show for its enormous casualties was a small amount of territory in the north of the salient, a modest area around the Vazuza, and Seleznev's salient in the Luchesa valley. The cost had been appalling. Model's Ninth Army gathered the reports from subordinate units and estimated total Soviet losses as over 1,600 tanks, 200,000 dead or wounded, and over 4,600 prisoners. Soviet figures confirm these German estimates. Twentieth Army lost over 58,000 men; Forty-First Army reported losses of over 50,000; I Mechanised Corps lost over 8,000; Thirty-Ninth Army lost over 36,000.[14] Daily casualties of the two Soviet Fronts during the operation exceeded over 8,200 men.[15]

German losses were serious, but nowhere near as high. Because of the different manner and timeframes in which the Wehrmacht reported its casualties, a direct comparison between the two sides is difficult, but total German casualties for Ninth Army between 25 November and the end of the year came to about 40,000–45,000 men.[16] But Model and his corps and division commanders were aware that these bare numbers hid two important facts. Firstly, the losses far exceeded the numbers of replacement drafts reaching the front line. Secondly, casualties among the experienced officers and NCOs had been particularly high. 1st Panzer Division reported the deaths of two battalion commanders, an acting battalion commander, nine company commanders and an acting company commander. In addition, two division doctors were killed; and three battalion commanders and 16 company commanders and acting company commanders were badly wounded.[17] On the other side of the salient, 5th Panzer Division lost 28 officers killed and another 38 wounded. Losses among lower ranks were also heavy – 510 dead or missing and another 1,064 wounded.[18] Ninth Army might have avoided the fate of Paulus' Sixth Army in Stalingrad, but it was still badly weakened by the savage fighting of the preceding weeks.

Throughout the battle, Model balanced personal involvement with allowing his corps commanders to do their jobs. He saw his role as ensuring that his subordinate formations received the resources they needed – thereafter, men like Harpe and Hilpert knew what was required and the manner in which their army commander wished them to operate. The successful defence of the Rzhev Salient owed much to the relatively fresh troops – 12th, 19th and 20th Panzer Divisions in particular – that Model was able to concentrate against the Red Army, but the conduct of most of the battle was carried out by corps and division commanders operating on well-established Wehrmacht principles.

The role of Zhukov in the fighting remains controversial, not least because his personal accounts distort the narrative so much. Few of his interventions directly hindered the development of operations, but nor did they improve matters for the Red Army. The failure of the Soviet forces to achieve the expected successes was due to many factors, but direct interference from senior commanders was not one of them. Rather, it was the original concept of the plan that doomed it to failure.

CHAPTER 14

BÜFFEL: THE END OF
THE SALIENT

The fate of the Rzhev Salient, the scene of so much bloodshed for so little gain on either side, was decided on other sectors of the Eastern Front.

The winter of 1942–43 saw a huge shift in the balance of power. The German Sixth Army – numerically the strongest army deployed by the Wehrmacht on the Eastern Front – was trapped in Stalingrad, where it died a slow death from starvation. The first attempts by the Red Army to break into the encirclement in early December were repulsed, with heavy losses on both sides – it was perhaps the first time that the Soviet high command realised just how many German troops they had surrounded. Thereafter, a more gradual approach was adopted, and the Germans were gradually forced back from the steppe to the west of Stalingrad into the ruins of the city itself. Finally, on 26 January, the Red Army attacked with greater force, splitting the encirclement in two. It was further subdivided into three separate groups two days later. The southern and central groups surrendered on 31 January, and the northern pocket two days later. It was perhaps a sign of how much had changed that General Karl Strecker, commander of XI Corps and the de facto commander of the northern pocket, took care in the deliberate wording of his last signal:

> XI Army Corps has with its six divisions performed its duty down to the last man in heavy fighting. Long live Germany![1]

It was almost unthinkable that such a signal could be transmitted without the customary acclamation to Hitler. When the message was received in the headquarters of Army Group Don, someone decided that it would be best to add the words 'Long live the Führer!' before transmitting it on to Hitler's headquarters in East Prussia.

A total of about 91,000 German soldiers were taken prisoner. Many thousands died of disease and malnutrition in the weeks that followed – they were starved and exhausted, and the Red Army struggled to provide adequate medical support for its own forces, let alone for such an unexpectedly large haul of prisoners. Ultimately, fewer than 6,000 survived to be repatriated to Germany after the war.[2] The total surrounded in Stalingrad has been estimated at over 260,000 Germans, Romanians and Italians, with perhaps as many as 65,000 former Red Army personnel serving as *Hilfswillige* with the German units. About 35,000 wounded were evacuated by air before the final surrender. These losses would have been devastating enough for the Wehrmacht, but the true scale of the catastrophe in the southern sector was far greater. Fourth Panzer Army, which attempted to fight its way through to the encirclement, suffered heavy casualties as it first advanced towards the perimeter and then fell back under heavy counterattack. The two Romanian armies on the flanks of Sixth Army were almost completely destroyed during *Uranus*, the operation overseen by Vasilevsky to encircle Stalingrad. To the northwest, the Axis front line disintegrated under a series of blows with the Italian Eighth Army and the Hungarian Second Army, effectively ceasing to exist; to their north, the German Second Army was also forced into precipitate retreat, suffering heavy losses.[3] The defeat of Second Army was almost overlooked in the midst of the overall disaster, but it was significant in that the German infantry divisions proved to be every bit as brittle in the face of Soviet attacks as their Hungarian, Italian and Romanian allies further south.

The consequence of these disasters was that, for a few heady weeks, the Red Army believed that it was on the verge of winning the war. With no semblance of a continuous front line, large formations moved steadily west and southwest, threatening a multitude of encirclements: German forces in the Caucasus might be cut off; a drive to the coast of the Sea of Azov might isolate the German units trying to establish a new defensive line in the Donets valley; and a thrust towards central Ukraine might reach and sever the rail link to the only intact railway bridge over the Dnepr, over which nearly all the supplies to Axis forces in the south had to pass. If the Wehrmacht was to avoid a defeat that would cost Germany the war, it was essential that troops be sent to Ukraine to permit a new front line. Even if troops could be made available, stabilisation of the front line would require consummate skill.

The main source of troops to shore up the broken front line was the west, where several German divisions had spent a relatively comfortable few months on garrison duty in France, Norway and Denmark. A steady stream of these reinforcements arrived throughout the winter, though the German commanders frequently complained that these units, particularly the invaluable panzer divisions, were repeatedly delayed due to interference by Hitler. But other sectors of the Eastern Front were also required to release units for deployment in the south. The first battlegroup of 19th Panzer Division had already left for Ukraine before the completion of the fighting in the Rzhev Salient in December 1942, and the rest of the division followed in the first few days of 1943; other units would follow.

Ultimately, Field Marshal Erich von Manstein, who had taken command of Army Group Don during the crisis, was able to use both the reinforcements and the units he freed up by persuading Hitler to permit the evacuation of First Panzer Army from the Caucasus to mount a series of astonishing counterstrikes in March 1943.[4] The over-extended Red Army units suddenly found themselves caught in a series of encounter battles with fast-moving German armour, the sort of fighting at which the Germans excelled, and Manstein was able to restore the situation.

The consequence of this for Kluge's Army Group Centre was that there was no prospect whatever of it receiving any significant reinforcements in coming months. After suffering heavy losses in the winter fighting, it would now have to fend for itself with its remaining weakened units. To make matters worse, there was a further development that had a detrimental effect. In addition to the assault on the western and northern sides of the Rzhev Salient, Kalinin Front also conducted an operation to encircle the German forces holding Velikiye Luki to the west. Galitsky's Third Shock Army made an initial attack on 24 November, advancing about a mile into the German positions; in anticipation of an assault, the German defences, mainly made up of 83rd Infantry Division, had established a series of forward positions that could be abandoned when the Red Army attacked. The following day, Galitsky's troops assaulted the main German defensive line. In heavy fighting, they pressed forward both to the north and south of Velikiye Luki. Despite the commitment of German reinforcements – 8th Panzer Division against the northern Soviet thrust and 291st Infantry Division and 20th Motorised Infantry Division from the south – the two Soviet groups linked up on 28 November, encircling 83rd Infantry Division in the city.[5]

This development, unwelcome at any time, was particularly difficult for the Germans at the same time that Sixth Army was being encircled in the south and Zhukov was unleashing his bloody assault on the Rzhev Salient. Generalleutnant Theodor Scherer, commander of 83rd Infantry Division, promptly contacted his superior, General Kurt von der Chevallerie, at the headquarters of LIX Corps. The encirclement was still porous, and an immediate breakout was almost certain to succeed. This would allow the German division to pull back towards the west, where a new defensive line could be established. Chevallerie agreed with this assessment, as did Kluge at Army Group Centre; characteristically, Hitler did not. Scherer's request was refused, and he was ordered to hold the city while Chevallerie formed a relief group and broke through to Velikiye Luki.

While Sixth Army endured its siege in Stalingrad, 83rd Infantry Division fought a similar though smaller battle further north throughout December. Repeated Soviet attempts to reduce the city's defences were beaten off, but supplies rapidly ran short – the Luftwaffe's aerial transport capacity was fully stretched trying to keep Sixth Army alive in the south and few aircraft could be spared. Finally, Chevallerie's relief column managed to fight its way to within five miles (eight km) of the encirclement in the first week of January, though every attempt to push closer was beaten back. At the same time, the Red Army finally succeeded in penetrating 83rd Infantry Division's defences, breaking the division in two. The smaller pocket, located in the western part of the city, attempted to break out to reach Chevallerie's column late on 14 January; about 150 men managed to reach German lines. The larger group was forced to surrender.[6] Scherer was one of those who escaped.

At a time when Sixth Army was in its death throes, the escape of such a small group of men was a source of some solace to the Germans. As was so often the case, the battle cost the Red Army more casualties than the Wehrmacht – about 104,000 dead, wounded or missing compared with 60,000 on the German side – but the outcome of the fighting was a major setback for Germany. The direct rail link between Army Group Centre and Army Group North was now within artillery range and could be interdicted by the Red Army. Just as importantly, the capture of Velikiye Luki gave the Red Army a new rail link to concentrate forces against the northwest face of the Rzhev Salient. Since the preceding winter, the Red Army forces between Rzhev and Velikiye Luki had been unable to pose any major threat of an advance towards the south against Smolensk, due partly to logistic difficulties and partly because the German position at Velikiye Luki meant that the Red Army constantly feared that the Wehrmacht could easily concentrate forces against the rear of any Red Army operation towards Smolensk. The recapture of Velikiye Luki, therefore, removed any such constraint from the Red Army. With the threat of a Soviet strike towards Smolensk now a real possibility, there was a danger that Model's Ninth Army in the Rzhev Salient might be encircled by operations beyond its flanks, much as had been the case for Paulus' Sixth Army.

Although the weather had interfered greatly with the movement of troops on both sides in the recent fighting, the winter of 1942–43 was less severe than the preceding year. With the usual mix of labour – local troops, construction battalions, prisoners of war, and forcibly conscripted civilians – the units of Ninth Army began the task of repairing the fortifications that had been tested in the preceding weeks. In order to reduce persisting partisan activity, Model issued orders for an operation codenamed *Sternlauf* ('Star run') under the control of XXXI Panzer Corps. As had been the case in the summer fighting, Model intended to create an improvised cavalry formation in an attempt to deal with the difficulties of the terrain, and this force would be used to sweep through the densely forested areas, driving the partisan bands into waiting infantry formations. In addition, a second operation codenamed *Sewastopol 505* was planned for XXXIX Panzer Corps, intended to push back the Red Army on the eastern side of the salient.

With the ongoing crisis in Ukraine continuing to unfold and German resources already stretched to the limit, Model can't have been surprised when both Zeitzler and Hitler rejected the plans for *Sewastopol 505*. Not only would such an operation require logistic support that was badly needed for the southern sector; there were also fears that, despite the successes of Ninth Army in the preceding weeks, a new surge in fighting might lead to unexpected reversals and further victories for the Red Army. Undaunted, Model devised a more restricted operation codenamed *Schachturnier* ('Chess tournament') – backed by the massed artillery assets of Ninth Army, local attacks were made to straighten the line.

Sternlauf ultimately involved elements of Bittrich's SS Cavalry Division, other improvised mounted units, and detachments from four infantry divisions, together with a small number of SS police units and Russian volunteer formations. The sweep continued for two weeks, at the end of which the units reported that they had killed about 3,000 partisans. However, they also noted that many of the 'partisans' were unarmed, and a total of only 277 rifles, 41 pistols, 61 machine-guns, 17 mortars, nine anti-tank rifles and 16 small-calibre guns were seized.[7] Many of these weapons, particularly the mortars, anti-tank rifles and light field guns, would have been items left behind during the Red Army's retreat from the area in earlier fighting; this means that only a total of 379 personal weapons were captured, and that about 88 per cent of those killed were unarmed. Many – perhaps the majority – were ordinary civilians, who may or may not have been assisting the partisans. The extent to which this suppressed partisan activity is debatable, and the modest successes of *Schachturnier* were no substitute for a proper reordering of the front line. Quietly and without fuss, Kluge started preparation of a new defensive line further west, which would require the abandonment of the Rzhev Salient.

The first documents relating to a withdrawal appeared in Kluge's headquarters at the beginning of the third week of January, but given the complexity of what was proposed, it is highly likely that Kluge and his staff had been discussing such a withdrawal for some time beforehand.[8] It seems that at this stage, the main discussion about this plan was between Zeitzler and Generalleutnant Adolf Heusinger (head of operations) at *OKH* and Kluge at Army Group Centre; Model was not consulted. This appears to have been a deliberate measure on the part of Kluge. During the difficult days of the previous winter, he had negotiated sufficient freedom of action to save his army group, and the interventions of subordinate commanders in the constant discussions with Hitler had rarely been conducive; it seems that on this occasion, Kluge wished to ensure that there would be no undermining of his case when it was presented to Hitler. Securing permission for withdrawals was difficult at the best of times, and this would involve the voluntary abandonment of a large tract of territory that the Wehrmacht had defended with great determination. If Model were to suggest to Hitler that it was possible to retain the salient, Kluge knew that Hitler would grasp that opportunity to reject any talk of a withdrawal.

As had been the case in the first winter of the war on the Eastern Front, Kluge painstakingly built his case for the withdrawal. By doing so in a timely manner, he explained, it would be possible to release substantial forces from the front line. These could be used either to shore up other sectors of the Eastern Front or – his preferred solution – held in reserve in Army Group Centre, where they would be available either to deal with any renewed Soviet attacks or could be used in a new offensive operation in the summer. Armed with Kluge's arguments, Zeitzler then took up the matter, repeatedly urging Hitler to adopt the plan. At first, there was a characteristic refusal to accept the necessity for such a major withdrawal, but given the difficulty of extracting permission from Hitler for far more modest withdrawals in the past, Kluge must have been pleasantly surprised at the manner in which Hitler then rapidly agreed to the proposals drawn up by Army Group Centre. It should be remembered that at this time, Sixth Army was dying in terrible circumstances on the shores of the Volga and the entire southern sector remained fluid; it wasn't at all clear that Manstein would be able to salvage the situation. Consequently, the thought of releasing battle-hardened troops from Army Group Centre must have been particularly attractive to the Führer.

The orders for the evacuation of the Rzhev Salient reached Ninth Army headquarters on 26 January. At this stage, they described the overall plan, but a start date had yet to be decided. Whatever his views on the abandonment of a salient that his troops had defended with such tenacity, Model immediately took steps to comply with the new plan. He promptly dispatched two officers to the planned position for the new defensive line in order to draw up plans for how it was to be fortified. The first of these officers was Generalleutnant Max Lindig, who held the post of *Höher Artillerie-Kommandeur 307* ('Artillery High Commander 307'); in this role, he oversaw the artillery assets held by Ninth Army under its direct control. He was an experienced artilleryman; he served as a junior artillery officer throughout the First World War and remained in the Reichswehr in the inter-war years. He was accompanied by Oberst Otto Meyer, head of Ninth Army's pioneers. After three days, they submitted their first report, and immediately seven pioneer battalions were ordered to move to the new line. On the first day of February, Model ordered the creation of a special staff group to oversee ongoing preparations.

In addition to preparing new fortifications, Model and his staff looked at the actual process of withdrawal. They anticipated that regardless of their attempts at secrecy, it would be impossible to disguise preparations from the Red Army. If the Germans had detected preparations for such a large withdrawal by their opponents, they would immediately have launched attacks, seeking to try to pin down their enemies before they could withdraw or to take advantage of any opportunities that might arise during the withdrawal. It was therefore highly likely that the Red Army would attempt something similar. The planning for the withdrawal had to take this into account, and Model's special team of staff officers recommended a multi-phased operation, with units falling back from one intermediate line to another. At each stage, Ninth Army would have to be prepared to make a stand and fight off any pursuing Soviet units.

Preparations for the withdrawal were complicated by the departure of Generalmajor Hans Krebs, Model's chief of staff. Newly promoted to Generalleutnant, he moved to Army Group Centre, where he became Kluge's chief of staff. He and Model had worked closely and had a good personal relationship, which would of course be of great value in future, as Krebs would be an important contact for Model in the headquarters of his superior. But if Krebs' new role was to Model's liking, the new chief of staff at Ninth Army was not. Oberst Harald Freiherr von Elverfeldt had held a series of command and staff posts since the beginning of the war, most recently overseeing two major anti-partisan operations in Belarus.[9] Whereas Krebs had been an extroverted and self-confident figure, Elverfeldt gave the impression of being neither. The staff officers in Model's headquarters had the strong impression that the new chief of staff was more scared of Model than he was of the enemy. Never one to make any secret of his views, Model made no attempt to hide his dissatisfaction with Elverfeldt, but for the moment he had no choice and would have to work as best he could with the new appointee.

Some units had already departed for duties elsewhere. *Grossdeutschland* began to withdraw in the second week of January; after a short period to recuperate, it was to be deployed in Ukraine. The rest period was badly needed. One company of the division's Fusilier Regiment reported that its strength was just a single officer, two NCOs and eight men; similarly, a company from the Grenadier Regiment had been reduced to one officer, one NCO and 16 men. Since 6 August, the Grenadier Regiment had recorded the loss of over 2,600 men of all ranks killed, wounded or missing. Another of the divisions involved in the bitter fighting around Bely, 1st Panzer Division, recorded the loss of nearly 1,800 men during the battles. This division was also pulled out of line in January, but unlike *Grossdeutschland*, it enjoyed a better assignment: it was sent to Normandy for a prolonged period of recuperation.

The plans for the abandonment of the Rzhev Salient became known as Operation *Büffel* ('Buffalo'), and the new defensive line would be the *Büffelstellung* ('Buffalo line' or 'Buffalo position'). Work continued on preparations, and orders were finally issued by Kluge on 22 February that the operation was to commence on 1 March. The plans were on a massive scale. In order to permit a rapid withdrawal, about 120 miles (200km) of new roads would have to be constructed for motorised vehicles and an additional 360 miles (600km) of tracks cleared for non-motorised traffic. As they withdrew, the Germans intended to destroy about 600 miles (1,000km) of railway lines and recover over 600 miles of telegraph cables. In addition to the units and equipment of Ninth Army, the Wehrmacht planned the evacuation of several thousand Soviet prisoners of war and most of the local population, numbering about 60,000 people. Some German accounts describe how these people were to be moved because they didn't welcome the return of Soviet rule and wished to flee to the west; the reality is that the Wehrmacht intended to create a 'dead zone' as it pulled back, to hinder the future activity of the Red Army in the region. As a result, civilians were to be moved together with their livestock, regardless of any wishes they may have had.[10]

Given the dreadful casualties of the preceding months, it might have been natural for Kalinin and Western Fronts to pause and lick their wounds. Instead, the entire Red Army was seized by growing confidence that the war had turned decisively in its favour. The rout of the Wehrmacht in Ukraine showed no sign of stopping, and Soviet troops took Kharkov on 12 February, narrowly failing to encircle a substantial part of the SS Panzer Corps in the city. Consequently, further plans were drawn up for offensive operations to accelerate the collapse of the entire German position in the east. In mid-February, Rokossovsky was moved from command of Don Front to the new Central Front:

> At *Stavka* I was shown the general plan of the offensive on the Kursk sector. It was to be carried out by the new Central Front, comprising Twenty-First and Sixty-Fifth Armies and Sixteenth Air Army from Don Front, and Second Tank Army and Seventieth Army and a number of units from *Stavka* reserve.
>
> This new Front was to be deployed between Bryansk and Voronezh Fronts, which were continuing the offensive on the Kursk and Kharkov sectors. In cooperation with Bryansk Front it was to execute a deep turning movement in the general direction of Gomel, Smolensk, aimed at the flank and rear of the enemy's Orel group.
>
> The beginning of this beautifully planned operation had been timed for 15 February. However, it was first necessary to deploy the troops, the bulk of which were, with their rear services, still in the neighbourhood of Stalingrad ...
>
> From the outset we encountered tremendous difficulties. There was only one single-track railway functioning – the only one that had been restored by then. Naturally, it couldn't handle such heavy traffic. Our transportation plans were bursting at the seams. Traffic schedules collapsed, there were not enough troop trains, and in those that were available the trucks were, as often as not, unsuited for varying personnel or horses.[11]

This was the legacy of the death throes of the German Sixth Army: its prolonged resistance in Stalingrad had tied down substantial Soviet forces. It would take time for the units to move to new sectors, and most had suffered substantial casualties in the fighting in and around Stalingrad. Rokossovsky mentions that accelerating the redeployment was handed to the NKVD with unfortunate results:

> Its men pitched into it with such zeal, clamping down so hard on the railway authorities that the latter lost their heads completely and whatever timetables and schedules had existed until then now went up in smoke. Troops began to arrive at the concentration area all mixed up. Artillery units came without draught horses or tractors, which as often as not were still at the entraining point. Or a unit's materiel might have been unloaded at one station while the men were detrained at another. Troop trains were held up at stations and sidings for days on end. Owing to train shortages, 169 logistical establishments and units remained stuck at Stalingrad.[12]

In addition to the offensive planned for Rokossovsky's new Central Front, Western and Kalinin Fronts were also to resume offensive operations. Western

Front was to advance towards Smolensk, while Kalinin Front attacked towards Vitebsk, Orsha and Smolensk. The result, it was expected, would be the fragmentation of Army Group Centre and its destruction in a series of encirclements. Even if all the units involved had been in position when the plans were drawn up, it was a hugely ambitious undertaking. With weakened units arriving in a haphazard fashion, the plan had no chance of success, particularly as many of the attacks would take place against strong defensive positions. On 12 February, Bryansk Front launched widespread attacks in an attempt to turn the southern flank of the German positions at Orel. At considerable cost, it managed to advance as much as 18 miles (30km) before exhaustion brought the offensive to an end. Western Front was able to attack with Sixteenth Army a few days later, and enjoyed even less success.

Rokossovsky made repeated requests to *Stavka* for his planned offensive to be abandoned, or at least postponed to a more realistic start date. The best that he could secure was that it was put off until 25 February. With many of his units still awaiting the arrival of all their elements, Rokossovsky's Central Front duly attacked as ordered and, perhaps to Rokossovsky's surprise, enjoyed some early success. When they attacked, Sixty-Fifth and Seventieth Armies swiftly pushed aside the opposing German units, and Central Front's exploitation forces were let loose. Second Tank Army underwent a change of command on the very eve of the operation. When it was first formed in January 1943, it was commanded by Lieutenant General Prokofiy Logvinovich Romanenko, who had previously commanded Fifth Tank Army in the fighting near Stalingrad. During the unfolding of *Uranus*, Vatutin was critical about the manner in which Romanenko led his army. Lieutenant General Semen Pavlovich Ivanov, who was chief of staff with First Guards Army and was about to be appointed Vatutin's chief of staff, later wrote that Romanenko didn't respond well to criticism by his superior:

A little later, Vatutin received a telephone call from Prokofiy Logvinovich. It was a difficult conversation. The commander of Fifth Tank Army was offended by the fact that the Front had effectively transferred control of one of his tank corps from him. In addition, he believed that [his units] should help close the encirclement [of the Germans in Stalingrad].

With the tacit approval of Vasilevsky, Vatutin responded in an unexpectedly harsh manner. He criticised [Romanenko] for never being in his command post and constantly moving from one formation to another, leaving his headquarters to its own devices. He also reproached Prokofiy Logvinovich for losing control of I Tank Corps and III Cavalry Corps. The usually taciturn [Major General Grigorii

Davidovich] Stelmakh [Vatutin's chief of staff, killed in action shortly after this incident] commented that the army had fulfilled its overall mission well and that flaws in the command and control of troops during mobile operations were inevitable. Vatutin, however, judging by his scowl, was not convinced.[13]

Despite the dissatisfaction of Vatutin – and the implied dissatisfaction of Vasilevsky – Romanenko was transferred to the new Second Tank Army, only to be moved on once more to take command of Forty-Eighth Army. In his place, Second Tank Army was led during Rokossovsky's new offensive by one of his former subordinates, Major General Georgii Semenovich Rodin, who had commanded XXVI Tank Corps and had led it to capture the vital town of Kalach on the Don, cutting the supply lines of the German Sixth Army in Stalingrad; for this operation, he received the award of 'Hero of the Soviet Union', and the tank corps was renamed I Guards Tank Corps. He now inherited a new tank army that was far from fully ready for a major operation. Many of its units, like other parts of Central Front, were still en route to their forming-up points, and the entire army had fewer than half its establishment of 408 tanks.

Notwithstanding this handicap, Rodin pushed forward with his tanks through the breach secured by Rokossovsky's infantry and captured the town of Sevsk before driving on to Seredina-Buda, 19 miles (30km) further west. Here he was forced to halt, largely due to fuel shortages and the weakness of his army, but nonetheless the important railway line between Bryansk in the north and Konotop in the south was cut, hindering the movement of German troops between Army Group Centre and Army Group South. II Guards Cavalry Corps, Rokossovsky's other exploitation force, pushed on further. Led by Kryukov, the corps – reinforced with three ski brigades of riflemen and collectively termed the 'cavalry-rifle group' – was committed on Rodin's northern flank. Kryukov found itself operating in open space and rapidly reached the town of Trubchevsk, about 60 miles (100km) from his start line.

Rokossovsky was struggling to keep his various armies under tight control, with Twenty-First Army only beginning to concentrate after the offensive had already begun. The delay in moving logistic units from the Stalingrad area now began to make itself felt, and the failure of the Fronts on either flank to make comparable progress left Central Front in a somewhat exposed salient. Increasingly worried about his exposed flanks, particularly to the north, Rokossovsky ordered Kryukov to halt his advance and prepare defences against a potential German counterattack – both aerial reconnaissance and partisan reports indicated that substantial German forces were gathering in the area.

The reports were correct. In addition to two Hungarian divisions from the Hungarian Army's VIII Corps, the Germans moved 137th Infantry Division from the north to block any further advance by Rodin's Second Tank Army. In addition, 9th Panzer Division and Bittrich's SS Cavalry Division began to gather against the northern flank of Rokossovsky's salient, while 4th Panzer Division and two infantry divisions concentrated against the southern flank.

Meanwhile, the plans for *Büffel* continued to develop. Trains operated at all hours, moving equipment and supplies back from the Rzhev Salient – it was later estimated that over 110,000 tons of material was brought back.[14] The Red Army couldn't help but be aware that a withdrawal was being planned, and orders were issued as early as the second week of February to Thirtieth Army:

> The army's task is to detect in a timely manner the commencement of the enemy's withdrawal or partial withdrawal of forces from the front line of Thirtieth Army. Once the withdrawal of the main forces has been detected, [Thirtieth Army is to] break through the rearguard left by the enemy with strong formations and pursue resolutely.[15]

Similar orders were sent to other armies in the region, and all were ordered to carry out active reconnaissance.

The weather grew warmer in mid-February, resulting in a partial thaw, which made all movement much more difficult. While they struggled to prepare for their withdrawal, the Germans were aware that their opponents were watching closely:

> In mid-February, reconnaissance patrols reported lively enemy activity. Ski units and their movements in the rear of the enemy front line were detected. Russian officers could be seen conducting reconnaissance and observation of the area. They were driven off by machine-gun fire. The enemy's air activity increased and enemy artillery fired repeatedly at German command posts. Did the Russians suspect something? On numerous occasions enemy attacks took place on the front line. The troops fought them off and inflicted heavy casualties ... On 17 February, the headquarters of 251st Infantry Division informed its regiments that the enemy was urging his divisions to be especially alert and to begin an immediate pursuit of the Germans with tanks at the first opportunity.

Using a loudspeaker, the Russians broadcast on 18 February: 'Ninth Army, pack your bags and get ready to leave!' They had therefore certainly noticed something. The thaw continued and small patches of earth peeped through the snow. The sappers began mining trenches and putting 'surprises' in dugouts and buildings – the insidious way of waging war that the German soldier had learned from the Russians.[16]

At the headquarters of Zygin's Thirty-Ninth Army in the northern sector of the Rzhev Salient, Voloshin – Zygin's chief of intelligence – was increasingly aware of unusual activity on the German side of the line but was unsure of how to interpret it. Was this activity a precursor to a withdrawal, or preparations for a German offensive? Despite the huge setback inflicted upon the Wehrmacht at Stalingrad and in Ukraine, Voloshin seems to have believed that the Germans retained the capability of attacking towards Moscow, and it is unlikely that he was alone in this assessment, which lay behind much of the obsession with destroying the Rzhev Salient. He organised an extended reconnaissance mission, led by a lieutenant named Korogodov, with the intention of probing into the depth of the salient. After six days, the patrol returned with confirmation that the German rear area units were withdrawing. Voloshin presented the findings from the patrol and from other sources of intelligence, such as partisan reports, to the army's military council. A few officers doubted the information, but at the end of February came further confirmation:

> A group headed by Sergeant A.V. Khoroshilov burst into the enemy's trenches and brought back three prisoners. They were soldiers of 459th Regiment, 251st Infantry Division, and during interrogation they indicated that their unit would soon begin to withdraw to the south. All non-essential materiel had already been handed over to rear area units. Heavy weapons were being mounted on sleds and other means of transportation.
>
> A day later, it was noted that here and there, enemy signalmen were removing communications lines. This spoke volumes. No unit in wartime can exist without secure communications.[17]

There were widespread demolitions, and there could be no doubt that a withdrawal was imminent. Soviet units reported a sudden increase in brief artillery bombardments at various points of the front line, and staff officers correctly interpreted this as units firing off their surplus ammunition in preparation for departure. Orders were issued by some army commanders for front-line units to mount raids in order to capture a German 'tongue', ideally an officer, so that more details might be obtained, and Gorbachevsky was assigned to such a task. Major

General Stanislav Giliarovich Poplavsky, the division commander, toured the front line and offered whatever inducements he could to motivate his men:

'Guys,' he said bluntly, 'we need a "tongue"! Help me. We must bring in a German officer. Whoever succeeds will be nominated for an award. Further, if you want a woman, you'll get one. If you want some home leave, we'll organise it. You can have as much vodka as you want. I'm putting all my hopes on you! We urgently need a "tongue". Pick some volunteers and get organised.'[18]

Gorbachevsky came up with a plan for a small group of men to pretend to be deserters, but his regiment commander rejected the suggestion. But before he could mount a raid, Gorbachevsky learned that a neighbouring company had succeeded in killing a senior German NCO and had brought back his documents, and Gorbachevsky and his comrades watched with envy as the successful raiders departed on their promised home leave, but the incident had an unexpected conclusion. When Shevchenko – the leader of the successful raid – returned from leave, Poplavsky summoned the officers of Gorbachevsky's regiment:

Poplavsky asked the reconnaissance platoon commander just one question: 'Who are you? A Soviet officer or a piece of shit?' Shevchenko turned deathly pale and seemed to shrink. He tried to say something, perhaps in his defence, but the division commander stepped forward. His heavy hand tore the epaulets from his shoulders and punched the now former officer on the jaw. Spitting out teeth and blood, he fell to the floor, howling like a wounded animal. But it wasn't a cry of pain or protest, but rather a plea.

'Get up, you bastard!' commanded the general.

Shevchenko got up with difficulty and immediately received another blow on the jaw. We stood around the walls of the dugout silently, not understanding what was happening or what the accusation was. He crawled like a worm on the floor around the general, mechanically mumbling the same thing: 'Sorry, sorry.'

From a mixture of despair, pain and fear, he didn't dare get to his feet, dreading that the general would strike him again. He reached for the general's boots and tried to hug them. Poplavsky grimaced in disgust. Another blow followed, a boot to the face ... The general's voice sounded loud as it broke the silence: 'A person without character is not a person, but a non-entity! This bastard has committed a grave crime. We will judge him. He has besmirched the honour of an officer. I have other things to attend to. The regiment commander will accompany me. My reconnaissance commander will tell you what has happened.'

Special officers [i.e. NKVD] seized Shevchenko by the arms and pulled the barely conscious, bloody man from the dugout and took him away. Captain Mishchenko [the reconnaissance commander] was brief: 'The general believed Shevchenko's reports. I sent them to the army and from there they went to the Front. They always double-check information, as they have agents behind enemy lines. So it became known that the German unit allegedly standing in front of us is currently in France. Your Shevchenko never captured any senior Feldwebel. All the allegedly captured documents were taken by him from a stash he secretly created during the summer offensive.'[19]

Shevchenko was brought before a tribunal two days later, was found guilty, and was promptly executed in front of the other officers of the regiment. His accomplices in the ruse were sent to a penal battalion. But other units captured genuine prisoners, who informed their interrogators that new boots had been issued, surplus ammunition and non-essential personnel had been evacuated, and men had been given four days' rations for an imminent withdrawal. However, attempts by the Soviet troops to probe the German lines were still repulsed energetically. On the eve of the evacuation, a reconnaissance group of 22 men attempted to slip into Rzhev from the north; only the platoon commander survived when the Germans spotted the group and ambushed it.[20] Another larger attack was conducted by the Soviet Fifth Army to the east of Vyazma a week before *Büffel* commenced. The first two lines of German trenches were overrun, and a small exploitation group of tanks and a ski brigade attempted to take advantage of the success, as a veteran later described:

Tanks moved towards the front, dozens of tanks of an American model. The powerful machines surged by along a snowy road. Later I learned that almost all of them were knocked out and set ablaze. And the tankers? How often we witnessed the unkind fate of the tankers in those days![21]

The ski brigade managed to penetrate into the rear of the German lines, but a local counterattack sealed off the Soviet penetration, and the brigade was wiped out. Fifth Army suffered major losses in this attack, with the consequence that Colonel-General Iakov Timofeevich Cherevichenko, the army commander, was dismissed, as were several lower-ranking officers. A more prominent fall from favour occurred at the headquarters of Western Front, where Konev was summoned back to Moscow. There, he was informed that he too was dismissed from command of the Front, as *Stavka* – which in this context was largely a cipher for Stalin – had concluded that he was unable to cope with leading the Front. But instead of being demoted, he was transferred to command of Northwest Front and returned to favour during the summer when he led Steppe Front during and after the Battle of Kursk. Had his ability to command a Front been seriously in doubt, it seems highly unlikely that he would have been given this new appointment. Rather, this is likely to have been at the instigation of Zhukov, and the manner in which Stalin agreed to it suggests that the Soviet dictator still held Zhukov in high regard and was prepared to take the necessary steps for Zhukov to retain face. Despite the failures of the offensives against the Rzhev Salient throughout 1942, Zhukov remained untouched. During the first months of 1943, he was overseeing operations further north, near Demyansk. Konev's replacement at Western Front was Colonel General Vasily Danilovich Sokolovsky, who had been Konev's chief of staff.

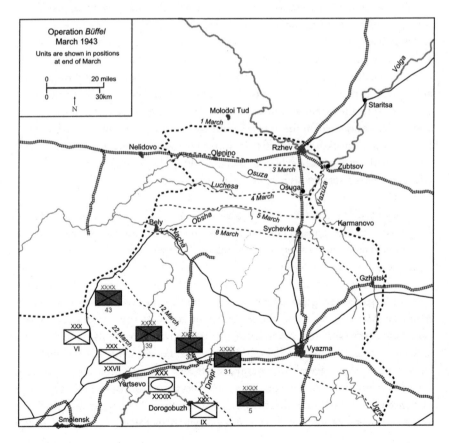

The first German unit to pull out of the front line near Rzhev was 251st Infantry Division, which quietly moved out of its trenches late on 28 February. It seems that this departure went unobserved by the opposing Soviet forces, with a small German rearguard firing from time to time at the opposing lines to simulate the continuing presence of the entire division. The unseasonal warm weather continued, with running water on most of the roads; many German units had prepared the evacuation of much of their equipment using sleds, and there were now doubts whether this would be possible. But late on 1 March, the temperature dropped below freezing again and fresh snow began to fall. More troops began to pull out, dragging heavy loads behind them:

> Exhausted limbs felt as heavy as lead. Men were no longer used to marching after weeks of digging in, keeping watch, fighting, and sleeping now and then. Rifles felt heavier and heavier. Ration packs, gas masks, entrenching tools, rain capes, ammunition, helmets and hand grenades seemed to want to drag us down. Vehicles became stuck. The march continued in starts and stops as it wasn't possible to move past stoppages and everything would come to a halt. 'All hands to the vehicle!' 'Heave ho! Heave ho!' We had to put aside out fatigue, everyone had to join in, nothing was to be left behind, or we would lose valuable materiel. Nobody could help us, we had no towing vehicles or tractors, just our feet, arms, hands and the will that this withdrawal was carried out with as little loss of men and equipment as possible, but with bloody losses for the enemy.
>
> Morning dawned, our winter uniforms were soaking and we were bitterly cold. Nobody spoke a word. We dragged ourselves on. Two men pulled a sled with a machine-gun and ammunition. Our bodies were like machines – after a long period of positional warfare, a 30km [18 mile] march was no small thing. The column stretched out ever longer. Overnight, the companies reached the prepared position of a snow wall. The front remained quiet.[22]

A powerful Soviet attack at this stage could have created chaos, but the Soviet lines remained inexplicably silent. It is possible that after the dismissal of Konev and Cherevichenko for their failed attacks a week earlier, other commanders were cautious of making the same mistake, but a great opportunity to achieve a decisive success was slipping away before their eyes. Along the Volga, German rearguards were subjected to intermittent heavy bombardments, but the only significant probing attack by Soviet infantry was repulsed. Late on 2 March, the Germans abandoned the Volga line at the same time as a general withdrawal from the ruins of Rzhev. Scouting groups from the Soviet Thirtieth Army reported that the German trenches were no longer manned, but Lieutenant General Vladimir Iakovlevich Kolpachki, who took command of Thirtieth Army in November 1942, remained cautious and issued no orders for a pursuit. Prior to taking command of Thirtieth Army, Kolpachki had led Sixty-Second Army in the fighting in the great bend of the Don River against the German Sixth Army; his army was effectively destroyed in the battles near Kalach, and he was dismissed in August, having been criticised for losing contact with his units. Perhaps this experience contributed to his caution in front of Rzhev.

The neighbouring Thirty-First Army showed a little more energy. Lieutenant General Vitaly Sergeevich Polenov, who had commanded the army through the fighting of November and December, had been replaced by Major General Vladimir Alekseevich Gluzdovsky, and he ordered his troops forward as soon as the German retreat was detected. His men captured the first line of German trenches almost without a shot being fired but then came under intense fire from what seemed like a substantial body of German troops; in reality, it was the rearguard of the German infantry, conducting an energetic defence. Despite this check, Gluzdovsky ordered the divisions on his right flank – nearest Rzhev – to attempt to enter the city from the south, but they too ran into defensive fire and were driven to ground.

Despite the order sent out in mid-February warning army commanders in Kalinin and Western Fronts to be ready to pursue the Wehrmacht in the event of a withdrawal, *Stavka* issued a new order late on 2 March ordering the armies to create strong combined arms detachments for such a pursuit – effectively a repetition of the previous order. Purkaev and Sokolovsky at the headquarters of Kalinin and Western Fronts respectively were ordered to produce plans by midnight for a joint operation involving their adjacent flanks to take advantage of the German retreat; cryptically, the requirement was not for a simple pursuit:

> The general pursuit of the enemy must not follow the routes of his withdrawal, but according to our offensive plan.[23]

It isn't clear what 'offensive plan' was to be followed, and many documents relating to the orders issued to and by the two Fronts during this period continue to be unavailable.

Major General Andrei Filiminovich Kupryanov, commander of 215th Rifle Division to which Gorbachevsky had now been transferred, was receiving a steady stream of reports from the front line that the Germans were leaving. A platoon commander later described the scene as it grew light on 3 March:

There was a certain strange silence. There wasn't a sound, either from the direction of the Germans or from our side. Gradually, soldiers began to climb out of the trenches and bunkers; these courageous individuals grew in number slowly but steadily. Then I heard someone shout: 'Fritz has run away!'[24]

During the preceding night, Stalin personally telephoned Kolpachki and urged him to move forward. In any event, Kupryanov ran out of patience with his army commander and ordered his division to move forward into Rzhev. His troops slipped through the abandoned German trenches, showing increasing caution after they triggered a few booby traps, and took possession of Rzhev on 3 March. For Kupryanov, it was a moment of personal victory. He had been offered promotion and a transfer to take command of a rifle corps in the Far East but had refused, insisting that he wished to remain in the Rzhev sector until the city was captured, and he now stood on the banks of the Volga in the centre of the ruins, surveying the remains of the city for which so much blood had been spilled. Even if Kolpachki remained cautious, Kupryanov had no doubt that the Germans were withdrawing and ordered his division to pursue energetically; as a native of Smolensk, he wanted his division to play a leading part in the liberation of his home city. Just 17 days later, he was killed in a German artillery bombardment a few miles to the south of Rzhev. His body was brought back to Rzhev where he was buried; a small monument was erected in his honour. Gorbachevsky and his comrades took part in the offensive of late summer 1943 which took them to the gates of Smolensk. For its role in the recapture of the city on 25 September, the division was given the honorific title of 'Red Banner Smolensk' division, a fitting epitaph to Kupryanov.

On 3 March, *Sovinformburo* (the information department of the USSR) issued a hugely misleading communiqué:

A few days ago, our troops began a decisive assault on the city of Rzhev. Long ago, the Germans turned the city and the approaches to it into a heavily fortified area. Today, 3 March, after a long and fierce battle, our troops captured Rzhev.[25]

The order of the day in the German Ninth Army was in some respects at least rather more accurate:

On the evening of 2 March 1943, the last German rearguards, with no pressure from the enemy, left the long-abandoned city ... The army thus surrendered the ground that had been won in fierce fighting without enemy pressure, having successfully defended it for more than a year, bloodily repulsing the massive onslaught of countless enemy units ... The fighters of Rzhev left undefeated a sector of the front whose name alone remains for them the embodiment of a soldier's trial and in future will become a watchword for military self-sacrifice.[26]

Despite the recapture of Rzhev, the Soviet pursuit remained hesitant. From Rzhev, the Wehrmacht units pulled back about three miles to the south, where they took up temporary positions along a convenient ridge until the rearguard caught up; late on 3 March, the retreat resumed. German artillery units continued to fire at the Soviet troops with considerable effect – ammunition had been prepositioned along the line of retreat, and the gunners were able to take advantage of poor radio discipline by the Red Army:

> Russian radio transmissions were monitored. In one, a Russian commander complained angrily about a large concentration of troops from various units in his village and warned that if the Germans fired on it, there would be dreadful losses. As he had given the name of the village, our entire artillery fired a coordinated bombardment.[27]

Together with continuing casualties from German mines and booby traps, such incidents further fed the Red Army's caution. A large German column was detected by aerial reconnaissance, moving south from Olenino on 3 March, and the following day Soviet troops moved into the town. A little belatedly, Purkaev ordered his armies to mount attacks with the intention of encircling and destroying German forces in Bely, but despite a few sharp local attacks, there was little coordinated effort and the German retreat continued almost unhindered.

By 5 March, the German infantry had reached Sychevka. The following day saw the first major attack by the pursuing Soviet troops. For the Germans, there was a brief shock when they saw a new weapon being used against them: *aerosani* or aerosleds, lightly armoured sleds with a large propeller mounted on the back. They were usually equipped with two machine-guns and deployed in groups of up to battalion strength, often accompanied by riflemen on skis, and their appearance near Sychevka caused some momentary consternation. Within a few minutes, the German infantry realised that they were easily disabled with machine-gun fire or by the use of light anti-tank guns, and the moment of alarm rapidly passed. The first Soviet attack was repulsed, as was a second attack on 7 March. A little to the south, Gzhatsk was taken by the southern wing of the Soviet Twenty-Ninth Army, but still there was no urgency in the Soviet pursuit.

Despite the repeated attempts to suppress partisan activity, German columns continued to report hit-and-run attacks that disrupted the withdrawal, albeit briefly. Sychevka was abandoned on 8 March, the Wehrmacht's withdrawal marked by a series of explosions as a few remaining key installations were demolished. Soviet troops cautiously moved into Sychevka the following day, and once again *Sovinformburo* announced the capture of the town as a conspicuous success for the Red Army in a communiqué with the title of *Nashi Voiska Zanyali Gorod Sychevka* ('Our army has captured the town of Sychevka'):

> On 8 March, after two days of fighting our troops broke the resistance of the enemy and took possession of the town and railway station of Sychevka (to the north of Vyazma).
>
> During the battles on the Sychevka axis and for the town of Sychevka, our troops seized the following trophies: eight aircraft, 310 tanks, 40 guns of assorted calibres, 250 machine-guns, 22 steam locomotives, 215 railway wagons and boxcars, as well as numerous shells, mines, bullets and other military equipment.
>
> The enemy lost 8,000 officers and men killed.[28]

One imagines that Model would have welcomed having 310 tanks available for his army.

Finally, on 10 March the retreating German infantry reported the first attacks by significant numbers of Soviet tanks. Several tanks were destroyed or disabled through a combination of anti-tank guns and mines.[29] The following day, there occurred perhaps the first error made by the Wehrmacht during this complex operation: a gap of over a mile appeared in the retreating line following the premature withdrawal of an infantry unit. The pursuers swiftly moved into the gap, but a determined German counterattack pushed them back. On 12 March, Vyazma was abandoned.

On the same day, the Wehrmacht opened its counteroffensive against Rokossovsky's penetration further south. The advance of II Guards Cavalry Corps and the accompanying ski infantry left the group exposed to a pincer attack, but there was a growing dissonance between the fears of front-line commanders and *Stavka*, as Rokossovsky described:

> In the hurry of getting the troops to the new area we had failed to study the terrain in advance; nor had we brought up our road and transport units and their machines together with the combat troops. The higher bodies who had planned the operation for the newly created Front had also overlooked this.

Their only thought had been of redeploying the fighting units as quickly as possible, and the result was that they had been left without roads or transport. The necessary adjustments had had to be made in the course of the concentration and actual fighting.

I reported to Stalin that in the circumstances the Front would be unable to carry out its task. Shortly afterwards the task was changed and we were ordered to strike northwards towards Orel with Twenty-First and Seventieth Armies and with Second Tank Army. The aim was to rout the enemy's Orel grouping in coordination with Bryansk Front and the left wing of Western Front. However, as things stood, this operation too held no promise of success: the enemy was considerably superior to us in strength.[30]

Rokossovsky was increasingly concerned about the exposed position of II Guards Cavalry Corps and reiterated his orders for Kryukov to adopt a defensive stance. Kryukov had already ordered a partial withdrawal to the east, with the ski battalions tasked with setting up a defensive line facing south, but 4th Panzer Division's battlegroups pushed aside the thin screen in their path without difficulty. As they advanced, the Germans encountered and largely destroyed the Soviet 3rd Guards Cavalry Division; by the end of the day, the panzer division reported that it had suffered just 13 wounded and no dead.[31] Fighting continued at a low tempo for several days; 4th Panzer Division established contact with the northern pincer, effectively completing the encirclement of II Guards Cavalry Corps, but a combination of terrain and the advent of the spring thaw made any concerted operation against the trapped cavalry almost impossible. Kryukov and his men endured some difficult days before they broke out to the east on 28 March, leaving behind most of their heavy equipment and several thousand dead. The abortive operation cost Rokossovsky's Central Front nearly 70,000 dead or wounded. German losses were estimated to be about 23,000.

The brief cold spell that had refrozen the roads in the Rzhev Salient was over by mid-March, and the landscape turned once more to mud. The stream of instructions emanating from *Stavka* show the growing frustration of senior Soviet commanders: army commanders were ordered to avoid costly frontal attacks and were instead to attempt to outflank the withdrawing German units and cut their line of retreat. Sokolovsky attempted to insert some urgency into the pursuit by ordering V Tank Corps to attack towards Yelnya, while I Tank Corps was to attempt to move past the retreating German formations and drive south, isolating the forces facing Rokossovsky's front, but neither tank corps came remotely close to fulfilling its mission. Several powerful attacks were attempted but all were repulsed by the Germans, and after losing more than 130 tanks and assault guns, the attacks were abandoned.

The German retreat ended on 22 March when the last of the rearguards reached the *Büffel* line constructed according to the instructions issued by Lindig and Meyer. The Wehrmacht units enjoyed the benefits of a withdrawal towards their depots and supply dumps, whereas the pursuing Soviet troops had to struggle with German minefields and booby traps, a devastated landscape, and the difficulties of bringing forward their supplies and artillery. There was no question of an attack against the new German line, and the exhausted rifle divisions merely came to a halt before the new German positions. To a large extent, their 'pursuit' of the retreating Wehrmacht was hampered by structural problems. The longstanding lack of attention to adequate support services for front-line troops meant that they lacked the supplies to conduct more energetic and aggressive actions. A captain in Gorbachevsky's division described the end of the operation:

> We attempted to attack, but the Germans had entrenched. We were played out. On 30 March we received an order to take up a defensive stance. Hard work on constructing defensive fortifications began. The muddy season brought all transport to a halt until 22 April. We sustained ourselves on whatever we received by air-drops. There was no tobacco and just 100–150g of sugar and 100g of flour for soup. It was a tough time.[32]

The annual punctuation of operations due to the spring thaw was now underway. The Germans might have been forced by circumstance to abandon the salient that they had defended so tenaciously throughout 1942, but they left on their own terms, and the withdrawal was almost a textbook example of how to conduct such a complex and potentially dangerous operation; morale in the units that retreated was high, with a general feeling of a difficult task accomplished satisfactorily. Remarkably, the Soviet troops that plodded in the wake of the German Ninth Army suffered substantial losses from the sudden German artillery bombardments, from encounters with mines and booby traps, and from other causes – one estimate puts the figure for Red Army casualties in this sector during March at over 138,000 killed, wounded, sick or missing.[33] The new shortened line – almost 120 miles (200km) shorter than before *Büffel* – permitted the withdrawal of three German corps headquarters and eight divisions for deployment elsewhere. In recognition of the successful defence of the Rzhev Salient and the equally successful evacuation, Model was awarded the Knight's

Cross with Oak Leaves and Crossed Swords on 3 April. For a brief period he was sent south to act as a temporary replacement for Manstein, who had been forced to return to Germany due to illness, but he then returned to his Ninth Army in mid-April and was issued orders to plan for a new summer offensive: Model was to lead the northern part of the planned strike against the Soviet-held salient around Kursk.

Others were also awarded for their roles in the recent fighting. Harpe, Hilpert and Martinek, the three corps commanders who had held the line during *Mars*, were awarded the German Cross in Gold. Hörnlein, the commander of *Grossdeutschland*, was promoted to Generalleutnant as well as receiving the German Cross in Gold; at the conclusion of the spring fighting in Ukraine, in which *Grossdeutschland* played a key part, he was awarded the Knight's Cross with Oak Leaves. Generalmajor Eduard Metz, whose 5th Panzer Division defended the northern part of the line facing Konev's assault, was awarded the Knight's Cross. Unlike the Red Army, which renamed formations as 'Guards' units in honour of their successes or added the name of a city for which they had fought with distinction, the Wehrmacht had no tradition of awarding units with name changes, but this battle was an exception. For their role in the obdurate defence against Konev's Western Front, 78th Infantry Division was renamed 78th *Sturm* ('Assault') Division. Generalleutnant Paul Völckers, the commander of the division, was awarded the Knight's Cross. Oberst Wend von Wietersheim, whose battlegroup from 1st Panzer Division stubbornly defended the southern approaches of Bely, was awarded the Knight's Cross with Oak Leaves. Hundreds of men at lower levels also received medals in recognition of their personal achievements.

For the Red Army, there was little sense of victory in the front line. Thirtieth Army was renamed Tenth Guards Army in recognition of its efforts over the preceding months, but only a single air force division received the honorific title of 'Rzhevskaya' – no ground unit received such recognition for the huge sacrifices that had been made. Zhukov was conspicuously absent from the sector during the German withdrawal. On 13 December, he sent gifts of engraved watches to Zygin, commander of Thirty-Ninth Army, and Vasily Romanovich Boyko, a member of Zygin's military council, with a note that read:

I am awarding you with watches for taking the city of Olenino and wish you further successes.[34]

At the time, Zygin had just been given new orders to reach and capture Olenino, and perhaps these gifts were intended to spur the command of Thirty-Ninth

Army on to success. Instead, the failure to advance to Olenino left these gifts as a reminder of the failed ambitions of Zhukov.

The ruthless efficiency of the German withdrawal left the Red Army occupying a desolate stretch of territory, as Gorbachevsky recalled:

> The first spring warmth melted almost all the snow, turning it into slush, which swept away the soil and the roads soon turned into swampy mud. We could barely move our legs when we tried to walk. The ground was chewed up by the explosions of bombs and shells and strewn with mines; these caused a lot of difficulties and slowed our movement further. In addition, we had to carry everything we needed – a rifle, ammunition, a duffel bag, gas mask, an entrenching tool, helmet, grenades – and some men discarded some of their equipment. It was especially difficult for the machine-gunners, anti-tank men and mortar crews. Even the horses could barely shift the stranded guns. We walked all day. When we halted, it was rare to find a dry spot …
>
> The Germans retreated quickly, leaving a desert behind them. They blew up everything they could, destroying it and turning it into ash, leaving mines everywhere: here you are, Ivan, presents for you! There were mines on the roads that we had to use and many people were blown up by them. Just between Gzhatsk and Vyazma [36 miles or 58km] 14 bridges were destroyed. We passed many wounded men, lying on the scorched earth that reeked of the smoke of conflagrations and the stench of the dead … Hearts were filled with hatred for the enemy, and increasingly men were heard to say, 'We will reach your homeland, you bastards, and we will repay you in full!' It was particularly distressing to encounter old people and women, and especially the children who gathered in the ashes of villages. When we met these victims we gave them all we had – some bread, biscuits, sugar, clothing, towels – and our cooks fed them from our field kitchens. The division marched on, leaving the victims behind and taking with us hatred for the enemy in our hearts.[35]

The scale of devastation was immense, a deliberate policy on the part of the Wehrmacht, similar to the events of the previous winter. The 'dead zone' that the Germans wished to create for the area that would fall under Soviet control was largely achieved. A Soviet report drawn up in April 1943 recorded that barely 1 per cent of the buildings in Vyazma were still intact. Over half the villages in the Sychevka area were completely destroyed, and this was largely due to deliberate arson by the retreating Germans rather than as a consequence of any combat, and the water supplies in many villages were deliberately poisoned.

As they advanced, the Soviet soldiers were met by dispossessed, bereaved civilians; their livestock had been taken from them, and many of their family members had either been taken away forcibly or shot out of hand. It is worth noting that all of this was through the action of regular army formations – there was no involvement of SS or other bodies often blamed for such behaviour.[36] Moreover, all men of military service age were removed from the 'dead zone' regardless of their wishes, on Model's explicit orders to prevent them from being conscripted into the Red Army at a later date. While some may have left willingly, there can be little doubt that many were forced to leave. Together with civilians from other parts of the Soviet Union, most were forced to work for the Germans, either building fortifications and roads or working in factories in the Reich. Few returned to their homes.

CHAPTER 15

LESSONS IMPERFECTLY LEARNED

The year 1942 saw the fortunes of war shift between the two sides facing each other across the battle lines of the Eastern Front. At the beginning of the year, the Wehrmacht was still reeling from the Soviet winter counteroffensive, but within a few weeks this crisis had passed. Overly ambitious attempts by the Red Army to continue offensive operations ended largely in failure, in some areas actually facilitating new German offensives, and during the summer it seemed as if the Wehrmacht was once more in full flood, pouring towards the Volga and the Caucasus Mountains. Autumn brought a change, with fighting in the south degenerating into a brutal slaughter in the ruins of Stalingrad; similarly, renewed attempts by the Red Army to destroy the Rzhev Salient floundered to a halt with huge losses for little or no gain. Then, as winter began, the Soviet forces launched *Uranus*, the operation that encircled the German Sixth Army in Stalingrad, and at the same time made yet another attempt to eliminate the Rzhev Salient in Operation *Mars*. *Uranus* was a great success, but *Mars* failed as badly as previous attempts.

Analysis of the failures in the central sector raises several questions. Firstly, this sector had seen major and swift advances by the Wehrmacht in late 1941, and equally swift advances by the Red Army in its winter counteroffensive, yet every attempt by the Red Army to repeat these advances in 1942 ended in huge bloodshed and failure – why was it impossible to repeat the movements of earlier months? Secondly, what lessons were learned from those failures?

Given the difficulty experienced by Kalinin and Western Fronts during 1942, the speed of the German advance through the region in 1941 seems all the more remarkable. When *Taifun* began in early October 1941, the German attack groups burst through the Red Army's defences with little or no difficulty. Led by

Reinhardt, Third Panzer Group easily overcame the Red Army's defences in two thrusts, one advancing down the road and rail corridor from Velikiye Luki to Olenino and Rzhev, the other commencing to the southwest of Bely and rapidly penetrating to the Sychevka area. The Soviet units facing the two thrusts by Third Panzer Group at the start of the offensive were, from north to south, Twenty-Ninth Army, Thirtieth Army, Nineteenth Army and Sixteenth Army. Of these, the latter two, together with three further armies, were caught in an encirclement immediately to the west of Vyazma, while the others were driven east and northeast in great disarray. The failure of the Soviet defences even to delay the German advance contributed greatly to the threat that the Wehrmacht created to Moscow, and perhaps left commanders on both sides with an impression that swift advances in this sector were not only possible but could be achieved relatively easily. There seems to have been little analysis of the manner in which the Soviet defences collapsed.

The reality was that the armies facing Reinhardt's divisions were very weak. Nineteenth Army was commanded by Lieutenant General Mikhail Fedorovich Lukin. Its divisions had been badly mauled in fighting earlier in the year, and although large replacement drafts were brought in during the autumn, the army remained weak in terms of guns and ammunition. The defences that it had been ordered to prepare were incomplete, and the Germans made skilful use of reconnaissance to direct their main attacks at particularly weak points of the line.[1] The neighbouring Sixteenth Army had been encircled in the fighting near Smolensk, and although it subsequently escaped as a result of Rokossovsky's efforts, it was so weak that it was effectively disbanded and its remaining personnel transferred to Twentieth Army. Sixteenth Army was then rebuilt with fresh, untried units; these endured a difficult baptism of fire when they were thrown into a counteroffensive against the Wehrmacht in the second week of August 1941, but although it was ordered to prepare defences in anticipation of a renewed German attack towards Moscow, these preparations were far from complete, not least because of shortages of anti-tank mines, barbed wire and other construction material. The armies facing the northern thrust by the German Third Panzer Group survived the initial battle and avoided both destruction and encirclement, but only by retreating rapidly.

The lesson to be learned from this was that rapid advances in this area occurred because one side was far stronger than the other, and perhaps more critically the defences of the weaker side were incomplete and inadequate. The same factors played a major part in the success of the Soviet winter counteroffensive, where the greatest advances were made not by frontal assaults on German positions but by taking advantage of the fact that the German lines were not configured for defence; with so much of their strength tied up in the stalled spearheads close to Moscow, there were significant gaps through which Soviet units could advance effectively unopposed. Indeed, the winter fighting showed that on almost every occasion that the Red Army attempted to make frontal attacks on even improvised German defences, the attacks failed with heavy losses.

In early 1942, Zhukov and others repeatedly tried to resume the counteroffensive that had effectively stalled by the end of 1941, with very limited success. Once again, attacks against prepared German defences almost always failed, but it was still possible to introduce mobile units through the gaps in the German line, as was the case with Belov's cavalry corps. However, the penetration through which the cavalry was deployed was too narrow and closed immediately after Belov and his men had passed through. This failure to achieve an adequate initial breach and, perhaps more importantly, to ensure that it remained open, was something that was barely recognised in the analyses after the battle.

The Red Army had experimented extensively with the use of airborne troops in the years before the war, but attempts to reproduce these exercises once the war began repeatedly failed, largely due to the unavailability of sufficient transport aircraft to deliver the paratroopers in as short a time as possible – the nature of airborne forces is that they are relatively lightly armed and therefore must make the most of surprise, and must link up with ground forces soon after their initial deployment. In an attempt to mitigate the effect of the limited airlift capacity of the Soviet Air Force, plans were made for the paratroopers to be flown from airfields immediately behind the front line, allowing aircraft to make repeated drops, but this proved to be a failure. The preparation of the airborne units in terms of briefings, orders, reconnaissance etc. was almost non-existent; the result was an operation that faced huge difficulties from the outset. Again, as was the case with the deployment of Belov's cavalry, it seems that little was learned from this mistake. When airborne forces were used at the Bukrin bridgehead over the Dnepr in 1943, almost all of the mistakes of the operations in the Rzhev Salient were repeated, once again dooming the operation to failure.

In a similar manner to the fighting of the winter of 1941–42, the German Operation *Seydlitz* to eliminate Soviet forces in the 'salient within a salient' to the northeast of Bely during the summer of 1942 was successful largely because the Soviet defences were so weak. With limited supplies, the forces of Kalinin Front made inadequate preparations to defend against German attacks that should have been anticipated, but the impression gained by both sides was that despite the terrain being very difficult for attacking forces, such attacks could achieve success.

The Soviet analysis of the failed winter attacks, and of the failure to re-energise the offensive in early 1942, correctly identified many of the shortcomings of the Red Army: the lack of initiative among officers; the poor use of tactics; the lack of cooperation between different arms; inadequate reconnaissance; and logistic weaknesses. These shortcomings applied to every level of the Red Army, from the individual infantrymen in the front line to Zhukov and other senior figures, but as is so often the case, it seems that the tendency among higher commands was to attribute all of these failures to lower levels. Even on occasions where deficiencies were correctly identified at a specific level, there is little evidence of any comprehensive or systematic analysis of what measures needed to be taken to remedy the problems in future. Consequently, it was almost inevitable that the same mistakes would be made again.

There appears to have been a large element of drawing up plans based upon the situation that seemed to be displayed on maps, with too little consideration for the reality on the ground. On the maps in *Stavka* or the headquarters of each Front, even at each army headquarters, it seemed as if matters would be straightforward. In early 1942, the Germans seemed to be on the verge of collapse and there were widespread gaps in the front line – surely, it would be possible to break up the German defences and overwhelm small units, thus creating further gaps that could be exploited. The distances that needed to be covered to achieve a spectacular success were modest – similar advances had already been achieved when the Wehrmacht was driven back from the outskirts of Moscow. A substantial drive now would result in the destruction of the German forces in the Rzhev Salient, a position that positively invited the Red Army to cut it off. Once Belov's force had been deployed and reinforced by airborne units, the maps suggested that an even shorter advance would allow ground units to link up with this large group of Soviet troops and then advance swiftly through the terrain controlled by the cavalry. But perhaps because of the appalling losses suffered by the Red Army in the opening weeks of 1942, there was little energy in the attacks by Western Front to link up with the isolated units. Plans were made repeatedly and often failed to reach implementation; on other occasions, the attacks were abandoned when an early breakthrough was not achieved. Yet in August and November, such attacks were doggedly continued in the face of huge losses and clear evidence that they were not going to succeed.

The summer offensive against the Rzhev Salient enjoyed some initial success, and the assumptions made by Zhukov and others seemed justified – despite the difficult terrain and the strength of the German lines, success could be achieved. But every attempt to exploit this ended in failure, and it proved impossible to replicate the early advance. In many cases, the Red Army showed astonishing stubbornness in throwing its resources against German defences that had already withstood repeated attacks. It seems that the lessons of the Chinese strategist and philosopher Sun Tzu were either ignored or forgotten:

> Appear at points which the enemy must hasten to defend; march swiftly to places where you are not expected.
>
> An army may march great distances without distress if it marches through country where the enemy is not.
>
> You can be sure of succeeding in your attacks if you only attack places that are undefended.[2]

Even the most rudimentary analysis should have shown that, if the German lines were intact, they were simply too strong to be overcome, and Khlebnikov's account of the repeated attempts to capture Polunino shows how division commanders seemed paralysed by the demands from higher levels to deliver results, and responded to setbacks with repetition and rigidity. It seems that the attitude of Zhukov's deputy commander at Western Front during the winter of 1941–42, Zakharov, was widespread throughout the Red Army's command structure: the task of the front-line units had been decided by higher commands, and it was the task of those units either to achieve these objectives or die in the attempt. Tens of thousands of Soviet soldiers were sacrificed in futile efforts to accomplish tasks that were simply impossible.

The fighting in the region throughout the year was significantly affected by the weather. The German operations to eliminate Belov's group and to destroy the Red Army units between Bely and Olenino were greatly handicapped by rain that made the difficult terrain almost impassable, and the Soviet summer offensive was also badly affected by the rain that turned already inadequate roads into quagmires. Although the weather was unseasonably wet, it wasn't unusual, something that can be deduced from the swampy nature of the terrain; and even if it can be argued that the rain took the Red Army by surprise, the poor road network was surely something that should have been taken into account. In the days before the Germans launched *Taifun*, partisans and aerial reconnaissance reported considerable German activity to improve roads behind their front line to ensure that, once the offensive began, they would be able to move supplies and reinforcements forward to sustain the offensive. By contrast, despite Solomatin's assertions that such measures were normal practice in mechanised units, the Red Army made few attempts to assess the road capacity that they would need, or to improve the roads that were available. Nor was there any consideration of the road network when Zhukov drew up his plans.

When the August offensive began, the Germans had been occupying their defensive positions for several months. The experience of the winter fighting was that, even if the Germans had a short time to prepare their defences, they were almost impossible to dislodge. Indeed, experiences of the First World War showed that German defensive positions survived major artillery bombardments, and subsequent attacks failed with heavy losses; the only conclusion drawn at the time was that even heavier bombardments would be needed in future, with little regard for the accuracy of the bombardment.[3] The Red Army seems to have inherited much of this doctrine, believing that it could impose its operations on the enemy with little regard for the dispositions of the enemy's defences. While there was repeated use of reconnaissance to identify key defensive positions, there seems to have been little assessment of the efficacy of this reconnaissance and no measures to improve reconnaissance in future.

To a large extent, the Red Army was still struggling to catch up with the realities of mechanised warfare, and was further hamstrung by the purges inflicted by Stalin in the preceding years. The experiences of Gorbachevsky in his baptism of fire show the clumsy tactics used by Soviet troops, and this was due to shortcomings at every level. The losses of the preceding months cost the Red Army many experienced men, and the need to shore up front-line units resulted in men being rushed through their basic training. Soldiers lacked vital tactical skills; officers, too, had little understanding of how to modify their tactics to overcome their enemies. By the standards of the Wehrmacht, there was little or no cooperation between tanks and infantry once an attack began, with both the foot soldiers and tanks continuing doggedly to pursue their set objectives, with little ability to react to events on the ground. When attacking units came across intact defences, it was difficult – often impossible – for front-line units to get fresh, targeted artillery support. In short, the ability of the Red Army to react to events on the ground was very limited. The dictum of Helmuth von Moltke, the father of the German General Staff, that no plans survive contact with the enemy ensured that the Red Army was doomed to throw itself in clumsy, costly attacks against a tough and experienced opponent. The lack of expertise and experience in the Red Army, and the need to adhere to pre-existing plans, made careful preparation and accurate reconnaissance all the more important, making it all the more regrettable that there was so little analysis of the efficacy of reconnaissance and how it might be improved in future.

The account left by Gorbachevsky of his first experience of combat demonstrates so many of the failings of the Red Army at this stage of the war. The initial artillery bombardment was visually impressive, but as soon as they advanced the Soviet riflemen realised that the German bunkers and trenches were largely intact. The rapid onset of German artillery fire showed that the bombardment had failed to suppress German heavy weapon positions, and the defensive shelling and machine-gun fire rapidly separated the infantry from their supporting tanks. Gorbachevsky and his comrades could only watch as the tanks pressed on into the German positions without infantry support – every attempt to follow them merely resulted in further slaughter, and without infantry the tanks were doomed to be picked off. All of these shortcomings were known to the Red Army after the failures earlier in the year, yet there had been no attempt to adapt training to take account of the changes that were needed. The failings were often identified and reported; but responsibility for remedying them was never discussed or agreed.

While the analysis of the failures of the first half of 1942 was in many respects incomplete, the reports that followed the failed summer offensive were remarkable for reporting almost exactly the same shortcomings. As the *Stavka* representative for the sector, Zhukov must have known that the same mistakes had been repeated, but there is little to suggest that he ordered comprehensive interventions to prevent further repetition. The changes that were made in preparation for *Mars* were incomplete – there was considerable attention to improving logistic support, but no allowances were made for the simple fact that the road network that had been inadequate in the summer was hardly going to be any better in November 1942, especially with increased logistic traffic. The Red Army merely channelled larger volumes of trucks and wagons down the same roads, which were now badly degraded as a consequence of earlier use. Far from making matters better, this merely added to congestion and provided the Germans with irresistible targets for artillery and air attacks.

After *Mars* finally floundered to a halt in a jumble of snow, bloody corpses and wrecked vehicles, there was once again an attempt by the Red Army to consider the reasons for its failure. Writing his memoirs after the war, Zhukov gave a hugely misleading account of the entire operation, and his analysis of the reasons why it failed was extraordinarily dishonest:

> When we analysed the reasons for the unsuccessful offensive by the troops of
> Western Front, we concluded that the main factor was the underestimation of the

difficulties of the terrain that was selected by the Front command to deliver the main attack.

War experience teaches that if the enemy's defence is located in terrain with good lines of vision, where there is no natural cover from artillery fire, such a defence can easily be destroyed with artillery and mortar fire and thereafter an offensive will most likely succeed. If the enemy's defence is located in poorly observed terrain, where there is good shelter on reverse slopes of hills and ridges, with ravines running parallel to the front, it is difficult to break up such a defence with artillery and then break through, especially when the use of tanks is limited.

In this particular case, the influence of the terrain on which the German defence was located, carefully concealed on reverse slopes in rough terrain, was not taken into account.

Another reason for the failure was the lack of tanks, artillery, mortars and air power to ensure a breakthrough of the enemy's defence. The Front command tried to correct all of this during the offensive, but failed to do so. The situation was complicated by the fact that contrary to our calculations, the German command significantly strengthened its troops in this area, transferring them from other fronts.[4]

Firstly, the terrain that was selected was largely imposed upon Konev, the Front commander, by Zhukov himself. It seems inconceivable that Zhukov was not aware of the difficult terrain in the area – after all, he grew up in a village in the region, and in any case he had experience of fighting here in late 1941 and early 1942. Despite this, he chose to attack in this area first in the summer offensive, then again in late November. The initial success of the summer attacks may have left him with a belief that the German positions could be overcome, but the failure to exploit those early gains owed a great deal to the difficult terrain, and to ignore this when he drew up the plans for *Mars* was a remarkable oversight. Nor did he show any recognition of the manner in which the Red Army continued to make the same tactical mistakes throughout 1942.

It wasn't merely a matter of terrain that favoured defensive fighting. The road network of the region was completely unsuitable for rapid advances, both by attacking troops and their vital support services. While some army commanders were clearly aware of the poor road network over which they would be operating, Zhukov and his Front commanders do not appear to have taken such limitations into account. As was consistently the case throughout 1942, they seem to have been fixated by the apparent proximity of objectives on their maps. To an extent, it can be argued that the multiplicity of Soviet attacks was a reflection of the poor road network and the inability to concentrate efforts in fewer sectors, but if this was the case, the lack of any major effort to improve the vital roads is all the more striking.

Nor, it seems, was sufficient consideration given to trying to prevent the Germans from becoming aware of the impending attack. Voloshin, who was Zygin's intelligence officer on the northern side of the salient, later wrote:

> The fact is that preparations for the offensive were carried out over a relatively long time. This was due to the shortages of vehicles and the poor condition of the roads. In all honesty, we must admit that not all commanders and staff officers attached sufficient importance to concealing transportation. In some cases, people simply neglected to camouflage the forces already preparing for the offensive, together with their military equipment and ammunition. And German reconnaissance planes made long flights over the location of our troops almost every day. There was nothing to drive them away, no means of destroying them. At that time, the units did not have sufficient air defence assets. Logic suggests that aerial reconnaissance provided the Fascists with extensive information.
>
> As for the specific timing of the impending offensive, it is highly likely that other sources played a role too. Our signalmen would sometimes discover 'taps' on telephone lines, which were used by the enemy to eavesdrop on conversations. Radio interception could not be ruled out either. Moreover, some commanders used almost plain language in conversations: shells might be called cucumbers, tanks might be called boxes, and so on. It is quite likely that the Nazis could easily guess such a 'cipher'.[5]

In later phases of the war, some Soviet commanders took considerable steps to improve camouflage, including personally flying over their units to see how easily they could be spotted. There was nothing new about the presence of German reconnaissance flights, yet it seems that there was little attempt to try to achieve local air superiority to deny them easy access, or to ensure that all commanders camouflaged their units properly.

The difficult terrain was bad enough, but Zhukov makes no mention of the additional problems created by the weather. An advance through the region during winter was always going to be a difficult undertaking, yet the objectives set by Zhukov for *Mars* took little account of this. Instead, it seems that he simply assumed that, because the Red Army had been able to advance quickly in the previous winter, it would be possible to repeat that achievement – after all, considerable strength had been gathered for a new assault. His inability to understand that he was about to replicate the errors of the summer and autumn offensive is remarkable.

The suggestion by Zhukov and others that there was insufficient materiel for a successful attack is misleading. In terms of artillery and tanks, the Red Army enjoyed a considerable superiority both at the beginning of the summer attack and again in November. German accounts of the Soviet artillery bombardments repeatedly describe their intensity, but the shelling simply failed to achieve its objectives, leaving most of the German defences intact. To a large extent, this was due to failures of reconnaissance. Some officers might have been enthusiastic proponents of 'reconnaissance in force' as a means of forcing the Germans into revealing the positions of their heavy weapons, but the experience of fighting around the Rzhev Salient throughout 1942 suggests that this tactic was, at best, of limited value. The Germans also used reconnaissance in force, as the US Army noted:

> The Germans stress aggressiveness, attempt to obtain superiority in the area to be reconnoitred, and strive for continuous observation of the enemy. They believe in employing reconnaissance units in force as a rule. They expect and are prepared to fight to obtain the desired information …
>
> Only enough reconnaissance troops are sent on a mission to assure superiority in the area to be reconnoitred. Reserves are kept on hand to be committed when the reconnaissance must be intensified, when the original force meets strong enemy opposition, or when the direction and area to be reconnoitred are changed. The Germans encourage aggressive action against enemy security forces. When their reconnaissance units meet superior enemy forces, they fight a delaying action while other units attempt to flank the enemy.[6]

It is important to note that German divisions had dedicated reconnaissance battalions, often equipped and trained differently from other troops. These battalions were used to operating independently and were frequently used to create ad hoc battlegroups to intercept enemy formations that had broken through, as was the case in the fighting to stop Solomatin's mechanised corps to the southeast of Bely in November. By contrast, the accounts of Gorbachevsky and others show that the Red Army assigned the task of reconnaissance in force to ordinary line battalions, which were simply ordered to attack and provoke the German defences to respond. Voloshin's description of preparatory training is not replicated by accounts of men like Gorbachevsky, suggesting that in many – perhaps most – cases the reconnaissance in force was conducted by men with little or no experience in such operations. The usefulness of these reconnaissance probes does not seem to have been assessed objectively. As the war progressed, the strength of the units deployed in such missions steadily increased, but this was in parallel with the increasing strength of all Soviet units – it doesn't seem to have been a specific response to the failures of previous reconnaissances in force.

Zhukov's comments that the Germans unexpectedly brought up reserves is also misleading. The units that intervened during *Mars* were largely from reserves held either by Ninth Army or Army Group Centre. Far from being surprised by their deployment, Zhukov and his Front commanders should have expected such reserves to be committed. The numerous channels by which the Soviet Union could gather intelligence have already been described, but it seems that on this occasion at least, either Soviet intelligence operations failed to identify the reserves held by Model and Kluge, or this information wasn't passed on to Front commanders for them to take into account in their plans. Voloshin acknowledges his failure to identify the presence of the German 14th Motorised Infantry Division, which had been in that sector since the failed German attack on Moscow, but gives no explanation for his failure.

The individual armies involved in the failed operation were also required to produce reports about the failure to deliver results. Twentieth Army's analysis after *Mars* could have been written after any of the failed attacks in 1942:

> The attacking infantry crowded together, their support weapons were often inactive; the attacking tanks, which became separated from the infantry ... would come to a halt, didn't manoeuvre on the battlefield, and didn't seek out the enemy firing points to destroy [them] ... The units had a sufficiently complete picture of the enemy's first line of defence [but] there was almost no information available about the second line of defence ... During the offensive, reconnaissance was not conducted. There was no clear notion of the enemy's troop strength. Cooperation among all the types of forces ... has been insufficiently rehearsed and organised ... There is no common language between the infantry and aviation, the infantry and tanks, or between aviation and tanks.[7]

All of these criticisms are correct, but they repeat the comments made after the failed summer and autumn offensive, and there is no attempt to analyse why the previous recognition of these failings produced no action to remedy matters. The analysis of the performance of Twentieth Army's tanks was just as accurate, and – again – almost identical to the reports after the previous failed operation:

Commanders of tank subunits didn't understand their actions with the infantry, didn't familiarise themselves with the terrain, as a result of which tanks repeatedly blew up on our own minefields ... Tank units didn't know the enemy [and] his weapons ... During combat the tanks were poorly supported by artillery fire ... The tanks often became exposed and lacked infantry support.[8]

It seems remarkable that tanks assigned to support the infantry in the initial attack were so poorly led that the commanders of platoons and companies blundered into Soviet minefields, but it would be unfair to apply the same criticism to tank units that were held back in anticipation of being used as an exploitation force. When the initial attacks failed, these units suddenly found themselves thrust into the front line to help create the breach that they were meant to exploit, and in many cases the commanders were given little or no time to familiarise themselves with the lie of the land. Furthermore, given that their role in the operation was meant to be deep penetration and exploitation, it is perhaps understandable that these tanks tended to press on into the depth of the German position instead of helping the infantry to secure the breakthrough. This, at least, led to growing recognition of the need for specific 'breakthrough' units of tanks that were equipped and trained for that particular task; the exploitation forces could then be unleashed once a breakthrough was achieved.

The performance of the assault on the Vazuza line during *Mars*, particularly the deployment of the exploitation forces, came in for severe criticism in a report produced by the Soviet General Staff in the months that followed. Once again, the failure of rifle regiments to cooperate with tanks was noted, and almost all aspects of Twentieth Army's conduct of the battle were found to fall short of what was required:

The blow on the right flank of Western Front was targeted at a narrow front. There were no powerful supporting assaults in other sectors. The offensive on the left wing of Kalinin Front also failed. All of this gave the enemy the opportunity to manoeuvre his reserves without any restrictions. There was no element of surprise because of poor camouflage discipline, and consequently the enemy knew about offensive operations before they occurred and was able to bring forward necessary reserves.

The shock group of Twentieth Army failed to penetrate the full depth of the enemy's defence because of poorly organised cooperation between infantry, artillery and aviation ... The enemy's fire system was not suppressed during the artillery bombardment. The units of Twentieth Army operated with hesitation and indecision. The offensive of Twentieth Army's cavalry-mechanised group did not get the required level of air support.

It is also important to note that the deployment of the cavalry-mechanised group into a wedge created by the infantry to a depth of 4km and on a narrow front was unwise. Attempts to deploy the cavalry-mechanised group despite incomplete penetration of the enemy defences resulted in heavy casualties. The tank corps lost about 60 per cent of its strength attempting to penetrate the enemy defences and the powerful cavalry-mechanised group was effectively exhausted in pointless attacks on the enemy's unsuppressed defences.[9]

Overt criticism of Zhukov and other senior officers was almost non-existent at the time, but many men involved in the battles were less reticent after the war when they wrote their memoirs. Solomatin blamed Tarasov for the encirclement and near-destruction of his I Mechanised Corps:

One must bear in mind that the encirclement of the corps and several rifle brigades of VI Rifle Corps need not have taken place. These forces could still have been withdrawn when the clear danger of encirclement became apparent. However, the commander of Forty-First Army clearly believed that without the instructions of the Front commander, it was important to hold the region we had secured until the resumption of offensive operations, and he relied on destroying the counterattacking enemy and once more restoring contact with the corps. In the course of offensive operations, such a decision is quite acceptable if the gain is sufficient and the command has sufficient forces and resources to break through the enemy's encirclement ring. However, in this case, the commander's plan was not fully implemented due to the significant numerical superiority of the German forces operating against Forty-First Army.[10]

Solomatin offers a critique of the failure of the Bely penetration to be developed to complete success:

Firstly, [the failure] was due to the fact that in the area of operations of Forty-First Army south of the town of Bely the enemy had large armoured reserves, and after we broke through their defences and penetrated to Bolinovo, Matrenino and Klimovo, the Hitlerites brought up fresh panzer divisions, creating a significant superiority in forces and resources against Forty-First Army.

In addition, it should be acknowledged that there were mistakes made by our side.

For example, our troops did not conduct manoeuvres where the enemy's defence was not completely overcome in a timely manner.

There were other mistakes too. One of these was that on 26 November, when I Mechanised Corps achieved significant success and began to deploy into the depths of the enemy's defences, 19th Mechanised Brigade was removed from its command, depleting its second echelon and was thrown into battle against a strong enemy point of resistance, greatly weakening the striking power of the corps.

Another mistake was that the independent mechanised brigades of Forty-First Army were used on diverging axes in an uncoordinated manner, without taking into account their proper purpose or capabilities. Had they been deployed in a timely manner for exploitation towards Matrenino and Kanyutino, then it would have been possible to overrun the metalled road from Bogolyubovo to Manyutino [i.e. the vital supply road along the Nacha valley] on a broad front. The capture of this road by our troops would have restricted the enemy in the Razdobarino and Bely areas as there were no other metalled roads in the region, and off-road movement was very difficult due to the deep snowdrifts.[11]

In addition, Solomatin was critical of the manner in which two tank brigades were sent towards the Vladimirskoye–Bely highway, where they were immediately tied down in a defensive battle against superior enemy tank formations. It would have been better, he concluded, if this task had been conducted by combined arms formations; the tank brigades would then have been free to manoeuvre against the rear of the German units concentrated in Bely. But it was the stubborn defence of Bely, which tied down so much of Forty-First Army, that ultimately doomed Tarasov's attack to failure, and Solomatin's account perhaps fails to give sufficient credit to the Germans for the tenacious resistance in the ring of shattered villages to the south of the town.

It is noteworthy that all of Solomatin's comments are directed at those above him, or at the terrain and weather. He has nothing but praise for his subordinates. As was often the case with memoirs written during the Soviet era, he repeatedly describes the heroic exploits of individuals, stressing the Komsomol credentials of many of those who fought with distinction, but he speaks highly of the performance of all his men:

In difficult and complex circumstances, the personnel of the corps passed a serious trial of combat with honour, showing cohesion, resilience, and high morale. This was of great merit to the command staff, the political workers, Communists, and

Komsomol members. The diligent officers of the corps' headquarters carried out a great deal of organisational work during combat. Colonel [Ivan Vasilevich] Dubovoy, the chief of staff, constantly demonstrated strong leadership of the troops, going to the front-line units involved in executing major combat tasks. Major Kurnosov, chief of the headquarters operational department, remained in the ranks despite being wounded twice ...

Colonel Ershov, the commander of 19th [Mechanised] Brigade, and Lieutenant Colonel Kuzmenko, commander of 35th [Mechanised] Brigade, led their troops with courage and skill. Despite being wounded, Lieutenant Colonel Gukov, chief of staff of 35th Brigade, refused to be evacuated and remained in the ranks.

Lieutenant Colonel Shanaurin, commander of 37th [Mechanised] Brigade, was always at the most difficult and dangerous areas of battle and inspired his subordinates with his personal conduct in combat. On 8 December, Lieutenant Colonel Shanaurin and Lieutenant Colonel Panfilov, his deputy for political affairs, died heroic deaths leading their men into battle. Command of the brigade passed temporarily to the chief of staff, Captain Ugriomov. He proved to be a worthy successor to his commander. Despite being wounded, Captain Ugriomov continued to lead the brigade in battle until the corps escaped the encirclement ...

Many other officers of the corps and its subdivisions showed similar dedication to military duty in the severe battle. For their courage and bravery, 600 officers and other ranks of I Mechanised Corps were awarded orders and medals of the Soviet Union ...

The troops of I Mechanised Corps gained rich and comprehensive experience during these battles. The personnel of the corps believed even more in the strength of their weapons and were increasingly convinced of our superiority over the Fascist German Army and of our ultimate victory over the enemy.[12]

Precisely the same sentiments were expressed by German commanders involved in the fighting – they too had nothing but praise for the resilience and determination of their officers and men, and were confident that their successes in the defensive fighting showed their ability to prevail. As the exhausted battlegroups of 1st Panzer Division handed over their positions to infantry units and left the sector, they received a message from Model at the headquarters of Ninth Army:

1st Panzer Division leaves the ranks of Ninth Army after playing a role in the events of almost a year of tough but glorious battle.

When the winter battles of 1941–42 reached their dramatic climax in January of this year, the division was assigned to the army and – thrown into battle at the last minute at Sychevka – was able to secure this vital location for the army in swift, powerful attacks.

In the subsequent winter battle at Rzhev [i.e. early 1942], the outstanding offensive spirit of the division made decisive contributions to the destruction of the two enemy armies that had penetrated our lines. After hard defensive fighting in the first months of the year, the division was once more in the front line, helping to destroy remnants of the enemy in the forests between Sychevka and Bely. In the encirclement battle southwest of Rzhev, 1st and 2nd Panzer Divisions worked together to close a ring of iron around the enemy. They held this line against all assaults from inside and outside until the encircled foe was destroyed.

The ordeal that the division had to endure in the great defensive battles at Rzhev and southwest of Kalinin at the key points east of Sychevka in August and south of Bely in November and December in the past year were tough and difficult ... Together with 12th Panzer Division, the division secured the vital supply road to Bely and later closed the ring of encirclement that destroyed the powerful enemy forces that had broken through.

For this outstanding effort by the officers and troops, I offer once more my thanks and particular recognition to the division and its leadership as they depart. The division will live in the annals of the army as the division which even in the most severe situation never failed. We remember with respect the men of the division who sacrificed their lives or health in these battles.[13]

Despite Solomatin's high praise for his subordinates, the inexperience of some Soviet officers, particularly those who found themselves commanding units of a type that was new to them, also contributed to the failures of the Red Army. The chief of staff of 1st Mechanised Brigade, part of Katukov's III Mechanised Corps, later wrote:

The commander of the brigade, Colonel Ivan Vasilevich Melnikov, was an infantryman and clearly underestimated the advantages that could be gained by the use of tank and mechanised forces. In addition, the brigade's chief of staff was not well organised. Control of the battle was disrupted. The brigade's tank regiment operated in isolation from the motorised rifle battalions, and the latter, without tank or artillery support, got stuck in the snow. Communication with the two battalions was lost. All of these facts had a negative influence on the corps' conduct.[14]

Some of the most perceptive criticisms of the performance of an army are made by its opponents, and the fighting around Rzhev gave further examples of this. In mid-December 1942, even before the fighting around the salient had come to an exhausted end, Ninth Army's intelligence staff produced an analysis of the Red Army's conduct of the campaign:

> After showing skill and innovation in the preparation and initial implementation of the offensive ... the enemy leadership once again demonstrated earlier weaknesses as the operation unfolded. It is clear that the enemy has learned a great deal but once more he showed himself unable to exploit critical favourable situations. There were repeated occasions of operations beginning with great intentions and local successes but then, after encountering heavy losses and unforeseen situations, degenerating into mindless, furious assaults on solid front-line positions. This incomprehensible phenomenon is seen repeatedly. Even in extreme situations, the Russians fail to behave logically – they fall back on their basic instinct and their tendency to use massed steamroller attacks, adhering to given objectives without any regard to the changed situation ...
>
> The enemy's combat reliability is generally poor. In November, half the replacement drafts were from national minorities. In many units, poor leadership and treatment have repeatedly resulted in distrust between officers and men ...
>
> Cooperation between infantry and tanks remains poor. The enemy's poor leadership of tanks is demonstrated by the manner in which after an attack fails or is repulsed, attacks are repeated at the same point after a predictable pause with no change in tactics ... Tank commanders [who have been interrogated] say that orders for company commanders to no longer lead from the front but rather to remain in observation posts to the rear results in a loss of attack momentum. It makes leadership difficult because only the company commander has a radio, and thus has no means of communicating with his forces. The attacks therefore often break down into small actions.[15]

As the Red Army slowly pursued the retreating Germans, and perhaps more importantly in the weeks that followed, Soviet personnel had their first opportunity to study the defensive positions that had defied them throughout 1942. There was considerable surprise at the strength and depth of the positions; it seems that many had not been identified, even once fighting began. As the failures of *Mars* were analysed, particularly in light of better knowledge of how German defences were prepared, the Red Army finally began to learn how to avoid such failures in future. As had been the case in the First World War, there were repeated calls for ever heavier artillery preparation before assaults, but the interaction of reconnaissance – particularly reconnaissance in force, favoured by intelligence officers like Voloshin but hated by front-line soldiers like Gorbachevsky – with the use of artillery resulted in more success in coming years. As the German attacks on the Kursk Salient faltered in the summer of 1942, the Soviet armies on the central sector launched a major attack on the positions that the Wehrmacht had constructed after its withdrawal from the Rzhev Salient. The operation – codenamed *Kutuzov* – was as bloody as some of the attacks on the Rzhev Salient, resulting in the loss of over 400,000 Soviet soldiers killed, wounded or missing, compared with German losses of about 86,000, but the city of Orel was recaptured, and for the first time since the end of the counteroffensive outside Moscow, Soviet troops on this axis succeeded in overcoming German troops defending prepared positions.[16] It was a modest degree of progress, and some of this success was due to the lessons painfully learned at the cost of the hundreds of thousands of men killed or maimed in 1942. Writing nearly 60 years after the terrible battles of 1942, a former artillery platoon commander looked back on his experiences:

The Rzhev–Sychevka Operation of 30 July to 23 August 1942 was the baptism of fire for our 52nd Rifle Division. We had attacked Rzhev head-on from the north … In five months of fighting between August and December 1942, the division lost its entire personnel *three times over* [emphasis in original] suffering casualties of up to 4–5,000 killed and up to 13,000 wounded. Through superhuman effort, we had managed to advance all of 6km [3.6 miles] to the northern outskirts of Rzhev at the cost of staggering losses. Such was the result of a five-month battle of attrition at Rzhev. But we failed to capture the city itself …

In spite of the weather and enemy resistance we continued to push forward. On the one hand, we learned to fight, and on the other hand, we no longer feared death. We had already fatefully placed our lives on the altar of victory, because our experience was telling us that the end of the war was nowhere in sight, yet all the same it was impossible to survive it. You were going to be killed anyway, sooner or later, so what was there to fear? …

Our great commanders learned how to execute their forthcoming victories at our expense. For 15 months we battled for Rzhev and accomplished almost nothing, until the Germans left it themselves. Let us assume that these were victories for the enemy, but these were also our most terrible tragedies. The war didn't develop on success alone. But the history of it should be complete and credible, no matter how bitter it was. War was this bitterness after all, so costly to many, who passed through the 'Rzhev meat grinder'. The Germans were turning the handle, and we poured and poured thousands and thousands of soldiers into it.[17]

The German units involved in the Rzhev fighting drew up their after-action reports, but the Wehrmacht had a less structured way of reviewing such reports and sharing experiences than the Red Army. These reports repeatedly highlighted the failings of the Red Army, the predictability of their attacks, and the lack of flexibility in tactics. Shortcomings of German equipment were also often described, and these points at least resulted in changes, but the overall impression is that the Wehrmacht was satisfied with its performance. Nonetheless, the battles around the Rzhev Salient cost it substantial casualties. The Red Army's losses might have been greater, and by defending their positions the Germans had avoided a disastrous encirclement of their forces in the central sector, but many felt that if the battles of 1942 were German successes, they represented something of a Pyrrhic victory. The loss of so many experienced soldiers of all ranks could not be replaced, particularly given the destruction of Sixth Army at Stalingrad. To a large extent, the German successes were achieved because of the tactical superiority of German soldiers and units in the front line; the loss of these experienced men, at a time when the Red Army was slowly and painfully learning how to fight a modern war, tilted the balance further against Germany.

There is another possible narrative for the battles and their legacy. In 1941, the Wehrmacht came close to capturing Moscow, though had it succeeded, its ability to hold the city is questionable. Nonetheless, it was in many senses superior to its opponent, and the Red Army rapidly discovered that even if the Germans hadn't been strong enough to win the war in 1941, they were easily strong enough to avoid defeat in the months that followed. The terrible attrition and slaughter that characterised much of 1942 – outside Leningrad, around the Rzhev Salient, and ultimately in Stalingrad – can be seen as an essential part of wearing down the Wehrmacht to the point where the Red Army could prevail against it. It would be a step too far to suggest that this attrition was a deliberate Soviet policy, but in retrospect it was an almost inevitable part of the war. Faced with a life-or-death struggle, the Soviet Union had no option but to use its two great assets, space and manpower, and when the pace of German advances came close to exhausting the first, the second became even more crucial in what was ultimately a struggle for existence. But to draw such conclusions publicly after the war would have been to admit both the scale of the slaughter and the tactical futility of the sacrifice.

One of the consequences of the fighting was that Model's reputation as a master of defensive warfare was greatly strengthened. As the war increasingly turned against Germany, Hitler relied on this reputation and dispatched Model to take command of sectors where the Wehrmacht was in retreat. Given what he had achieved in the Rzhev Salient, he could surely repeat this on battlefields. This reputation as a defensive genius deserves further analysis.

Model took command of Ninth Army at a moment of crisis and oversaw the restoration of the front line. His personal strength of character undoubtedly helped bolster the resolve of his subordinates, and that is of course a vital role for an army commander. His innovative use of an ad hoc cavalry group during *Seydlitz* contributed considerably to the success of the German operation, and he is often credited with organising the defences that proved so obdurate through 1942; the use of local reserves in aggressive counterattacks is also a tactic for which Model has been praised. Further analysis of the German defensive fighting around Rzhev suggests that – with the exception of the improvised cavalry group – none of these factors were innovations created by Model. Local counterattacks to recover lost positions were a long-established part of German doctrine, and this automatically required the availability of local reserves. The increasing fragility of German infantry as the war progressed was at least in part due to the requirement imposed upon the units to defend ever larger sections of front line; in combination with irreplaceable casualties, this meant that it was almost impossible to hold back adequate reserves both to shore up the defences and to mount counterattacks. The development of tactics during the year to deal with Red Army attacks – the infantry would allow Soviet armour to move past them and in combination with German artillery would separate accompanying infantry, leaving the tanks to be dealt with by a deeper line of defence – owed little to Model's personal intervention. It is arguable that Model's reputation benefited greatly from his assignment to a defensive sector where the existing doctrine of the Wehrmacht, in combination with the terrain, provided a very favourable combination of circumstances, particularly when combined with local innovations that would have occurred regardless of who was in command of Ninth Army.

The legacy of this was a further strengthening of Hitler's belief, first seen in the winter of 1941–42, that strength of will was as important a factor as numerical strength, firepower and terrain. Throughout 1944, Model was dispatched from one sector of the front line to another, where it seemed as if the Wehrmacht was in full retreat; often, his arrival coincided with the Red Army reaching the end of its logistic leash, resulting in an inevitable pause in Soviet attacks, but Model was often credited with bringing the Red Army's advance to a halt. Then, a new crisis would arise elsewhere and Model would move on, with the consequence that he was rarely in command of a sector when it first came under attack. It is an example of how the Germans as well as their Soviet opponents often learned lessons imperfectly.

Nonetheless, Model's reputation was firmly established. He continued to command Ninth Army through 1943; the following January, when the Wehrmacht seemed to be retreating precipitately from the outskirts of Leningrad, he was dispatched by Hitler to take command of Army Group North. When he arrived, the Red Army had reached the frontier with Estonia along the Narva River and was caught in an increasingly costly and futile series of attempts to force its way across the river; the Soviet forces were heavily disadvantaged by their supply lines running across an area devastated by the retreating Wehrmacht, and as had been the case in the Rzhev Salient, the terrain was favourable for defensive operations. Nonetheless, Model was credited with stopping the Red Army's offensive. When Hitler dismissed Manstein from command in the southern sector, Model was assigned as his replacement at the newly created Army Group North Ukraine. Once more, his arrival coincided with the rolling Soviet offensive that had driven the Germans back to and across the Dniester, running out of steam, but again he seemed to be the man who was able to halt the retreat. In the summer of 1944, the Red Army launched Operation *Bagration*, the great offensive that tore apart Army Group Centre. Kluge had been replaced as commander of the army group by Field Marshal Ernst Busch, who was dismissed, and Model took command. Ultimately, the Soviet offensive was brought to a halt to the east of Warsaw, through a mixture of skilful counterattacks and the Red Army's exhaustion; but again, Hitler credited Model with stopping the Soviet onslaught and awarded him the Diamonds to the Knight's Cross.

Kluge, Model's former superior, was by then supreme commander in the west, having replaced Field Marshal Gerd von Rundstedt in early July. He was involved at least peripherally in the July Plot to kill Hitler, and on 15 August, after the failure of the plot, Hitler was alarmed when it proved impossible to contact Kluge by radio. By this stage, the investigations into the plot had revealed Kluge's possible involvement, and Hitler feared that Kluge was attempting to negotiate a surrender of his forces to the Western Allies – Udo Esche, Kluge's son-in-law, later claimed that this was in fact the case and that Kluge was thwarted only because he couldn't make contact with the Americans. That evening, when Kluge returned to his headquarters, he was dismissed by Hitler and ordered back to Berlin. Fearing that his involvement in the plot had been revealed, Kluge took cyanide (provided for him by Esche).[18]

Model was now sent to take command of Kluge's forces, and it seems that even his self-belief was shaken by the general chaos that he found. His panzer divisions had fewer than a dozen tanks each and the infantry divisions were badly worn down, unable to cope with the constant attacks of their more mobile and powerfully armed opponents. He sent an assessment to Hitler that the front could only be restored if he was provided with at least 30 infantry divisions and 12 panzer divisions as reinforcements; given that he had commanded almost every army group on the Eastern Front in the preceding months, he knew from personal experience that such reinforcements were unavailable, and in early September he informed Hitler that what he described as an unequal struggle could not be sustained. He knew that those around Hitler often withheld reports that they suspected the Führer would find unpalatable, and he took to adding a sentence to many of his reports: 'For submission to the Führer in the original.'[19]

Model managed to restore some semblance of order to his shattered Army Group B as it pulled back into Belgium and the Netherlands, and was involved in organising the defence against the attempt by Allied airborne forces to secure sufficient bridges to achieve a bridgehead across the Rhine at Arnhem. As had been the case during *Mars* in late 1942, he had Bittrich as a subordinate; this time, the SS officer was in command of II SS Panzer Corps. The two men disagreed strongly when British ground forces managed to advance as far as Nijmegen; Bittrich wanted to destroy the bridge over the Waal River, but Model remained true to his previous policy and wanted the bridge intact so that he could mount a counterattack to drive back the British units. This insistence nearly ended in disaster when US troops managed to capture the bridge intact, permitting British tanks to cross and move closer to Arnhem. He had overall command of the failed German offensive in the Ardennes in December 1944, an operation that he believed from the outset was doomed to failure. His Army Group B was encircled in the Ruhr in late March 1945 and split in two a fortnight later. Model refused to implement Hitler's orders to destroy all German infrastructure but couldn't bring himself to order his men to surrender. By now, he was aware that the Soviet Union intended to charge him with numerous war crimes, particularly the use of forced labour to help the Germans construct defences and roads. He was also charged with the deaths of over half a million Latvians in concentration camps, though these killings, undertaken by the SS, may have been unknown to Model at the time. He issued orders that he was disbanding his army group, leaving the decision to surrender or fight on to the commanders of its various units, and shot himself on 21 April 1945.[20]

The German officers who deserved the most credit for the defence of the Rzhev Salient were those below Model in the command chain. Hilpert, Harpe, Martinek and Fretter-Pico, the corps commanders who shuffled their modest resources to hold back the Red Army, were all recognised for their skilful leadership. Hilpert was assigned to command several different corps in the following months. In the summer of 1944, he was commander of I Corps and succeeded in extracting it from near-encirclement to the north of Polotsk, for which he was awarded the Oak Leaves to the Knight's Cross. He took command of Sixteenth Army in September 1944; this force was isolated in the Courland Peninsula with Eighteenth Army, and in March 1945 the combined armies were designated 'Army Group Courland' under Hilpert's overall control. He surrendered to the Red Army at the end of the war and was charged with war crimes. He was sentenced to death and executed in February 1947.[21]

Harpe became commander of Ninth Army in late 1943 and was then assigned to command of Fourth Panzer Army in northern Ukraine in May 1944. His former army commander, Model, was now once more his superior, and when Model was transferred to Army Group Centre, Harpe became commander of Army Group North Ukraine and then Army Group A. The defeats suffered by the Wehrmacht in the closing months of 1944 led to him being dismissed, but in March 1945 he was assigned to command of Fifth Panzer Army in the west; he surrendered to American forces in April.

Martinek remained in command of XXXIX Panzer Corps, leading it through a series of battles in 1943 and 1944. He was killed in late June 1944 when he was caught in a Soviet air raid near his headquarters.

Fretter-Pico and his headquarters were dispatched to the huge crisis in the southern sector even before the counterattacks near Bely were completed; Fretter-Pico took command of an eponymous 'army detachment' made up of units that had been badly mauled by the Red Army or had been improvised from rear area units and used them to help restore the front line. This group of soldiers was then redesignated XXX Corps in February 1943. In the summer of 1944, he took command of Sixth Army on the Romanian frontier, where it was almost destroyed in the Soviet offensive in August 1944.[22] Thereafter, in addition to Sixth Army, he commanded the neighbouring Hungarian Third Army as 'Army Group Fretter-Pico'. He ended the war as commander of a military district in Germany.

The fates of many of the commanders on the Soviet side during the fighting around the Rzhev Salient have already been described. There can be little doubt that Zhukov was personally responsible for many of the disasters suffered by the Red Army during the fighting, but Stalin chose not to censure him. The reasons for this are debatable. Zhukov had repeatedly demonstrated his ability to fight with great – sometimes ruthless – determination and, the setbacks around the Rzhev Salient notwithstanding, he was clearly capable of handling the command of large groups of subordinate units. Stalin probably recognised in Zhukov a man who could lead the Red Army to future victories, and in any event the days of summary dismissal and punishment were over: the Soviet Union would have to fight the war with the leadership resources that it had. Zhukov remained in favour and was permitted to take much of the credit for the Red Army's huge success at Stalingrad; the reticent Vasilevsky characteristically accepted the diminution of his personal credit for the operation without a murmur of complaint.

CHAPTER 16

REMEMBERING THE PAST

The repeated futile attacks on the Rzhev Salient can be seen in many respects as a manifestation of an obsession on the part of the Soviet leadership to destroy a threat to Moscow. As 1942 unfolded, Zhukov made two major attempts to eliminate the salient in addition to the counteroffensive that opened the year, but the obsession extended beyond him – Stalin, too, must have shared Zhukov's desire to retake Rzhev, or he would not have agreed to repeated assaults. However, a narrative based upon obsessive attacks against the salient is far from the manner in which the battles have been portrayed in the years that have followed. This raises questions about the original intentions of the operations, their actual consequences, and the manner in which the events of 1942 were remembered.

Soviet historiography repeatedly described Operation *Mars* as a deliberate attempt to tie down German troops that could be deployed elsewhere, particularly in the critical Stalingrad sector. The earlier attempts to reduce or cut off the salient were largely downplayed or ignored entirely. This narrative often portrayed *Mars* as a 'deception', which successfully prevented the Wehrmacht from dispatching significant forces to the south. Indeed, the transfer of *Grossdeutschland* from the southern sector to the salient prior to *Mars* has been used not only to justify this argument, but to extend it further: *Mars* forced the Germans to transfer troops from elsewhere, thus helping to create the weaknesses that were exploited so devastatingly during *Uranus*.

Most of the senior figures in the Red Army who survived to write their memoirs, such as Zhukov and Konev, have left incomplete and in many cases misleading accounts of the events of 1942 around the Rzhev Salient. Zhukov barely mentions the August offensive, and his account of the timing of decisions about carrying out *Mars* is manifestly incorrect. The only reason that can be offered for this is that he wished to downplay his personal involvement in planning such a costly and unsuccessful operation. He acknowledges the failure of the operation to penetrate the German lines, but implies strongly that its true purpose – to prevent the transfer of German forces to other sectors – was achieved, and that the operation therefore was a success. How much justification is there for such a point of view?

Writing in 2003, Makhmut Akhmetovich Gareev, a veteran of the Second World War who rose to the rank of general, asserted strongly that *Uranus* and *Mars* should not be considered as entirely independent strategic operations; rather, they should be seen as part of a single overall strategic vision. He wrote:

> In the fall of 1942, taking into account the experience of previous campaigns in the first period of the war, *Stavka* abandoned the simultaneous conduct of large offensive operations on several different strategic axes. The State Defence Committee and *Stavka* recognised that it was necessary 'to consider the upcoming operation in the Stalingrad region as the main event until the end of 1942 on the entire Soviet–German front, focusing on it the main attention and efforts of the Party, government and the entire Soviet people.'
>
> The plan of *Stavka* was 'first to crush the enemy grouping in the region between the Volga and Don Rivers, and then to strike in the northern Caucasus, the upper Don, near Leningrad, at Velikiye Luki, at Rzhev, and at Vyazma.'
>
> The main goal of the operation in the region of the Rzhev–Vyazma Salient was, therefore, to prevent the transfer of reserves from the [German] Army Group Centre to the southern axis, and if possible to attract additional enemy forces into the area and thereby ensure the success of the Stalingrad operation.[1]

This is a re-articulation of the conventional view that was promulgated after the war, but it provides several key points for discussion.

A persuasive case can be made that the policy of the previous winter, in which individual Fronts were given permission to organise local counteroffensives, almost always with poor results, had been formally abandoned by the second half of 1942. Prior to this, the overall strategic drive was to put pressure upon the entire Eastern Front in the confident expectation that, after being defeated before Moscow, the Wehrmacht was close to breaking point and would collapse at one point or another; such a local collapse could then be exploited to bring about the decisive defeat of Germany. This approach was further enhanced by a number of factors. In the north, the lifting of the siege of Leningrad seemed to be an urgent need; in the centre, the Germans remained worryingly close to Moscow; and in the south, the presence of Timoshenko, an old comrade of Stalin, led to a desire on the part of the former to mount an eye-catching successful operation against the German forces near Kharkov.

The new strategy was for tighter central control, with awareness that individual Fronts would probably lack the strength to achieve a decisive success on their own. Rather, they would have to work in cooperation with neighbouring Fronts. The equivalence of forces is worth considering. Until mid-1943, it was reasonable to assess the combat strength of Wehrmacht units as being the equivalent of Red Army units of a higher level: thus, a German regiment was equivalent to a Soviet division; a German division was equivalent to a Soviet corps; a German corps was equivalent to a Soviet army; and a German army was equivalent to a Soviet Front. It should also be noted that, partly due to the catastrophic losses of officers in 1941, the Red Army briefly dispensed with the use of corps headquarters during 1942, with divisions directly controlled by army headquarters. With all operations now requiring *Stavka* approval, the intention was to ensure that future assaults would involve the use of more than one Front in order to overwhelm the German forces opposing them. Therefore, the combined forces of two or more Fronts could be directed at a single German army, creating sufficient local superiority for success.

This new policy can be seen to have been in place during the renewed Soviet attacks of August 1942, when Kalinin Front and Western Fronts combined their resources to attack the Rzhev Salient from the north and east. However, this offensive failed to put any pressure on the western side of the salient. Had it done so, the Germans would surely have been forced to divert resources from the bitter fighting elsewhere. It is arguable that the Red Army lacked the resources for such attacks, but the manner in which troops were repeatedly thrown into the meat grinder around Rzhev and the Sychevka sector suggests that at least some of these units might have been used profitably to attack in other sectors. But during the attacks of August and September, it seems that the Red Army still believed that, just as it had advanced quickly during the winter counteroffensive of December 1941, it would be able to push aside the German defences and strike deep into the salient from the north and east.

There can be little doubt that the operations of November and December 1942 against the Rzhev Salient and the German Sixth Army in Stalingrad were intended to take place in parallel. A similar strategy had been adopted on a larger scale in the First World War, when the Entente Powers agreed to launch major attacks on the Germans on all fronts in order to prevent the German Army from transferring troops from one sector to another, and in the expectation that by stretching German resources to breaking point, a breakthrough would be achieved by at least one of the attacks. This raises a possibility that *Uranus* and *Mars* may have been launched in the hope that one or other would open the way for a decisive victory, and would then be declared the 'main axis'. When *Mars* failed and *Uranus* succeeded, this is perhaps what happened: Stalin, Zhukov and Vasilevsky concluded that the remaining reserves were to be committed in the southern sector to maximise the victory that had been achieved. Had *Mars* succeeded in breaking into the depths of the salient, resulting in the encirclement of much of Model's Ninth Army in Rzhev, the deployment of reserves in this area would have led to *Jupiter*, the drive to and beyond Vyazma and Smolensk, perhaps necessitating the abandonment of plans for *Saturn*.

But this is not the narrative that Soviet historiography followed, nor is it what is described in the memoirs of senior officers who took part in these operations. The manner in which the Soviet Union chose to remember and commemorate the Great Patriotic War imposed limits on how events could be interpreted, and the details of this are worth consideration.

Almost as soon as the war was over, there was a deliberate policy of portraying the war in a manner that was different from the accounts that were emerging in the West. While other nations might see their wartime exploits as being part of a long history of military endeavours, such an approach was problematic for the Soviet Union. Prior to 1917, Russian armies might have been successful in historic wars – in particular in defeating Napoleon's invasion of Russia in 1812 – but any attempt to link recent Soviet successes to this past raised two problems. Firstly, the armies of Russia in the past had been acting on behalf of the tsars, and were undeniably part of an imperialistic past that was anathema to Soviet thinking. Secondly, the Soviet leadership was concerned that drawing such links with Russian military history risked alienating the large non-Russian populations of the Soviet Union.

Moreover, Stalin and other senior Soviet leaders saw an opportunity to use the recent past to highlight the uniqueness of the Soviet state. The victory over Nazi Germany was due to the special qualities brought out by the Soviet system, and would not have been possible without this system and in particular the leadership of the Communist Party. The Soviet Union was born out of the 1917 Revolution, but it was tested and tempered in the fire of the Great Patriotic War. This narrative required the portrayal of the Soviet leadership to be entirely positive and sought to stress the importance of pan-Soviet cooperation and unity. A letter written by senior officials in the Communist Party about political work in Belarus in 1945, for example, called for the publication of articles in local newspapers to promote 'the role of the Soviet state and the Party of Lenin and Stalin during the Great Patriotic War'.[2] As part of this narrative, it was important to bolster the confidence of the Soviet people in their leadership. Even the terrible purges of the 1930s and the deliberate starvation of parts of Ukraine had to be interpreted in this light; a document drawn up in May 1945 by Georgy Fyodorovich Aleksandrov, head of Agitprop (the Soviet Department of Agitation and Propaganda), stressed this:

> [Party workers should] every day explain to the working people … [that prior to the war,] the Central Committee of the Communist Party of the Soviet Union and Comrade Stalin warned that the coming war will be severe, prolonged and bloody, and stressed the need in this context to prepare all peoples of the country for the upcoming war.[3]

If the events of the 1930s could be justified in order to show Stalin's foresight, it was unthinkable to acknowledge that any of the battles of the war itself had failed because of Stalin.

As western historians began to write about the conflict, there was concern and anger in Soviet circles about the influence of Germans in helping to shape the western narrative, which stressed the importance of the vastness of the Soviet Union, the terrible weather, the poor roads, and the indiscriminate use of manpower to bludgeon the Germans into defeat, and gave little or no credit to the Red Army or the Soviet people. Franz Halder, who was chief of the German General Staff for much of 1942, successfully escaped prosecution in the post-war trials of suspected criminals even though there was ample evidence that he had helped draw up many of the controversial orders issued to the Wehrmacht before the invasion, particularly those relating to the treatment of suspected commissars. When this information came to light, he was cooperating with the US Army's Center of Military History, and the US government refused to support his prosecution. He and other senior Wehrmacht figures – sometimes referred to as the 'Halder Group' – helped draw up a narrative that to some extent persists to this day, in which the technically and tactically superior Wehrmacht fought a clean war and was not involved in atrocities, but was defeated through a combination of Hitler's errors and the numberless Soviet hordes.[4]

The Soviet Union rejected this entire narrative and sought to oppose it for several reasons. Firstly, the narrative was manifestly incorrect, and almost every aspect of it has been unpicked in recent years: far from being 'clean', many – perhaps most – major units in the German Army were involved in atrocities in the Soviet Union and elsewhere; while Hitler's errors contributed considerably to the German defeat, such an argument ignores the manner in which the Red Army's pressure often forced those errors; and ultimately, the Soviet war machine evolved from a clumsy blunt instrument into a force capable of defeating its opponent. Furthermore, with the development of the Cold War, it was inevitable that the Soviet Union would reject a less than complimentary narrative from its new opponents, just as the West largely ignored the Soviet narrative of the war. But from an ideological point of view, the biggest problem for the Soviet Union with the historiography of the West was that it failed to recognise what was a self-evident fact for the Soviet leadership: that their victory was unique, possible only due to the superiority of the Soviet system and the leadership of Stalin and the Communist Party.

After the death of Stalin and the gradual reappraisal of his 'personality cult', the narrative of flawless Communist Party leadership during the war was so well established that it was almost impossible to question it. In his landmark speech to the Twentieth Congress of the Communist Party of the Soviet Union in 1956, Nikita Sergeyevich Khrushchev denounced Stalin and his record, and offered a modified explanation for Soviet victory:

> Not Stalin, but the Party as a whole, the Soviet government, our heroic army, its talented generals and valiant warriors, the whole Soviet people – that's who ensured victory in the Great Patriotic War.[5]

Even with Stalin no longer regarded as infallible, his role in the Second World War remained almost above challenge; in any case, if success in the war was now being attributed to the entire Soviet people, it was equally impossible to regard them as being at fault.

Writing at various phases of this period, the Soviet generals who fought in the battles around the Rzhev Salient were bound by the requirement to adhere to the orthodox point of view that rapidly developed, which was without question that *Mars* had always been intended to be a diversion, designed to tie down German reserves. Gareev's account – and the accounts written in the years of Soviet rule after the war – suggest that, from the outset, the intention was always to concentrate first on the Stalingrad encirclement, and then to widen operations. The extract from Gareev's publication detailed previously contains a degree of contradiction – if *Stavka* had genuinely abandoned independent operations on different strategic axes, is it entirely consistent to suggest that the overall plan following success at Stalingrad was to mount operations along the entire Eastern

Front, from the Caucasus to Leningrad? This would immediately create the same dilution of strength that doomed the counteroffensives of the previous winter to failure. Such wide-scale offensive operations could only be regarded as appropriate if German forces had suffered so catastrophic a defeat that their entire front line was about to collapse.

Nor does the positioning of combat units necessarily reflect the strategy described by Gareev and others. If *Uranus* and the Stalingrad sector were the main priorities, the retention of Second Guards Army and Third Tank Army in the Moscow area seems anomalous. The success of the 'main event' in the south should surely have been supported by positioning these powerful units in readiness for their deployment as *Uranus* unfolded, and both armies were in fact deployed in the south. Their presence in the central sector suggests as a minimum that even before *Uranus* was started, Stalin wished to hold back substantial reserves to commence major operations elsewhere.

In the rest of his article, Gareev made further comments that are open to challenge:

> It must be acknowledged, of course, that there were serious omissions and errors in the preparation and conduct of Operation *Mars* ... Ammunition stocks were low; reconnaissance was not always effective. Because of this, infantry and tanks were forced to break through heavily fortified and insufficiently suppressed enemy defensive positions. They had to operate on very unfavourable terrain, which greatly favoured defensive fighting. *Stavka* and the Front commanders demanded that the troops make continuous attacks in order to pin down the enemy and keep him under constant pressure, not giving him the time and opportunity to prepare thoroughly for a new offensive. All of this led to heavy human losses.[6]

It is difficult to reconcile this with the accounts of Khlebnikov and others, none of whom make any mention of ammunition being in short supply, though moving ammunition and artillery posed great problems. There is no doubt that the terrain was highly unfavourable for an offensive operation in this sector, which begs the question: if the intention was to tie down German forces, surely a sector more favourable for offensive operations might have been selected, where the attackers would at least have some chance of success? German units were indeed tied down in the fighting, but had Kluge's Army Group Centre come under attack elsewhere, it would have been forced to send those same reserves to counter the Soviet attack. In short, the choice of the Rzhev Salient for a winter offensive, regardless of whether it was intended as a serious attempt to defeat the

Wehrmacht or was purely intended to tie down German forces, was a bad decision, particularly as previous Soviet offensive operations in this precise sector had already failed. The difficulties caused by the terrain and lack of adequate roads were already well known. To throw troops into a new operation was almost certain to result in the same outcome as before: heavy casualties for no significant gain of ground.

An attack on more favourable terrain – for example, to the south, where Rokossovsky ultimately attacked with his ill-prepared Central Front – would have encountered fewer natural obstacles. Such an operation would, just like the winter attack on the Rzhev Salient, have required the Germans to commit reserves to prevent a Soviet breakthrough, thus preventing those units from being deployed in the Stalingrad sector. Instead, Zhukov selected Rzhev. This strongly suggests that he remained determined to destroy the salient at all costs – for him, this was not merely an attack to tie down German reserves. Much as Hitler became obsessed with the physical capture of the city that bore Stalin's name, Zhukov and perhaps Stalin were determined to eliminate the German salient to the west of Moscow.

The comment that the operation was intended to keep the Germans under pressure and prevent them preparing for a new offensive is curious. There is nothing to suggest that the Wehrmacht planned any new offensive in late 1942, and although the Germans had mounted *Kremlin* in an attempt to persuade the Soviet leadership that their main effort would be against Moscow rather than in the south, the events of the second half of 1942 should have made clear to Stalin and Zhukov that this had been a deception on the part of the Germans.

Gareev continued:

> It should be borne in mind that since *Stavka* saw its main task as leading the operation in the Stalingrad sector, this was the main focus of attention for Deputy Supreme Commander Zhukov. Suffice to say that both during the defensive battles [in Stalingrad] and during the preparation of the counteroffensive, he worked with the troops of Southwest and Don Fronts until mid-November 1942. During the Stalingrad counteroffensive operation, Zhukov participated in the development of the decision of *Stavka* to defeat Field Marshal Manstein's army group, which was trying to relieve the Nazi troops of Generaloberst Paulus who were encircled in Stalingrad …
>
> Despite certain miscalculations, Zhukov essentially fulfilled his task of coordinating the actions of the fronts on the western direction [i.e. Kalinin and Western Fronts].[7]

Much of this is manifestly false. Zhukov spent a great deal of time in the central sector in the weeks before the onset of *Mars* and *Uranus*, with Vasilevsky largely overseeing operations in the south.

There is the odd matter of the manner in which details of *Mars* were revealed to the Germans. Using 'Max' as a conduit, the Soviet intelligence services warned the Germans that the main effort of the Red Army in November 1942 would be in the central sector rather than the south. Gareev asserts that Zhukov was unaware of this, which raises a possibility that at some level, there was a deliberate attempt to make the Germans aware of the impending attack purely to tie down reserves, exactly as Soviet historiography described. If this was the case, then *Mars* was indeed a huge deception, but among those deceived was Zhukov, and the deception was carried out in such a manner that it ensured the deaths of tens of thousands of Soviet soldiers. It is difficult to imagine that such a decision could have been made by anyone other than Stalin. There is no direct documentary evidence that Stalin ever ordered such a deception.

There is further evidence that for Zhukov at least, this was not primarily a deception. In January and February 1943, when Model and Kluge were beginning their planning for an evacuation of the salient, Zhukov was proposing further attacks in the central sector. He argued repeatedly that the German divisions in the salient were badly weakened by the winter fighting, and a renewed offensive would succeed where previous attacks had failed. This was surely wishful thinking – the terrain would be precisely the same ground where previous offensives had failed so badly, and despite their losses, the Germans remained in their fortified positions. Ultimately, Zhukov's desire for a new offensive led to Rokossovsky's operation, but there was surely no prospect of any renewed offensive against the Rzhev Salient succeeding. The episode merely shows Zhukov's continuing obsession with an objective that had defied him on several occasions.[8]

Mars was therefore either part of a plan to deceive the Germans into believing that the main effort of the Red Army would be made here, on the Moscow axis, or it was an attempt to inflict a defeat on the Germans of the same scale as the fighting in the Stalingrad sector. While either case can be put forward, there is less doubt about the outcome of the fighting. *Grossdeutschland* spent much of 1942 in the southern sector but was transferred to the Rzhev Salient shortly before the onset of *Mars*; had this powerful division still been in the southern sector, it would have made the encirclement of Stalingrad and the operations that followed far more difficult to achieve. The intensity of the fighting around the salient during the winter tied down 1st, 2nd, 5th, 9th, 12th and 20th Panzer Divisions for at least part of the critical period that the Red Army secured its huge victory in the south, and the transfer of one or more of these divisions to the southern sector would undoubtedly have been of great benefit to the Wehrmacht.

Furthermore, the losses that Ninth Army suffered during *Mars* had serious consequences. As fighting died down in the spring muddy season of 1943, thoughts turned to the coming summer. Hitler had already decided that he would launch *Zitadelle*, an offensive against the great bulge that the Red Army seized around Kursk, and Model's Ninth Army was to lead the assault against the northern side of the bulge – indeed, the evacuation of the Rzhev Salient was at least in part intended to release sufficient forces for such an operation, and this was one of the reasons why Hitler was persuaded to permit the withdrawal. But after suffering such heavy losses, Model's divisions were in no state to mount an offensive as the ground began to dry out in May. The need to improve the strength of these divisions was a major reason for the repeated delays in commencing *Zitadelle*. These delays allowed the Red Army to build up its strength in anticipation of the German attack, and undoubtedly contributed to the final failure of the operation.

The generals wrote their memoirs, turning a blind eye to events that didn't suit their narratives and further reinforcing the official view of the war, but it was left to the ordinary soldiers on both sides who fought in the front line to remember the terrible price that was paid by their comrades. Gorbachevsky looked back on what he and his fellow Red Army soldiers endured:

The battles in the Rzhev–Vyazma sector lasted for 502 days. According to many historians, these battles were the most brutal and bloody in the history of the Great Patriotic War. The losses in the battles for Rzhev, for example, were twice as large as those at Stalingrad. Each reclaimed kilometre of our soil cost about 10,000 lives. No battle in the history of mankind has known such huge losses.

This tragedy consisted not only of unparalleled casualties, but also in the fact that all of these offensive battles failed to bring success. Death and unthinkable suffering were not rewarded with the joy of victory in battle, but caused bitter despair and unbearable resentment ...

In the Rzhev region there are 42 mass graves, in which lie the remains of soldiers from more than 140 rifle divisions, 50 independent rifle brigades and 50 tank brigades. And how many more have never been formally buried! ...

How many people died near Rzhev, Vyazma, Sychevka, Bely, and Polunino? 'We have not seen this anywhere else and will never see it again' – so say front-line soldiers who miraculously got out alive from that inhuman massacre, remembering the battles near Rzhev in which more than 3 million men took part. During the battles near Rzhev, 215th Rifle Division, which entered the battle in August 1942 with a strength of 14,000, lost between 7,000 and 8,000 men, mainly young recruits ...

Rzhev became a bloody meat grinder not just for the Soviet troops, but also for the Germans ... More than 72 per cent of all German casualties in the Second World War [were on the Eastern Front]. Many of their units were 'gutted' near Rzhev.[9]

Regardless of the true purpose of *Mars*, or the culpability of Zhukov and others in the mindless mass attacks against tough German defences, there was a need to remember the dead and to make sense of their sacrifice that was not addressed for many years. It is understandable that many found it impossible to regard such huge casualty figures as futile. This undoubtedly helped shape the manner in which the terrible battles were remembered, emphasising their contribution to the decisive victory in the Stalingrad sector, whether this had ever been the true intention of the assaults.

After the war, monuments appeared in many Soviet cities to commemorate the fighting that had taken place, and to remind people of the great sacrifices made to defeat the Germans, but it is noteworthy that in the first decade after the war, more memorials were built in the new client states of Eastern Europe than in the Soviet Union itself. There were several small memorials in the Rzhev region, but throughout the Soviet era, unlike in Leningrad or Stalingrad, there was no major monument to remember the terrible fighting that raged in the Rzhev area for so many bloodstained weeks and months. It was only in 2017, in response to repeated pressure from Red Army veterans and following a major public fundraising campaign, that the Russian government took the decision to create a memorial. Following a competition that resulted in 19 submissions, a design by the sculptor Andrey Korobtsov and the architect Konstantin Formin was selected. A foundation stone was laid in November 2018, and construction began in earnest the following summer. The great central figure that dominates the memorial was cast in the second half of 2019, and the memorial was finally inaugurated at the end of June 2020. At the ceremony where the memorial was officially unveiled, President Vladimir Putin gave a speech:

Today we pay tribute to everyone who fought here on the battlefields near Rzhev, who selflessly defended our Motherland and gave their lives for the great victory.

Not so long ago, the battles near Rzhev were hardly ever mentioned in official historical sources. Participants had written just a few scarce words. It was too difficult to remember that terrible Rzhev Meat Grinder as it is sometimes called. Fierce, exhausting, bitter fighting continued in this area for months. Soldiers fought for every single grove, hill, every square metre of land.

It is impossible to think about the Red Army's losses in those battles without pain. More than 1.3 million people were killed, injured or recorded as missing. It is a horrifying, unimaginable number.

The significance of that long and bloody victory for the victory of the Soviet people over Nazism is huge. The Soviet Army finally demonstrated that the enemy would not be able to turn and advance towards Moscow once more; nor would it be able to break and subjugate the people who stood firm for the defence of their Motherland. Every time a soldier fell, another rose up behind him. The unbelievable intensity of that battle exhausted the enemy, crushing and slowly destroying the giant military machine of the Third Reich.

Step by step, day after day, the battles near Rzhev brought closer the triumphant outcome of the Battle of Stalingrad and the long-awaited lifting of the Siege of Leningrad, the liberation of Belarus, Ukraine and the Baltic States – and the final and critical change in the course of the entire Second World War ...

The Rzhev Memorial is another symbol of our collective memory, a symbol of our veneration for the great and selfless, valiant deeds of the heroic soldier, the liberating soldier, the victorious solder, the soldier who saved Europe and the entire world from Nazism. Time has no grip on this deed and it cannot and must not be forgotten or erased or besmirched by lies and falsifications. We will not allow this to happen.

Lives destroyed in the war will always remain with us like an open wound. Even now, the valour and endurance of our fathers, grandfathers and great grandfathers as well as their bottomless love and loyalty to the Motherland will serve as vital moral guidance to us. We must be worthy of this highest moral standard in our deeds and actions today, and we must protect and preserve the historical truth that unites generations both in Russia and abroad like a living thread.[10]

Even in this speech, some of the myths of the past persist: the suggestion that 'the battles near Rzhev brought closer the triumphant outcome of the Battle of Stalingrad' and other successes suggests a causal link, much as the official historiography has always attempted to portray.

Of all the sectors of the blood-soaked Eastern Front, the Rzhev Salient was perhaps one of the worst, yet the story of the battles fought there remains largely unknown. Had the extraordinary 'raid' mounted by Belov's cavalry corps and the accompanying paratroopers occurred on almost any other front of the war, it would surely have been marked by a profusion of books and movies, but this remarkable episode is almost forgotten. The sculpture in the Rzhev Memorial, 25m tall, stands on a grassy mound and portrays a young soldier; the lower parts of his uniform gradually transform into birds, and it is a fitting and poignant memorial to the men who died in the region in the 502 days of fighting. For the Germans who fought and died in the Rzhev Salient, there is no memorial. The devastation of the region was so great that, like in many parts of the former Soviet Union, many villages were left depopulated and simply vanished after the war. Many of the mass graves in the region lie in desolate areas of swamp or woodland, and the remains of the dead and dozens of military artefacts are found every year by people exploring the region. While many of the fallen lie in mass graves, tens of thousands from both sides have never been formally buried, or even had their remains identified. The terrible fields of slaughter on the banks of the Vazuza River are now submerged under the Vazuza Reservoir, and it is certain that hundreds, probably thousands, of the fallen lie beneath its waters. Other battlefields have reverted to farmland, and here, too, the past lies below the surface, as the poet Boris Slutsky wrote in his poem 'Kropotovo':

This is Kropotovo, near Rzhev, turn left from the road.
There were no more than twenty houses there. I don't know how much is left.
In the vast Russian land, that village is like a deep wound through the chest ...
And there is no medal for Kropotovo? No, no medals were given for it ...
And probably, the combine harvests the rye, or the tractor turns the soil,
And they all pass freely over the lines, and they don't know, they don't hear, they don't smell.[11]

NOTES

MEAT GRINDER

1   B. Gorbachevsky, *Rzhevskaya Myasorubka. Vremya Otvagi. Zadacha – Vyzhit'!*
     (Eksmo, Moscow, 2007), p.4
2   W. Dunn, *Stalin's Keys to Victory: The Rebirth of the Red Army* (Stackpole,
     Mechanicsburg, PA, 2007), p.36–38

CHAPTER 1

1   G. Buchheit, *Der Deutsche Geheimdienst. Geschichte der Militärischen Abwehr*
     (Munich, 1966), p.255
2   H. Höhne and J. Brownjohn (trans.), *Canaris* (Doubleday, New York, 1979),
     p.441
3   For an overview of *FHO*, see D. Thomas, 'Foreign Armies East and German
     Military Intelligence in Russia 1941–45' in *Journal of Contemporary History* 22,
     No. 2 (1987), p.261–301
4   Quoted in Thomas, 'Foreign Armies', p.277
5   Bundesarchiv-Militärarchiv Freiburg, *FHO Feindbeurteilung Stand 20/5/41*
     T-78/479/6465470
6   J. Bradley and T. Buell, *Why Was Barbarossa Delayed? The Second World War:
     Europe and the Mediterranean* (Square One, Garden City, NY, 2010), p.35–40
7   G. Heinrici, J. Hürter and C. Brocks (trans.), *A German General on the Eastern
     Front: The Letters and Diaries of Gotthard Heinrici 1941–1942* (Pen & Sword,
     Barnsley, 2014), p.69
8   D. Glantz, *Barbarossa Derailed: The Battle for Smolensk 10 July–10 September 1941*
     (Helion, Warwick, 2010), p.576
9   A. Hitler, *Mein Kampf* (Houghton Mifflin, Boston, 1971), p.646
10 M. Rössler and S. Schleiermacher, 'Hauptlinien der NationalSozialistischen
     Planungs- und Vernichtungspolitik' in *Central European History Journal*, Vol. 29:2
     (Cambridge University Press, 1996), p.270–274
11 T. Snyder, *Bloodlands: Europe Between Hitler and Stalin* (Vintage, London, 2011),
     p.161–162
12 A. Kay, *Exploitation, Resettlement, Mass Murder: Political and Economic Planning
     for German Occupation Policy in the Soviet Union* (Berghahn, New York, 2006),

p.164; I. Ehrenburg, V. Grossman and D. Patterson (trans.), *The Complete Black Book of Russian Jewry* (Transaction, New Brunswick, NJ, 2003), p.562

13   C. Burdick and H.-A. Jacobsen (eds), *The Halder War Diary 1939–1942* (Greenhill, Novato, CA, 1988), p.346

14   H.-A. Jacobsen, 'The Kommissarbefehl and Mass Executions of Soviet Russian Prisoners of War' in H. Krausnick, H. Buchheim, M. Broszat and H.-A. Jacobsen, *Anatomy of the SS State* (Walter, New York, 1968), p.518–519

15   C. Ingrao and A. Brown (trans.), *Believe and Destroy: Intellectuals in the SS War Machine* (Polity, Cambridge, 2013), p.140

16   Heinrici, Hürter and Brocks, *A German General*, p.79

17   Ibid., p.74–75

18   D. Glantz, *When Titans Clashed: How the Red Army Stopped Hitler* (University Press of Kansas, Lawrence, 1995), p.293

19   H. Schäufler, *So Lebten und so Starben Sie: Das Buch vom Panzerregiment-35* (Kameradschaft Ehemaliger Panzer-Regiment 35 e.V, Bamberg, 1983), p.76–77

20   Quoted in H. Boog, *Der Angriff auf die Sowjetunion* (Fischer-Taschenbuch Verlag, Frankfurt am Main, 1996), p.498–503

21   Burdick and Jacobsen, *The Halder War Diary*, p.506

22   N. Zetterling and A. Frankson, *The Drive on Moscow, 1941. Operation Taifun and Germany's First Great Crisis of World War II* (Casemate, Havertown, PA, 2012), p.253

23   For a detailed discussion of the Soviet concept of deep operations, see R. Harrison, *The Russian Way of War: The Operational Art 1904–1940* (University of Kansas Press, Lawrence, 2001), p.123–200; R. Simpkin, *Deep Battle: The Brainchild of Marshal Tukhachevsky* (Brassey, London, 1987)

24   Heinrici, Hürter and Brocks, *A German General*, p.85

25   Schäufler, *So Lebten*, p.96–97

26   G. Jukes, *The Second World War – The Eastern Front 1941–1945* (Osprey, Oxford, 2002), p.29–31

27   From https://www.jewishvirtuallibrary.org/adolf-hitler-broadcast-to-the-german-people-on-the-winter-help-scheme-october-1941

28   V. Krasnov, *G Zhukov. Marshal Velikoy Impreii. Lavry I Ternii Polkovodtsa* (Olma, Moscow, 2005), p.88

29   P. Grigorenko, *V Podpol'e Možno Vstretit' Tol'ko Krys* (Zven'ja, Moscow, 1997), p.82

30   G. Zhukov, *Vospomimaniya I Razmyshleniya* (Olma, Moscow, 2002), Vol. II, p.12–13

31   O. von Knobelsdorff, *Geschichte der Niedersächsischen 19. Panzer-Division 1939–1945* (Podzun-Pallas, Friedberg, 1958), p.121–122

32   H. Grossmann, *Die Geschichte der Rheinisch-Westfälischen 6. Infanterie-Division 1939–1945* (Dörfler, Eggolsheim, 2005), p.80

33   P. Rotmistrov, *Stalnaya Gvardiya* (Voyenizdat, Moscow, 1984), p.78–79

34   Grossmann, *Die Geschichte*, p.82

35   Burdick and Jacobsen, *The Halder War Diary*, p.553

36   Heinrici, Hürter and Brocks, *A German General*, p.102

37   Ibid., p106

38   Grossmann, *Die Geschichte*, p.85

39   Zhukov, Vol. II, p.26

40   K. Rokossovsky, *A Soldier's Duty* (Lancer, New Delhi, 1992), p.70

41   R. Harrison (ed. and trans.), *The Battle of Moscow 1941–1942: The Red Army's Defensive Operations and Counteroffensive along the Moscow Strategic Direction – The Soviet General Staff Study* (Helion, Warwick, 2015), p.57

42   Quoted in H. von Manteuffel, *Die 7. Panzer-Division im Zweiten Weltkrieg* (Josef Broich, Uerdingen am Rhein, 1965), p.221

43   Schäufler, *So Lebten*, p.118–119

44   Manteuffel, *Die 7. Panzer-Division*, p.225–226

45   M. Abdullin, *Stranits iz Soldatskogo Dnevnika* (Molodaya Gvardiya, Moscow, 1985), p.35

46   F. Strauss, *Geschichte der 2. (Wiener) Panzer-Division* (Dörfler, Eggolsheim, 2005), p.98

47   Ibid., p.100–101

48   H. Schäufler, *Der Weg war Weit: Panzer Zwischen Weichsel und Wolga* (Vowinckel, Neckargemünd, 1973), p.60

49   Heinrici, Hürter and Brocks, *A German General*, p.115

50   M. Pahl and D. Hammond, *Hitler's Fremde Heere Ost: German Military Intelligence on the Eastern Front 1942–1945* (Helion, Warwick, 2016), p.87

51   M. Jones, *The Retreat: Hitler's First Defeat* (John Murray, London, 2010), p.135

52   Quoted in Harrison, *The Battle of Moscow*, p.155

53   *Izvestia*, Moscow, 19 November 1941

54   *Krasnaya Zvezda*, 27 November 1941

CHAPTER 2

1   Zhukov, Vol. II, p.37

2   For an excellent account of the Soviet counteroffensive mainly from the German perspective, see D. Stahel, *Retreat from Moscow: A New History of Germany's Winter Campaign, 1941–1942* (Picador, New York, 2019)

3   Heinrici, Hürter and Brocks, *A German General*, p.111

4   Manteuffel, *Die 7. Panzer-Division*, p.243–244

5   Harrison, *The Battle of Moscow*, p.41–42

6   Quoted in Stahel, *Retreat*, p.24

7   Grossmann, *Die Geschichte*, p.87

8   Strauss, *Geschichte*, p.106

9   Schäufler, *So Lebten*, p.130–132

10   Burdick and Jacobsen, *The Halder War Diary*, p.581–582

11   Grossmann, *Die Geschichte*, p.90

12 D. Lelyushenko, *Moskva-Stalingrad-Berlin-Praga. Zapiski Komandarma* (Nauka, Berlin, 1971), p.70
13 Ibid., p.75
14 Bundesarchiv-Militärarchiv Freiburg, *Tagebuch Reinhardts*, N245/3-16, 7/12/41
15 Grossmann, *Die Geschichte*, p.93
16 Letter from Private Meyer quoted in *True to Type: A Selection From Letters and Diaries of German Soldiers and Civilians Collected on the Soviet-German Front* (Hutchinson, London, 1945), p.99
17 I. Lykov, *V Groznyy Chas* (Voyenizdat, Moscow, 1986), p.106–108
18 Schäufler, *Der Weg*, p.43–45
19 R. Stoves, *Die 1. Panzer-Division 1935–1945* (Podzun, Bad Neuheim, 1961), p.313–316; Lelyushenko, *Moskva-Stalingrad-Berlin-Praga*, p.78
20 Rotmistrov, *Stalnaya Gvardiya*, p.108–109
21 T. Wray, *Standing Fast: German Defensive Doctrine on the Russian Front During World War II* (Combat Studies Institute, Fort Leavenworth, KS, 2004), p.90–91
22 Rokossovsky, *A Soldier's Duty*, p.95
23 S. Sevryugov, *Tak Eto Bylo …* (Voenizdat, Moscow, 1957), p.115
24 Strauss, *Geschichte*, p.110
25 Quoted in W. Richardson, *The Fatal Decisions: The Decisive Battles of the Second World War from the Viewpoint of the Vanquished* (Pen and Sword, Barnsley, 2012), p.66–67
26 Stahel, *Retreat*, p.110ff
27 K. Gerbet (ed.), *Generalfeldmarschall Fedor von Bock: The War Diary 1939–1945* (Schiffer, Atglen, PA, 1996), p.399
28 Grossmann, *Die Geschichte*, p.93
29 Ibid., p.95–97
30 Heinrici, Hürter and Brocks, *A German General*, p.122–124
31 Burdick and Jacobsen, *The Halder War Diary*, p.594; H. Guderian, *Panzer Leader* (Da Capo, New York, 1996), p.265
32 G. Schreiber, B. Stegemann and D. Vogel, *Germany and the Second World War* (Clarendon, Oxford, 1998), Vol. IV, p.723–724
33 Knobelsdorff, *Geschichte*, p.137–138
34 Ibid., p.138–139
35 Heinrici, Hürter and Brocks, *A German General*, p.127

CHAPTER 3

1 Grossmann, *Die Geschichte*, p.100–102
2 K. Reinhardt, *Moscow – The Turning Point: The Failure of Hitler's Strategy in the Winter of 1941–1942* (Berg, New York, 1992), p.300
3 Bundesarchiv-Militärarchiv Freiburg, *Kriegstagebuch des Oberkommandos der Heeresgruppe Mitte* 29/12/41, RH 19-II/122, 234

4   Grossmann, *Die Geschichte*, p.103
5   For further information about Fegelein and his unit's operations in Poland and the Soviet Union, see M. Miller, *Leaders of the SS and German Police* (Bender, San Jose, CA, 2006), Vol. I, p.308; A. Krüger and S. Scharenberg, *Zeiten für Helden – Zeiten für Berümtheiten im Sport* (LIT, Münster, 2014), p.85; H. Peiper, *Fegelein's Horsemen and Genocidal Warfare: The SS Cavalry Brigade in the Soviet Union* (Palgrave Macmillan, Basingstoke, 2015)
6   H. Grossmann, *Rshew, Eckpfeiler der Front* (Podzun, Bad Neuheim, 1962), p.144
7   Grossmann, *Die Geschichte*, p.105
8   Knobelsdorff, *Geschichte*, p.140
9   Zhukov, Vol. II, p.43–44
10 Harrison, *The Battle of Moscow*, p.306
11 M. Katukov, *Na Ostriye Glavnogo Udara* (Voyenizdat, Moscow, 1974), p.139
12 H. Bücheler, *Hoepner: Ein Deutsches Soldatenschiksal des 20. Jahrhunderts* (Mittler, Herford, 1980), p.169
13 Bundesarchiv-Militärarchiv Freiburg, *Kriegstagebuch Pz.AOK IV*, RH 21-4/50-110, 9/1/42
14 Knobelsdorff, *Geschichte*, p.143–144
15 W. Görlitz, *Model. Strategie der Defensive* (Limes, Wiesbaden, 1975), p.124
16 I. Starchak, *S Neba, V Boy* (Voyenizdat, Moscow, 1965), p.131–132
17 P. Belov, *Za Nami Moskva* (Voyenizdat, Moscow, 1963), p.178
18 Ibid., p.180
19 Ibid., p.182
20 Ibid.
21 A. Eremenko, *V Nachale Voyny* (Nauka, Moscow, 1965), p.94
22 S. Newton, *Hitler's Commander: Field Marshal Walter Model, Hitler's Favorite General* (Da Capo, Cambridge MA, 2006), p.181–182
23 Zhukov, Vol. II, p.54

CHAPTER 4

1   Stahel, *Retreat*, p.423; R. Forczyk and A. Hook, *Walther Model* (Osprey, Oxford, 2011), p.19
2   Starchak, *S Neba, V Boy*, p.86–88
3   Grossmann, *Die Geschichte*, p.108
4   *Grazami Detei: Rasskazyi Detei v Rzheva o Zberstvach Nemetsko-Fachistskich Zachvatchikov* (Izdanie Kalininskogo Ovkoma, Kalinin, 1944), p.5
5   Ibid., p.7
6   Ibid., p.22–23
7   Ibid., p.23
8   A. Von Plato, *Die Geschichte der 5. Panzerdivision 1938 bis 1945* (Walhalla und Praetoria, Regensburg, 1978), p.211–212

9   R. Khisamutdinova and V. Zolotarev, *Velikaia Otechestvennaia Voiny 1941–1945: Voyenno-Istoricheskie Ocherki* (Nauka, Moscow 1998–1999, 4 volumes), Vol. I, p.295

10 I. Lykov, *V Groznyy Chas* (Voyenizdat, Moscow, 1986), p.146

11 Strauss, *Geschichte*, p.116–117

12 Plato, *Die Geschichte der 5. Panzerdivision*, p.212–213

13 Ibid., p.214

14 Belov, *Za Nami Moskva*, p.205–206

15 S. Gerasimova, *Rzhev Slaughterhouse* (Helion, Warwick, 2012), p.31

16 Belov, *Za Nami Moskva*, p.210–211

17 D. Sukhorukov, *Sovetskie Vozdushno-Desantnye* (Voyenizdat, Moscow, 1980), p.85–86

18 D. Glantz, *The Soviet Airborne Experience* (US Army Command and General Staff College, Fort Leavenworth, KS, 1984), p.63

19 Quoted in Belov, *Za Nami Moskva*, p.215

20 Ibid.

21 Tsentral'nyy Arkhiv Ministerstva Oborony RF/F388 Op. 5879D 27L, p.453–454

22 V. Melnikov, *Ikh Poslal na Smert' Zhukov? Gibel' Armii Generala Efremova* (Eksmo, Moscow, 2009), p.660–662

23 S. Mikheyenkov, *Armiya, Kotoruyu Predali. Tragediya 33-y Armii Generala M G Efremova* (Tsentrpoligraf, Moscow, 2010), p.341

24 Ibid., p.257–258

25 F. Sverdlov, *Tragediya 33-y Armii. Oshibki G K Zhukova* (Monolit, Moscow, 2002), p.22

26 Glantz, *The Soviet Airborne Experience*, p.74–79

27 Tsentral'nyy Arkhiv Ministerstva Oborony Pub. 3 (1988)

28 Schäufler, *So Lebten*, p.149

29 Y. Gordon, *Soviet Air Power in World War 2* (Midland, Herssham, 2008), p.285

30 G. Krivosheev, *Rossiya I SSSR Voynakh XX Veka: Poteri Vooruzhennykh Sil, Statisticheskoye Issledovaniye* (Olma, Moscow, 2001), p.101

31 Bundesarchiv-Militärarchiv Freiburg, RW 6/556, 6/558

32 Heinrici, Hürter and Brocks, *A German General*, p.146

33 Zhukov, Vol. II, p.51

34 Quoted in F. Sverdlov, *Oshibki G K Zhukova God 1942* (self-published, available at 1942.ru/Zhukov.1942.htm)

35 Quoted in Sverdlov, *Oshibki G K Zhukova God 1942*

36 S. Mitiagin, *Boevye Deistviya pod Viazmoi v Ianvare-Aprele 1942: Operatsiia ili Imitatsiia?* (Voyenno-Istoricheskii Archiv, Moscow, 1988), No. 3, p.87

CHAPTER 5

1   A. Vasilevsky, *A Lifelong Cause* (Progress, Moscow, 1973), p.153–157

2   Führer Directive 41, retrieved from www2db.com/doc.php?q=419

3   Burdick and Jacobsen, *The Halder War Diary*, p.613–614
4   Gerasimova, *Rzhev Slaughterhouse*, p.88
5   Gorbachevsky, *Rzhevskaya Myasorubka*, p.7
6   Ibid., p.10
7   Ibid., p.15
8   Ibid., p.27
9   Belov, *Za Nami Moskva*, p.234–235
10 Ibid., p.290–292
11 *Grazami Detei*, p.8
12 Interview with M. Bogatsky, available at https://iremember.ru/memoirs/desantniki/bogatskiy-mikhail-moiseevich/
13 Plato, *Die Geschichte der 5. Panzerdivision*, p.222
14 Sukhorukov, *Sovetskie Vozdushno-Desantnye*, p.122
15 Belov, *Za Nami Moskva*, p.298
16 Bogatsky interview
17 Belov, *Za Nami Moskva*, p.301
18 Ibid., p.302–303
19 Ibid., p.305

CHAPTER 6

1   Bundesarchiv-Militärarchiv Freiburg, *Kriegstagebuch 5. Panzer Division 8-9/6/42*, RH-27-5
2   Krivosheev, *Rossiya*, p.312
3   Grossmann, *Rshew*, p.48
4   Tsentral'nyy Arkhiv Ministerstva Oborony, Moscow F.213 Op.2002 D.327, p.71–91
5   Görlitz, *Model*, p.122
6   For Belov's account of the breakout, see Belov, *Za Nami Moskva*, p.306–320
7   Ibid., p.309–310
8   Bogatsky interview
9   Sukhorukov, *Sovetskie Vozdushno-Desantnye*, p.126–127
10 H. Reinhardt, 'Russian Air Landings in the Area of German Army Group Center' in *Foreign Military Studies* (Historical Division, US Army Europe, 1955), P-116, p.26–27
11 G. Blumentritt, 'Operations Against Rear Lines of Communications' in *Foreign Military Studies* (Historical Division, US Army Europe, 1947), B-684, p.6–7
12 Burdick and Jacobsen, *The Halder War Diary*, p.623
13 Bogatsky interview
14 Stoves, *Die 1. Panzer-Division*, p.347–348
15 Strauss, *Geschichte*, p.342–343

16   Gerasimova, *Rzhev Slaughterhouse*, p.97
17   L. Mylnikov and O. Kondratev, *Eto Bylo na Rzhevsko-Viazemskom Platsdarme* (Rzhevskiy Knizhyy Klub, 1998), Vol. I, p.62
18   Ibid., p.63
19   Ibid., p.65–66
20   Ibid., p.66–68
21   Strauss, *Geschichte*, p.125
22   Stoves, *Die 1. Panzer-Division*, p.352–356
23   M. Vorobev and V. Usov, *Za Kazhdyi Klochok Zemli* (Moskovskii Rabochii, Smolensk, 1989), p.91
24   Interview with M. Lukinov, available at https://iremember.ru/memoirs/artilleristi/lukinov-mikhail-ivanovich/
25   Ibid.
26   Ibid.
27   Plato, *Die Geschichte der 5. Panzerdivision*, p.230
28   Strauss, *Geschichte*, p.128
29   I. Konev, 'Vospominaniia' in *Znamia* (Pravda, Moscow, 1987), 12, p.101

CHAPTER 7

1   Zhukov, Vol. II, p.70
2   V. Zolotarev (ed.), *Russkii Arkhiv. Velikaia Otechestvennaia Voina 1941–1945* (Nauka, Moscow, 1998, 4 volumes), Vol. III, p.311–312
3   Voyenno-Nauchnoye Upravleniye Generalnogo Shtaba, Voyenno-Istoricheskiy Otdel, *Boevoi Sostav Sovetskoi Armii 1942 Goda* (Voyenizdat, Moscow, 1966, 4 volumes), Vol. II, p.41
4   A. Kazaryan, *Prisyaga na vsio Zhizn* (Voenizdat, Moscow, 1988), p.84–86
5   Ibid., p.95–97
6   N. Khlebnikov, *Pod Grokhot Soten Batarey* (Voyenizdat, Moscow, 1974), p.173–174
7   Ibid., p.177
8   N. Belov and T. Mikhailova, *Rzhev 1942: Bitva za Vysotu 200* (self-published, Tver, 2000), p.3
9   Khlebnikov, *Pod Grokhot Soten Batarey*, p.180
10   Interview with M. Bogopolsky, available at https://iremember.ru/memoirs/artilleristi/bogopolskiy-mikhail-petrovich/
11   Tsentral'nyy Arkhiv Ministerstva Oborony, Moscow F384 Op.8629 D130, L27
12   V. Boyko, *S Dumoy O Rodine* (Voenizdat, Moscow, 1982), p.4
13   Kazaryan, *Prisyaga na vsio Zhizn*, p.108–110
14   L. Sandalov, *Pogorelo-Gorodishchenskaia Operatsiia. Nastupatelnaia Operatsiia 20-Armii Zapadnogo Fronta v Avguste 1942 Goda* (Voyenizdat, Moscow, 1960), p.74
15   Stoves, *Die 1. Panzer-Division*, p.360
16   Strauss, *Geschichte*, p.343–344

17 Plato, *Die Geschichte der 5. Panzerdivision*, p.232

18 Ibid., p.234

19 P. Chamberlain and H. Doyle, *Encyclopaedia of German Tanks of World War Two* (Arms & Armour, London, 1978), p.66, 245

20 Plato, *Die Geschichte der 5. Panzerdivision*, p.234–235

21 Sevryugov, *Tak Eto Bylo …*, p.137–138

22 Interview with A. Stepenskiy, available at https://iremember.ru/memoirs/kavaleristi/stepenskiy-aleksandr-borisovich/

23 Interview with A. Gorodinskiy, available at https://iremember.ru/memoirs/minometchiki/gorodinskiy-aron-semenovich/

24 Stoves, *Die 1. Panzer-Division*, p.363–364

25 A. Drabkin, *Ya Dralsya s Pantservaffe 'Dvoynoy Oklad – Troynaya Smert!'* (Eksmo, Moscow, 2007), p.5–15

26 Stoves, *Die 1. Panzer-Division*, p.264–265

CHAPTER 8

1   Tsentral'nyy Arkhiv Ministerstva Oborony, Moscow F208 Op.2511 D1466, L9-12

2   Zhukov, Vol. II, p.72

3   Burdick and Jacobsen, *The Halder War Diary*, p.657

4   Quoted in E. Ziemke and M. Bauer, *Moscow to Stalingrad: Decision in the East* (Military Heritage Press, New York, 1988), p.405

5   Stoves, *Die 1. Panzer-Division*, p.365–366

6   Interview with A. Schvebig, available at https://iremember.ru/memoirs/tankisti/shvebig-anatoliy-petrovich/

7   Ibid.

8   Grossmann, *Die Geschichte*, p.119–120

9   Belov and Mikhailova, *Rzhev 1942*, p.58

10 Khlebnikov, *Pod Grokhot Soten Batarey*, p.182–183

11 Belov and Mikhailova, *Rzhev 1942*, p.62

12 Grossmann, *Die Geschichte*, p.126–129

13 Quoted in Gerasimova, *Rzhev Slaughterhouse*, p.146

14 G. Roberts, *Wars: From World War to Cold War, 1939–1952* (Yale University Press, New Haven, CT, 2006), p.132–134

15 A. Toptygin, *Lavrentij Beria: Neizvestny Marsal Gosbezopasnosti* (Eksmo, Moscow, 2005), p.121

16 Interview with A. Solodov, available at https://iremember.ru/memoirs/minometchiki/solodov-anatoliy-andreevich/

17 Interview with B. Aiushiev, available at https://iremember.ru/memoirs/kavaleristi/aiushiev-batomunko-aiushievich/

18 Gorbachevsky, *Rzhevskaya Myasorubka*, p.76

19 Zolotarev, *Russkii Arkhiv*, Vol. III, p.341–342
20 Interview with N. Guzhva, available at https://iremember.ru/memoirs/pekhotintsi/guzhva-nikolay-avraamovich/
21 Gorbachevsky, *Rzhevskaya Myasorubka*, p.68
22 Ibid., p.87–88
23 Ibid., p.96, 102
24 Stoves, *Die 1. Panzer-Division*, p.367–368
25 Ziemke and Bauer, *Moscow to Stalingrad*, p.455–457
26 Plato, *Die Geschichte der 5. Panzerdivision*, p.239
27 Interview with N. Vershinin, available at https://iremember.ru/memoirs/tankisti/vershinin-nikolay-petrovich/
28 Interview with A. Bodnar, available at https://iremember.ru/memoirs/tankisti/bodnar-aleksandr-vasilevich/
29 Ibid.
30 Strauss, *Geschichte*, p.132

CHAPTER 9

1   Zolotarev, *Russkii Arkhiv*, Vol. IV, p.394
2   Zhukov, Vol. II, p.79–80
3   Gorbachevsky, *Rzhevskaya Myasorubka*, p.116–117
4   Ibid., p.118–125
5   V. Shavrov, *Istoriya Konstruktsiy Samolotov v SSSR do 1938g* (Mashinostroyenie, Moscow, 1985), p.752
6   Ibid., p.752–753
7   J. Smith and A. Kay, *German Aircraft of the Second World War* (Putnam, London, 1978), p.165–172
8   For a good overview of German signals intelligence in the Second World War, see A. Praun, *German Radio Intelligence* (US Army Office of the Chief of Military History, Washington, DC, 1950)
9   Gorbachevsky, *Rzhevskaya Myasorubka*, p.139–142
10 P. Buttar, *The Reckoning: The Defeat of Army Group South, 1944* (Osprey, Oxford, 2020), p.136–137; P. Buttar, *Retribution: The Soviet Reconquest of Central Ukraine, 1943* (Osprey, Oxford, 2019), p.308–310
11 H. Höhne, *Canaris: Hitler's Master Spy* (Doubleday, New York, 1979), p.216–217
12 L. Delattre, *A Spy in the Heart of the Third Reich* (Grove, New York, 2006), p.79
13 Public Records Office, Kew, London, KV-2-1593_1, p.16
14 This account is based upon: Public Records Office, Kew, London, KV-2-1498, KV-2-1593_1, KV-2-1593_2, and KV-2-1631
15 H. Höhne and H. Zolling, *The General Was a Spy: The Truth About General Gehlen and his Spy Ring* (Coward, McCann & Geoghegan, New York, 1972), p.13

16   Burdick and Jacobsen, *The Halder War Diary*, p.664

17   Quoted in E. Ziemke, *Stalingrad to Berlin: The German Defeat in the East* (US Army Office of the Chief of Military History, Washington, DC, 1968), p.47

18   D. Kahn, 'An Intelligence Case History: The Defense of Osuga, 1942' in *Aerospace Historian* (US Air Force Historical Foundation, Clinton, MD, 1981), Vol. 28.4, p.245

19   V. Tarrant, *The Red Orchestra* (J Wiley, London, 1995), p.166–170

20   S. Radó, *Sous le Pseudonyme Dora* (Julliard, Paris, 1972), p.144

21   A. Foote, *Handbook for Spies* (Museum, London, 1964), p.92–95

22   W. Adam, O. Rühle and T. le Tissier (trans.), *With Paulus at Stalingrad* (Pen and Sword, Barnsley, 2015), p.22–23

23   Kahn, 'An Intelligence Case History', p.245

24   Gorbachevsky, *Rzhevskaya Myasorubka*, p.129–133

25   D. Glantz, *Zhukov's Greatest Defeat: The Red Army's Epic Disaster in Operation Mars, 1942* (University Press of Kansas, Lawrence, 1999), p.325–326

26   Khlebnikov, *Pod Grokhot Soten Batarey*, p.186

27   A. Sinitsky, *Razvedchikam Oshibatsya Nelzya* (Voyenizdat, Moscow, 1987), p.67

28   A. Isaev, *Poteriannoe Zveno* (foreword to Russian language edition of D. Glantz, *Zhukov's Greatest Defeat*), quoted in Gerasimova, *Rzhev Slaughterhouse*, p.185

29   Zhukov, Vol. II, p.105

30   Gorbachevsky, *Rzhevskaya Myasorubka*, p.135–136

31   M. Voloshin, *Razvedchiki Vsegda Vperedi* (Voyenizdat, Moscow, 1977), p.43–44

32   Bundesarchiv-Militärarchiv Freiburg, *Kriegstagebuch Armeeoberkommando 9*, 20/11/42, 31624/3

33   For the evolution of *Grossdeutschland*, see H. Spaeter, *The History of the Panzerkorps Grossdeutschland* (Fedorowicz, Winnipeg, 1992), Vol. I, p.20–156, 293–295

34   Spaeter, Vol. I, p.395–396

35   Glantz, *Zhukov's Greatest Defeat*, p.53–54

36   M. Solomatin, *Krasnogradtsky* (Voyenizdat, Moscow, 1963), p.8–9

37   Ibid., p.13

38   Katukov, *Na Ostriye Glavnogo Udara*, p.175–176

39   K. Malygin, *V Tsentre Boyevogo Poryadka* (Voyenizdat, Moscow, 1986), p.67

40   For a full history of the Luftwaffe field divisions, see K. Ruffner, *Luftwaffe Field Divisions 1941–1945* (Osprey, Oxford, 1990); A. Munõz, *Goering's Grenadiers: The Luftwaffe Field Divisions 1942–1945* (Axis Europa, Bayside, NY, 2002)

41   E. von Manstein and G. Powell (trans.), *Lost Victories: The War Memoirs of Hitler's Most Brilliant General* (Presidio, Novato, CA, 1994), p.268

CHAPTER 10

1   Plato, *Die Geschichte der 5. Panzerdivision*, p.245

2   Tsentral'nyy Arkhiv Ministerstva Oborony, Moscow, RF F.208, Op.2511, D1097, L.272

3   Glantz, *Zhukov's Greatest Defeat*, p.92–94

4   Plato, *Die Geschichte der 5. Panzerdivision*, p.246–247

5   Sevryugov, *Tak Eto Bylo …*, p.145–146

6   A. Getman, *Tanki Idut na Berlin* (Nauka, Moscow, 1973), p.72–73

7   Interview with L. Plonskiy, available at http://iremember.ru/memoirs/svyazisti/plonskiy-lev-markovich/

8   Sevryugov, *Tak Eto Bylo …*, p.150

9   Plato, *Die Geschichte der 5. Panzerdivision*, p.248

10 'Vvod v Proryv Konnemekhanizirovannykh Grupp' in *Sbornik Materialov po Izucheniiu Opijta Voimj* (Voyenizdat, Moscow, 1944), No.9, p.145

11 Sevryugov, *Tak Eto Bylo …*, p.151

12 Statement of G. Platonov, available at 1942.ru/book/mars_2gvkk.htm

13 Plato, *Die Geschichte der 5. Panzerdivision*, p.249–250

14 Interview with A. Gorodinskiy, available at https://iremember.ru/memoirs/minometchiki/gorodinskiy-aron-semenovich/

15 Getman, *Tanki Idut na Berlin*, p.73–74

16 Plato, *Die Geschichte der 5. Panzerdivision*, p.251–252

17 Ibid., p.254

18 Getman, *Tanki Idut na Berlin*, p.74

19 Interview with A. Barash, available at https://iremember.ru/memoirs/tankisti/barash-anatoliy-mikhaylovich/

20 Sevryugov, *Tak Eto Bylo …*, p.154

21 Glantz, *Zhukov's Greatest Defeat*, p.189

CHAPTER 11

1   A. Babadzhanian, *Dorogi Pobedy* (Molodaya Gvardiya, Moscow, 1975), p.77

2   A. Petrukhin, 'Spetsdobrovoltsy' in *Rodina* (FGBU Redaktsiya Rossiyskoy Gazety, Moscow, 2000), No. 5, p.154

3   Spaeter, Vol. I, p.437

4   Malygin, *V Tsentre Boyevogo Poryadka*, p.70

5   Solomatin, *Krasnogradtsky*, p.19

6   Glantz, *Zhukov's Greatest Defeat*, p.121–122

7   Görlitz, *Model*, p.130

8   Voloshin, *Razvedchiki Vsegda Vperedi*, p.46

9   Spaeter, Vol. I, p.447

10 Solomatin, *Krasnogradtsky*, p.22–23

11 Malygin, *V Tsentre Boyevogo Poryadka*, p.71–72

12 Spaeter, Vol. I, p.451–452

13 Stoves, *Die 1. Panzer-Division*, p.385

Chapter 12

1 Zolotarev, *Russkii Arkhiv*, Vol. IV, p.244
2 D. Volkogonov, *Stalin: Politicheskiy Portret* (Novosti, Moscow, 1992), Vol. II, p.844–845
3 Stoves, *Die 1. Panzer-Division*, p.391
4 Khlebnikov, *Pod Grokhot Soten Batarey*, p.194
5 Stoves, *Die 1. Panzer-Division*, p.395
6 Glantz, *Zhukov's Greatest Defeat*, p.225–227
7 A. Kochetkov, *Dvinskii Tankovyi: Boevoi Put 5-go Tankovogo Dvinskogo Korpusa* (Voyenizdat, Moscow, 1989), p.10–11
8 Plato, *Die Geschichte der 5. Panzerdivision*, p.466–469
9 Khlebnikov, *Pod Grokhot Soten Batarey*, p.195
10 Ibid., p.195–196
11 Stoves, *Die 1. Panzer-Division*, p.400
12 Spaeter, Vol. I, p.470
13 P. Buttar, *On a Knife's Edge: The Ukraine, November 1942–March 1943* (Osprey, Oxford, 2018), p.115–168
14 Solomatin, *Krasnogradtsky*, p.33
15 *Russkaya Starina* (St Petersburg, 1872), Vol. VI, p.450–451
16 Khlebnikov, *Pod Grokhot Soten Batarey*, p.197
17 Solomatin, *Krasnogradtsky*, p.37–39
18 Stoves, *Die 1. Panzer-Division*, p.403
19 Kochetkov, *Dvinskii Tankovyi*, p.13–14
20 Glantz, *Zhukov's Greatest Defeat*, p.264
21 Quoted in Gerasimova, *Rzhev Slaughterhouse*, p.202
22 Tsentral'nyy Arkhiv Ministerstva Oborony, Moscow, F3404, op.1, d.12, 1.55
23 Kochetkov, *Dvinskii Tankovyi*, p.13
24 Ibid., p.12
25 Bundesarchiv-Militärarchiv Freiburg, *Kriegstagbuch Armee Oberkommando 9* 15/12/41, RH20-9
26 Sevryugov, *Tak Eto Bylo …*, p.155
27 Glantz, *When Titans Clashed*, p.293
28 Sevryugov, *Tak Eto Bylo …*, p.156
29 Ibid., p.157

Chapter 13

1 Spaeter, Vol. I, p.458
2 Ibid., p.459–461
3 Ibid., p.467–468
4 Grossmann, *Rshew*, p.62

5 Malygin, *V Tsentre Boyevogo Poryadka*, p.72
6 Grossmann, *Rshew*, p.63
7 Grossmann, *Die Geschichte*, p.135
8 Kazaryan, *Prisyaga na vsio Zhizn*, p.127–128
9 Gorbachevsky, *Rzhevskaya Myasorubka*, p.151–152
10 Ibid., p.152–154
11 Stoves, *Die 1. Panzer-Division*, p.406
12 Grossmann, *Die Geschichte*, p.136–137
13 *Grazami Detei*, p.18–19
14 V. Gurkin, 'Mars v Orbite Urana I Saturna' in *Voyenno-Istoricheskiy Zhurnal* (Russian Ministry of Defence, Moscow, 2000), Vol. IV, p.18
15 Krivosheev, *Rossiya*, p.312
16 Grossmann, *Rshew*, p.66
17 Stoves, *Die 1. Panzer-Division*, p.408
18 Plato, *Die Geschichte der 5. Panzerdivision*, p.256

CHAPTER 14

1 Quoted in A. Beevor, *Stalingrad* (Penguin, Harmondsworth, 1999), p.393
2 G. MacDonagh, *After the Reich: From the Liberation of Vienna to the Berlin Airlift* (John Murray, London, 2007), p.421
3 Buttar, *On a Knife's Edge*, p.146–168; 214–250
4 Ibid., p.338–411
5 A. Beloborodov, *Vsevda v Boio* (Ekonomika, Moscow, 1984), p.176
6 For a full account of the Battle of Velikiye Luki, see R. Forczyk, *Velikiye Luki 1942–1943: The Doomed Fortress* (Osprey, Oxford, 2020)
7 S. Newton, p.507
8 Görlitz, *Model*, p.133; Bundesarchiv-Militärarchiv Freiburg, *Kriegstagebuch Heersgruppe Mitte 26/01/43*
9 D. Bradley (ed.), *Die Generale des Heeres 1921–1945* (Biblio, Osnabrück, 1994), p.329–330
10 Görlitz, *Model*, p.136; Grossmann, *Rshew*, p.127
11 Rokossovsky, *A Soldier's Duty*, p.175–176
12 Ibid., p.176
13 S. Ivanov, 'General Armii N F Vatutin (K 80-letiyo Dnya Pozhdeniya)' in *Voyenno-Istoricheskiy Zhurnal* (Russian Ministry of Defence, Moscow, 1980), Vol. 12, p.78
14 Görlitz, *Model*, p.136
15 Tsentral'nyy Arkhiv Ministerstva Oborony, Moscow, F.354, Op.5806, D.256
16 Grossmann, *Rshew*, p.129
17 Voloshin, *Razvedchiki Vsegda Vperedi*, p.53–55
18 Gorbachevsky, *Rzhevskaya Myasorubka*, p.173

19 Ibid., p.176

20 Ibid., p.177

21 G. Denisenko, 'Zapiski Pozhilogo Soldata' in *Voyenno-Istoricheskiy Zhurnal* (Moscow, 2005), Vol. I, p.106

22 Grossmann, *Die Geschichte*, p.141–142

23 Zolotarev, *Russkii Arkhiv*, Vol. IV, p. 87

24 Mylnikov and Kondratev, Vol. I, p.49

25 *Sovinformburo* bulletin 3 March 1943, quoted in Gorbachevsky, *Rzhevskaya Myasorubka*, p.179

26 Grossmann, *Rshew*, p.162

27 Grossmann, *Die Geschichte*, p.143

28 *Sovinformburo* bulletin 9 March 1943, quoted in Gorbachevsky, *Rzhevskaya Myasorubka*, p.241

29 Grossmann, *Die Geschichte*, p.145

30 Rokossovsky, *A Soldier's Duty*, p.179

31 J. Neumann, *Die 4. Panzer-Division 1938–1943* (Verlag und Antiquariat für Zeitgeschichte, Bad Dürkheim, 1989), p.587–588

32 Mylnikov and Kondratev, Vol. II, p.46

33 Krivosheev, *Rossiya*, p.313

34 Boyko, *S Dumoy O Rodine*, p.48

35 Gorbachevsky, *Rzhevskaya Myasorubka*, p.181

36 A. Werth, *Russia at War 1941–1945* (Dutton, New York, 1964), p.630–631

CHAPTER 15

1 L. Lopukhovsky, *Na Glavnom Napravleniy* (Super, Moscow, 2017), p.40

2 Sun Tzu and T. Butler-Brown, *The Art of War: The Ancient Classic* (Capstone, Mankato Min, 2020), p.141–142

3 See, for example, P. Buttar, *Russia's Last Gasp: The Eastern Front 1916–17* (Osprey, Oxford, 2016), p.82–117

4 Zhukov, Vol. II, p.113–114

5 Voloshin, *Razvedchiki Vsegda Vperedi*, p.48–49

6 *Handbook on German Military Forces* (United States Department of War, Washington, DC, 1945), p.82–83

7 Quoted in Gerasimova, *Rzhev Slaughterhouse*, p.213

8 Ibid., p.214

9 'Vvod v Prooyv Konno-Mekhanizirovannykh Grupp' in *Sbornik Materialov po Izucheniiu Opiyta Voiny* (Voyenizdat, Moscow, 1944), No. 9, p.149

10 Solomatin, *Krasnogradtsky*, p.39–40

11 Ibid., p.40–41

12 Ibid., p.41–42, 44

13 Stoves, *Die 1. Panzer-Division*, p.409–410

14 D. Dragunsky, *Gody v Brone* (Voyenizdat, Moscow, 1973), p.85
15 Bundesarchiv-Militärarchiv Freiburg, *Armeeoberkommando 9 Feindnachrichtenblatt 139*, p.3–6 RH 20-9
16 K.-H. Frieser, K. Schmider, K. Schönherr, G. Schreiber, K. Ungváry and B. Wegner, *Das Deutsche Reich und der Zweite Weltkrieg* (Deutsche Verlags-Anstalt, Munich, 2007), Vol. VIII, p.154; Krivosheev, *Rossiya*, p.133
17 P. Mikhin, *Voyna, Kakoy Ona Byla: Rasskazy* (Slavyanka, Kursk, 2012), p.47–48, 150–151
18 C. Barnett, *Hitler's Generals* (Weidenfeld & Nicholson, New York, 1989), p.406
19 C. Wilmot, *The Struggle for Europe* (Wordsworth, Ware, 2003), p.486
20 Barnett, *Hitler's Generals*, p.328–330
21 A. Weigelt, K.-D. Müller, T. Schaarschmidt and M. Schmeitzner, *Todesurteile Sowjetischer Militärtribunale gegen Deutsche (1944–1947): Eine Historisch-Biographische Studie* (Vandenhoeck & Ruprecht, Göttingen, 2015), p.263–264
22 Buttar, *The Reckoning*, p.429–449

CHAPTER 16

1   M. Gareev, 'Operatsiya "Mars" y Sovremennyi "Marsyani"' in *Voyenno-Historicheskiy Zhurnal* (Moscow, 2003), Vol. 10, p.22
2   Quoted in J. Brunstedt, *The Soviet Myth of World War II: Patriotic Memory and the Russian Question in the USSR* (Cambridge University Press, 2021), p.50
3   Rossiiskii Gosudarstvennyi Arkhiv Sotsialno-Politicheskoi Istorii, Moscow, 17/125/311, p.51–60
4   R. Smelser, *The Myth of the Eastern Front: The Nazi-Soviet War in American Popular Culture* (Cambridge University Press, 2008), p.64–89
5   K. Aimermakher, *Doklad N S Khrushcheva o Kultse Lichnosti Stalina na XXsezde KPSS: Dokumenty* (Rosspen, Moscow, 2002), p.93–94
6   Gareev, 'Operatsiya "Mars"', p.23
7   Ibid., p.24
8   Glantz, *Zhukov's Greatest Defeat*, p.312–313
9   Gorbachevsky, *Rzhevskaya Myasorubka*, p.179–180
10 Speech of President V. Putin at the unveiling of the Rzhev Memorial, 30 June 2020, available at en.kremlin.ru/events/president/news/63585
11 Excerpt from 'Kropotovo' by Boris Slutsky; entire poem available at www.1942.ru /mars.htm

BIBLIOGRAPHY

Bundesarchiv-Militärarchiv, Freiburg
Public Records Office, Kew, London
Rossiiskii Gosudarstvennyi Arkhiv Sotsialno-Politicheskoi Istorii, Moscow
Tsentral'nyy Arkhiv Ministerstva Oborony, Moscow

Aerospace Historian (US Air Force Historical Foundation, Clinton, MD)
Central European History Journal (Cambridge University Press)
Foreign Military Studies (Historical Division, US Army Europe)
Izvestia (Moscow)
Journal of Contemporary History (Sage, CA)
Krasnaya Zvezda (Moscow)
Rodina (FGBU Redaktsiya Rossiyskoy Gazety, Moscow)
Russkaya Starina (St Petersburg)
Sbornik Materialov po Izucheniiu Opijta Voimj (Voyenizdat, Moscow)
Voyenno-Istoricheskiy Zhurnal (Russian Ministry of Defence, Moscow)
Znamia (Pravda, Moscow)

Abdullin, M., *Stranits iz Soldatskogo Dnevnika* (Molodaya Gvardiya, Moscow, 1985)
Adam, W., Rühle, O. and le Tissier, T. (trans.), *With Paulus at Stalingrad* (Pen and Sword, Barnsley, 2015)
Babadzhanian, A., *Dorogi Pobedy* (Molodaya Gvardiya, Moscow, 1975)
Barnett, C., *Hitler's Generals* (Weidenfeld & Nicholson, New York, 1989)
Beevor, A., *Stalingrad* (Penguin, Harmondsworth, 1999)
Beloborodov, A., *Vsevda v Boio* (Ekonomika, Moscow, 1984)
Belov, N. and Mikhailova, T., *Rzhev 1942: Bitva za Vysotu 200* (self-published, Tver, 2000)
Belov, P., *Za Nami Moskva* (Voyenizdat, Moscow, 1963)
Boog, H., *Der Angriff auf die Sowjetunion* (Fischer-Taschenbuch Verlag, Frankfurt am Main, 1996)
Boyko, V., *S Dumoy O Rodine* (Voyenizdat, Moscow, 1982)
Bradley, D. (ed.), *Die Generale des Heeres 1921–1945* (Biblio, Osnabrück, 1994)

Bradley, J. and Buell, T., *Why Was Barbarossa Delayed? The Second World War: Europe and the Mediterranean* (Square One, Garden City, NY, 2010)

Brunstedt, J., *The Soviet Myth of World War II: Patriotic Memory and the Russian Question in the USSR* (Cambridge University Press, 2021)

Bücheler, H., *Hoepner: Ein Deutsches Soldatenschiksal des 20. Jahrhunderts* (Mittler, Herford, 1980)

Buchheit, G., *Der Deutsche Geheimdienst. Geschichte der Militärischen Abwehr* (Munich, 1966)

Burdick, C. and Jacobsen, H.-A. (eds), *The Halder War Diary 1939–1942* (Greenhill, Novato, CA, 1988)

Buttar, P., *Russia's Last Gasp: The Eastern Front 1916–17* (Osprey, Oxford, 2016)

Buttar, P., *On a Knife's Edge: The Ukraine, November 1942–March 1943* (Osprey, Oxford, 2018)

Buttar, P., *Retribution: The Soviet Reconquest of Central Ukraine, 1943* (Osprey, Oxford, 2019)

Buttar, P., *The Reckoning: The Defeat of Army Group South, 1944* (Osprey, Oxford, 2020)

Chamberlain, P. and Doyle, H., *Encyclopaedia of German Tanks of World War Two* (Arms & Armour, London, 1978)

Delattre, L., *A Spy in the Heart of the Third Reich* (Grove, New York, 2006)

Drabkin, A., *Ya Dralsya s Pantservaffe 'Dvoynoy Oklad – Troynaya Smert!'* (Eksmo, Moscow, 2007)

Dragunsky, D., *Gody v Brone* (Voyenizdat, Moscow, 1973)

Dunn, W., *Stalin's Keys to Victory: The Rebirth of the Red Army* (Stackpole, Mechanicsburg, PA, 2007)

Ehrenburg, I., Grossman, V. and Patterson, D. (trans.), *The Complete Black Book of Russian Jewry* (Transaction, New Brunswick, NJ, 2003)

Eremenko, A., *V Nachale Voyny* (Nauka, Moscow, 1965)

Foote, A., *Handbook for Spies* (Museum, London, 1964)

Forczyk, R., *Velikiye Luki 1942–1943: The Doomed Fortress* (Osprey, Oxford, 2020)

Forczyk, R. and Hook, A., *Walther Model* (Osprey, Oxford, 2011)

Frieser, K.-H., Schmider, K., Schönherr, K., Schreiber, G., Ungváry, K. and Wegner, B., *Das Deutsche Reich und der Zweite Weltkrieg* (Deutsche Verlags-Anstalt, Munich, 2007), 10 volumes

Gerasimova, S., *Rzhev Slaughterhouse* (Helion, Warwick, 2012)

Gerbet, K. (ed.), *Generalfeldmarschall Fedor von Bock: The War Diary 1939–1945* (Schiffer, Atglen, PA, 1996)

Getman, A., *Tanki Idut na Berlin* (Nauka, Moscow, 1973)

Glantz, D., *The Soviet Airborne Experience* (US Army Command and General Staff College, Fort Leavenworth, KS, 1984)

Glantz, D., *When Titans Clashed: How the Red Army Stopped Hitler* (University Press of Kansas, Lawrence, 1995)

Glantz, D., *Zhukov's Greatest Defeat: The Red Army's Epic Disaster in Operation Mars, 1942* (University Press of Kansas, Lawrence, 1999)

Glantz, D., *Barbarossa Derailed: The Battle for Smolensk 10 July–10 September 1941* (Helion, Warwick, 2010)

Gorbachevsky, B., *Rzhevskaya Myasorubka. Vremya Otvagi. Zadacha – Vyzhit'!* (Eksmo, Moscow, 2007)

Gordon, Y., *Soviet Air Power in World War 2* (Midland, Herssham, 2008)

Görlitz, W., *Model. Strategie der Defensive* (Limes, Wiesbaden, 1975)

Grigorenko, P., *V Podpol'e Možno Vstretit' Tol'ko Krys* (Zven'ja, Moscow, 1997)

Grossmann, H., *Rshew, Eckpfeiler der Front* (Podzun, Bad Neuheim, 1962)

Grossmann, H., *Die Geschichte der Rheinisch-Westfälischen 6. Infanterie-Division 1939–1945* (Dörfler, Eggolsheim, 2005)

Guderian, H., *Panzer Leader* (Da Capo, New York, 1996)

Harrison, R., *The Russian Way of War: The Operational Art 1904–1940* (University of Kansas Press, Lawrence, 2001)

Harrison, R. (ed. and trans.), *The Battle of Moscow 1941–1942: The Red Army's Defensive Operations and Counteroffensive along the Moscow Strategic Direction – The Soviet General Staff Study* (Helion, Warwick, 2015)

Heinrici, G., Hürter, J. and Brocks, C. (trans.), *A German General on the Eastern Front: The Letters and Diaries of Gotthard Heinrici 1941–1942* (Pen & Sword, Barnsley, 2014)

Hitler, A., *Mein Kampf* (Houghton Mifflin, Boston, 1971)

Höhne, H., *Canaris: Hitler's Master Spy* (Doubleday, New York, 1979)

Höhne, H. and Brownjohn, J. (trans.), *Canaris* (Doubleday, New York, 1979)

Höhne, H. and Zolling, H., *The General Was a Spy: The Truth About General Gehlen and his Spy Ring* (Coward, McCann & Geoghegan, New York, 1972)

Ingrao, C. and Brown, A. (trans.), *Believe and Destroy: Intellectuals in the SS War Machine* (Polity, Cambridge, 2013)

Jones, M., *The Retreat: Hitler's First Defeat* (John Murray, London, 2010)

Jukes, G., *The Second World War – The Eastern Front 1941–1945* (Osprey, Oxford, 2002)

Katukov, M., *Na Ostriye Glavnogo Udara* (Voyenizdat, Moscow, 1974)

Kay, A., *Exploitation, Resettlement, Mass Murder: Political and Economic Planning for German Occupation Policy in the Soviet Union* (Berghahn, New York, 2006)

Kazaryan, A., *Prisyaga na vsio Zhizn* (Voenizdat, Moscow, 1988)

Khisamutdinova, R. and Zolotarev, V., *Velikaia Otechestvennaia Voiny 1941–1945: Voyenno-Istoricheskie Ocherki* (Nauka, Moscow, 1998–1999), 4 volumes

Khlebnikov, N., *Pod Grokhot Soten Batarey* (Voyenizdat, Moscow, 1974)

Knobelsdorff, O. von, *Geschichte der Niedersächsischen 19. Panzer-Division 1939–1945* (Podzun-Pallas, Friedberg, 1958)

Kochetkov, A., *Dvinskii Tankovyi: Boevoi Put 5-go Tankovogo Dvinskogo Korpusa* (Voyenizdat, Moscow, 1989)

Krasnov, V., *G Zhukov. Marshal Velikoy Impreii. Lavry I Ternii Polkovodtsa* (Olma, Moscow, 2005)

Krausnick, H., Buchheim, H., Broszat, M. and Jacobsen, H.-A., *Anatomy of the SS State* (Walter, New York, 1968)

Krivosheev, G., *Rossiya I SSSR Voynakh XX Veka: Poteri Vooruzhennykh Sil, Statisticheskoye Issledovaniye* (Olma, Moscow, 2001)

Krüger, A. and Scharenberg, S., *Zeiten für Helden – Zeiten für Berümtheiten im Sport* (LIT, Münster, 2014)

Lelyushenko, D., *Moskva-Stalingrad-Berlin-Praga. Zapiski Komandarma* (Nauka, Moscow, 1971)

Lopukhovsky, L., *Na Glavnom Napravleniy* (Super, Moscow, 2017)

Lykov, I., *V Groznyy Chas* (Voyenizdat, Moscow, 1986)

MacDonagh, G., *After the Reich: From the Liberation of Vienna to the Berlin Airlift* (John Murray, London, 2007)

Malygin, K., *V Tsentre Boyevogo Poryadka* (Voyenizdat, Moscow, 1986)

Manstein, E. von and Powell, G. (trans.), *Lost Victories: The War Memoirs of Hitler's Most Brilliant General* (Presidio, Novato, CA, 1994)

Manteuffel, H. von, *Die 7. Panzer-Division im Zweiten Weltkrieg* (Josef Broich, Uerdingen am Rhein, 1965)

Melnikov, V., *Ikh Poslal na Smert' Zhukov? Gibel' Armii Generala Efremova* (Eksmo, Moscow, 2009)

Mikheyenkov, S., *Armiya, Kotoruyu Predali. Tragediya 33-y Armii Generala M G Efremova* (Tsentrpoligraf, Moscow, 2010)

Mikhin, P., *Voyna, Kakoy Ona Byla: Rasskazy* (Slavyanka, Kursk, 2012)

Miller, M., *Leaders of the SS and German Police* (Bender, San Jose, CA, 2006), 2 volumes

Mitiagin, S., *Boevye Deistviya pod Viaz'moi v Ianvare-Aprele 1942: Operatsiia ili Imitatsiia?* (Voyenno-Istoricheskii Archiv, Moscow, 1988)

Munõz, A., *Goering's Grenadiers: The Luftwaffe Field Divisions 1942-1945* (Axis Europa, Bayside, NY, 2002)

Mylnikov, L. and Kondratev, O., *Eto Bylo na Rzhevsko-Viazemskom Platsdarme* (Rzhevskiy Knizhyy Klub, 1998), 3 volumes

Neumann, J., *Die 4. Panzer-Division 1938–1943* (Verlag und Antiquariat für Zeitgeschichte, Bad Dürkheim, 1989)

Newton, S., *Hitler's Commander: Field Marshal Walter Model, Hitler's Favorite General* (Da Capo, Cambridge, MA, 2006)

Pahl, M. and Hammond, D., *Hitler's Fremde Heere Ost: German Military Intelligence on the Eastern Front 1942–1945* (Helion, Warwick, 2016)

Peiper, H., *Fegelein's Horsemen and Genocidal Warfare: The SS Cavalry Brigade in the Soviet Union* (Palgrave Macmillan, Basingstoke, 2015)

Plato, A. Von, *Die Geschichte der 5. Panzerdivision 1938 bis 1945* (Walhalla und Praetoria, Regensburg, 1978)

Praun, A., *German Radio Intelligence* (US Army Office of the Chief of Military History, Washington, DC, 1950)

Radó, S., *Sous le Pseudonyme Dora* (Julliard, Paris, 1972)

Reinhardt, K., *Moscow – The Turning Point: The Failure of Hitler's Strategy in the Winter of 1941–1942* (Berg, New York, 1992)

Richardson, W., *The Fatal Decisions: The Decisive Battles of the Second World War from the Viewpoint of the Vanquished* (Pen and Sword, Barnsley, 2012)

Roberts, G., *Wars: From World War to Cold War, 1939–1952* (Yale University Press, New Haven, CT, 2006)

Rokossovsky, K., *A Soldier's Duty* (Lancer, New Delhi, 1992)

Rotmistrov, P., *Stalnaya Gvardiya* (Voyenizdat, Moscow, 1984)

Ruffner, K., *Luftwaffe Field Divisions 1941–1945* (Osprey, Oxford, 1990)

Sandalov, L., *Pogorelo-Gorodishchenskaia Operatsiia. Nastupatelnaia Operatsiia 20-Armii Zapadnogo Fronta v Avguste 1942 Goda* (Voyenizdat, Moscow, 1960)

Schäufler, H., *Der Weg war Weit: Panzer Zwischen Weichsel und Wolga* (Vowinckel, Neckargemünd, 1973)

Schäufler, H., *So Lebten und so Starben Sie: Das Buch vom Panzerregiment-35* (Kameradschaft Ehemaliger Panzer-Regiment 35 e.V, Bamberg, 1983)

Schreiber, G., Stegemann, B. and Vogel, D., *Germany and the Second World War* (Clarendon, Oxford, 1998), 9 volumes

Sevryugov, S., *Tak Eto Bylo …* (Voenizdat, Moscow, 1957)

Shavrov, V., *Istoriya Konstruktsiy Samolotov v SSSR do 1938g* (Mashinostroyenie, Moscow, 1985)

Simpkin, R., *Deep Battle: The Brainchild of Marshal Tukhachevsky* (Brassey, London, 1987)

Sinitsky, A., *Razvedchikam Oshibatsya Nelzya* (Voyenizdat, Moscow, 1987)

Smelser, R., *The Myth of the Eastern Front: The Nazi-Soviet War in American Popular Culture* (Cambridge University Press, 2008)

Smith, J. and Kay, A., *German Aircraft of the Second World War* (Putnam, London, 1978)

Snyder, T., *Bloodlands: Europe Between Hitler and Stalin* (Vintage, London, 2011)

Solomatin, M., *Krasnogradtsky* (Voyenizdat, Moscow, 1963)

Spaeter, H., *The History of the Panzerkorps Grossdeutschland* (Fedorowicz, Winnipeg, 1992), 3 volumes

Stahel, D., *Retreat from Moscow: A New History of Germany's Winter Campaign, 1941–1942* (Picador, New York, 2019)

Starchak, I., *S Neba, V Boy* (Voyenizdat, Moscow, 1965)

Stoves, R., *Die 1. Panzer-Division 1935–1945* (Podzun, Bad Neuheim, 1961)

Strauss, F., *Geschichte der 2. (Wiener) Panzer-Division* (Dörfler, Eggolsheim, 2005)

Sukhorukov, D., *Sovetskie Vozdushno-Desantnye* (Voyenizdat, Moscow, 1980)

Sun Tzu and Butler-Brown, T., *The Art of War: The Ancient Classic* (Capstone, Mankato Min, 2020)

Sverdlov, F., *Tragediya 33-y Armii. Oshibki G K Zhukova* (Monolit, Moscow, 2002)

Sverdlov, F., *Oshibki G K Zhukova God 1942* (self-published, available at 1942.ru/Zhukov .1942.htm)

Tarrant, V., *The Red Orchestra* (J. Wiley, London, 1995)

Toptygin, A., *Lavrentij Beria: Neizvestny Marsal Gosbezopasnosti* (Eksmo, Moscow, 2005)

Vasilevsky, A., *A Lifelong Cause* (Progress, Moscow, 1973)

Volkogonov, D., *Stalin: Politicheskiy Portret* (Novosti, Moscow, 1992), 2 volumes

Voloshin, M., *Razvedchiki Vsegda Vperedi* (Voyenizdat, Moscow, 1977)

Vorobev, M. and Usov, V., *Za Kazhdyi Klochok Zemli* (Moskovskii Rabochii, Smolensk, 1989)

Voyenno-Nauchnoye Upravleniye Generalnogo Shtaba, Voyenno-Istoricheskiy Otdel, *Boevoi Sostav Sovetskoi Armii 1942 Goda* (Voyenizdat, Moscow, 1966), 4 volumes

Weigelt, A., Müller, K.-D., Schaarschmidt, T. and Schmeitzner, M., *Todesurteile Sowjetischer Militärtribunale gegen Deutsche (1944–1947): Eine Historisch-Biographische Studie* (Vandenhoeck & Ruprecht, Göttingen, 2015)

Werth, A., *Russia at War 1941–1945* (Dutton, New York, 1964)

Wilmot, C., *The Struggle for Europe* (Wordsworth, Ware, 2003)

Wray, T., *Standing Fast: German Defensive Doctrine on the Russian Front During World War II* (Combat Studies Institute, Fort Leavenworth, KS, 2004)

Zetterling, N. and Frankson, A., *The Drive on Moscow, 1941. Operation Taifun and Germany's First Great Crisis of World War II* (Casemate, Havertown, PA, 2012)

Zhukov, G., *Vospomimaniya I Razmyshleniya* (Olma, Moscow, 2002), 2 volumes

Ziemke, E., *Stalingrad to Berlin: The German Defeat in the East* (US Army Office of the Chief of Military History, Washington, DC, 1968)

Ziemke, E. and Bauer, M., *Moscow to Stalingrad: Decision in the East* (Military Heritage Press, New York, 1988)

Zolotarev, V. (ed.), *Russkii Arkhiv. Velikaia Otechestvennaia Voina 1941–1945* (Nauka, Moscow, 1998), 4 volumes

Grazami Detei: Rasskazyi Detei v Rzheva o Zberstvach Nemetsko-Fachistskich Zachvatchikov (Izdanie Kalininskogo Ovkoma, Kalinin, 1944)

Handbook on German Military Forces (United States Department of War, Washington, DC, 1945)

True to Type: A Selection From Letters and Diaries of German Soldiers and Civilians Collected on the Soviet-German Front (Hutchinson, London, 1945)

INDEX